MAJOR CRISES IN
AMERICAN HISTORY

UNDER THE GENERAL EDITORSHIP OF

Leonard W. Levy &
Merrill D. Peterson

Brandeis University

THE EDITORS

JAMES MacGREGOR BURNS
JANET THOMPSON BURNS
Williams College

ALFRED D. CHANDLER, JR.
Massachusetts Institute of Technology

HOLMAN HAMILTON
University of Kentucky

SAMUEL P. HUNTINGTON
Columbia University

GORDON JENSEN
Massachusetts Institute of Technology

LEONARD W. LEVY
Brandeis University

DAVID S. LOVEJOY
University of Wisconsin

ERIC McKITRICK
Columbia University

ERNEST R. MAY
Harvard University

MERRILL D. PETERSON
Brandeis University

T. HARRY WILLIAMS
Louisiana State University

MAJOR CRISES
IN
AMERICAN
HISTORY

Documentary Problems

I

1689–1861

New York ⚏ Burlingame

HARCOURT, BRACE & WORLD, INC.

Library of Congress Catalog Card Number: 62–15960

CONTENTS

The Ratification of the Constitution:
The Crisis of 1787–1789

LEONARD W. LEVY
MERRILL D. PETERSON

Freedom in Turmoil,
Era of the Sedition Act:
The Crisis of 1797–1800

LEONARD W. LEVY

Contents

Nationalism and Sectionalism:
The Crisis of 1819–1820
MERRILL D. PETERSON

Jacksonian Democracy and the Bank War:
The Crisis of 1830–1834
ALFRED D. CHANDLER, JR.

Slavery and Expansion:
The Crisis and Compromise of 1850
HOLMAN HAMILTON

Disruption of the Union:
The Secession Crisis, 1860–1861
T. HARRY WILLIAMS

PREFACE

M*ajor Crises in American History* offers a documentary approach in depth to the first college course in American history. It possesses a unifying theme in the general idea of historical crisis. Sixteen crucial events, episodes, or experiences in the history of the United States are treated intensively through primary sources, the raw data of historical knowledge. The eight topics grouped in Volume I range in time from the seventeenth century to the Civil War; the eight topics in Volume II begin with Reconstruction and end with the Korean War. While each topic has great intrinsic importance, it also offers a perspective on larger issues and developments. Utilizing different kinds of data, and calling for different kinds of analysis, each topic locates a problem, a problem that has a distinctly decisive aspect and that, from its focus in time, is subject to reasonably comprehensive, as well as intensive, coverage. Taken together, and within themselves, these chapters exhibit the standard fields of historical study—social, political, economic, diplomatic, constitutional, intellectual—and raise perennial questions of analysis and interpretation.

The structure of the present work has several distinguishing marks. *First*, it combines the interest in controversial problems and issues with the historian's fundamental responsibility to the record of events. Except as problems are delineated and explored in the thick, baffling context of specific situations and events, they cannot be grasped historically. As elementary as this truth is, the obligation to exchange the telescope, with its panoramic sweep, for the microscope, with its faithful attention to characteristic local contour and complexity, and so to examine the historical record in considerable depth and detail, needs to be brought home repeatedly. Narrative textbooks with centuries to account for are necessarily telescopic and if relied upon too heavily may convey the impression that history is a well-ordered march rather than a disheveled and spreading battle in which there are few certainties. The difficulty is but partially overcome by confronting students with issues and problems as sweeping in their scope as those disclosed in the chapters of the one- or even two-volume narrative text, since, in such a scheme, the contexts are vague and the quality of concreteness, so essential to historical understanding, is necessarily neglected. In the present volumes, the objectives of depth, fullness, and concreteness are sought through the study of a carefully selected series of critical cases as turning points in American history. No attempt is

made to fill out an entire chronology; on the contrary, the deliberate intention
is to place in focus a relatively few great moments in American history, each
as dramatic as it is charged with significance.

Second, the method employed throughout the book makes a strong claim
on the intelligence and initiative of the student in the reconstruction, analysis,
and interpretation of the data. The aim is to provide the student not so much
with a book of knowledge as with a tool of historical inquiry. Within reasonable limits, the goal is to make him the "doer" rather than the "taker." Only
primary sources are used. The documents are accompanied by such editorial
guidance and interpretation as may be necessary to assure coherence, but they
are neither predigested nor prejudged for the student.

Confronted with primary sources—most of them entirely new to him—the
student must work with their uncertainties and yield to their discipline, without the benefit or the hindrance of what historians have said at second hand
about the events in question. He will learn from conflicting evidence, interest, and opinion that great historical events are susceptible to a number of
interpretations, which are better or worse not according to their rightness or
wrongness but according to their cogency in treating all the complexities of
the problem at hand. It is no part of the editors' intention to create around
the student what is as manifestly impossible as it is undesirable: a vacuum of
accumulated historical knowledge. Classroom instruction and additional
reading, either in standard texts or in specialized studies, may be relied upon
to furnish this knowledge so far as it is wanted. But there is no substitute for
the student making discoveries for himself; and in the instance of historical
study this means there is no substitute for each student becoming, if only on
a rudimentary level, his own historian.

Third, the work's focus on crises should convey to the student that American history is not lacking in turbulence and passion, that it has its share of
dramatic conflict, great debate, and great decision, and that many contingencies attended the outcome. The editors believe that this emphasis is both
pedagogically sound and a welcome antidote to the current tendency to view
American history as one mellifluous and more or less predestined flow along
an inevitable path of consensus. Without supposing that American history
is adequately comprehended solely as a sequence of crises, they aim through
these volumes to enrich the student's knowledge of the past, to give him a
heightened awareness of the grave disturbances and dislocations that successive generations of Americans have experienced and of the responses they have
made.

A number of considerations played a part in the actual choice of the topics
included in each volume: the preferences of the general and contributing
editors; the desire for freshness and variety and originality; the obvious needs

of the course, both in terms of content and of coverage. Since it is assumed that the book will generally, if not exclusively, be used in conjunction with a standard text, efforts have been made to minimize repetition and to phase the topics chronologically so as to permit their assignment on a fairly regular basis —weekly in one semester courses, biweekly in two semester courses.

Each topic composes a chapter, and each chapter follows a uniform plan. The Chronology provides a useful guide to the progression of events in the particular crisis. The Introduction supplies, in narrative form, the immediate background and context of the crisis. The Documents, reproduced as they appear in the sources cited, are arranged in logical sequence, prefaced by Headnotes that explain the source or authorship and add other significant details. The Conclusion rounds out the documentary treatment in narrative fashion. The Study Questions, all of the essay type, are intended to contribute to the book's usefulness as a vehicle of undergraduate research. Each chapter is completed by a concise bibliography, Recommended Readings, which students may use most effectively in the writing of brief, critical essays or longer research papers. Maps, statistical tables, and similar aids are provided in so far as they seemed necessary. At the end of each volume there is a brief discussion—"Historical Aids"—of the chief standard bibliographical and historiographical works that facilitate the study of American history.

Within the limits of the format described, the historians responsible for the several chapters were free to make their own decisions. They wrote the original narratives, selected and edited the documents, and shaped each chapter. The general editors consider themselves fortunate to have obtained such excellent collaborators. They entered heartily into the spirit of the book, discharged their responsibilities cheerfully and skillfully, and responded to our gentle proddings and suggestions in a most gratifying fashion. The general editors shared equally in the responsibility of overseeing the entire work, from initial planning to final completion.

L. W. L.

M. D. P.

Brandeis University
March 1, 1962

The Glorious Revolution
in America:
The Crisis of
1689

DAVID S. LOVEJOY

UNIVERSITY OF WISCONSIN

CONTENTS

CHRONOLOGY

1684

OCTOBER 23   Revocation of Massachusetts charter.

1685

FEBRUARY 6   Charles II dies; James II becomes king.

1686

MAY 25   Dominion of New England established under President Joseph Dudley.

DECEMBER 20   Sir Edmund Andros, governor-general of the Dominion, arrives in Boston.

1688

APRIL 7   New York and New Jersey added to the Dominion.

JUNE   The Glorious Revolution commences in England.

NOVEMBER 5   Prince William lands at Torbay.

DECEMBER 23   James II flees England for last time.

1689

JANUARY 22   Convention Parliament meets.

APRIL 18   Bay colonists overthrow Andros in Boston.

MAY 31   Leisler's Rebellion begins in New York; fort seized.

JULY 25   Protestants in Maryland issue Declaration.

AUGUST 1   John Coode and rebels seize Maryland government.

1690

FEBRUARY 9   Massacre at Schenectady, New York.

JULY 28   Unsuccessful invasion of Canada begins.

1691

MARCH 20   Leisler surrenders fort to Governor Henry Sloughter and is imprisoned.

MAY 16   Jacob Leisler and Jacob Milborne hanged for murder and treason.

1692

MAY 10   Governor Sir Lionel Copley meets first assembly under royal government in Maryland.

MAY 14   Governor Sir William Phips arrives in Boston with royal charter for Massachusetts.

INTRODUCTION

THE RESTORATION of Charles II in 1660 and the Glorious Revolution of 1688, two major landmarks in the history of England, had an equally historic impact upon England's American colonies. The very year Englishmen restored Charles to the throne, their Parliament commenced a series of navigation acts which helped to shape the course of American history for the next hundred years. Poorer in cash than in friends, Charles paid off debts to the faithful with a wave of proprietary grants—the Carolinas, New York, New Jersey, and Pennsylvania—almost doubling the number of colonies in America. In the 1680's Charles's brother, James II, drastically altered the political aspects of colonial policy and established arbitrary government in America as well as in England. The Glorious Revolution wrecked James's plans in both places and precipitated a crisis in the colonies second only to the conflict of 1776.

When it became apparent that American colonists were not as sympathetic to trade regulation as the mercantilists in England thought they should be, the crown, through the Privy Council and the Lords of Trade, decided that closer political control over colonial governments was absolutely necessary. Massachusetts, a charter colony since 1630, was doubtless the worst offender and already at odds with the king over a long list of offenses; therefore she was subject to the first attention. In 1684 the crown revoked the Bay Colony's charter and representative government in the Puritan interest collapsed, marking the end of the Saints' rule in Zion. Other colonies and governments were suspect too; but Charles's action was only a beginning, for James II, who succeeded to the throne in 1685, effected a more vigorous policy of colonial control than merely revoking charters and establishing royal governments.

To bring the northern colonies more into line with imperial policy and at the same time to unite them against an imminent threat from New France, James II imposed the Dominion of New England on Massachusetts, Plymouth, New Hampshire, Connecticut, and Rhode Island. After about a year of provisionary administration under President Joseph Dudley, James commissioned Sir Edmund Andros, his former governor of New York, as governor-general. Connecticut and Rhode Island feebly surrendered their independence by admitting the authority of Andros, and he, with a council alone, proceeded to govern New England from Boston. In 1688 James added New York and New Jersey to the Dominion, extending Andros' rule from Maine to the Delaware.

But James proved to be a bad king. His Catholicism offended Protestant England; his filling royal offices with Catholics scandalized both Whigs and Tories; his use of the Declaration of Indulgence antagonized the established church; his attempt to rule without Parliament violated the rights of Englishmen; and his queen gave birth to a son, guaranteeing a Catholic succession. All this and more was sufficient to arouse Englishmen to revolt. From Holland they invited Prince William of Orange and his wife Mary—a Protestant daughter of James—to accept the Crown. William landed at Torbay in November, 1688, and James soon fled—abdicated, the legalists said—to France. A Convention Parliament in February, 1689, offered the vacant throne to William and Mary and the Revolution was well begun, although it took a number of Englishmen several years to learn to live with it. News of the historic event reached America in the early spring of 1689. In four months' time it had provoked major rebellions in Massachusetts, New York, and Maryland, and sent ripples of revolt as far south as the Carolinas.

There were several general causes for the crisis in America in 1689. James II was no more liked in the colonies than in England, and his arbitrary ideas about government were reflected, the colonists believed, in Andros' high-handed treatment of New England, New York, and New Jersey, the proprietor's Catholic control in Maryland, and a general stiffening of the royal prerogative all along the line. In turning out their governments and proclaiming William, these colonists claimed to denounce Stuart tyranny and strike a blow for Protestantism and the rights of Englishmen throughout the empire. That Protestant William had replaced Catholic James was a major triumph, according to the colonists, and although Catholic influence had not heavily touched their lives, except in Maryland, there were instances in New York when Catholics had held several offices, including the governorship. Despite the devotion of Andros and his followers to the Church of England, their closeness to James made their religion suspect, particularly among the virulently anti-Catholic Puritans.

But the immediate Catholic issue was not as important by itself as it was in combination with the colonists' fear of the French in Canada and their Indian allies, archrivals of England's imperial schemes in America with whom the colonists had frequently skirmished. Their fear had a good deal of substance. William's success in England upset the customary balance of power in Europe and brought on a major war with France, an important part of which was fought in America close to the colonists' homes. More specifically, official news of William's landing was slow to reach America (although rumors of it had circulated as early as February, 1689), and the colonists had become aware of the momentous events in England before their governments took notice. The delay, which many interpreted as a deliberate scheme to oppose the Revolution and keep them loyal to James, inflamed imaginations already excited. James's flight to France gave some basis, it seemed, to wild rumors that he, Andros, and the Catholics of Maryland, along with Louis XIV and the French and Indians of Canada, were deep in a Popish plot to hold the colonies for James and enslave the Protestants.

Hindsight renders such a conspiracy absurd, but there is no doubt that many colonists believed in it then. In justifying rebellion, the leaders in Massachusetts, New York, and Maryland listed these general grievances as they pertained to each colony, joyously declared their loyalty to William and Mary, and hoped that the new king would accept their rebellions as an integral part of the Glorious Revolution. In two of the three colonies they were successful.

Protestations of loyalty to their majesties in England, although sincere, were also exaggerated. The overturning of governments in Massachusetts, New York, and Maryland had origins deeper than Stuart tyranny, the threat of Catholicism, and fear of the French and Indians. Local conflicts and cleavages, intensifying the crisis, doubtless had more to do with the rebellions in America than a change of monarchs in England.

The decline of Puritanism in New England had begun long before Sir Edmund set foot on sacred Massachusetts soil. Second and third generation Puritans had already fallen away from the zeal of their fathers and grandfathers. Moreover, economic prosperity had blunted the rough edges of the wilderness and helped to erode whatever zeal remained. Failing to reform England, let alone Christendom, in accordance with the original purposes of their "Citty upon a Hill" at Boston, the Puritans were forced to provide a solution in the world of their own community. By the time Andros took over their government even this looked hopeless. The Puritans of the latter half of the seventeenth century had made several compromises with original principles; from their midst, supported by newcomers from England, emerged a group of moderates who objected to religious qualifications for voting, resented the church's restrictions on their business ways, and looked more kindly than did the old guard on closer economic and political ties to England. The loss of the charter and the arrival of Andros were staggering blows to what was left of the Puritan oligarchy.

Andros' rule in New England was both a manifestation of Puritan decline and a cause of it. According to the doctrine of the hard-core Saints, God was already displeased with their experiment in Massachusetts, and He inflicted upon them a tyrannical government for the same reason He had incited the Indians against them a few years earlier in King Philip's War— in punishment for their evil ways. But good Puritans did not surrender to calamities. God was not with the Indians nor behind Andros; He merely used them to show His displeasure. The Puritans eventually defeated the Indians, and they struggled against Andros in the best way they knew. The fact that Andros was James's governor made opposition easier; the people of Massachusetts fought against the Dominion in the name of Englishmen as well as in the name of God.

What is more, they believed their charter was illegally revoked and Andros' rule unconstitutional and tyrannical. He and his council taxed them without their consent; he altered their system of justice, introducing strange ways and customs. He attempted to revise the system of landholding, demanding that all property owners reapply for patents under the crown and pay him fees for the service. He planted the king's church in Boston despite the Saints' hatred of Anglicanism. To protect the frontier from the Indians, he led an expedition to Maine where forts were built and the Indians discouraged. But the efforts were wasted, said the colonists: no Indians were killed, and the soldiers needlessly suffered and died in the winter's cold and snow. And certainly not least of their grievances, although they registered no official complaint, was that Andros enforced the Acts of Trade and scattered the pirates who were a source of hard money.

For relief from this "tyranny," Increase Mather, Boston's foremost minister, "escaped" to London in 1688 to lay their grievances before the king and beg for the restoration of the charter. James seemed sympathetic, but before he acted one way or another he lost his throne, and Mather had to begin all over again with William. Mather did succeed in delaying the new king's instructions to Andros and the Dominion; these would have confirmed colonial officers in their places until the crown had time to decide upon the disposition of colonial governments. Meanwhile, news of the Revolution reached the Bay Colony.

With only a whimper, Peter Stuyvesant had surrendered New Netherland to the English in 1664—and Charles gave the colony to his younger brother to govern as he pleased. James's pleasure was to rule New York through a governor and council, without an assembly. The proprietor's rule was interrupted only during the Third Dutch War (1672–74), when the Dutch recaptured and then returned New York to the English. James's policy of no assembly weakened in 1683 when Governor Thomas Dongan, after frequent demands from New Yorkers and with James's reluctant permission, called a meeting of representatives who drafted a frame of government which included a permanent legislature. Before he gave final approval, if he had ever intended to, James ascended the throne of England (1685) and carried New York with him as a royal colony without an assembly. Three years later New York and New Jersey were added to the Dominion; Catholic Governor Dongan was relieved of his post, and James commissioned Francis Nicholson to govern New York as lieutenant governor under Andros.

While the specific and local causes of the overthrow of the Dominion in Massachusetts had accumulated only since the loss of the charter in 1684, several of the grievances behind the rebellion in New York were almost a generation old. New York was a good deal more heterogeneous than either Massachusetts or Virginia. It contained Dutch Calvinists from before the conquest, Puritans from New England (chiefly on Long Island), Anglicans (in New York City, in Albany, and in outlying towns), and small groups of Quakers and Germans. Out of this mixture emerged an aristocracy of merchants and landholders which won commercial monopolies, political privileges, and large, landed estates through favor with the proprietary and royal governors—on whose councils several of them sat. New York City's control over the colony's trade discriminated against the Long Islanders who would rather have done business directly with their friends in Connecticut and Boston than through the city as the laws demanded. Bolting and packing of flour was a city monopoly which infuriated farmers forced to send their grain there, and the Albany fur trade was in the hands of a privileged few, discouraging competition. An economic depression and tax increases, particularly hard on the lower classes, aggravated conditions, but effective opposition was stifled by lack of an assembly.

The shift to the Dominion in 1688 changed little in New York, for several of the aristocrats, including Nicholas Bayard, Stephen Courtlandt, and Frederick Philips, were invited by Andros to serve on his council and thus to help him govern New England and particularly New York under the new Lieutenant Governor Nicholson. To the disaffected, alleviation of their grievances looked more and more remote. Among the discontented was Jacob Leisler, a German-born merchant, who represented a formidable group of well-to-do but socially inferior New Yorkers who bitterly resented the favored position of the commercial, landed, and social elite. Although most of the colonists were Protestant, scattered here and there were several Catholics, including the collector of customs and former Governor Dongan. Albany's vulnerability to French and Indian attack made New Yorkers particularly sensitive to rumors that the Catholics about them and their enemies to the North were plotting together to do them in.

The causes of the rebellion in Maryland were closer in nature to Leisler's in New York than to the overthrow of Andros in Massachusetts where royal government had only recently been imposed upon the Bay Colony. The similarity stemmed from the fact that in Maryland, as in New York, a discontented and ambitious group, in its own behalf and in the broader interests of equally discontented inhabitants, took advantage of the upheaval in England to rid the colony of a long-entrenched party of privilege. Maryland had an assembly, to be sure, but it was repeatedly frustrated by the proprietor's council which favored the Catholics and whose members and president governed according to Baltimore's wishes and their own. The proprietor himself, by this time Charles Calvert, third Lord Baltimore, regarded the colony as his private domain, which indeed it was in a legal sense. But representatives of the Protestant majority in the lower house found Baltimore's notions of proprietary rule repugnant to what they claimed were the will of the people and the rights of Englishmen.

The grievances were many and, as in New York, a number were of long standing. They varied in kind from arbitrary restrictions on suffrage, representation, and lawmaking, to courts dominated by the proprietor's council, tobacco laws favoring Baltimore's customs, and illegal punishments and "extroordinary fees." Catalyst for the outburst was the sharp issue of Catholicism which underlined most conflicts and differences between council and house, the proprietor's favorites—many his relatives—and most of the people. Maryland suffered from Indian difficulties too, and these were easily blown up as proof of a plot between Catholics and French to wipe out the Protestants.

Such was the state of affairs in the three colonies when news of William's invasion reached America in the spring of 1689. That the news first came unofficially heightened the rumors of conspiracy. That it was for so long unconfirmed wore out the patience of the discontented.

The sequence of events leading to the explosion in Massachusetts began early in January. Governor Andros, on instructions from James, published a warning of a "great and sudden Invasion from *Holland*" and girded the colony against trouble from abroad. In March, when at Pemaquid in Maine, Andros first learned of William's landing in England, and he sped to Boston to quell any uprising the spread of such information might provoke among the people. On April 4 John Winslow arrived from Nevis in the West Indies, spilling the news wholesale to the inhabitants and bearing a copy of the prince's declaration from The Hague. For two uneasy weeks the people of Boston lived with the news and saw Winslow jailed by Andros for treasonable libel. Moreover, they looked back with a good deal of suspicion upon Andros' proclamation in January, commanding the colonists to defend the empire against a Dutch invasion. Meantime, the troops left by Andros at Pemaquid mutinied and started for Boston, arriving in the middle of April. The colony was ready for action.

Fearing that Andros might oppose William's conquest and carry the colony for France and the Pope with the help of the French and the Indians, apprehensive, at the same time, that Andros might declare for William and be confirmed in his office without offering them any relief from what they believed was tyrannical rule, the Bay colonists on April 18, almost unanimously and with a firm show of force, seized the government and threw Andros and his retinue into jail. Some of the moderates, who had earlier accepted places in Andros' council, deserted the governor and joined ranks with the Saints. A few weeks after setting up a committee of safety and after serious debate as to how they should proceed, the people of Massachusetts reinstated their former magistrates, including Simon Bradstreet, the last elected governor, declared their loyalty to William and Mary, and hoped for the best. Not to be outdone, the colonists at Plymouth sent a Dominion councilor to jail and carried on as before.

Lieutenant Governor Nicholson and his council at New York learned of London events on March 1, 1689, and tried to keep them secret for several weeks to come. But news of the arrest of Andros and the fall of the Dominion could not be suppressed. To hold things together until instructions from England arrived, Nicholson hastily called a convention made up of available council members, the city officers, and militia captains, forming, he hoped, a stable body of leaders. Despite the governor's efforts to avoid a crisis, fear among the people of a Catholic plot, Nicholson's and the council's apparent reluctance to proclaim the Prince of Orange, and the governor's few ill-chosen and inflammatory words to an officer of the militia precipitated sudden revolt on May 31. The militia quickly defected from governor and council and seized the fort. Jacob Leisler emerged as commander of the rebels, to be confirmed later by a committee of safety. Not long afterwards Nicholson fled to England to report the debacle, leaving the field to Leisler and his supporters, who were opposed by the council, particularly Nicholas Bayard, and a loyal faction.

The crisis in New York did not end with Leisler's seizure of power, owing to the strength of the opposition to him within the colony and the outbreak of war between England and France. During his regime Leisler called a representative assembly, revoked some of the commercial monopolies so offensive to the people, and planned and attempted, with the help of several other colonies, a military campaign against Canada in defense of all British America. Although loyal to William, Albany opposed Leisler until

a French and Indian massacre at nearby Schenectady in early 1690 convinced the people of Albany they would do better with Leisler than against
him. New England and Maryland, if not Nicholas Bayard and the council,
recognized Leisler as governor of New York almost from the outset; for the
fate of one was the fate of all, or so it seemed at the time of crisis.

Many Protestants in Maryland believed themselves to have suffered heavy
burdens for some time. But the arrival of William Joseph in October, 1688,
with Baltimore's commission as president of the council, helped bring matters to a head even before Prince William made his dash for England.
Joseph was as impolitic a governor as they come. Within a short time he had
alienated a good many people by lecturing the Assembly on the divine
right of government, proclaiming the birth of the Prince of Wales, for
whom he demanded an annual birthday celebration, and insisting that members of the Assembly take a fresh oath of fidelity to the proprietor alone
without reference to the king.

In January, 1689, as in Massachusetts, James's warning of a Dutch invasion reached Maryland, and the council reacted by calling in all public
arms for repair—an act later regarded with considerable suspicion by the
rebels. In March a "greate uproar and Tumult" arose owing to countless
rumors of a pending "coup" by the Catholics and Indians. The council added
to the uproar by proroguing the Assembly to October when it should have
met in April. The intense excitement continued through May and June,
aggravated by the people's knowledge of what had occurred to the northward. Ironically, Baltimore's messenger, bearing news of William's success
and instructions to proclaim the new king, died just before he was to leave
England, delaying an official communication of events in London. The council's failure to declare for William convinced its enemies that the government had deliberately suppressed the news.

Late in July, under Protestant John Coode, a member of the Assembly
and a notorious malcontent, the disaffected armed themselves and by declaration dissolved their allegiance to Baltimore's government. Coode and his
followers set out for St. Mary's City, gathering forces as they marched. On
August 1 they demanded and received the surrender of the president and
council and their friends; two days later they petitioned the king to establish a royal government in Maryland. By early September Coode and his
supporters had organized the Associators' Assembly and proceeded to govern,
hopefully waiting for confirmation of their actions from England.

Between the middle of April and early August, 1689, William and Mary
were presented with three colonial governments they never knew they had
lost. Busy at war and in keeping his throne, William took his time about
re-establishing the rebellious colonies, and Massachusetts, New York, and
Maryland limped along as best they could. The delay only tended to string
out the crisis and add to the confusion.

DOCUMENTS

1] A Boston Saint Explains the Rebellion Against Andros

"A. B." 's account of what happened in Boston, written three weeks after the overthrow of Andros, has considerable merit since it not only describes the crisis but implies that the uprising was contemplated earlier and that the leaders were determined not just to forestall an attack upon them from Andros and the French but to prevent, if necessary, an unmanageable revolt on the part of their friends. "A. B." has not been identified but was doubtless a Massachusetts patriot who wanted to set the "facts" straight and get the jump on any "False Reports" which might be sent home to England. Italics are omitted.*

SIR,

. . . Since the Illegal Subversion of our Ancient Government, this Great, but poor people have been in the Hands of men skilful to destroy, and all our Concerns both Civil and Sacred, have suffered by the Arbitrary Oppressions of Unreasonable Men. I believe, no part of the English America, so powerful and united as New-England was, could have endured half so many Abuses as we have bin harrassed withal, with a tenth part of our Patience; but our Conscience was that which gave metal to our Patience, and kept us Quiet; for though our foul-mouth'd Enemies have treated us a Rebellious, because we are a Religious people, they may be pleased now to understand, That if we had not been Religious, we had long since been what they would, if they durst, have called Rebellious. The very Form of Government imposed upon us, was among the worst of Treasons, even a Treasonable Invasion of the Rights which the whole English Nation lays claim unto; every true English-man must justifie our Dissatisfaction at it, and believe that we have not so much Resisted the Ordinance of God, as we have Resisted an intollerabel Violation of His Ordinance. . . .

Sir, I own, that we Argue simply about the Affairs of Government; but we Feel True. I have sometimes challenged any man to mention so much as One Thing done by our Late Superiors for the welfare of the Country; a thousand things we all Felt every day doing for the Ruine of it. . . . However I confess (and I know not whether you will count it our Honour or our Blemish) we should have born the Grievances without any Attempts for our own Relief, but our own Supplications to the Great God; for our Applications to the Late King, our only remaining Remedy on earth, we had found ineffectual. But there

---

* A BOSTON SAINT EXPLAINS THE REBELLION AGAINST ANDROS: "An Account of the Late Revolutions in New-England; in a Letter," by A. B. (Boston, 1689). From W. H. Whitmore, ed., *The Andros Tracts*, II, 189–201, in *The Publications of the Prince Society*, VI (Boston, 1869).

happened one Provocation to our people more, which had more than an hundred in it, and such was their Infirmity, if you will call it so, that this they could not bear. A small Body of our Eastern Indians had begun a War upon us: the Occasion of which was as doubtful to us all at first, as the whole Management of it was afterwards mysterious. A Party of Indians which were affirm'd to belong unto that crew of Murderers were seiz'd by the English; but Governour Andros with many favours to them, ordered them to be set at Liberty again: and it's affirmed Those very men have done great part of the mischief sustained by us. An Army of near a Thousand English (and the flower of our Youth) was raised for the subduing of our Enemies, which I believe were much fewer than an Hundred Indians. This Army goes through the tedious Fatigues of a long and cold Winter, many scores of miles to the Northward; and underwent such Hardships that very many or our poor Souldiers perished on the Spot; and it is justly fear'd, That not a few more of them have got their bane, that they will never be strong men again: but not one Indian killed all the while: only Garrisons were here and there planted in the wild woods on a pretence, To keep the Indians from Fishing; which project of Hedging in the Cuckow's, our dull New-Englanders could not understand. . . . In the mean time the Country was wonderfully surprised, with Evidences coming in, from Indians and others, in several parts, which very Strangely concurred in their Testimonies, That there was a Plot to bring in the Indians upon us; and it was easy unto us to conceive, How serviceable another Indian War might have been to the Designs which we saw working for us. These Evidences were so far from being duly enquired into, that the English-men,—who had been inquisitive after them, were put unto all manner of trouble, and must have been destroyed if a Turn had not happend,—thought nothing in the World was more natural than the Agreement between such a Plot and the whole conduct of our Eastern Affairs. . . . While these things were going on, by way of the West-Indies there arrived unto us a few small Intimations, That the Prince of Orange had prospered in his Noble Undertaking to rescue the English Nation from imminent POPERY and SLAVERY. But Sir Edmond Andross took all imaginable care to keep us ignorant of the News, which yet he himself could not be unacquainted with; and one that brought the Princes Declaration with him, was imprisoned for bringing Seditious and Treasonable Papers into the Country with him; and our Oppressors went on without Fear or Wit, in all the methods that could inflame the people to the highest exasperation. The Reports continually coming in from our Eastern Army now caused the Relations of those that were there perishing, here a little to bestir themselves; and they could not forbear forming themselves here and there in the Country unto some Body, that they might consider what should be done for their poor Children, whom they thought bound for a bloody Sacrifice. While this was doing, the people of Boston were Alarmed with Suspicions buzz'd about the Town, by some belonging to the Ship, That the *Rose Frigat* now in our Harbour was intended to carry off our Late Governour for France, & to take any of our English Vessels that might be coming in unto us; and we apprehended our selves in the mean time very ill provided, if an Attacque from any of the French Fleet in the West Indies were perfidiously made upon us. 'T is impossible to express the Agonies which filled the minds of both Town and Country; but the considertion of the extream Ferment which we were boiling in, caused several very leserving Gentlemen in Boston, about the middle of April, to enter into a Consultation, how they might best serve the Distressed Land in its present Discomposures. They considered the Directions given in the Princes Declarations (of which at last we had stolen a sight) and the Examples which the whole Kingdom of England (as far as we could learn) had set before us. They also considered, that the Governour being mov'd to call a General Council in his extraordinary juncture, instead of this, he never so much as called his Council here at hand to communicate unto them any part of the Intelligence relating to the Late Affairs in England. They likewise considered, That though they were above all things inclinable to stay a little, hoping that every day might bring some Orders from England for our safety, yet they could not undertake for such a Temper in all their provoked Neighbours. Wherefore they Resolved, That if either the outragious madness of our Foes, or the impatient motion of our Friends, did necessitate any Action, they would put themselves in the Head of it, and endeavour to prevent what ill effects an Unform'd Tumult might produce.

By that time the Eighteenth of April had given a few Hours of Light unto us, things were push'd on to such extremities that Bostons part in Action seem'd loudly enough and hastily called for. Accordingly, the Captain of the Frigat being then on Shoar, it was determined that he must be made incapable either to Obstruct, or to Revenge the Action, by Firing on, or Sailing from the Town; him therefore, they immediately seized. There were not very many acquainted with the measures that were to be taken; but the Action was now begun, and the Rumour of it running like Lightning through the Town, all sorts of people were presently inspired with the most unanimous Resolution, I believe, that was ever seen. Drums were beaten, and the whole Town was immediately up in Arms.

The first work done, was by small parties here and there about the Town to seize upon these unworthy Men who by repeated Extortions and Abuses had made themselves the objects of Universal Hatred and Indignation. These were many of them secured and confined; but the principal of them, at the First Noise of the Action, fled into the Garrison on Fort-Hill, where the Governours Lodgings were; a place very Commodiously Scituated to Command the whole Town, but not sufficiently Fortify'd.

The Army had no sooner got well together, but a Declaration was Read unto them, unto which they gave an Assent by a very considerable Shout. And upon this, the Gentlemen with such as had come in to their Assistance in the Townhouse, apprehending the Resolutions of the people, drew up a short Letter to Sir Edmond Andross, and dispatched away a couple of their Number with it; the whole armed Body attend them unto the Fortification, whither they Marched with all the Alacrity in the world, and yet with so composed a Sobriety, that I question whether America has ever seen what might equal it. It was expected, That the Garrison might make some Resistance: but they intended to be Owners of it within one-half hour, or perish in the Attempt. When they were just come to beset the Fort, they met the Governour and his Creatures, going down the Hill to the Man-of-Wars Pinace, which was come to fetch them off;

had they not come thither just at that Neck of time, our Adversaries would have got down to the Castle, which is a League below the Town; and in spite of us all, the Frigat would have gone unto them: but our Houses on shore and our Vessels at Sea, must have paid all the satisfaction they could have demanded of us. However, now at the sight of our Forces, the Gentlemen ran back into their Hold; whither the two Gentlemen our Messengers, now advancing, were presented at by the Red-coat Centinels; our Souldiers warned them on pain of Death, to forbear firing; upon which they fled into the Fort, and (as 'tis affirmed) had very terrible Reprimands, for not firing on them. The Gentlemen being admitted, Sir Edmond Andross read what was written to him, and now better understanding his own circumstances, there was a safe conduct given to him, and he with his Associates were brought into the Chamber where he had formerly himself been hatching the Things that now procur'd his more humble Appearance there. He was treated with all the Respect that could be due unto his Character; but he was confined for that Night unto the House of the Late Treasurer, with Guards upon him; and the Rest had their several confinements alotted unto them in such places as were most agreeable to their Quality. With much ado, the Governour gave Order for the surrender of the Fort; and the ceremonies of the surrender were performed by Secretary Randolph, the very man whose lyes and clamours and malicious unwearied Applications had the greatest influence in the overthrow of our former Government.

All the Country round about now began to flock in, and by the next day some Thousands of Horse and Foot were come in from the Towns Adjacent, to express the unanimous content they took in the Action, and offer their utmost Assistance in what yet remained for the compleating of it. The obtaining of the Castle was the main thing that yet called for our cares; but after some stomachful Reluctances the Late Governour gave Order also for the surrender of That; and himself was by the people removed unto the Fort to be kept as a Prisoner there. Thus was the Action managed; and through the singular Providence of God, not one mans Life was lost in the whole Undertaking: There was no Bloodshed, nor so much as any Plunder committed in all the Action; and setting aside the intemperate Speeches of some inconsiderable men (if there were any such) the people generally gave a Demonstration, That they designed nothing but the securing of some great Malefactors, for the Justice which a course of Law would expose them to, and they were loath to treate them with any incivility beyond the bare keeping of them in sufficient custody. No man underwent any Confinement, but such as the people counted the Enemies of the Prince of Orange, and of our English Liberties; it was not any passion for the Service of the Church of England, that exposed any man to hardship; no, even some of that Communion did appear in their Arms to assist the enterprise; tho' the Worship of the Church of England had the disadvantage with us, that most of our Late Oppressors were the great and sole Pillars of it there. The principal Delinquents being now in durance, and the Frigat secured for the Crown of England, our main difficulty was yet behind: Namely what Form we should put our selves into, that the Peace might be kept among us.

A great part of the Country was for an immediate Reassumption of our old Government, conceiving that the vacating of our Charter was a most illegal and injurious thing, and that tho' a Form of Law had cast us out of it, yet we might now return to it at least as a *Vacuum Domicilium*.[1] Others were of the Opinion, That since Judgment was entred against our Charter, and we did not know what Consequence a wrong step at this time might have, therefore 'twas best for the Affairs of the Country to continue in the Hands of a Committee for the Conservation of the Peace, till the daily expected Directions from England should arrive unto us. The latter Expedient was condescended unto, but the Sword yet continued in every man's hands, and for divers weeks the Colony continued without any pretence to Civil Government; yet thro' the mercy of God, all things were under such good Inclinations among us, that every man gave himself the Laws of good Neighbourhood, and little or nothing extravagant was all that while done, besides the seizure of a few more persons who had made themselves obnoxious to the Displeasure of the People. The Gentlemen of the Committee laid their Country under great Obligations by their Studies for the Conservation of our Peace, and it mostly consisted of such as were ever worthy of our esteem. It was made up of them whose Hap 'twas to be in the Head of the late Action; but there were added unto them the most of our old Magistrates, who had not so far concerned themselves in the Affair. Our former Governour, the Honourable Simon Bradstreet, Esq; was Chosen by them for their President: Who tho' he be well towards Ninety Years of Age, has his Intellectual Force hardly abated, but retains a vigour and Wisdom that would recommend a younger man to the Government of a greater Colony.

But when the Day which our ancient Charter appoints for our Anniversary Election drew near, our people grew more and more set upon a Return to the Basis on which our Charter formerly had placed us; and of those who were thus disposed, some were for an Election on the proper Day; others judged that could not be so honestly attended, because a whole County in the Colony was too far to have a Vote in it, and they therefore were for a Re-assumption the Day following. These Two Opinions, with a Third which was for the continuing of their Committee just as it was, filled the Country; and very potent Numbers espoused each of these three opinions: only we all agreed in joyful expectations of having our Charter restored unto us. This Variety of Apprehension was the occasion of much needless Discourse and of many Heart burnings that might as well have been spared. But the Towns on the Eighth and Ninth of May sent in their Representatives at the Desire of the Committee to adjust the matters that concerned a further Necessary Settlement; and after many Debates and some Delays they came to this Temper: That our Ancient Magistrates should apply themselves unto the Conservation of our Peace, and exercise what acts of Government the Emergencies might make needful for us, and thus wait for further Directions from the Authority of England.

The country being put into this posture, all things tended unto a good settlement both of Minds and Things; which were again too much disturbed by a Fire, too justly fear'd to be maliciously kindled (by some that made themselves parties to our Late Enemies) . . . But our people being in a good measure again composed, the World mov'd on in its old orderly pace, until the last week in May when two Ships arrived unto us from England with more perfect News than we had yet been owners of; the first effect thereof was, our Pro-

1 *Vacuum Domicilium*: empty or abandoned residence.

claiming of King William and Queen Mary, with such a Joy, Splendour, Appearance and Unanimity, as had never before been seen in these Territories. The other Colonies are now settling on their old Foundations; and We, according to the Advice now brought us, hasten to put our selves into such a condition as may best answer the performance of our Allegiance to their Majesties.

SIR,

This Relation of our State will doubtless give New-England an interest in the Prayers of all Good Men to whom you shall Communicate it: And Yours I hope will not be wanting for the Wellfare of

Sir,

BOSTON, JUNE 6   Your Servant
1689   A. B. . . .

2] John Palmer Defends Andros' Administration

> When the Massachusetts people toppled Andros' government on April 18, 1689, their leaders published a Declaration listing their grievances and justifying their action. *An Impartial Account*, an answer to the Declaration, was written by John Palmer, a judge and council member under Andros. It challenged most of the Bay colonists' assumptions: that their charter was illegally revoked; that Andros' government was unconstitutional and tyrannical; and that the colonists were equal to subjects in the realm and therefore entitled to the rights of Englishmen. That Palmer was in jail with the rest of the Dominion officers at the time of writing, may have prejudiced somewhat his argument. Still, his was an acceptable point of view if one were a Tory, and he argued it with learning and wit. Italics are omitted.*

REVEREND SIRS,

Two Months have already passed away, since, with Astonishment, I have beheld the most deplorable Condition of this Country; into what a Chaos of Confusion and Distraction have this People run themselves; and in what a labyrinth of Miserys and Perplexitys are they involved! 'Tis high time now to make some serious Reflections on the State of Affairs. . . .

Although 'tis not a doubt but a prevailing Party among you, to gratifie their Malice, Ambition or Revenge, have been the Plotters and Contrivers of these unhappy Troubles; and the better to carry it on, have made use of the deluded Countrymen, as the Monkey did the Cats Foot, to pluck the Chesnut out of the Fire: Yet I shall not meddle in that matter; I will only instance such things as Conversation and Report have brought to my Knowledge, or as I shall find obvious in the *Declaration;* the sum of which is . . . [Here follows a precise summary of the Massachusetts Declaration of April 18, 1689, omitted here since Palmer answers it point by point repeating the charges.]

---

* JOHN PALMER DEFENDS ANDROS' ADMINISTRATION: "An Impartial Account of the State of New England: or, the Late Government there, Vindicated . . . in a Letter to the Clergy there," by John Palmer (London, 1690). From W. H. Whitmore, ed., *The Andros Tracts,* I, 21–62, in *The Publications of the Prince Society,* V (Boston, 1868).

. . . 2. That the Charter was injuriously and illegally Condemned, without giving them timely notice of it, or allowing them to answer for themselves, might bear some weight with it, if true; but it will appear quite otherwise, and that they had opportunity enough to have made Defence on behalf of their Charter, if they had thought fit: For several Years before the proceedings to the Condemnation thereof, our late Soveraign King Charles the Second, by His Letters signified to them the many Complaints that were made to him of their Encroachments, and ill Administration of the Government . . . And when His Majesty was pleased to cause a Writ of *Quo Warranto*[1] to be sued forth against the Charter . . . the General Court would not submit to, or comply therewith. . . .

His Majesty by this, finding that all the easie means he had used, could not bring them to any answer for the Crimes and Misdemeanors laid to their charge, nor produce any thing else but baffles and delays, gave Order to his Attorney-General, to sue out a Writ of *Scire Facias*[2] from the High Court of Chancery, against the Governour and Company; which was accordingly done . . . upon which Writ the said Governour and Company not appearing, another Writ of *Scire Facias,* of the same Tenor issued forth, returnable in Trinity-Term, then next following, when the said Governor and Company appeared by their constituted Attorney and Council; but refused to Plead to the said Writ, only moved for time to send to New England, which not being agreeable with the Rules and Practice of the Court in such Cases, could not be allowed; but in Favour to them a Rule was made, That unless they Pleaded by the first day of the then next Michaelmas-Term, Judgment should be entered by Default: And in that Term, for default of Pleading, Judgment was entered on His Majesty's behalf, and the said Charter adjudged to be void, null, and cancell'd, and that the Liberties and Privileges of the said Governour and Company be Seiz'd into the King's Hands; which was accordingly done. . . . All which Proceedings are most just and legal, according to the Rules and Practice of the Law of England, and agreeable with many Precedents of the like Nature, both ancient and modern.

Besides, all Companies, Corporations, or Bodies Politick, made or granted by Letters Patents, or Charter, from His Majesty, for any part of places beyond the Seas, are by themselves or Agents to be alwaies ready to answer His Majesty in any of his Courts at Westminster . . . as the East-India, Royal African, Bermoodos, and Hudsons-bay Companys are, who have their Trade, Factories, Colonys, and Plantations, abroad in Asia, Africa, and America: And in the like state or condition were the Company or Corporation of Massathusetts-Bay in New England to be . . . wherein if they have neglected their Duty, as well as exceeded their Powers and Privileges granted, and would not put themselves into a condition to be heard, when they ought and might, it is not His Majesty, nor the proceedings of His Courts that are to be blamed, but themselves.

3. That there was a Commission sent to the President, and the successive one, to Sir Edmond Andros, are both true; but that they were Illegal, is a Position too confidently asserted by the Pen-man, who seems to be more a Clergyman

---

1 *Quo Warranto:* a writ requiring demonstration of the right to hold any office or exercise any franchise.

2 *Scire Facias:* a writ requiring that the party proceeded against show cause why a judgment or record should not be enforced.

than a Lawyer; but because the well clearing up of this point will be of great service to the subsequent Discourse, 'twill not be amiss that it be thoroughly considered. I shall therefore lay down this as a certain Maxime, both consonant to Reason and the Laws of the Land, That those Kingdoms, Principalities, and Collonies, which are of the Dominion of the Crown of England, and not of Empire of the King of England, are subject to such Laws, Ordinances, and Forms of Government, as the Crown shall think fit to establish. New England, and all the Plantations are subject to the Dominion of the Crown of England, and not to the Empire of the King of England: Therefore the Crown of England may Rule and Govern them in such manner, as it shall think most fit. . . . [For proof of these points Palmer cites precedents in the history of Wales, Ireland, and several foreign nations.]

The next thing then to be proved is, That New England, and all the English Colonies, are subject to the Dominion of the Crown of England, as Wales and Ireland are, and not to the Empire of the King of England, as Scotland is.

'Tis a fundamental point, consented unto by all Christian Nations, that the first Discovery of a Countrey inhabited by Infidels, gives a Right and Dominion of that Countrey to the Prince, in whose Service and Imployment the Discoverers was sent: Thus the Spaniard claims the West-Indies; the Portugals Brasile: and thus the English these Northern parts of America . . . which being granted, the Conclusion must necessarily be good, and it will follow; That Englishmen permitted to be Transported into the Plantations (for thither without the Kings Licence we cannot come) can pretend to no other Liberties, Privileges, or Immunities there, than anciently the Subjects of England, who removed themselves into Ireland could have done: For it is from the Grace and Favour of the Crown alone that all these Flow, and are dispenced at the pleasure of him that sits upon the Throne; which is plain in the great Charter it self; where, after the Liberties therein granted by the King, it concludes thus . . . To have and to hold of Us, and Our Heirs for ever; which by the Learned Sir Edward Coke is thus explained: These words (saith he) are not inserted to make a Legal Tenure of the King, but to intimate that all Liberties were at first derived from the Crown . . . Barbados, Jamaica, the Leeward Islands, and Virginia have their Assemblies: but it is not *sui juris*,[3] 'tis from the grace and favour of the Crown, signified by Letters Patents under the Broad Seal. But the Laws made by these Assemblies with the consent of the Governour, are no longer in force than till the King is pleased to signifie his Disapprobation of them, which power he hath always reserved to himself, and can, whenever he thinks fit, Repeal and Annul all such as have not been before confirmed by him, or some of his Predecessors.

New England had a Charter, but no one will be so stupid to imagine that the King was bound to grant it them . . . They owe it only to the Grace and Favour of their Sovereign; and if they had made better use of it, to promote the Ends for which it was granted, the weight of those Afflictions under which the People of this Country now groans, would not have lain so heavy upon them, at least they would have less deserved them.

Besides, the Parliament of England have never by any Act of theirs favoured

3 *sui juris*: of their own right.

the Plantations, or declared or inlarged their Privileges; but have all along demonstrated, that they were much differenced from England, and not to have those Privileges and Liberties which England enjoyed, being in all Acts relating to the Plantations, restrained and burthened beyond any in England, as appears by the several Acts made for the increasing of Navigation, and for regulating and securing the Plantation Trade.

I think I have both by good Authority, Practice and Precedent made it plain, That the Plantations are of the Dominion of the Crown of England, and without any regard to *Magna Charta,* may be rul'd and govern'd by such ways and methods as the Person who wears that Crown, for the good and advancement of those Settlements, shall think most proper and convenient: therefore neither the Commission to the President, nor that to Sir Edmond Andros, can be said to be Illegal.

Since then such an one might lawfully be granted, you have great reason to commend the Moderation of the Gentleman who was intrusted with it, and to return Thanks to Almighty God, for placing over you a Person indued with that Prudence and Integrity, that he was so far from exceeding his Commission, that he never put in execution the powers therein granted him. Have there been any Taxes laid upon the People, but such as were settled fifty years since, and made perpetual by Laws of their own making? Any part whereof might be retained, and in force, after the condemnation of their Charter, that the King thought fit. Who hath been transferr'd out of this Territory? Or were ever fewer Rates paid than under him?

And whereas it is also alleaged in the Declaration, That there were courses taken to damp and spoil their Trade, while neither the Honour nor Treasure of the King were advanced: Give me leave to tell you, the same is altogether false, and mistaken, for the very considerable increase of Their Majesties Revenue arising by Customs (not at all altered under Sir Edmond's government) doth sufficiently demonstrate that the regular and lawful Trade of this Territory was exceedingly improved under him: 'Tis true, the Acts for Regulating the Plantation-Trade, and Navigation (little regarded under the Massathusets Government, to the great prejudice of the Revenues of the Crown, and detriment of its European Subjects) were carefully inforced, and their constant and profitable correspondence with Foreigners and Pyrats diligently obstructed, (which was very disagreeable to many Persons who had even grown old in that way of Trade, and was I believe one chief cause of the Revolution, which seems evident by their falling again upon the same measures since that change.) By this is meant Courses taken do damp and spoil their Trade, for which I hope the Government will not lie under any imputations in the Judgment of considering Men. . . .

And 'tis as plain that the King's Subjects, which for many years had groaned under the severity of a Tyrannical and Arbitrary Constitution, deprived of the Laws and Liberties of English-men, forced in their Consciences, suffered death for Religion, and denied Appeals to the King, were eased of those intollerable Burthens, and allowed the free Exercise of their Religion, and the benefit of the Laws of England, which were duly and truly administered unto them, by which the Honour of the King is advanced to the highest pitch. . . .

9. That the Privileges of *Magna Charta,* and other Liberties of English-men

were denied them, is a thing which can never be made appear; however, admitting it, I have sufficiently discuss'd that Point in the Third Article. By the Persons said to be severely Fined, for peaceably objecting against raising of Taxes without an Assembly, I conjecture are meant the Ipswich-men, who were so far from a peaceable objecting, that they assembled themselves in a riotous manner, and by an Instrument conceived in Writing, did Associate and oblige themselves to stand by each other in opposition to the Government; and by their Example, influenced their Neighbours to do the like. And this by the Law is esteemed an Offence of that Nature, that it is next door to Rebellion; for which they were Indicted, Tryed, and Convicted, either by Verdict or their own Confession. . . .

11. That any one hath been Imprisoned, without being charged with Crime or Misdemeanor, is an Allegation which I dare be bold to say can never be proved; I have heard indeed an *Habeas Corpus* demanded upon the Statute of the 31. C. 2. was denied in Major Appleton's Case, (who was one of the Ipswich-men before-mentioned;) but let any considering Man peruse the Act, and I believe he will be easily convinced, that it is particularly limitted to the Kingdom of England; besides, he was committed only because he would not find Sureties for the good Behaviour, and the question was not whether he should be Bailed; for upon finding the said Sureties, he must have been discharged of course; so that it was not the want of an *Habeas Corpus* detain'd him in Prison, but his own wilful and obstinate Humour; if they do but consider well how many Gentlemen lie now in stinking Goals, and close Prisons, without either Mittimus or Crime laid to their charge, and without the allowance of an *Habeas Corpus,* although demanded; I am sure they cannot but blush, when they read that part of the Declaration.

12. That Jurymen were fined and imprisoned for refusing to lay their hands to the Book, I presume is a mistake; probably they may have been fined for their contempt, and sent to Prison for not paying that Fine, which by the Law may be Justified: for every Court may fine any man for a contempt in open Court, and they themselves are Judges of the Contempt.

. . . Prescription is a good and sufficient Law, the form of laying the Hand upon the Book hath been the only modus of Swearing time out of mind; therefore the laying the Hand on the Book in Swearing, is a good Law, and the Judges cannot dispence with it, *Salvo Sacramento;* [4] if they did, a Judgment in such a case would be erroneous and reversible, and 'tis dangerous to admit of Innovations.

The Common Law of New England is brought in, to Warrant the lifting up the Hand; but I take that to be *rara Avis in Terris;* [5] for I challenge the whole Territory to produce one Precedent of such a resolved case; but perhaps by it, Prescription is intended; if it be, that will as illy serve the turn as th'other; for the Colony hath not been long enough settled, to claim any advantage by that Right; neither if it had, would it be admitted without apparent violation of their Charter, being absolutely repugnant to the Laws of England. . . .

21. That your Churches and Ministers have been discouraged, is so general

---

4 *Salvo Sacramento:* without breaking their own oaths.
5 *rara Avis in Terris:* a rare bird in these lands; unique or unprecedented.

an Head, and the rest of the Declaration so particular, that it gives me cause to suspect the truth of it; and I shall hardly alter my Opinion, until any one of you be instanced, who kept himself within his Province, and only medled with that which belong'd to him.

'Tis the Church of England that hath most reason to complain, only you cry Whore first: For at Sir Edmond's Arrival, they were the only People destitute of a Place to Worship in, until, by Advice and Consent of the Council, the New Meeting House, in Boston, was borrowed, and made use of by them, but at inconvenient Hours; in the Morning after Eleven, and sometimes as their Service was prolong'd at Twelve; and after Four in the Afternoon, which with patience was endured, tho' the Enmity of that People, to the Church of England, was such, that they grudged them that small Accomodation, and shewed their uneasiness therein; which was soon removed, by the Governour's encouraging a Church to be built, and compleated in Boston, at the Charge of those of that Communion, where the Publick Worship, and Service of God hath been attended, until the late Insurrection, when the Minister was forced to leave the Countrey, and Church, for his own safety; And has not the Minister been before this publickly affronted, and hindred from doing of his Duty? What scandalous Pamphlets have been Printed to villifie the Liturgy? And are not all of that Communion daily called Papist Doggs, and Rogues, to their Faces? How often has the plucking down the Church been threatned? One while, it was to be converted to a School, and anon, 'twas to be given to the French Protestants. And whoso will but take the Pains to survey the Glass Windows, will easily discover the Marks of a Malice not common; I believe 'tis the first National Church, that ever lay under such great Disadvantages, in a Place, where those that dissent from her, ought to expect all things from her Grace and Favour.

22. Should I undertake to recount all the particulars of the late Indian Rebellion, this would swell to a bulk bigger than ever I designed it; I shall only tell you, you must look at home; for the reasons of those troubles, which is well known, began when his Excellency was above Five Hundred Miles off at New-York, and that the Folly and Rashness of the People, drew it on their own Heads. The Governours Conduct in that Affair has been so prudent and discreet, that I have no reason to doubt but your Council of Safety, &c. Into whose hands, all the Papers relating to that business did fall, are very well satisfied with it . . . To what a degree of Madness and Impiety are we then grown, so Falsly and Maliciously, to Recriminate a Person, who for your Defence and Security, hath so generously exposed himself to the Hardships of that Cold and Uncomfortable Clymate, and the Fatigues of War, against a Barbarous and Savage People? . . .

24. That it was either their Duty to God [to overthrow Andros' government], or that they had the Nobility, Gentry, and Commons of England, for their Presedent, I cannot by any means allow; and I am amaz'd to see Christians call that a Duty, which God has so remarkably shewed his Displeasure against, in all Countries, and Ages; Is not Rebellion, as the Sin of Witchcraft? . . . And as it is far from being their Duty to God, so there is no Parallel between the Proceedings of the Lords Spiritual and Temporal in England, and theirs here; for the Design of Establishing Popery and Arbitrary Government,

in this Colony, is altogether Ridiculous and Incredible; for, who was to have effected it? Could those few of the Church of England, that with the hazard of their Lives and Fortunes, so lately opposed it in Europe; and that in all Ages have been the only Bulwark against it? Or were the Presbyterians, Independants, or Anabaptists, to have brought this about? It must have been one of those, for I dare be bold to say, there are not Two Roman Catholicks betwixt this and New-York.

I have sufficiently demonstrated, in the third Article, the little Right we have to any other Government in the Plantations; and that we cannot justly call that Arbitrary, which by the Law we are obliged to submit to: So that betwixt their Condition and ours, there can be no Parity.

As their Reasons and yours were different, so are the Measures which have been taken; for his late Highness the Prince of Orange, having well-weighed and considered the tottering Condition of the Protestant Religion all over Europe, thought it was high time for him to take up Arms, as well for his own Preservation, as that of his Neighbours and Allies. We do not find, that notwithstanding the Danger that hung over their heads, the People of England took up Arms to right themselves; but instead thereof, they became humble Suppliants to his Highness for his Favour and Protection, which he was pleased to grant them: Neither do we find, that the Lords Spiritual and Temporal, assumed any Authority, for which they had no colour of Law: As they are Peers, they are invested with the highest Authority, and are the grand Conservators of the Peace of the Nation; they never left their Duty and Allegiance to his late M A J E S T Y, until he first left the Kingdom; and all Things were transacted in his Name, and by his Authority, until the very minute the Prince was proclaimed; who came not by force to Conquer and Subject the Nation to a foreign Power, nor to Subvert and Destroy the lawful Government, but to Maintain and Support the same, in a peaceable manner, by a Free Parliament: The Prince, nor Peers, never abrogated nor altered any of the lawful Powers of the Nation, but strengthned and confirmed all that were capable of bearing Office, by which there was always a due Administration of Justice. The Sword was never said to Rule and Sway; and by consequence that Confusion and Disorder avoided, which their Illegal and Arbitrary Proceedings have precipitated us into.

As to the fanciful Stories of Macquas, Subterranean Vaults, Fire-Works, French Frigats, poisoning the Soldiers to the Eastward, &c. they are so apparently false, and strangely ridiculous, that by this time, no Man in his Wits can believe them; and I need no Argument to confute the Credit of those monstrous Follies, since Time and Experience have sufficiently demonstrated them to be meer Lyes and Inventions.

And now I hope all sober thinking Men are convinced, That the before-alledged Reasons, are in themselves either absolutely false, or of little moment; and consequently no sufficient ground for taking up Arms. . . .

But, perhaps, they may fancy, that this Action of theirs, hath extreamly obliged their Majesties, and that all things now are become justly due to the Merits of their Services: 'Twill do very well if it be so understood; but I cannot see the least probability of such a Construction, for they have sufficiently manifested in their *Declaration;* that Self-Interest, fondness of their former popular Government, and aversion to the Government establish'd from England, was the first and principal Motive to their Undertakings; and their Progress doth plainly demonstrate, that they have only made use of their Majesties Names, the better to effect their own Designs, whilst every thing that hath any relation to them lies neglected and unregarded, without any Recognition of their Authority over those Dominions, or the least acknowledgment of their submission to such Orders as should come from them, saving what particularly related to some few ill Men, (as they call them,) whom they have imprisoned and detained, without any Law or Reason: So that they have rashly and imprudently adventured their A L L upon a Chance, (not an equal one,). . . .

I hope every good Man will seriously consider the foregoing Discourse, and suffer himself to be guided by the Dictates of Reason, and not of Humor and Prejudice; and then I am well assured, it will be evident enough that they have mistaken their Measures, and that a due sence thereof, and a timely recess, will more advantage them, than an obstinate and wilful perseverance; and that nothing but such a Remedy can restore their almost-perishing and undone Country, to a lasting Peace and happy Settlement; for which, shall ever be the hearty Prayers of

Your humble Servant,

J. PALMER. . . .

3] Nicholas Bayard Describes Leisler's Rule by the Sword

> Nicholas Bayard was nephew of old Peter Stuyvesant and an officeholder in New York since before the conquest of 1664. A member of Andros' council at New York and a colonel of the militia, Bayard epitomized the faction of privileged favorites against whom Leisler and his supporters rebelled. He frequently refers to himself in the account as "the Collonell." Jacob Milborne, who attempted unsuccessfully to bring Albany into line with the rebel government, was Leisler's chief aide.*

A Brief Deduction and Narrative of the Severall Disorders, Abuses, Enormities, & Insolencies lately Committed by JACOB LEYSELER and severall of his Associatts att New Yorke, since the 27th day of Aprill A° 1689.

No SOONER came the news at New Yorke that Boston and some of the neighbouring Collonies had by violence and force of armes subverted the Governement setled over them by the authority from the Crowne of England, and had imprisoned the Governour Sr Edmund Andros, and other chief Ministers; but immediately thereuppon Itt was Resolved by the Leftent Governour ffrancis

---

* NICHOLAS BAYARD DESCRIBES LEISLER'S RULE BY THE SWORD: "Colonel Bayard's Narrative of Occurrences in New-York, from April to December, 1689." From *Documents Relative to the Colonial History of the State of New-York*, III (Albany, 1853), 636–48.

Nicholson and the few members of the Councell left at New Yorke for to conveane the Mayor, Aldermen Common Councell, and all the Military Officers of the Citty of New Yorke, to acquaint them thereof; and withall to desire them for to joyne with the Councel in one boddy and convention, for to consult and advise from time to time what might conduce for the common peace of ye people, and the safety of the Governm^t.

In pursuance to wch s^d resolve the s^d Convention being conveaned att the Citty Hall accepted thereof; and since as occasion offered did frequently meete and make severall suitable Resolves, Orders and Proclamations for the Preservation of the peace of the Inhabitants, and the most speedy satisfying of the Citty of New Yorke, and of the ffort, against any Invasion either of the ffrench or other fforreigne Ennemy untill due orders should arrive from the authority of ye Crowne of England, as by the Minutes of the s^d Convention will more fully & att large appeare.

Itt was alsoo Resolved and accordingly putt in practice, that in regard the ffort was but weakly provided of Souldiers in pay that a competent number of the citty's Militia should supply that defect, either by whole companies or lesser quantities as the danger Required, att the discretion of the Collonell of the Regiment, regulated by the Major Vote of the Captens of the severall companies.

The orders for the s^d ffortifications where no sooner made but wth all possible speed the materialls where provided by the s^d Collonell and the Committy with him appointed, and thereuppon wth all vigour the worke was begun by the labour of the inhabitans and in few dayes brought to a very great perfection; Although verry much obstructed by the many discords and divisions promoted by the ill contrivances of Jacob Leiseler and his associatts, both in the convention and elsewhere, endeavouring to stirr up the minds of the people to sedition and rebellion agst the established Authority, and to destroy the Revenue, uppon hopes thereby to be exalted, and reipe some particular benefitt, he the said Leiseler having a shipp loaden with Wines in the port for which he refused to pay the customes and enticed others to do the same.

This continues untill the 31th of May when the Mabble [Rabble?] by ye instigation of ye s^d Jacob Leiseler and severall of his associatts, under ye command of Joost Stool being a Sergeant, roose in actuall rebellion, and by a mad and franticq humour (without any cause they then could give) took to armes, and with force and violence entred and seized the ffort, which was surrendered them without the least opposition by the Lt Henry Cuyler who was intrusted to guard the same, whilst the Lt Governour and the s^d Convention where in Councell att the Citty Hall to settle some disorders lately happened.

Collonell Bayard with severall of the Commission officers att the desire of the Convention went up to the ffort endeavouring to putt a stop to their rebellious proceedings; and upon enquiry for what reasons they had soo entred the ffort, answer was made by the s^d Joost Stoll their Speaker (being in drinck as most of the rest alsoo where) that they disowned all the Authority of the Governement, and in particular denyed any obedience to ye lawfull commands of their s^d Collonell: saying, wee are long enough deluded, and led by the noaze, wee have now secured the ffort, and will have the Kayes of the ffort and of the stores alsoo; and told the s^d Collonell in a scornfull manner that it was best for him to depart, etz,—

Whereuppon the Collonell with the rest of the Commission Officers (except Capt. Leyseler who disobeyed the s^d Collonell's commands) returned towards the Citty Hall, for to give the Convention an account of what past at ye ffort. But immediatly thereuppon one Serg^t William Churcher, with a party of armed men, went up to the Citty hall, whilst the full convention was sitting and by threatening words forced the Lt Governor to deliver up the s^d kayes to Capt. Lodewick.

The Convention considering that this currant of the people's furie was not to be stopt att present without hazard of great Bloodshead Resolved to be passive; only desired the Capt^ns not to head their men during this Rebellion, and Ordered that the Monny of the Revenue and Country Tax etz. amounting to the summe of £773.12. then in Tresury at ye fort should be removed att ye howse of M^r ffredrick Phillips. . . .

But Jacob Leyseler and his associatts seing that none did approve of his rebellious proceedings only a few hot headed and meane sort of people, and that hardly a man of repute or sence was seene amongst them, neither than any of the Authority or Magestracy of the Civill Governm^t nor any of the rest of the Commission Officers did acquies or concurre therein, but had absolutely protested against the same; and for feare that their hot headed men would recant and leave them in the lurch, the s^d Jacob Leyseler and his associatts took in hand their former practice, to invent lyes and falcetyes, noising abroad that all those that would not be of his rebellious faction where ill affected men and persons not to be trusted, that the Lt Governor and all the Members of the Councell where papists, that they were roages and traitors who intended to secure the Governm^t for the late King James, whoose wicked Creatures and Pensionaries they where, that they had defrauded the Citty and Government of itts Revenue, with a multitude of such and the like falceties, which they too blazed abroad by verball words, and pamphlets in writing, throughout the Citty and Governm^t that some of the ignorant and innocent sort of people where deluded, infested and poisoned thereby.

And to the end this Rebellion still might not lye only at the ye door of the s^d Leyseler and a few of his associatts, butt to encrease the number of their faction; he the s^d Leyseler first noysed in his owne company, then being on the guard in the ffort, that (since the Protestant Religion and the safety of the Governm^t was in eminent danger) he would have all the Inhabitants to meete, and to signe and prevente the same and therefore would have all the Militia in the ffort, and gave warning accordingly over night to severall of his faction in the other companies, together with a signe when they should all come into the ffort att the first allarm, intising them not to obey their Commission Officers, if any should hinder them to march into the ffort, at the signe given.

Whereuppon he the s^d Leyseler on the 3^d day of June made a falls allarm to have all the Militia in Armes, wch accordingly was effected, butt as soone itt was discovered only to be a falce allarm and a contrivance of the s^d Leyseler, orders where given by the Collonel to the severall Captens not to march to the usuall place of Parade before the ffort, who alsoo gave their commands accordingly, but where disobeyed by the instigation of severall of s^d Leyseler's faction who where instructed in every company and pressed first to appeare in the s^d place of Paraade before the ffort, and when alsoo the like commands where given there to the severall companies for to move from thence, the s^d commands where, by the pressures of the s^d Jacob Leyseler, Joost Stoll, Wm Churcher and severall of their associatts, in contempt of the authority, not only disobeyed, but openly contradicted, untill an absolute Muteny and uproare was occasioned in wch most part of the souldiers left their coullers, Captens and Commission officers and fled to the ffort, for what reason most could not tell, unlesse to follow the greatest number.

Att the s^d Souldiers comming to the ffort great signes of Joy where given by Shouts and Hozars, where they found a paper prepared by the s^d Leyseler for to be signed unto by the Souldiers, tending for to approve of their rebellious proceedings, only guilded with a speciall pretence, that the same was for the preservation of the protestant Religion, and of the ffort and Citty, till orders should arrive from his Royall Highnesse the Prince of Orange, truely a fair pretence to raise a Rebellion, falce alarme, muteny, and uproare in which severall of the Magistracy and Commission officers, besides many others of their Majesties loyall subjects where exposed to the uttermost danger of their lives, and undoubtedly no lesse thing was intended, for it's evedent that the s^d Leyseler since has boasted that he had charged all the great gunns & small armes in ye ffort, on purpose to fire upon the Towne unlesse they had come in otherwise, and that it had been good some had been slayne in that furie for itt would not be at quiet before five or six were despatched, etz.

Notwithstanding all these contrivances itt could only delude and ensnare a parcel of ignorant and innocent people, almost none but of the Dutch Nation, the tenth man not knowing what he had signed, a notion being put in many of there heads that by a Voate of Parliament, all Chartres and Priviledges where to be restored to all places of the Dominions, and they be put in the same state as they were in the year 1660. And by consequence this Governm^t to be restored to the Dutch, and therefore no orders from the authority or Crowne of England, but only from his Royall Highnesse the Prince of Orange would serve their termes, as their printed Proclamation likewise intimates.

But to bring in alsoo some men of note & repute for to signe, severall Messengers where sent to some of the Captens, with horrible threatenings that night to plunder all their howses, except they came in the ffort and signed alsoo to s^d Leyseler's dictated Proclamation, in soo much that the said Captens at last went to the ffort, intending to passify the mad and violent temper of the s^d Leyseler and his associatts, but where forced to signe unlesse they would run the hazard of being killed as threatenings where made.

In all this time no cause or reason could be given for any of the s^d irregular proceedings only some days after a pamphlet was published but not affixed, or no Coppy allowed to be had, intituled, A DECLARATION OF THE INHABITANTS AND SOULDIERS BELONGING UNDER THE SEVERALL COMPANIES OF THE TRAINE BANDS OF NEW YORKE, which said Declaration severall weekes after came out in print antidated the 31th day of May, and found to be grounded on a Deposition which Hendrick Cuyler severall dayes after should give and sweare unto, which s^d Deposition and Declaration in themselves most nonsensicall and rediculous being cramd up with severall contradictions and falceties must needs expose all concerned therein to be rash and foolish medlers wth that wch did not concerne them. . . .

But that the Lt Govern^r Nicholson (as is falsly alledged) or any of the Councel or Magestracy where any wicked Creatures or Pensionaries of the late Govern^r Dongan, is a most notorious and malicious falshood, since they have sufficiently manifested in all their actions & proceedings their uttermost zeal for the Protestant cause and their loyalty for the safety of the Governm^t under ye present authority of ye Crowne of England.

And for the second part of their s^d pamphlet or Declaration, alledging that they were cajolled and terrified out of their reason may be true enough, since their actions and proceedings are more becoming such then otherwise, but only occasioned by their owne false notions & feares. But that the Lieu^t Governour ever made any infringement on their Libertyes, Properties, or Laws (as is alledged) is utterly denyed, and will be found to be a falce and mallicious aspersion, Wherefore all the authority and Magestracy must do the Lt Govr that common justice, and certify that ever since the power of Governm^t by the disabling of Sr Edmund Andros devolved into his hands nothing was acted in the affaires of the Government, but what was concluded and agreed unto by the generall convention . . .

And relating the alledged threatnings of ye s^d Lt Govr (which are utterly denyed by him) tho' tenne dayes after ye date of their said pamphlet sworne to by Hendrick Kuyler before a person not duly qualified; The first part thereof is disowned by the Corporall and Interpreter himselfe, and for the other part that the Lt Govern^r had said only to him ye said Kuyler, that he was not sure of his life, nor to walke the streetes, because there where soo many Roagues in the Towne, and that therefore before it should go longer after that manner he would sett the Towne in fire, to wch the Lt Govr denyed the latter words, to sett the Town in fire, to be spoken Butt affirmed that the words where, that before he should live longer after that manner, he would rather see their Towne burnt or sunck; and why or for what reason the words of s^d Kuyler (whoos weaknesse in the English language is evident to all, and owned by himselfe, and who is of that timerous temper y^t he often is troubled in his mind with most strange imaginations) should be of any more credit then the words of the Lt Govern^r will by no man of sence, to whom the persons, parts and conversations of both are knowne, be thought reasonable. . . .

. . . Now that all these false Notions and feares raised & occasioned only by the malice & ambition of a few hot headed men, should be of that import, vallidity & consequence for any subject, without the least Comission or authority, to subvert and unhinge their Mayesties sole Governm^t by Law established, will now be thought reasonable, unlesse by such as for their owne ambition mallice and particular ends expect to reipe some benefitt thereby.

For wch reason, and no other, the s^d Leyseler and those of his faction have subverted their Mayesties s^d Governm^t and introduced an arbitrary Power, rueling absolute by the sword which they exercized for severall weekes blindfolding the ignorant and innocent people with that speciall and guilded pretence, the same to be for their Mayesties service and for the safety of the Governm^t and of the Protestant Religion, tho none was in any danger, but secure under an established government; with further exclamations against the Authority, that in regard the late King James was departed out of the Kingdom that therefore all the Commissions of the Authority and Mayestracy where utterly void, and that those in power where creatures and Pensionaries of the late King, who had created themselves, and for those reasons not to be trusted nor obeyed. Whereby the s^d Leyseler and those of this faction assumed the absolute power in an arbitrarie manner, to hector and domineere over the lives, liberties and properties of the people, dayly committing all manner of enormities and insolencies whatsoever.

The civill authority and Magestracy of the Governm^t and Citty perceiving the eminent danger & possibility of stopping the furie & currant of the rebellion resolved to be passive, and continued soo untill the 22th of June, when Information was given that Mayor Gold and Capt. fitz where come with orders for to proclaime their May^{ties} Wherefore the Mayor, Aldermen & Common Councill endeavoured to procure the s^d orders & proclamations to the end they might enjoy that happines and honour to proclaime their s^d Mayesties as in duty they thought to be obliged; but it being denyed them that Ceremony was observed (tho verry disorderly) by the s^d Leyseler & his associatts; Yett by what order or authority unknowne.

And tho' their s^d Mayes^{ties} where thus disorderly proclaimed yett no care was taken for the safety and security of the subject, to publish their Mayesties gracious proclamation of the 14th of ffeb^r last confirming all Protestant Sheriffs, Justices of ye peace Collectors and receivors of the Revenue etz. Wherefore the s^d Mayor, Aldermen and Common Councel, with much difficulty having procured the s^d proclamation made publication thereof.

And in regard the Collect^r Matthew Plowman being a Roman Catholicq was exempted by the s^d proclamation for to continue in that office, the Councel (who were intrusted to secure their May^{ties} Revenue) imediatly thereuppon suspended the said Plowman from officiating any longer, and on the following day by and with the advice of the Mayor, Aldermen and Common Councell made a Resolve for the securing of the s^d Revenue, and did appoint, commissionate, and accordingly sweare four Commissioners, vizt Côll Nicholas Bayard one of the Councell, Mr Paullus Richard, one of the Aldermen and Justice of the peace, Mr John Haynes & Mr Thomas Wenham, Marchants, for to collect and secure the s^d Revenue, wthout any fee or sallary for themselves, untill the arrival of orders from s^d May^{ties}, and made publication thereof by affixing their s^d Resolve at the usuall place before the Custom howse doore; In pursuance to wch said resolve, and by vertue of that Power and authority, the s^d Commissioners did meete that afternoone at the Custom house in order to settle the affaires of the s^d Customs & Revenue: But the said Commissioners where suddanly obstructed and stop^t in ye prosecution of their s^d duty, by Jacob Leyseler, Joost Stoll and some of their associatts, who with a party of armed souldiers entred the Custom howse with most horrible thretnings and exclamations against the s^d Comissioners, and the authority that established them, that they where all Roagues, Rascalls, Villans & Divells, that had created themselves, and stood up for the late King James etz: with many other filthy aspersions, as p^r the Journall of the Collonell Bayard may more at large appeare; And altho the s^d Comissioners moderatly answered that the s^d Leyseler was under a mistake and did alsoo convince him thereof; Yett since the s^d Comissioners perceived that not their May^{ties} Authority and Lawes, but y^t the sword now ruled, they offered to be passive and depart the Custom howse, if he the s^d Leyseler would only command the same: Yett notwithstanding he the s^d Leyseler, Joost Stoll and some of their associatts not only aiming for to destroy the s^d Revenue but alsoo to massakre some of the Cômission^rs and especially the Collonell, whom they suspected to be the most forward and zelous for the securing of the s^d Revenue, and had often thwarted & crost their irregular Proceedings. Wherefore all pressures where made, by the s^d Leyseler, to exasperate his drunken crue for to massakre the s^d Collonell, and severall more of their May^ties loyall subjects, causing forthwith an allarme & uproare to be raised throughout the Citty, Crying out Treason, Treason, wth the like exasperating expressions and thô the s^d Coll by providence was rescued from their bloody designes, Yett a strict search and enquiry was made for severall dayes, with severe and horrible thretnings to cut him and others in peeces, with severall other barbarous expressions; In soo much that the s^d Collonell, and many of the Magestrates, gentry, chief Marchants, and Cittizens where forced to obscund themselves, but especially the s^d Coll: who by the advice of the Councel and Magestracy retired for safety to Albany, where he was forced to continue for the space of severall months, in regard the s^d thretnings where still continued to be executed against him by the s^d Leyseler and his associatts; and no protextion of their Mayt^ies Laws could be obtained, since the s^d Leyseler now ruled absolute by ye sword as afores^d. . . .

Att this deplorable conjuncture the s^d Leyseler and his associatts haveing in this manner subdued (as much in them lay) all the authority and Magestracy of the Governm^t destroyed the revenue, and raised an absolute rebellion. Yett did not stop there, but in contempt of their Mayesties authority soo lately proclaimed and in particular and expresse opposition ag^st their May^ties s^d proclamation of the 14th of ffeb. last, proceeded further for to moddel and fraame a new sort of an arbitrary power and Government, and by the Votes of a few of their faction in a riotous manner made a choice and election of some few ill affected and factious men, for to be their Representatives & Governours, under the Titull, Stile & Denomination of A Committee of Safety, a power and authority never suffered or exercised in any of the reigns of their May^ties most glorious ancestors, unles in times of rebellion; wch said pretended committy together with the s^d Leyseler and some of his associatts, ever since the 28th day of June, have usurped and exercized all manner of Jurisdiction and Government, even over the lives, liberties, properties Lawes & Religion of their May^ties liege people, dayly committing by themselves and their Officers and Souldiers all manner of enormities, abuses & Insolensies . . .

Coll. Bayard (as being the Chief Ey sore of the s^d Leyseler & his faction) continued all this time at Albany, wayting only for the happy arrivall of their Mayesties Govern^r. Wherefore severall threatnings where made by the s^d Leyseler & his crue forcebly to fetch the s^d Collonel wth severall of the Chief Magestrates & officers from Albany, and by sending of severall of his Creatures and seditious letters made all pressures & endeavors to desquiet and unhinge all manner of Governm^t in that County of Albany and in the County of Ulstor, insinuating and intising the ignorant & meane people of those Counties to the like sedition and rebellion against the established authority, But was (during ye s^d Coll's aboade there) prevented by the Watchfull endevors of the Authority and chief Inhabitants of the s^d Counties, which alsoo quietted the five Cantons Indian Nations who being entred into a Warre against Canida by any such Revolution would undoubtedly have bene verry much disturbed (haveing their Chief Dependancy uppon the present Authority there) if not soly recanted to accept of the great offers of the ffrench to the uttermost ruyne of all their May[ties] Collonies on this continent. But in regard of the approaching winter and other pressing occurrances the s[d] Coll. Bayard was necessitated to return from Albany to New Yorke, where he arrived on y[e] 29th of October, and at his landing being about two houres before day he received Informations . . . that the s[d] Leyseler had made severall thretnings against some of the chief Inhabitants and especially against the Coll. and his son, that he wished they had bene destroyed and massakred in his former furies and false allarmes. . . . Wherefore the s[d] Coll. further resolved to obscunde himselfe till releefe from England.

Some few dayes after the Coll's returne from Albany, a party of about 60 armed men under the Command of Jacob Milborn, where sent up to Albany by the s[d] Leyseler and his associatts under a faire pretence of assisting that County ag[st] any incursions from Canida, but as it afterwards appeared only contrived for to unhinge all manner of Governm[t] there, and to inthrall that County, and the County of Ulstor, with the like tiranny & slavery, equall wth some parts of the County of New Yorke, King's County, Queen's County and the Counties of Berge and Weschester most part of whose Inhabitants are concerned in the Rebellion (whilst all the rest of this Province and New Yarsie still do maintaine their established Authority and abhor the s[d] Leyseler's rebellious proceedings) ffor soo it is, that the s[d] Jacob Milborn at his arivall at Albany endeavored imedeatly to raise all the people into a Rebellion against the authority, whoose Commissions, he declared, where utterly void & of no effect, since they were graunted under that unlawfull King James (altho' the s[d] authority had newly sworne faith & allegiance to their now May[ties] King W[m] and Queen Mary, and where confirmed by their s[d] May[ties] gracious proclamation of the 14th of ffeb. last) and did further send his seditious letters to the severall Townes of the s[d] County inviting the people to meet him in the Citty of Albany for to receive their Rights Priviledges and Liberties as by his s[d] letters more fully appeares . . .

Uppon receipt of these and other the like seditious letters from those of his faction the Country people for a great part flockt to him in the Citty hall, where he made them a long speech, and enticed them to a new Election of Magestrates & officers, which being prevented by the endeavours of the authority, he the s[d] Milborn presumed further in a hostile manner to attempt the invading of their May[ties] ffort then under the command of the Mayor of Albany, marching with his men in arms up to the ffort, demanding the surrender thereof into his hands from the s[d] Mayor; But was shamefully defeated and hurried not only from the s[d] ffort, but even out of y[e] s[d] Citty of Albany in soo much that he was forced to leave there all, or most part, of his men. . . .

Coll. Bayard (who had bene forced to obscund himselfe from his habitation at New Yorke upwards the space of foure months to escape the danger of being massakred) received Intelligence that his only son was in a dying Condition, after an extream sickness of about 3 months past, sent thereupon a letter to y[e] Justices of y[e] Peace in New Yorke, desiring the protextion of their May[ties]

Lawes and Governm^t ag^st the s^d Leyseler, offering to give in security, to what vallue they pleased to appoint, for to answer the law to any complaint or accusation that could be alledged ag^st him. But received only for answer tho' they knew of no crime or accusation that could be laid to his charge, yett since the sword now ruled in their Citty, they where obstructed in the executing of their Commissions, and could not give him any releefe ag^st the s^d Leyseler therein.

Whereuppon the s^d Coll: sent his warrant to Capt. Abram De Peyster, and Capt. Jno De Bruyn, renewing his former Commands unto them, to beare good faith & allegeance to o^r Soveraigne Lord and Lady King William and Queen Mary, and to be obedient to the lawful Commands of the Civill Authority within the s^d Citty and in particular to those of the Justices of the Peace, and to desist from councelling, abetting, or assisting the illegall and unwarrantable proceedings of the s^d Leyseler and his associatts, as they would answer the contrary att their perrills; which s^d warrant the s^d Capt^s saw cawse to send up to the s^d Leyseler, who thereuppon caused all those of his faction outt of the Citty and County of New Yorke, King's County, & Bergen County to appeare at the ffort with their armes, where he blazed amongst them his old newes, that the Lieu^t Govern^r Nicholson, that Popish dogg, was turned a Privateer, and would never show his face in England, etz. And that he had discovered a plott, in which Bayard with about 300 men would attempt to retake ye ffort for the late King James, and that a great party of lathers, and other materialls where alreddy prepared etz. Whereby he perswaded the Country people by turnes to watch in the fort besides some of the Cittizens, and caused them to make a new subscription, in substance for to be true & ffaithfull to King W^m and Queen Mary and to be obedient to the Committy of Safety as the Supream authority, and him the s^d Leyseler as their Commander in Chief, which if any person did but scrupple to signe such were horribly thretned, and cryed out for King James' creatures and soo turned out of the fort, a notion being put into the ignorant peoples heads, that a great number of subscriptions would enduce a Govern^r at his arrivall to give them better articles & Priviledges, yea some of the worser sort had the confidence to vapor, that if a new Govern^r would not approve of their actions, or should not behave himselfe as he ought to ye minds of ye people, they knew now the way how to lay the Govern^r aside and to send them from whence they came, or words to that effect. . . .

In this confusion was the Governm^t inthraled without any hopes of resettlem^t unlesse by the arrival of their May^ties orders; When Mr John Riggs as an Expresse from their May^ties arrived here on the 8th of this instant month of Decemb^r with two packetts directed as followeth. *To our Trusty and well Beloved Francis Nicholson Esqr o^r Lt Govern^r & Comander in Chief of o^r Province of New Yorke in America, or in his absence to such as for ye time being take care for ye preservation of the peace, & administring the Lawes in o^r s^d province of New Yorke in America,* wch said two packetts the said Jno Riggs declared that he should deliver to their May^ties Council as soone the Members thereof, that where absent & fled, could be sent for out of ye Country (it being undoubtedly an answer from their Mayesties uppon the letters & complaints of the s^d Lt Govern^r & Council sent by him the s^d Riggs in May last p^r ye shipp Beaver) But before the s^d Councel could meete, the said Jno Riggs was comanded to the fort and forced to deliver the s^d Packetts to Jacob Leyseler as by his Certificate will appeare; whereby the s^d Leyseler since has taken uppon him the titull of Lt Govern^r and Comander in Chief of the Province of New Yorke, by their May^ties Commands, tho' no such command appeares, nor as yet no proclamation thereof being made according to custome, it being now the 13th of December and five days after the arrivall of the s^d packetts, when this Narrative of the Chief Occurrances since the beginning of the Rebellion to this date, was sent for England to his Lordship the Secretary of Staate and the Secretary of the Plantations by one of their May^ties most loyall thô suffering subjects.

N. BAYARD

New Yorke
13 Xber 1689.

4] Leisler's "Martyrdom for King William and Queen Mary"

> For several years after the death of Leisler, New York was rent by a bitter
> factional struggle between those who defended and those who opposed him
> and his two-year regime. Just prior to the arrival of a new governor in 1698,
> the anti-Leislerians published a pamphlet severely critical of Leisler's govern-
> ment. *Loyalty Vindicated*, published at Boston, was the Leislerians' answer.
> It remains the best defense of the rebel leader and his administration.*

. . . It was with great dread known, that the late King James was bound in Conscience to indeavour to Damn the English Nation to Popery and Slavery, and therefore no wonder (since he made such large steps towards it in his Kingdom's) that he took a particular care of this Province, of which he was Proprietor, and at one jump leapt over all the bounds, and Laws of English Right and Government; and appointed a Governour of this Province of New York, who (although he was a person of large indowments of mind yet) gave active Obedience to his Prince without reserve; and accepted of a Commission now on record in the Secretarys Office, giving him power with consent of any Seven of his Council to make Laws and to raise Taxes (as the French King doth) without consent of the People, (for the Council are no body, but whom [he] pleases to name, and therefore could represent nothing but the Kings pleasure). Hereby the will of the Prince became the Law; and the estates of the subjects became the Kings property. And this Governour and Council were the tools to inslave their Country, who pursuant to their Commission did make Laws and Assessed Taxes accordingly, without any Representatives of the People, as appears by the Records of the Council book.

This French Government being thus (by Commission) introduced, it was

---

* LEISLER'S "MARTYRDOM FOR KING WILLIAM AND QUEEN MARY": "Loyalty Vindicated from the Reflections of a Virulent Pamphlet . . ." (Boston, 1698). From Charles M. Andrews, ed., *Narratives of the Insurrections, 1675–1690* (New York, 1915), pp. 375–401. Reprinted by permission of Barnes and Noble, Inc.

natural that Papists should be employed in the highest Trusts; such as the Council, the Revenue, and the Military Forces; and since no Law was left alive to make them unqualifyed, therefore this obedient Governour admitted major Brockholse and major Baxter into the Council, Matthew Plowman to be Collector of the Revenue, and said Baxter and Russel to Command Military Forces; all professed Papists to assist in making Arbitrary Placats, and forcing obedience to them from a Protestant free People.

This was the condition of New York, the Slavery and Popery that it lay under, until the Hand of Heaven sent the glorious King William to break those chains, which would otherwise have fetter'd all Europe. And these were the reasons that moved the Gentlemen concerned in the Revolution of New York to be early in shaking off their Tyrants, and declaring for their Deliverer. . . .

In the third page which is the first of the Letter, he declares that Jacob Leisler and his accomplices committed great disorders in the Revolution. And was ever Revolution made without them? What, must the noxious humours of the body natural be loosned and put a float, and very often with pangs and gripes, before the Medicament can officiate the discharge? and must not the body politick suffer a Convulsion to pluck up Spiritual and Temporal Tyranny that was taking root in it? But I pray explain yourself, was not the Revolution it self the greatest disorder that could be given to you and the Jacobite party? and therefore you need not admire nor wonder that all those that have a good opinion of the Revolution, have so likewise of Jacob Leisler, and other early Instruments of it in this Province: Nor is it a wonder that it should be credited, that the persons then in Commission in New York were Jacobites, and persons ill affected to the Revolution (which now the Libeller dare not say otherwise than call happy) for their very Commissions from King James were expresly contrary to Law, and their persons unqualified to serve in any Capacity in any English Government and so that as Jacobites (*i.e.* obeyers of King James's Arbitrary Government) and as Papists they must naturally be ill affected to the happy Revolution in England, and implacable Enemies to the well wishers thereof in New York. . . .

We are told the Lieutenant Governour and Council were Protestants, and perhaps they were; and so were Friend, Perkins, Jefferys, Herbert, Bishop of Chester, and Brian Haynes the player; therefore that is no infallible Test that they were well affected to the Revolution, if they had no other. But they resolved Thereupon to suspend all Roman Catholicks from Command and places of trust in the Government. Well resolved, though they did not perform it, as the Libeller afterwards owns. But what means the word "Thereupon"? *i.e.*, King James was fled into France, the Prince of Orange was Armed with considerable Forces in England, and by consent and voice of the Nation declared their Deliverer and King: and since King James could not stand by them, and the Arbitrary Commissions he had given them, and Old England would be sure to Command New-York: *Thereupon* they, etc. No thanks to them for their Thereupon. . . . But we do not find that *Thereupon* they declared for the Prince of Orange, or the Protestant Religion. No, these Gentlemen had submitted so intirely to such a blind Obedience to their Prince as (notwithstanding their Profession) was never practis'd by any Christians, but the Papists; and think to hide their nakedness by the fig leaf of turning a single Papist out of the Council, just as their Master King James did, when the Prince of Orange was landing, the Nations hearts alienated from him, and his standing Army likely to run over to the Prince: *Thereupon,* he restored the Charters of Corporations, and Magdalen Colledge of Oxford, and declared to call a free Parliament: Just with the same good will as these New York Thereuponmen. . . .

. . . He adds, that the said Lieutenant Governour and Council Convened to their Assistance all the Justices of the Peace and Civil Magistrates, and Military Officers. But they had quite forgot the English Constitution of calling the Representatives of the People: and whereas several of this Convention were the Persons that were pitched upon, and thought fit by the then Arbitrary Government to have Commission, Office and Power to enslave the subject, No wonder the People did not think themselves safe in their hands, to be managed by the major Vote of such a Convention.

Neither was the first thing they ordered, *viz.* Fortifying the City of New York, any wise satisfactory; since it was most proper that those persons who gave occasion for a Revolution, were most probable to make themselves strong to oppose it. And therefore Coll. Bayard, made Coll. of the Militia by King James, was most liable to obey and execute King James's order, and an unsure Security for the Fort; Especially having so often declared in Words, and Letters, under his own hand to Mr. West, etc., That those who were in Arms for the Prince of Orange were Rebels. But it is absolutely false, that Coll. Bayards industry fortifyed the Fort; for Capt. Leisler opened the Well, which was closed up; he it was ordered the Batteries, that were made about the Town, he mended the Breast works of the Fort, as likewise the Platforms, and Powder Room, all which were in a miserable Condition . . . Besides when the Militia Forces were on guard in the Fort, the Lieutenant Governour in Passion altered their Orders given by their Officers, and told them, if they gave him any farther trouble he would set the City on fire. This prooved by the Depositions of Albort Bosch and Henry Coyler. . . .

It matters not what Letters were sent home by the Lieutenant Governour, for it is plain neither Governour nor Council would declare for the Prince of Orange, pretending they wanted Orders; No, they wanted good will; for without Orders this Libeller pretends they turned out Baxter and Russel out of Commission. I wonder how they dared to go so far, and no farther. But no body but themselves know or care whither they wrote or no, for it signifyed nothing, except to excuse themselves from declaring till an answer came, and they knew who was uppermost. I suppose they had a mind to stay to see who got the better in Ireland, before they would declare.

A Lying building must have a lying foundation, and therefore the Libeller says, That Capt. Leisler, unwilling to pay the Duty of his Wines, stirred up the People to Rebellion. The case was thus, the Popish Collector Plowman was then continued in Office, and Capt. Leisler did, even with him, make entry in the Custom house for his Wines, and ingaged to pay the Customs to such as should be legally qualified to receive them, which the Papist Plowman was not.

And now the people being exasperated by the delay of the Governour and Council to declare for the Prince, the greater body of the Militia with their Officers did Seize on the Fort, and did send and demand the Keyes from the

Lieutenant Governour; and since they had taken the Government on them, they did Seize what Publick Moneys they could find; and took the Seven hundred Seventy three Pounds from Coll. Nicholson, which with great prudence they did Expend for the safety and defence of the Revolution: nor were the People Drunk or Mad: for no Man, Woman, or Child, was hurt by them even in the very Convulsion of changing the Government; nay the very Papists then in Office, and others who were justly suspected of designs of betraying the Country to King James's faithful Allie, the French King, had not a hair hurt, except by the fright their own guilt occasioned; and these Revolutioners must either be very sober or loving in their drink, or these Jacobites had never scap'd being Dewitted by a sufficiently provoked People, who had the Power, but more grace than to use it.

False Assertions without proof are sufficiently answered by denying them. This northern forehead answers himself: for the Libeller says, the people cry'd out that they disowned all Government, and in the next line tells you, they proclaimed Capt. Leisler their Commander. But I suppose, he gives the contradiction as a proof of the Peoples being drunk; to be against all manner of Government, and choose a Governour in the same breath. 'Tis likewise notoriously false, that no other Commission'd Officer was amongst them: for most of the Officers of the Militia of the City joyned therein: But had it been true, then Capt. Leisler as the only Commission Officer ought to Command them; and they were just and sober in their choice, as well as prudent in their Trust of so good and faithful a Person. But the fact of this was false, for Capt Leisler. though instrumental in shaking off the Tyrannical Government, did not believe he had a Title to govern longer than the Peoples Resolutions were known; and therefore, circular Letters were carried by Coll. Depeyster and Capt. De Brayn to the several Counties; whose Freeholders chose their Representatives, who being met appointed Capt. Leisler Commander in Chief under their Hands and Seals, and appointed several to be of his Council, under the name of a Committee of Safety to preserve the Publick Peace of the Province: who did it so effectually, that those divested of the Governing power had no other harm done to their persons; and the late Lieutenant Governour was permitted to withdraw himself whither he pleased. And here I must remark that he fared much better than Sir Edmund Andross at Boston, who was made close Prisoner and sent home to England, and yet no man was Executed or attainted there for that act of Loyal Violence.

Boston having proclaimed King William and Queen Mary, and New York Fort and Government possess'd by Loyal Leisler and his party, and the Lieutenant Governour withdrawn out of the Province, then the Libeller saith, That the late Council and their Convention of Justices of the Peace and Officers, had a great mind to proclaim the King and Queen, whom they never had declared for, and we must take his word for it: but he owns the Loyalists did proclame them, but saith, it was very disorderly. I observe whatever made for the Revolution, or against the late King James, is very displeasing to the Scribler: For when the People took the Government out of their Arbitrary betrayers hands, he saith, they were drunk or mad; and now the proclaiming of the King and Queen was very disorderly, in neither of which he gives one instance: But thank God, they were proclaimed, and their goodness will pardon small disorders which were the effects of Loyal Zeal, Although the Jacobites will never forgive them for it. Some of which Council and Magistrates went to Coll. Bayards house and drank and rejoyced that Leisler had done what they never could have the heart to do, nor made one step towards. And we may know what kidney these drinkers were of, by whose Wine they drank: For Coll. Bayard having been a complying tool all King James's Arbitrary Reign, you shall judge of the rest by his opinion of the happy Revolution, in his letter to Mr. West of the 14th of January 1689/90, Wherein he calls them Philistines, calls Leisler and his Loyal party, the Arch Rebel and his hellish crew, wishes he had a sufficient number to suppress the Rebels, calls them usurpers of the Government, and Sir Edmund Andross, his Excellency, and calls his friends Loyal, and the whole tenour of the Letter is to keep up King James's title, to admit his Commissions of Government to be of force, to brand all that declared for the Prince of Orange with the black name of Rebels; by which he owned King James was still in his heart, and had he power equal to his will, would have kept him still on the Throne, and therefore we may judge of his and his Companies joy, on this occasion, and whose Health they drank: which, eight years after, they tell us was King William's and Queen Mary's. . . .

These worthy Commissioners of the Revenue sate in the Custom-house, but Capt. Leisler with the Inhabitants who had possession of the Government and Fort, demanded of them by what Authority they pretended to act; who refusing to give Capt. Leisler any Account they offered to turn him out of the Custom-house by force; on which tumult (made by three Jacobites) a guard of Inhabitants from the Fort came to defend their Captain. And the People in the Streets were so enraged at Coll. Bayard (who they knew was as inveterate as any Papist against the Revolution) that they certainly had tore him to pieces, had not the good temper of Capt. Leisler been his protector, who was the only person capable of saving him in that extremity, and favored his escape, and let him live to have afterwards a hand in the Murdering his deliverer: So that the Violence of Armed men and naked Swords, beating the Commissioners from the Custom-house, was very modestly done, for no man was hurt, not so much as a skin broke of those who deserved the halter; but they are still alive; some of them to watch another occasion to betray their Country, when they can get a Popish King of England to assist them.

Captain Leisler finding several Papists and false Protestants in the Town, like a prudent Officer kept good guards, sent parties to prevent any Conspiracy they might make to resume the Government, and to preserve the Peace, which was dayly attempted to be broke by declaring for King James, and his Governour Sir Edmund Andross, and denying the Authority of the People, and Capt. Leisler intrusted by them, on which it was wisely done of Capt. Leisler to secure in the Fort those whom he found so troublesome to the publick Peace, and as the heads of them he Imprisoned the afore-mentioned famous Coll. Bayard and Mr. Nichols, but without barbarity they were confined, and not in a nasty Goal, but in handsome lodgings, such as now are thought proper for the Captain of the Guard, the Store keeper and the Secretary of the Province to lodge and keep Office in. It is true that Coll. Bayard was put in Irons, as he well deserved for his aversion to the Revolution, disturbing the Peace, and attacking Capt. Leisler (then Commander in Chief) in the open Street, as appears by several credible Oaths. Nor could it be safe to admit such fire brands to Bail; and therefore they were kept close from doing mischief, which is the part of all good Governments to do, and was most necessary in this Revolution.

Captain Leisler with the Committee of safety (appointed by the Representatives of the Freeholders of the several Counties of the Province) having published their Declaration for the Prince of Orange, the Protestant Religion, and the English Laws and Liberties, they thought it prudent to discriminate the Well affected from the Enemy, and therefore Summoned all the Inhabitants of the City to the Fort, to sign their names to such a Declaration as owned the Authority of the Prince of Orange. And the refusers must justly by him and all mankind be deemed Enemies to the Revolution, to His Majesty, and their Country. And is this a crime to know the Sheep from the Goats, or to take all Reasonable methods for the safety of the then Government: but the Libeller is angry at every prudent step was taken, nor is he satisfyed, although it is above Seven years since he was gorg'd with their innocent blood which he had a hand in shedding. . . .

On the tenth of December one Riggs brought his Majesties Letters which were delivered to Capt. Leisler, as they ought according to their direction; for Coll. Nicholson (to whom they were first directed) had withdrawn himself out of the Province, and in his absence the Letters were directed to such as for the time being took care for the preservation of the Peace and Administring the laws; which was none other but Capt. Leisler, who was appointed thereto by the Representatives of the Freeholders of the several Countyes of the Province and had the Command of the Fort; nor could those who called themselves of the Council be intituled thereto, for they were the Persons that were made use of in the late Arbitrary and Tyrannical Government, to the overturning of all Laws, and Civil Rights, and who gave Occasion for the Revolution in New York, and did never declare for the Prince of Orange.

These Letters from His Majesty fully confirming Capt. Leisler in the Government, whereto he was chosen by the People's Representatives, he indeavoured to execute his trust faithfully, and on such an Emergency it was the greatest wisdom and prudence to find Money to support the Government, which he did as regularly as the time would permit, by and with the consent of the General Assembly of the Province fairly chosen by the Freeholders; which this seducer falsely insinuates were only Selected and Appointed by Capt. Leisler. And by and with their advice and consent Taxes were raised and properly applyed. . . . But the Revenue was not sufficient to defray so great a charge, had not Capt. Leisler expended great Sums out of his own private Estate, as others concerned with him likewise did, for which he was repayed with a barbarous Death, through the means of men who will never venture their Lives or Estates to serve their Prince, Country, or Protestant Religion. . . .

The Protestant Ministers, the Libeller saith, could not scape Capt. Leislers Malice and Cruelty: I am afraid those Ministers he mentioned, were Popish Trumpets, to Preach up the damn'd Doctrins of Passive Obedience and Non Resistance, and to noise in our Ears with their accursed breath, that we ought patiently to hold our Protestant Throats to be cut by the Command of a Popish King: and when Capt. Leisler with his friends had taken hold of that wonderful Deliverance offered immediately from God to Redeem His People from Slavery upon Earth, and Popish Damnation in Hell, to have false Priests of Baal get up, and use their wicked Eloquence to make the People believe a lye, even in the house of the God of Truth, and from the Pulpit, to tell these Captains of our Temporal Salvation to their faces, that being faithful to their God, their Country, and their Laws, in the defence of the Holy Protestant Religion, and the Rights and Liberties of English men, and their thankful declaring for the most glorious Prince upon Earth their Deliverer: was the blackest of Treason and Rebellion. . . .

'Tis true Capt. Leisler sent to the Merchants of the Town to supply the Garrison with Provisions and other necessaries, and sent without distinction to all People who had Stores, otherwise the Garrison might have perished: but he honestly gave them Credit in the Kings Books, and they have since (for the greatest part) been satisfyed; and Capt. Leisler (as he ought) did order forcibly to break their Ware-houses open, where they were refractory, and refused on so great Emergency to afford support to the Government; but exact Accompts were kept of all such goods, and Entries made in Books kept for that purpose; so that it was not plunder, (as the Libeller falsely calls it) but they were to be satisfyed, and paid for the same. And I believe it was never known in the Memory of man, that ever a Revolution, or change of Government, was more regular: or where Military power would not force Victuals where it was denyed them, when they wanted it: and therefore it was for the special Service of King William and Queen Mary, to keep alive those that were the only persons in that Province who declared early for Them, and owned Their Authority. Nor can any proof upon Earth be brought (except such as the Libeller) that one Farthings Value of goods was ever converted to the private use of Capt. Leisler, or Transported by him to the West Indies, but the imposture of the whole book depends on such positive falsehoods. . . .

And thus the Libeller expatiates on Capt. Leislers Arbitrary proceedings over his Majesties Subjects, Persons and Estates, against the fundamental Laws of the Land; but he should have considered that all the fundamental Laws of the Land were wholly subverted and trampled upon by the Hellish, Popish, Arbitrary Government, Established by King James's Commission; so that Capt. Leisler found no fundamental Laws to transgress; and was forced in discharge of his trust from the People, and by and with the consent of those appointed by their Representatives, to use these violent methods which Heaven gave him the power to make use of to restore those fundamental Laws, which were abolished by tools of the same temper with the Libeller.

Major Ingoldsby, a Captain of a foot Company, arrives near two years after, saith the Libeller, "And with several Gentlemen of the Council sends to Capt. Leisler, that for the preservation of the Peace he might continue to command in the Fort, until Coll. Slaughter's Arrival, and only desired that major Ingoldesby and the Kings Souldiers might be permitted to quarter, and refresh themselves in the City: but instead of complying, he in passion told Mr. Brooke, on his acquainting him, that Mr. Phillips, Coll. Bayard, Coll. Cortland were of the Council, that they were Papist Dogs, and if the King should send Three Thousand of them, he would cut them off; and without cause Proclaimed open War; on which said major Ingoldesby perswaded several of the Inhabitants to joyn with him merely for self preservation. On which several great and small Shot from the Fort killed and wounded several of His Majesties good Subjects, who made no opposition."

This whole Paragraph I shall shew to be the greatest complication of Iniquity, and fit to be the production of a Monster begat by an Incubus on a Scotch Witch, who had kindled his malice against Truth from the flames he put to the holy Bible, thereby to become the Adopted Son of the father of Lyes.

For major Ingoldesby, having no Commission, nor Authority to Command, on his Arrival took on him the Title of Commander in Chief, usurp'd a shew of Government, calling a Council, and Issuing peremptory orders, as appears by the Records of the Council Book: nay, quite contrary to the Romantick Account of the Libeller, he sent a demand under his own hand, which I have seen, wherein he acknowledges Capt. Leislers offer to him of his own Houses in the City for the Accommodation of himself and Officers, and to appoint fit Quarters for the Souldiers; which major Ingoldesby under his hand denyes to accept of, saying, he demanded the Fort from him, which unless Capt. Leisler would deliver up to him, he would esteem him as an Enemy to King William and Queen Mary. I have likewise seen Capt. Leislers Letter to Major Ingoldesby, full of Civility and true Reason, wherein he acquaints him, that he held the Fort and Commanded by Virtue of a trust reposed in him by the People, and confirmed by His Majesty, and assuring him, that if he had any Commission from His Majesty, or any Instruction or Order from Coll. Slaughter appointed Governour of the Province, on his producing it, The Fort should be immediately delivered to him, but desired to be excused from resigning his trust, till he found one qualifyed and authorized to receive it from him. But this was not satisfaction to major Ingoldesby, who was prevailed with to take the Government on him in opposition to Capt. Leisler, and as Governour in Chief (although never impowered by King or People) he issues orders to the several Counties to be ready to attend and assist in opposing Leisler and his party with Arms; which was the proclaiming open War; and pursuant thereto he sends his Rounds in the night, and ordered or permitted his Rounds at all hours to pass the guards and centrys on the Walls of the Fort, and not to make answer, but by reproachful Language, when challenged by them, in order to provoke the drawing of blood, and ingaging the People in a Civil War: and farther, major Ingoldesby ordered all the men under his Command to wear Marks on their Arms, to distinguish them from those who joyned with Capt. Leisler.

During this Revolution and Civil War, I am told not above two persons were killed, which happiness attended the moderate temper of Capt. Leisler and the Committee of Safety, who could not be raised to punish the Insolence of the Tory party, suitable to what they gave just occasion for.

Soon after, *viz.* in March, about a Month or five Weeks after major Ingoldesby's usurpation, Coll. Slaughter Arrived, who Summoned the Fort late at night, and, contrary to the Libellers assertion, it was never denyed to be delivered: but the delivery suspended till next Morning, it not being proper (according to Military Rules) to deliver a Fort in the night, and then it was Surrendered by Capt. Leisler, who waiting on the Captain General Coll. Slaughter, instead of thanks for the faithful Service he had done His Majesty in defending the Fort and Province from the French (our professed Enemies) and the Treachery of Papists and Jacobites amongst ourselves, was immediately by his order Seized with Mr. Milbourn, and others of the Loyal party, and bound over to answer at the next Supream Court of Judicature; where Capt. Leisler and Mr. Milbourn pleaded to the Jurisdiction of the Court, That whereas he was in possession of the Government by the choice of the People, and confirmed in it by the Kings Majesties Letters, that he was not bound by Law to answer for his Mal Administration in Government, to any Court or Authority, but to His Majesty, who had intrusted him: but this was overruled by the Violence of the Court, without reason or Law, and as Mutes they were found guilty of High Treason and Murder; and although a Reprieve was granted them by Coll. Slaughter, untill His Majesties pleasure should be known in the Matter: yet the Violence of the Jacobite party (of which sort were most of Capt. Leislers Judges and Officers of the Court) was such that they gave no rest to Coll. Slaughter, untill by their Importunity they prevailed with him to sign the Dead Warrant. And they were Executed accordingly. So that the representation of the matter, with an account of their Reprieve, reached His Majesty at the same time with the account of their Execution and Death. So fell Capt. Leisler and Mr. Milbourn, men of known Integrity, Honesty and Loyalty, and by a pretended course of Law, contrary to all Law, condemned, where their Judges were most of them violent Enemies of the happy Revolution, and therefore resolved to revenge themselves on these Gentlemen who were the most Early and Zealous Instruments of it; and who had first expended great part of their Estates, and then suffered Martyrdom for King William and Queen Mary, their Religion and Laws. . . .

5] "The Injustice and Tyranny Under Which We Groan": The Maryland Declaration

> If the date on the document is accurate, Coode and his followers justified their rebellion before it was actually completed. Their Declaration of July 25, 1689, renounced allegiance to the proprietor's government and defended their taking arms against the proprietary party. A week later they forced the president and council at St. Mary's City to surrender the government. Eight of the rebel leaders signed the Declaration; four of them, John Coode, Henry Jowles, Kenelm Cheseldyn, and Nehemiah Blackiston, members of the lower house under Baltimore, continued to be prominent in the government set up by the Association.*

ALTHOUGH the nature and state of Affairs relating to the government of this Province is so well and notoriously known to all persons any way con-

---

* "THE INJUSTICE AND TYRANNY UNDER WHICH WE GROAN": "The Declaration Of the reason and motive for the prest appearing in arms of His Majtys Protestant Subjects in the Province of Maryland." From William H. Browne, ed., *Archives of Maryland,* VIII (Baltimore, 1890), 101–07.

cerned in the same, as to the people Inhabitants here, who are more imediately interested, as might excuse any declaracōn or apologie for this pres^nt inevitable appearance; Yet forasmuch as (by the plotte contrivances insinuacōns remonstrances and subscriptions carryed on, suggested, extorted and obtained, by the Lord Baltemore, his Deputys Representatives and officers here) the injustice and tyranny under which we groan, is palliated and most if not all the particulars of our grievances shrowded from the eyes of observacōn and the hand of redress, Wee thought fitt for general satisfaccōn, and particularly to undeceive those that may have a sinister account of our proceedings to publish this Declaracōn of the reasons and motives inducing us thereunto. His Lordships right and title to the Government is by virtue of a Charter to his father Cecilius from King Charles the first of blessed memory how his present Lordship has managed the power and authority given and granted in the same wee could mourn and lament onely in silence, would our duty to God, our allegiance to his Vicegerent, and the care & welfare of ourselves and posterity permit us.

In the first place in the said Charter is a reservation of the fayth and allegiance due to the Crown of England (the Province and Inhabitants being imediately subject thereunto) but how little that is manifested is too obvious, to all unbyasted persons that ever had anything to do here the very name and owning of that Sovereign power is some times crime enough to incurr the frownes of our superiors and to render our persons obnoxious and suspected to be ill-affected to the government[.] The ill usage of and affronts to the Kings Officers belonging to the customes here, were a sufficient argument of this. Wee need but instance the busines of Mr Badcock and Mr Rousby, of whom the former was terribly detained by his Lordshipp from going home to make his just complaints in England upon which he was soon taken sick, and t'was more then probably conjectur'd that the conceit of his confinement was the chief cause of his death which soon after happened. The latter was barbarously murthered upon the execucōn of his office by one that was an Irish papist and our Cheif Governor.

Allegiance here by those persons under whom wee suffer is little talked of, other then what they would have done and sworn to, to his Lordship the Lord Proprietary, for it was very lately owned by the President himselfe, openly enough in the Upper House of Assembly, that fidelity to his Lordshipp was allegiance and that the denying of the One was the same thing with the refusall or denyall of the other. In that very Oath of Fidelity, that was then imposed under the penalty of banishment there is not so much as the least word or intimation of any duty, fayth or allegiance to be reserved to our Sovereign Lord the King of England.

How the jus regale is improved here, and made the prorogative of his Lordshipp, is so sensibly felt by us all in that absolute authority exercised over us, and by the greatest part of the Inhabitants in the service of their persons, forfeiture and loss of their goods, chatteles, freeholdes and inheritances.

In the next place Churches and Chappels, which by the said Charter should be built and consecrated according to the Ecclesiastical lawes of the Kingdom of England, to our greate regrett and discouragement of our religion, are erected and converted to the use of popish Idolatary and superstition, Jesuits and seminarie preists are the only incumbents; (for which there is a supply provided by sending our popish youth to be educated at St Omers) as also the Chief Advisers and Councellors in affaires of Government, and the richest and most fertile land sett apart for their use and maintenance, while other lands that are piously intended, and given for the maintenance of the Protestant Ministry, become escheats, and are taken as forfeit, the ministers themselves discouraged, and noe care taken for their subsistance.

The power to enact Laws is another branch of his Lordshipp's authority, but how well that has been executed and circumstances is too notorious. His present Lordshipp, upon the death of his father, in order thereunto, sent out writts for four (as was over the usage) for each County to serve as Representatives of the people, but when elected there were two of each respective four pickt out and sumoned to that convencōn, whereby many Laws were made, and the greatest leavy yet known layd upon the Inhabitants. The next Session the house was filled up, with the remaining two that was left out of the former in which there were many and the best of our Laws enacted to the great benefit and satisfacōn of the people but his Lordship soon after dissolved and declared the best of these Laws, such as he thought fit, null and voyd by Proclamacōn: Notwithstanding they were assented to in his Lordshipps name, by the Governor in his absence, and he himselfe some time personally acted and governed by the same, soe that the question in our Courts of Judicature, in any point that relates to many of our Laws, is not so much the relacōn it has to the said Laws, but whether the Laws themselves be agreable to the pleasure and approbacōn of his Lordshipp. Whereby our liberty and property is become uncertain and under the arbitary disposition of the Judge and Commissioners of our Courts of Justice.

The said Assembly being some time after dissolved by proclamacōn another was elected and mett consisting only of two members for each County, directly opposite to an Act of Assembly for four (in which severall laws with his Lordships personal assent were enacted, among the which one for the Encouragement of Trade and erecting of Towns, but the Execucōn of that Act was soon after by Proclamacōn from his Lordshipp out of England suspended the last year, and all officers Military and Civil severely prohibited executing and inflicting the penaltys of the same. Notwithstanding which suspension being in effect a dissolution and abrogateing of the whole Act, the income of three pence per hoggshead to the government (by the said Act payable for every hogshead of tobacco exported[ )] is carefully exacted & collected. How fatall and of what pernicious consequence that unlimited and arbitary pretended authority may be to the Inhabitants, is too apparent, but by considering that by the same reason all the use of the laws whereby our liberties and properties subsiste are subject to the same arbitary disposition, and if timely remedy be not had must stand or fall according to his Lordshipps good will and pleasure.

Nor is this nullyfyeing and suspending power the only grievance that doth perplex and burthen us in relacōn to Laws, but these laws that are of a certain and unquestioned acceptacōn are executed and countenanced, as they are more or less agreable to the good liking of our Govr in particular, one very good lawe provides that orphan children should be disposed of to persons of the same religion with that of their dead parents. In direct opposition to which several children of protestants have been committed to the tutlage of papists, and brought up in the Romish Superstition. Wee could instance in a young woman that has been lately forced by order of Council from her husband committed to the custody of a papist, and brought up in his religion.

T'is endless to enumerate the particulars of this nature, while on the contrary those laws that enhance the grandeur and income of his said Lordshipp are severely imposed and executed especially one that is against all sense, equity, reason and law punishes all speeches, practices and attempts relating to his Lordship and Government that shall be thought mutinous and seditious by the Judge of the provincial Court, with either whipping, branding, boreing through the Tongue, fines, imprisonments, banishment or death, all or either of the said punishments at the discretion of the said Judges, who have given a very recent and remarkable proof of their authority in each particular punishment aforesaid, upon several the good people of this Province, while the rest are in the same danger to have their words and acōns lyable to the construction & punishment of the said Judges, and their lives and fortunes to the mercy of their arbitary fancies, opinions and sentences.

To these Grievances are added

Excessive Officers Fees, and that too under Execucōn directly against the Law made & provided to redress the same, wherein there is no probability of a legall remedy, the Officers themselves that are partys and culpable being Judges. The like Fee being imposed upon and extorted from Masters and Owners of Vessels trading into this Province, without any Law to justifie the same, and directly against the plaine words of the said Charter that say there shall be no imposition or assessment without the consent of the Freemen in the Assembly to the great obstruccōn of trade and prejudice of the Inhabitants.

The like excessive Fees imposed upon and extorted from the owners of Vessels that are built here or do really belong to the Inhabitants contrary to an Act of Assembly made and provided for the same, wherein moderate and reasonable Fees are ascertained for the promoting and incouragement of Shipping and navigation amongst ourselves.

The frequent pressing of men, horses, boats, provisions and other necessarys in time of peace and often to gratifie private designs and occations, to the great burthen and regrett of the Inhabitants contrary to Law and several Acts of Assembly in that case made and provided.

The seirvice and apprehending of Protestants in their houses with armed force consisting of Pap^sts and that in time of peace, thence hurrying them away to Prisons without Warrant or cause of comittment these kept and confined with popish guards a long time without tryall.

Not only private but publick outrages, & murthers committed and done by papists upon Protestants without redress, but rather conived at and tolerated by the cheif in authority, and indeed it were in vain to desire or expect any help or other measures from them being papists and guided by the Councills and instigacōn of the Jesuits, either in these or any other grievances or oppresions, and yet these are the men that are our Cheif Judges at the Comon Law in Chancery of the Probat of Wills and the Affairs of Administration in the Upper House of Assembly, and Cheif military Officers and Commanders of our forces, being still the same individuall persons, in all these particular qualifications & places.

These and many more even infinit pressures and Calamitys, wee have hitherto layne with patience under and submitted to, hoping that the same hand of providence that hath sustained us under them would at length in due time release us. And now at length for as much as it hath pleased Almighty God, by meanes of the great prudence and conduct of the best of Princes our most gracious King William to putt a check to that great inu[n]dation of Slavery and Popery, that had like to overwhelm their Majestys Protestant Subjects in all their Territorys and Dominions (of which none have suffered more or are in greater danger than ourselves) Wee hoped and expected in our particular Stations and qualifications, a proportionable shew in soe great a blessing.

But our greatest grief and consternation, upon the first news of the great overture and happy change in England, wee found ourselves surrounded with strong and violent endeavours from our Governors here (being the Lord Baltemores Deputys and Representatives) to defeat us of the same.

Wee still find all the meanes used by these very persons and their Agents, Jesuits, Priests, and lay papists that are of malice can suggest to devise the obedience and loyalty of the inhabitants from their most sacred Majestys to that height of impudence that solemn masses and prayers are used (as we have very good informacōn) in their Chappells and Oratorys for the prosperous success of the popish forces in Ireland, and the French designs against England, whereby they would involve us, in the same crime of disloyalty with themselves and render us obnoxious to the insupportable displeasure of their Majesties.

Wee every where have not only publick protestations against their Majesties rights and possessions of the Crown of England, but their most illustrious persons vilefied and aspected with the worst and most trayterous expressions of obloquie and detraction.

Wee are every day threatened with the loss of our lives, libertys and Estates of which wee have great reason to think ourselves in eminent danger by the practises and machinacōns that are on foot to betray us to the French, Northern and other Indians of which some have been dealt withall, and others invited to assist in our distruccōn, well remembering the incursion and invade of the said Northern Indians in the year 1681, who were conducted into the heart of this Province by French Jesuits, and lay sore upon us while the Representatives of the Country, then in the Assembly were severely prest upon by our superiours to yield them an unlimited and tyrannicall power in the Affairs of the Militia[.] As so great a piece of villany cannot be the result but of the worst of principles, soe wee should with the greatest difficulty believe it to be true if undeniable evidence and circumstances did not convince Us.

Together with the promises we have with all due thinking and deliberacōn considered the endeavours that are making to disunite us among ourselves, to make and inflame differences in our neighbour Collony of Virginia, from whose friendshipp, vicinity great loyalty and samenes of Religion wee may expect assistance in our greatest necessity. Wee have considered that all the other branches of their Majesty's Dominions in this part of the world (as well as wee could be informed) have done their duty in proclaiming and asserting their undoubted right in these & all other their Majesties Territoryes & Countys.

But above all with due and mature deliberacōn wee have reflected upon that vast gratitude and duty incumbent likewise upon us, to our Sovereign Lord and Lady the King and Queene's most Excellent Majesty's in which as it would not be safe for us, soe it will not suffer us to be silent in soe great and general a Jubilee, withall considering and looking upon ourselves, discharged, dissolved and free from all manner of duty, obligacōn or fidelity to the Deputy Gov[r] or Chief Magistrate here as such they having departed from their Allegiance (upon which alone our said duty and fidelity to them depends) and by their Complices and Agents aforesaid endeavoured the destruccōn of our religion, lives, libertys, and propertys all which they are bound to protect.

These are the reasons, motives and considerraccōns which wee doe declare have induced us to take up Arms to preserve, vindicate and assert the sovereign Dominion and right of King William and Queen Mary to this Province; to defend the Protest[t] Religion among us, and to protect and chelter the Inhabitants from all manner of violence, oppression and destruccōn, that is plotted and designed against them, the which wee doe solemnly declare and protest wee have noe designes or intentions whatsoever.

For the more effectual Accomplishment of which, wee will take due care that a full and free Assembly be called and conven'd with all possible expedicōn by whom we may likewise have our condicōn circumstances, and our most dutyfull addresses represented and tendered to their Majesties, from whose great wisdom, justice and special care of the protestant religion wee may reasonably and comfortably hope to be delivered from our present calamity and for the future be secured under a just and legall Administracōn from being ever more subjected to the yoke of arbitrary government of tyranny and popery.

In the   of   wee will take care, and doe promise that no person now in armes with us, or that shall come to assist us shall committ any outrage or doe any violence to any person whatsoever that shall be found peaceable and quiet and not oppose us in our said just and necessary designes, and that there shall be a just and due satisfaccōn made for provisions and other necessarys had and received from the Inhabitants and the souldiers punctually and duely payed in such wayes and methodes as have been formerly accustomed or by Law ought to bee.

And wee doe lastly invite and require all manner of persons whatsoever residing or Inhabiting in this Province, as they tender their Allegiance, the Protestant Religion, their Lives, fortunes and Families, to ayd and assist us in this our undertaking.

Given under our hands, Maryland the 25th day of July in the first year of their Majesties Reign Anno Dom: 1689.

JOHN COODE
HEN. JOWLES
J[no] CAMBELL
HUM: WARREN
KENELM CHESELDYN
W[m] PURLING
W[la] BLACKISTON
RIC[d] CLOUDS.

6] "There Has Not Bin a More Tragick Comedy of Rebellion Acted": A Letter to Lord Baltimore

Most Catholics and a number of Protestants remained loyal to the proprietor and his council. Peter Sayer, a devoted Catholic, officer in the militia, and sheriff of Talbot County, refused to accept the revolution. He was drinking the health of James II and damning the Protestants in both England and America as late as 1693. Here is Sayer's letter to Baltimore describing what took place in the summer of 1689. He twice calls Coode "Massinella," a reference to Massienello, an Italian fisherman, later assassinated, who led a short-lived revolt in Naples against the Spanish Viceroy in 1647. The English figures were principals in the exciting events during the reign of James and the revolutionary crisis of 1688–89—some for James, some against James, and some turncoats.*

Mr Sayer to Lord Baltemore

31. December 1689.

MY LORD,

Since my last to your Lordship (which was in Johnson the verriest rogue that ever crost saltwater) there has not bin a more tragick comedy of rebellion acted, since the royall bounty of King James and King Charles of blessed memory bestowed upon your Ancestors the Charter of this Province of Maryland; to lay itt downe in all its acts, and scenes would be too tedious, there being some of the actors (whom God send safely to arrive) will give your Lordship an orall relation of all. I shall onely trouble your Lordship with some few particulars, which they (being forc'd to abscond) may not have notice of. As soon as the noise came into our County, that our Masinella Coade had gott at the head of five or six hundred men, Griff Jones sends a note to Clayland (then preaching) that he and his auditory must come away presently to the Court house which they did; where this villanous rascal persuaded the poor silly mobile that if they did not sign to that paper (a copy of which your Ldpp hath) they should all certainly loose their estates: Upon this our County (who were before as quiet as lambs) gott to such a head, and crying that all their throats should be cutt by the Papists, that if Coade's order for disbandeing of everybody then in armes had not come to Will: Combes, our timorous Magistrates could never have quietted 'em. With this order came up his declaration, which was read att our Court house the fourth day following which was the 15th of August, all people being warned to come and hear it by the cleark of our County Nicholas Lowe; Coll: Coursey being likewise invited for his advice by Mr Robotham who accordingly came, and advised them to lett no papers be read that came from any of the rebells, except they would permitt him, or that Mr Robotham himself would paraphrase, and lett the people know what damn'd falsities were contained in 'em; butt Mr

---

* "THERE HAS NOT BIN A MORE TRAGICK COMEDY OF REBELLION ACTED": "Mr Sayer's Letter to My Lord Baltemore," December 31, 1689. From William H. Browne, ed., *Archives of Maryland*, VIII (Baltimore, 1890), 158–62.

Robotham reply'd, that if any body should contradict anything, in that humor the people were in, they should have all their braines knockt out; says Coll: Coursey, what did you send for me for, if you won't take my advice; would you have me hear a company of lyes tould against My Lord Baltemore, to whom I have sworn fidelity, and so have you; if your conscience will, mine won't permitt me to doe itt. After a great many arguments the Court was call'd, but noe Coll: would appeare with 'em; In short, my Lord, the declaration was read, with Coad's other orders by Nick Lowe, after which Mr Robotham (without mentioning the goodness or badness of the things read) asks them how they would dispose of the County Arms, and who should be their Officers, never mentioning the duty or faithfulness they owed to your Lordship, and your substitutes (which I believe was forgettfulness, butt hoped that none of 'em (by what they heard read) would act anything against your Lordship, or your Countrey, and to be quiet and peaceable & in a small time all would be well. Two or three dayes after came up Coad's circular letters commanding every County to choose four delegates, who were to be ready at St Maries on the 26th August. The 24th they sent, for my arms and ammunition & Mad^m Lloyd's; betwixt thirty and forty men headed by Sweatnam, who had a warrant (in their Majestys' names) from Edward Man, Willm Combes, and J^no Edmondson to take what arms, and amunition they could find for the country's use; for that our Indians (haveing fled from the towne, and cutt up their corne) had reported, that they onely staid till the two great men came from the North, meaning Coll: Darnall and Major Sewall, who the day before parted from my house. I was resolved to find out who was the Inventor of those falsities, and rid down to Oxford to our Burgesses, who were just then takeing boat, where I mett a great Company of people, who askt me whether I knew not of Coll: Darnall and Major Sewalls being at our Indian towne: No, said I; but I know they were last night att Coll: Lowe's, and are now gone home. Upon this I desired the Burgesses to send some people to the Indians, to know the cause why they deserted the Towne, and betook themselves to that swamp; they said, it was a folly to goe, for the Indians would not come out except Coll: Coursey came; I tould 'em a Jackahick[1] from him would doe, and I would frame one, and send Mr John Hawkins with itt, Att last they pickt out four or five men (who knew best where the Indians were) and signed instructions for 'em to enquire as above; they went, and brought the answer which your Ldp has a Copy off. This was the Tuesday; & because Will: Combes was to muster by Coade's order on Thursday, I stay'd with him, to see how my old souldiers would look upon me being cashier'd. On Thursday night I came home. The Wednesday following came a Justice of peace and three or four more, who had a kindness for me, and askt me where I was last Saterday where, sayes I, here: Lord Jesus! said they, what lyes goes abroad? why, what's the matter? said I; Begod, said the Justice, Dick Sweatnam had much adoe to keep Capt: Hatfield and his Company from comeing to take you; take me, said I; for what? why, sayes he, there's two men att old Watts' will swear that last Saturday they see you over against the Indian towne, where you shot of two pistols, and three or four cannows full of In-

---

[1] Jackahick: a contrivance or device used in place of a man—in this instance, a message.

dians came over to you, to whom you tould that within ten days you would
be with 'em at the head of a thousand other Indians. I asked the fellows names;
& they tould me, and that they lived by the Indian Towne, and desired me
withall to make hast to Major Combes, for th^t Sweatnam was gone to tell
him the story. The next day I went to Combes's, where meeting his wife att
the door, she imediately cryed out; O Lord! Coll: I was always glad to see
you, but now am ten times gladder than ever I was; why? says I, why, says
she there's a parcell of lying devills would persuade the people that you were
att the Indian Towne last Saturday, butt that I tould 'em you were a Thursday att our house, they would all come to your house. My husband's gone to
the Indian Towne to know the certainty. Well, sayes I, I'le stay till he comes
back, and he sha'nt be hanged for your sake; nay gad, sayes she, if I knew
this would have excused him, I had not spoke a word. I stay'd till they came
back, and tould me that the fellows said they were tould so by an Indian, and
the Indian being questioned said, he heard it from two of the Nanticoke Indians, and so itt was put of from one to t'other till itt was lost, and they all
say now (being deceived so many times by these sham reports) that if I should
really deal with the Indians against the Protestants (which God forbid I should
be so wicked) they would never believe itt, yett those damned malitious stories
was in a fair way to pull my house downe about my ears; and which has
really turned your Lordship's Government out of the Province; for they doe
not pretend to meddle with your Lordship's title to itt. Coll: Darnall and
Major Sewall wont come so well off about their treaties with the Northern
Indians, altho' there is as much truth in one as t'other.

Last Saturday Jack Llewellin came up to my house, and gives me this brief
account of the Assembly[.] The first thing they did (after they voted themselves a full house, tho' there were ten of the forty two absent, vizt Anarun-
dell, Somersett, and two of Cecill, but Somersett came over the last day, and
excused their delay, saying, they heard all things were done in your Lordship's name, but indeed they intended to own no other power but their Majesties which excuse was readly accepted of nemine contradicente. Little Jen-
kins was chief, whom your Lordship may remember, and I hope will. They
fixed upon the State house Doore a prohibition that no Papist should come
into the citty dureing the Assembly. The rest of the transactions your Lordship will see in the papers, which Jack Llewellin has promised to give to my
man who's goeing down with him; Onely I must tell your Lordship that the
Committee of Secrecy appointed for the discovery of Coll: Darnalls and Major
Sewall's dealing with the Northern Indians is kept on foot still; It's composed
of Blacstone, Jowles, Gilbert Clark, and one or two more I forgott: Upon their
report to the House (which was presently voted to be entered) a vote past
that letters should be sent to each neighbouring Government, as farr as new
England, that the house had found by severall substantiall evidences that your
Lordship's deputies have been tampering with the Northern Indians to come
in and cut off the Protestants, and therefore desires all of 'em to hold a strict
correspondency with this Government and to take up all persons of this Colony that shall seem any way suspicious; This is the purport, but I'me promised a copy of the letter ittselfe. The grand Ordinance is not yett come up,
which must give the measures to all their actions both civill and millitary.

Your Lordship will see in itt all the Officers, and by that know that those that have gott Estates under your Lordship, are as ready to serve Jack Coade as your Lordship, butt there are some entered that I'me sure will never comply with itt. People in debt think itt the bravest time that ever was, no Courts open, nor no law proceedings, which they pray may continue, as long as they live. I asked why Coade & his Councill divested themselves of that supream power wch they usurped att first; and t'was tould me that Coade proposed to the House to have a standing Committee to receive all appeals, and be as the Grand Councill of the Countrey; but the house would be all alike in power; that the Officers civill & millitary of each respective County should give definitive sentences in all matters whatsoever, till further Orders out of Engl^d so that Coade & his adherents now have no more power out of their County than we cashiered Officers. They have drawne many impeachments against severall, which are not sent home, and which they keep untill the King sends or orders Comm^rs. It's a pleasant thing to see the rascals in their cupps, Coade calls himself Massinella, but vaunts he has outraigned him, & little Taylard is his Higgins; Jowles will be Count Scamburgh & Vivian Beal, Argyle; Furlin, glories in the name of Ferguson, and Cheseldyn is speaker Williams, but the Dog will never have so much witt; & I believe that if those persons of honour whose names they usurp did but know what villians they were, instead of a recompence (which they expect from His Majestie) would gett an order that they may be try'd & hanged. And now I think I have given your Lordship trouble enough to spoile your next meale; yett, my Lord, this comfort remains still, that the best men & best Protestants such as Coll: Coursey, Coll: Codd, Coll: Wells, and a great many others (men of the best Estates, & real professors of the Protestant Religion) stand stifly up for your Lordship's interests.

This onely more I have to say in my own behalf, being att present much afflicted with the Gout, as I have been this pretty while, which will be enough (I hope) to gain your Ldp's pardon for all faults committed in this relation. Comitting your Ldp and family to the Protection of Allmighty God, presenting my humble duty to your Ldp, & Lady, & my humble service to little Master, & the young ladies, I am, My Lord

Your Lordship's
most humble servant
PETER SAYER.

CONCLUSION

WILLIAM accepted the downfall of the Dominion and asked for the return of Andros and his friends, while Rhode Island and Connecticut quietly reassumed their charters as if nothing had happened. But the Bay Colony people settled for a good deal less than the restoration of their charter, one of the goals of rebellion; for in 1691 Massachusetts, including Plymouth, became a royal colony with a governor appointed by the king. Yet things might have been worse. The new charter, which relaxed voting restrictions, did guarantee religious toleration, a representative government, and a council elected by the lower house—a privilege unheard of in Virginia or in any other royal colony. Not everyone was satisfied by the new arrangement, nor, given their pride, could satisfaction be expected.

The arrival of Governor Henry Sloughter in the spring of 1691 abruptly signaled the end of Leisler's rebellion. It signaled, too, the end of Leisler, whose enemies promptly persuaded the new governor that what the rebels would get away with in Massachusetts and Maryland was treason in New York. Indeed, Leisler and his faction had failed to root out, and take the places of, the Bayards, the Courtlandts, and the rest of the privileged elite. Yet, like Massachusetts, the colony was rid of the Dominion, and William sent Governor Sloughter armed with instructions to call a permanent assembly. What Leisler had failed to do by revolution, his friends might now accomplish through politics.

John Coode and the Associators governed Maryland for almost three years, but in contrast to Leisler they convinced the king of their enemy's disloyalty and their own devotion. The crisis ended in the spring of 1692 with the arrival of Governor Lionel Copley who accepted the revolution as an accomplished fact. Doubtless the Associators owed some of their success to William, who was suspicious of proprietary governments and was already prepared to bind them closer to the crown. Baltimore lost political control of his colony for a generation, and the Catholics were stripped of any role in politics. The royal government established by William absorbed the rebels and gave the Protestants the political power and privileges they claimed they lacked under the proprietor. It was in Maryland, then, that the situation gave ground for the greatest expectations. In fact the revolution there was a complete success.

The Revolution in England, in overthrowing the Stuarts, freed Parliament from the dictates of the king and the burden of divine right. But as the sovereignty of Parliament eclipsed that of the king in the realm, the scheme to draw the colonies closer under the wing of the crown—begun earlier by Charles and exaggerated by James—was continued by William. The fruits of the Revolution, however, were not all lost to America. In the colonies, as well as in England, the revolt against James preserved the principle of representative government wherein the rights of Englishmen could best be protected. The colonial assemblies, rescued in Massachusetts, New York, and Maryland by overt rebellion, were reconfirmed by William as part of the imperial system; they throve and proved a vigorous match for the king's governors in the years to come.

A study of the Glorious Revolution in America, however, demonstrates a good deal more than the colonists' sensitivity to the rights of Englishmen, loyalty to the crown, and devotion to Protestantism. It affords the historian a magnificent opportunity to look under the rug and to examine firsthand an unexposed side of colonial society, a side revealed only in time of crisis.

STUDY QUESTIONS

1] Was the Glorious Revolution in the American colonies a single crisis or three separate crises?
2] In what way were the techniques of revolution similar in the three colonies discussed?
3] Discuss the relationship between local self-interest and the appeal to the rights of Englishmen during the crisis in America in 1689.
4] Can you equate the rebellions in 1689 with a democratic movement? Explain your answer.

RECOMMENDED READINGS

PRIMARY SOURCES

ANDREWS, CHARLES M., ed. *Narratives of the Insurrections, 1675–1690* (New York, 1915).
BROWNE, WILLIAM H., ed. *Archives of Maryland*, VIII, *Proceedings of the Council of Maryland, 1688–1693* (Baltimore, 1890); ibid., XIII, *Proceedings and Acts of the General Assembly of Maryland, April, 1684–June, 1692* (Baltimore, 1894).
Documents Relating to the Administration of Leisler, New York Historical Society *Collections for the Year 1868* (New York, 1868), pp. 241–426.
Documents Relative to the Colonial History of the State of New-York, III, *London Documents, 1614–1692* (Albany, 1853).
McANEAR, BEVERLY, ed. "Mariland's Grevances Wiy The Have Taken Op Arms," *Journal of Southern History*, VIII (1942), 392–409.
O'CALLAGHAN, EDMUND B., ed. *The Documentary History of the State of New-York*, II, *Papers Relating to the Administration of Lieut. Gov. Leisler, 1689–1691* (Albany, 1850), pp. 1–250.
WHITMORE, W. H., ed. *The Andros Tracts*, 3 vols. (Boston, 1868–74), in *The Publications of the Prince Society*, Vols. V–VII.

SECONDARY SOURCES

ANDREWS, CHARLES M. *The Colonial Period of American History*, 4 vols. (New Haven, 1934–38), Vols. II–III.

BAILYN, BERNARD. *The New England Merchants in the Seventeenth Century* (Cambridge, Mass., 1955).

BARNES, VIOLA F. *The Dominion of New England* (New Haven, 1923).

CRAVEN, WESLEY FRANK. *The Southern Colonies in the Seventeenth Century, 1607–1689* (Baton Rouge, La., 1949).

HALL, MICHAEL G. *Edward Randolph and the American Colonies, 1676–1703* (Chapel Hill, N.C., 1960).

KAMMEN, MICHAEL G. "The Causes of the Maryland Revolution of 1689," *Maryland Historical Magazine*, LV (December, 1960), 293–333.

LEDER, LAWRENCE H. *Robert Livingston, 1654–1728, and the Politics of Colonial New York* (Chapel Hill, N.C., 1961).

MASON, BERNARD. "Aspects of the New York Revolt of 1689," *New York History*, XXX (April, 1949), 165–80.

MILLER, PERRY. *The New England Mind: From Colony to Province* (Cambridge, Mass., 1953).

MORTON, RICHARD L. *Colonial Virginia*, 2 vols. (Chapel Hill, N.C., 1960), Vol. I.

MURDOCK, KENNETH B. *Increase Mather, the Foremost American Puritan* (Cambridge, Mass., 1925).

OGG, DAVID. *England in the Reigns of James II and William III* (Oxford, 1955).

OSGOOD, HERBERT L. *The American Colonies in the Seventeenth Century*, 3 vols. (New York, 1904–07), Vol. III.

PINKHAM, LUCILE, *William III and the Respectable Revolution* (Cambridge, Mass., 1954).

REICH, JEROME R. *Leisler's Rebellion: A Study of Democracy in New York, 1664–1720* (Chicago, 1953).

SPARKS, FRANCIS E. *Causes of the Maryland Revolution of 1689*, Johns Hopkins University Studies, ser. 14 (Baltimore, 1896), pp. 471–578.

STEINER, BERNARD C. *The Protestant Revolution in Maryland*, in *Annual Report of the American Historical Association for the Year 1897* (Washington, 1898), pp. 279–353.

WERTENBAKER, THOMAS JEFFERSON. *Virginia Under the Stuarts, 1607–1688* (Princeton, 1914).

The Road to Independence: The Crisis of 1775–1776

DAVID S. LOVEJOY

UNIVERSITY OF WISCONSIN

CONTENTS

CHRONOLOGY

1775

APRIL 19 Skirmishes at Lexington and Concord.

MAY 10 Second Continental Congress meets at Philadelphia.

JUNE 15 Washington appointed commander of the Continental Army and departs for Boston a week later.

JUNE 17 The Battle of Bunker Hill.

JULY 6 Congress issues the "Declaration of the Causes . . . for Taking Up Arms."

JULY 8 Congress approves the Olive Branch Petition to the king.

AUGUST 23 The king proclaims the colonies in a state of rebellion.

OCTOBER Continental troops invade Canada.

NOVEMBER 9 Pennsylvania instructs its delegates in Congress to oppose independence.

NOVEMBER 29 Congress appoints Committee of Secret Correspondence to seek foreign alliances.

DECEMBER 22 Parliament prohibits all intercourse with colonies; authorizes seizure of American ships.

1776

JANUARY *Common Sense* published at Philadelphia.

JANUARY 5 New Hampshire completes draft of first state constitution.

JANUARY 16 Congress refuses to consider Franklin's plan of union, first submitted in July, 1775.

MARCH 17 British forces evacuate Boston.

MARCH 26 South Carolina adopts state constitution.

APRIL 12 North Carolina instructs delegates in Congress to vote for independence.

MAY 4 Rhode Island declares its own independence.

MAY 10, 15 Congress recommends colonies form state governments.

MAY 15 Virginia convention instructs delegates in Congress to propose independence.

JUNE 7 Richard Henry Lee introduces resolution for independence in Congress.

JUNE 12 Virginia adopts Declaration of Rights.

JUNE 12 Congress appoints committee to draft Articles of Confederation.

JUNE 29 Virginia adopts first permanent state constitution.

JULY 2 Congress approves resolution for independence.

JULY 4 Declaration of Independence approved.

INTRODUCTION

Between April 19, 1775, and July 4, 1776, the Revolutionary generation met a major crisis. Within fifteen months American colonists resolved first to go to war to protect what they believed were the rights of colonists within the British empire and then, when this defense proved ineffective, declared their independence from the government which denied these rights. The decision to fight and to break loose from England stirred up a host of related problems, problems as diverse as establishing new governments and controlling the Tories, all of which intensified the crucial character of this period—and made brave men despair.

With the close of the Seven Years' War in 1763, Americans expected to resume their lucrative trade with the West Indies and to expand into the vast areas taken from the French. New British policy in that year and the next opposed both these assumptions. The cost of defending the conquests of war was staggering to England, whose debt had already soared as a consequence of the fight. Determined to leave several regiments of redcoats in the colonies to protect Americans from the Indians and to dampen any thoughts of disobedience, the British government looked to the colonies for relief. Hoping to increase the customs, Parliament tightened the trade laws and stimulated their enforcement through new use of admiralty courts and His Majesty's Navy. In a departure from customary policy, the British legislature initiated a system of taxing the colonists—their trade (Sugar Act, 1764) and their use of paper (Stamp Act, 1765)—in order to force them to pay something toward their own defense.

The response to Parliamentary taxation was almost unanimous, and from this opposition dates the revolutionary movement. Although the colonists had been subject to trade regulation since the seventeenth century, Parliament had never directly taxed their trade nor imposed an excise such as the Stamp Tax. The colonists fought the new policy on the basis of the English constitution and because new taxes would cost them money. British subjects, they said, could be taxed only by a legislature in which they were represented, and colonists were represented only in their local assemblies. Any attempt by Parliament to upset this arrangement was an innovation and unconstitutional.

Distinguishing between Parliament's legislative capacity (regulation of trade) and its taxing power, Americans in 1765 accepted one and denied the other. To bring Parliament to reason they boycotted English manufactures, successfully persuading English merchants, who felt the pinch, to force Parliament to back down. In 1766 the Stamp Act was repealed and the Sugar Act modified, not on the colonists' terms (although most of them thought so) but for expediency's sake. Repeal was accompanied by a Declaratory Act which explicitly expressed Parliament's right to bind the colonies in all cases whatsoever. The constitutional issue remained to plague both sides of the water for some time to come.

The next year Charles Townshend, the chancellor of the exchequer, persuaded Parliament to embark again on a program of taxes, this time on certain goods imported into America from England. The controversy flared anew and nonimportation was resumed. But the Townshend Acts were more than another attempt to tax Americans; since they authorized new admiralty courts, provided salaries for royal officials out of the revenue, and established an American Board of Customs to enforce the new taxes and trade regulations, they drew the colonists' attention to the legislative power of Parliament.

With the Townshend Acts began a shift in American attitudes toward Parliamentary power. In 1765 the colonists had denied Parliament's right to tax them but accepted its legislative authority, which had never been particularly onerous. With new statutes that went beyond the issue of taxation staring them in the face, some colonists took a second look at the authority of Parliament in general and began to redefine their interpretation of the empire. John Adams was one of these, and he joined Benjamin Franklin, who had been thinking about the problem for some time. Despite the repeal of most of the Townshend taxes in 1770, a series of incidents, such as customs racketeering and the Boston "Massacre," culminating in the Coercive and Quebec Acts of 1774, convinced a majority of Americans that Parliament had no authority over them at all.

The delegates to the First Continental Congress, which met at Philadelphia in September, 1774, in response to the Coercive Acts, gave notice in a Declaration and Resolves that the colonists owed allegiance to the king alone, whom they petitioned, and not Parliament. Regulation of trade might continue, they went on, but only because the colonists consented to it for the general good. Although the Congress was only a voluntary meeting of delegates, it authorized another nonimportation of English goods to be enforced through local committees, condemned the Coercive Acts in round terms, and agreed to meet again the next spring if Parliament had not repealed them. Congress achieved a kind of union despite the fact that it had no legal authority—indeed it was damned as illegal and rebellious in England. According to the colonists the empire had taken on a new character since 1765 and now was a commonwealth of equals, each owing allegiance to George III and its own legislature.

The Glorious Revolution of 1689 had proved to the English the supremacy of Parliament. Whig politicians of the eighteenth century, whose rise to eminence was owing to the ascendancy of that body, believed it meant supremacy over the colonies as well. Americans were good Whigs, too, and just as happy with the Glorious Revolution. To them, however, it signaled the supremacy of representative government as a principle, not just the victory of the English Parliament, and colonists were represented in their own local legislatures—although not always equally. There existed, then, two interpretations of the British constitution, and the colonists prepared to defend by force if necessary the one which best represented their interests.

Englishmen, and George III above all, demanded the constitution be respected abroad according to old Whig lights, and this meant subjection to Parliament. And so it stood, a kind of stalemate, in the winter and spring of 1774–75—until the middle of April when General Thomas Gage, aware of the colonists' military preparations, ordered out his troops from Boston to destroy stores of war at Lexington and Concord.

Revolutions are never simple historical events, and the American Revolution was no exception. Conflicts within each colony had a good deal to do with the twists and turns of the revolutionary movement. An understanding of local conditions helps to explain the colonists' response to encroachment by the British government and to the demands of the crisis.

Probably the extreme example demonstrating the effect of local issues on the course of events can be found in Pennsylvania, where conservative easterners, many of them Quakers, had for some time discriminated against the Scotch-Irish and Germans of the west in matters of suffrage, representation, and protection against the Indians. Militant westerners along with disaffected Philadelphians welcomed the revolutionary movement as a means to combat the conservative east and its control of the colony's government. The eastern oligarchy stubbornly resisted the westerners' challenge and opposed separation from Great Britain for fear it would lead to a political revolution in Pennsylvania. Their fears were fully borne out.

There were conflicts in other colonies too: between merchant groups which sought economic favors through politics; between political factions which struggled for supremacy and the spoils of office. In the South the general pattern was conflict between west and east, pitting back-country farmers against tidewater planters, involving representation, suffrage, courts of justice, and often religion. Some factions exploited the revolutionary movement to push their particular interests while others courted king and Parliament for the same reason and remained loyal. When union was necessary and the crisis imminent, some conflicts subsided, some were transcended; others were sharpened and added to the complicated character of the Revolution.

The shots exchanged at Lexington Green and Concord Bridge turned into open hostilities what had been since 1764 a resistance movement based on self-interest and political and constitutional principles. Again the colonists claimed it was a struggle to defend their assumption that British subjects anywhere were entitled equally to the rights of Englishmen. For the king's troops in America and Parliament and the ministry at home, it was a struggle to enforce the laws and suppress rebellion.

The Second Continental Congress met three weeks after the skirmishes in Massachusetts (May 10) and attempted to come to terms with the crisis. But the Congress was divided, as were most Americans—Tories excepted—between those who would push extreme measures to assert their liberty without fear of the outcome and the more cautious individuals who, without shirking their rights, sought conciliation and shrank from offending the king. It was this split in means to an end which seriously thwarted Congress' success in either approach and magnified the crisis. But even the slow-movers could not deny that the colonists were at war and the battlefield was Boston. The Declaration of Causes of Taking Up Arms, although a compromise between the two groups, combined the talents of Thomas Jefferson and John Dickinson and was still a strong step toward revolution. It was balanced, however, by a soft-spoken petition that the conservatives persuaded Congress to send to the king. More decisively Congress voted to adopt the militia surrounding Boston as a Continental Army and chose George Washington its commander in chief. Debate over his selection, and over every issue at stake, indicated that crisis did not produce unity even in Congress.

Cooping up the British in Boston was an inglorious and enervating job, punctuated in June by the militarily unwise yet encouraging Battle of Bunker Hill. The arrival of Washington in the middle of July improved matters somewhat, but it abruptly introduced him to the critical problems of a civilian army, some of which he never succeeded in solving. The frustrating siege wore on for almost a year, reaching a nadir the last of December when a number of troops departed at the end of their enlistments.

Congress' Olive Branch Petition of July, 1775, was dismissed with contempt in August, and two days later George III proclaimed the colonists in a state of rebellion. Urged by the king to suppress revolt forcefully, Parliament cut the colonists off altogether from trade with the mother country, authorized the capture of their ships at sea, and withdrew the government's protection. Such actions played into the hands of the patriot extremists and, said John Adams gleefully, practically forced America out of the empire in spite of itself.

It became increasingly obvious to many thinking Americans that Congress' policy of military action to defend the rights of Englishmen was a dismal failure. Not only had the king refused to answer their earlier petition; he and his ministry had openly hired Hessian mercenaries to help subdue the Americans. Hope of convincing the British government of the rightness of the colonists' cause had faded considerably by the end of 1775. A new approach was necessary, and although the possibility of independence had been noised about by the extremists, it was not yet a respectable solution. It was not respectable, at least, until January, 1776, when Tom Paine's *Common Sense* burst into view and shifted attention from Parliament and ministry to George III himself.

Hitherto the colonists' grievances had been laid at the door of Parliament and, although its authority had been denied since 1774, it was still, said the colonists, Parliament and the ministry who had brought the war to America. So far the king, at the head of the empire, remained for the most part unscathed, and it was to him that the colonists were accustomed to appeal in their struggle against treacherous government. *Common Sense* helped knock these notions from the heads of Americans and opened their eyes to the fact that the king above all was responsible for their troubles. Paine's expert piece of propaganda shook the colonists' confidence in monarchy in general and George III in particular; it strengthened their faith in their own resources and described the America dilemma in terms that made independence the only solution. It is a "masterly, irresistible performance," wrote Charles Lee to General Washington, and will "give the Coup-de-grace to Great Britain." The conservatives in Congress, unless convinced by his arguments, had little to thank Paine for, since the sentiment for independence spread like a flood.

Besides the countless problems of war and the increasing determination of the English to keep America subject to Parliament, Congress and local governments were confronted with the critical question of the Tories. It was the patriots' job, so they believed, to render the Tories useless to the British forces and to punish them for their treasonable beliefs and actions. The methods attempted to accomplish these ends varied from colony to colony: threats, disarmament, imprisonment, tests and oaths, and confiscation of estates. Congress voted to limit severely their activities, local governments passed resolves which their citizens enforced, and the army itself was called in on occasion. Moreover, some individuals took matters into their own hands, leading often to violent injustice and just as violent reprisal. The problem of the Tories was major, laced as it was with passion and vindictiveness, and dangerously worsened the crisis.

When the British resolved to suppress the revolt with whatever force was necessary, they authorized commissioners to negotiate with Americans "on the spot" for a settlement, which, of course, meant submission. The colonists got wind of this in the spring of 1776 at the very time the movement for independence was gaining momentum. Ardent patriots fought the possibility of negotiation with all their powers lest reluctant revolutionaries yield to temptation and delay the decision for independence until the commissioners' terms were known. Since the commissioners would deal with individuals and colonies and not with Congress, their activity might seriously undermine what union and determination the extremists had achieved. Luckily for John and Sam Adams and their cohorts, the commissioners were slow to organize, therefore depriving those sympathetic to England of any firm footing. Again events helped the advocates of independence when the British evacuated Boston in March and took several hundred Tories with them.

While Congress struggled with the problems of war, union, Tories, and commissioners, local governments slipped from under the thumb of the king and his governors and, through popularly elected provincial congresses and conventions, moved hesitatingly toward independence and freedom. Generally there was no wholesale reversal of political tradition except in Pennsylvania and possibly North Carolina. Although government was unhinged by the shock of revolution, most Americans were content to build upon what they knew rather than chuck all and start over. This was particularly true in Massachusetts, where patriots formed a temporary government based on the colonial charter—with the governor's chair vacant—until Congress could bring about an honorable reconciliation. When reconciliation still seemed possible, provisionary governments answered many needs. But as 1775 turned into 1776 and the movement for independence quickened, there was a general stir throughout America toward more permanent political establishments which would adequately protect rights and property.

New Hampshire led the way after a nudge from Congress and by January 5, 1776, its revolutionary convention had drafted a simple constitution. South Carolina followed in March, Virginia and New Jersey both late in June. The hasty work of the people of New Hampshire and South Carolina was short-lived; both their constitutions were replaced and improved before the end of the Revolution. But Virginia's and New Jersey's survived for several generations.

Although these early constitutions were not submitted to the people for ratification—a technique developed later and used successfully by Massachusetts—they were drafted by popularly elected congresses or conventions and were firmly based upon the principle that political power derives from the people. Most famous of the early constitutions, providing a model for several to follow, was that of Virginia. George Mason, who guided its drafting, prefaced it with an eloquent Declaration of Rights that set the tone of American political ideals for some time to come. Virginia's constitution, however, changed little in Virginia respecting participation in government. The tidewater oligarchy continued to rule at the expense of the westerners who were underrepresented, and property qualifications for voting remained intact; the same was true for South Carolina. And although the legislatures became ruling bodies in both states, unencumbered by strong executives, sovereignty in the people meant certain people, mostly easterners. Rhode Island and Connecticut, satisfied with the government outlined in their liberal seventeenth-century charters, converted these quickly into state constitutions which endured well into the nineteenth century.

Besides the establishing of independent governments during this period of transition, there were several hopeful signs of democratic reform. Discussion mounted as to what shape good government should take. Drawing on their political experience as colonists, on their knowledge of the British constitution, and on the writings of continental theorists, Americans came to several significant conclusions about the nature of government and began to work them out in practical ways. Although less was accomplished before independence than after, suffrage requirements were reduced in a number of states, opportunity to hold office was made easier, and representation became more equitable—particularly in Pennsylvania, North Carolina, and Georgia. In the few months just prior to independence, instructions to delegates and petitions to congresses and legislatures indicated a decided interest in bringing government closer to the people by direct elections for a host of offices, which had the effect of preventing encroachment by privileged groups.

The liberating tendencies of the revolutionary crisis, felt outside politics and government, provided opportunity for an attack on social evils and outright oppression. An antislavery movement, begun earlier by Quakers and other humanitarians, received impetus from some patriots—South as well as North—who found it hypocritical to demand liberty from an allegedly tyrannical English government and at the same time deny it to Negroes. Congress resolved to stop the slave trade in its nonimportation agreement, and Rhode Island as early as June, 1774, citing revolutionary principles, declared free all slaves entering the colony thereafter. Connecticut soon followed, and several colonies provided for gradual emancipation in the next few years.

Established churches felt the restlessness of reform too. Strong-minded Baptists, such as Isaac Backus of Massachusetts and his counterparts in Virginia, exploited revolutionary arguments to promote separation of church and state and total religious freedom for Protestants. The Virginia Baptists, who boldly hinted that religious freedom was the price of unanimity, were more successful than the Yankees; the Old Dominion's Bill of Rights of 1776 contained a magnificent statement declaring all men "equally entitled to the free exercise of religion according to the dictates of conscience." Backus had trouble in Massachusetts where the Puritan legacy was strong and the people overwhelmingly Congregationalist. Ignoring his appeal, they continued a church-state relationship for another half-century. Equalitarianism was not a widespread revolutionary principle, but it did affect some patriots who, like Tom Paine, saw in the crisis a chance to construct a better world.

While town meetings, county conventions, and provincial congresses discussed forms of government and the essence of liberty, they discussed, too, the merits of independence. As sentiment rose in its favor, the debates in Congress grew sharper. Conservatives, like Carter Braxton of Virginia, held out as long as possible against it, arguing that independence was a "delusive Bait" which should be pursued only when it could be "obtained with Safety and Honor." The time was not ripe, they claimed, and if Americans cut loose at this juncture, the "Continent would be torn in pieces by Intestine Wars and Convulsions." The middle colonies were slow to come around, Pennsylvania in particular, where the conservative assembly opposed the move. Congress came to the rebels' rescue there and elsewhere and strongly recommended in May the formation of independent governments in all states where "no government sufficient to the exigencies of their affairs have been hitherto established"—a resolution John Adams believed virtually cut the ties with England. Encouraged, the Pennsylvania rebels struck fast and took the issue to the people; in a well-managed mass meeting in Philadelphia, they bypassed their assembly, claiming it was powerless to act, and called a convention to plan a new government.

But despite the pleas of the conservatives and the discouraging news of the failure of American troops to capture Quebec, "Independence like a Torrent" engulfed all the arguments its enemies could muster. Late in May John Adams could foresee the end. Early the next month, Richard Henry Lee, acting on instructions from Virginia, introduced his famous resolution for independence, a plan of confederation, and the taking of "effectual measures" toward "forming foreign Alliances."

It was generally agreed that independence without satisfactory union would get nowhere. Benjamin Franklin, as early as July, 1775, had read to the Congress a plan of union which he believed might answer the need, or at least stimulate interest in something better. Nothing was done then; when the plan was later introduced in January, 1776, Congress was balky and refused to consider it. Tom Paine's *Common Sense* contained several suggestions on how a simple unicameral government might be formed—so simple, in fact, naïve, thought John Adams, that he answered that part of Paine's pamphlet with *Thoughts on Government*. With this persuasive exposition of separation of powers and bicameralism he hoped to counteract Paine's invitation to anarchy. (Adams' tract was published in time to affect the drafting of both the Virginia and New Jersey constitutions.) On June 12, when independence seemed assured, Congress appointed a committee headed by John Dickinson that drafted the Articles of Confederation. (After some revisions it was later accepted by Congress and much later by the states.) In November, 1775, Congress had selected a Committee of Secret Correspondence, including Benjamin Franklin, to investigate the possibility of foreign aid. In March, 1776, Silas Deane was commissioned its agent and shortly left for France.

Congress postponed the vote on Richard Henry Lee's resolution for independence for almost a month, allowing several colonies, Pennsylvania among them, to alter instructions to their delegates. Meantime, a committee was appointed to draft a declaration. The great debate continued indoors and out. On the first day of July John Dickinson made a last plea for delay in vain. The final vote occurred on July 2 and Congress adopted the Declaration on the fourth.

If the rights of Englishmen, which the colonists went to war to preserve, could not be won within the empire, then Americans would seize and enjoy those rights as an independent nation. If Americans could not be equal to Englishmen as British subjects, they would be equal to all men, let alone Englishmen, as human beings; for, said Jefferson, in the document which boldly expanded the principle of revolution and made it a model for generations to come: "all men are created equal." With the vote for independence and the adoption of the Declaration, members of Congress put the first major crisis of their generation behind them.

DOCUMENTS

1] Congress Justifies Resistance by Force

> After hostilities commenced at Lexington and even after the Battle of Bunker
> Hill, reluctant, as opposed to eager, patriots in Congress had difficulty agree-
> ing on a statement justifying the fact that the colonists were already at war
> with the mother country. The Declaration which Congress voted on July 6,
> 1775, was a compromise between the views of John Dickinson and Thomas
> Jefferson—actually a Jefferson draft modified by Dickinson. George Washing-
> ton had the Declaration read upon his taking command of the Continental
> Army on the Cambridge common outside Boston.*

A DECLARATION by the Representatives of the United Colonies of North
America, now met in General Congress at Philadelphia, setting forth the causes
and necessity of their taking up arms.

If it was possible for men, who exercise their reason, to believe, that the
Divine Author of our existence intended a part of the human race to hold
an absolute property in, and an unbounded power over others, marked out
by his infinite goodness and wisdom, as the objects of a legal domination never
rightfully resistible, however severe and oppressive, the Inhabitants of these Colonies might at least require from the Parliament of Great Britain some evidence, that this dreadful authority over them, has been granted to that body.
But a reverence for our great Creator, principles of humanity, and the dictates of common sense, must convince all those who reflect upon the subject,
that government was instituted to promote the welfare of mankind, and ought
to be administered for the attainment of that end. The legislature of Great
Britain, however, stimulated by an inordinate passion for a power, not only
unjustifiable, but which they know to be peculiarly reprobated by the very
constitution of that kingdom, and desperate of success in any mode of contest, where regard should be had to truth, law, or right, have at length, de-
serting those, attempted to effect their cruel and impolitic purpose of enslaving these Colonies by violence, and have thereby rendered it necessary for us
to close with their last appeal from Reason to Arms.—Yet, however blinded
that assembly may be, by their intemperate rage for unlimited domination, so
to slight justice and the opinion of mankind, we esteem ourselves bound, by
obligations of respect to the rest of the world, to make known the justice of
our cause. . . . [Here follows a hasty review of the origins and development
of the colonies and the course of events from 1763 to 1774.]

But why should we enumerate our injuries in detail? By one statute it is declared, that parliament can "of right make laws to bind us IN ALL CASES WHAT-

---

* CONGRESS JUSTIFIES RESISTANCE BY FORCE: "Declaration of the Causes and Necessity
for Taking Up Arms." From Worthington C. Ford, ed., *Journals of the Continental
Congress, 1774–1789* (Washington, 1904–37), II, 140–57.

oever." What is to defend us against so enormous, so unlimited a power? Not a single man of those who assume it, is chosen by us; or is subject to our conroul or influence; but, on the contrary, they are all of them exempt from the operation of such laws, and an American revenue, if not diverted from the ostensible purposes for which it is raised, would actually lighten their own burdens in proportion as they increase ours. We saw the misery to which such despotism would reduce us. We for ten years incessantly and ineffectually besieged the Throne as supplicants; we reasoned, we remonstrated with parliament, in the most mild and decent language. But Administration, sensible that we should regard these oppressive measures as freemen ought to do, sent over fleets and armies to enforce them. The indignation of the Americans was roused, it is true; but it was the indignation of a virtuous, loyal, and affectionate people. A Congress of Delegates from the United Colonies was assembled at Philadelphia, on the fifth day of last September. We resolved again to offer an humble and dutiful petition to the King, and also addressed our fellow-subjects of Great Britain. We have pursued every temperate, every respectful measure: we have even proceeded to break off our commercial intercourse with our fellow-subjects, as the last peaceable admonition, that our attachment to no nation upon earth should supplant our attachment to liberty.—This, we flattered ourselves, was the ultimate step of the controversy: But subsequent events have shewn, how vain was this hope of finding moderation in our enemies.

Several threatening expressions against the colonies were inserted in his Majesty's speech; our petition, though we were told it was a decent one, and that his Majesty had been pleased to receive it graciously, and to promise laying it before his Parliament, was huddled into both houses amongst a bundle of American papers, and there neglected. The Lords and Commons in their address, in the month of February, said, that "a rebellion at that time actually existed within the province of Massachusetts bay; and that those concerned in it, had been countenanced and encouraged by unlawful combinations and engagements, entered into by his Majesty's subjects in several of the other colonies; and therefore they besought his Majesty, that he would take the most effectual measures to enforce due obedience to the laws and authority of the supreme legislature."—Soon after, the commercial intercourse of whole colonies, with foreign countries, and with each other, was cut off by an act of Parliament; by another, several of them were entirely prohibited from the fisheries in the seas near their coasts, on which they always depended for their sustenance; and large re-inforcements of ships and troops were immediately sent over to General Gage. . . .

Soon after the intelligence of these proceedings arrived on this continent, General Gage, who in the course of the last year had taken possession of the town of Boston, in the province of Massachusetts Bay, and still occupied it as a garrison, on the 19th day of April, sent out from that place a large detachment of his army, who made an unprovoked assault on the inhabitants of the said province, at the town of Lexington, as appears by the affidavits of a great number of persons, some of whom were officers and soldiers of that detachment, murdered eight of the inhabitants, and wounded many others. From thence the troops proceeded in warlike array to the town of Concord, where they set upon another party of the inhabitants of the same province, killing several and wounding more, until compelled to retreat by the country people suddenly assembled to repel this cruel aggression. Hostilities, thus commenced by the British troops, have been since prosecuted by them without regard to faith or reputation.—The inhabitants of Boston being confined within that town by the General their Governor, and having, in order to procure their dismission, entered into a treaty with him, it was stipulated that the said inhabitants having deposited their arms with their own magistrates, should have liberty to depart, taking with them their other effects. They accordingly delivered up their arms, but in open violation of honor, in defiance of the obligation of treaties, which even savage nations esteemed sacred, the Governor ordered the arms deposited as aforesaid, that they might be preserved for their owners, to be seized by a body of soldiers; detained the greatest part of the inhabitants in the town, and compelled the few who were permitted to retire, to leave their most valuable effects behind.

By this perfidy wives are separated from their husbands, children from their parents, the aged and the sick from their relations and friends, who wish to attend and comfort them; and those who have been used to live in plenty and even elegance, are reduced to deplorable distress. . . .

. . . His troops have butchered our countrymen, have wantonly burnt Charles-Town, besides a considerable number of houses in other places; our ships and vessels are seized; the necessary supplies of provisions are intercepted, and he is exerting his utmost power to spread destruction and devastation around him.

We have received certain intelligence that General Carleton, the Governor of Canada, is instigating the people of that province and the Indians to fall upon us; and we have but too much reason to apprehend, that schemes have been formed to excite domestic enemies against us. In brief, a part of these colonies now feels, and all of them are sure of feeling, as far as the vengance of administration can inflict them, the complicated calamities of fire, sword, and famine.—We are reduced to the alternative of chusing an unconditional submission to the tyranny of irritated ministers, or resistance by force.—The latter is our choice.—We have counted the cost of this contest, and find nothing so dreadful as voluntary slavery.—Honor, justice, and humanity, forbid us tamely to surrender that freedom which we received from our gallant ancestors, and which our innocent posterity have a right to receive from us. We cannot endure the infamy and guilt of resigning succeeding generations to that wretchedness which inevitably awaits them, if we basely entail hereditary bondage upon them.

Our cause is just. Our union is perfect. Our internal resources are great, and, if necessary, foreign assistance is undoubtedly attainable.—We gratefully acknowledge, as signal instances of the Divine favour towards us, that his Providence would not permit us to be called into this severe controversy, until we were grown up to our present strength, had been previously exercised in warlike operation, and possessed of the means of defending ourselves.—With hearts fortified with these animating reflections, we most solemnly, before God and the world, declare, that, exerting the utmost energy of those powers, which our beneficent Creator hath graciously bestowed upon us, the arms we have been compelled by our enemies to assume, we will, in defiance of every hazard, with unabating firmness and perseverance, employ for the presevation of our liberties; being with our [one] mind resolved to dye Free-men rather than live Slaves.

Lest this declaration should disquiet the minds of our friends and fellow-subjects in any part of the empire, we assure them that we mean not to dissolve that Union which has so long and so happily subsisted between us, and which we sincerely wish to see restored.—Necessity has not yet driven us into that desperate measure, or induced us to excite any other nation to war against them.—We have not raised armies with ambitious designs of separating from Great Britain, and establishing independent states. We fight not for glory or for conquest. We exhibit to mankind the remarkable spectacle of a people attacked by unprovoked enemies, without any imputation or even suspicion of offence. They boast of their privileges and civilization, and yet proffer no milder conditions than servitude or death.

In our own native land, in defence of the freedom that is our birth-right, and which we ever enjoyed till the late violation of it—for the protection of our property, acquired solely by the honest industry of our fore-fathers and ourselves, against violence actually offered, we have taken up arms. We shall lay them down when hostilities shall cease on the part of the aggressors, and all danger of their being renewed shall be removed, and not before.

With an humble confidence in the mercies of the supreme and impartial Judge and Ruler of the universe, we most devoutly implore his divine goodness to protect us happily through this great conflict, to dispose our adversaries to reconciliation on reasonable terms, and thereby to relieve the empire from the calamities of civil war.

By order of Congress,
JOHN HANCOCK,
President.
Attested,
CHARLES THOMSON,
Secretary.

Philadelphia, July 6th, 1775.

2] An American Commander Advises a Congressman

After the "embattled farmers" had chased General Gage's troops from Lexington to Boston, the siege of that city began, interrupted only by the Battle of Bunker Hill in June. By December morale was disastrously low, the enthusiasm immediately following Lexington and Concord having worn off, and Washington found himself surrounded by serious problems and a motley army of provincials. Nathanael Greene of Rhode Island rose to be quarter-

master general and later took over the command of the Army of the South.
Here is his letter from the field to former Governor of Rhode Island Samuel
Ward, then a delegate to Congress, describing some difficulties faced by the
American army during the siege of Boston.*

Camp on Prospect Hill December 31. 1775

DEAR SIR

Yours of the 9th came to hand before that of the 7th; the former was a little
unintelligible untill I receiv[d] the latter—You entreat the General Officers to
recommend to the Congress the giveing a bounty—I wish we dare do it. But
his Excellency General Washington has often assur[d] us that the Congress would
not give a Bounty, and before they would give a bounty they would give up
the dispute—The Cement between the Southern and Northern Colonies is not
very strong if Forty thousand Lawful will induce the Congress to give us up
—Altho I dont immagin that the necessity of allowing a bounty would have
broken the Union yet it was a sufficient Intimation that the bare mention was
disagreeable—Can you think we should hesitate a Moment to recommend a
Bounty if we thought ourselves [at liber]ty—We should then have an Opportunity of picking the best men, filling the Army soon, keeping up a proper
decipline and preserveing good order and Government in the Camp, while we
are now Obligd to relax the very Sinews of Military Government and give a
latitude of indulgence to the Soldiery incompatible withe security of the Camp
or Country—What Reason have you to think A proposition of that sort if it
came Recommended by the General Officers would be acceded too by the
Congress—Most of the Generals belong to the Northern Governments, if the
Congress refuse to hear their Delegates, I apprehend they would the Generals
also—The Congress cannot suppose that the Generals are better acquainted
with the temper and Genius of this People than the Delegates are from these
Colonies, and why they should refuse to hear you and not us I cannot immagin—A good politician will ever have an Eye to Oeconomy, but to form
an extensive plan, and not provide the means for its execution, betrays a defect in Council and a want of Resolution to procecute—There is nothing that
will encourage our Enimies both External and Internal like the difficulties we
meet in raising a new Army; if we had given a good bounty and raisd the
Troops speedy it would have struck the Ministry with Asstonishment to see
that four Colonies could raise such a prodegious large Army in so short a time
—They could not expect to conquer a people so United, firm and resolutely
determind to defend their Rights and Privileges, but from the difficulties we
meet, the confusion and disorder we are in, the large number of the Soldiery
that are going home—Our Enemies will draw a conclusion we are like a Rope
of Sand and that we shall soon break to pieces—God grant it may not be the
case.

You misunderstood me Dear Sir or I wrote what I did not mean; it was

* AN AMERICAN COMMANDER ADVISES A CONGRESSMAN: Nathanael Greene to Samuel
Ward, December 31, 1775. From Bernhard Knollenberg, ed., *Correspondence of Governor
Samuel Ward, May 1775–March 1776* (Providence, 1952), pp. 152–57. Reprinted by
permission of the Rhode Island Historical Society.

ot the lower Class of People that I meant to complain of but the Merchants
nd wealthy Planters, who I think does not exert themselves as they ought—
'his is no time for giting Riches but to secure what we have got—Every
aadow of Oppresseon and Extortion ought to disappear, but instead of that
'e find many Articles of Merchandise multiplied four fold their original Value,
nd most Cent p Cent [100%]. The Farmers are Extortionate where ever their
tuation furnishes them with an Opportunity—These are the People that I
omplain mostly of; they are wounding the cause—When People are in dis-
ess its natural for them to try every thing and every where to get relief, and
 find Oppresseon instead of relief from these two orders of men will go near
 driving the poorer sort to desperation—It will be good policey in the United
olonies to render the poorer sort of people as easy and happy under their
resent circumstances as possible, for they are Creatures of a Day, and present
ain and gratification, tho small, has more weight with them, than much
reater advantagies at a distance—A good politician must & will consider the
mper of the times and the prejudice of the People he has to deal with, when
e takes his measures to execute any great design—The current Sentiment in
ae New England Colonies greatly favors the Opposition but if the distresses
 the People are multiplied their Oppinions may change, Theyl naturally look
ack upon their former happy Situation and contrast that with there present
retched condition, and conclude that the source of all their Misery Originates
 the despute with Great Britain.
If all the Maritime Towns throughout the United Colonies had a body of
'roops in Continental pay it would in a great measure remidy this Evil; Pro-
sion must be made for those that are thrown out of employ by the decay of
'rade; if they are not engag^d for us, necessity will drive them to engag against
s, for they cannot live upon the Air—What signifies our being freighte[n]d
. the Expence; if we succeed, we gain all, but if we are conquerd we loos
l; not only our present possessions, but all our future Labours will be Ap-
ropriated to the support of a Haughty Proud, Insolent, set of Puppies, whose
reatest merit with the Crown will be to render the People as compleatly mis-
rable as possible.
I agree with you that the Congress should embody Seventy thousand men—
ll the Troops raisd in the different Colonies to be under Continental pay and
here there are any stationd for the Security of any particular Province to be
onsiderd as a detachment from the Grand Army and all in every Province to
 subject to the commander in chief and at his desposal and direction—A
ody of Troops in each Colony would support the spirited, confirm the weak
nd wavering, and awe our Opposers into submision, for there are no Argu-
aents however well supported by Reason, that carries such conviction with
aem as those that are enforced from the Muzzle of a Gun or the Point of a
ayonet.
If the Southern and Nothern Troops were exchang'd it would be serviceable
 the cause; it would in a great measure cure the itch for going home on
urlough and save the Continent a needless expence of paying a large body of
roops that are Absent from Camp.
You complain and say the New England Colonies are treated ill; why are
aey treated so, You think there ought to have been a bounty given. The

Congress always had it in thier power to give a bounty if they pleasd. Why were not the New England Delegates sent to establish the plan, for the constitution of the New Army; why were strangers sent at so critical a period—History dont Afford so dangerous a Manaeuvre as that of disbanding an old Army and forming a new one within fine Blank shot of the Enemy the whole time—This task was renderd very difficult by the reduction of Eleven Regiments and the descharge of such a number of Officers, who has done every thing to Obstruct and retard the filling the new Army in hopes to ruin the Establishment and bring themselves into place again.

From whence Orgenates that groundless Jealosy of the New England Colonies. I believe there is nothing more remote from their thoughts; for my own part I abhor the thought and cannot help thinking it highly injurious to the New Engl. People who ever have been distinguisht for their Justice and Moderation—I mentioned this subject to M.ʳ Lynch and Col Harrison who assurd me there was no such Sentiment prevaild in Congress nor amongst the Southern Inhabitants that was of any consequence—I am sorry to find they were mistaken; it grieves me to find such Jealousies prevail; if they are nourisht they will sooner or lateer sap the foundation of the Union and dissolve the Connexeon; God in mercy avert so dreadful an Evil—How unhappy for the Interest of America that such Coloneal Prejudices prevail and personal Motives influences her councels. The Interest of one Colony is no way incompatible with that of another, We have all one common Interest & one common wish; to be free from Parliamentary Jurisdiction and Taxation. The different Climates and produce of the Colonies will ever preserve a harmony amongst them by a circuitous Trade and commerce—Each Colony will have the benefits of its own staples whether they are Independent or connected with Great Britain. . . .

This is the last day of the old enlisted Soldiers service. Nothing but confusion and disorder Reigns. We are Obligd to retain their Guns whether Private or Publick property—They are prized [appraised] and the Owners paid, but as Guns last Spring run very high, the Committee that values them sets them much lower than the price they were purchast At—This is lookt upon to be both Tyrannical and unjust—I am very sorry that necessity forces his Excellency [Washington] to adopt any Measures disagreeable to the Populace. But the Army cannot be provided for any other way. And those we retain are very indifferent, generally without Bayonets and of different Sizd Bores—Twenty thousand Troops with such Arms as we are provided with are not equal in an Engagement to fifteen thousand with as good Arms as the Kings Troops. I wish our Troops were better furnisht; the Enemy has a great Advantage over us.

We have sufferd prodigeously for want of Wood; many Regiments has been Obligd to Eat their Provision Raw for want of fireing to Cook, and notwithstanding we have burnt up all the fences and cut down all the Trees for a mile round the Camp, our suffering has been inconceivable—The Barracks has been greatly delayd for want of Stuff; many of the Troops are yet in their Tents and will be for some time, especially the Officers—The fatigues of the Campaign, the suffering for want of Wood and Cloathing, has made abundance of the Soldiers heartily sick of service—The Connecticut Troops went off in spite of all that could be done to prevent it; but they met with such an un-

favorable Reception at Home that many are returning to Camp again already
—The People upon the Roads exprest so much abhorrence at their conduct for
quiting the Army that it was with difficulty they got Provisions. I wish all the
Troops now going Home may meet with the same contempt—I expect the
Army not withstanding all the Obstacles we meet will be full in about Six
Weeks—Some Ships came in [to Boston] Yesterday and it is said brought
Troops in, but what grounds there is for the report am not Able to say.

We never have been so weak as we shall be to morrow when we dismiss the
old Troops; we growing weaker and the Enemy geting stronger, renders our
situation disagreeable—However if they Attack any of our Posts I hope theyl
meet with a severe repuls. They can scarcely make a movement on this side
Cambridge Bay, but that we on this Hill shall have a slap at them.

General Lee has Just returnd from Rhode Island; he has taken the Tories in
hand and swore them by a very Solemn Oath that they would not for the
future grant Any supplies to the Enemy directly nor indirectly nor give them
any kind of Intelligence nor suffer it to be done by others without giveing
Information—Joseph Wanton [son of the ex-Governor] & Doctor [William]
Hunter were the Principals; he gives a very good Account of the Spirit and
Resolution of the People, but thinks the Colony at too great an Expence for its
present defence—the Minute men are a very heavy charge—General Lee got
intimately acquainted with your brother and is prodegeously pleasd with him
—I beg leave to congratulate you on the recovery of your health, which May
God in his Provedence long Preserve that you may enjoy happiness your self
and continue a blessing to your Country—Make my Compliments agreeable to
your Colleague [Hopkins], Col Harrison, M.ʳ Lynch & Doctor Franklin, and
believe me to be your most Obedeint Humble Servant

NATH GREENE

3] Connecticut Acts Against the Tories

The problem of the Tories was attacked in various ways by the patriot governments, which severely limited their freedom of speech and action. Western
Connecticut, particularly Fairfield County, in the southwest corner, contained a large number of Americans who remained loyal to the crown. Although often more a potential than an actual menace, their presence and
their proximity to Tories in New York made the patriots uneasy. After
rumors of plots and counterplots, the Connecticut Assembly in December,
1775, legislated against them.*

*Be it enacted by the Governor, Council and Representatives, in General Court
assembled, and by the authority of the same,* That if any person within this
Colony shall directly or indirectly supply the ministerial army or navy with

* CONNECTICUT ACTS AGAINST THE TORIES: *An Act for Restraining and Punishing Persons who are Inimical to the Liberties of this and the Rest of the United Colonies, and
for Directing Proceedings therein.* From Charles J. Hoadly, ed., *The Public Records of the
Colony of Connecticut,* XV (Hartford, 1890), 192–95.

provisions, military or naval stores, or shall give any intelligence to the officers, soldiers or mariners belonging to said army or navy, or shall inlist or procure any others to inlist into the service of said army or navy, or shall take up arms against this or either of the United Colonies, or shall undertake to pilot any of the vessels belonging to said navy, or in any other ways shall aid or assist them, and be thereof duly convicted before the superior court, shall forfeit all his estate, which shall be accordingly seized by order of said court for the use of this Colony; and such person shall be further punished by imprisonment in any of the gaols in this Colony at the discretion of said court, for a term not exceeding three years.

And be it further enacted by the authority aforesaid, That if any person by writing or speaking, or by any overt act, shall libel or defame any of the resolves of the Honorable Congress of the United Colonies, or the acts and proceedings of the General Assembly of this Colony, made or which hereafter shall be made for the defence or security of the rights and privileges of the same, and be thereof duly convicted before the superior court, shall be disarmed and not allowed to have or keep any arms, and rendered incapable to hold or serve in any office civil or military, and shall be further punished either by fine, imprisonment, or disfranchisement, or find surety of the peace and good behaviour, as said court shall order, and shall pay the cost of prosecution.

And be it further enacted by the authority aforesaid, That on complaint being made to the civil authority, selectmen and committee of inspection of the respective towns in this Colony against any person or persons dwelling or residing in such town, or any adjoining town in the same county where there is not a committee of inspection, that he or they are inimical to the liberties of this Colony and the other United Colonies in America, it shall be the duty of such civil authority, selectmen and committee, to cause every such person or persons to appear before them to be examined, and if on examination they shall not be able to satisfy the said authority, selectmen and committee, or the major part of them, that they are not inimical to this or the other United American Colonies, then such person or persons shall be by order of said authority, selectmen and committee, or the major part of them, disarmed and not allowed to have or keep any arms until they shall satisfy said authority, selectmen and committee, or the major part of them, that such person or persons are friendly to this and the other United Colonies.

And for the more effectual carrying into execution this act according to the true intent and meaning thereof,

Be it further enacted by the authority aforesaid, That when any person shall be duly convicted and ordered to be disarmed as aforesaid, the superior court, or civil authority, selectmen and committee aforesaid, as the case may happen, are hereby impowered and fully authorized to issue a warrant, signed by the clerk of the superior court or by one or more of the said civil authority, directed to the sheriff of the county, his deputy, or to the constables of the town wherein such person or persons dwell, directing and ordering such officer forthwith to disarm such person or persons; and in case he or they shall refuse to resign up his or their arms, said officer by and with the advice of any one Assistant and justice of the peace, or two justices of the peace, is hereby authorized to raise the militia of the county, or so many of them as they shall judge needful, for the purpose of carrying into execution such warrant; and all military officers and soldiers, being duly required, who shall neglect or refuse to obey the command of such sheriff, his deputy, or constable, shall be subject to the same penalty as by law is provided for commission officers and soldiers who refuse to obey the sheriff in the execution of his office. And all informing officers are directed to enquire after and due presentment make of all the breaches of the foregoing paragraphs of this act.

And be it further enacted by the authority aforesaid, That on information being made to any of the county courts within this Colony by the selectmen of any towns, or the major part of them, that there are real estates in such town belonging to any person or persons who have since the making of this act put, or shall continue to hold and screen themselves under the protection of the ministerial army or navy, or have aided or assisted in carrying into execution the present ministerial measures against America, such county court within the county wherein such estate lyeth are hereby authorized and impowered to issue a warrant to attach such estate; an attested copy thereof with the officer's doings thereon shall be left at the last usual place of abode of such person or persons, if within this Colony, at least twelve days before the sitting of the next county court in such county; and if on enquiry by said court said information shall be found true, said court are directed to order said estate so attached to be held under the care of such person or persons as said court shall appoint, who shall improve said estate or estates for the use of this Colony and be accountable for the rents and profits thereof.

4] Tom Paine Awakens a Nation

> Paine, born in England, arrived in the colonies in 1774. Immediately sympathetic to the patriots' cause, he quickly mastered the revolutionary arguments. At Philadelphia in January, 1776, he published *Common Sense,* which, probably more than any other single factor, brought the crisis to a head that year. Eager patriots were delighted with his cogent arguments for independence. Serious statesmen like John Adams deplored the fuzzy thinking behind his suggestions for local and national government, believing Paine's recommendations could lead only to anarchy and chaos. The pamphlet is in four sections; following is the third, in which he argues for independence.*

In the following pages I offer nothing more than simple facts, plain arguments, and common sense: and have no other preliminaries to settle with the reader, than that he will divest himself of prejudice and prepossession, and suffer his reason and his feelings to determine for themselves: that he will put on, or rather that he will not put off, the true character of a man, and generously enlarge his views beyond the present day.

* TOM PAINE AWAKENS A NATION: "Thoughts on the Present State of American Affairs," *Common Sense.* From Moncure D. Conway, ed., *The Writings of Thomas Paine* (New York, 1894–96), I, 84–101.

Volumes have been written on the subject of the struggle between England and America. Men of all ranks have embarked in the controversy, from different motives, and with various designs; but all have been ineffectual, and the period of debate is closed. Arms as the last resource decide the contest; the appeal was the choice of the King, and the Continent has accepted the challenge. . . .

The Sun never shined on a cause of greater worth. 'Tis not the affair of a City, a County, a Province, or a Kingdom; but of a Continent—of at least one eighth part of the habitable Globe. 'Tis not the concern of a day, a year, or an age; posterity are virtually involved in the contest, and will be more or less affected even to the end of time, by the proceedings now. Now is the seed-time of Continental union, faith and honour. The least fracture now will be like a name engraved with the point of a pin on the tender rind of a young oak; the wound would enlarge with the tree, and posterity read it in full grown characters.

By referring the matter from argument to arms, a new aera for politics is struck—a new method of thinking hath arisen. All plans, proposals, &c. prior to the nineteenth of April, *i.e.* to the commencement of hostilities, are like the almanacks of the last year; which tho' proper then, are superceded and useless now. Whatever was advanced by the advocates on either side of the question then, terminated in one and the same point, viz. a union with Great Britain; the only difference between the parties was the method of effecting it; the one proposing force, the other friendship; but it hath so far happened that the first hath failed, and the second hath withdrawn her influence.

As much hath been said of the advantages of reconciliation, which, like an agreeable dream, hath passed away and left us as we were, it is but right that we should examine the contrary side of the argument, and enquire into some of the many material injuries which these Colonies sustain, and always will sustain, by being connected with and dependant on Great-Britain. To examine that connection and dependance, on the principles of nature and common sense, to see what we have to trust to, if separated, and what we are to expect, if dependant.

I have heard it asserted by some, that as America has flourished under her former connection with Great-Britain, the same connection is necessary towards her future happiness, and will always have the same effect. Nothing can be more fallacious than this kind of argument. We may as well assert that because a child has thrived upon milk, that it is never to have meat, or that the first twenty years of our lives is to become a precedent for the next twenty. But even this is admitting more than is true; for I answer roundly, that America would have flourished as much, and probably much more, had no European power taken any notice of her. The commerce by which she hath enriched herself are the necessaries of life, and will always have a market while eating is the custom of Europe.

But she has protected us, say some. That she hath engrossed us is true, and defended the Continent at our expense as well as her own, is admitted; and she would have defended Turkey from the same motive, *viz.* for the sake of trade and dominion.

Alas! we have been long led away by ancient prejudices and made large sacrifices to superstition. We have boasted the protection of Great Britain, without considering, that her motive was *interest* not *attachment;* and that she did not protect us from *our enemies* on *our account;* but from *her enemies* on *her own account,* from those who had no quarrel with us on any *other account,* and who will always be our enemies on the *same account.* Let Britain waive her pretensions to the Continent, or the Continent throw off the dependance, and we should be at peace with France and Spain, were they at war with Britain. The miseries of Hanover last war ought to warn us against connections. . . .

But Britain is the parent country, say some. Then the more shame upon her conduct. Even brutes do not devour their young, nor savages make war upon their families; Wherefore, the assertion, if true, turns to her reproach; but it happens not to be true, or only partly so, and the phrase *parent* or *mother country* hath been jesuitically adopted by the King and his parasites, with a low papistical design of gaining an unfair bias on the credulous weakness of our minds. Europe, and not England, is the parent country of America. This new World hath been the asylum for the persecuted lovers of civil and religious liberty from *every part* of Europe. Hither have they fled, not from the tender embraces of the mother, but from the cruelty of the monster; and it is so far true of England, that the same tyranny which drove the first emigrants from home, pursues their descendants still. . . .

Much hath been said of the united strength of Britain and the Colonies, that in conjunction they might bid defiance to the world: But this is mere presumption; the fate of war is uncertain, neither do the expressions mean any thing; for this continent would never suffer itself to be drained of inhabitants, to support the British arms in either Asia, Africa, or Europe.

Besides, what have we to do with setting the world at defiance? Our plan is commerce, and that, well attended to, will secure us the peace and friendship of all Europe; because it is the interest of all Europe to have America a free port. Her trade will always be a protection, and her barrenness of gold and silver secure her from invaders.

I challenge the warmest advocate for reconciliation to show a single advantage that this continent can reap by being connected with Great Britain. I repeat the challenge; not a single advantage is derived. Our corn will fetch its price in any market in Europe, and our imported goods must be paid for buy them where we will.

But the injuries and disadvantages which we sustain by that connection, are without number; and our duty to mankind at large, as well as to ourselves, instruct us to renounce the alliance: because, any submission to, or dependance on, Great Britain, tends directly to involve this Continent in European wars and quarrels, and set us at variance with nations who would otherwise seek our friendship, and against whom we have neither anger nor complaint. As Europe is our market for trade, we ought to form no partial connection with any part of it. It is the true interest of America to steer clear of European contentions, which she never can do, while, by her dependance on Britain, she is made the make-weight in the scale of British politics.

Europe is too thickly planted with Kingdoms to be long at peace, and whenever a war breaks out between England and any foreign power, the trade of

America goes to ruin, *because of her connection with Britain*. The next war
may not turn out like the last, and should it not, the advocates for reconciliation
now will be wishing for separation then, because neutrality in that case would
be a safer convoy than a man of war. Every thing that is right or reasonable
pleads for separation. The blood of the slain, the weeping voice of nature cries,
'TIS TIME TO PART. Even the distance at which the Almighty hath placed
England and America is a strong and natural proof that the authority of the
one over the other, was never the design of Heaven. The time likewise at which
the Continent was discovered, adds weight to the argument, and the manner
in which it was peopled, encreases the force of it. The Reformation was preceded
by the discovery of America: As if the Almighty graciously meant to open a
sanctuary to the persecuted in future years, when home should afford neither
friendship nor safety. . . .

Though I would carefully avoid giving unnecessary offence, yet I am inclined to believe, that all those who espouse the doctrine of reconciliation, may
be included within the following descriptions.

Interested men, who are not to be trusted, weak men who *cannot* see, prej-
udiced men who will not see, and a certain set of moderate men who think
better of the European world than it deserves; and this last class, by an ill-
judged deliberation, will be the cause of more calamities to this Continent than
all the other three.

It is the good fortune of many to live distant from the scene of present
sorrow; the evil is not sufficiently brought to their doors to make them feel the
precariousness with which all American property is possessed. But let our imaginations transport us a few moments to Boston; that seat of wretchedness
will teach us wisdom, and instruct us for ever to renounce a power in whom
we can have no trust. The inhabitants of that unfortunate city who but a few
months ago were in ease and affluence, have now no other alternative than
to stay and starve, or turn out to beg. Endangered by the fire of their friends
if they continue within the city, and plundered by the soldiery if they leave it, in
their present situation they are prisoners without the hope of redemption, and
in a general attack for their relief they would be exposed to the fury of both
armies.

Men of passive tempers look somewhat lightly over the offences of Great
Britain, and, still hoping for the best, are apt to call out, *Come, come, we shall
be friends again for all this*. But examine the passions and feelings of mankind:
bring the doctrine of reconciliation to the touchstone of nature, and then tell
me whether you can hereafter love, honour, and faithfully serve the power
that hath carried fire and sword into your land? If you cannot do all these,
then are you only deceiving yourselves, and by your delay bringing ruin upon
posterity. Your future connection with Britain, whom you can neither love
nor honour, will be forced and unnatural, and being formed only on the plan of
present convenience, will in a little time fall into a relapse more wretched than
the first. But if you say, you can still pass the violations over, then I ask, hath
your house been burnt? Hath your property been destroyed before your face?
Are your wife and children destitute of a bed to lie on, or bread to live on?
Have you lost a parent or a child by their hands, and yourself the ruined and

retched survivor? If you have not, then are you not a judge of those who have. ut if you have, and can still shake hands with the murderers, then are you nworthy the name of husband, father, friend, or lover, and whatever may be ur rank or title in life, you have the heart of a coward, and the spirit of a ycophant.

This is not inflaming or exaggerating matters, but trying them by those feel- gs and affections which nature justifies, and without which we should be capable of discharging the social duties of life, or enjoying the felicities of it. mean not to exhibit horror for the purpose of provoking revenge, but to waken us from fatal and unmanly slumbers, that we may pursue determinately me fixed object. 'Tis not in the power of Britain or of Europe to conquer merica, if she doth not conquer herself by delay and timidity. The present inter is worth an age if rightly employed, but if lost or neglected the whole ontinent will partake of the misfortune; and there is no punishment which at man doth not deserve, be he who, or what, or where he will, that may be e means of sacrificing a season so precious and useful.

'Tis repugnant to reason, to the universal order of things, to all examples from rmer ages, to suppose that this Continent can long remain subject to any xternal power. The most sanguine in Britain doth not think so. The utmost retch of human wisdom cannot, at this time, compass a plan, short of sepa- tion, which can promise the continent even a year's security. Reconciliation is ow a fallacious dream. Nature hath deserted the connection, and art cannot pply her place. For, as Milton wisely expresses, "never can true reconcilement ow where wounds of deadly hate have pierced so deep."

Every quiet method for peace hath been ineffectual. Our prayers have been jected with disdain; and hath tended to convince us that nothing flatters nity or confirms obstinacy in Kings more than repeated petitioning—and thing hath contributed more than that very measure to make the Kings of urope absolute. Witness Denmark and Sweden. Wherefore, since nothing but ows will do, for God's sake let us come to a final separation, and not leave e next generation to be cutting throats under the violated unmeaning names parent and child.

To say they will never attempt it again is idle and visionary; we thought so the repeal of the stamp act, yet a year or two undeceived us; as well may we ppose that nations which have been once defeated will never renew the arrel.

As to government matters, 'tis not in the power of Britain to do this continent stice: the business of it will soon be too weighty and intricate to be managed th any tolerable degree of convenience, by a power so distant from us, and very ignorant of us; for if they cannot conquer us, they cannot govern us. be always running three or four thousand miles with a tale or a petition, aiting four or five months for an answer, which, when obtained, requires e or six more to explain it in, will in a few years be looked upon as folly and ildishness. There was a time when it was proper, and there is a proper time r it to cease.

Small islands not capable of protecting themselves are the proper objects for vernment to take under their care; but there is something absurd, in supposing a Continent to be perpetually governed by an island. In no instance hath nature made the satellite larger than its primary planet; and as England and America, with respect to each other, reverse the common order of nature, it is evident that they belong to different systems. England to Europe: America to itself.

I am not induced by motives of pride, party, or resentment to espouse the doctrine of separation and independence; I am clearly, positively, and conscientiously persuaded that it is the true interest of this Continent to be so; that every thing short of *that* is mere patchwork, that it can afford no lasting felicity, —that it is leaving the sword to our children, and shrinking back at a time when a little more, a little further, would have rendered this Continent the glory of the earth.

As Britain hath not manifested the least inclination towards a compromise, we may be assured that no terms can be obtained worthy the acceptance of the Continent, or any ways equal to the expence of blood and treasure we have been already put to.

The object contended for, ought always to bear some just proportion to the expense. The removal of North, or the whole detestable junto, is a matter unworthy the millions we have expended. A temporary stoppage of trade was an inconvenience, which would have sufficiently ballanced the repeal of all the acts complained of, had such repeals been obtained; but if the whole Continent must take up arms, if every man must be a soldier, 'tis scarcely worth our while to fight against a contemptible ministry only. Dearly, dearly do we pay for the repeal of the acts, if that is all we fight for; for, in a just estimation 'tis as great a folly to pay a Bunker-hill price for law as for land. As I have always considered the independancy of this continent, as an event which sooner or later must arrive, so from the late rapid progress of the Continent to maturity, the event cannot be far off. Wherefore, on the breaking out of hostilities, it was not worth the while to have disputed a matter which time would have finally redressed, unless we meant to be in earnest: otherwise it is like wasting an estate on a suit at law, to regulate the trespasses of a tenant whose lease is just expiring. No man was a warmer wisher for a reconciliation than myself, before the fatal nineteenth of April, 1775, but the moment the event of that day was made known, I rejected the hardened, sullen-tempered Pharaoh of England for ever; and disdain the wretch, that with the pretended title of FATHER OF HIS PEOPLE can unfeelingly hear of their slaughter, and composedly sleep with their blood upon his soul.

But admitting that matters were now made up, what would be the event? I answer, the ruin of the Continent. And that for several reasons.

First. The powers of governing still remaining in the hands of the King, he will have a negative over the whole legislation of this Continent. And as he hath shown himself such an inveterate enemy to liberty, and discovered such a thirst for arbitrary power, is he, or is he not, a proper person to say to these colonies, *You shall make no laws but what I please!?* And is there any inhabitant of America so ignorant as not to know, that according to what is called the *present constitution,* this Continent can make no laws but what the king gives leave to; and is there any man so unwise as not to see, that (considering what has happened) he will suffer no law to be made here but such as suits *his* purpose? We may be as effectually enslaved by the want of laws in America, as by submitting to laws made for us in England. After matters are made up (as it is called) can there be any doubt, but the whole power of the crown will be exerted to keep this continent as low and humble as possible? Instead of going forward we shall go backward, or be perpetually quarrelling, or ridiculously petitioning. We are already greater than the King wishes us to be, and will he not hereafter endeavor to make us less? To bring the matter to one point, Is the power who is jealous of our prosperity, a proper power to govern us? Whoever says *No*, to this question, is an Independant for independency means no more than this, whether we shall make our own laws, or, whether the King, the greatest enemy this continent hath, or can have, shall tell us *there shall be no laws but such as I like. . . .*

America is only a secondary object in the system of British politics. England consults the good of this country no further than it answers her own purpose. Wherefore, her own interest leads her to suppress the growth of ours in every case which doth not promote her advantage, or in the least interferes with it. A pretty state we should soon be in under such a second hand government, considering what has happened! Men do not change from enemies to friends by the alteration of a name: And in order to show that reconciliation now is a dangerous doctrine, I affirm, *that it would be policy in the King at this time to repeal the acts, for the sake of reinstating himself in the government of the provinces;* In order that HE MAY ACCOMPLISH BY CRAFT AND SUBTLETY, IN THE LONG RUN, WHAT HE CANNOT DO BY FORCE AND VIOLENCE IN THE SHORT ONE. Reconciliation and ruin are nearly related.

Secondly. That as even the best terms which we can expect to obtain can amount to no more than a temporary expedient, or a kind of government by guardianship, which can last no longer than till the Colonies come of age, so the general face and state of things in the interim will be unsettled and unpromising. Emigrants of property will not choose to come to a country whose form of government hangs but by a thread, and who is every day tottering on the brink of commotion and disturbance; and numbers of the present inhabitants would lay hold of the interval to dispose of their effects, and quit the Continent.

But the most powerful of all arguments is, that nothing but independance, *i.e.* a Continental form of government, can keep the peace of the Continent and preserve it inviolate from civil wars. I dread the event of a reconciliation with Britain now, as it is more than probable that it will be followed by a revolt some where or other, the consequences of which may be far more fatal than all the malice of Britain.

Thousands are already ruined by British barbarity; (thousands more will probably suffer the same fate.) Those men have other feelings than us who have nothing suffered. All they now possess is liberty; what they before enjoyed is sacrificed to its service, and having nothing more to lose they disdain submission. Besides, the general temper of the Colonies, towards a British government will be like that of a youth who is nearly out of his time; they will care very little about her: And a government which cannot preserve the peace is no government at all, and in that case we pay our money for nothing; and pray what is it that Britain can do, whose power will be wholly on paper, should a civil tumult break out the very day after reconciliation? I have heard some men say, many of whom I believe spoke without thinking, that they dreaded an independance, fearing that it would produce civil wars: It is but seldom that our first thoughts are truly correct, and that is the case here; for there is ten times more to dread from a patched up connection than from independance. I make the sufferer's case my own, and I protest, that were I driven from house and home, my property destroyed, and my circumstances ruined, that as a man, sensible of injuries, I could never relish the doctrine of reconciliation, or consider myself bound thereby.

The Colonies have manifested such a spirit of good order and obedience to Continental government, as is sufficient to make every reasonable person easy and happy on that head. No man can assign the least pretence for his fears, on any other grounds, than such as are truly childish and ridiculous, viz., that one colony will be striving for superiority over another.

Where there are no distinctions there can be no superiority; perfect equality affords no temptation. The Republics of Europe are all (and we may say always) in peace. Holland and Switzerland are without wars, foreign or domestic: Monarchical governments, it is true, are never long at rest: the crown itself is a temptation to enterprising ruffians at home; and that degree of pride and insolence ever attendant on regal authority, swells into a rupture with foreign powers in instances where a republican government, by being formed on more natural principles, would negociate the mistake.

If there is any true cause of fear respecting independance, it is because no plan is yet laid down. Men do not see their way out. Wherefore, as an opening into that business I offer the following hints; at the same time modestly affirming, that I have no other opinion of them myself, than that they may be the means of giving rise to something better. Could the straggling thoughts of individuals be collected, they would frequently form materials for wise and able men to improve into useful matter.

Let the assemblies be annual, with a president only. The representation more equal, their business wholly domestic, and subject to the authority of a Continental Congress.

Let each Colony be divided into six, eight, or ten, convenient districts, each district to send a proper number of Delegates to Congress, so that each Colony send at least thirty. The whole number in Congress will be at least 390. Each congress to sit   and to choose a President by the following method. When the Delegates are met, let a Colony be taken from the whole thirteen Colonies by lot, after which let the Congress choose (by ballot) a president from out of the Delegates of that Province. In the next Congress, let a Colony be taken by lot from twelve only, omitting that Colony from which the president was taken in the former Congress, and so proceeding on till the whole thirteen shall have had their proper rotation. And in order that nothing may pass into a law but what is satisfactorily just, not less than three fifths of the Congress to be called a majority. He that will promote discord, under a government so equally formed as this, would have joined Lucifer in his revolt.

But as there is a peculiar delicacy from whom, or in what manner, this business must first arise, and as it seems most agreeable and consistent that it should come from some intermediate body between the governed and the governors, that is, between the Congress and the People, let a Continental Conference be held in the following manner, and for the following purpose,

A Committee of twenty six members of congress, *viz.* Two for each Colony. Two Members from each House of Assembly, or Provincial Convention; and five Representatives of the people at large, to be chosen in the capital city or town of each Province, for, and in behalf of the whole Province, by as many qualified voters as shall think proper to attend from all parts of the Province for that purpose; or, if more convenient, the Representatives may be chosen in two or three of the most populous parts thereof. In this conference, thus assembled, will be united the two grand principles of business, *knowledge* and *power*. The Members of Congress, Assemblies, or Conventions, by having had experience in national concerns, will be able and useful counsellors, and the whole, being impowered by the people, will have a truly legal authority.

The conferring members being met, let their business be to frame a Continental Charter, or Charter of the United Colonies; (answering to what is called the Magna Charta of England) fixing the number and manner of choosing Members of Congress, Members of Assembly, with their date of sitting; and drawing the line of business and jurisdiction between them: Always remembering, that our strength is Continental, not Provincial. Securing freedom and property to all men, and above all things, the free exercise of religion, according to the dictates of conscience; with such other matter as it is necessary for a charter to contain. Immediately after which, the said conference to dissolve, and the bodies which shall be chosen conformable to the said charter, to be the Legislators and Governors of this Continent for the time being: Whose peace and happiness, may GOD preserve. AMEN. . . .

But where, say some, is the King of America? I'll tell you, friend, he reigns above, and doth not make havoc of mankind like the Royal Brute of Great Britain. Yet that we may not appear to be defective even in earthly honours, let a day be solemnly set apart for proclaiming the Charter; let it be brought forth placed on the Divine Law, the Word of God; let a crown be placed thereon, by which the world may know, that so far as we approve of monarchy, that in America the law is king. For as in absolute governments the King is law, so in free countries the law ought to be king; and there ought to be no other. But lest any ill use should afterwards arise, let the Crown at the conclusion of the ceremony be demolished, and scattered among the people whose right it is.

A government of our own is our natural right: and when a man seriously reflects on the precariousness of human affairs, he will become convinced, that it is infinitely wiser and safer, to form a constitution of our own in a cool deliberate manner, while we have it in our power, than to trust such an interesting event to time and chance. If we omit it now, some Massanello [1] may

---

1 Massanello: or Masaniello; Tommaso Aniello (1623?–47), a fisherman of Naples who led his countrymen in a spontaneous and unsuccessful revolt against the oppressive rule of their Spanish overlords. After a few days in power he was assassinated.

hereafter arise, who, laying hold of popular disquietudes, may collect together the desperate and the discontented, and by assuming to themselves the powers of government, finally sweep away the liberties of the Continent like a deluge. Should the government of America return again into the hands of Britain, the tottering situation of things will be a temptation for some desperate adventurer to try his fortune; and in such a case, what relief can Britain give? Ere she could hear the news, the fatal business might be done; and ourselves suffering like the wretched Britons under the oppression of the Conqueror. Ye that oppose independance now, ye know not what ye do: ye are opening a door to eternal tyranny, by keeping vacant the seat of government. There are thousands and tens of thousands, who would think it glorious to expel from the Continent, that barbarous and hellish power, which hath stirred up the Indians and the Negroes to destroy us; the cruelty hath a double guilt, it is dealing brutally by us, and treacherously by them.

To talk of friendship with those in whom our reason forbids us to have faith, and our affections wounded thro' a thousand pores instruct us to detest, is madness and folly. Every day wears out the little remains of kindred between us and them; and can there be any reason to hope, that as the relationship expires, the affection will encrease, or that we shall agree better when we have ten times more and greater concerns to quarrel over than ever?

Ye that tell us of harmony and reconciliation, can ye restore to us the time that is past? Can ye give to prostitution its former innocence? neither can ye reconcile Britain and America. The last cord now is broken, the people of England are presenting addresses against us. There are injuries which nature cannot forgive; she would cease to be nature if she did. As well can the lover forgive the ravisher of his mistress, as the Continent forgive the murders of Britain. The Almighty hath implanted in us these unextinguishable feelings for good and wise purposes. They are the Guardians of his Image in our hearts. They distinguish us from the herd of common animals. The social compact would dissolve, and justice be extirpated from the earth, or have only a casual existence were we callous to the touches of affection. The robber and the murderer would often escape unpunished, did not the injuries which our tempers sustain, provoke us into justice.

O! ye that love mankind! Ye that dare oppose not only the tyranny but the tyrant, stand forth! Every spot of the old world is overrun with oppression. Freedom hath been hunted round the Globe. Asia and Africa have long expelled her. Europe regards her like a stranger, and England hath given her warning to depart. O! receive the fugitive, and prepare in time an asylum for mankind.

5] A Virginia Aristocrat Drags His Feet

Carter Braxton, a moderate patriot, doubted American unity and opposed independence in the spring of 1776 because of countless conflicts between colonies and sections. His letter to Landon Carter demonstrates the distrust of a Virginia gentleman for the "democracy" of New England. Moreover, he suspected that the self-interest of most other colonies would undermine any chance of union. Braxton later came around and signed the Declaration of Independence.*

PHILA. April. 14, 1776.

DEAR SIR,

. . . Independency and total seperation from Great Britain are the interesting Subjects of all ranks of men and often agitate our Body. It is in truth a delusive Bait which men inconsiderately catch at, without knowing the hook to which it is affixed. It is an Object to be wished for by every American, when it can be obtained with Safety and Honor. That this is not the moment I will prove by Arguments that to me are decisive, and which exist with certainty. Your refined notion of our publick Honor being engaged to await the terms offered by Commissioners operates strongly with me and many others and makes the first reason I would offer. My next is that America is in too defenceless a State for the declaration, having no Alliance with a naval Power nor as yet any Fleet of consequence of her own to protect that trade which is so essential to the prosecution of the War, without which I know we cannot go on much longer. It is said by the Advocates for Seperation that France will undoubtedly assist us after we have asserted the State, and therefore they urge us to make the experiment. Would such a blind precipitate measure as this be justified by Prudence, first to throw off our connexion with G. Britain and then give ourselves up to the Arms of France? Would not the Court so famous for Intrigues and Deception avail herself of our situation and from it exact much severer terms than if we were to treat with her (G. B.) before hand and settle the terms of any future Alliance. Surely she would, but the truth of the matter is, there are some who are affraid to await the Arrival of Commissioners, lest the dispute should be accomodated much agt their Will even upon the Admission of our own terms. For however strange it may appear I am satisfied that the eastern Colonies do not mean to have a Reconciliation and in this I am justified by publick and private Reasons. To illustrate my Opinion I will beg leave to mention them. Two of the New England Colonies enjoy a Government purely democratical the Nature and Principle of which both civil and religious are so totally incompatible with Monarchy, that they have ever lived in a restless state under it. The other two tho' not so popular in their frame bordered so near upon it that Monarchical Influence hung very heavy on them. The best opportunity in the World being now offered them to throw off all subjection and embrace their darling Democracy they are determined to accept it. These are aided by those of a private Nature, but not less cogent. The Colonies of Massachusetts, and Connecticut who rule the other two, have Claims on the Province of Pennsylvania in the whole for near one third of the Land within their Provincial Bounds and indeed the claim ex-

* A VIRGINIA ARISTOCRAT DRAGS HIS FEET: Carter Braxton to Landon Carter, April 14, 1776. From Edmund C. Burnett, ed., *Letters of Members of the Continental Congress* (Washington, 1921–36), I, 420–21. Reprinted by permission of the Carnegie Institution of Washington.

tended to its full extent comes within four miles of this City. This dispute was carried to the King and Council, and with them it now lies. The Eastern Colonies unwilling they should now be the Arbiter have asserted their Claims by force, and have at this time eight hundred men in arms upon the upper part of this Land called Wyoming, where they are peaceable at present only through the Influence of the Congress. Then naturally, there arises a heart burning and jealousy between these people and they must have two very different Objects in View. The Province of New York is not without her Fears and apprehensions from the Temper of her Neighbors, their great swarms and small Territory. Even Virginia is not free from Claim on Pennsylvania nor Maryland from those on Virginia. Some of the Delegates from our Colony carry their Ideas of right to lands so far to the Eastward that the middle Colonies dread their being swallowed up between the Claims of them and those from the East. And yet without any Adjustment of those disputes and a variety of other matters, some are for Lugging us into Independence. But so long as these remain unsettled and men act upon the Principles they ever have done, you may rely, no such thing will be generally agreed on. Upon reviewing the secret movements of Men and things I am convinced the Assertion of Independence is far off. If it was to be now asserted, the Continent would be torn in pieces by Intestine Wars and Convulsions. Previous to Independence all disputes must be healed and Harmony prevail. A grand Continental league must be formed and a superintending Power also. When these necessary Steps are taken and I see a Coalition formed sufficient to withstand the Power of Britain, or any other, then am I for an independent State and all its Consequences, as then I think they will produce Happiness to America. It is a true saying of a Wit—We must hang together or separately. I will not beg your pardon for intruding this long letter upon your old Age w^h I judged necessary in my situation and to conclude by assuring you I am with great regard

Your affect Nephew

CARTER BRAXTON

[P. S.] If any of our Newspapers will be agreeable say so in your next.

6] Mecklenburg County Demands a Democratic Government

Settlers in western North Carolina had been sadly underrepresented in the colonial legislature and discriminated against by easterners who controlled the government. When revolution came to the back country it was twofold. a drive for independence from Great Britain, to be sure, but also a drive to bring state and local government "under the authority of the People." The Scotch-Irish of Mecklenburg County already enjoyed a reputation for militancy and independence. As early as May 31, 1775, they had drafted a set of bold resolves declaring British government virtually suspended in America. They followed these on September 1 with instructions for their county delegates to the provincial congress advocating, besides independence, several democratic reforms including "equal Representation," suffrage rights to freemen, election of local officers—particularly clerks and sheriffs—and the "full, free and peaceable enjoyment" of the Protestant religion.*

1. YOU ARE instructed to vote that the late Province of North Carolina is and of right ought to be a free and independent state invested with all the power of Legislation capable of making laws to regulate all its internal policy subject only in its external connections and foreign commerce to a negative of a continental Senate.

2. You are instructed to vote for the Execution of a civil Government under the authority of the People for the future security of all the Rights Privileges and Prerogatives of the State and the private natural and unalienable Rights of the constituting members thereof either as Men or Christians.

If this should not be confirmed in Congress or Convention—protest.

3. You are instructed to vote that an equal Representation be established and that the qualifications required to enable any person or persons to have a voice in Legislation may not be secured to[o] high but that every Freeman who shall be called upon to support Government either in person or property may be admitted thereto. If this should not be confirmed protest and remonstrate.

4. You are instructed to vote that Legislation be not a divided right, and that no man or body of men be invested with a negative on the voice of the People duly collected and that no honors or dignities be conferred for life or made hereditary on any person or persons either legislative or executive. If this should not be confirmed—protest and remonstrate.

5. You are instructed to vote that all and every person or persons seized or possessed of any estate real or personal agreeable to the last establishment be confirmed in their seizures and possession to all intents and purposes in law who have not forfeited their right to the protection of the State by their Criminal practice towards the same. If this should not be confirmed—protest.

6. You are instructed to vote that Deputies to represent this State in a Continental Congress be appointed in and by the supreme Legislative body of the State the form of nomination to be submitted to if free and also that all officers the influence of whose office is equally to extend to every part of the State be appointed in the same manner and form—likewise give your consent to the establishing the old political divisions if it should be voted in convention or to new ones if similar. On such establishments taking place you are instructed to vote in the general that all officers who are to exercise their authority in any of the said districts be recommended to the trust only by the freemen of the said division—to be subject however to the general laws and regulations of the State. If this should not be substantially confirmed—protest.

7. You are instructed to move and insist that the people you immediately represent be acknowledged to be a distinct county of this State, as formerly of the late province with the additional privilege of annually electing their own officers both civil and military, together with the elections of Clerks and

---

* MECKLENBURG COUNTY DEMANDS A DEMOCRATIC GOVERNMENT: "Instructions for the Delegates of Mecklenburg County proposed to the Consideration of the County." From William L. Saunders, ed., *Colonial Records of North Carolina*, X (Raleigh, 1890), 239–42.

Sheriffs by the freemen of the same. The choice to be confirmed by the sovereign authority of the State, and the officers so invested to be under the jurisdiction of the State and liable to its cognizance and inflictions in case of malpractice. If this should not be confirmed—protest and remonstrate.

8. You are instructed to vote that no Chief Justice, no Secretary of State, no Auditor General, no Surveyor General, no practicing lawyer, no clerk of any court of record, no sheriff and no person holding a military office in this State shall be a representative of the people in Congress or Convention. If this should not be confirmed—contend for it.

9. You are instructed to vote that all claims against the public, except such as accrue upon attendance upon Congress or Convention, be first submitted to the inspection of a committee of nine or more men, inhabitants of the county where said claimant is a resident, and without the approbation of said committee it shall not be accepted by the public; for which purpose you are to move and insist that a law be enacted to empower the freemen of each county to choose a committee of not less than nine men, of whom none are to be military officers. If this should not be confirmed, protest and remonstrate.

10. You are instructed to refuse to enter into any combinations of secrecy as members of Congress or Convention and also to refuse to subscribe any ensnaring tests binding you to an unlimited subjection to the determination of Congress or Convention.

11. You are instructed to move and insist that the public accounts fairly stated shall be regularly kept in proper books open to the inspection of all persons whom it may concern. If this should not be confirmed—contend for it.

12. You are instructed to move and insist that the power of County Courts be much more extensive than under the former constitution, both with respect to matters of property and breaches of the peace[.] If not confirmed—contend for it.

13. You are instructed to assert and consent to the establishment of the Christian Religion as contained in the Scriptures of the Old and New Testaments and more briefly comprised in the 39 Articles of the Church of England excluding the 37th Article together with all the Articles excepted, and not to be imposed on dissenters, by the act of toleration and clearly held forth in the confession of faith compiled by the Assembly of divines at Westminster, to be the Religion of the State to the utter exclusion forever of all and every other (falsely so called) Religion, whether Pagan or Papal, and that the full, free and peaceable enjoyment thereof be secured to all and every constituent member of the State as their unalienable right as Freemen without the imposition of rites and ceremonies whether claiming civil or ecclesiastic power for their source and that a confession and profession of the Religion so established shall be necessary in qualifying any person for public trust in the State. If this should not be confirmed, protest and remonstrate.

14. You are instructed to oppose to the utmost any particular church or set of Clergymen being invested with power to decree rites and ceremonies and to decide in controversies of faith to be submitted to under the influence of penal laws. You are also to oppose the establishment of any mode of worship to be supported to the opposition of the rights of conscience together with the destruction of private property. You are to understand that under modes of worship

are comprehended the different forms of swearing by law required. You are moreover to oppose the establishing an ecclesiastic supremacy in the sovereign authority of the State. You are to oppose the toleration of the popish idolatrous worship. If this should not be confirmed, protest and remonstrate.

15. You are instructed to move and insist that not less than four fifths of the body of which you are members shall in voting be deemed a majority. If this should not be confirmed, contend for it[.]

16. You are instructed to give your voices to and for every motion and bill made or brought into the Congress or Convention where they appear to be for public utility and in no ways repugnant to the above instruction.

17. Gentlemen the foregoing instructions you are not only to look on as instructions but as charges to which you are desired to take special heed as the general rule of your conduct as our Representatives and we expect you will exert yourselves to the utmost of your ability to obtain the purposes given you in charge and wherein you fail either in obtaining or opposing you are hereby ordered to enter your protest against the vote of the Congress or Convention as is pointed out to you in the above instructions.

7] Governments Are Founded on Compact

> When royal government ceased in Massachusetts, at the suggestion of Congress the patriots reverted to their old charter and carried on with an assembly but no governor. This was a temporary arrangement and served the colonists' needs so long as reconciliation with England seemed possible. By the spring of 1776, when an accommodation was out of the question and independence imminent, Massachusetts was still under its old constitution—which ardent democrats hated, since it deprived them of electing some of their local officers, particularly judges. Pittsfield, in the heart of Berkshire County in the west, petitioned in May, 1776, in simple Lockean terms for a new constitution based on compact, so that the "foundation of government be well established" and the "Glory of the present Revolution remain untarnished." *

To THE Honourable Council, & the Honourable House of Representatives of the Colony of Massachusetts Bay in General Assembly met at Watertown May 29th. 1776——

The Petition & Memorial of the Inhabitants of the Town of Pittsfield in said Colony,

Humbly Showeth . . .

That 'till last fall your Memorialists had little or no Expectation of obtaining any new previleges beyound what our defective Charter secured to us.——

That when they came more maturely to ref[l]ect upon the nature of the present Contest, & the Spirit & obstinacy of Administration—What an amazing Ex-

---

* GOVERNMENTS ARE FOUNDED ON COMPACT: From Robert J. Taylor, ed., *Massachusetts, Colony to Commonwealth: Documents on the Formation of Its Constitution, 1775–1780* (Chapel Hill, N.C., 1961), pp. 26–29. Reprinted by permission of the University of North Carolina Press.

pence the united Colonies had incured? How many Towns had been burnt or
otherwise damaged? what Multitudes had turned out to beg & how many of
our valiant Heroes had been slain in the Defence of their Country & the
Impossibility of our being ever again dependant on Great Britain or in any
Measure subject to her Authority—When they further considered that the
Revolution in England affoarded the Nation but a very imperfect Redress of
Grievances the Nation being transported with extravagant Joy in getting rid
of one Tyrant forgot to provide against another—& how every Man by Nature
has the seeds of Tyranny deeply implanted within him so that nothing short of
Ommipotence can eradicate them—That when they attended to the Advice
given this Colony by the Continental Congress respecting the Assumption of
our antient Constitution, how early that Advice was given, the Reasons of it
& the principles upon which it was given which no longer exist, what a great
Change of Circumstances there has been in the Views & Designs of this whole
Continent since the giving said Advice—That when they considered, now is the
only Time we have reason ever to expect for securing our Liberty & the Liberties
of future posterity upon a permanent Foundation that no length of Time can
undermine—Tho' they were filled with pain & Anxiety at so much as seeming
to oppose public Councils yet with all these Considerations in our View, Love
of Virtue freedom & posterity prevailed upon us to suspend a second Time the
Courts of Justice in this County after the Judges of the Quarter Sessions had
in a pricipitate & clandestine Manner held one Court & granted out a Number
of Licences to Innholders at the rate of six shillings or more each & divided the
Money amongst themselves with this boast that now it was a going to be like
former Times & had discovered a Spirit of Independance of the People & a
Disposition triumphantly to ride over their heads & worse than renew all our
former Oppressions. . . . We beg leave to lay before your Honors our Principles real Views & Designs in what we have hitherto done & what Object we
are reaching after, with this Assurance if we have erred it is thro' Ignorance
& not bad Intention.——

We beg leave therefore to represent that we have always been persuaded that
the people are the fountain of power. That since the Dissolution of the power
of Great Britain over these Colonies they have fallen into a state of Nature.
That the first step to be taken by a people in such a state for the Enjoyment or
Restoration of Civil Government amongst them, is the formation of a fundamental Constitution as the Basis & ground work of Legislation.

That the Approbation of the Majority of the people of this fundamental
Constitution is absolutely necessary to give Life & being to it. That then & not
'till then is the foundation laid for Legislation. We often hear of the fundamental Constitution of Great Britain, which all political Writers (except
ministerial ones) set above the King Lords, & Commons, which they cannot
change, nothing short of the great rational Majority of the people being sufficient
for this.

That a Representative Body may form, but cannot impose said fundamental
Constitution upon a people. They being but servants of the people cannot be
greater than their Masters, & must be responsible to them. If this fundamental
Constitution is above the whole Legislature, the Legislature cannot certainly

make it, it must be the Approbation of the Majority which gives Life & being to it.——

That said fundamental Constitution has not been formed for this Province the Corner stone is not yet laid & whatever Building is reared without a foundation must fall into Ruins. That this can be instantly effected with the Approbation of the Continental Congress & Law subordination & good government flow in better than their antient Channels in a few Months Time.—That till this is done we are but beating the air & doing what will & must be undone afterwards, & all our labour is lost & on divers Accounts much worse than lost.

That a Doctrine lately broached in this County by several of the Justices newly created without the Voice of the People, that the Representatives of the People may form Just what fundamental Constitution they please & impose it upon the people & however obnoxious to them they can obtain no relief from it but by a New Election, & if our Representatives should never see fit to give the people one that pleases them there is no help for it appears to us to be the rankest kind of Toryism, the self same Monster we are now fighting against.

These are some of the Truths we firmly believe & are countenanced in believing them by the most respectable political Writers of the last & present Century, especially by Mr. Burgh in his political Disquisitions for the publication of which one half of the Continental Congress were subscribers.

We beg leave further to represent that we by no Means object to the most speedy Institution of Legal Government thro' this province & that we are as earnestly desirous as any others of this great Blessing.

That knowing the strong Byass of human Nature to Tyranny & Despotism we have Nothing else in View but to provide for Posterity against the wanton Exercise of power which cannot otherwise be done than by the formation of a fundamental Constitution. What is the fundamental Constitution of this province, what are the unalienable Rights of the people the power of the Rulers, how often to be elected by the people &c have any of these things been as yet ascertained. Let it not be said by future posterity that in this great this noble this glorious Contest we made no provision against Tyranny amongst ourselves[.]

We beg leave to assure your Honors that the purest & most disinterested Love of posterity & a fervent desire of transmitting to them a fundamental Constitution securing their sacred Rights & Immunities against all Tyrants that may spring up after us has moved us in what we have done. We have not been influenced by hope of Gain or Expectation of Preferment & Honor. We are no discontented faction we have no fellowship with Tories, we are the staunch friends of the Union of these Colonies & will support & maintain your Honors in opposing Great Britain with our Lives & Treasure.

But if Commissions should be recalled & the Kings Name struck out of them, if the Fee Table be reduced never so low, & multitudes of other things be done to still the people all is to us as Nothing whilst the foundation is unfixed the Corner stone of Government unlaid. We have heared much of Governments being founded in Compact. What Compact has been formed as the foundation of Government in this province?—We beg leave further to represent that we have undergone many grievous oppressions in this County & that now we wish a

Barrier might be set up against such oppressions, against which we can have no security long till the foundation of Government be well established.——

We beg leave further to represent these as the Sentiments of by far the Majority of the people in this County as far as we can Judge & being so agreeable to Reason Scripture & Common Sense, as soon as the Attention of people in this province is awakened we doubt not but the Majority will be with us.

We beg leave further to observe that if this Honourable Body shall find that we have embraced Errors dangerous to the safety of these Colonies it is our Petition that our Errors may be detected & you shall be put to no further Trouble from us but without an Alteration in our Judgment the Terrors of this World will not daunt us we are determined to resist Great Britain to the last Extremity & all others who may claim a similar Power over us. Yet we hold not to an Imperium in Imperio we will be determined by the Majority.——

Your Petitioners beg leave therefore to Request that this Honourable Body would form a fundamental Constitution for this province after leave is asked & obtained from the Honourable Continental Congress & that said Constitution be sent abroad for the Approbation of the Majority of the people in this Colony that in this way we may emerge from a state of Nature & enjoy again the Blessing of Civil Government in this way the Rights & Liberties of future Generations will be secured & the Glory of the present Revolution remain untarnished & future Posterity rise up & call this Honourable Council & House of Representatives blessed.

8] A Minister Urges Congress to Abolish Slavery

> The Reverend Samuel Hopkins, a Congregational minister from Newport, Rhode Island, was a Calvinist theologian and a disciple of Jonathan Edwards. His opposition to slavery was based on principles of the Revolution, Christian benevolence, and a Calvinist's strong sense of sin. The last he carried to the point where he believed, like an old Puritan, that the calamities which then confronted Americans were God's punishment for enslaving the Negroes. Hopkins and Moses Brown, a Providence Quaker, contributed nobly to Rhode Island's early lead in the antislavery movement. The *Dialogue*, from which the following is excerpted, was published in the spring of 1776.*

TO THE HONORABLE MEMBERS OF THE CONTINENTAL CONGRESS, REPRESENTATIVES OF THE THIRTEEN UNITED AMERICAN COLONIES.

MUCH-HONORED GENTLEMEN:

As God, the great Father of the universe, has made you the fathers of these colonies,—and in answer to the prayers of his people given you counsel, and that wisdom and integrity in the exertion of which you have been such great and

---

* A MINISTER URGES CONGRESS TO ABOLISH SLAVERY: Samuel Hopkins, *A Dialogue Concerning the Slavery of the Africans; Shewing it to be the Duty and Interest of the American States to Emancipate all their African Slaves . . . Dedicated to the Honorable the Continental Congress . . .* (Norwich, Conn., 1776). From Samuel Hopkins, *Timely Articles on Slavery* (Boston, 1854), pp. 547–88.

extensive blessings, and obtained the approbation and applause of your constituents and the respect and veneration of the nations in whose sight you have acted in the important, noble struggle for LIBERTY,—we naturally look to you in behalf of more than half a million of persons in these colonies, who are under such a degree of oppression and tyranny as to be wholly deprived of all civil and personal liberty, to which they have as good a right as any of their fellow-men, and are reduced to the most abject state of bondage and slavery without any just cause.

We have particular encouragement thus to apply to you, since you have had the honor and happiness of leading these colonies to resolve to stop the slave trade, and to buy no more slaves imported from Africa. We have the satisfaction of the best assurances that you have done this not merely from political reasons, but from a conviction of the unrighteousness and cruelty of that trade, and a regard to justice and benevolence,—deeply sensible of the inconsistence of promoting the slavery of the Africans, at the same time we are asserting our own civil liberty at the risk of our fortunes and lives. This leaves in our minds no doubt of your being sensible of the equal unrighteousness and oppression, as well as inconsistence with ourselves, in holding so many hundreds of thousands of blacks in slavery, who have an equal right to freedom with ourselves, while we are maintaining this struggle for our own and our children's liberty; and a hope and confidence that the cries and tears of these oppressed will be regarded by you, and that your wisdom and the great influence you have in these colonies will be so properly and effectually exerted as to bring about a total abolition of slavery, in such a manner as shall greatly promote the happiness of those oppressed strangers and the best interest of the public. . . .

May you judge the poor of the people, save the children of the needy, relieve the oppressed, and deliver the spoiled out of the hands of the oppressor, and be the happy instruments of procuring and establishing universal liberty to white and black, to be transmitted down to the latest posterity. . . .

The present situation of our public affairs and our struggle for liberty, and the abundant conversation this occasions in all companies, while the poor negroes look on and hear what an aversion we have to slavery and how much liberty is prized, they often hearing it declared publicly and in private, as the voice of all, that slavery is more to be dreaded than death, and we are resolved to live free or die, etc.; this, I say, necessarily leads them to attend to their own wretched situation more than otherwise they could. They see themselves deprived of all liberty and property, and their children after them, to the latest posterity, subject to the will of those who appear to have no feeling for their misery, and are guilty of many instances of hard-heartedness and cruelty towards them, while they think themselves very kind . . .

They see the slavery the Americans dread as worse than death is lighter than a feather compared to their heavy doom, and may be called liberty and happiness when contrasted with the most abject slavery and unutterable wretchedness to which they are subjected; and in this dark and dreadful situation they look round and find no help—no pity—no hope! And when they observe all this cry and struggle for liberty for ourselves and children, and see themselves and their children wholly overlooked by us, and behold the sons of liberty oppressing and tyrannizing over many thousands of poor blacks who have as good a claim to liberty as themselves, they are shocked with the glaring inconsistence, and wonder they themselves do not see it. You must not, therefore, lay it to the few who are pleading the cause of these friendless, distressed poor, that they are more uneasy than they used to be in a sense of their wretched state and from a desire of liberty: there is a more mighty and irresistible cause than this, viz., all that passes before them in our public struggle for liberty. . . .

No wonder there are many and great difficulties in reforming an evil practice of this kind, which has got such deep root by length of time and is become so common. . . . This matter ought, doubtless, to be attended to by the general assemblies, and continental and provincial congresses; and if they were as much united and engaged in devising ways and means to set at liberty these injured slaves as they are to defend themselves from tyranny, it would soon be effected. There were, without doubt, many difficulties and impediments in the way of the Jews liberating those of their brethren they had brought into bondage in the days of Jeremiah. But when they were besieged by the Chaldeans, and this their sin was laid before them, and they were threatened with desolation if they did not reform, they broke through every difficulty, and set their servants at liberty. . . .

Let this iniquity be viewed in its true magnitude, and in the shocking light in which it has been set in this conversation; let the wretched case of the poor blacks be considered with proper pity and benevolence, together with the probably dreadful consequence to this land of retaining them in bondage, and all objections against liberating them would vanish. The mountains that are now raised up in the imagination of many would become a plain, and every difficulty surmounted.

. . . And why are we not as much affected with the slavery of the many thousands of blacks among ourselves whose miserable state is before our eyes? And why should we not be as much engaged to relieve them? The reason is obvious. It is because they are negroes, and fit for nothing but slaves, and we have been used to look on them in a mean, contemptible light, and our education has filled us with strong prejudices against them, and led us to consider them, not as our brethren, or in any degree on a level with us, but as quite another species of animals, made only to serve us and our children, and as happy in bondage as in any other state. This has banished all attention to the injustice that is done them, and any proper sense of their misery or the exercise of benevolence towards them. If we could only divest ourselves of these strong prejudices which have insensibly fixed on our minds, and consider them as by nature and by right on a level with our brethren and children, and those of our neighbors, and that benevolence which loves our neighbor as ourselves, and is agreeable to truth and righteousness, we should begin to feel towards them, in some measure at least, as we should towards our children and neighbors . . .

This leads me to observe, that our distresses are come upon us in such a way, and the occasion of the present war is such, as in the most clear and striking manner to point out the sin of holding our blacks in slavery, and admonish us to reform, and render us shockingly inconsistent with ourselves, and amazingly guilty if we refuse. God has raised up men to attempt to deprive us of liberty, and the evil we are threatened with is slavery. This, with our vigorous attempts to avoid it, is the ground of all our distresses, and the general voice is, "We will die in the attempt, rather than submit to slavery." . . . O, the shocking, the intolerable inconsistence! And this gross, barefaced inconsistence is an open, practical condemnation of holding these our brethren in slavery; and in these circumstances the crime of persisting in it becomes unspeakably greater and more provoking in God's sight, so that all the former unrighteousness and cruelty exercised in this practice is innocence compared with the awful guilt that is now contracted. And in allusion to the words of our Savior, it may with great truth and propriety be said, "If he had not thus come in his providence, and spoken unto us, (comparatively speaking,) we had not had sin in making bondslaves of our brethren; but now, we have no cloak for our sin."

And if we continue in this evil practice and refuse to let the oppressed go free, under all this light and admonition suited to convince and reform us, and while God is evidently correcting us for it as well as for other sins, have we any reason to expect deliverance from the calamities we are under? May we not rather look for slavery and destruction like that which came upon the obstinate, unreformed Jews? In this light I think it ought to be considered by us; and viewed thus, it affords a most forcible, formidable argument not to put off liberating our slaves to a more convenient time, but to arise, all as one man, and do it with all our might, without delay, since delaying in this case is awfully dangerous as well as unspeakably criminal. . . .

9] A Massachusetts Dissenter Attacks the Established Church

The revolutionary movement gave the Reverend Isaac Backus of Middleborough a splendid opportunity to push the Baptists' demand that freedom from tyranny meant freedom from religious taxation for dissenters. Here is an excerpt from his memorial in behalf of the Warren Association to the Massachusetts Assembly in September, 1775, in which he echoes the arguments of Roger Williams for separation of church and state and pleads for an "entire freedom from being taxed by civil rulers to religious worship." The result was a bill that was read once in the Assembly but never enacted.*

OUR REAL grievances are, that we, as well as our fathers, have, from time to time, been taxed on religious accounts where we were not represented; and when we have sued for our rights, our causes have been tried by interested judges. That the Representatives in former Assemblies, as well as the present, were elected by virtue only of civil and worldly qualifications, is a truth so evident, that we presume it need not be proved to this Assembly; and for a civil Legislature to impose religious taxes, is, we conceive, a power which their constituents never had to give; and is therefore going entirely out of their jurisdiction.—Under the legal dispensation, where God himself prescribed the exact

* A MASSACHUSETTS DISSENTER ATTACKS THE ESTABLISHED CHURCH: Isaac Backus, *A History of New-England, with Particular Reference to the Denomination of Christians called Baptists* . . . , II (Providence, 1784), 304–05.

proportion of what the people were to give, yet none but persons of the worst characters ever attempted to *take it by force*. I Sam. ii. 12, 16. Mica. iii. 5-9. How daring then must it be for any to do it for Christ's ministers, who says, *my kingdom is not of this world!*—We beseech this honorable Assembly to take these matters into their wise and serious consideration, before him who has said, *with what measure ye mete it shall be measured to you again*. Is not all America now appealing to heaven, against the injustice of being taxed where we are not represented, and against being judged by men who are interested in getting away our money? And will heaven approve of your *doing the same thing* to your fellow servants! No, surely.—We have no desire of representing this government as the worst of any who have imposed religious taxes; we fully believe the contrary. Yet, as we are persuaded that an entire freedom from being taxed by civil rulers to religious worship, is not a mere favour, from any man or men in the world, but a right and property granted us by God, who commands us to *stand fast in it,* we have not only the same reason to refuse an acknowledgment of such a taxing power here, as America has the abovesaid power, but also, according to our present light, we should wrong our consciences in allowing that power to men, which we believe belongs only to God.

10] Virginia Sets the Pace with a Declaration of Rights and a Permanent Constitution

A] "THE BASIS AND FOUNDATION OF GOVERNMENT"

> Before drafting a constitution, the Virginia convention established a theoretical foundation for government by adopting on June 12, 1776, a Declaration of Rights written by George Mason. Soundly based on the principles of human rights, it set down succinctly what eighteenth-century Virginians believed an independent government ought to guarantee its people, including a section declaring all men "equally entitled to the free exercise of religion." *

A DECLARATION of rights made by the representatives of the good people of Virginia, assembled in full and free convention; which rights do pertain to them and their posterity, as the basis and foundation of government.

SECTION 1. That all men are by nature equally free and independent, and have certain inherent rights, of which, when they enter into a state of society, they cannot, by any compact, deprive or divest their posterity; namely, the enjoyment of life and liberty, with the means of acquiring and possessing property, and pursuing and obtaining happiness and safety.

SEC. 2. That all power is vested in, and consequently derived from, the people; that magistrates are their trustees and servants, and at all times amenable to them.

* "THE BASIS AND FOUNDATION OF GOVERNMENT": The Constitution of Virginia, 1776: Bill of Rights. From Francis N. Thorpe, ed., *The Federal and State Constitutions, Colonial Charters, and Other Organic Laws* . . . (Washington, 1909), VII, 3812–14.

Sec. 3. That government is, or ought to be, instituted for the common benefit, protection, and security of the people, nation, or community; of all the various modes and forms of government, that is best which is capable of producing the greatest degree of happiness and safety, and is most effectually secured against the danger of maladministration; and that, when any government shall be found inadequate or contrary to these purposes, a majority of the community hath an indubitable, inalienable, and indefeasible right to reform, alter, or abolish it, in such manner as shall be judged most conducive to the public weal.

Sec. 4. That no man, or set of men, are entitled to exclusive or separate emoluments or privileges from the community, but in consideration of public services; which, not being descendible, neither ought the offices of magistrate, legislator, or judge to be hereditary.

Sec. 5. That the legislative and executive powers of the State should be separate and distinct from the judiciary; and that the members of the two first may be restrained from oppression, by feeling and participating the burdens of the people, they should, at fixed periods, be reduced to a private station, return into that body from which they were originally taken, and the vacancies be supplied by frequent, certain, and regular elections, in which all, or any part of the former members, to be again eligible, or ineligible, as the laws shall direct.

Sec. 6. That elections of members to serve as representatives of the people, in assembly, ought to be free; and that all men, having sufficient evidence of permanent common interest with, and attachment to, the community, have the right of suffrage, and cannot be taxed or deprived of their property for public uses, without their own consent, or that of their represen[ta]tives so elected, nor bound by any law to which they have not, in like manner, assembled, for the public good.

Sec. 7. That all power of suspending laws, or the execution of laws, by any authority, without consent of the representatives of the people, is injurious to their rights, and ought not to be exercised.

Sec. 8. That in all capital or criminal prosecutions a man hath a right to demand the cause and nature of his accusation, to be confronted with the accusers and witnesses, to call for evidence in his favor, and to a speedy trial by an impartial jury of twelve men of his vicinage, without whose unanimous consent he cannot be found guilty; nor can he be compelled to give evidence against himself; that no man be deprived of his liberty, except by the law of the land or the judgment of his peers.

Sec. 9. That excessive bail ought not to be required, nor excessive fines imposed, nor cruel and unusual punishments inflicted.

Sec. 10. That general warrants, whereby an officer or messenger may be commanded to search suspected places without evidence of a fact committed, or to seize any person or persons not named, or whose offence is not particularly described and supported by evidence, are grievous and oppressive, and ought not to be granted.

Sec. 11. That in controversies respecting property, and in suits between man and man, the ancient trial by jury is preferable to any other, and ought to be held sacred.

Sec. 12. That the freedom of the press is one of the great bulwarks of liberty, and can never be restrained but by despotic governments.

Sec. 13. That a well-regulated militia, composed of the body of the people, trained to arms, is the proper, natural, and safe defence of a free State; that standing armies, in time of peace, should be avoided, as dangerous to liberty; and that in all cases the military should be under strict subordination to, and governed by, the civil power.

Sec. 14. That the people have a right to uniform government; and, therefore, that no government separate from, or independent of the government of Virginia, ought to be erected or established within the limits thereof.

Sec. 15. That no free government, or the blessings of liberty, can be preserved to any people, but by a firm adherence to justice, moderation, temperance, frugality, and virtue, and by frequent recurrence to fundamental principles.

Sec. 16. That religion, or the duty which we owe to our Creator, and the manner of discharging it, can be directed only by reason and conviction, not by force or violence; and therefore all men are equally entitled to the free exercise of religion, according to the dictates of conscience; and that it is the mutual duty of all to practise Christian forbearance, love, and charity towards each other.

B] "The Future Form of Government"

Virginia's constitution was a positive achievement: its preamble declared independence; it was the first permanent state constitution, serving as a model for others; and it established a bicameral legislature and a separation of powers (although, as Jefferson complained, the governor had too little power and the lower house too much). But the Revolution in Virginia was a moderate affair, under the thumb of the planter aristocracy which stomached no radical changes. These gentlemen accepted in theory the broad basis of human rights described earlier in the Declaration, but their implementation of these rights in a practical government was something else again. The constitution, which was adopted on June 29 but not submitted to the people, maintained the planter group in power. Representation still favored the tidewater, and suffrage requirements remained the same.*

. . . THE GOVERNMENT of this country, as formerly exercised under the crown of Great Britain, is TOTALLY DISSOLVED.

We therefore, the delegates and representatives of the good people of Virginia, having maturely considered the premises, and viewing with great concern the deplorable conditions to which this once happy country must be reduced, unless some regular, adequate mode of civil polity is speedily adopted, and in compliance with a recommendation of the General Congress, do ordain and declare the future form of government of Virginia to be as followeth:

The legislative, executive, and judiciary department, shall be separate and distinct, so that neither exercise the powers properly belonging to the other: nor

---

* "THE FUTURE FORM OF GOVERNMENT": *The Constitution or Form of Government, Agreed to and Resolved upon by the Delegates and Representatives of the several Counties and Corporations of Virginia.* From Francis N. Thorpe, ed., *The Federal and State Constitutions, Colonial Charters, and Other Organic Laws* . . . (Washington, 1909), VII, 3814–19.

shall any person exercise the powers of more than one of them, at the same time; except that the Justices of the County Courts shall be eligible to either House of Assembly.

The legislative shall be formed of two distinct branches, who, together, shall be a complete Legislature. They shall meet once, or oftener, every year, and shall be called, *The General Assembly of Virginia.* One of these shall be called, *The House of Delegates,* and consist of two Representatives, to be chosen for each county, and for the district of West-Augusta, annually, of such men as actually reside in, and are freeholders of the same, or duly qualified according to law, and also of one Delegate or Representative, to be chosen annually for the city of Williamsburgh, and one for the borough of Norfolk, and a Representative for each of such other cities and boroughs, as may hereafter be allowed particular representation by the legislature; but when any city or borough shall so decrease, as that the number of persons, having right of suffrage therein, shall have been, for the space of seven years successively, less than half the number of voters in some one county in Virginia, such city or borough thenceforward shall cease to send a Delegate or Representative to the Assembly.

The other shall be called *The Senate,* and consist of twenty-four members, of whom thirteen shall constitute a House to proceed on business; for whose election, the different counties shall be divided into twenty-four districts; and each county of the respective district, at the time of the election of its Delegates, shall vote for one Senator, who is actually a resident and freeholder within the district, or duly qualified according to law, and is upwards of twenty-five years of age; and the Sheriffs of each county, within five days at farthest, after the last county election in the district, shall meet at some convenient place, and from the poll, so taken in their respective counties, return, as a Senator, the man who shall have the greatest number of votes in the whole district. To keep up this Assembly by rotation, the districts shall be equally divided into four classes and numbered by lot. At the end of one year after the general election, the six members, elected by the first division, shall be displaced, and the vacancies thereby occasioned supplied from such class or division, by new election, in the manner aforesaid. This rotation shall be applied to each division, according to its number, and continued in due order annually.

The right of suffrage in the election of members for both Houses shall remain as exercised at present; and each House shall choose its own Speaker, appoint its own officers, settle its own rules of proceeding, and direct writs of election, for the supplying intermediate vacancies.

All laws shall originate in the House of Delegates, to be approved of or rejected by the Senate, or to be amended, with consent of the House of Delegates; except money-bills, which in no instance shall be altered by the Senate, but wholly approved or rejected.

A Governor, or chief magistrate, shall be chosen annually by joint ballot of both Houses (to be taken in each House respectively) deposited in the conference room; the boxes examined jointly by a committee of each House, and the numbers severally reported to them, that the appointments may be entered (which shall be the mode of taking the joint ballot of both Houses, in all cases) who shall not continue in that office longer than three years successively, nor be eligible, until the expiration of four years after he shall have been out of that office. An adequate, but moderate salary shall be settled on him, during his continuance in office; and he shall, with the advice of a Council of State, exercise the executive powers of government, according to the laws of this Commonwealth; and shall not, under any pretence, exercise any power or prerogative, by virtue of any law, statute or custom of England. But he shall, with the advice of the Council of State, have the power of granting reprieves or pardons, except where the prosecution shall have been carried on by the House of Delegates, or the law shall otherwise particularly direct; in which cases, no reprieve or pardon shall be granted, but by resolve of the House of Delegates.

Either House of the General Assembly may adjourn themselves respectively. The Governor shall not prorogue or adjourn the Assembly, during their sitting, nor dissolve them at any time; but he shall, if necessary, either by advice of the Council of State, or on application of a majority of the House of Delegates, call them before the time to which they shall stand prorogued or adjourned.

A Privy Council, or Council of State, consisting of eight members, shall be chosen, by joint ballot of both Houses of Assembly, either from their own members or the people at large, to assist in the administration of government. They shall annually choose, out of their own members, a President, who, in case of death, inability, or absence of the Governor from the government, shall act as Lieutenant-Governor. Four members shall be sufficient to act, and their advice and proceedings shall be entered on record, and signed by the members present, (to any part whereof, any member may enter his dissent) to be laid before the General Assembly, when called for by them. This Council may appoint their own Clerk, who shall have a salary settled by law, and take an oath of secrecy, in such matters as he shall be directed by the board to conceal. A sum of money, appropriated to that purpose, shall be divided annually among the members, in proportion to their attendance; and they shall be incapable, during their continuance in office, of sitting in either House of Assembly. Two members shall be removed, by joint ballot of both Houses of Assembly, at the end of every three years, and be ineligible for the three next years. These vacancies, as well as those occasioned by death or incapacity, shall be supplied by new elections, in the same manner.

The Delegates for Virginia to the Continental Congress shall be chosen annually, or superseded in the mean time, by joint ballot of both Houses of Assembly.

The present militia officers shall be continued, and vacancies supplied by appointment of the Governor, with the advice of the Privy-Council, on recommendations from the respective County Courts; but the Governor and Council shall have a power of suspending any officer, and ordering a Court Martial, on complaint of misbehaviour or inability, or to supply vacancies of officers, happening when in actual service.

The Governor may embody the militia, with the advice of the Privy Council; and when embodied, shall alone have the direction of the militia, under the laws of the country.

The two Houses of Assembly shall, by joint ballot, appoint Judges of the Supreme Court of Appeals, and General Court, Judges in Chancery, Judges of Admiralty, Secretary, and the Attorney-General, to be commissioned by the Governor, and continue in office during good behaviour. In case of death, incapacity, or resignation, the Governor, with the advice of the Privy Council, shall appoint persons to succeed in office, to be approved or displaced by both Houses. These officers shall have fixed and adequate salaries, and, together with all others, holding lucrative offices, and all ministers of the gospel, of every denomination, be incapable of being elected members of either House of Assembly or the Privy Council.

The Governor, with the advice of the Privy Council, shall appoint Justices of the Peace for the counties; and in case of vacancies, or a necessity of increasing the number hereafter, such appointments to be made upon the recommendation of the respective County Courts. The present acting Secretary in Virginia, and Clerks of all the County Courts, shall continue in office. In case of vacancies, either by death, incapacity, or resignation, a Secretary shall be appointed, as before directed; and the Clerks, by the respective Courts. The present and future Clerks shall hold their offices during good behaviour, to be judged of, and determined in the General Court. The Sheriffs and Coroners shall be nominated by the respective Courts, approved by the Governor, with the advice of the Privy Council, and commissioned by the Governor. The Justices shall appoint Constables; and all fees of the aforesaid officers be regulated by law.

The Governor, when he is out of office, and others, offending against the State, either by mal-administration, corruption, or other means, by which the safety of the State may be endangered, shall be impeachable by the House of Delegates. Such impeachment to be prosecuted by the Attorney-General, or such other person or persons, as the House may appoint in the General Court, according to the laws of the land. If found guilty, he or they shall be either forever disabled to hold any office under government, or be removed from such office *pro tempore,* or subjected to such pains or penalties as the laws shall direct.

If all or any of the Judges of the General Court should on good grounds (to be judged of by the House of Delegates) be accused of any of the crimes or offences above mentioned, such House of Delegates may, in like manner, impeach the Judge or Judges so accused, to be prosecuted in the Court of Appeals; and he or they, if found guilty, shall be punished in the same manner as is prescribed in the preceding clause.

Commissions and grants shall run, *"In the name of the Commonwealth of Virginia,"* and bear test by the Governor, with the seal of the Commonwealth annexed. Writs shall run in the same manner, and bear test by the Clerks of the several Courts. Indictments shall conclude, *"Against the peace and dignity of the Commonwealth."*

A Treasurer shall be appointed annually, by joint ballot of both Houses.

All escheats, penalties, and forfeitures, heretofore going to the King, shall go to the Commonwealth, save only such as the Legislature may abolish, or otherwise provide for.

The territories, contained within the Charters, erecting the Colonies of Maryland, Pennsylvania, North and South Carolina, are hereby ceded, released, and forever confirmed, to the people of these Colonies respectively, with all the rights of property, jurisdiction and government, and all other rights whatsoever, which might, at any time heretofore, have been claimed by Virginia, except the free navigation and use of the rivers Patomaque and Pokomoke, with the property of the Virginia shores and strands, bordering on either of the said rivers, and all improvements, which have been, or shall be made thereon. The western and northern extent of Virginia shall, in all other respects, stand as fixed by the Charter of King James I. in the year one thousand six hundred and nine, and by the public treaty of peace between the Courts of Britain and France, in the year one thousand seven hundred and sixty-three; unless by act of this Legislature, one or more governments be established westward of the Alleghany mountains. And no purchases of lands shall be made of the Indian natives, but on behalf of the public, by authority of the General Assembly.

In order to introduce this government, the Representatives of the people met in the convention shall choose a Governor and Privy Council, also such other officers directed to be chosen by both Houses as may be judged necessary to be immediately appointed. The Senate to be first chosen by the people, to continue until the last day of March next, and the other officers until the end of the succeeding session of Assembly. In case of vacancies, the Speaker of either House shall issue writs for new elections.

11] Adams Hails the Coming of "Independence Like a Torrent"

No one worked harder for independence than John Adams, and yet no one was more aware of the difficulties independence would provoke. He was impatient with conservatives who had for so long thwarted his revolutionary views, and he shows it in a letter to an old friend, James Warren of Massachusetts. (The "Farmer" referred to here is John Dickinson.) As a member of Congress, Adams had a ringside seat during the political revolution in Pennsylvania which put that state in the independence camp. The resolve read at the Philadelphia meeting was Congress' recommendation that the states form governments. Adams had drafted the preamble.*

May 20, 1776

MY DEAR SIR,—Every Post and every Day rolls in upon Us. Independence like a Torrent. The Delegates from Georgia made their Appearance this Day in Congress with unlimited Powers and these Gentlemen themselves are very firm. South Carolina, has erected her Government and given her Delegates ample Powers, and they are firm enough. North Carolina have given theirs full Powers, after repealing an Instruction given last August against Confederation and Independence. This Days Post, has brought a Multitude of Letters from Virginia, all of which breath the same Spirit. They agree they shall institute a Government—all are agreed in this they say. Here are four Colonies to the Southward who are perfectly agreed now with the four to the Northward. Five

* ADAMS HAILS THE COMING OF "INDEPENDENCE LIKE A TORRENT": John Adams to James Warren, May 20, 1776. From *Warren–Adams Letters*, I, Massachusetts Historical Society *Collections*, LXXII (1917), 249–51. Reprinted by permission of the Massachusetts Historical Society.

in the Middle are not yet quite so ripe; but they are very near it. I expect that New York will come to a fresh Election of Delegates in the Course of this Week, give them full Powers, and determine to institute a Government.

The Convention of New Jersey, is about Meeting and will assume a Government.

Pennsylvania Assembly meets this Day and it is said will repeal their Instruction to their Delegates which has made them so exceedingly obnoxious to America in General, and their own Constituents in particular.

We have had an entertaining Maneuvre this Morning in the State House Yard. The Committee of the City summoned a Meeting at Nine O'Clock in the State House Yard to consider of the Resolve of Congress of the fifteenth instant. The Weather was very rainy, and the Meeting was in the open air like the Comitia of the Romans, a Stage was erected, *extempore* for the Moderator, and the few orators to ascend—Coll. Roberdeau was the Moderator; Coll. McKean, Coll. Cadwallader and Coll. Matlack the principal orators. It was the very first Town Meeting I ever saw in Philadelphia and it was conducted with great order, Decency and Propriety.

The first step taken was this: the Moderator produced the Resolve of Congress of the 15th inst. and read it with a loud stentorian Voice that might be heard a Quarter of a Mile. "Whereas his Britannic Majesty, etc." As soon as this was read, the Multitude, several Thousands, some say, tho so wett rended the Welkin with three Cheers, Hatts flying as usual, etc.

Then a Number of Resolutions were produced, and moved, and determined with great Unanimity. These Resolutions I will send you as soon as published. The Drift of the whole was that the Assembly was not a Body properly constituted, authorized, and qualified to carry the Resolve for instituting a new Government into Execution and therefore that a Convention should be called. And at last they voted to support and defend the Measure of a Convention, at the Utmost Hazard and at all Events, etc.

The Delaware Government, generally, is of the same Opinion with the best Americans, very orthodox in their Faith and very exemplary in their Practice. Maryland remains to be mentioned. That is so eccentric a Colony—sometimes so hot, sometimes so cold; now so high, then so low—that I know not what to say about it or to expect from it. I have often wished it could exchange Places with Hallifax. When they get agoing I expect some wild extravagant Flight or other from it. To be sure they must go beyond every body else when they begin to go.

Thus I have rambled through the Continent, and you will perceive by this state of it, that We can't be very remote from the most decisive Measures and the most critical events. What do you think must be my Sensations when I see the Congress now daily passing Resolutions, which I most earnestly pressed for against Wind and Tide Twelve Months ago? and which I have not omitted to labour for a Month together from that Time to this? What do you think must be my Reflections, when I see the Farmer himself now confessing the Falsehood of all his Prophecies, and the Truth of mine, and confessing himself, now for instituting Governments, forming a Continental Constitution, making Alliances, with foreigners, opening Ports and all that—and confessing that the defence of the Colonies, and Preparations for defence have been neglected, in Consequence of fond delusive hopes and deceitfull Expectations?

I assure you this is no Gratification of my Vanity.

The gloomy Prospect of Carnage and Devastation that now presents itself in every Part of the Continent, and which has been in the most express and decisive nay dogmatical Terms foretold by me a thousand Times, is too affecting to give me Pleasure. It moves my keenest Indignation. Yet I dare not hint at these Things for I hate to give Pain to Gentlemen whom I believe sufficiently punished by their own Reflections.

12] "The People Wait for Us to Lead the Way"

Jefferson's is the best description of the debates in Congress, for and against independence, which followed Richard Henry Lee's motion. His "Notes," probably written in the summer or fall of 1776, demonstrate the fullness of the arguments on both sides. That Dickinson did not sign the Declaration is well known; that anyone but the President and secretary signed on July 4 is a debatable point, Jefferson's claim to the contrary notwithstanding.*

[7 June to 1 August 1776]

In Congress. FRIDAY June 7. 1776. the Delegates from Virginia moved in obedience to instructions from their constituents that the Congress should declare that these United colonies are & of right ought to be free & independant states, that they are absolved from all allegiance to the British crown, and that all political connection between them and the state of Great Britain is & ought to be totally dissolved; that measures should be immediately taken for procuring the assistance of foreign powers, and a Confederation be formed to bind the colonies more closely together.

The house being obliged to attend at that time to some other business, the [*resolution*] [1] proposition was referred to the next day when the members were ordered to attend punctually at ten o'clock.

Saturday June 8. they [*resolution proposed was*] [*house*] proceeded to take it into consideration and referred it to a committee of the whole, into which [*it*] they immediately resolved themselves, and passed that day & Monday the 10th. in debating on the subject.

It was argued by Wilson, Robert R. Livingston, [*the two*] E. Rutlege[*s*], Dickinson and others.

* "THE PEOPLE WAIT FOR US TO LEAD THE WAY": "Notes of Proceedings in the Continental Congress." From Julian P. Boyd, ed., *The Papers of Thomas Jefferson* (Princeton, 1950–   ), I, 309–15. Reprinted by permission of the Princeton University Press.

1 The italicized words in brackets are deletions that Jefferson made in correcting his original manuscript. For textual reasons they were retained in Julian P. Boyd's edition of the Jefferson papers.

That tho' they were friends to the measures themselves, and saw the impossibility that we should ever again be united with Gr. Britain, yet they were against adopting them at th[*at*]is time:

That the conduct we had formerly observed was wise & proper now, of deferring to take any capital step till the voice of the people drove us into it:

That they were our power, & without them our declarations could not be carried into effect:

That the people of the middle colonies ([*Pennsylvania*] Maryland, [*Dela*] Delaware, Pennsylva., the Jersies & N. York) were not yet ripe for bidding adieu to British connection but that they were fast ripening & in a short time would join in the general voice of America:

That the resolution entered into by this house on the 15th. of May for suppressing the exercise of all powers derived from the crown, had shewn, by the ferment into which it had thrown these middle colonies, that they had not yet accomodated their minds to a separation from the mother country:

That some of them had expressly forbidden their delegates to consent to such a declaration, and others had given no instructions, & consequently no powers to give such consent:

That if the delegates of any particular colony had no power to declare such colony independant, certain they were the others could not declare it for them; the colonies being as yet perfectly independant of each other:

That the assembly of Pennsylvania was now sitting above stairs, their convention would sit within a few days, the convention of New York was now sitting, & those of the Jersies & Delaware counties would meet on the Monday following & it was probable these bodies would take up the question of Independance & would declare to their delegates the voice of their state:

That if such a declaration should now be agreed to, these delegates must [*now*] retire & possibly their colonies might secede from the Union:

That such a secession would weaken us more than could be compensated by any foreign alliance:

That in the event of such a division, foreign powers would either refuse to join themselves to our fortunes, or having us so much in their power as that desperate declaration would place us, they would insist on terms proportionably more hard & prejudicial:

That we had little reason to expect an alliance with those to whom alone as yet we had cast our eyes:

That France & Spain had reason to be jealous of that rising power which would one day certainly strip them of all their American possessions:

That it was more likely they should form a connection with the British court, who, if they should find themselves unable otherwise to extricate themselves from their difficulties, would agree to a par-

tition of our territories, restoring Canada to France, & the Floridas
to Spain, to accomplish for themselves a recovery of these colonies:

That it would not be long before we should receive certain information of the disposition of the French court, from the agent
whom we had sent to Paris for that purpose:

That if this disposition should be favourable, by waiting the event
of [*another*] the present campaign, which we all hoped would be
[*favourable*] succesful, we should have reason to expect an alliance
on better terms:

That this would in fact work no delay of any effectual aid from
such ally, as, from the advance of the season & distance of our situation, it was impossible we could receive any assistance during this
campaign:

That it was prudent to fix among ourselves the terms on which
we would form alliance, before we declared we would form one at
all events:

And that if these were agreed on & our Declaration of Independance ready by the time our Ambassadour should be prepared to sail,
it would be as well, as to go into that Declaration at this day.

On the other side it was urged by J. Adams, Lee, Wythe and
others

That no gentleman had argued against the policy or the right of
separation from Britain, nor had supposed it possible we should ever
renew our connection: that they had only opposed it's being now
declared:

That the question was not whether, by a declaration of independance, we should make ourselves what we are not; but whether we
should declare a fact which already exists:

That as to the people or parliament of England, we had alwais
been independant of them, their restraints on our trade deriving
efficacy from our acquiescence only & not from any rights they possessed of imposing them, & that so far our connection had been
federal only, & was now dissolved by the commencement of hostilities:

That as to the king, we had been bound to him by allegiance,
but that this bond was now dissolved by his assent to the late act
of parliament, by which he declares us out of his protection, and
by his levying war on us, a fact which had long ago proved us
out of his protection; it being a certain position in law that allegiance & protection are reciprocal, the one ceasing when the other is
withdrawn:

That James the IId. never declared the people of England out of
his protection yet his actions proved it & the parliament declared it:

No delegates then can be denied, or ever want, a power of declaring an existent truth:

That the delegates from the Delaware counties having declared
their constituents ready to join, there are only two colonies Penn-

lvania & Maryland whose delegates are absolutely tied up, and
at these had by their instructions only reserved a right of con-
rming or rejecting the measure:

That the instructions from Pennsylvania might be accounted for
om the times in which they were drawn, near a twelvemonth ago,
nce which the face of affairs has totally changed:

That [*sin*] within that time it had become apparent that Britain
as determined to accept nothing less than a carte blanche, and
at the king's answer to the Lord Mayor Aldermen & common
uncil of London, which had come to hand four days ago, must
ave satisfied every one of this point:

That the people wait for us to lead the way [*in this step*]:

That *they* are in favour of the measure, tho' the instructions given
y some of their *representatives* are not:

That the voice of the representatives is not alwais consonant [*to*]
ith the voice of the people, and that this is remarkeably the case
these middle colonies:

That the effect of the resolution of the 15th. of May has proved
is, which, raising the murmurs of some in the colonies of Penn-
ylvania & Maryland, called forth the opposing voice of the freer
art of the people, & proved them to be the majority, even in these
olonies:

That the backwardness of these two colonies might be ascribed
artly to the influence of proprietary power & connections, & partly
their having not yet been attacked by the enemy:

That these causes were not likely to be soon removed, as there
eemed no probability that the enemy would make either of these
he seat of this summer's war:

That it would be vain to wait either weeks or months for perfect
nanimity, since it was impossible that all men should ever become
f one sentiment on any question:

That the conduct of some colonies from the beginning of this
ontest, had given reason to suspect it was their settled policy to
eep in the rear of the confederacy, that their particular prospect
night be better even in the worst event:

That therefore it was necessary for those colonies who had thrown
hemselves forward & hazarded all from the beginning, to come
orward now also, and put all again to their own hazard:

That the history of the Dutch revolution, of whom three states
nly confederated at first proved that a secession of some colonies
vould not be so dangerous as some apprehended:

That a declaration of Independance alone could render it con-
istent with European delicacy for European powers to treat with
s, or even to receive an Ambassador from us:

That till this they would not receive our vessels into their ports,
nor acknowledge the adjudications of our courts of Admiralty to
be legitimate, in cases of capture of British vessels:

That tho' France & Spain may be jealous of our rising power, they must think it will be much more formidable with the addition of Great Britain; and will therefore see it their interest to prevent a coalition; but should they refuse, we shall be but where we are; whereas without trying we shall never know whether they will aid us or not:

That the present campaign may be unsuccessful, & therefore we had better propose an alliance while our affairs wear a hopeful aspect:

That to wait the event of this campaign will certainly work delay, because during this summer France may assist us effectually by cutting off those supplies of provisions from England & Ireland on which the enemy's armies here are to depend; or by setting in motion the great power they have collected in the West Indies, & calling our enemy to the defence of the possessions they have there:

That it would be idle to lose time in settling the terms of alliance, till we had first determined we would enter into alliance:

That it is necessary to lose no time in opening a trade for our people, who will want clothes, and will want money too for the paiment of taxes:

And that the only misfortune is that we did not enter into alliance with France six months sooner, as besides opening their ports for the vent of our last year's produce, they might have marched an army into Germany and prevented the petty princes there from selling their unhappy subjects to subdue us.

It appearing in the course of these debates that the colonies of N. York, New Jersey, Pennsylvania, Delaware [&] Maryland [*had not yet advanced to*] & South Carolina were not yet matured for falling [*off*] from the parent stem, but that they were fast advancing to that state, it was thought most prudent to wait a while for them, and to postpone the final decision to July 1. but that this might occasion as little delay as possible, a committee was appointed to prepare a declaration of independance. the Commee. were J. Adams, Dr. Franklin, Roger Sherman, Robert R. Livingston & myself. committees were also appointed at the same time to prepare a plan of confederation for the colonies, and to state the terms proper to be proposed for foreign alliance. the committee for drawing the declaration of Independance desired me to [*prepare*] do it. [*I did so*] it was accordingly done and being approved by them,

June 28. I reported it to the house on Friday the 28th. of June when it was
July 1.   read and ordered to lie on the table. on Monday the 1st. of July the house resolved itself into a commee. of the whole & resumed the consideration of the original motion made by the delegates of Virginia, which being again debated through the day, was carried in the affirmative by the votes of N. Hampshire, Connecticut, Massachusets, Rhode island, N. Jersey, Maryland, Virginia, N. Carolina, & Georgia. S. Carolina and Pennsylvania voted against it. Delaware having but two members present, they were divided: the delegates for New York declared they were for it themselves, & were assured

their constituents were for it, but that their instructions having been drawn near a twelvemonth before, when reconciliation was still the general object, they were enjoined by them to do nothing which should impede that object. they therefore thought themselves not justifiable in voting on either side, and asked leave to withdraw from the question, which [*they had*] was given them. the Commee. rose & reported their resolution to the house. Mr. Rutlege of S. Carolina then [*desired*] requested the determination might be put off to the next day, as he beleived his collegues, tho' they disapproved of the resolution, would then join in it for the sake of unanimity. [*this was done*] the ultimate question whether the house would agree to the resolution of the committee was accordingly postponed to the next day, when it was again moved and S. Carolina concurred in voting for it. in the mean time a third member had come post from the Delaware counties and turned the vote of that colony in favour of the resolution. members of a different sentiment attending that morning from Pennsylvania also, their vote was changed, so that the whole 12. colonies, who were authorized to vote at all, gave their voices for it; and within a few days the convention of N. York approved of it [*by their votes to*] and thus supplied the void occasioned by the withdrawing of their delegates from the vote. *July 2.* *• July 9.*

Congress proceeded the same day to consider the declaration of Independance, which had been reported & laid on the table the Friday preceding, and on Monday referred to a commee. of the whole. the pusillanimous idea that we had friends in England worth keeping terms with, still haunted the minds of many. for this reason those passages which conveyed censures on the people of England were struck out, lest they should give them offence. the clause too, reprobating the enslaving the inhabitants of Africa, was struck out in complaisance to South Carolina & Georgia, who had never attempted to restrain the importation of slaves, and who on the contrary still wished to continue it. our Northern brethren also I believe felt a little tender [*on that*] under those censures; for tho' their people have very few slaves themselves yet they had been pretty considerable carriers of them to others. the debates having taken up the greater parts of the 2d. 3d. & 4th. days of July were, in the evening of the last closed. the declaration was reported by the commee., agreed to by the house, and signed by every member present except Mr. Dickinson. . . . *July 2.* *July 3. 4.*

13] Independence Is Declared: "Separate and Equal Station"

The task of drafting the Declaration was given to Jefferson, one of a committee of five appointed on June 11 by Congress. He submitted a draft to

the committee, which went over it carefully but made few changes. Between
July 2 and 4 Congress examined the document and, besides omitting the
attack on the slave trade, strengthened it elsewhere by deletion. On July 4
Congress adopted it. But the document needs no introduction; with grace
and majesty it speaks for itself.*

The unanimous Declaration of the thirteen United States of America.

𝔚𝔥𝔢𝔫, in the Course of human events, it becomes necessary for one people
to dissolve the political bands which have connected them with another, and
to assume, among the Powers of the earth, the separate and equal station to
which the Laws of Nature and of Nature's God entitle them, a decent respect
to the opinions of mankind requires that they should declare the causes which
impel them to the separation.

We hold these truths to be self-evident, that all men are created equal, that
they are endowed by their Creator with certain unalienable Rights, that among
these, are Life, Liberty, and the pursuit of Happiness. That, to secure these
rights, Governments are instituted among Men, deriving their just Powers from
the consent of the governed. That, whenever any form of Government becomes destructive of these ends, it is the Right of the People to alter or to
abolish it, and to institute new Government, laying its foundation on such
Principles, and organizing its Powers in such form, as to them shall seem most
likely to effect their Safety and Happiness. Prudence, indeed, will dictate that
Governments long established should not be changed for light and transient
causes; and, accordingly, all experience hath shewn, that mankind are more
disposed to suffer, while evils are sufferable, than to right themselves by abolishing the forms to which they are accustomed. But, when a long train of
abuses and usurpations, pursuing invariably the same Object, evinces a design
to reduce them under absolute Despotism, it is their right, it is their duty, to
throw off such Government, and to provide new Guards for their future Security. Such has been the patient sufferance of these Colonies; and such is now
the necessity which constrains them to alter their former Systems of Government. The history of the present King of Great Britain is a history of repeated
injuries and usurpations, all having in direct object the establishment of an
absolute Tyranny over these States. To prove this, let Facts be submitted to
a candid world.

He has refused his Assent to Laws the most wholesome and necessary for
the public good.

He has forbidden his Governors to pass Laws of immediate and pressing
importance, unless suspended in their operation till his Assent should be obtained; and when so suspended, he has utterly neglected to attend to them.

He has refused to pass other Laws for the accommodation of large districts
of People, unless those People would relinquish the right of Representation in
the legislature; a right inestimable to them and formidable to tyrants only.

---

* INDEPENDENCE IS DECLARED: "SEPARATE AND EQUAL STATION": *The unanimous Declaration of the thirteen United States of America.* From Worthington C. Ford, ed., *Journals
of the Continental Congress, 1774–1789* (Washington, 1904–37), V, 510–15.

He has called together legislative bodies at places unusual, uncomfortable, nd distant from the depository of their Public Records, for the sole Purpose f fatiguing them into compliance with his measures.

He has dissolved Representative Houses repeatedly, for opposing, with manly irmness, his invasions on the rights of the People.

He has refused for a long time, after such dissolutions, to cause others to e elected; whereby the Legislative Powers, incapable of Annihilation, have eturned to the People at large for their exercise; the State remaining in the nean time exposed to all the dangers of invasion from without, and convul- ions within.

He has endeavoured to prevent the Population of these States; for that pur- ose obstructing the Laws for Naturalization of Foreigners; refusing to pass thers to encourage their migrations hither, and raising the conditions of new Appropriations of Lands.

He has obstructed the Administration of Justice, by refusing his Assent to aws for establishing Judiciary Powers.

He has made Judges dependent on his Will alone, for the tenure of their ffices, and the amount and payment of their salaries.

He has erected a multitude of New Offices, and sent hither swarms of Of- icers to harrass our People, and eat out their substance.

He has kept among us, in times of Peace, Standing Armies, without the Consent of our legislatures.

He has affected to render the Military independent of and superior to the Civil Power.

He has combined with others to subject us to a jurisdiction foreign to our onstitution, and unacknowledged by our laws; giving his Assent to their Acts f pretended Legislation:

For quartering large bodies of armed troops among us:

For protecting them, by a mock Trial, from Punishment for any Murders vhich they should commit on the Inhabitants of these States:

For cutting off our Trade with all parts of the world:

For imposing Taxes on us without our Consent:

For depriving us, in many cases, of the benefits of Trial by Jury:

For transporting us beyond Seas to be tried for pretended offences:

For abolishing the free System of English Laws in a neighbouring province, stablishing therein an Arbitrary government, and enlarging its Boundaries, so s to render it at once an example and fit instrument for introducing the same bsolute rule into these Colonies:

For taking away our Charters, abolishing our most valuable Laws, and al- ering fundamentally the Forms of our Governments:

For suspending our own Legislatures, and declaring themselves invested with Power to legislate for us in all cases whatsoever.

He has abdicated Government here, by declaring us out of his protection, nd waging War against us.

He has plundered our seas, ravaged our Coasts, burnt our towns, and de- troyed the Lives of our People.

He is at this time transporting large Armies of foreign Mercenaries to compleat the works of death, desolation and tyranny, already begun with circumstances of Cruelty and perfidy scarcely paralleled in the most barbarous ages, and totally unworthy the Head of a civilized nation.

He has constrained our fellow Citizens, taken Captive on the high Seas, to bear Arms against their Country, to become the executioners of their friends and Brethren, or to fall themselves by their Hands.

He has excited domestic insurrections amongst us, and has endeavoured to bring on the inhabitants of our frontiers, the merciless Indian Savages, whose known rule of warfare, is an undistinguished destruction of all ages, sexes and conditions.

In every stage of these Oppressions, We have Petitioned for Redress, in the most humble terms: Our repeated Petitions, have been answered only by repeated injury. A Prince, whose character is thus marked by every act which may define a Tyrant, is unfit to be the ruler of a free People.

Nor have We been wanting in attentions to our Brittish brethren. We have warned them from time to time of attempts by their legislature to extend an unwarrantable jurisdiction over us. We have reminded them of the circumstances of our emigration and settlement here. We have appealed to their native justice and magnanimity, and we have conjured them by the ties of our common kindred, to disavow these usurpations, which, would inevitably interrupt our connexions and correspondence. They too have been deaf to the voice of justice and of consanguinity. We must, therefore, acquiesce in the necessity, which denounces our Separation, and hold them, as we hold the rest of mankind, Enemies in War, in Peace Friends.

We, therefore, the Representatives of the **united States of America**, in GENERAL CONGRESS assembled, appealing to the Supreme Judge of the World for the rectitude of our intentions, DO, in the Name, and by Authority of the good People of these Colonies, solemnly PUBLISH and DECLARE, That these United Colonies are, and of Right, ought to be **Free and Independent States;** that they are Absolved from all Allegiance to the British Crown, and that all political connexion between them and the State of Great Britain, is and ought to be totally dissolved; and that, as FREE and INDEPENDENT STATES, they have full Power to levy War, conclude Peace, contract Alliances, establish Commerce, and to do all other Acts and Things which INDEPENDENT STATES may of right do. AND for the support of this Declaration, with a firm reliance on the protection of divine Providence, we mutually pledge to each other our Lives, our Fortunes, and our sacred Honour.

CONCLUSION

THE BOLD stand taken by Congress was wholly insupportable without a decisive victory over British military forces. The crisis of 1775–76 only pointed out the immensity of the problems which the genius of George Washington, the courage of hard-core patriots, and the timely help of France came to solve. After the Alliance of 1778 France openly sent money, matériel, troops, and a navy; without them the war might never have been won.

Constitution-making continued during the war, guaranteeing rights for which the Revolution was fought and translating provisional governments into permanent institutions. The most orderly result was the constitution of Massachusetts, drafted by a specially elected convention in 1779. John Adams' hand was felt throughout, and the product was a sophisticated balance of powers which has served, with amendments, until today. Other state constitutions lacked Adams' deftness in their making and tended to lump power in the legislatures rather than divide it—a fault understandable after years of battle with royal governors.

By the time the Treaty of Paris was signed, the United States had established a central government under the Articles of Confederation. Drafted in 1776, the new instrument was approved by Congress with revisions the next year, and the thirteenth state ratified it in 1781. The Articles changed little as far as structure of government was concerned, but this first national constitution legalized the Congress, which had gradually emerged as a national legislature and established several precedents, making easier the next step in 1787.

The Revolution did not make the United States a democracy; but in some instances it led men's minds in that direction. Property qualifications for voting survived the Revolution and for some time afterward, yet in all states they were reduced—save in Massachusetts where most men could vote anyway. In Pennsylvania and Georgia one had only to be a taxpayer to vote. State governments, founded on the principle that power derived from the people, ideally should have established equal representation in their legislatures. But easterners who had controlled the assemblies were generally reluctant to relax their grasp, especially in the South, although some improvement was made. The most dramatic change came in Pennsylvania where back-country members outnumbered easterners in the unicameral legislature established by a liberal constitution of 1776.

The Revolution in general was a political and constitutional movement aimed primarily at independence from England and a restoration of rights which that nation had violated. But political revolutions are bound to have repercussions outside the scope of government. Several states outlawed the slave trade and commenced programs for manumission, encouraged by religious groups—particularly Quakers—and antislavery societies. Slavery, too, survived the Revolution, but progress was made against it as a result of the spirit of equality which the Revolution had stimulated. Nine colonies supported established churches in the early 1770's; with the exception of Massachusetts, New Hampshire, and Connecticut, where Congregationalists predominated, they disappeared during or soon after the Revolution. The most severe struggle occurred in Virginia, where the Anglican establishment died hard despite the Declaration of Rights. Thomas Jefferson and James Madison and a variety of dissenters combined their efforts against the church-state connection and were finally successful in 1785 when the Assembly enacted Jefferson's Statute of Religious Liberty. Liberating tendencies, already begun before independence, effected changes in American society not contemplated by patriots when the war began.

Although the Revolution did not end officially until 1783, certainly much was accomplished during the crisis of 1775–76. If, then, the times that tried men's souls lay ahead, at least the air was cleared and no one could doubt what Americans were fighting for. Out of the crisis came the promise of a new nation, for the Declaration symbolized the end of colonial status and the birth of an independent people. But it did more. Its appeal to the rights of man and the principle of equality struck a note of hope that has not stopped vibrating.

STUDY QUESTIONS

1] How do you explain the delay of fifteen months after the beginning of hostilities in declaring independence?

2] To what extent did a belief in the idea of equality precipitate the crisis of 1775–76?

3] Is there an inconsistency between the Virginia Declaration of Rights and the Virginia Constitution? Explain your answer.

4] To what extent do you think the period of crisis had important social consequences for Americans?

RECOMMENDED READINGS

PRIMARY SOURCES

ADAMS, CHARLES FRANCIS, ed. *The Works of John Adams*, 10 vols. (Boston, 1850–56), Vol. II.

BACKUS, ISAAC. *A History of New-England, with Particular Reference to the Denomination of Christians called Baptists* . . . , 3 vols. (Boston, 1777–96).

BOYD, JULIAN P., ed. *The Papers of Thomas Jefferson* (Princeton, 1950–   ), Vol. I.

BURNETT, EDMUND C., ed. *Letters of Members of the Continental Congress*, 8 vols. (Washington, 1921–36), Vol. I.

COMMAGER, HENRY STEELE, AND RICHARD B. MORRIS, eds. *The Spirit of 'Seventy-Six: The Story of the American Revolution as Told by Participants*, 2 vols. (Indianapolis and New York, 1958).

Conway, Moncure, D., ed. *The Writings of Thomas Paine*, 4 vols. (New York, 1894–96), Vol. I.

Force, Peter, ed. *American Archives, A Documentary History . . . of the Causes and Accomplishments of the American Revolution . . .* , 4th ser., 6 vols. (Washington, 1837–46), Vols. II–V.

Ford, Worthington C., ed. *Journals of the Continental Congress, 1774–1789*, 34 vols. (Washington, 1904–37), Vols. II–V.

Hoadly, Charles J., ed. *The Public Records of the Colony of Connecticut*, XV, (Hartford, 1890).

Jensen, Merrill, ed. *English Historical Documents*, IX, *American Colonial Documents to 1776*, Part VIII, "The Coming of the War for American Independence, 1773–1776" (New York, 1955).

Knollenberg, Bernhard, ed. *Correspondence of Governor Samuel Ward, May 1775–March 1776* (Providence, 1952).

Morison, Samuel Eliot, ed. *Sources and Documents Illustrating the American Revolution, 1764–1788, and the Formation of the Federal Constitution* (Oxford, 1923).

Niles, Hezekiah, ed. *Principles and Acts of the Revolution in America . . .* (Baltimore, 1822).

Saunders, William L., ed. *Colonial Records of North Carolina*, X (Raleigh, 1890).

Taylor, Robert J., ed. *Massachusetts, Colony to Commonwealth: Documents on the Formation of Its Constitution, 1775–1780* (Chapel Hill, N.C., 1961).

Thorpe, Francis N., ed. *The Federal and State Constitutions, Colonial Charters, and other Organic Laws . . .* , 7 vols. (Washington, 1909).

SECONDARY SOURCES

Adams, Randolph G. *Political Ideas of the American Revolution* (Durham, N.C., 1922).

Alden, John R. *The American Revolution, 1775–1783* (New York, 1954).

Becker, Carl. *The Declaration of Independence* (New York, 1922).

——————. *The History of Political Parties in the Province of New York, 1760–76* (Madison, Wis., 1909).

Burnett, Edmund C. *The Continental Congress* (New York, 1941).

Douglass, Elisha P. *Rebels and Democrats: The Struggle for Equal Political Rights and Majority Rule During the American Revolution* (Chapel Hill, N.C., 1955).

Freeman, Douglas S. *George Washington*, 7 vols. (New York, 1948–57) Vols. III–IV.

French, Allen. *The First Year of the American Revolution* (Boston, 1934).

Jameson, J. Franklin. *The American Revolution Considered as a Social Movement* (Princeton, 1926).

Jensen, Merrill. *The Articles of Confederation* (Madison, Wis., 1940).

Lovejoy, David S. *Rhode Island Politics and the American Revolution, 1760–1776* (Providence, 1958).

Malone, Dumas. *Jefferson the Virginian* (Boston, 1948).

Miller, John C. *The Origins of the American Revolution* (Boston, 1943).

NEVINS, ALLAN. *The American States During and After the Revolution, 1775–1789* (New York, 1924).

TYLER, MOSES COIT. *The Literary History of the American Revolution, 1763–1783*, 2 vols. (New York, 1897).

VAN DOREN, CARL. *Benjamin Franklin* (New York, 1938).

VAN TYNE, CLAUDE H. *The Loyalists in the American Revolution* (New York, 1902).

WILLIAMSON, CHILTON. *American Suffrage: From Property to Democracy, 1760–1860* (Princeton, 1960).

The Ratification of the Constitution: The Crisis of 1787–1789

LEONARD W. LEVY

MERRILL D. PETERSON

BRANDEIS UNIVERSITY

CONTENTS

CHRONOLOGY

1787

SEPTEMBER 17   The Constitution is unanimously approved by the Federal Convention and transmitted to Congress.

SEPTEMBER 28   Congress transmits the Constitution to the states for submission to ratification conventions.

OCTOBER 21   First number of *The Federalist* published.

DECEMBER 7–18   Ratification by Delaware, Pennsylvania, and New Jersey.

1788

JANUARY 2–   Ratification by Georgia, Connecticut, and Massa-
FEBRUARY 7   chusetts.

MARCH 24   Constitution defeated by vote of 2708–237 in Rhode Island's popular referendum.

APRIL 28   Ratification by Maryland.

MAY 23   Ratification by South Carolina.

JUNE 21   New Hampshire, the ninth state, ratifies.

JUNE 2–25   Virginia convention, ratification by vote of 89–78.

JULY 2   The President of Congress appoints a committee to prepare the change-over to the new government.

JULY 26   New York ratifies by vote of 30–27.

AUGUST 2   North Carolina rejects the Constitution, 184–83.

1789

APRIL 1–6   Organization of the First Congress.

APRIL 30   Washington takes oath of office as first President.

JUNE 8   Madison offers amendments to the Constitution.

SEPTEMBER 25   Congress submits amendments to the states for ratification.

NOVEMBER 21   Ratification of the Constitution by North Carolina.

1790

MAY 29   Ratification of the Constitution by Rhode Island.

1791

DECEMBER 15   The first ten amendments—Bill of Rights—having been duly ratified, become part of the Constitution.

INTRODUCTION

O N SEPTEMBER 17, 1787, the Constitutional Convention assembled for the last time in Independence Hall, Philadelphia, to put the finishing touches on its work. The roll was far from complete. In the course of four months' deliberations some of the fifty-five members had left to attend to affairs at home, while others had walked out in protest. But thirty-eight delegates, from all twelve of the states represented, were on hand for this final session. As the engrossed Constitution was read, few, if any, of them could take perfect satisfaction in the government they were about to propose to the people of the United States. A bundle of compromises, as it was later called, the Constitution conformed to no preconceived theory and realized the ambitions of no special group, class, or section. But if the delegates could not now suppress doubts and misgivings, they alone knew over what difficulties they had triumphed in producing this concededly imperfect frame of government.

The reading done, the aged Dr. Franklin rose to urge unanimous approval of the Constitution. "I consent, Sir, to this Constitution, because I expect no better, and because I am not sure, that it is not the best." He hoped every member would, with him, "doubt a little of his own infallibility, and to make manifest our unanimity, put his name to this instrument." On Franklin's motion it was agreed that the enrollment of the Constitution would be in the following form: "Done in Convention by the unanimous consent of the States present." It was this act, not necessarily endorsement of the instrument itself, that the delegates attested by their signatures. Nevertheless, Elbridge Gerry of Massachusetts and the Virginians George Mason and Edmund Randolph withheld their names. After the adoption of a resolution fixing the procedure by which the Constitution should be ratified and put into operation, the Convention adjourned. The next day the curtain of secrecy was lifted and the Constitution published to an anxious citizenry. George Washington, president of the Convention, departed for Mount Vernon. Before leaving he sent the Constitution to Lafayette with this stoic observation: "It is now a child of fortune, to be fostered by some and buffeted by others. . . . If it be good, I suppose it will work its way good—if bad it will recoil on the framers."

The momentous question was decided during the next nine months. Ratification proceeded in accordance with the plan worked out by the framers themselves. This plan consisted of several parts. First, that Congress, upon receiving the finished product of the Convention, should refer it to the states for action without in any way signifying approval or disapproval. Thus the body that had called the Philadelphia assemblage into being, "for the sole purpose of revising the Articles of Confederation," was to have no voice in the decision to be made on its fate other than submit the document to the states for ratification. Second, that the Constitution should be ratified

in conventions of delegates elected by the people under provision of the legislatures of the several states. It would be hard to overestimate the importance
of this recommendation. Nothing so clearly indicated the radical shift in the
groundwork of the Union. Whereas the existing government derived its authority from the state legislatures, the Federal Convention proposed to base
the new government on the people of the states. Even the state governments,
with but two exceptions, had been instituted without the benefit of popular
approval. Understandably, therefore, some of the delegates at first balked at
this "new set of ideas"—strangely democratic and unknown to the Articles
of Confederation—though finally assenting to the argument of James Madison and others that approval "by the supreme authority of the people themselves" was indispensable to establish the legitimacy of the new government.
Third, the Convention decided that the Constitution should become opera-
tive after ratification in *nine* states. This too was radical, for the Articles
could be changed only with the approval of the legislature of *each* state.
The remaining element of the plan was disclosed by the defeat, late in the
Convention, of Edmund Randolph's motion authorizing the ratification
bodies to offer amendments which could be submitted to a second federal
convention. In the absence of such a provision, the people of the states were
left with no alternative between swallowing the Constitution whole or not
at all. This was too much for Randolph and Mason.

The ratification provision emblazoned the political genius of the Founding
Fathers. Ratification was *by the people* (to the extent that they were en-
franchised) but *in the states*. It thus combined features of *democracy* and of
federalism, forestalling violent objection on either ground. Not only did the
procedure appeal to the political feelings of the American people; it was also
the best possible means of getting the Constitution adopted. The state legislatures were circumvented by special conventions in which the proponents of
the new system might be expected to carry greater weight. The crippling rule
of the unanimity of states was discarded for the rule of nine states. In this,
as in every part of the ratification plan, considerations of expediency mingled
with considerations of principle, and rarely have men managed so well to
accommodate their opportunities to the prevailing sentiments of the community.

The balance of forces between adoption and rejection being nearly equal
at the outset, the friends and the foes of the proffered Constitution waged
their campaigns in every avenue of public communication and debate.
Prominent figures in the various states donned literary masks—"Plebeian,"
"Fabius," "Aristides," "American Citizen"—and wrote pamphlets for or
against the new system. The newspapers teemed with letters and articles.
Even in remote settlements beyond the reach of the printed word the Constitution became the topic of heated discussion. The pulpit, the court green,
the country store, the muster field resounded to the din of politics. "Since
the world began," a Pennsylvanian remarked with some truth, "I believe no
question has ever been more repeatedly and strictly scrutinized or more fairly
and freely argued, than this proposed Constitution."

The advocates of the new system assumed the honorable name of Federalists and took the initiative that was theirs by virtue of having a concrete plan

to remedy the defects of the Articles of Confederation. Among the forces generally conceded to work in their favor were the weighty influence of the Philadelphia framers and, above all, the universal prestige of General Washington; the desires of key economic groups which, though varying from state to state, usually included large numbers interested in the expansion of commerce and the strengthening of credit, both public and private; and the conviction of many that a stronger national government was essential for the peace, good order, and welfare of the Union. Already accustomed to working together, the Federalists were better organized than their opponents for the country-wide campaign. They were comparatively more concentrated in the urban centers, from which influence radiated as spokes from a hub, and were the beneficiaries of the cohesive tendencies of the mercantile community.

The case for the Constitution was most thoroughly argued in a series of eighty-five letters contributed to the New York press by Alexander Hamilton, James Madison, and John Jay over the common signature "Publius" and later published collectively as *The Federalist*. Unquestionably the most distinguished product of the propaganda barrage—the classic commentary on the Constitution—*The Federalist* was both too lengthy and too sophisticated to exert much influence during the contest. It was not, as a North Carolina Federalist observed, "well calculated for the common people." Other Federalist writings, most of them emanating from New York and Philadelphia, were more widely read, though perhaps none as widely as the leading Anti-Federalist tract, *Letters from the Federal Farmer*, by Richard Henry Lee of Virginia.

The opposition began to organize in July, 1787, when two of the three New York delegates marched out of the Convention and reported to Governor George Clinton, the redoubtable champion of New York's autonomy within the Union. Working on the side of the Anti-Federalists (or Federal Republicans as they sometimes called themselves) were, in general, the following factors: the interest which leaders and officeholders in several of the state governments had in maintaining the *status quo*; the opposition of certain economic groups, mainly agrarian, to the powers of the new government to lay taxes, regulate commerce, enforce contractual obligations, and prohibit paper money issues by the states; the crucial omission of a Bill of Rights, which not only lent an air of credibility to Anti-Federalist fears for individual liberty but also became a convenient stalking-horse for opposition grounded in other and more mundane considerations; and finally, of paramount importance, the widespread apprehension that the Constitution foreshadowed the obliteration of the states and the establishment of a despotic central government.

Consolidation! This was the constant theme of the Anti-Federalist discourse. It was impossible, they said, to unite under one government a territory as varied and extensive as the United States without its soon sliding into tyranny or civil war. All history bore witness to this truth. Accustomed to look to local and state authorities for the protection of their liberties, many Americans instinctively distrusted the new, more centralized system. Nothing gave the Federalists more difficulty than the effort to explain the ingenious anatomy of a body politic some parts of which were *national*, some *federal*, and some *both*. "Were the states sovereign or not?" the opponents asked. The Federalists answered that they were sovereign in some matters though not in others. The distinction was subtle, the line of division blurred. Would the states, in any event, have adequate security for the rights and powers they retained? The Anti-Federalists had warrant for their belief that the Constitution shifted the preponderance of power from the states to the national government. Numerous veterans of the revolutionary struggle felt that Americans were now called upon to surrender themselves to an imperial authority of their own creation. "I confess," Sam Adams of Boston said on receiving the Constitution, "as I enter the Building I stumble at the threshold. I meet with a National Government, instead of a Federal union."

The Anti-Federalists made several attempts, all unsuccessful, to change the ratification plan of the framers. In Congress, Lee urged the addition of a Bill of Rights and several other amendments before transmission of the Constitution to the states. This failing, he corresponded with leaders of like mind, imploring them to seek amendments which could be woven into the proffered system by a second convention. His *Letters* in October carried the same plea. It was supported in Virginia by Governor Randolph and the veteran statesmen George Mason and Patrick Henry, who together persuaded the general assembly to communicate this plan, through the governor, to the executives of the states and to appropriate funds for sending delegates to another federal convention. But at the same time the Virginia legislature, like the legislature of every state except Rhode Island, issued the call for a ratification convention.

Thus, despite delaying tactics, the Anti-Federalists virtually acquiesced in the "rules of the game" laid down by their opponents. They might have fought, on their own principles, to send the Constitution back to Congress as a usurpation of the Articles of Confederation; or, choosing to regard it in the light of amendment to the Articles, they might have rejected it forthwith. Instead they appeared to concede the legitimacy of the proposed Constitution. Their complaint against the "unseemly haste" and the "all or nothing" attitude of the Federalists was not lacking in merit. A Constitution in some respects novel and perilous was before the people. Were the people to be barred from straightening the yoke before they surrendered to it? The proscription could not help but arouse fear and suspicion. "A Constitution," as one Anti-Federalist wrote, "ought to be like Caesar's wife, not only good but unsuspected."

There were, nevertheless, insuperable obstacles to the strategy advocated by Lee and others. With the further disintegration of the existing government, the Federalist specter of anarchy began to assume the frightening form of reality. To delay the establishment of the new government while the representatives of thirteen jealous sovereignties labored to adapt it to their clashing interests would be, in the Federalist opinion, to lose everything. "Clear I am," Washington wrote, "if another federal convention is attempted, that the sentiments of the members will be more discordant or less accommodating than the last." Had the Anti-Federalists been better organized, had they agreed upon specific amendments and conducted a coordinated campaign, they might possibly have overcome their foes. But such was not the case. Despite the efforts of the Clintonians and a few leaders like Lee, the Anti-Federalists were frustrated by the rapid pace of events, the scattered, intractable character of their sympathizers in the various states, and division within their own ranks. While most of them were unalterably opposed to a national government of any sort, others would sooner adopt the Constitution with all its deficiencies than jeopardize the Union. Perhaps the balance of forces lay with these moderate Anti-Federalists. They were subject to conversion. By zealously courting them, and then making modest concessions for their support, the Federalists obtained the margin of victory in several key states.

The ratification of the Constitution was one contest and thirteen contests. Most generalizations about the Union-wide contest must be modified for each of the states. The grant of power to Congress to lay imposts and regulate commerce, for example, was generally approved in the northern "carrying" states but vigorously opposed in the southern "producing" states. However, it is also true that this provision was of no discernible significance in Georgia, which ratified unanimously in order to obtain the protection of a strong national arm against the Indians; that the people in the Shenandoah Valley of Virginia, desiring free access to interstate markets, supported the Constitution largely because of this provision; and that the great landed interests of New York tended to oppose this provision—and the Constitution —because it would deprive the state of its lucrative impost and force resort to direct taxes on land. Similarly, the interest of public creditors, so much emphasized by Charles A. Beard in his *Economic Interpretation of the Constitution* (1913), worked for adoption in some areas, while in others it was neutralized or overset by more compelling considerations. Not only must the peculiar circumstances of each state be borne in mind, but also the status of the ratification movement at the time it swept over each of the states.

The movement leaped forward in December when Delaware, Pennsylvania, and New Jersey ratified in quick succession. The two smaller states, eager to throw off economic vassalage to their neighbors, adopted the Constitution without a dissenting vote. In Pennsylvania, however, the Federalist victory was gained by tactics that proved embarrassing to the cause. The pro-Federalist majority in the legislature was determined to call a convention before it adjourned at the end of September and proceeded to act even before it received the directive from Congress. When the opposition members absented themselves in order to prevent a quorum, hoping thus to deter the decision on the Constitution for many months, two of them— enough to make the quorum—were forcibly summoned and set upon by a mob who "broke into their lodgings, seized them, dragged them through the streets to the State House, and thrust them into the assembly room, with clothes torn and faces white with rage." By this time the resolution of Congress had arrived. The election of delegates was set only five weeks away. Before, during, and after the convention in the rabidly pro-Federalist metropolis, the opposition leaders were subjected to one indignity after another. Riot, effigy-burning, and suppression of information accompanied the ratification of the Constitution in Pennsylvania. The cause of this lay not alone in differences over the new government, but in the struggle that had convulsed the state for years between the partisans of the revolutionary state constitution of 1776 and the "conservatives" who wished to reform this unique and comparatively democratic instrument of government. Many of the "radicals" opposed the new federal model in the realization that the future of a state polity in which they took great pride was also at stake in the contest. Over this stout opposition, the Federalists adopted the Constitution 46–23. Within three years they had reformed the state system.

The Pennsylvania minority first raised the demand for amendments. Not until Massachusetts ratified on February 7, 1788, however, was this by now widespread demand partially met. The convention in Boston was thought to be the most completely representative body in the state's history. Early estimates of voting strength gave the Anti-Federalists a comfortable majority; but it was gradually whittled away by the superior leadership of the Federalists. They saw that if Sam Adams and John Hancock could be detached from the Anti-Federalist cause, it would become a tub without a bottom. Adams was nudged across the threshold by his political clients, the Boston merchants and tradesmen. Hancock was wooed by promises of political preferment: the Vice-Presidency was prominently mentioned. The conversion was made easier for them, and the battle was won, with the "conciliatory proposition" of the Federalists. This consisted of a formula whereby the Constitution would be ratified *unconditionally* but would be accompanied by amendments *recommended* for early adoption under the procedure authorized in Article V of the Constitution. The nine amendments were regarded as harmless by the Federalists and as fundamental guarantees by the Anti-Federalists. The convention voted 187–168 for the Constitution, with the "Federalist compromise" attached.

Eight states had come under the new roof when the Virginia convention assembled at Richmond on June 2. Federalists looked anxiously to Virginia, not simply because its ratification would make the necessary complement, but because without Virginia—the largest, richest, and most populous state —the Union would be impoverished, cut in two, deprived of Washington's leadership, rebuffed by New York, and left to waste away. (As it happened, the honor of becoming the ninth state went to New Hampshire, finally brought to ratify the Constitution by the example of Massachusetts, whose satellite that state was; but this was not known at Richmond when the Virginia convention adjourned.) The division in Virginia was expected to be very close, with the balance tipped against the Constitution. The Federalists' victory at the end of a protracted electoral campaign came as a genuine surprise. On the eve of the convention they were believed to be just shy of a majority. But there was a sizable block of uninstructed and undecided delegates, twelve of them from the Kentucky District, where the Constitution was little known. This fact, together with the influence commanded by the Anti-Federalist leaders, meant that the fate of the new government would be decided on the floor of the convention.

For more than three weeks one of the greatest assemblages in American history debated the momentous issue. Leading the Anti-Federalists was Patrick Henry, bespectacled, bewigged, slightly stooped, looking tired, but still flashing the oratorical brilliance that had inspired the colonists in 1765. Henry was the most powerful political figure in Virginia; the Federalists feared him as well for his power to charm, badger, and cajole his auditors by a flight of eloquence, a jab of irony, or a lapse into pathos. Henry was ably assisted by George Mason, author of the Virginia Declaration of Rights, William Grayson, a highly polished lawyer and a Virginia representative in Congress, and James Monroe, a young veteran of both the Continental Army and the Continental Congress. The Federalist command was more widely dispersed. Edmund Pendleton probably carried more prestige than any other man in the convention. Now sixty-seven, badly crippled, Judge Pendleton had stood opposed to Patrick Henry on most of the important issues in Virginia since the Stamp Act. James Madison, whose only eloquence consisted in unmatched powers of reasoned argument, George Nicholas, long a dominant figure in the House of Delegates, John Marshall, "Lighthorse Harry" Lee—such were the men responsible for the Federalist case. Thomas Jefferson followed the situation as best he could from France, where he had replaced Franklin as minister. On the whole, there was little to differentiate the two groups of delegates in respect to wealth, occupation, military service, slaveholding, ownership of public securities, and geographic section. It is worthy of remark, however, that the Constitution was carried by the votes of the two western sections: the Valley and the Trans-Allegheny.

The Federalists received an unexpected boon at the very outset. On Mason's motion, the convention agreed to discuss the Constitution "clause by clause" and to defer any voting until the end was reached. The object of the Anti-Federalists was to secure an unhurried, thoroughgoing investigation, which would bring into sharp relief those parts of the Constitution they disliked. But, as Madison at once saw, this strategy played into the Federalists' hands by precluding motions to amend in the heat of debate on particular clauses and by obliging the Anti-Federalists to address themselves to the Constitution rather than to their generalized political fears. The strategy may have suited Mason's talents but it did not suit Henry's; and this was only the most signal evidence of mismanagement by the Anti-Federalists.

One of the debate's most dramatic moments occurred on the third day. Governor Randolph, still hopefully relied upon by the Anti-Federalists, rose to address the delegates and the large audience that crowded every seat and passage in the convention hall. Hailing the Union as "the anchor of our political salvation," Randolph announced that despite his earlier misgivings he would sooner sever a limb from his body than see Virginia cut off from the Union. ("Young Arnold! Young Arnold!" Mason was heard to gasp.) Randolph had been patiently courted by Washington and Madison. His defection elated the Federalists.

Their severest trial came the following week when Henry introduced the question of the Jay-Gardoqui Treaty negotiations. This involved the American claim to the right of navigation of the Mississippi River, through Spanish territory, to its mouth. In 1786 Congress directed John Jay to disregard previous instructions for his negotiations with the Spanish minister, Gardoqui, and to seek in exchange for forbearance on the Mississippi claim a favorable commercial treaty with Spain. No treaty was made, but the Southern states, who had voted against the change of instructions, discovered in this action a design on the part of the "carrying" states to sacrifice Southern interests to Northern commerce. Airing this ominous affair in the convention, the Anti-Federalists aimed, first, to demonstrate the danger to Virginia and the South of permitting Congress to legislate on commerce by a simple majority vote; and second, to enlist the uncommitted Kentucky delegates under the Anti-Federalist banner. Ten enlisted. But this was not enough; and it is not likely that many votes were won or lost thereafter.

In the end the Virginia debate came down to the question of whether amendments should be demanded before or after ratification. The Anti-Federalist resolution for *prior* amendments lost by eight votes. The Constitution was then adopted on the plan of Massachusetts, 89–79. Some of the recommended amendments, such as those related to the federal tax power, were not acceptable to most of the Federalists. All, nevertheless, were referred to the First Congress, soon to convene.

DOCUMENTS

1] Lee Launches the Anti-Federalist Attack

> Within a month after the adjournment of the Constitutional Convention, Richard Henry Lee of Virginia, who had declined an appointment as a delegate to the Convention, published what immediately became the most popular and influential Anti-Federalist tract, *The Letters from the Federal Farmer*, in which he argued for prior amendments. Lee was a signer of the Declaration of Independence and a former President of the Continental Congress. He became the first United States senator from Virginia.*

. . . A FEDERAL government of some sort is necessary. We have suffered the present to languish; and whether the confederation was capable or not originally of answering any valuable purposes, it is now but of little importance. I will pass by the men, and states, who have been particularly instrumental in preparing the way for a change, and perhaps, for governments not very favourable to the people at large. A constitution is now presented which we may reject, or which we may accept with or without amendments, and to which point we ought to direct our exertions is the question. . . .

The first principal question that occurs, is, Whether, considering our situation, we ought to precipitate the adoption of the proposed constitution? If we remain cool and temperate, we are in no immediate danger of any commotions; we are in a state of perfect peace, and in no danger of invasions; the state governments are in the full exercise of their powers; and our governments answer all present exigencies, except the regulation of trade, securing credit, in some cases, and providing for the interest, in some instances, of the public debts; and whether we adopt a change three or nine months hence, can make but little odds with the private circumstances of individuals; their happiness and prosperity, after all, depend principally upon their own exertions. We are hardly recovered from a long and distressing war: The farmers, fishmen, &c. have not fully repaired the waste made by it. Industry and frugality are again assuming their proper station. Private debts are lessened, and public debts incurred by the war have been, by various ways, diminished; and the public lands have now become a productive source for diminishing them much more. I know uneasy men, who with very much to precipitate, do not admit all these facts; but they are facts well known to all men who are thoroughly informed in the affairs of this country. It must, however, be admitted, that our

---

* LEE LAUNCHES THE ANTI-FEDERALIST ATTACK: *Observations Leading to a Fair Examination of the System of Government, Proposed by the Late Convention: and to Several Essential and Necessary Alterations in It. In a Number of Letters from the Federal Farmer to the Republican* (Oct. 8–12, 1787). From Paul Leicester Ford, ed., *Pamphlets on the Constitution of the United States Published During Its Discussion by the People, 1787–1788* (Brooklyn, 1888), pp. 280–82, 286–88, 311–15, 317, 320–21, 324.

federal system is defective, and that some of the state governments are not well administered; but, then, we impute to the defects in our governments many evils and embarrassments which are most clearly the result of the late war. We must allow men to conduct on the present occasion, as on all similar ones. They will urge a thousand pretences to answer their purposes on both sides. When we want a man to change his condition, we describe it as wretched, miserable, and despised; and draw a pleasing picture of that which we would have him assume. . . . It is natural for men, who wish to hasten the adoption of a measure, to tell us, now is the crisis—now is the critical moment which must be seized or all will be lost; and to shut the door against free enquiry, whenever conscious the thing presented has defects in it, which time and investigation will probably discover. This has been the custom of tyrants, and their dependants in all ages. . . .

. . . The plan of government now proposed is evidently calculated totally to change, in time, our condition as a people. Instead of being thirteen republics, under a federal head, it is clearly designed to make us one consolidated government. . . .

There are three different forms of free government under which the United States may exist as one nation; and now is, perhaps, the time to determine to which we will direct our views. 1. Distinct republics connected under a federal head. In this case the respective state governments must be the principal guardians of the peoples rights, and exclusively regulate their internal police; in them must rest the balance of government. The congress of the states, or federal head, must consist of delegates amenable to, and removable by the respective states: This congress must have general directing powers; powers to require men and monies of the states; to make treaties; peace and war; to direct the operations of armies, &c. Under this federal modification of government, the powers of congress would be rather advisory or recommendatory than coercive. 2. We may do away the federal state governments, and form or consolidate all the states into one entire government, with one executive, one judiciary, and one legislature, consisting of senators and representatives collected from all parts of the union: In this case there would be a compleat consolidation of the states. 3. We may consolidate the states as to certain national objects, and leave them severally distinct independent republics, as to internal police generally. Let the general government consist of an executive, a judiciary, and balanced legislature, and its powers extend exclusively to all foreign concerns, causes arising on the seas to commerce, imports, armies, navies, Indian affairs, peace and war, and to a few internal concerns of the community; to the coin, post-offices, weights and measures, a general plan for the militia, to naturalization, *and, perhaps to bankruptcies,* leaving the internal police of the community, in other respects, exclusively to the state governments; as the administration of justice in all causes arising internally, the laying and collecting of internal taxes, and the forming of the militia according to a general plan prescribed. In this case there would be a compleat consolidation, *quoad* certain objects only.

Touching the first, or federal plan, I do not think much can be said in its favor: The sovereignty of the nation, without coercive and efficient powers to collect the strength of it, cannot always be depended on to answer the purposes of government; and in a congress of representatives of foreign states, there must necessarily be an unreasonable mixture of powers in the same hands.

As to the second, or compleat consolidating plan, it deserves to be carefully considered at this time by every American: If it be impracticable, it is a fatal error to model our governments, directing our views ultimately to it.

The third plan, or partial consolidation, is, in my opinion, the only one that can secure the freedom and happiness of this people. I once had some general ideas that the second plan was practicable, but from long attention, and the proceedings of the convention, I am fully satisfied, that this third plan is the only one we can with safety and propriety proceed upon. Making this the standard to point out, with candor and fairness, the parts of the new constitution which appear to be improper, is my object. The convention appears to have proposed the partial consolidation evidently with a view to collect all powers ultimately, in the United States into one entire government; and from its views in this respect, and from the tenacity of the small states to have an equal vote in the senate, probably originated the greatest defects in the proposed plan.

Independent of the opinions of many great authors, that a free elective government cannot be extended over large territories, a few reflections must evince, that one government and general legislation alone never can extend equal benefits to all parts of the United States: Different laws, customs, and opinions exist in the different states, which by a uniform system of laws would be unreasonably invaded. The United States contain about a million of square miles, and in half a century will, probably, contain ten millions of people; and from the center to the extremes is about 800 miles.

Before we do away the state governments or adopt measures that will tend to abolish them, and to consolidate the states into one entire government several principles should be considered and facts ascertained. . . .

. . . There are certain rights which we have always held sacred in the United States, and recognized in all our constitutions, and which, by the adoption of the new constitution in its present form, will be left unsecured. By article 6, the proposed constitution, and the laws of the United States, which shall be made in pursuance thereof; and all treaties made, or which shall be made under the authority of the United States, shall be the supreme law of the land; and the judges in every state shall be bound thereby; anything in the constitution or laws of any state to the contrary notwithstanding.

It is to be observed that when the people shall adopt the proposed constitution it will be their last and supreme act; it will be adopted not by the people of New Hampshire, Massachusetts, &c., but by the people of the United States; and wherever this constitution, or any part of it, shall be incompatible with the ancient customs, rights, the laws or the constitutions heretofore established in the United States, it will entirely abolish them and do them away: And not only this, but the laws of the United States which shall be made in pursuance of the federal constitution will be also supreme laws, and wherever they shall be incompatible with those customs, rights, laws or constitutions heretofore established, they will also entirely abolish them and do them away.

By the article before recited, treaties also made under the authority of the United States, shall be the supreme law: It is not said that these treaties shall be made in pursuance of the constitution—nor are there any constitutional bounds set to those who shall make them: The president and two-thirds of the senate will be empowered to make treaties indefinitely, and when these treaties shall be made, they will also abolish all laws and state constitutions incompatible with them. This power in the president and senate is absolute, and the judges will be bound to allow full force to whatever rule, article or thing the president and senate shall establish by treaty, whether it be practicable to set any bounds to those who make treaties, I am not able to say; if not, it proves that this power ought to be more safely lodged.

The federal constitution, the laws of congress made in pursuance of the constitution, and all treaties must have full force and effect in all parts of the United States; and all other laws, rights and constitutions which stand in their way must yield: It is proper the national laws should be supreme, and superior to state or district laws; but then the national laws ought to yield to unalienable or fundamental rights——and national laws, made by a few men, should extend only to a few national objects. This will not be the case with the laws of congress: To have any proper idea of their extent, we must carefully examine the legislative, executive and judicial powers proposed to be lodged in the general government, and consider them in connection with a general clause in art. 1, sect. 8, in these words (after enumerating a number of powers) "To make all laws which shall be necessary and proper for carrying into execution the foregoing powers, and all other powers vested by this constitution in the government of the United States, or in any department or officer thereof."——The powers of this government as has been observed, extend to internal as well as external objects, and to those objects to which all others are subordinate; it is almost impossible to have a just conception of their powers, or of the extent and number of the laws which may be deemed necessary and proper to carry them into effect . . . But the general presumption being, that men who govern, will in doubtful cases, construe laws and constitutions most favourably for increasing their own powers; all wise and prudent people, in forming constitutions, have drawn the line, and carefully described the powers parted with and the powers reserved. By the state constitutions, certain rights have been reserved in the people; or rather, they have been recognized and established in such a manner, that state legislatures are bound to respect them, and to make no laws infringing upon them. The state legislatures are obliged to take notice of the bills of rights of their respective states. The bills of rights, and the state constitutions, are fundamental compacts only between those who govern, and the people of the same state. . . .

. . . I think my opinion is not only founded in reason, but I think it is supported by the report of the convention itself. If there are a number of rights established by the state constitutions, and which will remain sacred, and the general government is bound to take notice of them—it must take notice of one as well as another; and if unnecessary to recognize or establish one by the federal constitution, it would be unnecessary to recognize or establish another by it. If the federal constitution is to be construed so far in connection with the state constitution, as to leave the trial by jury in civil causes, for instance, secured; on the same principles it would have left the trial by jury in criminal causes, the benefits of the writ of habeas corpus, &c. secured; they all stand on the same footing; they are the common rights of Americans, and have been recognized by the state constitutions: But the convention found it necessary to recognize or re-establish the benefits of that writ, and the jury trial in criminal cases. As to *expost facto* laws, the convention has done the same in one case, and gone further in another, It is a part of the compact between the people of each state and their rulers, that no *expost facto* laws shall be made. But the convention, by Art. 1, Sect. 10, have put a sanction upon this part even of the state compacts. In fact, the 9th and 10th Sections in Art. 1, in the proposed constitution, are no more nor less, than a partial bill of rights; they establish certain principles as part of the compact upon which the federal legislators and officers can never infringe. It is here wisely stipulated, that the federal legislature shall never pass a bill of attainder, or *expost facto* law; that no tax shall be laid on articles exported, &c. The establishing of one right implies the necessity of establishing another and similar one.

On the whole, the position appears to me to be undeniable, that this bill of rights ought to be carried farther, and some other principles established, as a part of this fundamental compact between the people of the United States and their federal rulers.

It is true, we are not disposed to differ much, at present, about religion; but when we are making a constitution, it is to be hoped, for ages and millions yet unborn, why not establish the free exercise of religion, as a part of the national compact. There are other essential rights, which we have justly understood to be the rights of freemen; as freedom from hasty and unreasonable search warrants, warrants not founded on oath, and not issued with due caution, for searching and seizing men's papers, property, and persons. The trials by jury in civil causes, it is said, varies so much in the several states, that no words could be found for the uniform establishment of it. If so, the federal legislation will not be able to establish it by any general laws. I confess I am of opinion it may be established, but not in that beneficial manner in which we may enjoy it, for the reasons beforementioned. When I speak of the jury trial of the vicinage, or the trial of the fact in the neighborhood, I do not lay so much stress upon the circumstance of our being tried by our neighbours: in this enlightened country men may be probably impartially tried by those who do not live very near them: but the trial of facts in the neighbourhood is of great importance in other respects. Nothing can be more essential than the cross examining witnesses, and generally before the triers of the facts in question. The common people can establish facts with much more ease with oral than written evidence; when trials of facts are removed to a distance from the homes of the parties and witnesses, oral evidence becomes intolerably expensive, and the parties must depend on written evidence, which to the common people is expensive and almost useless; it must be frequently taken ex parte, and but very seldom leads to the proper discovery of truth. . . .

It may also be worthy our examination, how far the provision for amending this plan, when it shall be adopted, is of any importance. No measures can be taken towards amendments, unless two-thirds of the congress, or two-thirds of the legislature of the several states shall agree.—While power is in the hands of the people, or democratic part of the community, more especially as at present, it is easy, according to the general course of human affairs, for the few influential men in the community, to obtain conventions, alterations in government, and to persuade the common people that they may change for the better, and to get from them a part of the power: But when power is once transferred from the many to the few, all changes become extremely difficult; the government, in this case, being beneficial to the few, they will be exceedingly artful and adroit in preventing any measures which may lead to a change; and nothing will produce it, but great exertions and severe struggles on the part of the common people. Every man of reflection must see, that the change now proposed, is a transfer of power from the many to the few, and the probability is, the artful and ever active aristocracy, will prevent all peaceful measures for changes, unless when they shall discover some favorable moment to increase their own influence. . . .

I have, in the course of these letters observed, that there are many good things in the proposed constitution, and I have endeavored to point out many important defects in it. I have admitted that we want a federal system—that we have a system presented, which, with several alterations may be made a tolerable good one—I have admitted there is a well founded uneasiness among creditors and mercantile men. In this situation of things, you ask me what I think ought to be done? My opinion in this case is only the opinion of an individual, and so far only as it corresponds with the opinions of the honest and substantial part of the community, is it entitled to consideration. Though I am fully satisfied that the state conventions ought most seriously to direct their exertions to altering and amending the system proposed before they shall adopt it—yet I have not sufficiently examined the subject, or formed an opinion, how far it will be practicable for those conventions to carry their amendments. As to the idea, that it will be in vain for those conventions to attempt amendments, it cannot be admitted; it is impossible to say whether they can or not until the attempt shall be made; and when it shall be determined, by experience, that the conventions cannot agree in amendments, it will then be an important question before the people of the United States, whether they will adopt or not the system proposed in its present form. This subject of consolidating the states is new: and because forty or fifty men have agreed in a system, to suppose the good sense of this country, an enlightened nation, must adopt it without examination, and though in a state of profound peace, without endeavouring to amend those parts they perceive are defective, dangerous to freedom, and destructive of the valuable principles of republican government—is truly humiliating. It is true there may be danger in delay; but there is danger in adopting the system in its present form; and I see the danger in either case will arise principally from the conduct and views of two very unprincipled parties in the United States—two fires, between which the honest and substantial people have long found themselves situated. One party is composed of little insurgents, men in debt, who want no law, and who want a share of the property of others; these are called levellers, Shayites, &c. The other party is composed of a few, but more dangerous men, with their servile dependents; these avariciously grasp at all power and property; you may discover in all the actions of these men, an evident dislike to free and equal government, and they will go systematically to work to change, essentially, the forms of government in this country; these are called aristocrats, m——ites,

&c. &c. Between these two parties is the weight of the community; the men of middling property, men not in debt on the one hand, and men, on the other, content with republican governments, and not aiming at immense fortunes, offices, and power. In 1786, the little insurgents, the levellers, came forth, invaded the rights of others, and attempted to establish governments according to their wills. Their movements evidently gave encouragement to the other party, which, in 1787, has taken the political field, and with its fashionable dependants, and the tongue and the pen, is endeavoring to establish in a great haste, a politer kind of government. These two parties, which will probably be opposed or united as it may suit their interests and views, are really insignificant, compared with the solid, free, and independent part of the community. . . .

In every point of view, therefore, in which I have been able, as yet, to contemplate this subject, I can discern but one rational mode of proceeding relative to it: and that is to examine it with freedom and candour, to have state conventions some months hence, which shall examine coolly every article, clause, and word in the system proposed, and to adopt it with such amendments as they shall think fit. How far the state conventions ought to pursue the mode prescribed by the federal convention of adopting or rejecting the plan in toto, I leave it to them to determine. . . .

2] Madison and Jefferson Discuss the Constitution

A] A Balance of Powers

In the following letter Madison reveals, in Jefferson's words, "the rich resources of his luminous and discriminating mind" that made him the architect of republican constitutionalism. The "digression" for which Madison apologizes, in his report to his friend in Paris, anticipated the ideas he was shortly to re-express in the famous tenth paper of *The Federalist.**

. . . You will herewith receive the result of the Convention, which continued its session till the 17th of September. I take the liberty of making some observations on the subject which will help to make up a letter, if they should answer no other purpose.

It appeared to be the sincere and unanimous wish of the Convention to cherish and preserve the Union of the States. . . .

It was generally agreed that the objects of the Union could not be secured by any system founded on the principle of a confederation of sovereign States. A voluntary observance of the federal law by all the members could never be hoped for. A compulsory one could evidently never be reduced to practice, and if it could, involved equal calamities to the innocent and the guilty, the neces-

---

* A balance of powers: James Madison to Thomas Jefferson, October 24, 1787. From Julian P. Boyd, ed., *The Papers of Thomas Jefferson* (Princeton, 1950–), XII, 271–79. Reprinted by permission of the Princeton University Press.

sity of a military force both obnoxious and dangerous, and in general, a scene resembling much more a civil war, than the administration of a regular Government.

Hence was embraced the alternative of a government which instead of operating, on the States, should operate without their intervention on the individuals composing them: and hence the change in the principle and proportion of representation.

This ground-work being laid, the great objects which presented themselves were 1. to unite a proper energy in the Executive and a proper stability in the Legislative departments, with the essential characters of Republican Government. 2. To draw a line of demarkation which would give to the General Government every power requisite for general purposes, and leave to the States every power which might be most beneficially administered by them. 3. To provide for the different interests of different parts of the Union. 4. To adjust the clashing pretensions of the large and small States. Each of these objects was pregnant with difficulties. The whole of them together formed a task more difficult than can be well conceived by those who were not concerned in the execution of it. Adding to these considerations the natural diversity of human opinions on all new and complicated subjects, it is impossible to consider the degree of concord which ultimately prevailed as less than a miracle.

The first of these objects as it respects the Executive, was peculiarly embarrassing. On the question whether it should consist of a single person, or a plurality of co-ordinate members, on the mode of appointment, on the duration in office, on the degree of power, on the re-eligibility, tedious and reiterated discussions took place. . . . It was much agitated whether a long term, seven years for example, with a subsequent and perpetual ineligibility, or a short term with a capacity to be re-elected, should be fixed. In favor of the first opinion were urged the danger of a gradual degeneracy of re-elections from time to time, into first a life and then a hereditary tenure, and the favorable effect of an incapacity to be reappointed, on the independent exercise of the Executive authority. On the other side it was contended that the prospect of necessary degradation would discourage the most dignified characters from aspiring to the office, would take away the principal motive to the faithful discharge of its duties. The hope of being rewarded with a reappointment, would stimulate ambition to violent efforts for holding over the constitutional term, and instead of producing an independent administration, and a firmer defence of the constitutional rights of the department, would render the officer more indifferent to the importance of a place which he would soon be obliged to quit for ever, and more ready to yield to the incroachments of the Legislature of which he might again be a member. . . .

The second object, the due partition of power, between the General and local Governments, was perhaps of all, the most nice and difficult. A few contended for an entire abolition of the States; Some for indefinite power of Legislation in the Congress, with a negative on the laws of the States, some for such a power without a negative, some for a limited power of legislation, with such a negative: the majority finally for a limited power without the negative. The question with regard to the Negative underwent repeated discussions, and was finally rejected by a bare majority. . . .

. . . A Constitutional negative on the laws of the States seems equally necessary to secure individuals against encroachments on their rights. The mutability
of the laws of the States is found to be a serious evil. The injustice of them has
been so frequent and so flagrant as to alarm the most stedfast friends of
Republicanism. I am persuaded I do not err in saying that the evils issuing
from these sources contributed more to that uneasiness which produced the
Convention, and prepared the public mind for a general reform, than those
which accrued to our national character and interest from the inadequacy of
the Confederation to its immediate objects. A reform therefore which does
not make provision for private rights, must be materially defective. The restraints against paper emissions, and violations of contracts are not sufficient.
Supposing them to be effectual as far as they go, they are short of the mark.
Injustice may be effected by such an infinitude of legislative expedients, that
where the disposition exists it can only be controuled by some provision which
reaches all cases whatsoever. The partial provision made, supposes the disposition which will evade it. It may be asked how private rights will be more
secure under the Guardianship of the General Government than under the
State Governments, since they are both founded on the republican principle
which refers the ultimate decision to the will of the majority, and are distinguished rather by the extent within which they will operate, than by any
material difference in their structure. A full discussion of this question would,
if I mistake not, unfold the true principles of Republican Government, and
prove in contradiction to the concurrent opinions of theoretical writers, that
this form of Government, in order to effect its purposes must operate not
within a small but an extensive sphere. I will state some of the ideas which
have occurred to me on this subject. Those who contend for a simple Democracy, or a pure republic, actuated by the sense of the majority, and operating
within narrow limits, assume or suppose a case which is altogether fictitious.
They found their reasoning on the idea, that the people composing the Society
enjoy not only an equality of political rights; but that they have all precisely
the same interests and the same feelings in every respect. Were this in reality
the case, their reasoning would be conclusive. The interest of the majority
would be that of the minority also; the decisions could only turn on mere
opinion concerning the good of the whole of which the major voice would be
the safest criterion; and within a small sphere, this voice could be most easily
collected and the public affairs most accurately managed. We know however
that no Society ever did or can consist of so homogeneous a mass of Citizens.
In the savage State indeed, an approach is made towards it; but in that state
little or no Government is necessary. In all civilized Societies, distinctions are
various and unavoidable. A distinction of property results from that very protection which a free Government gives to unequal faculties of acquiring it.
There will be rich and poor; creditors and debtors; a landed interest, a monied
interest, a mercantile interest, a manufacturing interest. These classes may again
be subdivided according to the different productions of different situations and
soils, and according to different branches of commerce and of manufactures.
In addition to these natural distinctions, artificial ones will be founded on
accidental differences in political, religious and other opinions, or an attachment to the persons of leading individuals. . . . If then there must be dif-

ferent interests and parties in Society; and a majority when united by a common interest or passion can not be restrained from oppressing the minority, what remedy can be found in a republican Government, where the majority must ultimately decide, but that of giving such an extent to its sphere, that no common interest or passion will be likely to unite a majority of the whole number in an unjust pursuit. In a large Society, the people are broken into so many interests and parties, that a common sentiment is less likely to be felt, and the requisite concert less likely to be formed, by a majority of the whole. The same security seems requisite for the civil as for the religious rights of individuals. If the same sect form a majority and have the power, other sects will be sure to be depressed. Divide et impera, the reprobated axiom of tyranny, is under certain qualifications, the only policy, by which a republic can be administered on just principles. It must be observed however that this doctrine can only hold within a sphere of a mean extent. As in too small a sphere oppressive combinations may be too easily formed against the weaker party; so in too extensive a one a defensive concert may be rendered too difficult against the oppression of those entrusted with the administration. The great desideratum in Government is, so to modify the sovereignty as that it may be sufficiently neutral between different parts of the Society to controul one part from invading the rights of another, and at the same time sufficiently controuled itself, from setting up an interest adverse to that of the entire Society. In absolute monarchies, the Prince may be tolerably neutral towards different classes of his subjects, but may sacrifice the happiness of all to his personal ambition or avarice. In small republics, the sovereign will is controuled from such a sacrifice of the entire Society, but it is not sufficiently neutral towards the parts composing it. In the extended Republic of the United States, the General Government would hold a pretty even balance between the parties of particular States, and be at the same time sufficiently restrained by its dependence on the community, from betraying its general interests.

Begging pardon for this immoderate digression, I return to the third object abovementioned, the adjustment of the different interests of different parts of the Continent. Some contended for an unlimited power over trade including exports as well as imports, and over slaves as well as other imports; some for such a power, provided the concurrence of two thirds of both Houses were required; some for such a qualification of the power, with an exemption of exports and slaves, others for an exemption of exports only. The result is seen in the Constitution. S. Carolina and Georgia were inflexible on the point of the slaves.

The remaining object, created more embarrassment, and a greater alarm for the issue of the Convention than all the rest put together. The little States insisted on retaining their equality in both branches, unless a compleat abolition of the State Governments should take place; and made an equality in the Senate a sine qua non. The large States on the other hand urged that as the new Government was to be drawn principally from the people immediately and was to operate directly on them, not on the States; and consequently as the States would lose that importance which is now proportioned to the importance of their voluntary compliances with the requisitions of Congress, it was necessary that the representation in both Houses should be in proportion to their size. It ended in the compromise which you will see, but very much to the dissatisfaction of several members from the large States. . . .

B] "What I Do Not Like"

On March 13, 1789, Jefferson wrote that he had been "dished up . . . as an anti-federalist," and commented: ". . . I am not of the party of the federalists. But I am much farther from that of the anti-federalists. I approved, from the first moment, of the great mass of what is in the new Constitution . . ." He had several reservations, however, chief among them the lack of guarantees for personal liberties. Replying to Madison, his skeptical but judicious friend, Jefferson insists that "a bill of rights is what the people are entitled to . . . "—a theme which he reiterated in subsequent letters, ultimately convincing Madison.*

. . . I LIKE much the general idea of framing a government which should go on of itself peaceably, without needing continual recurrence to the state legislatures. I like the organization of the government into Legislative, Judiciary and Executive. I like the power given the Legislature to levy taxes; and for that reason solely approve of the greater house being chosen by the people directly. For tho' I think a house chosen by them will be very illy qualified to legislate for the Union, for foreign nations &c. yet this evil does not weigh against the good of preserving inviolate the fundamental principle that the people are not to be taxed but by representatives chosen immediately by themselves. I am captivated by the compromise of the opposite claims of the great and little states, of the latter to equal, and the former to proportional influence. I am much pleased too with the substitution of the method of voting by persons, instead of that of voting by states: and I like the negative given to the Executive with a third of either house, though I should have liked it better had the Judiciary been associated for that purpose, or invested with a similar and separate power. There are other good things of less moment. I will now add what I do not like. First the omission of a bill of rights providing clearly and without the aid of sophisms for freedom of religion, freedom of the press, protection against standing armies, restriction against monopolies, the eternal and unremitting force of the habeas corpus laws, and trials by jury in all matters of fact triable by the laws of the land and not by the law of Nations. To say, as Mr. Wilson does that a bill of rights was not necessary because all is reserved in the case of the general government which is not given, while in the particular ones all is given which is not reserved might do for the Audience to whom it was addressed, but is surely gratis dictum, opposed by strong inferences from the body of the instrument, as well as from the omission of the clause of our present confederation which had declared that in express terms. It was a hard conclusion to say because there has been no uniformity among the states as to the cases triable by jury, because some have been so

* "WHAT I DO NOT LIKE": Thomas Jefferson to James Madison, December 20, 1787. From Julian P. Boyd, ed., The Papers of Thomas Jefferson (Princeton, 1950–   ), XII, 439–40. Reprinted by permission of the Princeton University Press.

incautious as to abandon this mode of trial, therefore the more prudent states shall be reduced to the same level of calamity. It would have been much more just and wise to have concluded the other way that as most of the states had judiciously preserved this palladium, those who had wandered should be brought back to it, and to have established general right instead of general wrong. Let me add that a bill of rights is what the people are entitled to against every government on earth, general or particular, and what no just government should refuse, or rest on inference. The second feature I dislike, and greatly dislike, is the abandonment in every instance of the necessity of rotation in office, and most particularly in the case of the President. Experience concurs with reason in concluding that the first magistrate will always be re-elected if the constitution permits it. He is then an officer for life. . . .

3] James Wilson Defends the Constitution

Next to Madison, the most constructive member of the Constitutional Convention had been James Wilson of Pennsylvania, a signer of the Declaration of Independence who became a member of the Supreme Court after the adoption of the Constitution. He completely dominated the Pennsylvania ratifying convention of 1787. The following extracts from his speeches at that convention reveal his nationalistic vision, his understanding of the problem of sovereignty, and his reasons for the omission of a Bill of Rights in the proposed Constitution. Wilson's argument on the latter point was widely adopted by Federalists in other states, most notably by Hamilton in *The Federalist*, No. 84.*

THE SYSTEM proposed, by the late Convention, for the government of the United States, is now before you. Of that Convention I had the honor to be a member. As I am the only member of that body who has the honor to be also a member of this, it may be expected that I should prepare the way for the deliberations of this assembly, by unfolding the difficulties which the late Convention were obliged to encounter; by pointing out the end which they proposed to accomplish; and by tracing the general principles which they have adopted for the accomplishment of that end.

To form a good system of government for a single city or state, however limited as to territory, or inconsiderable as to numbers, has been thought to require the strongest efforts of human genius. With what conscious diffidence, then, must the members of the Convention have revolved in their minds the immense undertaking which was before them. Their views could not be confined to a small or a single community, but were expanded to a great number of states; several of which contain an extent of territory, and resources of population, equal to those of some of the most respectable kingdoms on the other

* JAMES WILSON DEFENDS THE CONSTITUTION: The Pennsylvania Convention. From Jonathan Elliot, ed., *The Debates in the Several State Conventions on the Adoption of the Federal Constitution*, 2nd ed. (Philadelphia, 1836), I, 418–19, 435–37, 443–44, 455–58, 462–63.

side of the Atlantic. Nor were even these the only objects to be comprehended within their deliberations. Numerous states yet unformed, myriads of the human race, who will inhabit regions hitherto uncultivated, were to be affected by the result of their proceedings. It was necessary, therefore, to form their calculations on a scale commensurate to a large portion of the globe.

For my own part, I have been often lost in astonishment at the vastness of the prospect before us. To open the navigation of a single river was lately thought, in Europe, an enterprise equal to imperial glory. But could the commercial scenes of the Scheldt be compared with those that, under a good government, will be exhibited on the Hudson, the Delaware, the Potomac, and the numerous other rivers, that water and are intended to enrich the dominions of the United States?

The difficulty of the business was equal to its magnitude. No small share of wisdom and address is requisite to combine and reconcile the jarring interests that prevail, or seem to prevail, in a single community. The United States contain already thirteen governments mutually independent. Those governments present to the Atlantic a front of fifteen hundred miles in extent. Their soil, their climates, their productions, their dimensions, their numbers, are different. In many instances, a difference, and even an opposition, subsists among their interests; and a difference, and even an opposition, is imagined to subsist in many more. An apparent interest produces the same attachment as a real one, and is often pursued with no less perseverance and vigor. When all these circumstances are seen, and attentively considered, will any member of this honorable body be surprised that such a diversity of things produced a proportionate diversity of sentiment? Will he be surprised that such a diversity of sentiment rendered a spirit of mutual forbearance and conciliation indispensably necessary to the success of the great work? . . .

. . . I am called upon to give a reason why the Convention omitted to add a bill of rights to the work before you. I confess, sir, I did think that, in point of propriety, the honorable gentleman ought first to have furnished some reasons to show such an addition to be necessary; it is natural to prove the affirmative of a proposition; and, if he had established the propriety of this addition, he might then have asked why it was not made.

I cannot say, Mr. President, what were the reasons of every member of that Convention for not adding a bill of rights. I believe the truth is, that such an idea never entered the mind of many of them. I do not recollect to have heard the subject mentioned till within about three days of the time of our rising; and even then, there was no direct motion offered for any thing of the kind. I may be mistaken in this; but as far as my memory serves me, I believe it was the case. A proposition to adopt a measure that would have supposed that we were throwing into the general government every power not expressly reserved by the people, would have been spurned at, in that house, with the greatest indignation. Even in a single government, if the powers of the people rest on the same establishment as is expressed in this Constitution, a bill of rights is by no means a necessary measure. In a government possessed of enumerated powers, such a measure would be not only unnecessary, but preposterous and dangerous. Whence comes this notion, that in the United States there is no security without a bill of rights? Have the citizens of South Carolina no security for their liberties? They have no bill of rights. Are the citizens on the eastern side of the Delaware less free, or less secured in their liberties, than those on the western side? The state of New Jersey has no bill of rights. The state of New York has no bill of rights. The states of Connecticut and Rhode Island have no bill of rights. I know not whether I have exactly enumerated the states who have not thought it necessary to add *a bill of rights* to their constitutions; but this enumeration, sir, will serve to show by experience, as well as principle, that, even in single governments, a bill of rights is not an essential or necessary measure. But in a government consisting of enumerated powers, such as is proposed for the United States, a bill of rights would not only be unnecessary, but, in my humble judgment, highly imprudent. In all societies, there are many powers and rights which cannot be particularly enumerated. A bill of rights annexed to a constitution is *an enumeration of the powers* reserved. If we attempt an enumeration, every thing that is not enumerated is presumed to be given. The consequence is, that an imperfect enumeration would throw all implied power into the scale of the government, and the rights of the people would be rendered incomplete. On the other hand, an imperfect enumeration of the powers of government reserves all implied power to the people; and by that means the constitution becomes incomplete. But of the two, it is much safer to run the risk on the side of the constitution; for an omission in the enumeration of the powers of government is neither so dangerous nor important as an omission in the enumeration of the rights of the people. . . .

To every suggestion concerning a bill of rights, the citizens of the United States may always say, WE reserve the right to do what we please. . . .

The secret is now disclosed, and it is discovered to be a dread, that the boasted *state sovereignties* will, under this system, be disrobed of part of their power. Before I go into the examination of this point, let me ask one important question. Upon what principle is it contended that the sovereign power resides in the state governments? The honorable gentleman has said truly, that there can be no subordinate sovereignty. Now, if there cannot, my position is, that the sovereignty resides in the people; they have not parted with it; they have only dispensed such portions of power as were conceived necessary for the public welfare. This Constitution stands upon this broad principle. I know very well, sir, that the people have hitherto been shut out of the federal government; but it is not meant that they should any longer be dispossessed of their rights. In order to recognize this leading principle, the proposed system sets out with a declaration that its existence depends upon the supreme authority of the people alone. We have heard much about a consolidated government. I wish the honorable gentleman would condescend to give us a definition of what he meant by it. I think this the more necessary, because I apprehend that the term, in the numerous times it has been used, has not always been used in the same sense. It may be said, and I believe it has been said, that a consolidated government is such as will absorb and destroy the governments of the several states. If it is taken in this view, the plan before us is not a consolidated government, as I showed on a former day, and may, if necessary, show further on some future occasion. On the other hand, if it is meant that the general government will take from the state governments their power in some particulars, it is confessed, and evident, that this will be its operation and effect.

When the principle is once settled that *the people* are the source of authority, the consequence is, that they may take from the subordinate governments powers with which they have hitherto trusted them, and place those powers in the general government, if it is thought that there they will be productive of more good. They can distribute one portion of power to the more contracted circle, called *state governments;* they can also furnish another proportion to the government of the United States. Who will undertake to say, as a state officer, that the people may not give to the general government what powers, and for what purposes, they please? How comes it, sir, that these state governments dictate to their superiors—to the majesty of the people? When I say the *majesty of the people,* I mean the thing, and not a mere compliment to them. The honorable gentleman went further, and said that the state governments were kept out of this government altogether. The truth is,—and it is a leading principle in this system,—that not the states only, but the people also, shall be here represented. And if this is a crime, I confess the general government is chargeable with it; but I have no idea that a safe system of power in the government, sufficient to manage the general interest of the United States, could be drawn from any other source, or vested in any other authority, than that of the people at large; and I consider this authority as the rock on which this structure will stand. If this principle is unfounded, the system must fall. If the honorable gentlemen, before they undertake to oppose this principle, will show that the people have parted with their power to the state governments, then I confess I cannot support this Constitution. It is asked, Can there be *two taxing powers?* Will the people submit to two taxing powers? I think they will, when the taxes are required for the public welfare, by persons appointed immediately by their fellow-citizens. . . .

In this confederated republic, the sovereignty of the states it is said, is not preserved. We are told that there cannot be two sovereign powers, and that a subordinate sovereignty is no sovereignty.

It will be worth while, Mr. President, to consider this objection at large. When I had the honor of speaking formerly on this subject, I stated, in as concise a manner as possible, the leading ideas that occurred to me, to ascertain where the supreme and sovereign power resides. It has not been, nor, I presume, will it be denied, that somewhere there is, and of necessity must be, a supreme, absolute, and uncontrollable authority. This, I believe, may justly be termed the *sovereign* power; for, from that gentleman's (Mr. Findley) account of the matter, it cannot be sovereign unless it is supreme; for, says he, a subordinate sovereignty is no sovereignty at all. I had the honor of observing, that, if the question was asked, where the supreme power resided, different answers would be given by different writers. I mentioned that Blackstone will tell you that, in Britain, it is lodged in the British Parliament; and I believe there is no writer on this subject, on the other side of the Atlantic, but supposed it to be vested in that body. I stated, further, that, if the question was asked of some politician, who had not considered the subject with sufficient accuracy, where the supreme power resided in our governments, he would answer, that it was vested in the state constitutions. This opinion approaches near the truth, but does not reach it; for the truth is, that the supreme, absolute, and uncontrollable authority *remains* with the people. I mentioned, also, that the practical recognition of this truth was reserved for the honor of this country. I recollect no constitution founded on this principle; but we have witnessed the improvement, and enjoy the happiness of seeing it carried into practice. The great and penetrating mind of *Locke* seems to be the only one that pointed towards even the theory of this great truth.

When I made the observation that some politicians would say the supreme power was lodged in our state constitutions, I did not suspect that the honorable gentleman from Westmoreland (Mr. Findley) was included in that description, but I find myself disappointed; for I imagined his opposition would arise from another consideration. His position is, that the supreme power resides in the states, as governments; and mine is, that it *resides* in the people, as the fountain of government; that the people have not—that the people meant not—and that the people ought not—to part with it to any government whatsoever. In their hands it remains secure. They can delegate it in such proportions, to such bodies, on such terms, and under such limitations, as they think proper. I agree with the members in opposition, that there cannot be two sovereign powers on the same subject.

I consider the people of the United States as forming one great community; and I consider the people of the different states as forming communities, again, on a lesser scale. From this great division of the people into distinct communities, it will be found necessary that different proportions of legislative powers should be given to the governments, according to the nature, number, and magnitude of their objects.

Unless the people are considered in these two views, we shall never be able to understand the principle on which this system was constructed. I view the states as made *for* the people, as well as by them, and not the people as made for the states; the people, therefore, have a right, whilst enjoying the undeniable powers of society, to form either a general government, or state governments, in what manner they please, or to accommodate them to one another, and by this means preserve them all. This, I say, is the inherent and unalienable right of the people; and as an illustration of it, I beg to read a few words from the Declaration of Independence, made by the representatives of the United States, and recognized by the whole Union.

"We hold these truths to be self-evident, that all men are created equal; that they are endowed by their Creator with certain unalienable rights; that among these are life, liberty, and the pursuit of happiness; that, to secure these rights, *governments are instituted among men, deriving their just powers from the consent of the governed;* that, whenever any form of government becomes destructive of these ends, it is the right of the people to alter or abolish it, and institute new government, laying its foundation on such principles, and organzing its powers in such forms, as to them shall seem most likely to effect their safety and happiness."

This is the broad basis on which our independence was placed: on the same certain and solid foundation this system is erected.

State sovereignty, as it is called, is far from being able to support its weight. Nothing less than the authority of the people could either support it or give it efficacy. I cannot pass over this subject without noticing the different conduct pursued by the late federal Convention, and that observed by the Convention which framed the Constitution of Pennsylvania. On that occasion you find an attempt made to deprive the people of this right, so lately and so expressly asserted in the Declaration of Independence. We are told, in the preamble to the declaration of rights, and frame of government, that *we* "do, by virtue of the authority vested in *us,* ordain, declare, and establish, the following declaration of rights and frame of government, to be the Constitution of this commonwealth, and to remain in force therein unaltered, except in such articles as shall hereafter, on experience, be found to require improvement, and which shall, by the same authority of the people, fairly delegated *as this frame of government directs."*—An honorable gentleman (Mr. Chambers) was well warranted in saying that all that could be done was done, to cut off the people from the right of amending; for it cannot be amended by any other mode than that which it directs; then, any number more than one third may control any number less than two thirds.

But I return to my general reasoning. My position is, sir, that, in this country, the supreme, absolute, and uncontrollable power resides in the people at large; that they have vested certain proportions of this power in the state governments; but that the fee-simple continues, resides, and remains, with the body of the people. Under the practical influence of this great truth, we are now sitting and deliberating, and under its operation, we can sit as calmly and deliberate as coolly, in order to change a constitution, as a legislature can sit and deliberate under the power of a constitution, in order to alter or amend a law. It is true, the exercise of this power will not probably be so frequent, nor resorted to on so many occasions, in one case as in the other; but the recognition of the principle cannot fail to establish it more firmly. But, because this recognition is made in the proposed Constitution, an exception is taken to the whole of it; for we are told it is a violation of the present Confederation—*a Confederation of sovereign states.* I shall not enter into an investigation of the present Confederation, but shall just remark that its principle is not the principle of free governments. The people of the United States are not, as such, represented in the present Congress; and, considered even as the component parts of the several states, they are not represented in proportion to their numbers and importance. . . .

. . . Let us attend a moment to the situation of this country. It is a maxim of every government, and it ought to be a maxim with us, that the increase of numbers increases the dignity and security, and the respectability, of all governments. It is the first command given by the Deity to man, Increase and multiply. This applies with peculiar force to this country, the smaller part of whose territory is yet inhabited. We are representatives, sir, not merely of the present age, but of future times; not merely of the territory along the sea-coast, but of regions immensely extended westward. We should fill, as fast as possible, this extensive country, with men who shall live happy, free, and secure. To accomplish this great end ought to be the leading view of all our patriots and statesmen. But how is it to be accomplished, but by establishing peace and harmony among ourselves, and dignity and respectability among foreign nations? By these means, we may draw members from the other side of the

Atlantic, in addition to the natural sources of population. Can either of these objects be attained without a protecting head? When we examine history, we shall find an important fact, and almost the only fact which will apply to all confederacies:—

They have all fallen to pieces, and have not absorbed the government.

In order to keep republics together, they must have a strong binding force, which must be either external or internal. The situation of this country shows that no foreign force can press us together; the bonds of our union ought therefore to be indissolubly strong.

The *powers of the states,* I apprehend, will increase with the population and the happiness of their inhabitants. Unless we can establish a character abroad, we shall be unhappy from foreign restraints or internal violence. These reasons, I think, prove sufficiently the necessity of having a federal head. Under it, the advantages enjoyed by the whole Union would be participated by every state. I wish honorable gentlemen would think not only of themselves, not only of the present age, but of others, and of future times. . . .

4] The Pennsylvania Anti-Federalists Offer Their "Reasons of Dissent"

> Pennsylvania was the second state to ratify. The Anti-Federalist minority in the state ratifying convention indicated a willingness to accept the Constitution on condition that a number of amendments be approved. But the Federalist-dominated convention, by a vote of 46–23, rejected the minority propositions and even refused to enter them in the journal of the convention or in the reporter's account of the debates. Immediately after the convention adjourned, the minority, led by William Findley, John Smilie, and Robert Whitehall, published their "Reasons of Dissent." Their proposed amendments were thus given widespread publicity as the first emanating from any state convention.*

.   .   .   .

In the city of Philadelphia and some of the eastern counties the junto that took the lead in the business agreed to vote for none but such as would solemnly promise to adopt the system *in toto,* without exercising their judgment. In many of the counties the people did not attend the elections, as they had not an opportunity of judging of the plan. Others did not consider themselves bound by the call of a set of men who assembled at the State-house in Philadelphia and assumed the name of the legislature of Pennsylvania; and some were prevented from voting by the violence of the party who were determined at all events to force down the measure. To such lengths did the tools of despotism carry their outrage, that on the night of the election for members of

---

* THE PENNSYLVANIA ANTI-FEDERALISTS OFFER THEIR "REASONS OF DISSENT": "The Address and Reasons of Dissent of the Minority of the Convention of the State of Pennsylvania to Their Constituents," *The Pennsylvania Packet* (December 18, 1787). From John Bach McMaster and Frederic D. Stone, eds., *Pennsylvania and the Federal Constitution, 1787–1788* (Philadelphia, 1888), pp. 460–78, *passim.*

convention, in the city of Philadelphia, several of the subscribers (being then in the city to transact your business) were grossly abused, ill-treated and insulted while they were quiet in their lodgings, though they did not interfere nor had anything to do with the said election, but, as they apprehend, because they were supposed to be adverse to the proposed constitution, and would not tamely surrender those sacred rights which you had committed to their charge.

The convention met, and the same disposition was soon manifested in considering the proposed constitution, that had been exhibited in every other stage of the business. We were prohibited by an express vote of the convention from taking any questions on the separate articles of the plan, and reduced to the necessity of adopting or rejecting *in toto*. 'Tis true the majority permitted us to debate on each article, but restrained us from proposing amendments. They also determined not to permit us to enter on the minutes our reasons of dissent against any of the articles, nor even on the final question our reasons of dissent against the whole. Thus situated we entered on the examination of the proposed system of government, and found it to be such as we could not adopt, without, as we conceived, surrendering up your dearest rights. We offered our objections to the convention, and opposed those parts of the plan which, in our opinion, would be injurious to you, in the best manner we were able; and closed our arguments by offering the following propositions to the convention.

1. The right of conscience shall be held inviolable; and neither the legislative, executive nor judicial powers of the United States shall have authority to alter, abrogate or infringe any part of the constitution of the several States, which provide for the preservation of liberty in matters of religion.

2. That in controversies respecting property, and in suits between man and man, trial by jury shall remain as heretofore, as well in the federal courts as in those of the several States.

3. That in all capital and criminal prosecutions, a man has a right to demand the cause and nature of his accusation, as well in the federal courts as in those of the several States; to be heard by himself and his counsel; to be confronted with the accusers and witnesses; to call for evidence in his favor, and a speedy trial by an impartial jury of his vicinage, without whose unanimous consent he cannot be found guilty, nor can he be compelled to give evidence against himself; and, that no man be deprived of his liberty, except by the law of the land or the judgment of his peers.

4. That excessive bail ought not to be required, nor excessive fines imposed, nor cruel nor unusual punishments inflicted.

5. That warrants unsupported by evidence, whereby any officer or messenger may be commanded or required to search suspected places; or to seize any person or persons, his or their property not particularly described, are grievous and oppressive, and shall not be granted either by the magistrates of the federal government or others.

6. That the people have a right to the freedom of speech, of writing and publishing their sentiments; therefore the freedom of the press shall not be restrained by any law of the United States.

7. That the people have a right to bear arms for the defence of themselves and their own State or the United States, or for the purpose of killing game; and no law shall be passed for disarming the people or any of them unless for

crimes committed, or real danger of public injury from individuals; and as
standing armies in the time of peace are dangerous to liberty, they ought not
to be kept up; and that the military shall be kept under strict subordination
to, and be governed by the civil powers.

8. The inhabitants of the several States shall have liberty to fowl and hunt
in seasonable time on the lands they hold, and on all other lands in the United
States not inclosed, and in like manner to fish in all navigable waters, and
others not private property, without being restrained therein by any laws to
be passed by the legislature of the United States.

9. That no law shall be passed to restrain the legislatures of the several States
from enacting laws for imposing taxes, except imposts and duties on goods
imported or exported, and that no taxes, except imposts and duties upon goods
imported and exported, and postage on letters, shall be levied by the authority
of Congress.

10. That the house of representatives be properly increased in number; that
elections shall remain free; that the several States shall have power to regulate
the elections for senators and representatives, without being controlled either
directly or indirectly by any interference on the part of the Congress; and that
the elections of representatives be annual.

11. That the power of organizing, arming and disciplining the militia (the
manner of disciplining the militia to be prescribed by Congress), remain with
the individual States, and that Congress shall not have authority to call or
march any of the militia out of their own State, without the consent of such
State, and for such length of time only as such State shall agree.

That the sovereignty, freedom and independency of the several States shall
be retained, and every power, jurisdiction and right which is not by this Constitution expressly delegated to the United States in Congress assembled.

12. That the legislative, executive and judicial powers be kept separate; and
to this end that a constitutional council be appointed to advise and assist the
President, who shall be responsible for the advice they give—hereby the senators would be relieved from almost constant attendance; and also that the
judges be made completely independent.

13. That no treaty which shall be directly opposed to the existing laws of
the United States in Congress assembled, shall be valid until such laws shall
be repealed or made conformable to such treaty; neither shall any treaties be
valid which are in contradiction to the Constitution of the United States, or
the constitutions of the several States.

14. That the judiciary power of the United States shall be confined to cases
affecting ambassadors, other public ministers and consuls, to cases of admiralty
and maritime jurisdiction; to controversies to which the United States shall be
a party; to controversies between two or more States—between a State and citizens of different States—between citizens claiming lands under grants of different States, and between a State or the citizens thereof and foreign States;
and in criminal cases to such only as are expressly enumerated in the constitution; and that the United States in Congress assembled shall not have power
to enact laws which shall alter the laws of descent and distribution of the effects of deceased persons, the titles of lands or goods, or the regulation of contracts in the individual States.

After reading these propositions, we declared our willingness to agree to the plan, provided it was so amended as to meet those propositions or something similar to them, and finally moved the convention to adjourn, to give the people of Pennsylvania time to consider the subject and determine for themselves; but these were all rejected and the final vote taken, when our duty to you induced us to vote against the proposed plan and to decline signing the ratification of the same.

During the discussion we met with many insults and some personal abuse. We were not even treated with decency, during the sitting of the convention, by the persons in the gallery of the house. However, we flatter ourselves that in contending for the preservation of those invaluable rights you have thought proper to commit to our charge, we acted with a spirit becoming freemen; and being desirous that you might know the principles which actuated our conduct, and being prohibited from inserting our reasons of dissent on the minutes of the convention, we have subjoined them for your consideration, as to you alone we are accountable. It remains with you whether you will think those inestimable privileges, which you have so ably contended for, should be sacrificed at the shrine of despotism, or whether you mean to contend for them with the same spirit that has so often baffled the attempts of an aristocratic faction to rivet the shackles of slavery on you and your unborn posterity.

Our objections are comprised under three general heads of dissent, viz.:

We dissent, first, because it is the opinion of the most celebrated writers on government, and confirmed by uniform experience, that a very extensive territory cannot be governed on the principles of freedom, otherwise than by a confederation of republics, possessing all the powers of internal government, but united in the management of their general and foreign concerns. . . .

We dissent, secondly, because the powers vested in Congress by this constitution, must necessarily annihilate and absorb the legislative, executive, and judicial powers of the several States, and produce from their ruins one consolidated government, which from the nature of things will be *an iron handed despotism,* as nothing short of the supremacy of despotic sway could connect and govern these United States under one government.

As the truth of this position is of such decisive importance, it ought to be fully investigated, and if it is founded to be clearly ascertained; for, should it be demonstrated that the powers vested by this constitution in Congress will have such an effect as necessarily to produce one consolidated government, the question then will be reduced to this short issue, viz.: whether satiated with the blessings of liberty, whether repenting of the folly of so recently asserting their unalienable rights against foreign despots at the expense of so much blood and treasure, and such painful and arduous struggles, the people of America are now willing to resign every privilege of freemen, and submit to the dominion of an absolute government that will embrace all America in one chain of despotism; or whether they will, with virtuous indignation, spurn at the shackles prepared for them, and confirm their liberties by a conduct becoming freemen.

That the new government will not be a confederacy of States, as it ought, but one consolidated government, founded upon the destruction of the several governments of the States, we shall now show.

The powers of Congress under the new constitution are complete and un-limited over the *purse* and the *sword,* and are perfectly independent of and supreme over the State governments, whose intervention in these great points is entirely destroyed. By virtue of their power of taxation, Congress may com-mand the whole or any part of the property of the people. They may impose what imposts upon commerce, they may impose what land taxes, poll taxes, excises, duties on all written instruments and duties on every other article, that they may judge proper; in short, every species of taxation, whether of an external or internal nature, is comprised in section the eighth of article the first, viz.:

"The Congress shall have power to lay and collect taxes, duties, imposts, and excises, to pay the debts, and provide for the common defence and general welfare of the United States."

As there is no one article of taxation reserved to the State governments, the Congress may monopolize every source of revenue, and thus indirectly demolish the State governments, for without funds they could not exist; the taxes, duties and excises imposed by Congress may be so high as to render it impracticable to levy farther sums on the same articles; but whether this should be the case or not, if the State governments should presume to impose taxes, duties or excises on the same articles with Congress, the latter may abrogate and repeal the laws whereby they are imposed, upon the allegation that they interfere with the due collection of their taxes, duties or excises, by virtue of the following clause, part of section eighth, article first, viz.:

"To make all laws which shall be necessary and proper for carrying into execution the foregoing powers, and all other powers vested by this constitution in the government of the United States, or in any department or officer thereof."

The Congress might gloss over this conduct by construing every purpose for which the State legislatures now lay taxes, to be for the *"general welfare,"* and therefore as of their jurisdiction.

And the supremacy of the laws of the United States is established by article sixth, viz.: "That this constitution and the laws of the United States which shall be made in pursuance thereof, and *all treaties* made, or which shall be made under the authority of the United States, shall be the *supreme law* of the *land; and the judges in every State shall be bound thereby; anything in the constitution or laws of any State to the contrary notwithstanding."* It has been alleged that the words "pursuant to the constitution," are a restriction upon the authority of Congress; but when it is considered that by other sec-tions they are invested with every efficient power of government, and which may be exercised to the absolute destruction of the State governments, with-out any violation of even the forms of the constitution, this seeming restric-tion, as well as every other restriction in it, appears to us to be nugatory and delusive; and only introduced as a blind upon the real nature of the govern-ment. In our opinion, "pursuant to the constitution" will be co-extensive with the *will* and *pleasure* of Congress, which, indeed, will be the only limitation of their powers.

We apprehend that two co-ordinate sovereignties would be a solecism in politics; that, therefore, as there is no line of distinction drawn between the general and State governments, as the sphere of their jurisdiction is undefined, it would be contrary to the nature of things that both should exist together—one or the other would necessarily triumph in the fulness of dominion. However, the contest could not be of long continuance, as the State governments are divested of every means of defence, and will be obliged by "the supreme law of the land" *to yield at discretion.* . . .

Thus we have fully established the position, that the powers vested by this constitution in Congress will effect a consolidation of the States under one government, which even the advocates of this constitution admit could not be done without the sacrifice of all liberty.

. . . We dissent, thirdly, because if it were practicable to govern so extensive a territory as these United States include, on the plan of a consolidated government, consistent with the principles of liberty and the happiness of the people, yet the construction of this Constitution is not calculated to attain the object; for independent of the nature of the case, it would of itself necessarily produce a despotism, and that not by the usual gradations, but with the celerity that has hitherto only attended revolutions effected by the sword.

To establish the truth of this position, a cursory investigation of the principles and form of this constitution will suffice.

The first consideration that this review suggests, is the omission of a BILL OF RIGHTS ascertaining and fundamentally establishing those unalienable and personal rights of men, without the full, free and secure enjoyment of which there can be no liberty, and over which it is not necessary for a good government to have the control—the principal of which are the rights of conscience, personal liberty by the clear and unequivocal establishment of the writ of *habeas corpus,* jury trial in criminal and civil cases, by an impartial jury of the vicinage or county, with the common law proceedings for the safety of the accused in criminal prosecutions; and the liberty of the press, that scourge of tyrants, and the grand bulwark of every other liberty and privilege. The stipulations heretofore made in favor of them in the State constitutions, are entirely superseded by this Constitution.

The legislature of a free country should be so formed as to have a competent knowledge of its constituents, and enjoy their confidence. To produce these essential requisites, the representation ought to be fair, equal and sufficiently numerous to possess the same interests, feelings, opinions and views which the people themselves would possess, were they all assembled; and so numerous as to prevent bribery and undue influence, and so responsible to the people, by frequent and fair elections, as to prevent their neglecting or sacrificing the views and interests of their constituents to their own pursuits.

We will now bring the legislature under this Constitution to the test of the foregoing principles, which will demonstrate that it is deficient in every essential quality of a just and safe representation.

The House of Representatives is to consist of sixty-five members; that is one for about every 50,000 inhabitants, to be chosen every two years. Thirty-three members will form a quorum for doing business, and seventeen of these, being the majority, determine the sense of the house.

The Senate, the other constituent branch of the legislature, consists of twenty-six members, being *two* from each State, appointed by their legislatures every six years; fourteen senators make a quorum—the majority of whom, eight, determines the sense of that body, except in judging on impeachments, or in making treaties, or in expelling a member, when two-thirds of the senators present must concur.

The president is to have the control over the enacting of laws, so far as to make the concurrence of two-thirds of the representatives and senators present necessary, if he should object to the laws.

Thus it appears that the liberties, happiness, interests, and great concerns of the whole United States, may be dependent upon the integrity, virtue, wisdom, and knowledge of twenty-five or twenty-six men. How unadequate and unsafe a representation! Inadequate, because the sense and views of three or four millions of people, diffused over so extensive a territory, comprising such various climates, products, habits, interests, and opinions, cannot be collected in so small a body; and besides, it is not a fair and equal representation of the people even in proportion to its number, for the smallest State has as much weight in the Senate as the largest; and from the smallness of the number to be chosen for both branches of the legislature, and from the mode of election and appointment, which is under the control of Congress, and from the nature of the thing, men of the most elevated rank in life will alone be chosen. The other orders in the society, such as farmers, traders, and mechanics, who all ought to have a competent number of their best informed men in the legislature, shall be totally unrepresented.

The representation is unsafe, because in the exercise of such great powers and trusts, it is so exposed to corruption and undue influence, by the gift of the numerous places of honor and emolument at the disposal of the executive, by the arts and address of the great and designing, and by direct bribery.

The representation is moreover inadequate and unsafe, because of the long terms for which it is appointed, and the mode of its appointment, by which Congress may not only control the choice of the people, but may so manage as to divest the people of this fundamental right, and become self-elected. . . .

We have before considered internal taxation as it would effect the destruction of the State governments, and produce one consolidated government. We will now consider that subject as it affects the personal concerns of the people.

The power of direct taxation applies to every individual, as Congress, under this government, is expressly vested with the authority of laying a capitation or poll tax upon every person to any amount. This is a tax that, however oppressive in its nature, and unequal in its operation, is certain as to its produce and simple in its collection; it cannot be evaded like the objects of imposts or excise, and will be paid, because all that a man hath will he give for his head. This tax is so congenial to the nature of despotism, that it has ever been a favorite under such governments. Some of those who were in the late general convention from this State, have labored to introduce a poll tax among us.

The power of direct taxation will further apply to every individual, as Congress may tax land, cattle, trades, occupations, etc., to any amount, and every object of internal taxation is of that nature that however oppressive, the people will have but this alternative, either to pay the tax or let their property be taken, for all resistance will be vain. The standing army and select militia would enforce the collection.

For the moderate exercise of this power, there is no control left in the State governments, whose intervention is destroyed. No relief, or redress of grievances, can be extended as heretofore by them. There is not even a declaration of RIGHTS to which the people may appeal for the vindication of their wrongs in the court of justice. They must therefore, implicitly obey the most arbitrary laws, as the most of them will be pursuant to the principles and form of the constitution, and that strongest of all checks upon the conduct of administration, *responsibility to the people,* will not exist in this government. The permanency of the appointments of senators and representatives, and the control the congress have over their election, will place them independent of the sentiments and resentment of the people, and the administration having a greater interest in the government than in the community, there will be no consideration to restrain them from oppression and tyranny. . . .

5] Hancock, Adams, and the "Conciliatory Proposition"

> The Anti-Federalists entered the Massachusetts ratifying convention with a very substantial majority of the delegates, but the defeat of Elbridge Gerry for a seat in the convention and the noncommittal attitude of Governor John Hancock and Sam Adams injured their cause. The turning point in the proceedings came when Hancock, the very influential president of the convention, proposed what Sam Adams called a "conciliatory proposition," a motion to ratify with recommended amendments, drawn by Federalist leaders but presented to the convention by Hancock as his own. Adams then threw in his support, and the Constitution was ratified in the end by a narrow majority of nineteen out of three hundred and fifty-five votes.*

AFTER Gen. Heath sat down, his excellency, the PRESIDENT, rose, and observed, that he was conscious of the impropriety, situated as he was, of his entering into the deliberations of the Convention; that, unfortunately, through painful indisposition of body, he had been prevented from giving his attendance in his place, but, from the information he had received, and from the papers, there appeared to him to be a great dissimilarity of sentiments in the Convention. To remove the objections of some gentlemen, he felt himself induced, he said, to hazard a proposition for their consideration; which, with the permission of the Convention, he would offer in the afternoon.

Afternoon.—When the Convention met in the afternoon, his excellency, the PRESIDENT, observed, that a motion had been made and seconded, that this Convention do assent to and ratify the Constitution which had been under consideration; and that he had, in the former part of the day, intimated his intention of submitting a proposition to the Convention. My motive, says he, arises from my earnest desire to this Convention, my fellow-citizens, and the public at large, that this Convention may adopt such a form of government as

---

* HANCOCK, ADAMS, AND THE "CONCILIATORY PROPOSITION": The Massachusetts Convention. From Elliot, ed., *Debates,* II, 122–25, 177.

may extend its good influence to every part of the United States, and advance the prosperity of the whole world. His situation, his excellency said, had not permitted him to enter into the debates of this Convention: it, however, appeared to him necessary, from what had been advanced in them, to adopt the form of government proposed; but, observing a diversity of sentiment in the gentlemen of the Convention, he had frequently had conversation with them on the subject, and from this conversation he was induced to propose to them, whether the introduction of some general amendments would not be attended with the happiest consequences. For that purpose, he should, with the leave of the honorable Convention, submit to their consideration a proposition, in order to remove the doubts and quiet the apprehensions of gentlemen; and if, in any degree, the object should be acquired, he should feel himself perfectly satisfied. He should therefore submit them; for he was, he said, unable to go more largely into the subject, if his abilities would permit him; relying on the candor of the Convention to bear him witness that his wishes for a good constitution were sincere. [*His excellency then read his proposition.*] —This, gentlemen, concluded his excellency, is the proposition which I had to make; and I submit it to your consideration, with the sincere wish that it may have a tendency to promote a spirit of union. . . .

Hon. Mr. Adams. Mr. President, I feel myself happy in contemplating the idea that many benefits will result from your excellency's conciliatory proposition to this commonwealth and to the United States; and I think it ought to precede the motion made by the gentleman from Newburyport, and to be at this time considered by the Convention. I have said that I have had my doubts of this Constitution. I could not digest every part of it as readily as some gentlemen; but this, sir, is my misfortune, not my fault. Other gentlemen have had their doubts; but, in my opinion, the proposition submitted will have a tendency to remove such doubts, and to conciliate the minds of the Convention, and the people without doors. This subject, sir, is of the greatest magnitude, and has employed the attention of every rational man in the United States; but the minds of the people are not so well agreed on it as all of us could wish. A proposal of this sort, coming from Massachusetts, from her importance, will have its weight. Four or five states have considered and ratified the Constitution as it stands; but we know there is a diversity of opinion even in these states, and one of them is greatly agitated. If this Convention should particularize the amendments necessary to be proposed, it appears to me it must have weight in other states, where Conventions have not yet met. I have observed the sentiments of gentlemen on the subject as far as Virginia, and I have found that the objections were similar, in the newspapers, and in some of the Conventions. Considering these circumstances, it appears to me that such a measure will have the most salutary effect throughout the Union. It is of the greatest importance that *America* should still be united in sentiment. I think I have not, heretofore, been unmindful of the advantage of such a union. It is essential that the people should be united in the federal government, to withstand the common enemy, and to preserve their valuable rights and liberties. We find, in the great state of Pennsylvania, one third of the Convention are opposed to it: should, then, there be large minorities in the several states, I should fear the consequences of such disunion.

Sir, there are many parts of it I esteem as highly valuable, particularly the article which empowers Congress to regulate commerce, to form treaties, &c. For want of this power in our national head, our friends are grieved, and our enemies insult us. Our ambassador at the court of London is considered as a mere cipher, instead of the representative of the United States. Therefore it appears to me, that a power to remedy this evil should be given to Congress, and the remedy applied as soon as possible.

The only difficulty on gentlemen's minds is, whether it is best to accept this Constitution on conditional amendments, or to rely on amendments in future, as the Constitution provides. When I look over the article which provides for a revision, I have my doubts. Suppose, sir, nine states accept the Constitution without any conditions at all, and the four states should wish to have amendments,—where will you find nine states to propose, and the legislatures of nine states to agree to, the introduction of amendments? Therefore it seems to me that the expectation of amendments taking place at some future time, will be frustrated. This method, if we take it, will be the most likely to bring about the amendments, as the Conventions of New Hampshire, Rhode Island, New York, Maryland, Virginia, and South Carolina, have not yet met. I apprehend, sir, that these states will be influenced by the proposition which your excellency has submitted, as the resolutions of Massachusetts have ever had their influence. . . .

[The Proposition and Accompanying Amendments]

. . . as it is the opinion of this Convention, that certain amendments and alterations in the said Constitution would remove the fears and quiet the apprehensions of many of the good people of the commonwealth, and more effectually guard against an undue administration of the federal government, the Convention do therefore recommend that the following alterations and provisions be introduced into the said Constitution:—

First. That it be explicitly declared, that all powers not expressly delegated by the aforesaid Constitution are reserved to the several states, to be by them exercised.

Secondly. That there shall be one representative to every thirty thousand persons, according to the census mentioned in the Constitution, until the whole number of representatives amounts to two hundred.

Thirdly. That Congress do not exercise the powers vested in them by the 4th section of the 1st article, but in cases where a state shall neglect or refuse to make the regulations therein mentioned, or shall make regulations subversive of the rights of the people to a free and equal representation in Congress, agreeably to the Constitution.

Fourthly. That Congress do not lay direct taxes, but when the moneys arising from the impost and excise are insufficient for the public exigencies, nor then, until Congress shall have first made a requisition upon the states, to assess, levy, and pay their respective proportion of such requisitions, agreeably to the census fixed in the said Constitution, in such way and manner as the legislatures of the states shall think best, and, in such case, if any state shall neglect or refuse to pay its proportion, pursuant to such requisition, then Congress may assess and levy such state's proportion, together with interest thereon, at the rate of six per cent. per annum, from the time of payment prescribed in such requisitions.

Fifthly. That Congress erect no company with exclusive advantages of commerce.

Sixthly. That no person shall be tried for any crime, by which he may incur an infamous punishment, or loss of life, until he be first indicted by a grand jury, except in such cases as may arise in the government and regulation of the land and naval forces.

Seventhly. The Supreme Judicial Federal Court shall have no jurisdiction of causes between citizens of different states, unless the matter in dispute, whether it concern the realty or personalty, be of the value of three thousand dollars at the least; nor shall the federal judicial powers extend to any action between citizens of different states, where the matter in dispute, whether it concern the realty or personalty, is not of the value of fifteen hundred dollars at the least.

Eighthly. In civil actions between citizens of different states, every issue of fact, arising in actions at common law, shall be tried by a jury, if the parties, or either of them, request it.

Ninthly. Congress shall at no time consent that any person holding an office of trust or profit, under the United States, shall accept of a title of nobility, or any other title or office, from any king, prince, or foreign state.

6] Patrick Henry Fights Ratification

"Mr. Henry," wrote Madison, "is the great adversary who will render the event precarious." Madison's prediction was fully justified. When the Virginia ratifying convention met, Henry, the great idol of the people, relentlessly and passionately opposed ratification as if once again combating British "tyranny." The Constitution seemed to him a conspiracy against the liberties of the people, proof that he was right in turning down a seat in the Constitutional Convention because he had "smelt a rat." His speeches cover nearly one-fifth of the more than six hundred pages of the Virginia debates on the Constitution. The following extracts suggest the character of his opposition.*

MR. CHAIRMAN, the public mind, as well as my own, is extremely uneasy at the proposed change of government. Give me leave to form one of the number of those who wish to be thoroughly acquainted with the reasons of this perilous and uneasy situation, and why we are brought hither to decide on this great national question. I consider myself as the servant of the people of this commonwealth, as a sentinel over their rights, liberty, and happiness. I represent their feelings when I say that they are exceedingly uneasy at being brought from that state of full security, which they enjoyed, to the present delusive appearance of things. A year ago, the minds of our citizens were at perfect repose. Before the meeting of the late federal Convention at Philadelphia, a general peace and a universal tranquillity prevailed in this country; but, since that period, they are exceedingly uneasy and disquieted. When I wished for an appointment to this Convention, my mind was extremely agitated for the situation of public affairs. I conceived the republic to be in extreme danger. If our situation be thus uneasy, whence has arisen this fearful jeopardy? It

* PATRICK HENRY FIGHTS RATIFICATION: The Virginia Convention. From Elliot, ed., *Debates*, III, 21–23, 51, 54, 57–59, 151–52, 445–49, 590–91.

arises from this fatal system; it arises from a proposal to change our government—a proposal that goes to the utter annihilation of the most solemn engagements of the states—a proposal of establishing nine states into a confederacy, to the eventual exclusion of four states. It goes to the annihilation of those solemn treaties we have formed with foreign nations.

The present circumstances of France—the good offices rendered us by that kingdom—require our most faithful and most punctual adherence to our treaty with her. We are in alliance with the Spaniards, the Dutch, the Prussians; those treaties bound us as thirteen states confederated together. Yet here is a proposal to sever that confederacy. Is it possible that we shall abandon all our treaties and national engagements?—and for what? I expected to hear the reasons for an event so unexpected to my mind and many others. Was our civil polity, or public justice, endangered or sapped? Was the real existence of the country threatened, or was this preceded by a mournful progression of events? This proposal of altering our federal government is of a most alarming nature! Make the best of this new government—say it is composed by any thing but inspiration—you ought to be extremely cautious, watchful, jealous of your liberty; for, instead of securing your rights, you may lose them forever. If a wrong step be now made, the republic may be lost forever. If this new government will not come up to the expectation of the people, and they shall be disappointed, their liberty will be lost, and tyranny must and will arise. I repeat it again, and I beg gentlemen to consider, that a wrong step, made now, will plunge us into misery, and our republic will be lost. It will be necessary for this Convention to have a faithful historical detail of the facts that preceded the session of the federal Convention, and the reasons that actuated its members in proposing an entire alteration of government, and to demonstrate the dangers that awaited us. If they were of such awful magnitude as to warrant a proposal so extremely perilous as this, I must assert, that this Convention has an absolute right to a thorough discovery of every circumstance relative to this great event. And here I would make this inquiry of those worthy characters who composed a part of the late federal Convention. I am sure they were fully impressed with the necessity of forming a great consolidated government, instead of a confederation. That this is a consolidated government is demonstrably clear; and the danger of such a government is, to my mind, very striking. I have the highest veneration for those gentlemen; but, sir, give me leave to demand, What right had they to say, *We, the people?* My political curiosity, exclusive of my anxious solicitude for the public welfare, leads me to ask, Who authorized them to speak the language of, *We, the people,* instead of, *We, the states?* States are the characteristics and the soul of a confederation. If the states be not the agents of this compact, it must be one great, consolidated, national government, of the people of all the states. . . .

. . . The federal Convention ought to have amended the old system; for this purpose they were solely delegated; the object of their mission extended to no other consideration. You must, therefore, forgive the solicitation of one unworthy member to know what danger could have arisen under the present Confederation, and what are the causes of this proposal to change our government. . . .

A standing army we shall have, also, to execute the execrable commands of

tyranny; and how are you to punish them? Will you order them to be punished? Who shall obey these orders? Will your mace-bearer be a match for a
a disciplined regiment? In what situation are we to be? The clause before you
gives a power of direct taxation, unbounded and unlimited, exclusive power
of legislation, in all cases whatsoever, for ten miles square, and over all places
purchased for the erection of forts, magazines, arsenals, dockyards, &c. What
resistance could be made? The attempt would be madness. You will find all
the strength of this country in the hands of your enemies; their garrisons will
naturally be the strongest places in the country. Your militia is given up to
Congress, also, in another part of this plan: they will therefore act as they think
proper: all power will be in their own possession. . . .

. . . That country [England] is become a great, mighty, and splendid nation;
not because their government is strong and energetic, but, sir, because liberty
is its direct end and foundation. We drew the spirit of liberty from our British
ancestors: by that spirit we have triumphed over every difficulty. But now,
sir, the American spirit, assisted by the ropes and chains of consolidation, is
about to convert this country into a powerful and mighty empire. If you
make the citizens of this country agree to become the subjects of one great
consolidated empire of America, your government will not have sufficient
energy to keep them together. Such a government is incompatible with the
genius of republicanism. There will be no checks, no real balances, in this
government. What can avail your specious, imaginary balances, your rope-
dancing, chain-rattling, ridiculous ideal checks and contrivances? But, sir, we
are not feared by foreigners; we do not make nations tremble. Would this
constitute happiness, or secure liberty? I trust, sir, our political hemisphere
will ever direct their operations to the security of those objects.

Consider our situation, sir: go to the poor man, and ask him what he does.
He will inform you that he enjoys the fruits of his labor, under his own fig-
tree, with his wife and children around him, in peace and security. Go to every
other member of society,—you will find the same tranquil ease and content;
you will find no alarms or disturbances. Why, then, tell us of danger, to
terrify us into an adoption of this new form of government? And yet who
knows the dangers that this new system may produce? They are out of the
sight of the common people: they cannot foresee latent consequences. I dread
the operation of it on the middling and lower classes of people: it is for them
I fear the adoption of this system. I fear I tire the patience of the committee;
but I beg to be indulged with a few more observations. When I thus profess
myself an advocate for the liberty of the people, I shall be told I am a designing
man, that I am to be a great man, that I am to be a demagogue; and many
similar illiberal insinuations will be thrown out: but, sir, conscious rectitude
outweighs those things with me. I see great jeopardy in this new government.
I see none from our present one. . . .

In this scheme of energetic government, the people will find two sets of tax-
gatherers—the state and the federal sheriffs. This, it seems to me, will produce
such dreadful oppression as the people cannot possibly bear. The federal sheriff
may commit what oppression, make what distresses, he pleases, and ruin you
with impunity; for how are you to tie his hands? Have you any sufficiently
decided means of preventing him from sucking your blood by speculations,

commissions, and fees? Thus thousands of your people will be most shamefully robbed: our state sheriffs, those unfeeling bloodsuckers, have, under the watchful eye of our legislature, committed the most horrid and barbarous ravages on our people. It has required the most constant vigilance of the legislature to keep them from totally ruining the people; a repeated succession of laws has been made to suppress their iniquitous speculations and cruel extortions; and as often has their nefarious ingenuity devised methods of evading the force of those laws; in the struggle they have generally triumphed over the legislature. . . .

This Constitution is said to have beautiful features; but when I come to examine these features, sir, they appear to me horribly frightful. Among other deformities, it has an awful squinting; it squints towards monarchy; and does not this raise indignation in the breast of every true American?

Your President may easily become king. Your Senate is so imperfectly constructed that your dearest rights may be sacrificed by what may be a small minority; and a very small minority may continue forever unchangeably this government, although horridly defective. Where are your checks in this government? Your strongholds will be in the hands of your enemies. It is on a supposition that your American governors shall be honest, that all the good qualities of this government are founded; but its defective and imperfect construction puts it in their power to perpetrate the worst of mischiefs, should they be bad men; and, sir, would not all the world, from the eastern to the western hemisphere, blame our distracted folly in resting our rights upon the contingency of our rulers being good or bad? Show me that age and country where the rights and liberties of the people were placed on the sole chance of their rulers being good men, without a consequent loss of liberty! I say that the loss of that dearest privilege has ever followed, with absolute certainty, every such mad attempt.

If your American chief be a man of ambition and abilities, how easy is it for him to render himself absolute! The army is in his hands, and if he be a man of address, it will be attached to him, and it will be the subject of long meditation with him to seize the first auspicious moment to accomplish his design; and, sir, will the American spirit solely relieve you when this happens? I would rather infinitely—and I am sure most of this Convention are of the same opinion—have a king, lords, and commons, than a government so replete with such insupportable evils. If we make a king, we may prescribe the rules by which he shall rule his people, and interpose such checks as shall prevent him from infringing them; but the President, in the field, at the head of his army, can prescribe the terms on which he shall reign master, so far that it will puzzle any American ever to get his neck from under the galling yoke. . . .

. . . There is a dispute between us and the Spaniards about the right of navigating the Mississippi. This dispute has sprung from the federal government. I wish a great deal to be said on this subject. I wish to know the origin and progress of the business, as it would probably unfold great dangers. In my opinion, the preservation of that river calls for our most serious consideration. It has been agitated in Congress. Seven states have voted, so that it is known to the Spaniards that, under our existing system, the Mississippi shall be taken from them. Seven states wished to relinquish this river to them. The six

Southern States opposed it. Seven states not being sufficient to convey it away, it remains now ours. If I am wrong, there is a number on this floor who can contradict the facts; I will readily retract. This new government, I conceive, will enable those states who have already discovered their inclination that way, to give away this river. Will the honorable gentleman advise us to relinquish its inestimable navigation, and place formidable enemies on our backs? This weak, this poor Confederation cannot secure us. We are resolved to take shelter under the shield of federal authority in America. The southern parts of America have been protected by that weakness so much execrated. I hope this will be explained. I was not in Congress when these transactions took place. I may not have stated every fact. I may have misrepresented matters. I hope to be fully acquainted with every thing relative to the object. Let us hear how the great and important right of navigating that river has been attended to, and whether I am mistaken in my opinion that federal measures will lose it to us forever. If a bare majority of Congress can make laws, the situation of our western citizens is dreadful. . . .

Mr. Chairman, the necessity of a bill of rights appears to me to be greater in this government than ever it was in any government before. I have observed already, that the sense of the European nations, and particularly Great Britain, is against the construction of rights being retained which are not expressly relinquished. I repeat, that all nations have adopted this construction—that all rights not expressly and unequivocally reserved to the people are impliedly and incidentally relinquished to rulers, as necessarily inseparable from the delegated powers. It is so in Great Britain; for every possible right, which is not reserved to the people by some express provision or compact, is within the king's prerogative. It is so in that country which is said to be in such full possession of freedom. It is so in Spain, Germany, and other parts of the world. Let us consider the sentiments which have been entertained by the people of America on this subject. At the revolution, it must be admitted that it was their sense to set down those great rights which ought, in all countries, to be held inviolable and sacred. Virginia did so, we all remember. She made a compact to reserve, expressly, certain rights.

When fortified with full, adequate, and abundant representation, was she satisfied with that representation? No. She most cautiously and guardedly reserved and secured those invaluable, inestimable rights and privileges, which no people, inspired with the least glow of patriotic liberty, ever did, or ever can, abandon. She is called upon now to abandon them, and dissolve that compact which secured them to her. She is called upon to accede to another compact, which most infallibly supersedes and annihilates her present one. Will she do it? This is the question. If you intend to reserve your unalienable rights, you must have the most express stipulation; for, if implication be allowed, you are ousted of those rights. If the people do not think it necessary to reserve them, they will be supposed to be given up. How were the congressional rights defined when the people of America united by a confederacy to defend their liberties and rights against the tyrannical attempts of Great Britain? The states were not then contented with implied reservation. No, Mr. Chairman. It was expressly declared in our Confederation that every right was retained by the states, respectively, which was not given up to the government of the United States. But there is no such thing here. You, therefore, by a natural and unavoidable implication, give up your rights to the general government.

Your own example furnishes an argument against it. If you give up these powers, without a bill of rights, you will exhibit the most absurd thing to mankind that ever the world saw—a government that has abandoned all its powers—the powers of direct taxation, the sword, and the purse. You have disposed of them to Congress, without a bill of rights—without check, limitation, or control. And still you have checks and guards; still you keep barriers —pointed where? Pointed against your weakened, prostrated, enervated state government! You have a bill of rights to defend you against the state government, which is bereaved of all power, and yet you have none against Congress, though in full and exclusive possession of all power! You arm yourselves against the weak and defenceless, and expose yourselves naked to the armed and powerful. Is not this a conduct of unexampled absurdity? What barriers have you to oppose to this most strong, energetic government? To that government you have nothing to oppose. All your defence is given up. This is a real, actual defect. It must strike the mind of every gentleman. When our government was first instituted in Virginia, we declared the common law of England to be in force.

That system of law which has been admired, and has protected us and our ancestors, is excluded by that system. Added to this, we adopted a bill of rights. By this Constitution, some of the best barriers of human rights are thrown away. Is there not an additional reason to have a bill of rights? By the ancient common law, the trial of all facts is decided by a jury of impartial men from the immediate vicinage. This paper speaks of different juries from the common law in criminal cases; and in civil controversies excludes trial by jury altogether. There is, therefore, more occasion for the supplementary check of a bill of rights now than then. Congress, from their general powers, may fully go into business of human legislation. They may legislate, in criminal cases, from treason to the lowest offence—petty larceny. They may define crimes and prescribe punishments. In the definition of crimes, I trust they will be directed by what wise representatives ought to be governed by. But when we come to punishments, no latitude ought to be left, nor dependence put on the virtue of representatives. What says our bill of rights?—"that excessive bail ought not to be required, nor excessive fines imposed, nor cruel and unusual punishments inflicted." Are you not, therefore, now calling on those gentlemen who are to compose Congress, to prescribe trials and define punishments without this control? Will they find sentiments there similar to this bill of rights? You let them loose; you do more—you depart from the genius of your country. That paper tells you that the trial of crimes shall be by jury, and held in the state where the crime shall have been committed. Under this extensive provision, they may proceed in a manner extremely dangerous to liberty: a person accused may be carried from one extremity of the state to another, and be tried, not by an impartial jury of the vicinage, acquainted with his character and the circumstances of the fact, but by a jury unacquainted with both, and who may be biased against him. Is not this sufficient to alarm men? How different is this from the immemorial practice of your British ancestors, and your own!

I need not tell you that, by the common law, a number of hundredors were required on a jury, and that afterwards it was sufficient if the jurors came from the same county. With less than this the people of England have never been satisfied. That paper ought to have declared the common law in force.

In this business of legislation, your members of Congress will loose the restriction of not imposing excessive fines, demanding excessive bail, and inflicting cruel and unusual punishments. These are prohibited by your declaration of rights. What has distinguished our ancestors?—That they would not admit of tortures, or cruel and barbarous punishment. But Congress may introduce the practice of the civil law, in preference to that of the common law. They may introduce the practice of France, Spain, and Germany—of torturing, to extort a confession of the crime. They will say that they might as well draw examples from those countries as from Great Britain, and they will tell you that there is such a necessity of strengthening the arm of government, that they must have a criminal equity, and extort confession by torture, in order to punish with still more relentless severity. We are then lost and undone. And can any man think it troublesome, when we can, by a small interference, prevent our rights from being lost? If you will, like the Virginian government, give them knowledge of the extent of the rights retained by the people, and the powers of themselves, they will, if they be honest men, thank you for it. Will they not wish to go on sure grounds? But if you leave them otherwise, they will not know how to proceed; and, being in a state of uncertainty, they will assume rather than give up powers by implication.

A bill of rights may be summed up in a few words. What do they tell us? —That our rights are reserved. Why not say so? Is it because it will consume too much paper? Gentlemen's reasoning against a bill of rights does not satisfy me. Without saying which has the right side, it remains doubtful. A bill of rights is a favorite thing with the Virginians and the people of the other states likewise. It may be their prejudice, but the government ought to suit their geniuses; otherwise, its operation will be unhappy. A bill of rights, even if its necessity be doubtful, will exclude the possibility of dispute; and, with great submission, I think the best way is to have no dispute. In the present Constitution, they are restrained from issuing general warrants to search suspected places, or seize persons not named, without evidence of the commission of a fact, &c. There was certainly some celestial influence governing those who deliberated on that Constitution; for they have, with the most cautious and enlightened circumspection, guarded those indefeasible rights which ought ever to be held sacred! The officers of Congress may come upon you now, fortified with all the terrors of paramount federal authority. Excisemen may come in multitudes; for the limitation of their numbers no man knows. They may, unless the general government be restrained by a bill of rights, or some similar restriction, go into your cellars and rooms, and search, ransack, and measure, every thing you eat, drink, and wear. They ought to be restrained within proper bounds. With respect to the freedom of the press, I need say nothing; for it is hoped that the gentlemen who shall compose Congress will take care to infringe as little as possible the rights of human nature. This will result from their integrity. They should, from prudence, abstain from violating the rights of their constituents. They are not, however, expressly restrained. But whether they will intermeddle with that palladium of our liberties or not, I leave you to determine. . . .

. . . It has been repeatedly said here, that the great object of a national government was national defence. That power which is said to be intended for security and safety may be rendered detestable and oppressive. If they give power to the general government to provide for the *general defence,* the means must be commensurate to the end. All the means in the possession of the people must be given to the government which is intrusted with the public defence. In this state there are two hundred and thirty-six thousand blacks, and there are many in several other states. But there are few or none in the Northern States; and yet, if the Northern States shall be of opinion that our slaves are numberless, they may call forth every national resource. May Congress not say, *that every black man must fight?* Did we not see a little of this last war? We were not so hard pushed as to make emancipation general; but acts of Assembly passed that every slave who would go to the army should be free. Another thing will contribute to bring this event about. Slavery is detested. We feel its fatal effects—we deplore it with all the pity of humanity. Let all these considerations, at some future period, press with full force on the minds of Congress. Let that urbanity, which I trust will distinguish America, and the necessity of national defence,—let all these things operate on their minds; they will search that paper, and see if they have power of manumission. And have they not, sir? Have they not power to provide for the general defence and welfare? May they not think that these call for the abolition of slavery? May they not pronounce all slaves free, and will they not be warranted by that power? This is no ambiguous implication or logical deduction. The paper speaks to the point: they have the power in clear, unequivocal terms, and will clearly and certainly exercise it. As much as I deplore slavery, I see that prudence forbids its abolition. I deny that the general government ought to set them free, because a decided majority of the states have not the ties of sympathy and fellow-feeling for those whose interest would be affected by their emancipation. The majority of Congress is to the north, and the slaves are to the south.

In this situation, I see a great deal of the property of the people of Virginia in jeopardy, and their peace and tranquillity gone. I repeat it again, that it would rejoice my very soul that every one of my fellow-beings was emancipated. As we ought with gratitude to admire that decree of Heaven which has numbered us among the free, we ought to lament and deplore the necessity of holding our fellow-men in bondage. But is it practicable, by any human means, to liberate them without producing the most dreadful and ruinous consequences? We ought to possess them in the manner we inherited them from our ancestors, as their manumission is incompatible with the felicity of our country. But we ought to soften, as much as possible, the rigor of their unhappy fate. I know that, in a variety of particular instances, the legislature, listening to complaints, have admitted their emancipation. Let me not dwell on this subject. I will only add that this, as well as every other property of the people of Virginia, is in jeopardy, and put in the hands of those who have no similarity of situation with us. This is a local matter, and I can see no propriety in subjecting it to Congress.

With respect to subsequent amendments, proposed by the worthy member, I am distressed when I hear the expression. It is a new one altogether, and such a one as stands against every idea of fortitude and manliness in the states, or any one else. Evils admitted in order to be removed subsequently, and tyranny submitted to in order to be excluded by a subsequent alteration, are things totally new to me. But I am sure the gentleman meant nothing but to amuse the committee. I know his candor. His proposal is an idea dreadful to me. I ask, does experience warrant such a thing from the beginning of the world to this day? Do you enter into a compact first, and afterwards settle the terms of the government? . . .

7] Madison and Pendleton Reply to Henry

A] A GOVERNMENT PARTLY CONSOLIDATED, PARTLY FEDERAL

> Although some Federalists in the Virginia convention were quite as passionate in their advocacy of the new government as Henry was in opposing it, the dominant tone of the Federalist discourse was in marked contrast to that of their adversaries. The following extracts from speeches by Madison and Pendleton illustrate both the matter and manner of the Federalist argument. Discussing the power to tax, Madison seeks to allay fears that the new government will obliterate the states. His reasoned argument is refined in his great essay, *The Federalist*, No. 39.*

. . . HE [HENRY] informs us that the people of the country are at perfect repose,—that is, every man enjoys the fruits of his labor peaceably and securely, and that every thing is in perfect tranquillity and safety. I wish sincerely, sir, this were true. If this be their happy situation, why has every state acknowledged the contrary? Why were deputies from all the states sent to the general Convention? Why have complaints of national and individual distresses been echoed and reechoed throughout the continent? Why has our general government been so shamefully disgraced, and our Constitution violated? Wherefore have laws been made to authorize a change, and wherefore are we now assembled here? A federal government is formed for the protection of its individual members. Ours has attacked itself with impunity. Its authority has been disobeyed and despised. I think I perceive a glaring inconsistency in another of his arguments. He complains of this Constitution, because it requires the consent of at least three fourths of the states to introduce amendments which shall be necessary for the happiness of the people. The assent of so many he urges as too great an obstacle to the admission of salutary amendments, which, he strongly insists, ought to be at the will of a bare majority. We hear this argument, at the very moment we are called upon to assign reasons for

* A GOVERNMENT PARTLY CONSOLIDATED, PARTLY FEDERAL: The Virginia Convention. From Elliot, ed., *Debates*, III, 88–89, 93–96, 129.

proposing a constitution which puts it in the power of nine states to abolish the present inadequate, unsafe, and pernicious Confederation! In the first case, he asserts that a majority ought to have the power of altering the government, when found to be inadequate to the security of public happiness. In the last case, he affirms that even three fourths of the community have not a right to alter a government which experience has proved to be subversive of national felicity! nay, that the most necessary and urgent alterations cannot be made without the absolute unanimity of all the states! Does not the thirteenth article of the Confederation expressly require that no alteration shall be made without the unanimous consent of all the states? Could any thing in theory be more perniciously improvident and injudicious than this submission of the will of the majority to the most trifling minority? Have not experience and practice actually manifested this theoretical inconvenience to be extremely impolitic? Let me mention one fact, which I conceive must carry conviction to the mind of any one: the smallest state in the Union has obstructed every attempt to reform the government; that little member has repeatedly disobeyed and counteracted the general authority; nay, has even supplied the enemies of its country with provisions. Twelve states had agreed to certain improvements which were proposed, being thought absolutely necessary to preserve the existence of the general government; but as these improvements, though really indispensable, could not, by the Confederation, be introduced into it without the consent of every state, the refractory dissent of that little state prevented their adoption. The inconveniences resulting from this requisition, of unanimous concurrence in alterations in the Confederation, must be known to every member in this Convention; it is therefore needless to remind them of them. Is it not self-evident that a trifling minority ought not to bind the majority? Would not foreign influence be exerted with facility over a small minority? Would the honorable gentleman agree to continue the most radical defects in the old system, because the petty state of Rhode Island would not agree to remove them? . . .

Give me leave to say something of the nature of the government, and to show that it is safe and just to vest it with the power of taxation. There are a number of opinions; but the principal question is, whether it be a federal or consolidated government. In order to judge properly of the question before us, we must consider it minutely in its principal parts. I conceive myself that it is of a mixed nature; it is in a manner unprecedented; we cannot find one express example in the experience of the world. It stands by itself. In some respects it is a government of a federal nature; in others, it is of a consolidated nature. Even if we attend to the manner in which the Constitution is investigated, ratified, and made the act of the people of America, I can say, notwithstanding what the honorable gentleman has alleged, that this government is not completely consolidated, nor is it entirely federal. Who are parties to it? The people—but not the people as composing one great body; but the people as composing thirteen sovereignties. Were it, as the gentleman asserts, a consolidated government, the assent of a majority of the people would be sufficient for its establishment; and, as a majority have adopted it already, the remaining states would be bound by the act of the majority, even if they unanimously reprobated it. Were it such a government as is suggested, it would be now binding on the people of this state, without having had the privilege of deliberating upon it. But, sir, no state is bound by it, as it is, without its own consent. Should all the states adopt it, it will be then a government established by the thirteen states of America, not through the intervention of the legislatures, but by the people at large. In this particular respect, the distinction between the existing and proposed governments is very material. The existing system has been derived from the dependent derivative authority of the legislatures of the states; whereas this is derived from the superior power of the people. If we look at the manner in which alterations are to be made in it, the same idea is, in some degree, attended to. By the new system, a majority of the states cannot introduce amendments; nor are all the states required for that purpose: three fourths of them must concur in alterations; in this there is a departure from the federal idea. The members to the national House of Representatives are to be chosen by the people at large, in proportion to the numbers in the respective districts. When we come to the Senate, its members are elected by the states in their equal and political capacity. But had the government been completely consolidated, the Senate would have been chosen by the people in their individual capacity, in the same manner as the members of the other house. Thus it is of a complicated nature; and this complication, I trust, will be found to exclude the evils of absolute consolidation, as well as of a mere confederacy. If Virginia was separated from all the states, her power and authority would extend to all cases: in like manner, were all powers vested in the general government, it would be a consolidated government; but the powers of the federal government are enumerated; it can only operate in certain cases; it has legislative powers on defined and limited objects, beyond which it cannot extend its jurisdiction.

But the honorable member has satirized, with peculiar acrimony, the powers given to the general government by this Constitution. I conceive that the first question on this subject is, whether these powers be necessary; if they be, we are reduced to the dilemma of either submitting to the inconvenience or losing the Union. Let us consider the most important of these reprobated powers; that of direct taxation is most generally objected to. With respect to the exigencies of government, there is no question but the most easy mode of providing for them will be adopted. When, therefore, direct taxes are not necessary, they will not be recurred to. It can be of little advantage to those in power to raise money in a manner oppressive to the people. To consult the conveniences of the people will cost them nothing, and in many respects will be advantageous to them. Direct taxes will only be recurred to for great purposes. What has brought on other nations those immense debts, under the pressure of which many of them labor? Not the expenses of their governments, but war. If this country should be engaged in war,—and I conceive we ought to provide for the possibility of such a case,—how would it be carried on? By the usual means provided from year to year. As our imports will be necessary for the expenses of government and other common exigencies, how are we to carry on the means of defence? How is it possible a war could be supported without money or credit? And would it be possible for a government to have credit without having the power of raising money? No; it would be impossible for any government, in such a case, to defend itself. Then, I say, sir, that it is necessary to establish funds for extraordinary exigencies, and to give this power to the general government, for the utter inutility of previous requisitions on the states is too well known. Would it be possible for those countries, whose finances and revenues are carried to the highest perfection, to carry on the operations of government on great emergencies, such as the maintenance of a war, without an uncontrolled power of raising money? Has it not been necessary for Great Britain, notwithstanding the facility of the collection of her taxes, to have recourse very often to this and other extraordinary methods of procuring money? Would not her public credit have been ruined, if it was known that her power to raise money was limited? Has not France been obliged, on great occasions, to use unusual means to raise funds? It has been the case in many countries, and no government can exist unless its powers extend to make provisions for every contingency. If we were actually attacked by a powerful nation, and our general government had not the power of raising money, but depended solely on requisitions, our condition would be truly deplorable: if the revenue of this commonwealth were to depend on twenty distinct authorities, it would be impossible for it to carry on its operations. This must be obvious to every member here; I think, therefore, that it is necessary, for the preservation of the Union, that this power shall be given to the general government.

But it is urged that its consolidated nature, joined to the power of direct taxation, will give it a tendency to destroy all subordinate authority; that its increasing influence will speedily enable it to absorb the state governments. I cannot think this will be the case. If the general government were wholly independent of the governments of the particular states, then, indeed, usurpation might be expected to the fullest extent. But, sir, on whom does this general government depend? It derives its authority from these governments, and from the same sources from which their authority is derived. The members of the federal government are taken from the same men from whom those of the state legislatures are taken. If we consider the mode in which the federal representatives will be chosen, we shall be convinced that the general will never destroy the individual governments; and this conviction must be strengthened by an attention to the construction of the Senate. . . .

. . . A government which relies on thirteen independent sovereignties for the means of its existence, is a solecism in theory and a mere nullity in practice. Is it consistent with reason that such a government can promote the happiness of any people? It is subversive of every principle of sound policy, to trust the safety of a community with a government totally destitute of the means of protecting itself or its members. Can Congress, after the repeated unequivocal proofs it has experienced of the utter inutility and inefficacy of requisitions, reasonably expect that they would be hereafter effectual or productive? Will not the same local interests, and other causes, militate against a compliance? Whoever hopes the contrary must ever be disappointed. The effect, sir, cannot be changed without a removal of the cause. Let each county in this commonwealth be supposed free and independent; let your revenues depend on requisitions of proportionate quotas from them; let application be made to them repeatedly:—is it to be presumed that they would comply, or that an adequate collection could be made from partial compliances? It is now difficult to collect the taxes from them: how much would that difficulty be enhanced, were you to depend solely on their generosity! I appeal to the reason of every gentleman here, whether he is not persuaded that the present Confederation is as feeble as the government of Virginia would be in that case: to the same reason I appeal, whether it be compatible with prudence to continue a government of such manifest and palpable debility.

If we recur to history, and review the annals of mankind, I undertake to say that no instance can be produced, by the most learned man, of any confederate government that will justify a continuation of the present system, or that will not demonstrate the necessity of this change, and of substituting, for the present pernicious and fatal plan, the system now under consideration, or one equally energetic. The uniform conclusion drawn from a review of ancient and modern confederacies is, that, instead of promoting the public happiness, or securing public tranquillity, they have, in every instance, been productive of anarchy and confusion, ineffectual for the preservation of harmony, and a prey to their own dissensions and foreign invasions. . . .

B] A GENERAL GOVERNMENT FOR GREAT NATIONAL CONCERNS

Edmund Pendleton, elected president of the state ratifying convention by unanimous vote, was a cautious, respected conservative, experienced as a leader of Virginia conventions. He had been head of the provisional revolutionary government, president of the great convention of 1776 that framed the state constitution, speaker of the House of Burgesses, and since 1779 the head of the state judiciary. He took the floor on several occasions to defend the Constitution and here replies to Henry whom he regarded as a demagogue.*

MR. CHAIRMAN, my worthy friend [Mr. Henry] has expressed great uneasiness in his mind and informed us that a great many of our citizens are also extremely uneasy, at the proposal of changing our government; but that, a year ago, before this fatal system was thought of, the public mind was at perfect repose. It is necessary to inquire whether the public mind was at ease on the subject, and if it be since disturbed, what was the cause. What was the situation of this country before the meeting of the federal Convention? Our general government was totally inadequate to the purpose of its institution; our commerce decayed; our finances deranged; public and private credit destroyed: these and many other national evils rendered necessary the meeting of that Convention. If the public mind was then at ease, it did not result from a conviction of being in a happy and easy situation: it must have been an inactive, unaccountable stupor. The federal Convention devised the paper on

* A GENERAL GOVERNMENT FOR GREAT NATIONAL CONCERNS: The Virginia Convention. From Elliot, ed., *Debates*, III, 36–40, 301–02.

your table as a remedy to remove our political diseases. What has created the public uneasiness since? Not public reports, which are not to be depended upon; but mistaken apprehensions of danger, drawn from observations on government which do not apply to us. When we come to inquire into the origin of most governments of the world, we shall find that they are generally dictated by a conqueror, at the point of the sword, or are the offspring of confusion, when a great popular leader, taking advantage of circumstances, if not producing them, restores order at the expense of liberty, and becomes the tyrant over the people. It may well be supposed that, in forming a government of this sort, it will not be favorable to liberty: the conqueror will take care of his own emoluments, and have little concern for the interest of the people. In either case, the interest and ambition of a despot, and not the good of the people, have given the tone to the government. A government thus formed must necessarily create a continual war between the governors and governed.

Writers consider the two parties (the people and tyrants) as in a state of perpetual warfare, and sound the alarm to the people. But what is our case? We are perfectly free from sedition and war: we are not yet in confusion: we are left to consider our real happiness and security: we want to secure these objects: we know they cannot be attained without government. Is there a single man, in this committee, of a contrary opinion? What was it that brought us from a state of nature to society, but to secure happiness? And can society be formed without government? Personify government: apply to it as a friend to assist you, and it will grant your request. This is the only government founded in real compact. There is no quarrel between government and liberty; the former is the shield and protector of the latter. The war is between government and licentiousness, faction, turbulence, and other violations of the rules of society, to preserve liberty. Where is the cause of alarm? We, the people, possessing all power, form a government, such as we think will secure happiness: and suppose, in adopting this plan, we should be mistaken in the end; where is the cause of alarm on that quarter? In the same plan we point out an easy and quiet method of reforming what may be found amiss. No, but, say gentlemen, we have put the introduction of that method in the hands of our servants, who will interrupt it from motives of self-interest. What then? We will resist, did my friend say? conveying an idea of force. Who shall dare to resist the people? No, we will assemble in Convention; wholly recall our delegated powers, or reform them so as to prevent such abuse; and punish those servants who have perverted powers, designed for our happiness, to their own emolument. We ought to be extremely cautious not to be drawn into dispute with regular government, by faction and turbulence, its natural enemies. Here, then, sir, there is no cause of alarm on this side; but on the other side, rejecting of government, and dissolving of the Union, produce confusion and despotism.

But an objection is made to the form: the expression, We, the people, is thought improper. Permit me to ask the gentleman who made this objection, who but the people can delegate powers? Who but the people have a right to form government? The expression is a common one, and a favorite one with me. The representatives of the people, by their authority, is a mode wholly inessential. If the objection be, that the Union ought to be not of the people, but of the state governments, then I think the choice of the former very happy and proper. What have the state governments to do with it? Were they to determine, the people would not, in that case, be the judges upon what terms it was adopted.

But the power of the Convention is doubted. What is the power? To propose, not to determine. This power of proposing was very broad; it extended to remove all defects in government: the members of that Convention, who were to consider all the defects in our general government, were not confined to any particular plan. Were they deceived? This is the proper question here. Suppose the paper on your table dropped from one of the planets; the people found it, and sent us here to consider whether it was proper for their adoption; must we not obey them? Then the question must be between this government and the Confederation. The latter is no government at all. It has been said that it has carried us, through a dangerous war, to a happy issue. Not that Confederation, but common danger, and the spirit of America, were bonds of our union: union and unanimity, and not that insignificant paper, carried us through that dangerous war. "United, we stand—divided, we fall!" echoed and reechoed through America—from Congress to the drunken carpenter—was effectual, and procured the end of our wishes, though now forgotten by gentlemen, if such there be, who incline to let go this stronghold, to catch at feathers; for such all substituted projects may prove.

This spirit had nearly reached the end of its power when relieved by peace. It was the spirit of America, and not the Confederation, that carried us through the war: thus I prove it. The moment of peace showed the imbecility of the federal government: Congress was empowered to make war and peace; a peace they made, giving us the great object, independence, and yielding us a territory that exceeded my most sanguine expectations. Unfortunately, a single disagreeable clause, not the object of the war, has retarded the performance of the treaty on our part. Congress could only recommend its performance, not enforce it; our last Assembly (to their honor be it said) put this on its proper grounds—on honorable grounds; it was as much as they ought to have done. This single instance shows the imbecility of the Confederation; the debts contracted by the war were unpaid; demands were made on Congress; all that Congress was able to do was to make an estimate of the debt, and proportion it among the several states; they sent on the requisitions, from time to time, to the states, for their respective quotas. These were either complied with partially, or not at all. Repeated demands on Congress distressed that honorable body; but they were unable to fulfil those engagements, as they so earnestly wished. What was the idea of other nations respecting America? What was the idea entertained of us by those nations to whom we were so much indebted? The inefficacy of the general government warranted an idea that we had no government at all. Improvements were proposed, and agreed to by twelve states; but were interrupted, because the little state of Rhode Island refused to accede to them. This was a further proof of the imbecility of that government. Need I multiply instances to show that it is wholly ineffectual for the purposes of its institution? Its whole progress since the peace proves it.

Shall we then, sir, continue under such a government, or shall we introduce that kind of government which shall produce the real happiness and security of the people? When gentlemen say that we ought not to introduce this new government, but strengthen the hands of Congress, they ought to be explicit. In what manner shall this be done? If the union of the states be necessary, government must be equally so; for without the latter, the former cannot be effected. Government must then have its complete powers, or be ineffectual; a legislature to fix rules, impose sanctions, and point out the punishment of the transgressors of these rules; an executive to watch over officers, and bring them to punishment; a judiciary, to guard the innocent, and fix the guilty, by a fair trial. Without an executive, offenders would not be brought to punishment; without a judiciary, any man might be taken up, convicted, and punished without a trial. Hence the necessity of having these three branches. Would any gentleman in this committee agree to vest these three powers in one body—Congress? No. Hence the necessity of a new organization and distribution of those powers. If there be any feature in this government which is not republican, it would be exceptionable. From all the public servants responsibility is secured, by their being representatives, mediate or immediate, for short terms, and their powers defined. It is, on the whole complexion of it, a government of laws, not of men.

But it is represented to be a consolidated government, annihilating that of the states—a consolidated government, which so extensive a territory as the United States cannot admit of, without terminating in despotism. If this be such a government, I will confess, with my worthy friend, that it is inadmissible over such a territory as this country. Let us consider whether it be such a government or not. I should understand a consolidated government to be that which should have the sole and exclusive power, legislative, executive, and judicial, without any limitation. Is this such a government? Or can it be changed to such a one? It only extends to the general purposes of the Union. It does not intermeddle with the local, particular affairs of the states. Can Congress legislate for the state of Virginia? Can they make a law altering the form of transferring property, or the rule of descents, in Virginia? In one word, can they make a single law for the individual, exclusive purpose of any one state? It is the interest of the federal to preserve the state governments; upon the latter the existence of the former depends: the Senate derives its existence immediately from the state legislatures; and the representatives and President are elected under their direction and control; they also preserve order among the citizens of their respective states, and without order and peace no society can possibly exist. Unless, therefore, there be state legislatures to continue the existence of Congress, and preserve order and peace among the inhabitants, this general government, which gentlemen suppose will annihilate the state governments, must itself be destroyed. When, therefore, the federal government is, in so many respects, so absolutely dependent on the state governments, I wonder how any gentleman, reflecting on the subject, could have conceived an idea of a possibility of the former destroying the latter. . . .

But we are told that there will be a war between the two bodies equally our representatives, and that the state government will be destroyed, and consolidated into the general government. I stated before, that this could not be so. The two governments act in different manners, and for different purposes— the general government in great national concerns, in which we are interested in common with other members of the Union; the state legislature in our mere local concerns. Is it true, or merely imaginary, that the state legislatures will be confined to the care of bridges and roads? I think that they are still possessed of the highest powers. Our dearest rights,—life, liberty, and property,— as Virginians, are still in the hands of our state legislature. If they prove too feeble to protect us, we resort to the aid of the general government for security. The true distinction is, that the two governments are established for different purposes, and act on different objects; so that, notwithstanding what the worthy gentleman said, I believe I am still correct, and insist that, if each power is confined within its proper bounds, and to its proper objects, an interference can never happen. Being for two different purposes, as long as they are limited to the different objects, they can no more clash than two parallel lines can meet. Both lay taxes, but for different purposes. The same officers may be used by both governments, which will prevent a number of inconveniences. If an invasion, or insurrection, or other misfortune, should make it necessary for the general government to interpose, this will be for the general purposes of the Union, and for the manifest interest of the states.

I mentioned formerly that it would never be the interest of the general government to destroy the state governments. From these it will derive great strength: for if *they* be possessed of power, they will assist *it;* if *they* become feeble, or decay, the general government must likewise become weak, or moulder away.

But we are alarmed on account of Kentucky. We are told that the Mississippi is taken away. When gentlemen say that seven states are now disposed to give it up, and that it *will* be given up by the operation of this government, are they correct? It must be supposed that, on occasions of great moment, the senators from all the states will attend. If they do, there will be no difference between this Constitution and the Confederation in this point. When they are all present, two thirds of them will consist of the senators from nine states, which is the number required by the existing system to form treaties. The consent of the President, who is the representative of the Union, is also necessary. The right to that river must be settled by the sword, or negotiation. I understood that the purpose of that negotiation which has been on foot, was, that Spain should have the navigation of that river for twenty-five years, after which we were peaceably to retain it forever. This, I was told, was all that Spain required. If so, the gentleman who differed in opinion from others, in wishing to gratify Spain, must have been actuated by a conviction that it would be better to have the right fixed in that manner than trust to uncertainty. I think the inhabitants of that country, as well as of every other part of the Union, will be better protected by an efficient, firm government, than by the present feeble one. We shall have also a much better chance for a favorable negotiation, if our government be respectable, than we have now. . . .

8] Virginia's Recommended Amendments

Immediately after the Virginia convention ratified the Constitution by a ten-vote majority, the Federalists, having won their battle to prevent prior amendments, sought to "relieve the apprehensions" of the opposition by resolving that a committee be formed to frame recommended amendments for the guidance of the first Congress. The committee's recommendations substantially duplicated demands originally made by Patrick Henry during the debates. The influence of Virginia's amendments was apparent when Congress, under Madison's leadership, framed the Bill of Rights.*

MR. WYTHE reported, from the committee appointed, such *amendments* to the proposed Constitution of government for the United States as were by them deemed necessary to be recommended to the consideration of the Congress which shall first assemble under the said Constitution, to be acted upon according to the mode prescribed in the 5th article thereof; and he read the same in his place, and afterwards delivered them in at the clerk's table, where the same were again read, and are as follows:—

"That there be a declaration or bill of rights asserting, and securing from encroachment, the essential and unalienable rights of the people, in some such manner as the following:—

"1st. That there are certain natural rights, of which men, when they form a social compact, cannot deprive or divest their posterity; among which are the enjoyment of life and liberty, with the means of acquiring, possessing, and protecting property, and pursuing and obtaining happiness and safety.

"2d. That all power is naturally invested in, and consequently derived from, the people; that magistrates therefore are their *trustees* and *agents,* at all times amenable to them.

"3d. That government ought to be instituted for the common benefit, protection, and security of the people; and that the doctrine of non-resistance against arbitrary power and oppression is absurd, slavish, and destructive to the good and happiness of mankind.

"4th. That no man or set of men are entitled to separate or exclusive public emoluments or privileges from the community, but in consideration of public services, which not being descendible, neither ought the offices of magistrate, legislator, or judge, or any other public office, to be hereditary.

"5th. That the legislative, executive, and judicial powers of government should be separate and distinct; and, that the members of the two first may be restrained from oppression by feeling and participating the public burdens, they should, at fixed periods, be reduced to a private station, return into the mass of the people, and the vacancies be supplied by certain and regular elections, in which all or any part of the former members to be eligible or ineligible, as the rules of the Constitution of government, and the laws, shall direct.

"6th. That the elections of representatives in the legislature ought to be free

---

* VIRGINIA'S RECOMMENDED AMENDMENTS: The Virginia Convention. From Elliot, ed., *Debates,* III, 657–61.

and frequent, and all men having sufficient evidence of permanent common interest with, and attachment to, the community, ought to have the right of suffrage; and no aid, charge, tax, or fee, can be set, rated, or levied, upon the people without their own consent, or that of their representatives, so elected; nor can they be bound by any law to which they have not, in like manner, assented, for the public good.

"7th. That all power of suspending laws, or the execution of laws, by any authority, without the consent of the representatives of the people in the legislature, is injurious to their rights, and ought not to be exercised.

"8th. That, in all criminal and capital prosecutions, a man hath a right to demand the cause and nature of his accusation, to be confronted with the accusers and witnesses, to call for evidence, and be allowed counsel in his favor, and to a fair and speedy trial by an impartial jury of his vicinage, without whose unanimous consent he cannot be found guilty, (except in the government of the land and naval forces;) nor can he be compelled to give evidence against himself.

"9th. That no freeman ought to be taken, imprisoned, or disseized of his freehold, liberties, privileges, or franchises, or outlawed, or exiled, or in any manner destroyed, or deprived of his life, liberty, or property, but by the law of the land.

"10th. That every freeman restrained of his liberty is entitled to a remedy, to inquire into the lawfulness thereof, and to remove the same, if unlawful, and that such remedy ought not to be denied nor delayed.

"11th. That, in controversies respecting property, and in suits between man and man, the ancient trial by jury is one of the greatest securities to the rights of the people, and to remain sacred and inviolable.

"12th. That every freeman ought to find a certain remedy, by recourse to the laws, for all injuries and wrongs he may receive in his person, property, or character. He ought to obtain right and justice freely, without sale, completely and without denial, promptly and without delay, and that all establishments or regulations contravening these rights are oppressive and unjust.

"13th. That excessive bail ought not to be required, nor excessive fines imposed, nor cruel and unusual punishments inflicted.

"14th. That every freeman has a right to be secure from all unreasonable searches and seizures of his person, his papers, and property; all warrants, therefore, to search suspected places, or seize any freeman, his papers, or property, without information on oath (or affirmation of a person religiously scrupulous of taking an oath) of legal and sufficient cause, are grievous and oppressive; and all general warrants to search suspected places, or to apprehend any suspected person, without specially naming or describing the place or person, are dangerous, and ought not to be granted.

"15th. That the people have a right peaceably to assemble together to consult for the common good, or to instruct their representatives; and that every freeman has a right to petition or apply to the legislature for redress of grievances.

"16th. That the people have a right to freedom of speech, and of writing and publishing their sentiments; that the freedom of the press is one of the greatest bulwarks of liberty, and ought not to be violated.

"17th. That the people have a right to keep and bear arms; that a well-regulated militia, composed of the body of the people trained to arms, is the proper, natural, and safe defence of a free state; that standing armies, in time of peace, are dangerous to liberty, and therefore ought to be avoided, as far as the circumstances and protection of the community will admit; and that, in all cases, the military should be under strict subordination to, and governed by, the civil power.

"18th. That no soldier in time of peace ought to be quartered in any house without the consent of the owner, and in time of war in such manner only as the law directs.

"19th. That any person religiously scrupulous of bearing arms ought to be exempted, upon payment of an equivalent to employ another to bear arms in his stead.

"20th. That religion, or the duty which we owe to our Creator, and the manner of discharging it, can be directed only by reason and conviction, not by force or violence; and therefore all men have an equal, natural, and unalienable right to the free exercise of religion, according to the dictates of conscience, and that no particular religious sect or society ought to be favored or established, by law, in preference to others."

AMENDMENTS TO THE CONSTITUTION

"1st. That each state in the Union shall respectively retain every power, jurisdiction, and right, which is not by this Constitution delegated to the Congress of the United States, or to the departments of the federal government.

"2d. That there shall be one representative for every thirty thousand according to the enumeration or census mentioned in the Constitution until the whole number of representatives amounts to two hundred; after which, that number shall be continued or increased, as Congress shall direct, upon the principles fixed in the Constitution, by apportioning the representatives of each state to some greater number of people, from time to time, as population increases.

"3d. When the Congress shall lay direct taxes or excises, they shall immediately inform the executive power of each state, of the quota of such state, according to the census herein directed, which is proposed to be thereby raised; and if the legislature of any state shall pass a law which shall be effectual for raising such quota at the time required by Congress, the taxes and excises laid by Congress shall not be collected in such state.

"4th. That the members of the Senate and House of Representatives shall be ineligible to, and incapable of holding, any civil office under the authority of the United States, during the time for which they shall respectively be elected.

"5th. That the journals of the proceedings of the Senate and House of Representatives shall be published at least once in every year except such parts thereof, relating to treaties, alliances, or military operations, as, in their judgment, require secrecy.

"6th. That a regular statement and account of the receipts and expenditures of public money shall be published at least once a year.

"7th. That no commercial treaty shall be ratified without the concurrence of two thirds of the whole number of the members of the Senate; and no treaty ceding, contracting, restraining, or suspending, the territorial rights or claims of the United States, or any of them, or their, or any of their rights or claims to fishing in the American seas, or navigating the American rivers, shall be made, but in cases of the most urgent and extreme necessity; nor shall any such treaty be ratified without the concurrence of three fourths of the whole number of the members of both houses respectively.

"8th. That no navigation law, or law regulating commerce, shall be passed without the consent of two thirds of the members present, in both houses.

"9th. That no standing army, or regular troops, shall be raised, or kept up, in time of peace, without the consent of two thirds of the members present, in both houses.

"10th. That no soldier shall be enlisted for any longer term than four years, except in time of war, and then for no longer term than the continuance of the war.

"11th. That each state respectively shall have the power to provide for organizing, arming, and disciplining its own militia, whensoever Congress shall omit or neglect to provide for the same. That the militia shall not be subject to martial law, except when in actual service, in time of war, invasion, or rebellion; and when not in the actual service of the United States, shall be subject only to such fines, penalties, and punishments, as shall be directed or inflicted by the laws of its own state.

"12th. That the exclusive power of legislation given to Congress over the federal town and its adjacent district, and other places, purchased or to be purchased by Congress of any of the states, shall extend only to such regulations as respect the police and good government thereof.

"13th. That no person shall be capable of being President of the United States for more than eight years in any term of sixteen years.

"14th. That the judicial power of the United States shall be vested in one Supreme Court, and in such courts of admiralty as Congress may from time to time ordain and establish in any of the different states. The judicial power shall extend to all cases in law and equity arising under treaties made, or which shall be made, under the authority of the United States; to all cases affecting ambassadors, other foreign ministers, and consuls; to all cases of admiralty and maritime jurisdiction; to controversies to which the United States shall be a party; to controversies between two or more states, and between parties claiming lands under the grants of different states. In all cases affecting ambassadors, other foreign ministers, and consuls, and those in which a state shall be a party, the Supreme Court shall have original jurisdiction; in all other cases before mentioned, the Supreme Court shall have appellate jurisdiction, as to matters of law only, except in cases of equity, and of admiralty, and maritime jurisdiction, in which the Supreme Court shall have appellate jurisdiction both as to law and fact, with such exceptions and under such regulations as the Congress shall make; but the judicial power of the United States shall extend to no case where the cause of action shall have originated before the ratification of the Constitution, except in disputes between states about their territory, disputes between persons claiming lands under the grants of different states, and suits for debts due to the United States.

"15th. That, in criminal prosecutions, no man shall be restrained in the exercise of the usual and accustomed right of challenging or excepting to the jury.

"16th. That Congress shall not alter, modify, or interfere in the times, places, or manner of holding elections for senators and representatives, or either of them, except when the legislature of any state shall neglect, refuse, or be disabled, by invasion or rebellion, to prescribe the same.

"17th. That those clauses which declare that Congress shall not exercise certain powers, be not interpreted, in any manner whatsoever, to extend the powers of Congress; but that they be construed either as making exceptions to the specified powers where this shall be the case, or otherwise, as inserted merely for greater caution.

"18th. That the laws ascertaining the compensation of senators and representatives for their services, be postponed, in their operation, until after the election of representatives immediately succeeding the passing thereof; that excepted which shall first be passed on the subject.

"19th. That some tribunal other than the Senate be provided for trying impeachments of senators.

"20th. That the salary of a judge shall not be increased or diminished during his continuance in office, otherwise than by general regulations of salary, which may take place on a revision of the subject at stated periods of not less than seven years, to commence from the time such salaries shall be first ascertained by Congress."

9] A Bill of Rights to Complete the Constitution

A] "Parchment Barriers" Are of Some Use

When the new government was being organized, Madison sought a seat in Congress. With the Constitution unconditionally ratified and an election coming up in which the Anti-Federalists might capitalize on his opposition to amendments, he pledged his support for a Bill of Rights. At this stage, however, he had no enthusiasm for the project. In the following letter he explains himself to Jefferson in Paris.*

. . . My own opinion has always been in favor of a bill of rights; provided it be so framed as not to imply powers not meant to be included in the enumeration. At the same time I have never thought the omission a material defect, nor been anxious to supply it even by subsequent amendment, for any

---

* "Parchment barriers" are of some use: James Madison to Thomas Jefferson, October 17, 1788. From Julian P. Boyd, ed., The Papers of Thomas Jefferson (Princeton, 1950–), XIV, 18–21. Reprinted by permission of the Princeton University Press.

other reason than that it is anxiously desired by others. I have favored it because I supposed it might be of use, and if properly executed could not be of dis-service. I have not viewed it in an important light 1. Because I conceive that in a certain degree, though not in the extent argued by Mr. Wilson, the rights in question are reserved by the manner in which the federal powers are granted. 2. Because there is great reason to fear that a positive declaration of some of the most essential rights could not be obtained in the requisite latitude. I am sure that the rights of conscience in particular, if submitted to public definition would be narrowed much more than they are likely ever to be by an assumed power. One of the objections in New England was that the Con-stitution by prohibiting religious tests opened a door for Jews, Turks and infidels. 3. Because the limited powers of the federal Government and the jealousy of the subordinate Governments, afford a security which has not existed in the case of the State Governments, and exists in no other. 4. Because experience proves the inefficacy of a bill of rights on those occasions when its controul is most needed. Repeated violations of these parchment barriers have been committed by overbearing majorities in every State. In Virginia I have seen the bill of rights violated in every instance where it has been opposed to a popular current. Notwithstanding the explicit provision contained in that instrument for the rights of Conscience it is well known that a religious establishment would have taken place in that State, if the legislative majority had found as they expected, a majority of the people in favor of the measure; and I am persuaded that if a majority of the people were now of one sect, the measure would still take place and on narrower ground than was then proposed, notwithstanding the additional obstacle which the law has since created. Wherever the real power in a Government lies, there is the danger of oppres-sion. In our Governments the real power lies in the majority of the Com-munity, and the invasion of private rights is *chiefly* to be apprehended, not from acts of Government contrary to the sense of its constituents, but from acts in which the Government is the mere instrument of the major number of the constituents. This is a truth of great importance, but not yet sufficiently attended to: and is probably more strongly impressed on my mind by facts, and reflections suggested by them, than on yours which has contemplated abuses of power issuing from a very different quarter. Wherever there is an interest and power to do wrong, wrong will generally be done, and not less readily by a powerful and interested party than by a powerful and interested prince. The difference, so far as it relates to the superiority of republics over monarchies, lies in the less degree of probability that interest may prompt abuses of power in the former than in the latter; and in the security in the former against op-pression of more than the smaller part of the Society, whereas in the former it may be extended in a manner to the whole. The difference so far as it relates to the point in question—the efficacy of a bill of rights in controuling abuses of power—lies in this: that in a monarchy the latent force of the nation is superior to that of the Sovereign, and a solemn charter of popular rights must have a great effect, as a standard for trying the validity of public acts, and a signal for rousing and uniting the superior force of the community; whereas in a popular Government, the political and physical power may be considered as vested in the same hands, that is in a majority of the people, and consequently the tyrannical will of the sovereign is not to be controuled by the dread of an appeal to any other force within the community. What use then it may be asked can a bill of rights serve in popular Governments? I answer the two following which though less essential than in other Governments, sufficiently recommend the precaution. 1. The political truths declared in that solemn manner acquire by degrees the character of fundamental maxims of free Government, and as they become incorporated with the national sentiment, counteract the impulses of interest and passion. 2. Altho' it be generally true as above stated that the danger of oppression lies in the interested majorities of the people rather than in usurped acts of the Government, yet there may be occasions on which the evil may spring from the latter sources; and on such, a bill of rights will be a good ground for an appeal to the sense of the community. Perhaps too there may be a certain degree of danger, that a succession of artful and ambitious rulers, may by gradual and well-timed advances, finally erect an independent Government on the subversion of liberty. Should this danger exist at all, it is prudent to guard against it, especially when the precaution can do no injury. At the same time I must own that I see no tendency in our governments to danger on that side. It has been remarked that there is a tendency in all Governments to an augmentation of power at the expence of liberty. But the remark as usually understood does not appear to me well founded. Power when it has attained a certain degree of energy and independence goes on generally to further degrees. But when below that degree, the direct tendency is to further degrees of relaxation, until the abuses of liberty beget a sudden transition to an undue degree of power. With this explanation the remark may be true; and in the latter sense only is it in my opinion applicable to the Governments in America. It is a melancholy reflection that liberty should be equally exposed to danger whether the Government have too much or too little power; and that the line which divides these extremes should be so inaccurately defined by experience.

Supposing a bill of rights to be proper the articles which ought to compose it, admit of much discussion. I am inclined to think that absolute restrictions in cases that are doubtful, or where emergencies may overrule them, ought to be avoided. The restrictions however strongly marked on paper will never be regarded when opposed to the decided sense of the public; and after repeated violations in extraordinary cases, they will lose even their ordinary efficacy. Should a Rebellion or insurrection alarm the people as well as the Government, and a suspension of the Hab. Corp. be dictated by the alarm, no written prohibitions on earth would prevent the measure. Should an army in time of peace be gradually established in our neighbourhood by Britn: or Spain, declarations on paper would have as little effect in preventing a standing force for the public safety. The best security against these evils is to remove the pretext for them. . . .

b] THE PEOPLE ARE ENTITLED TO IT

Many Anti-Federalists soon realized that a Bill of Rights, by quieting the apprehensions of the people, would make unobtainable the crippling amendments they most wanted. Jefferson's brilliant reply to Madison unquestionably influenced him to carry out his pledge despite formidable apathy and opposition in both parties. Indeed, it is not too much to say that Jefferson "converted" him to the cause. The following letter is restrained and reasoned, lacking wholly in the intensity Jefferson really felt: he knew his man and was out to win him.*

. . . Your thoughts on the subject of the Declaration of rights in the letter of Oct. 17. I have weighed with great satisfaction. Some of them had not occurred to me before, but were acknoleged just in the moment they were presented to my mind. In the arguments in favor of a declaration of rights, you omit one which has great weight with me, the legal check which it puts into the hands of the judiciary. This is a body, which if rendered independent, and kept strictly to their own department merits great confidence for their learning and integrity. In fact what degree of confidence would be too much for a body composed of such men as Wythe, Blair, and Pendleton? On characters like these the 'civium ardor prava jubentium' [1] would make no impression. I am happy to find that on the whole you are a friend to this amendment. The Declaration of rights is like all other human blessings alloyed with some inconveniences, and not accomplishing fully it's object. But the good in this instance vastly overweighs the evil. I cannot refrain from making short answers to the objections which your letter states to have been raised. 1. That the rights in question are reserved by the manner in which the federal powers are granted. Answer. A constitutive act may certainly be so formed as to need no declaration of rights. The act itself has the force of a declaration as far as it goes: and if it goes to all material points nothing more is wanting. In the draught of a constitution which I had once a thought of proposing in Virginia, and printed afterwards, I endeavored to reach all the great objects of public liberty, and did not mean to add a declaration of rights. Probably the object was imperfectly executed: but the deficiencies would have been supplied by others in the course of discussion. But in a constitutive act which leaves some precious articles unnoticed, and raises implications against others, a declaration of rights becomes necessary by way of supplement. This is the case of our new federal constitution. This instrument forms us into one state as to certain objects, and gives us a legislative and executive body for these objects. It should therefore guard us against their abuses of power within the field submitted to them. 2. A positive declaration of some essential rights could not be obtained in the requisite latitude. Answer. Half a loaf is better than no bread. If we cannot secure all our rights, let us secure what we can. 3. The limited powers of the federal government and jealousy of the subordinate governments afford a security which exists in no other instance. Answer. The first member of this seems resolvable into the 1st. objection before stated. The jealousy of the subordinate governments is a precious reliance. But observe that those governments are only agents. They must have principles furnished

---

* THE PEOPLE ARE ENTITLED TO IT: Thomas Jefferson to James Madison, March 15, 1789. From Julian P. Boyd, ed., *The Papers of Thomas Jefferson* (Princeton, 1950–), XIV, 659–61. Reprinted by permission of the Princeton University Press.

1 'civium ardor prava jubentium': "the wayward zeal of the ruling citizens."

them whereon to found their opposition. The declaration of rights will be the text whereby they will try all the acts of the federal government. In this view it is necessary to the federal government also: as by the same text they may try the opposition of the subordinate governments. 4. Experience proves the inefficacy of a bill of rights. True. But tho it is not absolutely efficacious under all circumstances, it is of great potency always, and rarely inefficacious. A brace the more will often keep up the building which would have fallen with that brace the less. There is a remarkeable difference between the characters of the Inconveniencies which attend a Declaration of rights, and those which attend the want of it. The inconveniences of the Declaration are that it may cramp government in it's useful exertions. But the evil of this is shortlived, moderate, and reparable. The inconveniencies of the want of a Declaration are permanent, afflicting and irreparable: they are in constant progression from bad to worse. The executive in our governments is not the sole, it is scarcely the principal object of my jealousy. The tyranny of the legislatures is the most formidable dread at present, and will be for long years. That of the executive will come in it's turn, but it will be at a remote period. I know there are some among us who would now establish a monarchy. But they are inconsiderable in number and weight of character. The rising race are all republicans. We were educated in royalism: no wonder if some of us retain that idolatry still. Our young people are educated in republicanism. An apostacy from that to royalism is unprecedented and impossible. I am much pleased with the prospect that a declaration of rights will be added: and hope it will be done in that way which will not endanger the whole frame of the government, or any essential part of it. . . .

TABLES

1] Economic Interests of the Members of the Virginia Convention of 1788

	FEDERALISTS		ANTI-FEDERALISTS	
	number	per cent (89 = 100 per cent)	number	per cent (79 = 100 per cent)
a] *principal occupation*				
agricultural	64	72	60	75.9
professional	24	26.9	14	17.8
mercantile	1	1.1	4	5.0
unclassified	—	—	1	1.3
b] *security holdings*				
United States securities	28	31.4	20	25.3
state securities	7	7.9	1	1.3
state and national securities	1	1.1	6	7.6
c] *taxable value of land owned*				
under $1000	24	27	21	26.6
$1000–$5000	33	37	33	41.8
over $5000	9	10.1	11	13.9
unknown	23	25.9	14	17.7
d] *slaveholdings*				
none	11	12.4	1	1.3
under 10	21	23.6	23	29.1
10–49	48	42.6	37	46.8
50 or over	5	5.6	4	5
unknown	14	15.8	14	17.8
e] *sectional distribution*				
Tidewater	49	55.1	22	27.8
Piedmont	10	11.2	40	50.6
Valley	14	15.7	0	0
Trans–Allegheny (northwest)	13	14.6	1	1.3
Kentucky District	3	3.4	16	20.3

] Principal Occupations and Distribution of Security Holdings of the Members of the Ratification Conventions *

STATE	VOTE	PRINCIPAL OCCUPATION					PER CENT OWNING PUBLIC SECURITIES
		Unknown	Agricultural (including landholding)	Commercial and mercantile	Manufacturing and venture capitalism	Professional and unclassified	
elaware	30 for	—	23	—	—	7	16.6
nnsylvania	46 for	—	16	5	6	19	50.0
	23 against	—	6	2	7	8	73.9
ew Jersey	38 for	—	25	1	4	8	34.0
eorgia	26 for	2	13	3	—	8	0.26
onnecticut	128 for	—	74	13	—	41	35.1
	40 against	—	27	2	—	11	15.0
lassachusetts	187 for	38	40	25	27	57	31.0
	168 against	89	13	17	30	19	10.1
[aryland	63 for	—	60	1	—	2	17.4
	11 against	2	3	1	—	5	27.3
outh Carolina	149 for	2	106	11	—	30	41.6
	73 against	6	58	—	5	4	68.5
ew Hampshire	57 for	15	15	7	7	13	10.5
	47 against	19	9	2	8	9	2.2
irginia	89 for	—	64	1	—	24	40.4
	79 against	—	60	4	—	15	34.2
ew York	30 for	5	13	4	—	8	50.0
	27 against	10	8	—	1	8	63.0
orth Carolina							
FIRST CONVENTION	84 for	—	77	3	—	4	2.25
	184 against	—	176	3	1	4	1.09
SECOND CONVENTION	194 for	—	186	4	1	3	2.0
	77 against	—	74	—	1	3	3.9
hode Island	34 for	5	13	9	—	7	50.0
	32 against	7 †	12 †	6 †	1 †	6 †	47.0

* Where a member was engaged in two or more occupations he is assigned to the category that appears to principal. Column 2 includes farmers, planters, and wealthy landholders and land speculators. Column 3 cludes retail tradesmen, merchants in interstate and foreign commerce, factors, mariners, and shipowners. olumn 4 includes mill proprietors and other manufacturers, and men with substantial venture capital in

CONCLUSION

No MORE than a week after the adoption of the Constitution by Virginia, the wheels began turning for the new system. Only the uncertainty of the outcome in New York caused concern. Hamilton and the Federalist forces in New York had hoped that the favorable decision in Virginia would break the mighty phalanx of George Clinton's party at Poughkeepsie. But the convention dragged on for weeks after the special messenger arrived from Richmond. Slowly, however, the realization of the tremendous difficulties which must attend independence of the Union dawned upon many Anti-Federalists; and under the threat of the Federalist strongholds of New York City and the surrounding counties to secede from the state and find other means of joining the Union, Clinton's ranks broke. The Constitution was adopted unconditionally, with recommended amendments, 30–27. At the same time, the Federalists consented to a circular letter, addressed to the various states, urging support of a second convention to revise the Constitution in the light of the numerous amendments that had been offered. This act, seemingly unnecessary except as a face-saver for the defecting Anti-Federalists, was rebuked by Federalists throughout the Union. Washington feared the New York circular would "set every thing afloat again." But, despite the efforts of the Clintonians, nothing materialized. This was the last gasp of the stalwart Anti-Federalists. Meanwhile, in the First Congress, by submitting proposals that became the Bill of Rights, Madison almost singlehandedly moved to redeem the Federalist pledge to amend the Constitution. His proposals were coldly received by the Anti-Federalists, who realized that guarantees of personal liberty, once adopted, would allay popular fears of the new national government, thereby preventing the additional amendments that they most wanted—amendments that would hamstring national powers. The party that had first opposed a Bill of Rights, the Federalist, inadvertently wound up with the responsibility for its framing and ratification, while the party that had first professedly wanted it, the Anti-Federalist, discovered too late that its framing and ratification were politically inexpedient. Thus the Bill of Rights was, in the main, the chance result of certain Federalists having been forced to capitalize for their own cause the propaganda that had been originated by the Anti-Federalists for ulterior purposes. Even before North Carolina and Rhode Island entered the new union, the amendments were voted by Congress and submitted to the states. On December 13, 1791, the Bill of Rights became a part of the Constitution of the United States.

---

manufacturing and other enterprises. Column 5 includes lawyers, ministers, physicians, educators, and men in occupations not otherwise subject to classification. All kinds and amounts of security holdings, state and national, as near as can be ascertained, are represented in the percentage figures. The figures are compiled principally from Forrest McDonald, *We the People: The Economic Origins of the Constitution* (Chicago, 1958).

† Estimated.

STUDY QUESTIONS

1] What principles did the friends and enemies of the Constitution have in common and what principles divided them? Or was there any clear-cut division of principle in the ratification controversy?

2] What specific objections were made to the Constitution? How well grounded were they, and how were they answered by the Federalists?

3] Were the Federalists successful principally because of powerful economic and political forces which worked in their favor, or principally because of superior tactics and leadership in the ratification campaign?

4] In view of the "Federalist compromise," is it correct to say that the Anti-Federalists were defeated? How did this compromise, so called, affect the character and prospects of the new government under the Constitution?

5] How do you account for Virginia's ratification of the Constitution?

RECOMMENDED READINGS

PRIMARY SOURCES

ELLIOT, JONATHAN, ed. *The Debates in the Several State Conventions on the Adoption of the Federal Constitution*, 2nd ed., 5 vols. (Philadelphia, 1836).

FARRAND, MAX, ed. *The Records of the Federal Convention of 1787*, 4 vols. (New Haven, 1911–37), Vol. III.

FORD, PAUL LEICESTER, ed. *Essays on the Constitution of the United States, Published During Its Discussion by the People, 1787–1788* (Brooklyn, 1888).

————. *Pamphlets on the Constitution* (Brooklyn, 1888).

HAMILTON, ALEXANDER, ET AL. *The Federalist*.

McMASTER, JOHN B., AND FREDERICK D. STONE. *Pennsylvania and the Federal Constitution, 1787–1788* (Philadelphia, 1888).

SECONDARY SOURCES

BATES, FRANK G. *Rhode Island and the Formation of the Union* (New York, 1898).

BEARD, CHARLES A. *An Economic Interpretation of the Constitution of the United States* (New York, 1913).

BISHOP, HILLMAN M. *Why Rhode Island Opposed the Federal Constitution* (Providence, 1950). Reprinted from *Rhode Island History*, VIII (1949), 47 pp.

BRANT, IRVING. *James Madison, Father of the Constitution, 1787–1800* (Indianapolis, 1950).

BROWN, ROBERT E. *Charles Beard and the Constitution* (Princeton, 1956).

FORD, WORTHINGTON C. *The Federal Constitution in Virginia, 1787–1788* (Cambridge, Mass., 1903). Reprinted from *Proceedings of Massachusetts Historical Society*, 2nd ser., XVII, 450–510.

GRIGSBY, HUGH B. *The History of the Virginia Federal Convention of 1788, With Some Account of the Eminent Virginians of that Era Who Were Members of the Body*, 2 vols. (Richmond, 1890–91).

HARDING, SAMUEL B. *The Contest Over the Ratification of the Federal Constitution in the State of Massachusetts* (New York, 1896).

LIBBY, ORIN G. *The Geographical Distribution of the Vote of the Thirteen States on the Federal Constitution, 1787–1788* (Madison, Wis., 1894).

MCDONALD, FORREST. *We the People: The Economic Origins of the Constitution* (Chicago, 1958).

MAIN, JACKSON T. *The Anti-Federalists: Critics of the Constitution, 1781–1788* (Chapel Hill, N.C., 1961).

MAYS, DAVID J. *Edmund Pendleton, 1721–1803*, 2 vols. (Cambridge, Mass., 1952), Vol. II.

MINER, CLARENCE E. *The Ratification of the Federal Constitution by the State of New York* (New York, 1921).

ROCHE, JOHN P. "The Founding Fathers: A Reform Caucus in Action," *American Political Science Review*, LV (December, 1961), 799–816.

ROWLAND, KATE M. *The Life of George Mason*, 2 vols. (New York, 1892), Vol. II.

SMITH, EDWARD P. "The Movement Towards a Second Constitutional Convention in 1788," in Franklin J. Jameson, ed. *Essays on the Constitutional History of the United States in the Formative Period, 1775–1789* (Boston, 1889), pp. 46–115.

TRENHOLME, LOUISE I. *The Ratification of the Federal Constitution in North Carolina* (New York, 1932).

Freedom in Turmoil, Era of the Sedition Act: The Crisis of 1797–1800

LEONARD W. LEVY

BRANDEIS UNIVERSITY

CONTENTS

6] Federalist Schemes for War and Conquest
   a] "Wage War, and Call It Self-Defence"
                 (Ames to Pickering, July 10, 1798, *Works of Fisher Ames*)

   b] Senator Sedgwick Explains the Benefits of War
                 (Theodore Sedgwick to Rufus King, January 20, 1799,
                                    Correspondence of Rufus King)

   c] General Hamilton Dreams of Military Glory
                 (Letters to King, Otis, and McHenry, 1798–1799, *Works of
                                                  Alexander Hamilton*)

   d] The "Christian Cause": Conquest and Commerce
                 (J. W. Fenno, *Desultory Reflections*, 1800)

7] The Republican Attack on the Alien and Sedition Acts
   a] The Kentucky Resolutions of 1798
                                              (Elliot's *Debates*)

   b] Massachusetts Replies
                                              (Elliot's *Debates*)

   c] The Kentucky Resolutions of 1799
                                              (Elliot's *Debates*)

   d] Madison Argues for Freedom of the Press
                                    (*The Virginia Report of 1799–1800*)

8] The Republican Attack on the Army
   a] Resolutions of Dinwiddie County, Virginia
                         (Philadelphia *Aurora*, December 6, 1798)

   b] Gallatin Fears the "Standing Army"
                 (Letter to His Wife, December 7, 1798, Adams, *Gallatin*)

   c] Military Outrages on Civilians
                 (Philadelphia *Aurora*, June 25 and August 5, 1799)

   d] The Danger of the Army to a Free Press
                 (Philadelphia *Aurora*, April 27 and May 16, 1799)

9] The Economic Consequences of Federalist Political Policies
   a] The Tax Gatherer Eases Jefferson's Despair
                 (Letters to Archibald Rowan and John Taylor, 1798, *Writings of
                                                  Thomas Jefferson*)

   b] Dr. Ames and the "Great Sovereign" Grumble
                                    (Warren, *Jacobin and Junto*)

   c] The People's "Love for Pelf Was Roused"
                                    (Alexander Graydon, *Memoirs*)

CHRONOLOGY

1797

MARCH   Adams inaugurated; news received of France's refusal to recognize Minister Pinckney; President calls special session of Congress.

MAY   President's message to Congress; envoys to France nominated.

JUNE   Secretary Pickering reports that 316 American ships were sunk or captured by France within a year.

JUNE–JULY   Preliminary defense measures enacted; taxes increased —salt and stamp taxes enacted.

OCTOBER   Envoys in Paris begin negotiations.

DECEMBER   New French decrees against neutral vessels.

1798

MARCH   News received of the failure of the mission in Paris; President requests strong defense measures.

APRIL   Congress receives XYZ dispatches; wave of patriotism sweeps country; war seems imminent. Department of Navy established.

MAY   Speaker of House warns of French invasion; Congress authorizes fortifications, military supplies, provisional expansion of army and navy.

JUNE   Naturalization and Alien Friends Acts; arming of American merchant ships.

JULY   Alien Enemies and Sedition Acts; suspension of commercial intercourse with France; abrogation of all treaties with France; expansion of regular army; American vessels authorized to capture armed French ships; enactment of direct tax; Washington appointed commander of army.

SUMMER   Undeclared naval war with France commences; Hamilton corresponds with Miranda.

OCTOBER   Hamilton appointed second in command; Sedition Act prosecutions commence; Adams informed of French overtures to re-establish diplomatic relations.

NOVEMBER   Kentucky Resolutions.

DECEMBER   Virginia Resolutions.

1799

JANUARY   Hamilton plans on war by August.

FEBRUARY   Adams suddenly nominates envoy to France; victories at sea; federal budget reaches new high; more taxes, loans, expansion of military establishment.

MARCH   Fries's Rebellion.

SUMMER Hamilton and Cabinet delay departures of peace mission to France.
OCTOBER Adams orders departure of envoys.
NOVEMBER Second Kentucky Resolution.

1800

JANUARY Madison's *Virginia Report.*
FEBRUARY Continued American victories at sea.
MAY McHenry and Pickering dismissed from Cabinet; Marshall becomes head of the Cabinet.
SUMMER Open rift in Federalist party.
SEPTEMBER Franco-American Convention signed in Paris.
DECEMBER Late election returns clinch victory of Jefferson-Burr ticket.

1801

FEBRUARY Senate ratifies Convention of 1800.
MARCH Jefferson inaugurated.

INTRODUCTION

I n 1798 the Fourth of July was commemorated in rather sinister fashion. While the officers of a New York military company drank to the toast "One and but one party in the United States," Federalist partisans in Newburyport, Massachusetts, publicly burned copies of the leading Republican newspaper in New England. On that same festive day the Senate, in the hope of controlling public opinion and crushing the opposition party, passed a bill making it a crime to criticize the government. The sponsor of the bill, Senator Lloyd, expressed anxiety to Washington—the bill might not be severe enough to muzzle "the lovers of Liberty, or, in other words, the Jacobins"; moreover, complained Lloyd, "I fear Congress will close the session without a declaration of War, which I look upon as necessary to enable us to lay our hands on traitors . . ." In a similar spirit the president of Yale, in his Fourth of July Sermon, warned that if the author of the Declaration of Independence, then the Vice-President of the United States, were to have his way, the country would "see the Bible cast into a bonfire . . . our wives and daughters the victims of legal prostitution . . . our sons become the disciples of Voltaire, and the dragoons of Marat . . ." Within a fortnight and even before the Sedition Act became law, the impatient administration arrested two opposition editors, Burke of the New York *Time Piece* and Bache of the Philadelphia *Aurora*, the nation's foremost Republican newspaper. A spirit of vigilantism flashed like summer lightning over a divided land that girded itself for war—abroad against the legions of Napoleon, at home against the subversion of its Jeffersonian minions. A crisis was in the making that jeopardized the nation's policies and free institutions.

The foreign crisis had been caused by French aggressions against American commerce and aggravated by Jay's Treaty. France, at war with England, not unjustifiably viewed Jay's Treaty as a pro-British instrument, a rebuff to an old ally and benefactor, even as diplomatic treachery. For Monroe, the American minister to France, had been deceived by the State Department and unwittingly misled the French on the course of Jay's mission. He had also induced them to promise compensation for their spoilations and repeal of their maritime decrees against American shipping. News of the treaty provoked France to recall her American ambassador and reinstitute her decrees with greater rigor than before, on the theory that American commerce deserved from France no greater respect than offered by England and acquiesced in by the United States. Within a year the French sank or captured over three hundred American ships and refused recognition to Charles C. Pinckney, Monroe's successor—indeed, had ordered him out of France on threat of arrest. Such was the posture of Franco-American relations when John Adams was inaugurated.

President Adams, convinced that the differences with France, however serious, might be resolved by negotiation, resolutely determined upon a policy of peace with honor. He proposed a new diplomatic mission to Paris and wisely recommended defense measures during the emergency: an increased army (then only 3500 men), creation of a permanent navy, convoys, and the arming of merchant ships. But the Republicans, despite their recent bellicosity against Great Britain, opposed all preparedness measures as unnecessarily provocative and contrary to the pacific intent of the new mission. A fierce party battle ensued in Congress. The Federalists, spurred by a war faction, tarred the obstructionist Republicans with charges of disloyalty and indulged in jingoistic saber rattling. The session ended in July with the failure of most major defense measures, chiefly because Congress was so closely divided. But the party debate had been so vituperative that a residue of hate remained. Jefferson, presiding over the Senate, commented to a friend:

You and I have formerly seen warm debates and high political passions. But gentlemen of different politics would then speak to each other, and separate the business of the Senate from that of society. It is not so now. Men who have been intimate all their lives, cross the streets to avoid meeting, and turn their heads another way, lest they should be obliged to touch their hats.

When Congress reconvened in a tense atmosphere, partisan oratory was disrupted by a fistfight on the floor, and some Congressmen predicted "blood to be let" before the session ended.

In March of 1798 the President notified Congress that dispatches from the American envoys proved that the objects of the peace mission could not be accomplished "on terms compatible with the safety, the honor, or the essential interests of the nation." He would therefore permit merchant ships to arm for their own protection, and exhorted Congress speedily to enact defense measures proportionate to the dangers to national security. Adams neither wished war nor took any step that would provoke Congress to its declaration; but the Republicans fitfully described his message as "insane" and denounced him for incitement to belligerency on behalf of England's interests. The Republicans, however, were betrayed by their own distrust. Believing that the President had exaggerated the gravity of the situation, they induced Congress to request full disclosure of the envoys' dispatches. When Adams complied, the doubters were aghast to discover that he had muted the true state of affairs. The damning evidence of the humiliating and contumelious treatment of our envoys even alluded to a "French party in America." The envoys, after having been ignored for months, had been approached by unofficial agents of the French government—designated as Messrs. X, Y, and Z—who demanded outrageous gifts of money for high officials, an extravagant "loan" to France, and an apology for supposedly obnoxious statements made by President Adams. In addition the United States must pay all debts owed by France to American citizens and the cost of damages caused by French depredations on American commerce. Official negotiation would follow if these terms were met! After more months of degrading intrigue and diplomatic blackmail, the envoys gave up the mission as a hopeless failure.

France had been motivated by simple rapacity and arrogance, not by a desire to drive the United States into war, but she almost succeeded in doing just that. The "XYZ" disclosures, whose publication the Republicans sought to suppress, electrified the country. In the patriotic craze in support of the administration, "Millions for defense, but not one cent for tribute" became the national slogan, and the opposition dwindled to a distinctly beaten minority. War fever mounted, but no one lusted for hostilities except a small sect of ultra-Federalists who controlled the Senate. The President, the closely divided House, and the majority of the people would countenance only resistance against French aggression, not an offensive war.

Federalists of whatever hue shared a sinister understanding that national security and party supremacy might be insured if the country could be first frightened and then panicked. Both fear and panic, already present in the situation, were intensified by chilling stories in the Federalist press on the imminence of a French invasion and the dangers of subversive activities. The Republican opposition was identified as revolutionary Jacobins treasonably allied with the foreign enemy to overthrow the Constitution and cut the throats of true Americans. The Federalists were so obsessed with hate and convinced that anyone whose opinion differed must be a criminal subversive that they openly reviled even their fellow Congressmen.

For example, when Gallatin, the Republican leader of the House, discounted the possibility of an invasion, Speaker Dayton retorted that since his principles were those of "the furious hordes of democrats which threatened this country with subjugation," Gallatin could calmly watch "our dwellings burning, and might 'laugh at our calamities and mock when our fears came upon us.' " When Livingston of New York spoke against a Federalist system of tyranny that would destroy civil liberties, Allen of Connecticut lashed him for "intimate acquaintance with treason" and claimed that he "vomited" falsehood on "everything sacred, human and divine." The prime victim of abuse was the Vice-President himself, who observed: "It suffices for a man to be a philosopher and to believe that human affairs are susceptible of improvement, and to look forward, rather than back to the Gothic ages, for perfection, to mark him as an anarchist, disorganiser, atheist, and enemy of the government." To be an alien or even a naturalized citizen was equally stigmatizing. Was not Gallatin himself a Swiss, and were not Priestly, Cooper, Volney, Burk, Duane, Callender, and other foreign-born scholars and journalists the leaders of swarms of wild Irishmen, political refugees, and French apostles of sedition? It was necessary to "strike terror among these people," as Congressman Harper put it.

Between April and July of 1798, when Congress adjourned, the party program was adopted. In addition to mustering the forces of defense—enlisting an army, creating a navy, fortifying harbors, abrogating all treaties with France, authorizing the capture of armed French ships—Congress passed a series of repressive measures designed to intimidate the opposition, coerce conformity of opinion, and extend Federalist control of the government. The Naturalization Act increased the period of residence from five to fourteen years before citizenship could be granted to immigrants. The statute was a disappointment to ultra-Federalists who preferred "that nothing but birth should entitle a man to citizenship" or the right to vote and hold office. The Alien Act empowered the President to order, without assigning cause, the summary arrest and deportation of any foreigner, even the citizen of a friendly nation, whom he judged to be "dangerous" to the peace and safety of the nation or believed "suspect" of "secret machinations." A deported alien who returned without permission might be imprisoned indefinitely at the discretion of the President. The Republicans described the measure as a "refinement on despotism," while the Federalists claimed that "to *boggle* about slight forms" in time of danger courted national disaster.

The capstone of the new Federalist system was the Sedition Act, an expression of the easy rule of thumb offered by the party organ in the nation's capital, "He that is not for us, is against us." The same editor added: "Whatever American is a friend to the present administration of the American government, is undoubtedly a true republican, a true patriot . . . Whatever American opposes the administration is an anarchist, a jacobin and a traitor . . . It is *Patriotism* to write in favour of our government—it is Sedition to write against it." Given such a view of things, the Federalists believed that the government could be criminally assaulted merely by political opinions that had the supposed tendency of lowering the public esteem of the administration. Security lay in the elimination of political criticism and the creation of a one-party press, eventually a one-party system. Thus the Sedition Act made criminal any "false" or "malicious" statements against the President (but not the Vice-President), Congress, or the "government"—i.e., the administration—with intent to defame or excite the people's animosity. The Federalists had deliberately exploited the crisis in foreign relations for the sake of partisan advantage. To Jefferson, Madison explained that "the loss of liberty at home is to be charged to provisions against danger real or pretended from abroad."

As actually applied by the federal judges—all Federalists—the Sedition Act made criticism of the administration the test of criminality. Even in the course of the House debates, advocates of the measure clearly stated that the political opinion of the Republican opposition was to be outlawed. But only one congressman, Mathew Lyon of Vermont, was tried and convicted. For the crime of having published an address to his constituents in which he accused Adams of a "continual grasp for power" and an "unbounded thirst for ridiculous pomp," he was sentenced to four months and fined $1000. Lyon's cruel treatment in jail was vividly described by the editor of one of the few Jeffersonian newspapers in New England, with the result that he too became a victim of the Sedition Act.

Altogether there were only about twenty-five arrests under the Sedition Act, fourteen indictments, and a dozen trials—all ending in conviction. Though few in number the prosecutions were selectively important, for among the victims were major Jeffersonian publicists like Thomas Cooper and the editors of four of the five leading Republican papers in the nation. The administration's sedition-net also closed around several minor journalists and a few village radicals. In one farcical case a town drunk, upon hearing

a sixteen-gun salute in honor of the President who had just passed by, re-
marked: "I do not care if they fired through his ass." Another potential
Robespierre who was jailed was the itinerant speaker who so fired his
Dedham audience that they put up a liberty pole with a sign proclaiming:

> No Stamp Act, No sedition, No Alien Bills,
> No Land Tax; downfall to the Tyrants of
> America, peace and retirement to the
> President, Long Live the Vice President
> and the Minority.

The speaker and a local farmer who raised the liberty pole were convicted
for having erected a "rallying point of insurrection and civil war."

Despite these prosecutions the repressive impact of the Sedition Act has
been exaggerated. Countless citizens guarded their political expressions, but
the "witchhunt" and "reign of terror" decried by the Republicans existed
more by Federalist intention than by execution. Harassed Republican politicians and journalists simply refused to be intimidated and their popular support in the Middle Atlantic states and especially in the South was so great
that the administration did not dare close their presses or tamper with free
elections. By the time of the election of 1800 the number of Jeffersonian
newspapers had even increased substantially, in spite of the Sedition Act—
or perhaps because of it, as well as because of the high taxes accompanying
brink-of-war defense policies. The Sedition Act was a measure of abortive
tyranny. Its failure might have been predicted by any astute politician when
Congressman Lyon, its first victim, was re-elected while in prison.

The policies of the government—high taxes (even a stamp tax), repression,
a standing army—convinced Old Dominion leaders of the need to resist
another "Anglo-monarchic-aristocratic-military government." The nation
must be roused to the danger, brought to its senses. Mass petitions of protest
from many states were deluging Congress, but a more effective, statesmanly
appeal must be made to the voters. The device hit upon by Jefferson was
the adoption of formal resolutions by state legislatures. In *The Federalist*
Hamilton himself had once argued that the states were "bodies of perpetual
observation . . . capable of forming and conducting plans of regular opposition" should the central government exceed its powers and invade constitutional rights. The Vice-President secretly framed a series of resolutions which
were adopted by the legislature of Kentucky in November, 1798; a month
later Virginia passed companion resolutions drawn by James Madison.

The Kentucky and Virginia Resolves were classic expressions of the Republican creed. They consisted of a spirited denunciation of Federalist policies, particularly the Alien and Sedition Acts, a defense of civil liberties and of
the rights of a peaceable opposition, and an eloquent restatement of the
most orthodox American constitutional theory, based on the concept of
limited government. In a word they expressed the view that man is free because the government is not, is limited, rather, by regularized restraints upon
power. What was controversial about the resolutions was their assertion that
each state retained the right to judge for itself whether the central govern-

ment had exceeded its powers. The other states, which were invited to join in a declaration of the unconstitutionality of the Alien and Sedition Acts, either responded adversely or not at all. In the Southern states, where public opinion was agitated by the XYZ disclosures, a discreet silence was maintained rather than give the appearance of national disunity. In the North, where the Federalists viewed the Resolutions as little short of a declaration of war against the Union, the state legislatures censured their erring Southern sisters, defended Congressional policies, and maintained that the federal judiciary was the proper body to judge infractions of the Constitution—although judicial review over Congress was not yet established. A Supreme Court decision against the Sedition Act would have been welcomed by the Jeffersonians, obviating the need for their Resolutions; but the members of the Court, on circuit duty, had been enforcing the dread statute.

The disheartening state responses impelled counter-responses, lest silence be construed as the abandonment of doctrines considered vital for the preservation of constitutional liberty. The Second Kentucky Resolves, penned by Jefferson, contained the proposition that state "nullification" was the rightful remedy for an unconstitutional act of Congress. In later years Calhoun was to subvert the constitutional theories of Jefferson and Madison when he adopted them for a defense of slavery, whereas they had been reluctantly driven to "nullification" and "interposition" in defense of human rights.

General Alexander Hamilton, who was in actual command of the army, was certain—and even hopeful—that the Virginia Jacobins were about to rise in insurrection. Given the opportunity to "subdue a *refractory* and *powerful* State," he would head the army for Virginia, enforce the national laws, and "put Virginia to the Test of resistance." Hamilton, even before the XYZ disclosures that "delighted" him, had become the principal architect of American foreign and domestic policy because of his influence on the Federalist party and his control over a Cabinet which was disloyal to Adams. As soon as the United States was armed, Hamilton, echoed by his ultra-Federalist followers, wanted war, preferably as a result of French attack. War would unify the nation, make possible the execution of traitors and the electoral destruction of the opposition party, and in the event of "internal disorder" would justify the "subdivision" of Virginia into small states that could not menace the central government. A large army, whose officers were carefully screened for party loyalty, was the *sine qua non* of his plans. He got that army, although both he and it had to be "crammed" down Adams' throat by the Cabinet and Washington, the titular commander.

Virginia, however, failed to oblige Hamilton by rebellion, and Napoleon was equally uncooperative. As early as October, 1798, Adams had predicted that there was "no more prospect of seeing a French army here than there is in Heaven." As for General Hamilton's fellow citizens, only a few Pennsylvania farmers armed to resist payment of direct taxes for the army, and they fired merely dirty looks when "conquered" by four brigades. What little satisfaction could be gained when the leaders of "Fries's Rebellion" were sentenced to death for treason was robbed by Adams' pardon.

Notwithstanding disappointments Hamilton envisioned military glories and conquests more grandiose than those of the Conquistadors. His army was not to be unused. Adams justifiably thought of him as an "artful, indefatigable and unprincipled intriguer," while a Republican journalist shrewdly wrote, "When a *little Alexander* dreams himself to be ALEXANDER THE GREAT . . . he is very apt to fall into miserable intrigues." Hamilton's plan, in which he was joined by Rufus King, the American minister in Great Britain, and Timothy Pickering, the Secretary of State, was the conquest and annexation of Louisiana and the Floridas. Even "the riches of Mexico and Peru," perhaps all of Latin America, beckoned invitingly for a liberator. Spain, the hapless ally of France, was to be despoiled, France herself forestalled from expansion in the Americas. Great Britain, in alliance with the United States, would provide the naval cover, while the United States would furnish the whole land force. "The command in this case," Hamilton modestly confided to Ambassador King, "would naturally fall upon me, and I hope I shall disappoint no favorable expectation." The British were ready to cooperate; Miranda, a South American revolutionary, promised the aid of his insurrectionary constituents; Pickering and McHenry, the Secretary of War, consented; and Hamilton, who did not recognize a real traitor when confronted by one, had enlisted the western commander, General Wilkinson, in the plan—Wilkinson who was a spy in the pay of Spain! All was in readiness, but John Adams had been ignored.

In February, 1799, the President stunned the country, his Cabinet, the Congress, and most of all, Hamilton and the ultra-Federalists, by announcing his intention to make peace with France. Making public a letter from Talleyrand which stated France's desire to end "existing differences" and assured that an envoy would be received on the President's own terms, "with the respect due to the representative of a free, independent, and powerful nation," Adams nominated an envoy. Disbelief soured into consternation and rage among the Hamiltonians. Their leader had planned for a declaration of war by August, but peace with France signaled the end of everything— the crisis psychology which they had manipulated for party gain, the plans for new defense measures and more taxes, the thrilling little naval war that raged at sea, the British alliance, the glorious prospects of military conquest, the army itself, the expectation of victory in the next election. All fizzled like a soggy firecracker. Hamilton still wanted "to squint at South America," but the best that he and his followers could do was delay negotiations, first by pressing for a three-man mission, then by intriguing against the departure of the envoys. The President finally issued a personal order for their sailing and did all but place them aboard himself.

In later years he wrote, "I desire no other inscription over my gravestone than: 'Here lies John Adams, who took upon himself the responsibility of the peace with France . . .'" His bold and courageous stroke, placing country above partisanship, earned him the enmity of the ultras whose factiousness split the party and cost Adams his re-election. But the triumph of Jefferson and the restoration of national sanity represented the triumph of moderation. In that sense the triumph belonged also to Adams himself, a flinty, principled old patriot whom the British ambassador admitted was the last man to be "bullied into measures which he does not approve."

DOCUMENTS

1] Federalist Warnings of Invasion and Subversion

A] CONGRESSMAN HARPER CAUTIONS AGAINST PHILOSOPHERS

A brilliant and rabid partisan, Robert Goodloe Harper of South Carolina was chairman of the House Committee on Ways and Means and an author of the Sedition Act. A former leader of the Charlestown Jacobin Club, he adopted the aristocratic cause with all the enthusiasm of a convert. One of the most frequent and abusive Federalist speakers in Congress, he here replies to the Gallatin who had opposed the unrestricted arming of merchant ships.*

. . . LET NOT gentlemen, therefore, Mr. Chairman, accuse us of too much jealousy, when we zealously oppose these attempts, and charge them with supporting principles which lead to the utter overthrow of the Constitution. I view their principles in that light; and in this view I am fully confirmed by the most mature reflection, not only on the consequences of those principles, but on the manner in which they have been introduced and supported here.

But, say gentlemen, what interest can we have to subvert the Constitution? Why should we harbor designs of overthrowing the Government, and introducing anarchy and confusion? Have we not as much at stake, as much to lose, as you? Have we not equally concurred in the establishment of this Government? And what inducement can we have to wish for its destruction?

Since gentlemen, Mr. Chairman, make this appeal to their motives, I must be permitted to offer a few observations on that subject, before I dilate, as it is my intention to do, on the object and tendency of their political system. . . . For revolutions, Mr. Chairman, are brought about in all countries by three descriptions of men; philosophers, jacobins, and *sans-culottes*. They exist in all countries, and accordingly in all countries are to be found the materials of revolution; but they exist in different proportions, and according as these proportions are great or less in any country, so is the danger of revolution wherewith it is threatened.

The philosophers are the pioneers of revolution. They advance always in front, and prepare the way, by preaching infidelity, and weakening the respect of the people for ancient institutions. They are, for the most part, fanatics, of virtuous lives, and not unfrequently, of specious talents. They have always, according to the expression of an ancient writer, *"Satis eloquentia, parum sapientia;"* eloquence enough, but very little sense. They declaim with warmth on

* CONGRESSMAN HARPER CAUTIONS AGAINST PHILOSOPHERS: From the *Annals of Congress* (*Debates and Proceedings in the Congress of the United States*), 5 Cong., 2 Sess. (March 29, 1798), VIII, 1175–80.

the miseries of mankind, the abuses of government, and the vices of rulers; all of which they engage to remove, provided their theories should once be adopted. They talk of the perfectibility of man, of the dignity of his nature; and entirely forgetting what he is, declaim perpetually about what he should be. Thus they allure and seduce the visionary, the superficial, and the unthinking part of mankind. They are for the most part honest, always zealous, and always plausible, whereby they become exceedingly formidable. Of the three classes employed in the work of revolution, they are infinitely the most to be dreaded; for, until they have shaken the foundations of order, and infused a spirit of discontent and innovation into the community, neither the jacobins not the *sans-culottes* can produce any considerable effect. The army cannot find entrance until these forerunners have corrupted the garrison to open the gates. Of these men we, in this country, have enough and more than enough.

Of Jacobins we also have plenty. They follow close in the train of the philosophers, and profit by all their labours. This class is composed of that daring, ambitious, and unprincipled set of men, who, possessing much courage, considerable talents, but no character, are unable to obtain power, the object of all their designs, by regular means, and, therefore, perpetually attempt to seize it by violence. Tyrants when in power, and demagogues when out, they lay in wait for every opportunity of seizing on the Government, *per fas aut nefas,*[1] and for this purpose use all implements which come to their hands, neglect no means which promise success. Unable to enter at the door of the sheep-fold, they climb in at the windows, and devour the flock. Although they use the assistance of the philosophers in gaining entrance, they dread their honesty, their zeal, and their influence with the public, and accordingly the first use they make of power when they can obtain it, is to destroy the philosophers themselves.

As the philosophers are the pioneers, these men are the generals of the army of revolution; but both pioneers and generals are useless without an army; and, fortunately, the army does not exist in this country.

. . . We have Jacobins in plenty, and philosophers not a few; but while we are free from *sans-culottes,* and it is probable that the nature of our Government and the abundance of untilled land in our country will secure us from them for ages, we need not apprehend great danger. We ought, no doubt, to watch and withstand the enterprises of the pioneers and generals; but while they remain without troops they are not much to be dreaded.

Having made these observations on the purity of gentlemen's motives, observations which were due not only to candor and truth, but to the respect I feel for their personal characters, I hold myself at full liberty to explain the tendency of the present amendment, and of that system of policy whereof it is a part; and I mean not to impute any ill intentions to gentlemen when I declare, and attempt to prove, that this tendency is to the utter subversion of the present Government. It is my firm and most deliberate opinion, that the amendment now under consideration, and the principles of that system to which it belongs, lead directly to the introduction of anarchy and revolution in this country, and if not steadily opposed, must sooner or later produce that

---

1 *per fas aut nefas:* by right or wrong; *i.e.,* by any means.

effect. This opinion it is my purpose to support by the observations which I am about to offer; and it is by a full conviction of its truth that I have been induced to consider it as a most sacred duty, to combat the system at all times, and by all the means in my power.

B] SPEAKER DAYTON DEFINES THE DANGER

> Jonathan Dayton of New Jersey, who had been the youngest member of the Federal Convention, was Speaker of the House for the Fifth Congress. A former moderate, he joined the ultra-Federalist camp after the XYZ disclosures. In the following speech, which was triggered by Gallatin's opposition to a provisional army, Dayton brands the Republican leader as disloyal. Dayton himself was indicted for high treason in 1807 for complicity in the Burr conspiracy.*

... THE GENTLEMAN from Pennsylvania had now boldly erected his standard, and had invited all disposed like himself to rally round it. It was the ensign of opposition, not merely to the Administration or to the Government, but to the only effectual measures of protection, defence, and preservation: and what was the motto most proper to be engraved upon its party-colored field? ... "Weakness and Submission:" written, it was true, in faint characters, and with a trembling hand, but still too intelligible to escape observation. Let those who choose it resort to such a standard, but he should arrange himself under the opposite banners.

Having exhibited the tendency and character of the opposition to the principle of the bill, which the motion went entirely to destroy, he proceeded to remark with what art and industry the mover had labored to lull this country into a state of profound indifference, inactivity, and security. "I am not (says the member from Pennsylvania) apprehensive, for my own part, of an invasion." And why should that gentleman be under no apprehension from such an event? Was it that, secure in the perfect coincidence of the principles he avowed with those which actuated the furious hordes of democrats which threatened this country with subjugation, he felt a confidence of his own safety, even if they should overrun and revolutionize the States? Was it that, confiding in the remote distance of his residence from the seacoast, among the ridges of the Monongahela, he ... might, indeed, contemplate an invasion without alarm or apprehension; he might see, with the calmness of indifference, our dwellings burning, and might "laugh at our calamities and mock when our fears came upon us." ... It was known that the Directory must find employment for their armies, or that the armies would find employment for the Directory, and that their safety consisted in their ridding themselves in any way of at least forty or fifty thousand of the most restless, daring, and ambitious spirits. The interest of the whole people of France was, therefore, one thing, and that of those who governed was another very different and opposite consideration. To transport to other countries the men to whom millions had been solemnly promised at the time of their discharge, and who

* SPEAKER DAYTON DEFINES THE DANGER: From the *Annals of Congress*, 5 Cong., 2 Sess. (May 10, 1798), VIII, 1676–78.

might, therefore, become importunate and dangerous at home, would be the interest, and must be the wish of the French Pentarchy, whose heads would otherwise be made to skip from their shoulders. This would be their interest, even where there might be little prospect of success for the transported army, because the object would be equally answered, whether they should succeed and provide for themselves in a foreign country, or be vanquished and utterly destroyed.

As to the power and the means of invasion, it was known, he said, that there were already collected upon the coasts of France, bordering upon the English channel, a numerous army which, in gasconading style, was called the "Army of England." It was known that there were also collected and collecting at the various ports in that quarter, ships of war and transports of all descriptions. The same soldiers who were prepared to invade an island might certainly be employed upon the Main, and the same bayonets would pierce the breasts of the people inhabiting the latter as the former. Their larger transports, their frigates, their larger ships cut down and armed *en flute,* and their ships-of-the-line, might transport a considerable part of them across the Atlantic, and land them upon our shores, and would very possibly be thus employed in the event of a peace in Europe, or of their abandoning, from any cause whatever, their project against England. But the member from Pennsylvania, aware of the possibility of the attempt, had endeavored to divert the country from immediate preparation by the assurance that we should have timely intelligence of such a design, if it should be contemplated, and here, Mr. D. said, he entirely differed from that gentleman. As the same men, arms, artillery, and military stores, were calculated as well for the one expedition as the other; and as there was a sufficiency of shipping calculated for the navigation of the Atlantic, it would follow that there would be nothing in their preparations to evidence a change of purpose, and a design against the United States, but the additional quantity of provisions shipped in which it would not be easy to detect them, or certainly not possible to do it in season. . . .

c] "A Great Body of Domestic Traitors"

The *Gazette of the United States,* published in the capital city of Philadelphia by John Fenno, was the leading Federalist paper in the United States. Subsidized by members of the party, it was the semiofficial organ of Federalism and waged a daily battle against the "monster of Jacobinism." No newspaper in the country surpassed its viciousness nor did more to create an atmosphere of hysteria.*

We have authentic information from Europe, and have authority to state, that unless we unite as a band of brothers in defence of our independence, we shall be called to witness, and that soon, an open attempt to reduce us to the same disgrace and ruin, as the Swiss, Dutch and other free nations have experienced under the domination of the French in consequence of their attachment to foreign nations and internal divisions.

* "A great body of domestic traitors": From the *Gazette of the United States* (June 9, 1798).

The Directory have undoubtedly settled their plan respecting America, and this plan is not consistent with a reception of our Envoys and an accommodation of differences. They have been informed by their own agents who have been in this country, and by our own citizens, that we are a divided people; that our government does not possess the hearts of our citizens; that the great body of people are displeased with their rulers, and passionately attached to France; and that they could make a fourth of Sept. at Philadelphia with as much ease as at Paris. (Our readers will recollect this was the arrest and banishment of Barthelemy and Pichegru—The declaration, when uttered in plain language, is that, with the help of their friends and agents here, they could seize President Adams, the heads of departments and all the supporters of administration, send them into banishment, and put Jefferson, Madison, Monroe and Burr in their places.)

A Frenchman by the name of Bayard, who lately returned from America, has published his travels through the United States, which book has been printed in Paris, in which he says, 'That France wants only a footing upon the Continent to regulate the destinies of the United States.'

If any man can read these facts, without a glow of indignation, he must be a traitor to his country, and fitted to be the vile slave of a foreign despotism.

Our time, though delayed by the great projects of France in Europe, which occupy her forces, will certainly come, when we are to be invaded by a body of their troops, who are expected to be joined by their friends among us, our Jacobins, and when our 'destinies are to be regulated by the French Directory.' Our elections are to be annulled by an edict of some French commissary at the head of a few thousand foreign troops, and a great body of domestic traitors. These men will take possession of our forts and arsenals, as they have done in Switzerland, and we must receive a constitution of government from Paris, as the Dutch and Swedes have been compelled to do—This project is unquestionably settled in the French councils, and delayed only by the invasion of England and other revolutionary schemes. On these points we have to make up our minds and that very soon—We must soon be called upon to draw a line of distinction between patriots & traitors—to separate the wheat from the chaff.

D] "It Is Your Annihilation They Seek"

The political tract was a popular literary form in the eighteenth century. The anonymous author of *What Is Our Situation?*, a widely read tract, was Joseph Hopkinson, a young Federalist lawyer, later Congressman and federal judge, who is best remembered for composing "Hail Columbia," a patriotic anthem which was enthusiastically received in 1798.*

THE PEACE and safety of this country are assailed by two enemies mutually encouraging and enflaming each other. The FRENCH, who are invited to

---

* "IT IS YOUR ANNIHILATION THEY SEEK": From *What Is Our Situation and What Our Prospects? or A Demonstration of the Insidious Views of Republican France*, by an AMERICAN [Joseph Hopkinson] (1799), pp. 8, 29–30.

their hostility by an assurance that our Government is divided from the people, pursuing different wishes and different interests; and an INTERNAL FACTION, who finding themselves supported by the aggression and countenance of the French, aim at nothing short of universal uproar and plunder— These then are our foes—Let us understand them to be so, and no longer contend in the dark; no longer feel ourselves wasting away, and see our property and rights wrested from our hands, without knowing against whom we should repel the outrage, or to what point to direct our defence. These, AMERICANS, are the artful insidious foes that would really divide you from your best interests, that you may the more easily become their prey; that excite vile and groundless jealousies against your Government, that being no longer supported by you, it can no longer give you protection; and that conscious the strength of America is invincible when united, seek its overthrow by disunion. . . .

Believe me, Americans, the object of this faction is not to correct the abuses of government or defend your liberties: Your government despises such monitors, and you need no such defenders. They imagine and fabricate abuses that they may appear as the watchmen of your liberties—they roar about encroachments on your rights, that they may be looked up to as their guardians and vindicators; but although they would deceive you, they are not themselves deceived—they feel the vileness of their conduct, they understand the tendency of their measures, and the darkness of their views. It is the overthrow of your government and constitution, it is the disorder and ruin of your country, it is your annihilation as a nation, they seek.

E] THE PROPHECY OF JAMES WALKER, JR.

Omens and revelations, born of superstition and intolerance, spiced the news. During the frenzy over Jacobinism, it was not surprising that the Federalist press should publicize the frenetic forebodings of a five-year-old clairvoyant. "A little child shall lead them." *

A CHILD of James Walker, born blind, and only five years of age, is visited by crouds [*sic*] of people for his great sagacity and foresight. He foretold the coming, and the continuation of the Yellow Fever at York and Philadelphia last season, and also the present scarcity of bread in Europe.

He says that before the year 1803, the Jacobins are to swarm in this country to overthrow our present government, and to put to death all the Clergy and the religious of both sexes. That having effected this revolution, they will then fall out for the supremacy, and finally destroy each other with the sword; after which the present government will again be restored, and the country flourish for one hundred years, &c.

* THE PROPHECY OF JAMES WALKER, JR.: Extract of a Letter from Vermont. From the *Gazette of the United States* (June 4, 1800).

2] Congress Debates Loyalty-Security Measures

A] LIVINGSTON CALLS FOR RESISTANCE TO TYRANNY

Edward Livingston, a member of one of New York's most distinguished families, began his political career as a staunch Jeffersonian congressman. He was subsequently mayor of New York, senator from Louisiana, Secretary of State under Jackson, and one of the world's foremost penal reformers. The following extract is from his powerful speech against the Alien Act.*

... THE STATE of things, if we are to judge from the complexion of the bill, must be, that a number of aliens, enjoying the protection of our Government, were plotting its destruction; that they are engaged in treasonable machinations against a people who have given them an asylum and support, and that there is no provision to provide for their expulsion and punishment. If these things are so, and no remedy exists for the evil, one ought speedily to be provided, but even then it must be a remedy that is consistent with the Constitution under which we act; for, as by that instrument all powers not expressly given by it to the Union are reserved to the States; it follows that, unless an express authority can be found, vesting us with the power, be the evil ever so great, it can only be remedied by the several States who have never delegated the authority to Congress. But this point will be presently examined, and it will not be a difficult task to show that the provisions of this bill are not only unauthorized by the Constitution, but are in direct violation of its fundamental principles, and contradictory to some of its most express prohibitions; at present, it is only necessary to ask whether the state of things contemplated by the bill have any existence.

We must legislate upon facts, not on surmises; we must have evidence, not vague suspicions, if we meant to legislate with prudence. What facts have been produced? What evidence had been submitted to the House? I have heard, sir, of none; but if evidence of facts could not be procured, at least it might have been expected that reasonable cause of suspicion should be shown. Here, again, gentlemen were at fault; they could not show even a suspicion why aliens ought to be suspected. . . .

The first section provides, that it shall be lawful for the President "to order all such aliens as he shall judge dangerous to the peace and safety of the United States, or shall have reasonable grounds to suspect are concerned in any treasonable or secret machinations against the Government thereof, to depart out of the United States, in such time as shall be expressed in such order." . . . by it the President alone is empowered to make the law, to fix in his mind what acts, what words, what thoughts or looks, shall constitute the crime contem-

* LIVINGSTON CALLS FOR RESISTANCE TO TYRANNY: From the *Annals of Congress*, 5 Cong., 2 Sess. (June 21, 1798), VIII, 2006–14.

plated by the bill, that is, the crime of being "suspected to be dangerous to the peace and safety of the United States." He is not only authorized to make this law for his own conduct, but to vary it at pleasure, as every gust of passion, every cloud of suspicion, shall agitate or darken his mind. The same power that formed the law, then, applies it to the guilty or innocent victim, whom his own suspicions, or the secret whisper of a spy, have designated as its object. The President, then, having made the law, the President having construed and applied it, the same President is by the bill authorized to execute his sentence, in case of disobedience, by imprisonment during his pleasure. This, then, comes completely within the definition of despotism—an union of Legislative, Executive, and Judicial powers. But this bill, sir, does not stop here, its provisions are a refinement upon despotism, and present an image of the most fearful tyranny. Even in despotisms, though the monarch legislates, judges, and executes, yet he legislates openly; his laws, though oppressive, are known; they precede the offence, and every man who chooses may avoid the penalties of disobedience. Yet he judges and executes by proxy, and his private interests or passions do not inflame the mind of his deputy.

But here, the law is so closely concealed in the same mind that gave it birth —the crime is "exciting the suspicions of the President," but no man can tell what conduct will avoid that suspicion—a careless word, perhaps misrepresented, or never spoken, may be sufficient evidence; a look may destroy, an idle gesture may insure punishment; no innocence can protect, no circumspection can avoid the jealousy of suspicion; surrounded by spies, informers, and all that infamous herd which fatten under laws like this, the unfortunate stranger will never know either of the law, of the accusation, or of the judgment, until the moment it is put in execution; he will detest your tyranny, and fly from a land of desolators, inquisitions, and spies.

. . . Now, sir, what minute article in these several provisions of the Constitution is there that is not violated by this bill? All the bulwarks which it opposed to encroachments, fall before personal liberty, fall before this engine of oppression.

Judiciary power is taken from courts, and given to the Executive, the previous safeguard of a presentment by a grand inquest is removed; the trial by jury is abolished; the "public trial" required by the Constitution is changed into a secret and worse than inquisitorial tribunal; instead of giving "information on the nature and cause of the accusation," the criminal, ignorant of his offence and the danger to which he is exposed, never hears of either until the judgment is passed and the sentence is executed; instead of being "confronted with his accusers," he is kept alike ignorant of their names and their existence; and even the forms of a trial being dispensed with, it would be a mockery to talk of "proofs for witnesses," or the "assistance of counsel for defence"—thus are all the barriers which the wisdom and humanity of our country had placed between accused innocence and oppressed power, at once forced and broken down. Not a vestige even of their form remains. No indictment; no jury; no trial; no public procedure; no statement of the accusation; no examination of the witnesses in its support; no counsel for defence; all is darkness, silence, mystery, and suspicion. But, as if this were not enough, the unfortunate victims of this law are told in the next section, that if they can convince the President that his suspicions are unfounded, he may, if he pleases, give them a license to stay; but, how remove his suspicions, when they know not on what act they were founded? Miserable mockery of justice! appoint an arbitrary Judge armed with Legislative and Executive powers added to his own! let him condemn the unheard, the unaccused object of his suspicion; and, then, to cover the injustice of the scene, gravely tell him, you ought not to complain—you need only disprove facts that you have never heard—remove suspicions that have never been communicated to you; it will be easy to convince your Judge, whom you shall not approach, that he is tyrannical and unjust; and, having done this, we give him the power he had before, to pardon you, if he pleases.

So obviously do the Constitutional objections present themselves, that their existence cannot be denied. . . . I now ask, sir, whether the people of America are prepared for this? Whether they are willing to part with all the means which the wisdom of their ancestors discovered, and their own caution so lately adopted, to secure their own persons? Whether they are ready to submit to imprisonment or exile whenever suspicion, calumny, or vengeance, shall mark them for ruin? Are they base enough to be prepared for this? No, sir; they will, I repeat it, they will resist this tyrannic system; the people will oppose it—the States will not submit to its operation. They ought not to acquiesce, and I pray to God they never may.

My opinions, sir, on this subject, are explicit, and I wish they may be known; they are, that whenever our laws manifestly infringe the Constitution under which they were made, the people ought not to hesitate which they should obey. If we exceed our powers, we become tyrants, and our acts have no effect. Thus, sir, one of the first effects of measures such as this, if they be not acquiesced in, will be disaffection among the States, and opposition among the people to your Government—tumults, violations, and a recurrence to first revolutionary principles. If they are submitted to, the consequences will be worse. After such manifest violation of the principles of our Constitution, the form will not long be sacred; presently, every vestige of it will be lost and swallowed up in the gulf of despotism. But, should the evil proceed no further than the execution of the present law, what a fearful picture will our country present! The system of *espionage* being thus established, the country will swarm with informers, spies, delators, and all that odious reptile tribe that breed in the sunshine of despotic power; that suck the blood of the unfortunate, and creep into the bosom of sleeping innocence, only to awake it with a burning wound. The hours of the most unsuspecting confidence, the intimacies of friendship, or the recesses of domestic retirement, afford no security. The companion whom you must trust, the friend in whom you must confide, the domestic who waits in your chamber, are all tempted to betray your imprudence or unguarded follies; to misrepresent your words; to convey them, distorted by calumny, to the secret tribunal where jealousy presides—where fear officiates as accuser, and suspicion is the only evidence that is heard.

b] Otis Replies to Livingston

A social lion and wealthy young aristocrat from Boston, Congressman Harrison Gray Otis was a member of the Federalist war faction and a confidante of Hamilton. But for a term in the Senate, he spent most of his political career in state and local politics and was the leader of the state rights movement in Massachusetts and head of the Hartford Convention.*

THE GENTLEMAN complains most piteously of the conduct of the House, in undertaking to legislate, without evidence, upon the question before them, and implores them not to make a breach in the Constitution upon mere surmises, and vociferates for the evidence of plots and conspiracies against the Government.

Mr. O. never understood that it was necessary to examine witnesses in the ordinary course of legislation, and the gentleman should recollect that, in these cases, the full evidence does not appear until the explosion; the proof consists in the catastrophe, and when the enemy is in possession of the citadel, it is too late to inquire by what means the mine was sprung. But, if the gentleman is still clamorous for evidence, let him look, said he, at the "Ruins of Empires;" let him recollect the literati and journalists, the agents, official and unofficial, that have been in this country. Who, said he, is the present Minister of Foreign Affairs in France? Has he not made the tour of this Continent; has he not been naturalized under our laws, received, cherished, and domesticated in our families? Have not the French, heretofore, pushed their intrigues into some of the first offices of our Government? Do not our bad citizens correspond with the agents of the Directory, and does not that Directory boast of its diplomatic means, and, of course, calculate on individuals here to give efficiency to those means? Are not, in short, he said, the victories of France, her influence, and facility in revolution-making, to be imputed to the system of espionage which she has so well digested, rather than to any other cause? Most undoubtedly they were, or history was unfaithful, and the concurrent testimony of thousands and the evidence of the senses were unworthy of trust.

Further than this, if the gentleman insisted upon evidence of seditious dispositions in our country, he would refer him to his own speech which he had just uttered. That gentleman had just preached up the duty of insurrection in his place; he had called upon the people to resist the laws. Never had he expected to hear this French doctrine enforced as orthodox upon that floor. He could hardly believe his own ears. Good God! exclaimed he, what society has that gentleman frequented? what books has he read? He could not believe that the gentleman was himself ready to resist the laws or join in an insurrection. These were not his own principles; they were, however, evidence of the contagion of the French mania. When a mind like that of the gentleman is so easily infected, no better evidence need be required of the necessity of purifying the country from the sources of pollution.

* OTIS REPLIES TO LIVINGSTON: From the *Annals of Congress*, 5 Cong., 2 Sess. (June 21, 1798), VIII, 2017–18.

c] ALLEN PROVES THE NEED OF A SEDITION ACT

"Long John" Allen, a formidable six-and-a-half-footer, was a fanatical xenophobe, ferocious in his appearance, temper, and opinions. The House's foremost champion of repressive legislation, he enjoyed a brief but sensational career as congressman from Connecticut.*

. . . I HOPE this bill will not be rejected. If ever there was a nation which required a law of this kind, it is this. Let gentlemen look at certain papers printed in this city and elsewhere, and ask themselves whether an unwarrantable and dangerous combination does not exist to overturn and ruin the Government by publishing the most shameless falsehoods against the Representatives of the people of all denominations, that they are hostile to free Governments and genuine liberty, and of course to the welfare of this country; that they ought, therefore, to be displaced, and that the people ought to raise an *insurrection* against the Government.

In the *Aurora,* of the 28th of June last, we see this paragraph: "It is a curious fact, America is making war with France for *not* treating, at the very moment the Minister for Foreign Affairs fixes upon the very day for opening a negotiation with Mr. Gerry. What think you of this, Americans!"

Such paragraphs need but little comment. The public agents are charged with crimes, for which, if true, they ought to be hung. The intention here is to persuade the people that peace with France is in our power; nay, that she is sincerely desirous of it, on proper terms, but that we reject her offers, and proceed to plunge our country into a destructive war.

This combination against our peace is extensive; it embraces characters whose stations demand a different course. Is this House free from it? Recollect what a few days ago fell from the very gentleman (MR. LIVINGSTON,) who now so boldly and violently calls on us to reject this bill at the instant of its coming before us, without suffering it to be read a second time. The gentleman proposed a resolution requesting the President to instruct Mr. Gerry to conclude a treaty with the French Government; and declared that "he believed a negotiation might be opened, and that it was probable a treaty might be concluded which it would be honorable to the United States to accept. He did not wish to frustrate so happy an event by any punctilio, because they had refused to treat with three Envoys, but were willing to treat with one." This is in the very spirit of the malicious paragraph I just now read. It is pursuing the same systematic course of operations. . . . I mention these things to show what false ideas gentlemen endeavor to impress the public mind with on this subject.

I will take the liberty of reading to the House another paragraph from the same paper; and it comes from high authority. It is published as the speech of the same gentleman, (MR. LIVINGSTON,) when we were discussing the Alien bill a few days since, and I presume is correct. It is a precious disclosure of the principles of certain gentlemen. I will read but a part of it. . . . This, sir, was

* ALLEN PROVES THE NEED OF A SEDITION ACT: From the *Annals of Congress,* 5 Cong., 2 Sess. (July 5, 1798), VIII, 2093–2100.

a foul calumny on the good people of the United States, or the gentleman has a more intimate acquaintance with treason and traitors than I had been ever in the habit of ascribing to him. It is too manifest to admit of doubt or denial that the intention and tendency of such principles, are to produce divisions, tumults, violence, insurrection, and blood, all which are intended by the fashionable doctrine of modern times, which the gentlemen terms "a recurrence to first revolutionary principles," from which may God preserve us. Do we want another revolution in this country? But, sir, that a revolution is intended, I hope to convince you before I sit down. In the Aurora, of last Friday, we read the following:

"The period is now at hand when it will be a question difficult to determine, whether there is more safety and liberty to be enjoyed at Constantinople or Philadelphia?"

This, sir, is faithfully pursuing the system of the gentleman in announcing to the poor deluded readers of the factious prints, the rapid approach of Turkish slavery in this country. Who can doubt the existence of a combination against the real liberty, the real safety of the United States? I say, sir, a combination, a conspiracy against the Constitution, the Government, the peace and safety of this country, is formed, and is in full operation. It embraces members of all classes; the Representative of the people on this floor, the wild and visionary theorist in the bloody philosophy of the day, the learned and ignorant. And the paper from which I have so often read, with three or four others, furnish demonstrations without number of the truth of the accusation. Each acts its part: but all are in perfect unison. . . .

In the Aurora, of last Tuesday, is this paragraph:

"Where a law shall have been passed in violation of the Constitution, making it criminal to expose the crimes, the official vices or abuses, or the attempts of men in power to usurp a despotic authority, is there any alternative between an abandonment of the Constitution and resistance?"

The gentleman (Mr. Livingston) makes his proclamation of war on the Government in the House on Monday, and this infamous printer (Bache) follows it up with the tocsin of insurrection on Tuesday. While this bill was under consideration in the Senate, an attempt is made to render it odious among the people. "Is there any alternative," says this printer, "between an abandonment of the Constitution and resistance?" He declares what is unconstitutional, and then invites the people to "resistance." This is an awful, horrible example of "the liberty of opinion and freedom of the press." Can gentlemen hear these things and lie quietly on their pillows? Are we to see all these acts practised against the repose of our country, and remain passive? Are we bound hand and foot that we must be witnesses of these deadly thrusts at our liberty? Are we to be the unresisting spectators of these exertions to destroy all that we hold dear? Are these approaches to revolution and Jacobinic domination, to be observed with the eye of meek submission? No, sir, they are indeed terrible; they are calculated to freeze the very blood in our veins. Such liberty of the press and of opinion is calculated to destroy all confidence between man and man; it leads to a dissolution of every bond of union; it cuts asunder every ligament that unites man to his family, man to his neighbor, man to society, and to Government. God deliver us from such liberty, the liberty of vomiting on the public floods of falsehood and hatred to everything sacred, human and divine! . . .

I wish there were no other species of writings which aim at the overthrow of this Government, and calculated to excite the deeds of death. But, sir, members of this body are in the habit of writing to their constituents things which they cannot justify; or there are men wicked enough to forge such letters, and send them in their names, either of which I contend, is highly evidential of those treasonable combinations and calumnies which this law is intended to prevent or punish. . . .

D] GALLATIN EXPOSES FEDERALIST OBJECTIVES

> A Swiss aristocrat by birth, but an American by choice and a democrat by conviction, Albert Gallatin was one of our greatest statesmen. An incisive debater with a grasp of constitutional law rivaled only by that of Madison (whom he succeeded as the leader of the Republican minority in 1797), Gallatin was the intellectual peer of any of his contemporaries. A genius in the field of public finance, he became Secretary of the Treasury (1801–14), and served with equal distinction as a diplomat. In the stormy days of 1798 Congressman Gallatin fearlessly condemned repressive measures in speeches that helped to broaden libertarian principles.*

MR. GALLATIN wished that the bill had been committed before any debate had taken place, as, in its present stage, any observations on details susceptible of amendment would be out of order; and he must now confine himself to the general question "Does the situation of the country, at this time, require that any law of this kind should pass? Do there exist such new and alarming symptoms of sedition, as render it necessary to adopt, in addition to the existing laws, any extraordinary measure for the purpose of suppressing unlawful combinations, and of restricting the freedom of speech and of the press? For such were the objects of the bill, whatever modifications it might hereafter receive.

The manner in which the principle of the bill had been supported, was perhaps more extraordinary still than the bill itself. The gentleman from Connecticut, (MR. ALLEN,) in order to prove the existence of a combination against the Constitution and Government, had communicated to the House—what? a number of newspaper paragraphs; and even most of those were such as would not be punishable by the bill as it now stands. The object of that gentleman in wishing a bill of this nature to pass, extended far beyond the intention of the Senate who had sent down this bill; far beyond, he would venture to say, the idea of any other member upon this floor, besides himself. His idea was to punish men for stating facts which he happened to disbelieve, or for enacting and avowing opinions, not criminal, but perhaps erroneous. Thus one of the paragraphs most obnoxious to the gentleman from Connecticut, was that in

* GALLATIN EXPOSES FEDERALIST OBJECTIVES: From the *Annals of Congress*, 5 Cong., 2 Sess. (July 5 and 10, 1798), VIII, 2107–10, 2162–64.

which the writer expresses his belief that Mr. Gerry may yet make a treaty with the French Government, his powers being sufficient for that purpose. . . . When a paragraph of this nature was held out as criminal, what writings, what opinions, could escape the severity of the intended law, which did not coincide with the opinions, and which might counteract the secret views of a prevailing party?

The gentleman from Connecticut had also quoted an extract of a letter said to be written by a member of Congress from Virginia, and published in last Saturday's Aurora. The style and composition of that letter did the highest honor to its writer. It contained more information and more sense, and gave more proofs of a sound understanding and strong mind, than ever the gentleman from Connecticut had displayed, or could display on this floor. So far he would venture to say, although he had given but a cursory reading to the letter, and he was altogether at a loss to know what was criminal in it, though he might easily see why it was obnoxious. Was it erroneous or criminal to say that debts and taxes were the ruinous consequences of war? Or that some members in both Houses of Congress uniformly voted in favor of an extension of the powers of the Executive, and of every proposed expenditure of money? Was it not true? . . . Look at the laws passed during this session. Look at the alien bill, at the provisional army bill, look at the prodigious influence acquired by so many new offices, and then deny that the powers of the Executive have not been greatly increased. As to the increased rate of expenditure, and the propensity of these gentlemen to vote money, they would not themselves deny it. Was it criminal to say that the Executive is supported by a party? when gentlemen declared that it must be supported by a party. When the doctrine had been avowed on this floor that men of a certain political opinion, alone ought to be appointed to offices; and when the Executive had now adopted and carried into practice that doctrine in its fullest extent?

Mr. G. acknowledged that some of the newspaper paragraphs quoted by Mr. Allen were of a very different nature from that letter. . . . Yet in almost every one of them there was a mixture of truth and error; and what was the remedy proposed by the gentleman from Connecticut, in order to rectify and correct error? Coercion: a law inflicting fine and imprisonment for the publication of erroneous opinions.

Was the gentleman afraid, or rather was Administration afraid, that in this instance error could not be successfully opposed by truth? The American Government had heretofore subsisted, it had acquired strength, it had grown on the affection of the people, it had been fully supported without the assistance of laws similar to the bill now on the table. It had been able to repel opposition by the single weapon of argument. And at present, when out of ten presses in the country nine were employed on the side of Administration, such is their want of confidence in the purity of their own views and motives, that they even fear the unequal contest, and require the help of force in order to suppress the limited circulation of the opinions of those who did not approve all their measures. One of the paragraphs says, that it will soon become a question whether there will be more liberty at Philadelphia or Constantinople. The gentleman from Connecticut bitterly complains of this, as insinuating that some persons in Government intend to establish a despotic power; and in order to convince the writer of his error, that gentleman not only supports the bill, but avows principles perfectly calculated to justify the assertions contained in the paragraph. . . .

And how has that seditious spirit been exhibited? The only evidences brought by the supporters of this bill consist of writings expressing an opinion that certain measures of Government have been dictated by an unwise policy, or by improper motives, and that some of them were unconstitutional. This bill and its supporters suppose, in fact, that whoever dislikes the measures of Administration and of a temporary majority in Congress, and shall, either by speaking or writing, express his disapprobation and his want of confidence in the men now in power, is seditious, is an enemy, not of Administration, but of the Constitution, and is liable to punishment. That principle, Mr. G. said, was subversive of the principles of the Constitution itself. If you put the press under any restraint in respect to the measures of members of Government; if you thus deprive the people of the means of obtaining information of their conduct, you in fact render their right of electing nugatory; and this bill must be considered only as a weapon used by a party now in power, in order to perpetuate their authority and preserve their present places.

. . . the bill now under discussion justified the suspicions of those who, at the time of the adoption of the Constitution, had apprehended that the sense of that generally expressed clause might be distorted for that purpose. It was in order to remove these fears, that the amendment, which declares that Congress shall pass no law abridging the freedom of speech or the liberty of the press, was proposed and adopted—an amendment which was intended as an express exception to any supposed general power of *passing laws,* &c., vested in Congress by the other clause. The sense in which he and his friends understood this amendment, was that Congress could not pass any law to punish any real or supposed abuse of the press. The construction given to it by the supporters of the bill was, that it did not prevent them to punish what they called the licentiousness of the press, but merely forbade their laying any previous restraints upon it. It appeared to him preposterous to say, that to punish a certain act was not an abridgement of the liberty of doing that act. It appeared to him that it was an insulting evasion of the Constitution for gentlemen to say, "We claim no power to abridge the liberty of the press; *that,* you shall enjoy unrestrained. You may write and publish what you please, but if you publish anything against us, we will punish you for it. So long as we do not prevent, but only punish your writings, it is no abridgment of your liberty of writing and printing." Congress were by that amendment prohibited from passing any law abridging, &c.; they were, therefore, prohibited from adding any restraint, either by previous restrictions, or by subsequent punishment, or by any alteration of the proper jurisdiction, or of the mode of trial, which did not exist before; in short, they were under an obligation of leaving that subject where they found it—of passing no law, either directly or indirectly, affecting that liberty.

. . . Whilst, therefore, they [the Federalists] support the bill in its present shape, do they not avow that the true object of the law is to enable one party to oppress the other; that they mean to have the power to punish printers who may publish against them, whilst their opponents will remain alone, and without redress, exposed to the abuse of Ministerial prints? Is it not their object to frighten and suppress all presses which they consider as contrary to their views; to prevent a free circulation of opinion; to suffer the people at large to hear only partial accounts, and but one side of the question; to delude and deceive them by partial information, and, through those means, to perpetuate themselves in power?

In vain did those gentlemen attempt to shelter themselves under the different pleas that this bill could only affect the authors of false publications, since any man might justify his writings by giving in evidence the truth of his assertions; and that it created no new offence, but only re-enacted what had always been the common law of libels.

It was true that, so far as related merely to facts, a man would be acquitted by proving that what he asserted was true. But the bill was intended to punish solely writings of a political nature, libels against the Government, the President, or either branch of the Legislature; and it was well known that writings, containing animadversions on public measures, almost always contained not only facts but opinions. And how could the truth of opinions be proven by evidence? If an individual thinking, as he himself did, that the present bill was unconstitutional, and that it had been intended, not for the public good, but solely for party purposes, should avow and publish his opinion, and if the Administration thought fit to prosecute him for that supposed individual offence, would a jury, composed of the friends of that Administration, hesitate much in declaring the opinion ungrounded, or, in other words, false and scandalous, and its publication malicious? And by what kind of argument or evidence, in the present temper of parties, could the accused convince them that his opinion was true?

3] The Sedition Act

Although the Constitution details treason as the levying of war against the United States or the giving of aid and comfort to the enemy in time of war—and although war had not been declared—the original version of the Sedition Act defined adherence to the French cause as treason, carrying a penalty of death. The final version, passed by only a three-vote majority in the House, ironically incorporated the principal demands of libertarian theorists since the Zenger trial of 1735: demonstration of malicious intent, truth as a defense, and the power of the jury to decide the criminality of the defendant as well as the fact of authorship.*

Section 1. *Be it enacted by the Senate and House of Representatives of the United States of America, in Congress assembled,* That if any persons shall unlawfully combine or conspire together, with intent to oppose any measure

---

* THE SEDITION ACT: "An act in addition to the act, entitled 'An act for the punishment of certain crimes against the United States.'" From the *Statutes at Large of the United States of America, 1789–1873* (Boston, 1845–73), I, 596–97.

or measures of the government of the United States, which are or shall be directed by proper authority, or to impede the operation of any law of the United States, or to intimidate or prevent any person holding a place or office in or under the government of the United States, from undertaking, performing or executing his trust or duty; and if any person or persons, with intent as aforesaid, shall counsel, advise or attempt to procure any insurrection, riot, unlawful assembly, or combination, whether such conspiracy, threatening, counsel, advice, or attempt shall have the proposed effect or not, he or they shall be deemed guilty of a high misdemeanor, and on conviction, before any court of the United States having jurisdiction thereof, shall be punished by a fine not exceeding five thousand dollars, and by imprisonment during a term not less than six months nor exceeding five years; and further, at the discretion of the court may be holden to find sureties for his good behaviour in such sum, and for such time, as the said court may direct.

Sec. 2. *And be it further enacted,* That if any person shall write, print, utter or publish, or shall cause or procure to be written, printed, uttered or published, or shall knowingly and willingly assist or aid in writing, printing, uttering or publishing any false, scandalous and malicious writing or writings against the government of the United States, or either house of the Congress of the United States, or the President of the United States, with intent to defame the said government, or either house of the said Congress, or the said President, or to bring them, or either of them, into contempt or disrepute; or to excite against them, or either or any of them, the hatred of the good people of the United States, or to stir up sedition within the United States, or to excite any unlawful combinations therein, for opposing or resisting any law of the United States, or any act of the President of the United States, done in pursuance of any such law, or of the powers in him vested by the constitution of the United States, or to resist, oppose, or defeat any such law or act, or to aid, encourage or abet any hostile designs of any foreign nation against the United States, their people or government, then such person, being thereof convicted before any court of the United States having jurisdiction thereof, shall be punished by a fine not exceeding two thousand dollars, and by imprisonment not exceeding two years.

Sec. 3. *And be it further enacted and declared,* That if any person shall be prosecuted under this act, for the writing or publishing any libel aforesaid, it shall be lawful for the defendant, upon the trial of the cause, to give evidence in his defence, the truth of the matter contained in the publication charged as a libel. And the jury who shall try the cause, shall have a right to determine the law and the fact, under the direction of the court, as in other cases.

Sec. 4. *And be it further enacted,* That this act shall continue and be in force until the third day of March, one thousand eight hundred and one, and no longer: *Provided,* that the expiration of the act shall not prevent or defeat a prosecution and punishment of any offence against the law, during the time it shall be in force.

Approved, July 14, 1798.

4] Thomas Cooper Is Tried for Sedition

Cooper was an intellectual Jack-of-all-trades and a master of most: lawyer, editor, politician, author of scholarly treatises on legal, religious, scientific and political subjects, judge, professor of chemistry, and college president. He began his political career as a radical but ended as a leader of the South Carolina nullification movement and a conservative Whig. At the time of his trial he had published a volume entitled *Political Essays* (1799) and was the editor of a Pennsylvania country newspaper frequently quoted by the Philadelphia *Aurora*. His judge was Samuel Chase of Maryland, a vindictive extirpator of Jeffersonian Jacobinism whose disgraceful behavior while presiding over sedition trials tarnished a brilliant career as a revolutionary patriot, a signer of the Declaration of Independence, and the most constructive member of the Supreme Court previous to Marshall. The Republicans, who regarded Chase as the "hanging judge" and compared him to England's notorious Judge "Bloody" Jeffreys, impeached him for his judicial crimes in 1804, but the Senate failed to convict.*

THE LIBELLOUS matter complained of was as follows:—

"Nor do I see any impropriety in making this request of Mr. Adams. At that time he had just entered into office; he was hardly in the infancy of political mistake; even those who doubted his capacity thought well of his intentions. Nor were we yet saddled with the expense of a permanent navy, or threatened, under his auspices, with the existence of a standing army. Our credit was not yet reduced so low as to borrow money at eight per cent. in time of peace, while the unnecessary violence of official expressions might justly have provoked a war. Mr. Adams had not yet projected his embassies to Prussia, Russia and the Sublime Porte, nor had he yet interfered, as President of the United States, to influence the decisions of a court of justice—a stretch of authority which the monarch of Great Britain would have shrunk from—an interference without precedent, against law and against mercy. This melancholy case of Jonathan Robbins, a native citizen of America, forcibly impressed by the British, and delivered up, with the advice of Mr. Adams, to the mock trial of a British court-martial, had not yet astonished the republican citizens of this free country; a case too little known, but of which the people ought to be fully apprised, before the election, and they shall be." . . .

Mr. Rawle opened the case to the jury . . . MR. COOPER then addressed the jury as follows:—

. . . But I hope, in the course of this trial, I shall be enabled to prove to your satisfaction, that I have published nothing which truth will not justify. That the assertions for which I am indicted are free from malicious imputation, and that my motives have been honest and fair. . . .

You, and all who hear me, well know that this country is divided, and al-

---

* THOMAS COOPER IS TRIED FOR SEDITION: "Trial of Thomas Cooper, for a Seditious Libel. In the Circuit Court of the United States for the Pennsylvania District. Philadelphia, 1800." From Francis Wharton, ed., *State Trials of the United States* (Philadelphia, 1849), pp. 659–79.

most equally divided, into two grand parties; usually termed, whether properly or improperly, *Federalists* and *Anti-Federalists*: and that the governing powers of the country are ranked in public opinion under the former denomination—of these divisions, the one wishes to increase, the other to diminish, the powers of the executive; the one thinks that the people (the democracy of the country) has too much, the other too little, influence on the measures of government: the one is friendly, the other hostile, to a standing army and a permanent navy: the one thinks them necessary to repel invasions and aggressions from without, and commotions within; the other, that a well-organized militia is a sufficient safeguard for all that an army could protect, and that a navy is more dangerous and expensive than any benefit derived from it can compensate; the one thinks the liberties of our country endangered by the licentiousness, the other, by the restrictions of the press. Such are some among the leading features of these notorious divisions of political party. It is evident, Gentlemen of the Jury, that each will view with a jealous eye the positions of the other, and that there cannot but be a bias among the partisans of the one side, against the principles and doctrines inculcated by the other. . . .

But in the present state of affairs, the press is open to those who will praise, while the threats of the law hang over those who blame the conduct of the men in power. Indiscriminate approbation of the measures of the executive is not only unattacked, but fostered, and received with the utmost avidity; while those who venture to express a sentiment of opposition must do it in fear and trembling, and run the hazard of being dragged like myself before the frowning tribunal, erected by the Sedition Law. Be it so; but surely this anxiety to protect public character must arise from fear of attack.—That conduct which will not bear investigation will naturally shun it; and whether my opinions are right or wrong, as they are stated in the charge, I cannot help thinking they would have been better confuted by evidence and argument than by indictment. Fines and imprisonment will produce conviction neither in the mind of the sufferer nor of the public.

Nor do I see how the people can exercise on rational grounds their elective franchise, if perfect freedom of discussion of public characters be not allowed. Electors are bound in conscience to reflect and decide who best deserves their suffrages; but how can they do it, if these prosecutions in *terrorem* close all the avenues of information, and throw a veil over the grossest misconduct of our periodical rulers?

After having offered these preliminary remarks, I shall give an account of the paper on which I am accused, and then proceed to examine the charges of the indictment. . . .

The first article selected for accusation is, that, at the time I allude to, *he was but in the infancy of political mistake.* Why this expression should have been fixed on as seditious, I know not, unless it be that *quem deus vult perdere prius dementat;* [1] for have we advanced so far on the road to despotism in this republican country, that we dare not say our President may be mistaken? Is a plain citizen encircled at once by the mysterious attribute of political infallibility

1 *quem deus vult perdere prius dementat*: Whom God would destroy, he first maddens.

the instant he mounts the presidential chair? If so, then indeed may it be seditious to say he is mistaken; but before you can condemn me for this kind of sedition, you must become catholic believers in this new-fangled doctrine of infallibility. I know that in England the king can do no wrong, but I did not know till now that the President of the United States had the same attribute.

I have said (and I am accused for saying it) *"that even those who doubted his capacity thought well of his intentions."* Is it a crime to doubt the capacity of the President? Suppose I had said that there were some who did not give him credit for capacity sufficient for the office he holds, is that a crime? Or if in them, is it a crime in me, who have not said it? . . .

Nor had we yet, under his auspices, been saddled with the expense of a permanent navy.

Gentlemen, is it true or not that we are saddled with the expense of a permanent navy? Is it necessary that I should enter into a detail of authorities to prove that the sun shines at noon-day? But farther, is true that we incur this expense under his auspices and sanction? . . .

Mr. Cooper then went on to argue at great length, from a copious collection from the public documents of the day, that the policy of the President had been to saddle upon the country a permanent navy and army, and to keep down the liberties of the citizens by his arbitrary interference in the case of Jonathan Robbins.

Judge CHASE then charged the jury as follows:—Gentlemen of the jury— When men are found rash enough to commit an offence such as the traverser is charged with, it becomes the duty of the government to take care that they should not pass with impunity. It is my duty to state to you the law on which this indictment is preferred, and the substance of the accusation and defence.

Thomas Cooper, the traverser, stands charged with having published a false, scandalous and malicious libel against the President of the United States, in his official character as President. There is no civilized country that I know of, that does not punish such offences; and it is necessary to the peace and welfare of this country, that these offences should meet with their proper punishment, since ours is a government founded on the opinions and confidence of the people. . . .

All governments which I have ever read or heard of punish libels against themselves. If a man attempts to destroy the confidence of the people in their officers, their supreme magistrate, and their legislature, he effectually saps the foundation of the government. A republican government can only be destroyed in two ways; the introduction of luxury, or the licentiousness of the press. This latter is the more slow, but most sure and certain, means of bringing about the destruction of the government. The legislature of this country, knowing this maxim, has thought proper to pass a law to check this licentiousness of the press: by a clause in that law it is enacted—(Judge C. here read the second section of the Sedition Law.)

It must, therefore, be observed, gentlemen of the jury, that the *intent* must be plainly manifest: it is an important word in the law; for if there is no such intent to defame, &c., there is no offence created by that law.

Thomas Cooper, then, stands indicted for having published a false, scandalous and malicious libel upon the President of the United States, with *intent* to defame the President, to bring him into contempt and disrepute, and to excite against him the hatred of the good people of the United States. This is the charge. The traverser has pleaded not guilty, and that he has not published, &c., with these views: he has also pleaded in justification (which the law provides for), that the matters asserted by him are true, and that he will give the same in evidence.

It is incumbent on the part of the prosecution to prove two facts:

1st. That the traverser did publish the matters contained in the indictment.

2d. That he did publish with intent to defame, &c. . . .

First, then, as to the publication.

The fact of writing and publishing is clearly proved: nay, in fact, it is not denied. . . . This conduct showed that he intended to dare and defy the government, and to provoke them, and his subsequent conduct satisfies my mind that such was his disposition. For he justifies the publication in all its parts, and declares it to be founded in truth: it is proved most clearly to be his publication. It is your business to consider the intent as coupled with that, and view the whole together. You must take that publication, and compare it with the indictment; if there are doubts as to the motives of the traverser, he has removed them; for, though he states in his defence that he does not arraign the motives of the President, yet he has boldly avowed that his own motives in this publication were to censure the conduct of the President, which his conduct, as he thought, deserved. . . .

Now we will consider this libel as published by the defendant, and observe what were his motives. You will find the traverser speaking of the President in the following words: "Even those who doubted his capacity, thought well of his intentions." This the traverser might suppose would be considered as a compliment as to the intentions of the President; but I have no doubt that it was meant to carry a sting with it which should be felt; for it was in substance saying of the President, "you may have good intentions, but I doubt your capacity."

He then goes on to say, "Nor were we yet saddled with the expense of a permanent navy, nor threatened, under his (the President's) auspices, with the existence of a standing army. Our credit was not yet reduced so low as to borrow money at eight per cent. in *time of peace.*" Now, gentlemen, if these things were true, can any one doubt what effect they would have on the public mind? If the people believed those things, what would be the consequence? What! the President of the United States saddle us with a permanent navy, encourage a standing army, and borrow money at a large premium? And are we told, too, that this is in time of peace? If you believe this to be true, what opinion can you, gentlemen, form of the President? One observation must strike you, viz.: That these charges are made not only against the President, but against yourselves who elect the House of Representatives, for these acts cannot be done without first having been approved of by Congress. Can a navy be built, can an army be raised, or money borrowed, without the consent of Congress?

The President is further charged for that "the unnecessary violence of his official expressions might *justly* have provoked a war." This is a very serious charge indeed: what, the President, by unnecessary violence, plunge this country into a war! and that a *just* war? It cannot be—I say, gentlemen, again, if you believe this, what opinion can you form of the President? Certainly the worst you can form: you would certainly consider him totally unfit for the high station which he has so honourably filled, and with such benefit to his country.

The traverser states that, under the auspices of the President, "our credit is so low that we are obliged to borrow money at eight per cent. in time of peace." I cannot suppress my feelings at this gross attack upon the President. Can this be true? Can you believe it? Are we now in time of peace? Is there no war? No hostilities with France? Has she not captured our vessels and plundred us of our property to the amount of millions? Has not the intercourse been prohibited with her? Have we not armed our vessels to defend ourselves, and have we not captured several of her vessels of war? Although no formal declaration of war has been made, is it not notorious that actual hostilities have taken place? And is this, then, a time of peace? The very expense incurred, which rendered a loan necessary, was in consequence of the conduct of France. The traverser, therefore, has published an untruth, knowing it to be an untruth. . . .

The traverser goes on thus—"This melancholy case of Jonathan Robbins, a native of America, forcibly impressed by the British, and delivered, with the advice of Mr. Adams, to the mock trial of a British court-martial, had not yet astonished the republican citizens of this free country. A case too little known, but of which the people ought to be fully apprised before the election, and they SHALL be." Now, gentlemen, there are circumstances in this publication which greatly aggravate the offence. The traverser does not only tell you that the President interfered to influence a court of justice without precedent against law and against mercy; but that he so interfered in order to deliver up a native American citizen to be executed by a British court-martial *under a mock trial,* against law and against mercy. Another circumstance is adduced to complete the picture. He tells you that this Robbins was not only an American, but a native American, forcibly impressed by the British; and yet that the President of the United States, without precedent, against law and against mercy, interfered with a court of justice, and ordered this native American to be delivered up to a mock trial by a British court-martial. I can scarcely conceive a charge can be made against the President of so much consequence, or of a more heinous nature. But, says Mr. Cooper, he has done it; I will show you the case in which he has done it; it is the case of Jonathan Robbins. It appears then that this is a charge on the President, not only false and scandalous, but evidently made with intent to injure his character, and the manner in which it is made is well calculated to operate on the passions of Americans, and I fear such has been the effect. . . . Here, then, the evident design of the traverser was, to arouse the people against the President so as to influence their minds against him on the next election. I think it right to explain this to you, because it proves, that the traverser was actuated by improper motives to make this charge against the President. It is a very heavy charge, and made with intent to bring the President into contempt and disrepute, and excite against him the hatred of the people of the United States. . . .

Take this publication in all its parts, and it is the boldest attempt I have known to poison the minds of the people. He asserts that Mr. Adams has countenanced a navy, that he has brought forward measures for raising a standing army in the country. The traverser is certainly a scholar, and has shown himself a man of learning, and has read much on the subject of armies. But to assert, as he has done, that we have a standing army in this country, betrays the most egregious ignorance, or the most wilful intentions to deceive the public. We have two descriptions of armies in this country—we have an army which is generally called the Western army, enlisted for five years only —can this be a standing army? Who raises them? Congress. Who pays them? The people. We have also another army, called the provisional army, which is enlisted during the existence of the war with France—neither of these can, with any propriety, be called a standing army. In fact, we cannot have a standing army in this country, the Constitution having expressly declared that no appropriation shall be made for the support of an army longer than two years. Therefore, as Congress may appropriate money for the support of the army annually, and are obliged to do it only for two years, there can be no standing army in this country until the Constitution is first destroyed.

There is no subject on which the people of America feel more alarm, than the establishment of a standing army. Once persuade them that the government is attempting to promote such a measure, and you destroy their confidence in the government. Therefore, to say, that under the auspices of the President, we were saddled with a standing army, was directly calculated to bring him into contempt with the people, and excite their hatred against him.

It is too much to press this point on the traverser. But he deserves it. This publication is evidently intended to mislead the ignorant, and inflame their minds against the President, and to influence their votes on the next election. . . .

You will please to notice, gentlemen, that the traverser in his defence must prove every charge he has made to be true; he must prove it to the marrow. If he asserts three things, and proves but one, he fails; if he proves but two, he fails in his defence, for he must prove the whole of his assertions to be true. If he were to prove, that the President had done everything charged against him in the first paragraph of the publication—though he should prove to your satisfaction, that the President had interfered to influence the decisions of a court of justice, that he had delivered up Jonathan Robbins without precedent, against law and against mercy, this would not be sufficient, unless he proved at the same time, that Jonathan Robbins was a native American, and had been forcibly impressed, and compelled to serve on board a British ship of war. If he fails, therefore, gentlemen, in this proof, you must then consider whether his intention in making these charges against the President were malicious or not. It is not necessary for me to go more minutely into an investigation of the defence. You must judge for yourselves—you must find the publication, and judge of the intent with which that publication was made, whether it was malice or not? If you believe that he has published it without malice, or an

intent to defame the President of the United States, you must acquit him; if
he has proved the truth of the facts asserted by him, you must find him Not
Guilty.

After the jury had returned with a verdict of Guilty. . . . Mr. Cooper attended, and the court sentenced him to pay a fine of four hundred dollars;
to be imprisoned for six months, and, at the end of that period, to find surety
for his good behaviour, himself in a thousand, and two sureties in five hundred
dollars each.

5] Purging Disloyalty

A] COBBETT ON THE INVISIBLE JACOBIN MINE

> William Cobbett, publisher of *Porcupine's Gazette* and author of many
> political tracts, was the most talented of all Federalist editors, hated by the
> Jeffersonians for his incredibly savage scurrility and sardonic humor. He agi-
> tated for an English alliance, a war against France, and suppression of any-
> thing even remotely democratic.*

AN INVASION on the coast is a thing naturally to be expected, unless an alliance is formed with Great Britain; and from Louisiana or the Floridas is to
be expected, whether such an alliance takes place or not. This, then, would be
the *"case of URGENCY,"* and thus the conspirators would act. Before the first
panic would be over, the whole affiliation would be in movement. They would
thwart, threaten, or collect mobs; openly oppose, or secretly betray, just as it
suited their several situations. They are not visible now, but then they would
be seen and felt too. I make no doubt but they have members, in some capacity
or other, in every public department. I should not wonder if they had at this
time fifty in the different branches of the Post-office. Thus has it proved in
every country, which the infamous sans-culottes have invaded with success.
In Holland, for instance, few people feared the invaders. . . . But the for-
tresses fell, nobody could tell how; the French arrived as if it were *by appointment,* . . . the jacobin affiliation ran through all the United Provinces; its
members had crept into every department, civil and military; the mine was
completed, and, at the approach of the enemy it was sprung. Just so was it in
Italy, in Geneva, in Venice. . . .

* COBBETT ON THE INVISIBLE JACOBIN MINE: From *Detection of a Conspiracy Formed
By The United Irishmen, With the Evident Intention of Aiding the Tyrants of France in
Subverting the Government of the United States of America,* by Peter Porcupine [William
Cobbett] (May, 1798), p. 25 of 1799 ed.

B] WASHINGTON DISAPPROVES OF REPUBLICAN OFFICERS

Hamilton, playing Iago to the susceptible Washington, convinced him that
the Republicans would "go every length" with the French and "new-model
our Constitution . . . to make this country a province of France." Washington, in a letter to Lafayette, explained that the opposition party sought by
"Clogging its Wheels" to change the nature of the government "and to
Subvert the Constitution." It is not surprising, therefore, to find even the
moderate Washington, now the titular commanding general, recommending
against army commissions for Republicans.*

Mount Vernon, September 30, 1798.

DEAR SIR:

I have lately received information, which, in my opinion, merits attention.
It is that the brawlers against Governmental measures, in some of the most
discontented parts of this state, have, all of a sudden, become silent; and, it is
added, are very desirous of obtaining Commissions in the Army, about to be
raised.

This information did not fail to leave an impression upon my mind at the
time I received it; but it has acquired strength from a publication I have lately
seen in one of the Maryland Gazettes (between the Author of which and my
informant, there could have been no interchange of sentiments) to the same
effect. The motives ascribed to them are, that in such a situation they would
endeavour to divide, and contaminate the Army, by artful and seditious dis-
courses, and perhaps at a critical moment bring on confusion. What weight to
give to these conjectures you can judge of, as well as I. But, as there will be
characters enough of an opposite description, who are ready to receive appointments, circumspection is necessary; for my opinion of the first are, that you
could as soon scrub the blackamore white, as to change the principles of a
profest Democrat; and that he will leave nothing unattempted to overturn the
Government of this Country. Finding the resentment of the People at the
conduct of France too strong to be resisted, they have, in appearance, adopted
their sentiments; and pretend that, notwithstanding the misconduct of Government have brought it upon us, yet, if an Invasion should take place, it will
be found that *they* will be among the first to defend it. This is their story at
all Elections, and Election meetings, and told in many instances with effect. . . .

C] "SCRUTINIZE EVERY DEPARTMENT"

Noah Webster, the great lexicographer, was also a talented political pamphleteer, journalist, economist, and medical historian. His newspaper, the *Commercial Advertiser* of New York, supported President Adams after Fenno
and Cobbett had soured on him because of his peace policy. Webster, who

---

* WASHINGTON DISAPPROVES OF REPUBLICAN OFFICERS: To Secretary of War James Mc-
Henry. From John C. Fitzpatrick, ed., *The Writings of George Washington* (Washington, 1933–44), XXXVII, 474.

believed that any critic of the Sedition Act "deserves to be suspected," here advocates loyalty checks for government employees. His article begins with a description of the internal subversion that led to the overthrow of Naples.*

WHAT A lesson is this to all the governments, which by the protection of providence do yet exist!—Can any thing prove more strongly the necessity to scrutinize every department of Office, civil and military, but especially the latter?—to bring every man, as far as possible, to the ordeal, and where there is the smallest reason to suspect a collusion with the enemy, or a strong disposition to favor him, instantly to cashier the guilty person. No connection, no friendship, no consideration whatever, should screen the man, to whom the smallest suspicion is attached. But what shall we think, when there are many notorious characters fattening in public offices, at this awful crisis, who are unworthy of the smallest public trust even in times of profound peace.

Hear then, ye guardians of the public welfare!—Ye watchmen on the walls of our Zion!—and thou, great and much respected Chief! hear the voice of wisdom, speaking from the tombs of martyred monarchies and republics:

"PURGE YOUR COUNTRY, but especially all its Public Offices, BEFORE IT IS TOO LATE, OF DOMESTIC TRAITORS."

D] JACOBINISM IN CHILDREN'S BOOKS

Fenno's *Gazette* labored unremittingly to arouse the public against Jeffersonian policies and principles. Here, with unintended humor, the editor extends to fairy tales and primers his belief that all Jacobin ideas should be quarantined.†

. . . THE JACOBINS continue their criminal projects, undismayed by detection, unawed by defeat. . . . But, though not less desperate in their end, they display more caution and prudence in their means. Thus the difficulty of counteraction is enhanced, and the consequent necessity of increased vigilance and circumspection established. We are particularly anxious to press upon the attention of the public . . . the diffusion of Jacobinal principles, thro' the medium of Children's Books. This truly diabolical effort to corrupt the minds of the Rising Generation, to make them imbibe, with their very milk, as it were, the poison of atheism and disaffection, and so to contaminate the very sources of social order and social happiness, so to eradicate the very germs of public prosperity and public welfare, is strongly characteristic of the Genius of Jacobinism. . . .

Among the various modes of disseminating Jacobinism, or what directly leads to it, the principles of liberty and equality, there is one which, though in

---

* "SCRUTINIZE EVERY DEPARTMENT" From the *Commercial Advertiser* (June 4, 1799).
† JACOBINISM IN CHILDREN'S BOOKS: "Observations: Worthy the Attention of Parents." From the *Gazette of the United States* (June 4, 1800).

appearance may be less formidable, is no less pernicious in its tendency and
which has hitherto escaped your notice. It is well known what pains all writers
of that stamp, have taken to impress upon the minds of the young and unwary, the leading doctrines of their school, and under what artful disguises
and specious pretexts, they have endeavored to insinuate their poison into all
ranks and degrees of men. Even the misery is not exempt from the unremitting efforts of these disturbers of the human race. And the fact . . . will
shew the necessity of every parent's examining with care, every little penny-
book which may fall into the hands of their children, even of the most tender
age.

6] Federalist Schemes for War and Conquest

A] "Wage War, and Call It Self-Defence"

Fisher Ames, the "sage of Dedham," was probably the most charming and
cultivated reactionary in American history. A member of the first four Congresses, he retired from political office in 1796 because of ill health and an
icy contempt for the democratic process; but he remained enormously influential as the intellectual leader of the Essex Junto, the ultra-Federalist faction
in New England. Believing that the government must display its power "*in
terrorem*," Ames was instrumental in flushing out local disciples of the "devil
of sedition." In the following letter to Secretary of State Pickering he offers
a cynical stratagem for leading the "multitudes," whom he despised, into war
against France.*

. . . I CALCULATE on the eventual resort of Congress to measures of force.
Internal foes can do us twice as much harm as they could in an open war.
The hope of peace is yet strong enough to furnish the means of popular influence and delusion; at any rate, it chills the spirit of the citizens, and dis-
tracts them in the exercise of duty. I wish therefore, impatiently, to see Congress urged to proceed to steps which will have no such ambiguity in them.
A declaration of war would be such a step. But it is the very one that their
imbecility would reluct at; it is the very one that demands something like
unanimity. I think this very reluctance might be used to advantage. Instead
of *declaring* war in form, could they not be persuaded, even some of the
Demos, to *enact* penal laws, *as if* it was war? To do something short of duty,
something tamer than energy, suits the foible of the weak, temporizing, trim-
ming members.

I should imagine a number, who would flinch from a *declaration of war,*
would urge the enacting, one by one, the effects of a state of war. Not being
on the spot, I can judge only from my knowledge of some characters, and the

* "WAGE WAR, AND CALL IT SELF-DEFENCE": Fisher Ames to Timothy Pickering, July
10, 1798. From Seth Ames, ed., *Works of Fisher Ames* (Boston, 1854), I, 233–34.

color of their conduct and speeches; with such materials I may be deceived in my conclusion. I think it probable, however, that several votes could be gained for strong measures, from the dread of being urged to adopt still stronger. Energy is a word of comparison, and to vote *as if* we were in war, might seem a half-way business, compared with *a declaration* of war. In this way they may authorize the burning, sinking, and destroying French ships and property *gradatim,* till no case is left which is to shelter them from hostility. As every armed French vessel takes our vessels, every armed French vessel should be prize, every one on board a prisoner; correspondence with the French, adhering to our enemies, &c., &c. I need not detail the consequences of this idea, as they will occur to you, nor discriminate the odds between a formal declaration of war, which would instantly draw after it all the consequences of a state of war, and a series of acts of Congress, which would annex to our state of peace all those consequences, one by one.

The difference of effect on the public mind is also worth computation and deliberation.

To declare is to choose war; it is voluntarily changing our condition, which however urgent the reasons and motives of the change may be, leaves a door open for blame on the government; it is, no doubt, a change at all times involving a high responsibility. Disasters in the conduct of a war would aggravate first ill impressions, and give a malecontent party a specific text of sedition. Ripe as the citizens are for self-defence, they reluct at offence; they would yield much, far too much, for peace; and this hope would delude them, if proud France would condescend to hold it out. Now why should not we play off against our foe a part of their own policy? Wage war, and call it self-defence; forbear to call it war; on the contrary, let it be said that we deprecate war, and will desist from arms, as soon as her acts shall be repealed, &c., &c., grounding all we do on the necessity of self-preservation, &c. We should need no negotiation to restore peace; at least we should act, as the *salus Reipublicæ* [1] demands we should, instantly, and there would be little balancing among the citizens, and the spirit would grow warmer in its progress. But a formal declaration would perhaps engender discords; all the thinking would come first, the action after. I would reverse this order. Not that I would conceal from the country its duties or its dangers. No, they should be fully stated and enforced. I would, however, oppose art to art, and employ, in self-defence against French intrigue, some of those means of influence which we may lawfully use, and which her party will so much abuse if we do not first possess them.

My long letter amounts to this: we must make haste to *wage war,* or we shall be lost. . . .

B] SENATOR SEDGWICK EXPLAINS THE BENEFITS OF WAR

Senator Theodore Sedgwick of Massachusetts was a member of the Essex Junto. Instinctively a Tory, overbearing in manner to the common people whom he distrusted as "swinish *sans culottes,*" Sedgwick yearned for war

---

1 *salus Reipublicæ:* health of the Republic.

against France. In this letter to Ambassador King in England, he explains the policy that he and his faction advocated after the XYZ disclosures.*

. . . OUR MEASURES in themselves were not only feeble, but taken with that gradation and hesitation, which shewed a want of system, & of spirit & vigor. . . . We ought at once to have put an end to the cooperation of external & internal enemies—to have at once, as far as in our power, prevented the possibility of their carrying on that most dangerous species of warfare, for the seduction of our people, "diplomatic skill." This could not in my opinion have been done effectually but by a declaration of war. This would have conduced equally to the honor & interest of the U.S. To have taken advantage of that measure, it would have been necessary to consider Spain, as in fact she is, a Colony of france. Besides, acting under the orders of her principal, Spain had given us sufficient cause, by innumerable aggressions, to justify our conduct. Having assumed the character of Enemy, as such, I would have rendered myself respectable by a prompt and decided blow. The mouth of the Mississippi & the countries connected with and dependent on it should have been immediately seized. The immense benefits to have been derived from that position, whether for treaty, or a continuance of the war, are obvious. In the mean time we should have superseded the necessity of alien & sedition laws—without them we might have hanged traitors and exported frenchmen. This was the policy I would have pursued instantly after the publication of the dispatches. But it was ordered otherwise. . . .

c] GENERAL HAMILTON DREAMS OF MILITARY GLORY

Hamilton, who directed the Essex Junto during the crisis with France, advised Secretary of War McHenry, as early as January of 1798, that the proper strategy to be followed was for Ambassador King to sound out Great Britain on "cooperation in case of open rupture [with France], the furnishing us with naval force—the point'g the cooperation to the Floridas, Louisiana, & South American possessions of Spain . . ." In the following letters, to King, Otis, and McHenry, Hamilton reveals his hopes for a policy of aggressive expansionism. Miranda, mentioned in the conspiratorial letter to King, was a Venezuelan general who was in touch with King, Hamilton, and the British government, enlisting aid for his scheme to liberate South America from Spain.†

TO RUFUS KING

August 22, 1798

I HAVE received several letters from General Miranda. I have written an answer to some of them, which I send you to deliver or not, according to your

---

* SENATOR SEDGWICK EXPLAINS THE BENEFITS OF WAR: Theodore Sedgwick to Rufus King, January 20, 1799. From Charles R. King, ed., *The Life and Correspondence of Rufus King* (New York, 1894–1900), II, 515.

† GENERAL HAMILTON DREAMS OF MILITARY GLORY: Alexander Hamilton to Rufus King, August 22, 1798; to Harrison Gray Otis, January 26, 1799; and to James McHenry, June 27, 1799. From James C. Hamilton, ed., *The Works of Alexander Hamilton* (New York, 1850–51), VI, 347–48, 390; VII, 243.

estimate of what is passing in the scene where you are. Should you deem it expedient to suppress my letter you may do it, and say as much as you think fit on my part in the nature of a communication through you.

With regard to the enterprise in question, I wish it much to be undertaken, but I should be glad that the principal agency was in the United States,— they to furnish the whole land force if necessary. The command in this case would very naturally fall upon me, and I hope I shall disappoint no favorable anticipation. The independence of the separate territory under a moderate government, with the joint guaranty of the co-operating powers, stipulating equal privileges in commerce, would be the sum of the results to be accomplished. . . .

TO HARRISON GRAY OTIS

NEW YORK, Jan. 26, 1799.

DEAR SIR:

You will recollect that I reserved for a future answer part of a letter which I had the pleasure of receiving from you some time since. These are my ideas on that subject.

I should be glad to see, before the close of the session, a law empowering the President, at his discretion, in case a negotiation between the United States and France should not be on foot by the first of August next, or being on foot should terminate without an adjustment of differences, to declare that a state of war exists between the two countries, and thereupon to employ the land and naval forces of the United States in such manner as shall appear to him most effectual for annoying the enemy, and for preventing and frustrating hostile designs of France, either directly or *indirectly through any of her allies.*

This course of proceeding, by postponing the event, and giving time for the intervention of negotiation, would be a further proof of moderation in the government, and would tend to reconcile our citizens to the last extremity, if it shall ensue, gradually accustoming their minds to look forward to it. . . .

As it is every moment possible that the project of taking possession of the Floridas and Louisiana, long since attributed to France, may be attempted to be put in execution, it is very important that the Executive should be clothed with power to meet and defeat so dangerous an enterprise. Indeed, if it is the policy of France to leave us in a state of semihostility, 't is preferable to terminate it, and by taking possession of those countries for ourselves, to obviate the mischief of their falling into the hands of an active foreign power, and at the same time to secure to the United States the advantage of keeping the key to the Western country. I have been long in the habit of considering the acquisition of those countries as essential to the permanency of the Union which I consider as very important to the welfare of the whole.

If universal empire is still to be the pursuit of France, what can tend to defeat the purpose better than to detach South America from Spain, which is only the channel through which the riches of *Mexico and Peru* are conveyed to France? The Executive ought to be put in a situation to embrace favorable conjunctures for effecting that separation. 'T is to be regretted that the preparation of an adequate military force does not advance more rapidly. . . .

TO JAMES MC HENRY

NEW YORK, June 27, 1799

It is a pity, my dear sir, and a reproach, that our administration have no general plan. Certainly there ought to be one formed without delay. If the chief is too desultory, his ministry ought to be more united and steady, and well-settled in some reasonable system of measures.

Among other things, it should be agreed what precise force should be created, naval and land, and this proportioned to the state of our finances. It will be ridiculous to raise troops, and immediately after disband them. Six ships of the line and twenty frigates and sloops of war are desirable. More would not now be comparatively expedient. It is desirable to complete and prepare the land force which has been provided for by law. Besides eventual security against invasion, we ought certainly to look to the possession of the Floridas and Louisiana, and we ought to squint at South America.

Is it possible that the accomplishment of these objects can be attended with financial difficulty? I deny the possibility. Our revenue can be considerably reinforced. The progress of the country will quickly supply small deficiencies, and these can be temporarily satisfied by loans, provided our loans are made on the principle that we require the aliment of European capital,—that lenders are to gain, and their gains to be facilitated, not obstructed. . . .

D] THE "CHRISTIAN CAUSE": CONQUEST AND COMMERCE

The *Gazette of the United States,* spokesman for the ultra-Federalist faction, reflected Hamilton's policies. The ideas contained in this extract from a tract by the editor, John Ward Fenno, first appeared in the *Gazette* for March 4, 1799. In the first paragraph Fenno offers a suggestion for remodeling the government. He advocated abolition of the states and division of the country into a few large counties governed by appointed "Praefects" who should constitute the upper house. The tract, reported the British ambassador to his government, was published with "the advice and consent of some of the leading Federalists in New York . . ." *

UNDER the auspices of a wise and prudent ruler, the elective franchise might forever be cut off from all paupers, vagabonds and outlaws, and the Legislation of the country placed in those hands to which it belongs, the proprietors of the country. At present we are the vassals of foreign outlaws. The frequency of elections, those elections being now entrusted to men of sense, men of principle, and men having an interest connected with the interests of the country, declines of course; as the folly and danger of annual elections can now be securely remedied. . . .

The measure which most pressingly demands adoption, is, an immediate declaration of war against France, and her dependencies, Spain and Holland.

* THE "CHRISTIAN CAUSE": CONQUEST AND COMMERCE: From John Ward Fenno, *Desultory Reflections on the New Political Aspects of Public Affairs in the United States of America* (New York, 1800), pp. 54–57.

It is time, after having so long and so pusillanimously beheld England fighting our battles, while we have rather comforted and abetted the common enemy, than even wished well to the opposition to him; it is time, after having fattened so long upon the spoils of war, to bring our mite of contribution into the general chest, and to relieve, as we may effectually do, the generous assertors of the christian cause.

The conquest of the remaining possessions of France, Spain and Holland in the West Indies, might be effected by this country, with very little expence or inconvenience. The naval force already extant, is fully adequate, and the regular troops lately embodied, though its intervention would have atchieved [*sic*] the conquest, without difficulty. . . .

This country possesses such advantages for carrying on expeditions against the West India Islands, as must render her cooperation in the cause very acceptable. In short, the contingent we could bring into the coalition would be such as to entitle us to assume the rank of a first rate power, and to make stipulations, the fulfillment of which could not fail to fix us in a state of prosperity and to extend to our empire and renown. To instance, for our quota of 25,000 troops (which should act separately and independently) and a stipulated quantum of military stores, etc. Great Britain should guarantee to us the island of Cuba, or which would be more convenient to our commerce, that of Porto Rico. Either of these possessions would amply remunerate us for the most expensive exertions which the conquest of them could require. In the East, we might establish ourselves in the possession of Batavia or the Mauritius, and thus to secure a footing in the Indian Ocean, highly essential to us, but now depending on the most precarious tenure.

It is in vain to disguise the truth that America is essentially and naturally a commercial nation; and that from her location on the map of the world she must ever remain so. It ought therefore to be the undeviating care of the Government, whether it be Federal or Jacobinical, or true Columbian, to secure on the most advantageous footing possible, our commercial intercourse with foreign nations. To procure admission to our flag, in ports whence it is now excluded; to obtain it by right where it now rests on the ground of sufferance; and to establish it on a regular and permanent footing; in those cases where it is at present precarious and temporary; is not merely the province of the Government, but a duty, and obligation which its subjects have a right to hold it to. . . .

7] The Republican Attack on the Alien and Sedition Acts

A] The Kentucky Resolutions of 1798

The Kentucky Resolutions were sponsored in the state legislature by John Breckinridge, framer of the Kentucky Constitution of 1799, who became United States senator in 1801 and Attorney-General in 1805. After deleting

a clause proposing that "a nullification . . . is the rightful remedy," Breckinridge submitted the resolutions substantially as secretly drafted by Jefferson.
The resolutions, which were passed by the lower house with only three
opposing votes and unanimously adopted three days later by the state
senate, on November 13, 1798, were the first state protests specifying a remedy other than repeal by Congress of an "unconstitutional" act. The Virginia Resolutions, drafted by Madison and adopted December 21, 1798, were
similar in spirit and language to the Kentucky Resolutions, but were less
specific and detailed.*

1. *Resolved,* That the several states composing the United States of America
are not united on the principle of unlimited submission to their general government; but that, by compact, under the style and title of a Constitution for
the United States, and of amendments thereto, they constituted a general
government for special purposes, delegated to that government certain definite
powers, reserving, each state to itself, the residuary mass of right to their own
self-government; and that whensoever the general government assumes undelegated powers, its acts are unauthoritative, void, and of no force; that to
this compact each state acceded as a state, and is an integral party; that this
government, created by this compact, was not made the exclusive or final
judge of the extent of the powers delegated to itself, since that would have
made its discretion, and not the Constitution, the measure of its power; but
that, as in all other cases of compact among parties having no common judge,
*each party has an equal right to judge for itself, as well of infractions as of the
mode and measure of redress.*

2. *Resolved,* That the Constitution of the United States having delegated to
Congress a power to punish treason, counterfeiting the securities and current
coin of the United States, piracies and felonies committed on the high seas,
and offences against the laws of nations, and no other crimes whatever; and it
being true, as a general principle, and one of the amendments to the Constitution having also declared "that the powers not delegated to the United States
by the Constitution, nor prohibited by it to the states, are reserved to the states
respectively, or to the people,"—therefore, also, the same act of Congress, passed
on the 14th day of July, 1798, and entitled "An Act in Addition to the Act
entitled 'An Act for the Punishment of certain Crimes against the United
States;'" as also the act passed by them on the 27th day of June, 1798, entitled
"An Act to punish Frauds committed on the Bank of the United States," (and
all other their acts which assume to create, define, or punish crimes other
than those enumerated in the Constitution,) are altogether void, and of no
force; and that the power to create, define, and punish, such other crimes is
reserved, and of right appertains, solely and exclusively, to the respective states,
each within its own territory.

3. *Resolved,* That it is true, as a general principle, and is also expressly declared by one of the amendments to the Constitution, that "the powers not
delegated to the United States by the Constitution, nor prohibited by it to the

* THE KENTUCKY RESOLUTIONS OF 1798: From Jonathan Elliot, ed., *The Debates in the
Several State Conventions on the Adoption of the Federal Constitution*, 2nd ed. (Philadelphia, 1836), IV, 540–44.

states, are reserved to the states respectively, or to the people;" and that, no power over the freedom of religion, freedom of speech, or freedom of the press, being delegated to the United States by the Constitution, nor prohibited by it to the states, all lawful powers respecting the same did of right remain, and were reserved to the states, or to the people; that thus was manifested their determination to retain to themselves the right of judging how far the licentiousness of speech, and of the press, may be abridged without lessening their useful freedom, and how far those abuses which cannot be separated from their use, should be tolerated rather than the use be destroyed; and thus also they guarded against all abridgment, by the United States, of the freedom of religious principles and exercises, and retained to themselves the right of protecting the same, as this, stated by a law passed on the general demand of its citizens, had already protected them from all human restraint or interference; and that, in addition to this general principle and express declaration, another and more special provision has been made by one of the amendments to the Constitution, which expressly declares, that "Congress shall make no laws respecting an establishment of religion, or prohibiting the free exercise thereof, or abridging the freedom of speech, or of the press," thereby guarding, in the same sentence, and under the same words, the freedom of religion, of speech, and of the press, insomuch that whatever violates either throws down the sanctuary which covers the others,—and that libels, falsehood, and defamation, equally with heresy and false religion, are withheld from the cognizance of federal tribunals. That therefore the act of the Congress of the United States, passed on the 14th of July, 1798, entitled "An Act in Addition to the Act entitled 'An Act for the Punishment of certain Crimes against the United States,'" which does abridge the freedom of the press, is not law, but is altogether void, and of no force.

4. *Resolved,* That alien friends are under the jurisdiction and protection of the laws of the state wherein they are; that no power over them has been delegated to the United States, nor prohibited to the individual states, distinct from their power over citizens; and it being true, as a general principle, and one of the amendments to the Constitution having also declared, that "the powers not delegated to the United States by the Constitution, nor prohibited to the states, are reserved to the states, respectively, or to the people," the act of the Congress of the United States, passed the 22d day of June, 1798, entitled "An Act concerning Aliens," which assumes power over alien friends not delegated by the Constitution, is not law, but is altogether void and of no force.

5. *Resolved,* That, in addition to the general principle, as well as the express declaration, that powers not delegated are reserved, another and more special provision inserted in the Constitution from abundant caution, has declared, "that the migration or importation of such persons as any of the states now existing shall think proper to admit, shall not be prohibited by the Congress prior to the year 1808." That this commonwealth does admit the migration of alien friends described as the subject of the said act concerning aliens; that a provision against prohibiting their migration is a provision against all acts equivalent thereto, or it would be nugatory; that to remove them, when migrated, is equivalent to a prohibition of their migration, and is, therefore, contrary to the said provision of the Constitution, and *void.*

6. *Resolved,* That the imprisonment of a person under the protection of the laws of this commonwealth, on his failure to obey the simple order of the President to depart out of the United States, as is undertaken by the said act, entitled, "An Act concerning Aliens," is contrary to the Constitution, one amendment in which has provided, that "no person shall be deprived of liberty without due process of law;" and that another having provided, "that, in all criminal prosecutions, the accused shall enjoy the right of a public trial by an impartial jury, to be informed as to the nature and cause of the accusation, to be confronted with the witnesses against him, to have compulsory process for obtaining witnesses in his favor, and to have assistance of counsel for his defence," the same act undertaking to authorize the President to remove a person out of the United States who is under the protection of the law, on his own suspicion, without jury, without public trial, without confrontation of the witnesses against him, without having witnesses in his favor, without defence, without counsel—contrary to these provisions also of the Constitution—is therefore not law, but utterly void, and of no force.

That transferring the power of judging any person who is under the protection of the laws, from the courts to the President of the United States, as is undertaken by the same act concerning aliens, is against the article of the Constitution which provides, that "the judicial power of the United States shall be vested in the courts, the judges of which shall hold their office during good behavior," and that the said act is void for that reason also; and it is further to be noted that this transfer of judiciary power is to that magistrate of the general government who already possesses all the executive, and a qualified negative in all the legislative powers.

7. *Resolved,* That the construction applied by the general government (as is evident by sundry of their proceedings) to those parts of the Constitution of the United States which delegate to Congress power to lay and collect taxes, duties, imposts, excises; to pay the debts, and provide for the common defence and general welfare, of the United States, and to make all laws which shall be necessary and proper for carrying into execution the powers vested by the Constitution in the government of the United States, or any department thereof, goes to the destruction of all the limits prescribed to their power by the Constitution; that words meant by that instrument to be subsidiary only to the execution of the limited powers, ought not to be so construed as themselves to give unlimited powers, nor a part so to be taken as to destroy the whole residue of the instrument; that the proceedings of the general government, under color of those articles, will be a fit and necessary subject for revisal and correction at a time of greater tranquillity, while those specified in the preceding resolutions call for immediate redress.

8. *Resolved,* That the preceding resolutions be transmitted to the senators and representatives in Congress from this commonwealth, who are enjoined to present the same to their respective houses, and to use their best endeavors to procure, at the next session of Congress, a repeal of the aforesaid unconstitutional and obnoxious acts.

9. *Resolved,* lastly, That the governor of this commonwealth be, and is, authorized and requested to communicate the preceding resolutions to the legislatures of the several states, to assure them that this commonwealth considers

union for special national purposes, and particularly for those specified in their late federal compact, to be friendly to the peace, happiness, and prosperity, of all the states: that, faithful to that compact, according to the plain intent and meaning in which it was understood and acceded to by the several parties, it is sincerely anxious for its preservation; that it does also believe, that, to take from the states all the powers of self-government, and transfer them to a general and consolidated government, without regard to the special government, and reservations solemnly agreed to in that compact, is not for the peace, happiness, or prosperity of these states; and that, therefore, this commonwealth is determined, as it doubts not its co-states are, to submit to undelegated and consequently unlimited powers in no man, or body of men, on earth; that, if the acts before specified should stand, these conclusions would flow from them— that the general government may place any act they think proper on the list of crimes, and punish it themselves, whether enumerated or not enumerated by the Constitution as cognizable by them; that they may transfer its cognizance to the President, or any other person, who may himself be the accuser, counsel, judge, and jury, whose suspicions may be the evidence, his order the sentence, his officer the executioner, and his breast the sole record of the transaction; that a very numerous and valuable description of the inhabitants of these states, being, by this precedent, reduced, as outlaws, to absolute dominion of one man, and the barriers of the Constitution thus swept from us all, no rampart now remains against the passions and the power of a majority of Congress, to protect from a like exportation, or other grievous punishment, the minority of the same body, the legislatures, judges, governors, and counsellors of the states, nor their other peaceable inhabitants, who may venture to reclaim the constitutional rights and liberties of the states and people, or who, for other causes, good or bad, may be obnoxious to the view, or marked by the suspicions, of the President, or be thought dangerous to his or their elections, or other interests, public or personal; that the friendless alien has been selected as the safest subject of a first experiment; but the citizen will soon follow, or rather has already followed; for already has a Sedition Act marked him as a prey: That these and successive acts of the same character, unless arrested on the threshold, may tend to drive these states into revolution and blood, and will furnish new calumnies against republican governments, and new pretexts for those who wish it to be believed that man cannot be governed but by a rod of iron; that it would be a dangerous delusion were a confidence in the men of our choice to silence our fears for the safety of our rights; that confidence is every where the parent of despotism; free government is founded in jealousy, and not in confidence; it is jealousy, and not confidence, which prescribes limited constitutions to bind down those whom we are obliged to trust with power; that our Constitution has accordingly fixed the limits to which, and no farther, our confidence may go; and let the honest advocate of confidence read the Alien and Sedition Acts, and say if the Constitution has not been wise in fixing limits to the government it created, and whether we should be wise in destroying those limits; let him say what the government is, if it be not a tyranny, which the men of our choice have conferred on the President, and the President of our choice has assented to and accepted, over the friendly strangers, to whom the mild spirit of our country and its laws had pledged hospitality and protection; that the men of our choice have more respected the bare suspicions of the President than the solid rights of innocence, the claims of justification, the sacred force of truth, and the forms and substance of law and justice.

In questions of power, then, let no more be said of confidence in man, but bind him down from mischief by the chains of the Constitution. That this commonwealth does therefore call on its co-states for an expression of their sentiments on the acts concerning aliens, and for the punishment of certain crimes herein before specified, plainly declaring whether these acts are or are not authorized by the federal compact. And it doubts not that their sense will be so announced as to prove their attachment to limited government, whether general or particular, and that the rights and liberties of their co-states will be exposed to no dangers by remaining embarked on a common bottom with their own; but they will concur with this commonwealth in considering the said acts as so palpably against the Constitution as to amount to an undisguised declaration, that the compact is not meant to be the measure of the powers of the general government, but that it will proceed in the exercise over these states of all powers whatsoever. That they will view this as seizing the rights of the states, and consolidating them in the hands of the general government, with a power assumed to bind the states, not merely in cases made federal, but in all cases whatsoever, by laws made, not with their consent, but by others against their consent; that this would be to surrender the form of government we have chosen, and live under one deriving its powers from its own will, and not from our authority; and that the co-states, recurring to their natural rights not made federal, will concur in declaring these void and of no force, and will each unite with this commonwealth in requesting their repeal at the next session of Congress.

B] Massachusetts Replies

The five New England states, New York, and Delaware replied critically to the Kentucky and Virginia Resolutions of 1798; the other state legislatures remained silent. The reply from Federalist Massachusetts, which follows, was the longest and sharpest of all.*

In Senate, *February* 9, 1799

The legislature of Massachusetts, having taken into serious consideration the resolutions of the state of Virginia, passed the 21st day of December last, and communicated by his excellency the governor, relative to certain supposed infractions of the Constitution of the United States, by the government thereof; and being convinced that the Federal Constitution is calculated to promote the happiness, prosperity, and safety, of the people of these United States, and to maintain that union of the several states so essential to the welfare of the whole; and being bound by solemn oath to support and defend that Constitution,—feel it unnecessary to make any professions of their attachment to it, or of their

---

* MASSACHUSETTS REPLIES: From Elliot, ed., *Debates*, IV, 533–37.

firm determination to support it against every aggression, foreign or domestic.

But they deem it their duty solemnly to declare that, while they hold sacred the principle, that consent of the people is the only pure source of just and legitimate power, they cannot admit the right of the state legislatures to denounce the administration of that government to which the people themselves, by a solemn compact, have exclusively committed their national concerns. That, although a liberal and enlightened vigilance among the people is always to be cherished, yet an unreasonable jealousy of the men of their choice, and a recurrence to measures of extremity upon groundless or trivial pretexts, have a strong tendency to destroy all rational liberty at home, and to deprive the United States of the most essential advantages in relations abroad. That this legislature are persuaded that the decision of all cases in law and equity arising under the Constitution of the United States, and the construction of all laws made in pursuance thereof, are exclusively vested by the people in the judicial courts of the United States.

That the people, in that solemn compact which is declared to be the supreme law of the land, have not constituted the state legislatures the judges of the acts or measures of the federal government, but have confided to them the power of proposing such amendments of the Constitution as shall appear to them necessary to the interests, or conformable to the wishes, of the people whom they represent.

That, by this construction of the Constitution, an amicable and dispassionate remedy is pointed out for any evil which experience may prove to exist, and the peace and prosperity of the United States may be preserved without interruption.

But, should the respectable state of Virginia persist in the assumption of the right to declare the acts of the national government unconstitutional, and should she oppose successfully her force and will to those of the nation, the Constitution would be reduced to a mere cipher, to the form and pageantry of authority, without the energy of power; every act of the federal government which thwarted the views or checked the ambitious projects of a particular state, or of its leading and influential members, would be the object of opposition and of remonstrance; while the people, convulsed and confused by the conflict between two hostile jurisdictions, enjoying the protection of neither, would be wearied into a submission to some bold leader, who would establish himself on the ruins of both.

The legislature of Massachusetts, although they do not themselves claim the right, nor admit the authority of any of the state governments, to decide upon the constitutionality of the acts of the federal government, still, lest their silence should be construed into disapprobation, or at best into a doubt as to the constitutionality of the acts referred to by the state of Virginia; and as the General Assembly of Virginia has called for an expression of their sentiments, —do explicitly declare, that they consider the acts of Congress, commonly called "the Alien and Sedition Acts," not only constitutional, but expedient and necessary: That the former act respects a description of persons whose rights were not particularly contemplated in the Constitution of the United States, who are entitled only to a temporary protection while they yield a temporary allegiance—a protection which ought to be withdrawn whenever they become "dangerous to the public safety," or are found guilty of "treasonable machination" against the government: That Congress, having been especially intrusted by the people with the general defence of the nation, had not only the right, but were bound, to protect it against internal as well as external foes: That the United States, at the time of passing the *Act concerning Aliens,* were threatened with actual invasion; had been driven, by the unjust and ambitious conduct of the French government, into warlike preparations, expensive and burdensome; and had then, within the bosom of the country, thousands of aliens, who, we doubt not, were ready to coöperate in any external attack.

It cannot be seriously believed that the United States should have waited till the poniard had in fact been plunged. The removal of aliens is the usual preliminary of hostility, and is justified by the invariable usages of nations. Actual hostility had unhappily long been experienced, and a formal declaration of it the government had reason daily to expect. The law, therefore, was just and salutary; and no officer could with so much propriety be intrusted with the execution of it, as the one in whom the Constitution has reposed the executive power of the United States.

The *Sedition Act,* so called, is, in the opinion of this legislature, equally defensible. The General Assembly of Virginia, in their resolve under consideration, observe, that when that state, by its Convention, ratified the Federal Constitution, it expressly declared, "that, among other essential rights, the liberty of conscience and of the press cannot be cancelled, abridged, restrained, or modified, by any authority of the United States," and, from its extreme anxiety to guard these rights from every possible attack of sophistry or ambition, with other states, recommended an amendment for that purpose; which amendment was, in due time, annexed to the Constitution; but they did not surely expect that the proceedings of their state Convention were to explain the amendment adopted by the Union. The words of that amendment, on this subject, are, "Congress shall make no law abridging the freedom of speech or of the press."

The act complained of is no abridgment of the freedom of either. The genuine liberty of speech and the press is the liberty to utter and publish the truth; but the constitutional right of the citizen to utter and publish the truth is not to be confounded with the licentiousness, in speaking and writing, that is only employed in propagating falsehood and slander. This freedom of the press has been explicitly secured by most, if not all the state constitutions; and of this provision there has been generally but one construction among enlightened men—that it is a security for the rational use, and not the abuse of the press; of which the courts of law, the juries and people will judge; this right is not infringed, but confirmed and established, by the late act of Congress.

By the Constitution, the legislative, executive, and judicial departments of government are ordained and established; and general enumerated powers vested in them respectively, including those which are prohibited to the several states. Certain powers are granted, in general terms, by the people, to their general government, for the purposes of their safety and protection. The government is not only empowered, but it is made their duty, to repel invasions and suppress insurrections; to guaranty to the several states a republican form of government; to protect each state against invasion, and, when applied to, against domestic violence; to hear and decide all cases in law and equity arising under the Constitution, and under any treaty or law made in pursuance thereof; and all cases of admiralty and maritime jurisdiction, and relating to the law of nations. Whenever, therefore, it becomes necessary to effect any of the objects designated, it is perfectly consonant to all just rules of construction to infer that the usual means and powers necessary to the attainment of that object are also granted. But the Constitution has left no occasion to resort to implication for these powers; it has made an express grant of them, in the 8th section of the 1st article, which ordains, "that Congress shall have power to make all laws which shall be necessary and proper for carrying into execution the foregoing powers, and all other powers vested by the Constitution in the government of the United States, or in any department or officer thereof."

This Constitution has established a Supreme Court of the United States, but has made no provision for its protection, even against such improper conduct in its presence, as might disturb its proceedings, unless expressed in the section before recited. But as no statute has been passed on this subject, this protection is, and has been for nine years past, uniformly found in the application of the principles and usages of the common law. The same protection may unquestionably be afforded by a statute passed in virtue of the before-mentioned section, as necessary and proper for carrying into execution the powers vested in that department. A construction of the different parts of the Constitution, perfectly just and fair, will, on analogous principles, extend protection and security, against the offences in question, to the other departments of government, in discharge of their respective trusts.

The President of the United States is bound by his oath "to preserve, protect, and defend, the Constitution;" and it is expressly made his duty "to take care that the laws be faithfully executed." But this would be impracticable by any created being, if there could be no legal restraint of those scandalous misrepresentations of his measures and motives which directly tend to rob him of the public confidence; and equally impotent would be every other public officer, if thus left to the mercy of the seditious.

It is holden to be a truth most clear, that the important trusts before enumerated cannot be discharged by the government to which they are committed, without the power to restrain seditious practices and unlawful combinations against itself, and to protect the officers thereof from abusive misrepresentations. Had the Constitution withheld this power, it would have made the government responsible for the effects, without any control over the causes which naturally produce them, and would have essentially failed of answering the great ends for which the people of the United States declare, in the first clause of that instrument, that they establish the same—viz., "to form a more perfect union, establish justice, insure domestic tranquillity, provide for the common defence, promote the general welfare, and secure the blessings of liberty to ourselves and posterity."

Seditious practices and unlawful combinations against the federal government, or any officer thereof, in the performance of his duty, as well as licentiousness of speech and of the press, were punishable, on the principles of common law, in the courts of the United States, before the act in question was passed. This act, then, is an amelioration of that law in favor of the party accused, as it mitigates the punishment which that authorizes, and admits of any investigation of public men and measures which is regulated by truth. It is not intended to protect men in office, only as they are agents of the people. Its object is to afford legal security to public offices and trusts created for the safety and happiness of the people, and therefore the security derived from it is for the benefit of the people, and is their right.

This construction of the Constitution, and of the existing law of the land, as well as the act complained of, the legislature of Massachusetts most deliberately and firmly believe, results from a just and full view of the several parts of the Constitution; and they consider that act to be wise and necessary, as an audacious and unprincipled spirit of falsehood and abuse had been too long unremittingly exerted for the purpose of perverting public opinion, and threatened to undermine and destroy the whole fabric of government.

The legislature further declare, that in the foregoing sentiments they have expressed the general opinion of their constituents, who have not only acquiesced without complaint in those particular measures of the federal government, but have given their explicit approbation by reelecting those men who voted for the adoption of them. Nor is it apprehended that the citizens of this state will be accused of supineness, or of an indifference to their constitutional rights; for while, on the one hand, they regard with due vigilance the conduct of the government, on the other, their freedom, safety, and happiness require that they should defend that government and its constitutional measures against the open or insidious attacks of any foe, whether foreign or domestic.

And, lastly, that the legislature of Massachusetts feel a strong conviction, that the several United States are connected by a common interest, which ought to render their union indissoluble; and that this state will always cooperate with its confederate states in rendering that union productive of mutual security, freedom, and happiness.

c] THE KENTUCKY RESOLUTIONS OF 1799

The replies of the states and the trend of national affairs had a depressing effect upon Jefferson. On August 23, 1799, he stated that a counter-reply should include the point that "we . . . sever ourselves" from the Union rather than give up liberty and self-government. Under Madison's influence, however, the final draft submitted by Jefferson to Breckinridge was a temperate restatement of the constitutional nature of the Union with an ambiguous reference to "nullification." The resolutions were adopted without dissent by the Kentucky legislature on November 29. Three days earlier Jefferson, in a new statement of his policies to Madison, stressed "a sincere cultivation of the Union." *

HOUSE OF REPRESENTATIVES, *Thursday, Nov. 14, 1799.*
THE HOUSE, according to the standing order of the day, resolved itself into a committee of the whole house, on the state of the commonwealth, (Mr. Desha in the chair,) and, after some time spent therein, the speaker resumed the chair, and Mr. Desha reported, that the committee had taken under con-

---

* THE KENTUCKY RESOLUTIONS OF 1799: From Elliot, ed., *Debates*, IV, 544–45.

sideration sundry resolutions passed by several state legislatures, on the subject of the Alien and Sedition Laws, and had come to a resolution thereupon, which he delivered in at the clerk's table, where it was read and *unanimously* agreed to by the house, as follows:—

The representatives of the good people of this commonwealth, in General Assembly convened, having maturely considered the answers of sundry states in the Union to their resolutions, passed the last session, respecting certain unconstitutional laws of Congress, commonly called the Alien and Sedition Laws, would be faithless, indeed, to themselves, and to those they represent, were they silently to acquiesce in the principles and doctrines attempted to be maintained in all those answers, that of Virginia only excepted. To again enter the field of argument, and attempt more fully or forcibly to expose the unconstitutionality of those obnoxious laws, would, it is apprehended, be as unnecessary as unavailing. We cannot, however, but lament that, in the discussion of those interesting subjects by sundry of the legislatures of our sister states, unfounded suggestions and uncandid insinuations, derogatory to the true character and principles of this commonwealth, have been substituted in place of fair reasoning and sound argument. Our opinions of these alarming measures of the general government, together with our reasons for those opinions, were detailed with decency and with temper, and submitted to the discussion and judgment of our fellow-citizens throughout the Union. Whether the like decency and temper have been observed in the answers of most of those states who have denied, or attempted to obviate, the great truths contained in those resolutions, we have now only to submit to a candid world. Faithful to the true principles of the federal Union, unconscious of any designs to disturb the harmony of that Union, and anxious only to escape the fangs of despotism, the good people of this commonwealth are regardless of censure or calumniation. Lest, however, the silence of this commonwealth should be construed into an acquiescence in the doctrines and principles advanced, and attempted to be maintained, by the said answers; or at least those of our fellow-citizens, throughout the Union, who so widely differ from us on those important subjects, should be deluded by the expectation that we shall be deterred from what we conceive our duty, or shrink from the principles contained in those resolutions,—therefore,

Resolved, That this commonwealth considers the federal Union, upon the terms and for the purposes specified in the late compact, conducive to the liberty and happiness of the several states: That it does now unequivocally declare its attachment to the Union, and to that compact, agreeably to its obvious and real intention, and will be among the last to seek its dissolution: That, if those who administer the general government be permitted to transgress the limits fixed by that compact, by a total disregard to the special delegations of power therein contained, an annihilation of the state governments, and the creation, upon their ruins, of a general consolidated government, will be the inevitable consequence: That the principle and construction, contended for by sundry of the state legislatures, that the general government is the exclusive judge of the extent of the powers delegated to it, stop not short of *despotism*—since the discretion of those who administer the government, and not the *Constitution,* would be the measure of their powers: That the several states who formed that instrument, being sovereign and independent, have the unquestionable right to judge of the infraction; and, *That a nullification, by those sovereignties, of all unauthorized acts done under color of that instrument, is the rightful remedy:* That this commonwealth does, under the most deliberate reconsideration, declare, that the said Alien and Sedition Laws are, in their opinion, palpable violations of the said Constitution; and, however cheerfully it may be disposed to surrender its opinion to a majority of its sister states, in matters of ordinary or doubtful policy, yet, in momentous regulations like the present, which so vitally wound the best rights of the citizen, it would consider a silent acquiescence as highly criminal: That, although this commonwealth, as a party to the federal compact, will bow to the laws of the Union, yet it does, at the same time, declare, that it will not now, or ever hereafter, cease to oppose, in a constitutional manner, every attempt, at what quarter soever offered, to violate that compact: And finally, in order that no pretext or arguments may be drawn from a supposed acquiescence, on the part of this commonwealth, in the constitutionality of those laws, and be thereby used as precedents for similar future violations of the federal compact, this commonwealth does now enter against them its solemn PROTEST.

D] MADISON ARGUES FOR FREEDOM OF THE PRESS

As chairman of a committee appointed by the Virginia legislature to draft a rebuttal to the state replies opposing the resolutions of 1798, Madison wrote a superlative document, originally published as a tract of over eighty pages, outlining the principles of a free government, defending the Bill of Rights, and systematically attacking every argument that had been advanced on behalf of the wisdom or constitutionality of the Alien and Sedition Acts. The section reprinted here, only about half of Madison's analysis of the Sedition Act, represents the newly emerging libertarian theory of freedom of expression and an abandonment of earlier reliance on the principles of the Zenger case. The report was written in December of 1799 and approved January 11, 1800. Jefferson had it reprinted and circulated throughout the country.*

THE NEXT point . . . is, that the power over the press exercised by the sedition-act, is positively forbidden by one of the amendments to the Constitution.

The amendment stands in these words—"Congress shall make no law respecting an establishment of religion, or prohibiting the free exercise thereof, *or abridging the freedom of speech or of the press;* or the right of the people peaceably to assemble, and to petition the government for a redress of grievances."

In the attempts to vindicate the "sedition-act," it has been contended, 1. That the "freedom of the press" is to be determined by the meaning of these terms in the common law. 2. That the article supposes the power over the press to be in Congress, and prohibits them only from *abridging* the freedom allowed to it by the common law.

---

* MADISON ARGUES FOR FREEDOM OF THE PRESS: From *The Virginia Report of 1799–1800, Touching the Alien and Sedition Laws* (Richmond, 1850), pp. 219–29.

Although it will be shown, in examining the second of these positions, that the amendment is a denial to Congress of all power over the press, it may not be useless to make the following observations on the first of them.

It is deemed to be a sound opinion, that the sedition-act, in its definition of some of the crimes created, is an abridgment of the freedom of publication, recognised by principles of the common law in England.

The freedom of the press under the common law, is, in the defences of the sedition-act, made to consist in an exemption from all *previous* restraint on printed publications, by persons authorized to inspect and prohibit them. It appears to the committee, that this idea of the freedom of the press, can never be admitted to be the American idea of it: since a law inflicting penalties on printed publications, would have a similar effect with a law authorizing a previous restraint on them. It would seem a mockery to say, that no law should be passed, preventing publications from being made, but that laws might be passed for punishing them in case they should be made.

The essential difference between the British government, and the American constitutions, will place this subject in the clearest light.

In the British government, the danger of encroachments on the rights of the people, is understood to be confined to the executive magistrate. The representatives of the people in the legislature, are not only exempt themselves, from distrust, but are considered as sufficient guardians of the rights of their constituents against the danger from the executive. Hence it is a principle, that the parliament is unlimited in its power; or, in their own language, is omnipotent. Hence, too, all the ramparts for protecting the rights of the people, such as their magna charta, their bill of rights, &c., are not reared against the parliament, but against the royal prerogative. They are merely legislative precautions against executive usurpations. Under such a government as this, an exemption of the press from previous restraint by licensers appointed by the king, is all the freedom that can be secured to it.

In the United States, the case is altogether different. The people, not the government, possess the absolute sovereignty. The legislature, no less than the executive, is under limitations of power. Encroachments are regarded as possible from the one, as well as from the other. Hence, in the United States, the great and essential rights of the people are secured against legislative, as well as against executive ambition. They are secured, not by laws paramount to prerogative, but by constitutions paramount to laws. This security of the freedom of the press requires, that it should be exempt, not only from previous restraint by the executive, as in Great Britain, but from legislative restraint also; and this exemption, to be effectual, must be an exemption not only from the previous inspection of licensers, but from the subsequent penalty of laws.

The state of the press, therefore, under the common law, cannot, in this point of view, be the standard of its freedom in the United States.

But there is another view, under which it may be necessary to consider this subject. It may be alleged, that although the security for the freedom of the press, be different in Great Britain and in this country; being a legal security only in the former, and a constitutional security in the latter; and although there may be a further difference, in an extension of the freedom of the press here, beyond an exemption from previous restraint, to an exemption from subsequent penalties also; yet that the actual legal freedom of the press, under the common law, must determine the degree of freedom which is meant by the terms, and which is constitutionally secured against both previous and subsequent restraints.

The committee are not unaware of the difficulty of all general questions, which may turn on the proper boundary between the liberty and licentiousness of the press. They will leave it therefore for consideration only, how far the difference between the nature of the British government, and the nature of the American governments, and the practice under the latter, may show the degree of rigour in the former to be inapplicable to, and not obligatory in the latter.

The nature of governments elective, limited, and responsible, in all their branches, may well be supposed to require a greater freedom of animadversion than might be tolerated by the genius of such a government as that of Great Britain. In the latter, it is a maxim, that the king, an hereditary, not a responsible magistrate, can do no wrong; and that the legislature, which in two-thirds of its composition, is also hereditary, not responsible, can do what it pleases. In the United States, the executive magistrates are not held to be infallible, nor the legislatures to be omnipotent; and both being elective, are both responsible. Is it not natural and necessary, under such different circumstances, that a different degree of freedom, in the use of the press, should be contemplated?

Is not such an inference favoured by what is observable in Great Britain itself? Notwithstanding the general doctrine of the common law, on the subject of the press, and the occasional punishment of those who use it with a freedom offensive to the government; it is well known, that with respect to the responsible members of the government, where the reasons operating here, become applicable there, the freedom exercised by the press, and protected by the public opinion, far exceeds the limits prescribed by the ordinary rules of law. The ministry, who are responsible to impeachment, are at all times animadverted on, by the press, with peculiar freedom; and during the elections for the House of Commons, the other responsible part of the government, the press is employed with as little reserve towards the candidates.

The practice in America must be entitled to much more respect. In every state, probably, in the Union, the press has exerted a freedom in canvassing the merits and measures of public men, of every description, which has not been confined to the strict limits of the common law. On this footing, the freedom of the press has stood; on this footing it yet stands. And it will not be a breach, either of truth or of candour, to say, that no persons or presses are in the habit of more unrestrained animadversions on the proceedings and functionaries of the state governments, than the persons and presses most zealous in vindicating the act of Congress for punishing similar animadversions on the government of the United States.

The last remark will not be understood as claiming for the state governments an immunity greater than they have heretofore enjoyed. Some degree of abuse is inseparable from the proper use of everything; and in no instances is this more true, than in that of the press. It has accordingly been decided by the practice of the states, that it is better to leave a few of its noxious branches to their luxuriant growth, than by pruning them away, to injure the vigour of those yielding the proper fruits. And can the wisdom of this policy be doubted by any who reflect, that to the press alone, chequered as it is with abuses, the world is indebted for all the triumphs which have been gained by reason and humanity, over error and oppression; who reflect, that to the same beneficent source, the United States owe much of the lights which conducted them to the rank of a free and independent nation; and which have improved their political system into a shape so auspicious to their happiness. Had "sedition-acts," forbidding every publication that might bring the constituted agents into contempt or disrepute, or that might excite the hatred of the people against the authors of unjust or pernicious measures, been uniformly enforced against the press, might not the United States have been languishing at this day, under the infirmities of a sickly confederation? Might they not possibly be miserable colonies, groaning under a foreign yoke?

To these observations, one fact will be added, which demonstrates that the common law cannot be admitted as the *universal* expositor of American terms, which may be the same with those contained in that law. The freedom of conscience, and of religion, are found in the same instruments which assert the freedom of the press. It will never be admitted, that the meaning of the former, in the common law of England, is to limit their meaning in the United States.

Whatever weight may be allowed to these considerations, the committee do not, however, by any means intend to rest the question on them. They contend that the article of amendment, instead of supposing in Congress a power that might be exercised over the press, provided its freedom was not abridged, was meant as a positive denial to Congress, of any power whatever on the subject.

To demonstrate that this was the true object of the article, it will be sufficient to recall the circumstances which led to it, and to refer to the explanation accompanying the article.

When the Constitution was under the discussions which preceded its ratification, it is well known, that great apprehensions were expressed by many, lest the omission of some positive exception from the powers delegated, of certain rights, and of the freedom of the press particularly, might expose them to the danger of being drawn by construction within some of the powers vested in Congress; more especially of the power to make all laws necessary and proper for carrying their other powers into execution. In reply to this objection, it was invariably urged to be a fundamental and characteristic principle of the Constitution, that all powers not given by it, were reserved; that no powers were given beyond those enumerated in the Constitution, and such as were fairly incident to them; that the power over the rights in question, and particularly over the press, was neither among the enumerated powers, nor incident to any of them; and consequently that an exercise of any such power, would be a manifest usurpation. It is painful to remark, how much the arguments now employed in behalf of the sedition-act, are at variance with the reasoning which then justified the Constitution, and invited its ratification.

From this posture of the subject, resulted the interesting question in so many of the conventions, whether the doubts and dangers ascribed to the Constitution, should be removed by any amendments previous to the ratification, or be postponed, in confidence that as far as they might be proper, they would be introduced in the form provided by the Constitution. The latter course was adopted; and in most of the states, the ratifications were followed by propositions and instructions for rendering the Constitution more explicit, and more safe to the rights not meant to be delegated by it. Among those rights, the freedom of the press, in most instances, is particularly and emphatically mentioned. The firm and very pointed manner, in which it is asserted in the proceedings of the convention of this state, will be hereafter seen.

In pursuance of the wishes thus expressed, the first Congress that assembled under the Constitution, proposed certain amendments which have since, by the necessary ratifications, been made a part of it; among which amendments, is the article containing, among other prohibitions on the Congress, an express declaration that they should make no law abridging the freedom of the press.

Without tracing farther the evidence on this subject, it would seem scarcely possible to doubt, that no power whatever over the press was supposed to be delegated by the Constitution, as it originally stood; and that the amendment was intended as a positive and absolute reservation of it.

But the evidence is still stronger. The proposition of amendment as made by Congress, is introduced in the following terms: *"The conventions of a number of the states having at the time of their adopting the Constitution expressed a desire, in order to prevent misconstructions or abuse of its powers, that further declaratory and restrictive clauses should be added; and as extending the ground of public confidence in the government, will best ensure the beneficent ends of its institutions."*

Here is the most satisfactory and authentic proof, that the several amendments proposed, were to be considered as either declaratory or restrictive; and whether the one or the other, as corresponding with the desire expressed by a number of the states, and as extending the ground of public confidence in the government.

Under any other construction of the amendment relating to the press, than that it declared the press to be wholly exempt from the power of Congress, the amendment could neither be said to correspond with the desire expressed by a number of the states, nor be calculated to extend the ground of public confidence in the government.

Nay more; the construction employed to justify the "sedition-act," would exhibit a phenomenon, without a parallel in the political world. It would exhibit a number of respectable states, as denying first that any power over the press was delegated by the Constitution; as proposing next, that an amendment to it, should explicitly declare that no such power was delegated; and finally, as concurring in an amendment actually recognising or delegating such a power.

Is then the federal government, it will be asked, destitute of every authority for restraining the licentiousness of the press, and for shielding itself against the libellous attacks which may be made on those who administer it?

The Constitution alone can answer this question. If no such power be expressly delegated, and it be not both necessary and proper to carry into execution an express power; above all, if it be expressly forbidden by a declaratory amendment to the Constitution, the answer must be, that the federal government is destitute of all such authority.

And might it not be asked in turn, whether it is not more probable, under all the circumstances which have been reviewed, that the authority should be withheld by the Constitution, than that it should be left to a vague and violent construction; whilst so much pains were bestowed in enumerating other powers, and so many less important powers are included in the enumeration?

Might it not be likewise asked, whether the anxious circumspection which dictated so many *peculiar* limitations on the general authority, would be unlikely to exempt the press altogether from that authority? The peculiar magnitude of some of the powers necessarily committed to the federal government; the peculiar duration required for the functions of some of its departments; the peculiar distance of the seat of its proceedings from the great body of its constituents; and the peculiar difficulty of circulating an adequate knowledge of them through any other channel; will not these considerations, some or other of which produced other exceptions from the powers of ordinary governments, all together, account for the policy of binding the hand of the federal government, from touching the channel which alone can give efficacy to its responsibility to its constituents; and of leaving those who administer it, to a remedy for their injured reputations, under the same laws, and in the same tribunals, which protect their lives, their liberties, and their properties?

But the question does not turn either on the wisdom of the Constitution, or on the policy which gave rise to its particular organization. It turns on the actual meaning of the instrument; by which it has appeared, that a power over the press is clearly excluded, from the number of powers delegated to the federal government.

3. And in the opinion of the committee, well may it be said, as the resolution concludes with saying, that the unconstitutional power exercised over the press by the "sedition-act," ought "more than any other, to produce universal alarm; because it is levelled against that right of freely examining public characters and measures, and of free communication among the people thereon, which has ever been justly deemed the only effectual guardian of every other right."

Without scrutinizing minutely into all the provisions of the "sedition-act," it will be sufficient to cite so much of section 2, as follows: "And be it further enacted, that if any person shall write, print, utter, or publish, or shall cause or procure to be written, printed, uttered or published, or shall knowingly and willingly assist or aid in writing, printing, uttering or publishing any false, scandalous and malicious writing or writings against the government of the United States, or either house of the Congress of the United States, or the President of the United States, *with an intent to defame the said government, or either house of the said Congress, or the President, or to bring them, or either of them, into contempt or disrepute; or to excite against them, or either, or any of them, the hatred of the good people of the United States, &c. Then such person being thereof convicted before any court of the United States, having jurisdiction thereof, shall be punished by a fine not exceeding two thousand dollars, and by imprisonment not exceeding two years."*

On this part of the act, the following observations present themselves:

1. The Constitution supposes that the President, the Congress, and each of its houses may not discharge their trusts, either from defect of judgment or other causes. Hence, they are all made responsible to their constituents, at the returning periods of election; and the President, who is singly entrusted with very great powers, is, as a further guard, subjected to an intermediate impeachment.

2. Should it happen, as the Constitution supposes it may happen, that either of these branches of the government may not have duly discharged its trust, it is natural and proper that, according to the cause and degree of their faults, they should be brought into contempt or disrepute, and incur the hatred of the people.

3. Whether it has, in any case, happened that the proceedings of either, or all of those branches, evince such a violation of duty as to justify a contempt, a disrepute or hatred among the people, can only be determined by a free examination thereof, and a free communication among the people thereon.

4. Whenever it may have actually happened, that proceedings of this sort are chargeable on all or either of the branches of the government, it is the duty as well as right of intelligent and faithful citizens, to discuss and promulge them freely, as well to control them by the censorship of the public opinion, as to promote a remedy according to the rules of the Constitution. And it cannot be avoided, that those who are to apply the remedy must feel, in some degree, a contempt or hatred against the transgressing party.

5. As the act was passed on July 14, 1798, and is to be in force until March 3, 1801, it was of course, that during its continuance, two elections of the entire House of Representatives, an election of a part of the Senate, and an election of a President, were to take place.

6. That consequently, during all these elections, intended by the Constitution to preserve the purity, or to purge the faults of the administration, the great remedial rights of the people were to be exercised, and the responsibility of their public agents to be screened, under the penalties of this act.

May it not be asked of every intelligent friend to the liberties of his country, whether the power exercised in such an act as this, ought not to produce great and universal alarm? Whether a rigid execution of such an act, in time past, would not have repressed that information and communication among the people, which is indispensable to the just exercise of their electoral rights? And whether such an act, if made perpetual, and enforced with rigour, would not, in time to come, either destroy our free system of government, or prepare a convulsion that might prove equally fatal to it?

In answer to such questions, it has been pleaded that the writings and publications forbidden by the act, are those only which are false and malicious, and intended to defame; and merit is claimed for the privilege allowed to authors to justify, by proving the truth of their publications, and for the limitations to which the sentence of fine and imprisonment is subjected.

To those who concurred in the act, under the extraordinary belief that the option lay between the passing of such an act, and leaving in force the common law of libels, which punishes truth equally with falsehood, and submits the fine and imprisonment to the indefinite discretion of the court, the merit of good intentions ought surely not to be refused. A like merit may perhaps be due for the discontinuance of the *corporal punishment,* which the common law also leaves to the discretion of the court. This merit of *intention,* however, would have been greater, if the several mitigations had not been limited to so short a period; and the apparent inconsistency would have been avoided, between justifying the act at one time, by contrasting it with the rigors of the common law, otherwise in force, and at another time by appealing to the nature of the crisis, as requiring the temporary rigour exerted by the act.

But, whatever may have been the meritorious intentions of all or any who contributed to the sedition-act, a very few reflections will prove, that its baneful tendency is little diminished by the privilege of giving in evidence the truth of the matter contained in political writings.

In the first place, where simple and naked facts alone are in question, there is sufficient difficulty in some cases, and sufficient trouble and vexation in all, of meeting a prosecution from the government, with the full and formal proof necessary in a court of law.

But in the next place, it must be obvious to the plainest minds, that opinions, and inferences, and conjectural observations, are not only in many cases inseparable from the facts, but may often be more the objects of the prosecution than the facts themselves; or may even be altogether abstracted from particular facts; and that opinions and inferences, and conjectural observations, cannot be subjects of that kind of proof which appertains to facts, before a court of law.

Again: It is no less obvious, that the *intent* to defame or bring into contempt or disrepute, or hatred, which is made a condition of the offence created by the act, cannot prevent its pernicious influence on the freedom of the press. For, omitting the inquiry, how far the malice of the intent is an inference of the law from the mere publication, it is manifestly impossible to punish the intent to bring those who administer the government into disrepute or contempt, without striking at the right of freely discussing public characters and measures: because those who engage in such discussions, must expect and *intend* to excite these unfavourable sentiments, so far as they may be thought to be deserved. To prohibit, therefore, the intent to excite those unfavourable sentiments against those who administer the government, is equivalent to a prohibition of the actual excitement of them; and to prohibit the actual excitement of them, is equivalent to a prohibition of discussions having that tendency and effect; which, again, is equivalent to a protection of those who administer the government, if they should at any time deserve the contempt or hatred of the people, against being exposed to it, by free animadversions on their characters and conduct. Nor can there be a doubt, if those in public trust be shielded by penal laws from such strictures of the press, as may expose them to contempt or disrepute, or hatred, where they may deserve it, in exact proportion as they may deserve to be exposed, will be the certainty and criminality of the intent to expose them, and the vigilance of prosecuting and punishing it; nor a doubt, that a government thus intrenched in penal statutes, against the just and natural effects of a culpable administration, will easily evade the responsibility, which is essential to a faithful discharge of its duty.

Let it be recollected, lastly, that the right of electing the members of the government, constitutes more particularly the essence of a free and responsible government. The value and efficacy of this right, depends on the knowledge of the comparative merits and demerits of the candidates for public trust; and on the equal freedom, consequently, of examining and discussing these merits and demerits of the candidates respectively. It has been seen, that a number of important elections will take place whilst the act is in force, although it should not be continued beyond the term to which it is limited. Should there happen, then, as is extremely probable in relation to some or other of the branches of the government, to be competitions between those who are, and those who are not, members of the government, what will be the situations of the competitors? Not equal; because the characters of the former will be covered by the "sedition-act" from animadversions exposing them to disrepute among the people; whilst the latter may be exposed to the contempt and hatred of the people, without a violation of the act. What will be the situation of the people? Not free; because they will be compelled to make their election between competitors, whose pretensions they are not permitted, by the act, equally to examine, to discuss, and to ascertain. And from both these situations, will not those in power derive an undue advantage for continuing themselves in it; which by impairing the right of election, endangers the blessings of the government founded on it?

It is with justice, therefore, that the General Assembly have affirmed in the resolution, as well that the right of freely examining public characters and measures, and free communication thereon, is the only effectual guardian of every other right, as that this particular right is levelled at, by the power exercised in the "sedition-act."

The resolution next in order is as follows:

That this state having by its convention, which ratified the federal Constitution, expressly declared, that among other essential rights, "the liberty of conscience and of the press cannot be cancelled, abridged, restrained or modified by any authority of the United States," and from its extreme anxiety to guard these rights from every possible attack of sophistry and ambition, having, with other states, recommended an amendment for that purpose, which amendment was, in due time, annexed to the Constitution, it would mark a reproachful inconsistency, and criminal degeneracy, if an indifference were now shown to the most palpable violation of one of the rights thus declared and secured; and the establishment of a precedent, which may be fatal to the other.

To place this resolution in its just light, it will be necessary to recur to the act of ratification by Virginia, which stands in the ensuing form:

We, the delegates of the people of Virginia, duly elected in pursuance of a recommendation from the General Assembly, and now met in convention, having fully and freely investigated and discussed the proceedings of the federal convention, and being prepared as well as the most mature deliberation hath enabled us to decide thereon, do, in the name and in behalf of the people of Virginia, declare and make known, that the powers granted under the Constitution, being derived from the people of the United States, may be resumed by them, whensoever the same shall be perverted to their injury or oppression; and that every power not granted thereby, remains with them, and at their will. That, therefore, no right of any denomination can be cancelled, abridged, restrained, or modified, by the Congress, by the Senate, or House of Representatives, acting in any capacity, by the President, or any department or officer of the United States, except in those instances in which power is given by the Constitution for those purposes; and that, among other essential rights, the liberty of conscience and of the press, cannot be cancelled, abridged, restrained, or modified, by any authority of the United States.

Here is an express and solemn declaration by the convention of the state, that they ratified the Constitution in the sense, that no right of any denomination can be cancelled, abridged, restrained, or modified by the government of the United States or any part of it; except in those instances in which power is given by the Constitution; and in the sense particularly, "that among other essential rights, the liberty of conscience and freedom of the press cannot be cancelled, abridged, restrained, or modified, by any authority of the United States."

Words could not well express, in a fuller or more forcible manner, the understanding of the convention, that the liberty of conscience and the freedom of the press, were *equally* and *completely* exempted from all authority whatever of the United States.

Under an anxiety to guard more effectually these rights against every possible danger, the convention, after ratifying the Constitution, proceeded to prefix to certain amendments proposed by them, a declaration of rights, in which are two articles providing, the one for the liberty of conscience, the other for the freedom of speech and of the press.

Similar recommendations having proceeded from a number of other states, and Congress, as has been seen, having in consequence thereof, and with a view to extend the ground of public confidence, proposed, among other declaratory and restrictive clauses, a clause expressly securing the liberty of conscience and of the press; and Virginia having concurred in the ratifications which made them a part of the Constitution, it will remain with a candid public to decide, whether it would not mark an inconsistency and degeneracy, if an indifference were now shown to a palpable violation of one of those rights, the freedom of the press; and to a precedent therein, which may be fatal to the other, the free exercise of religion.

That the precedent established by the violation of the former of these rights, may, as is affirmed by the resolution, be fatal to the latter, appears to be demonstrable, by a comparison of the grounds on which they respectively rest; and from the scope of reasoning, by which the power over the former has been vindicated.

First. Both of these rights, the liberty of conscience and of the press, rest equally on the original ground of not being delegated by the Constitution, and consequently withheld from the government. Any construction, therefore, that would attack this original security for the one, must have the like effect on the other.

Secondly. They are both equally secured by the supplement to the Constitution; being both included in the same amendment, made at the same time, and by the same authority. Any construction or argument, then, which would turn the amendment into a grant or acknowledgment of power with respect to the press, might be equally applied to the freedom of religion.

Thirdly. If it be admitted that the extent of the freedom of the press, secured by the amendment, is to be measured by the common law on this subject, the same authority may be resorted to, for the standard which is to fix the extent of the "free exercise of religion." It cannot be necessary to say what this standard would be; whether the common law be taken solely as the unwritten, or as varied by the written law of England.

Fourthly. If the words and phrases in the amendment, are to be considered as chosen with a studied discrimination, which yields an argument for a power over the press, under the limitation that its freedom be not abridged, the same argument results from the same consideration, for a power over the exercise of religion, under the limitation that its freedom be not prohibited.

For, if Congress may regulate the freedom of the press, provided they do not abridge it, because it is said only "they shall not abridge it," and is not said, "they shall make no law respecting it," the analogy of reasoning is conclusive, that Congress may *regulate* and even *abridge* the free exercise of religion, provided they do not *prohibit* it, because it is said only "they shall not prohibit it," and is *not* said, "they shall make no law *respecting,* or no law *abridging* it."

The General Assembly were governed by the clearest reason, then, in considering the "sedition-act," which legislates on the freedom of the press, as establishing a precedent that may be fatal to the liberty of conscience; and it will be the duty of all, in proportion as they value the security of the latter, to take the alarm at every encroachment on the former. . . .

8] The Republican Attack on the Army

A] RESOLUTIONS OF DINWIDDIE COUNTY, VIRGINIA

On Hamilton, the army, and high taxes, President Adams and the Republicans differed little. Adams, a strong navy man, turned against the army when Hamilton was forced upon him as second to Washington. The President, who discovered that he could not even appoint his own generals, later expostulated, ". . . I was only Viceroy under Washington and he was only Viceroy under Hamilton and Hamilton was Viceroy under the Tories . . ." Senator Sedgwick reported to Hamilton that the President once burst out: ". . . if you must have an army, I will give it to you, but remember, it will make the government more unpopular than all their other acts." The following resolutions of Dinwiddie County, Virginia, representative of the many that were adopted at mass meetings throughout the country, indicate the accuracy of Adams' views.*

Resolved, as the opinion of this meeting, that a militia, composed of the body of the people, is the proper, natural and safe defence of a free state,

---

* RESOLUTIONS OF DINWIDDIE COUNTY, VIRGINIA: From the Philadelphia *Aurora* (December 6, 1798).

and that regular armies, except in case of an invasion, or the certain prospect of an invasion, are not only highly detrimental to the public welfare, but dangerous to liberty.

Detrimental to the public welfare; because industrious men are heavily taxed to support those who do nothing; because indolence among the poor is publicly encouraged; *the army being an asylum for all who do not choose to labor* . . . because the same object, immediate defence against a sudden invasion, might be attained infinitely cheaper, by putting arms into the hands of every man capable of bearing them; and because, *the spirit which leads to war, the cause and the disgrace of humanity,* is greatly augmented by standing armies, to whose leaders it opens a prospect of greater wealth, and higher military honors: and,—

Dangerous to liberty; because, when numerous, they have tyrannized, as the experience of all ages has proved, both over the people & the government; and when limited, have always been subservient to the views of the *executive department, from which they derive their honors and emoluments;* because these honors and emoluments furnish an ample fund, by means of which the executive is enabled to *reward its partizans, and increase the number of its adherents;* because a people accustomed to look for protection from external violence, to a standing army, become *abject, debased,* and *gradually enslaved;* but knowing themselves to be the only defenders of their country, soon acquire that discipline and courage, which insure safety, not only from *foreign enemies, but domestic tyrants;* and because military establishments are in their nature progressive, the vast expence attending them, producing discontent and disturbances, and these furnishing a pretext for providing a force still more formidable; thus finally occasioning the *oppression,* the *ruin,* the SLAVERY *of the people.* . . .

B] GALLATIN FEARS THE "STANDING ARMY"

> In 1798 Congress authorized an expansion of the army from 3500 men to over 12,000, plus a provisional army of 20,000 to be called out by the President in case of emergency. Federalist newspapers spoke so stridently about the need to hang traitors, enforce the Sedition Act, and suppress domestic riot that Republicans were confirmed in their worst suspicions: the invasion scare was a mask to cover an intent to use the army against them. Here Gallatin, in a letter to his wife, displays a sincere alarm that was reflected in the Republican press.*

. . . As to politics, you know the destruction of the French fleet in Egypt. The news of peace being made by them at Radstat with the Empire and Emperor is generally believed. That they have found it their interest to change their measures with all neutrals, and that an honorable accommodation is in the power of our Administration is, in my opinion, a certain fact. We are to

---

* GALLATIN FEARS THE "STANDING ARMY": Albert Gallatin to Mrs. Gallatin, December 7, 1798. From Henry Adams, *The Life of Albert Gallatin* (Philadelphia, 1880), p. 223.

have the speech only to-morrow (Saturday). I expect it will be extremely violent against an insidious enemy and a domestic faction. They (the Federals) avow a design of keeping up a standing army for *domestic* purposes, for since the French fleet is destroyed they cannot even affect to believe that there is any danger of French invasion. General Washington, Hamilton, Pinckney, are still in town. In their presence and at the table of Governor Mifflin, Hamilton declared that a standing army was necessary, that the aspect of Virginia was threatening, and that he had the most correct and authentic information that the ferment in the western counties of Pennsylvania was greater than previous to the insurrection of 1794. You know this to be an abominable lie. But I suppose that Addison & Co. have informed him that the people turning out on an election day was a symptom of insurrection. Pickering says that militia are good for nothing unless they have 50,000 men of regular troops around which to rally. . . .

c] MILITARY OUTRAGES ON CIVILIANS

The Republican press did its best to give the military establishment a bad name by avidly exploiting every incident involving a drunken soldier or sailor. Uniformed men engaged in enough brawls, and even crimes, to make the army seem like an occupying force of Hessians to Republican editors. One copied from another so that an incident in Charleston made news in Boston and New York. The following items from the *Aurora* are typical.*

June 25, 1799

MARTIAL LAW

THE following article was handed to us by a very respectable citizen, and we have had it corroborated by several others—if the people cannot see in the outrages committed on all occasions in various parts of these States, by persons holding military authority under the United States—the danger to which the public liberties are exposed they deserve to be dragooned into military subjection.—

BE ON YOUR GUARD FELLOW-CITIZENS.

Last Saturday night, about 11 o'clock, a number of the officers of the United States Frigate, together with several others, in and out of uniform, among whom was an officer of the District Court of the United States for the State of Pennsylvania, were walking down Southstreet, committing every act of outrage upon the citizens whom they met with—they began with upsetting a cart, then to upset a chair before James Carr, the coach-maker's door—from thence they proceeded on a little farther where they attacked *Three Women,* who were sitting before their doors, by pulling up their clothes and laying hold of them—[decency forbids any further remarks here] They took with them

* MILITARY OUTRAGES ON CIVILIANS: From the Philadelphia *Aurora* (June 25 and August 5, 1799).

a chair, and went a little further, when one of them cried out—"*a sail!* a sail!" and immediately crossed the street to two women, and committed like indecencies; they then proceeded a little further and overtook a Mr. Cornelius and ordered him into the street, which he refused, upon which one of the officers drew his dirk and made a lounge [sic] at him. Mr. Luke Caffin was also obliged to fly. Mr. Durnell, a constable, who lives in the neighbourhood, hearing a noise came out and demanded that the peace of the city should not be disturbed, when he was immediately attacked in a furious manner and stabbed with a dirk—by this time a number of citizens gathered round, and had them all carried before Alderman Jennings. . . .

August 5, 1799

A circumstance transpired on Friday night last, which must eminently tend to convince the citizens of the danger in which they will be exposed, as soon as a mercenary *standing army* is quartered among them. It is a convincing proof that the *privates* who exchange the price of honest industry, for the *humiliating duties* of soldiers, are, "villains more desperate, and cut-throats equally bloody minded, with the soldiery of the British monarchy." About eleven o'clock, two of STAATS MORRIS's soldiers went into the tavern of Mr. *Davis,* near the Fell's Point market-house; they appeared to be intoxicated, and pressed a man in the house to play at cards for money—Mr. Davis assured them that he would not allow gambling in his house; the soldiers insisted, and on D. ordering them out of his house, one of them drew his bayonet from the belt, and stabbed Mr. D. in the left side; another person interfered, and the second soldier made a lunge with his bayonet, which, by the man's dodging took him on the left temple, and laid the flesh open to the extremity of the back of his head.

These men, with a number of others, we understand, were detached from the fort, *to support the dignity of government,* in guarding the sloops of war, in the very neighbourhood of the mechanics that built them, and of the citizens that suscribed largely towards their building. If such a delusion as national dignity is thus to endanger the lives of the quiet and peaceable citizens; if such bloodhounds are to be let loose at the dead hour of the night, what man who estimates the liberty and safety which our constitution guarantees, but must join in execrating an establishment that must multiply a set of men who have ever conceived themselves superior to civil law. . . . (From the Baltimore *American*)

D] THE DANGER OF THE ARMY TO A FREE PRESS

The Republican press had a field day in depicting the tyranny of the army in crushing Fries's Rebellion and pacifying the Northampton countryside of Pennsylvania in March of 1799. Lurid reports of the mistreatment of prisoners by the military provoked a few arrogant soldiers to take revenge, first on the editor of a German-language newspaper, and then on William Duane of the *Aurora,* the foremost Republican editor in the nation. For his offensive remarks about the conduct of federal troops, Duane was indicted under the Sedition Act. Jefferson, on becoming President, dismissed the indictment and all others pending under the hated statute; he also pardoned all persons convicted.*

April 27, 1799

FEDERAL LIGHT HORSE
Translated from 'THE READING ADLER,' or Eagle of April 23.

ON SATURDAY afternoon last, the troops who were sent to seize upon some people in Northampton, called insurgents, on their return from that expedition arrived in this town. . . . This army was small yet it was not without its rotten members, and some extremely so. But among the whole there were none that exceeded *Captain Montgomery's* troop of Lancaster light horse. . . .

As for example, a part of them came to my printing-office on Saturday last . . . like a banditti of robbers and assasins; they tore the clothes off my body, and forcibly dragged me from my house before their captain, who certainly proved himself worthy to command his corps. He ordered his troopers to take me to the Market-House and give me *twenty-five* lashes on the bare back, and they proceeded to obey his orders accordingly, and certainly would have fulfilled them exactly had not some of Captain Leiper's troop of Philadelphia, interfered, reproached them for their illegal and tyrannical conduct, in consequence of which only a part of the sentence of Captain Montgomery [*six lashes*] was inflicted.

These, my dear fellow citizens, are the friends of good order,—this is the mode of conduct which they pursue whose mouths are always full of a regard for the laws, and who have been called forth to support the government and suppress Insurrection, but who it is evident would much rather create one. So much for the present, but soon more; from

JACOB SCHNEIDER.

May 16, 1799

MORE OF GOOD ORDER AND REGULAR GOVERNMENT!

AFTER the conduct of the *Lancaster troop* towards Mr. Schnyder [*sic*], printer, of Reading—after the vindication of that conduct by general Macpherson's aid-de-camps, it was hardly to be expected that any *republican* printer or editor should be exempt from similar violence.

The Aurora has been long an object of dread and abhorrence to the detestable *faction* that has laboured with so much violence and dishonor to subject these free states to principles and institutions subversive of the republican form of government. . . .

Yesterday *a band* of those *friends of good order and regular government;* to the amount of near THIRTY, entered the Office of the Aurora—and while the the [*sic*] editor was pursuing his business, assaulted him; while some of

* THE DANGER OF THE ARMY TO A FREE PRESS: From the Philadelphia *Aurora* (April 27 and May 16, 1799)

the band acted as centinels on the Compositors and Pressmen—and others with presented pistols kept some persons who chanced to be in the office at bay, *Peter Merkin* who was the principal of those dastards with several others seized the Editor by violence, struck him several times on the head, while others held his hands. By force they dragged him down stairs into Franklin court, and there repeated their violence by reiterated blows, from above TEN different persons.

It was in vain that the Editor offered personal satisfaction to any or to all of them successively, equally disregardful of the *principles of honor* as of the *established laws*—they had neither the courage to attack him singly—nor to accept the resort of men of honor.

After having satiated their malice, by blows which the Editor was no longer able, and could not from their number either effectually retaliate or repel; they sought to add what they conceived to be dishonor on the Editor, by several blows with a whip—upon whom the dishonor rests the public will determine, the Editor neither feels it nor fears them either collectively or individually. . . .

WM. DUANE,
Editor of the Aurora.

9] The Economic Consequences of Federalist Political Policies

A] THE TAX GATHERER EASES JEFFERSON'S DESPAIR

President Adams himself thought "this damned army will be the ruin of this country" and predicted in 1800 that the government would be bankrupt within a year. Expensive defense preparations almost doubled the federal budget during the Adams administration. Taxes were *"liberally laid on,"* complained the President, and the people were losing patience. There was a stamp tax, a salt tax, an increased carriage tax, a direct tax, additional duties on imports, and still the government had to borrow at 8 per cent to meet deficits. Jefferson, as the following letters to friends demonstrate, very early sensed what Adams saw belatedly.*

TO ARCHIBALD HAMILTON ROWAN

MONTICELLO, Sep. 26, 98.

SIR,—

To avoid the suspicions & curiosity of the post office, which would have been excited by seeing your name and mine on the back of a letter, I have delayed acknoleging the receipt of your favor of July last, till an occasion to write to

---

* THE TAX GATHERER EASES JEFFERSON'S DESPAIR: Letters to Archibald Hamilton Rowan, September 26, 1798, and John Taylor, November 26, 1798. From Paul Leicester Ford, ed., *The Writings of Thomas Jefferson* (New York, 1892–99), VII, 280–81, 309–10.

an inhabitant of Wilmington gives me an opportunity of putting my letter under cover to him. The system of alarm & jealousy which has been so powerfully played off in England, has been mimicked here, not entirely without success. The most long-sighted politician could not, seven years ago, have imagined that the people of this wide-extended country could have been enveloped in such delusion, and made so much afraid of themselves and their own power, as to surrender it spontaneously to those who are manœuvring them into a form of government, the principal branches of which may be beyond their control. The commerce of England, however, has spread its roots over the whole face of our country. This is a real source of all the obliquities of the public mind; and I should have had doubts of the ultimate term they might attain; but happily, the game, to be worth the playing of those engaged in it, must flush them with money. The authorized expenses of this year are beyond those of any year in the late war for independence, & they are of a nature to beget great & constant expenses. The purse of the people is the real seat of sensibility. It is to be drawn upon largely, and they will then listen to truths which could not excite them through any other organ. . . .

TO JOHN TAYLOR

November 26, 98.

Dear Sir,

. . . I owe you a political letter. Yet the infidelities of the post office and the circumstances of the times are against my writing fully & freely, whilst my own dispositions are as much against mysteries, innuendos & half-confidences. I know not which mortifies me most, that I should fear to write what I think, or my country bear such a state of things. Yet Lyon's judges, and a jury of all nations, are objects of rational fear. We agree in all the essential ideas of your letter. We agree particularly in the necessity of some reform, and of some better security for civil liberty. . . . But there is a most respectable part of our State who have been enveloped in the X. Y. Z. delusion, and who destroy our unanimity for the present moment. This disease of the imagination will pass over, because the patients are essentially republican. Indeed, the Doctor is now on his way to cure it, in the guise of a tax gatherer. But give time for the medicine to work, & for the repetition of stronger doses, which must be administered. The principle of the present majority is *excessive expense,* money enough to fill all their maws, or it will not be worth the risk of their supporting. They cannot borrow a dollar in Europe, or above 2. or 3. millions in America. This is not the fourth of the expences of this year, unprovided for. Paper money would be perillous even to the paper men. Nothing then but excessive taxation can get us along; and this will carry reason & reflection to every man's door, and particularly in the hour of election. . . .

b] Dr. Ames and the "Great Sovereign" Grumble

When Fisher Ames died in 1808, his brother Dr. Nathaniel Ames refused to attend the funeral, though they had lived in the same little town. Nathaniel, as partisan in his politics as Fisher, was a passionate, pugnacious Republi-

can—a "Jacobin of Jacobins" his brother called him. In the following entries
in his diary, Nathaniel recorded with characteristic vehemence a Republican
reaction to the direct tax on dwellings, houses, and slaves. No other tax
aroused so much opposition. Its collection caused Fries's Rebellion and converted a Federalist stronghold to Republicanism.*

December 2, 1798. New occasions to pity the weakness of human nature.
Seeing N. Kingsberry, etc., accept assessment foreign tax! ! ! In Milton, December, I am informed they have begun to take the valuation of houses and
land under Act of Congress, and Col. Jon. Vose refused them admittance to
his house, for that Congress have no authority to take a Valuation, but only to
lay direct taxes according to numbers, which implies such tax shall be assessed
and collected under State Authority and town privileges of choosing our own
Assessors and Collectors without consolidation by having them fixed perpetual
and inexorable over us to increase Executive influence by infinite multiplication of officers—but Might will overcome Right.

January, 1799. House and land tax of Congress goes on heavily, causing
great uneasiness. Some refuse and then to avoid the penalty have to conform.
No assessor in Dedham will yet take office but N. Kingsberry, Esq. Silent indignation hath not yet exploded—tho' hard threatened. I fear civil war must
be the result of Government measures. But now, January 20, I hear that
Nehemiah Fales and Oliver Guild of Dedham have taken and begun to
officiate as understrappers tools to the Perpetual Assessors to number and
measure houses for High Fed. Government. Their names ought to be execrated
by all Posterity.

But possibly, seeing many will accept, and do, in other towns that have
been most bitter against the arbitrary British influence, for the sake of the
pay accept, it may be an easement not to be assessed by strangers, if any of our
own people will submit to the infamy of the office.

January 23, 1799. Called on by Nehemiah Fales for dimensions of my house
and windows, and list of land for direct tax of High Federalist tyrant Government. I introduce it thus:

"Nat. Ames (regretting the short dawn of rational liberty under the Confederation—deploring the blindness and apathy of that People who once dared
to defy and trample on the minions of foreign tyrants, only to be trampled
on by domestic traitors, in impudent junto, breaking the limits of their Sovereign—greeted with the tyrant songs of 'Energy of the Government'—'Tighten
the Reins of Government,' only to stifle the cheering sound of the great Sovereign's voice—forced to yield, instead of to Law, to the mighty powers that be),
exhibits this list and description of his house and land on the first day of
October, 1798:

"1 Dwelling House 40 feet long—two stories high—30 feet wide—glass, etc.—
198 feet glass—453 squares.

---

* DR. AMES AND THE "GREAT SOVEREIGN" GRUMBLE: From Charles Warren, ed., *Jacobin
and Junto, Or Early American Politics as Viewed in the Diary of Dr. Nathaniel Ames,
1758–1822* (Cambridge, Mass., 1931), pp. 123–24. Reprinted by permission of the editor
and the Harvard University Press.

"1 Barn, 24 × 35. 7¾ acres Lot and Bog Meadow. Woodland, 10 acres Rocks and Bushes. 1 corn house 10 feet square."

January 29. The great Sovereign grumbles at unconstitutional tax.

June 1, 1800. My direct High Fed. tax—House $5.60; other estate $1.43–$7.03.

c] THE PEOPLE'S "LOVE FOR PELF WAS ROUSED'

Alexander Graydon was a staunch conservative, prominent in Pennsylvania politics and literary circles. He was an early and important advocate of the adoption of the Constitution and served in the state ratifying convention and in the convention of 1790 that framed a new state constitution. He is best remembered for his charming and informative *Memoirs*, first published in 1811. Here is his view of the reasons for the defeat of his party in 1800. Jefferson carried Pennsylvania by only one electoral vote, but his popular support was probably about three to one.*

IT WAS to have been expected, that the unexampled profligacy and insolence of the ruling power in France, would have considerably depressed their Democratic adherents in America, and strengthened the Federalists in the same proportion; but the consequences were directly the reverse. Alarmed much more than necessary at the menace of the Directory, and relying more upon the addresses from the people, than a considerate attention to their sentiments would warrant; (as, although they all expressed a warm regard for the honour of the country, they, for the most part, drivelled about the unkindness of the *dear* Sister-Republic,) the administration and its friends in Congress, seemed to think, that they were assured of the public support, in any measures against France, however energetic they might be. In this persuasion, such as deemed a state of hostility preferable to a state of fraternity with her, probably thought the occasion too favourable to be suffered to pass away; and in this view, an attitude unequivocally hostile, was taken by the government. A provisional army was voted, volunteer corps invited, ships of war equipped, and as a part of the system of defence, against a foe, which was well known to have numerous partisans among us, the *alien* and *sedition* laws were enacted. But the most volcanic ground of all was yet to be trodden. Money was to be raised, and not a little would suffice. The ordinary revenues were insufficient; and the adherents of the foreign power, already exulted in the anticipated ruin of their adversaries, who vainly flattered themselves with a public confidence, which could not be shaken. With less ability, the intriguers had vastly more cunning than the federalists; and from their better acquaintance with the human heart in its selfishness and littlenesses, they well knew, that a direct and sensible application to the pocket, would be more likely to blow up the prevailing party than any thing else. It has been well said, that a disorderly people will suffer a *robbery* with more patience than an *impost*. Under this conviction, the patriots had long sickened at perceiving that the community was satisfied; and that the current expenses of government were so easily raised. This was truly

* THE PEOPLE'S "LOVE FOR PELF WAS ROUSED": From Alexander Graydon, *Memoirs of His Own Time* (Philadelphia, 1846), pp. 388–91.

provoking. They wished the people to feel, they said. It was not right that they should pay without knowing it; and hence, a furious and persevering clamour against indirect taxation. It was reprobated as hateful and anti-republican in the extreme; it was not to be endured; and, inasmuch as it aimed at deceiving the people (wicked thing!) by cheating them into contributions, which their love of country would always most cheerfully afford when necessary, it was represented to be unworthy of freemen; and to imply a suspicion both of the virtue and understanding of the community, which, about the same time was voted by the democratic part of congress, to be the most enlightened on the globe, France herself scarcely excepted. All this was vastly fine and highly pleasing, no doubt, to the galleries; a charming material too, for the *republican* editors to cook up a most savoury dish for their customers. The simple, well meaning federalists were, in their turn pleased also, at finding that their opponents were smoothing the way to a measure, that, in the present conjuncture, would be exceedingly eligible for them; and therefore, with no small degree of self-complacency for their supposed address, took the tricksters at their word, and passed a law for a direct tax. Its operation was on houses and lands; but still keeping in view, the policy of favouring the industrious and frugal at the expense of the luxurious, the farmer paid very little for his property in proportion to the idle gentleman or inhabitant of a city, who gratified himself in the enjoyment of a sumptuous house. In the same spirit, a tax had been laid upon carriages kept for comfort and pleasure; an article which, beyond all others, made manifest the discrimination in behalf of *the mouth of labour.* Nevertheless, it was the mouth that from the hollow, pretended solicitude of its parasites that it might not be "deprived of the bread that it earned," was brought to clamour the loudest against taxes which did not effect it, and had, in fact, a tendency to relieve it; another proof of the inconsiderateness of the multitude, and of the superior potency of words to things, and consequently, of the very little chance indeed of honesty and fair dealing in a contest with knavery and hypocrisy, before "the bar of public reason."

This tax on real property, was the fatal blow to federalism in Pennsylvania. The Stamp Act was, indeed, bad enough, because it was a Stamp Act that first excited our displeasure with the mother country: The very name of an excise was hateful to freemen: The alien law, set at naught one of the inherent rights of man, that is, the right of *impatriation* and *expatriation,* of coming and going and saying and doing whatever the love of liberty prompted; and the sedition law was still more execrable, since, in permitting the truth to be given in evidence in exculpation of a libeller, it gagged the mouths alone of patriotic liars and calumniators, the only species of partisans whose labours could be efficient in a cause, emphatically that of falsehood. But, though all these sad doings had been carefully impressed upon the sensory of the great Germanic body of Pennsylvania, they had not fully wrought the desired effect. Their pockets had hitherto been spared, and wheat had borne a good price. But now their vulnerable part was touched, and they began to look about them. Nor were there wanting "friends of the people" to sympathize in their oppression, and to put them in mind, that it was to avoid the payment of taxes we went to war with Great Britain; that the federalists, therefore, were as tyrannical as she had been, and that this tax upon farms, houses and *windows,* was but the beginning of a system, which would soon extend to every thing; and that we should have at length a tax upon horses, wagons and ploughs; or as it was expressed in a handbill, circulated in favour of the election of Thomas M'Kean, "a horse tax, a cart tax, a plough tax, &c. &c." The love of pelf was completely roused . . .

CONCLUSION

THE CRISIS of 1798–99 took shape when the latent authoritarianism within the Federalist party threatened to abort the development of a free and responsible government in the United States. Deterioration of relations with France created the opportunity and the cover for a thrust for power by a high-placed political elite with little or no faith in the capacity of the people for self-government. These men, who composed the ultra-Federalist faction, conceived of themselves as an aristocracy not of land and bloodline but of political virtue and fitness to rule—rule rather than govern. Impatient with political compromise and incapable of distinguishing dissent from disloyalty, they were prepared to use legal and military coercion to control public opinion for party purposes. They were prepared, too, to abandon a foreign policy of neutrality and nonintervention in exchange for foreign intrigues and military conquest. Even war was planned as an instrument of party policy. Distrustful of free elections, they were intolerant of free speech, freedom of the press, and a free political opposition. Their efforts to institutionalize vigilantism and repression were noxiously at variance with the elementary principles of an open society and the development of a political democracy.

The party had been in continuous mastery since the organization of the government under the Constitution. But Washington's retirement from politics had been followed by a hairline victory in the election of 1796, jarring the Hamiltonians into a realization that their personal power and domination of the nation's destiny faced a precarious future. Unable to accept gracefully the possibility of defeat, they exploited a crisis in foreign relations by advancing an extremist program calculated to burke the opposition.

When President Adams suddenly made peace with France, he broke the Hamiltonians by destroying the basis of their program. Their savage campaign against him ended public confidence in the party which had already been weakened by the public reaction against the high cost of military preparations. A few instances of outrageous conduct on the part of soldiers against civilians gave substance to Republican propaganda which played on the popular fear of a standing army. Taxes and soldiers probably alienated more moderate voters from Federalism than the Sedition Act prosecutions.

Adams deserved the credit for the Franco-American Convention of 1800, ratified in 1801, which gave the United States a desperately needed period of peace and re-established the principle of neutrality in American foreign relations. He also paved the way for the return of national sanity. It was Jefferson, however, who reaped the credit. Certainly his election meant the conclusive repudiation of militarism and of a one-party system by the young American nation. The new President's inaugural address rechartered the national course. The will of the majority, he declared, must prevail, but to be rightful it must be reasonable, respectful of the equal rights of the political opposition.

Let us, then, fellow-citizens [said Jefferson], unite with one heart and one mind. Let us restore to social intercourse that harmony and affection without which liberty and even life itself are but dreary things. And let us reflect that, having banished from our land that religious intolerance under which mankind so long bled and suffered, we have yet gained little if we countenance a political intolerance as despotic, as wicked, and capable of as bitter and bloody persecutions . . . every difference of opinion is not a difference of principle. We have called by different names brethren of the same principle. We are all Republicans, we are all Federalists. If there be any among us who would wish to dissolve this Union or change its republican form, let them stand undisturbed as monuments of the safety with which error of opinion may be tolerated where reason is left free to combat it. . . . Let us, then, with courage and confidence pursue our Federal and Republican principles, our attachment to the Union and representative government.

STUDY QUESTIONS

1] Given the diplomatic crisis with France and her military strength, were not the administration's preparedness measures justified? Which, if any, would you criticize? Why? How do you account for the opposition to preparedness measures by the Republicans? Would the national interest have best been served had the Republican policies been adopted?

2] What is your opinion of Madison's statement that the federal government should be "destitute of every authority for restraining the licentiousness of the press, and for shielding itself against the libellous attacks which may be made on those who administer it"? What, if any, limits should be placed on freedom of political expression during a period of national crisis such as 1798?

3] How do you account for President Adams' sudden decision to accept French overtures for the re-establishment of diplomatic relations and the resolution of Franco-American differences? Why did he adhere to his peace policy in the face of strenuous opposition from his own Cabinet and influential party leaders?

4] Jefferson's election is often referred to as the "Revolution of 1800." In what respects, if any, was his election a revolution, and how do you account for his victory over Adams, who was responsible for making peace with France?

RECOMMENDED READINGS

PRIMARY SOURCES

ADAMS, CHARLES FRANCIS, ed. *Works of John Adams with a Life*, 10 vols. (Boston, 1850–56), Vols. VIII–IX.

ADAMS, HENRY, ed. *Writings of Albert Gallatin*, 3 vols. (Philadelphia, 1879), Vol. I.

AMES, SETH, ed. *Works of Fisher Ames*, 2 vols. (Boston, 1854), Vol. I.

FITZPATRICK, JOHN C., ed. *The Writings of George Washington*, 39 vols. (Washington, 1933–44), Vol. XXXVII.

FORD, PAUL LEICESTER, ed. *The Writings of Thomas Jefferson*, 10 vols. (New York, 1892–99), Vol. VII.

GIBBS, GEORGE. *Memoirs of the Administrations of Washington and John Adams*, The Papers of Oliver Wolcott, 2 vols. (New York, 1846), Vol. II.

HAMILTON, JOHN C., ed. *Works of Alexander Hamilton*, 7 vols. (New York, 1850–51), Vols. VI–VII.

HUNT, GAILLARD, ed. *Writings of James Madison*, 9 vols. (New York, 1900–10), Vol. VI.

KING, CHARLES R., ed. *The Life and Correspondence of Rufus King, Comprising His Letters* . . . , 6 vols. (New York, 1894–1900), Vol. II.

U.S. CONGRESS. *Annals of Congress (Debates and Proceedings in the Congress of the United States)*, 5 Cong., 1797–99 (Washington, 1851).

The Virginia Report of 1799–1800, Touching the Alien and Sedition Laws; Together with the Virginia Resolutions of December 21, 1798, The Debates and Proceedings Thereon in the House of Delegates of Virginia, and Several Other Documents (Richmond, 1850).

WHARTON, FRANCIS, ed. *State Trials of the United States During the Administrations of Washington and Adams* (Philadelphia, 1849).

SECONDARY SOURCES

ANDERSON, FRANK M. "Enforcement of the Alien and Sedition Acts," American Historical Association, *Annual Report for 1912*, pp. 113–27.

DARLING, ARTHUR B. *Our Rising Empire, 1763–1803* (New Haven, 1940).

DAUER, MANNING J. *The Adams Federalists* (Baltimore, 1953).

KOCH, ADRIENNE, AND HARRY AMMON. "The Virginia and Kentucky Resolutions: An Episode in Jefferson's and Madison's Defense of Civil Liberties," *William and Mary Quarterly* (1948), 145–76.

KURZ, STEPHEN G. *The Presidency of John Adams: The Collapse of Federalism 1795–1800* (Philadelphia, 1957).

LEVY, LEONARD W. *Legacy of Suppression: Freedom of Speech and Press in Early American History* (Cambridge, Mass., 1960).

LYON, E. WILSON. "The Franco-American Convention of 1800," *Journal of Modern History*, XII (1940), 305–33.

MALONE, DUMAS. *The Public Life of Thomas Cooper* (New Haven, 1926).

MILLER, JOHN C. *Crisis in Freedom: The Alien and Sedition Acts* (Boston, 1952).

Perkins, Bradford. *The First Rapprochement: England and the United States, 1795–1805* (Philadelphia, 1955).

Smelser, Marshall. "The Jacobin Phrenzy: Federalism and the Menace of Liberty, Equality, and Fraternity," *Review of Politics*, XIII (1951), 457–82.

Smith, James Morton. *Freedom's Fetters: The Alien and Sedition Laws and American Civil Liberties* (Ithaca, N.Y., 1956).

Warfield, Ethelbert D. *The Kentucky Resolutions of 1798* (New York, 1887).

Warren, Charles, ed. *Jacobin and Junto, Or Early American Politics as Viewed in the Diary of Dr. Nathaniel Ames, 1758–1822* (Cambridge, Mass., 1931).

Nationalism and Sectionalism: The Crisis of 1819–1820

MERRILL D. PETERSON

BRANDEIS UNIVERSITY

CONTENTS

CHRONOLOGY

1815

FEBRUARY 15   Treaty of Ghent ratified by the United States Senate.

1816

APRIL 10   Second Bank of the United States chartered by Congress.

APRIL 27   Tariff of 1816 enacted by Congress.

1817

MARCH 3   President Madison vetoes the Bonus Bill.

MARCH 4   James Monroe inaugurated fifth President of the United States.

APRIL 15   Commencement of Erie Canal authorized by New York legislature.

1818

APRIL 18   The Navigation Act closes American ports to British vessels from colonies (e.g., the British West Indies) legally closed to American vessels.

JULY 20   Policy of contraction commenced by the Bank of the United States.

1819

JANUARY   Cotton prices plunge downward.

JANUARY–
FEBRUARY   The House of Representatives receives and debates report of its investigating committee on the Bank.

FEBRUARY 2–
MARCH 6   Supreme Court announces decisions in the cases of *Dartmouth College* v. *Woodward, Sturges* v. *Crowninshield,* and *McCulloch* v. *Maryland.*

FEBRUARY 13   James Tallmadge introduces amendment to restrict slavery in Missouri.

MARCH 6   Langdon Cheves succeeds William Jones as president of the Bank of the United States.

1820

MARCH 3   The Missouri Compromise adopted by Congress.

APRIL 24   Land Act of 1820 abolishes the credit system, reduces the minimum price from $2.00 to $1.25 an acre, and reduces the minimum purchase from 320 to 80 acres.

APRIL 29   Proposed Tariff of 1820 adopted in the House, lost in the Senate, and postponed to succeeding session.

DECEMBER 6   Monroe re-elected President with only one electoral vote cast against him.

INTRODUCTION

T HE UNITED STATES emerged from the dubious glories of the War of 1812 in a mood of exuberant optimism. "In 1815 for the first time," as Henry Adams later wrote, "Americans ceased to doubt the path they were to follow." The war, so meager in victories, was rich in patriotic symbols, songs, and slogans—the affectionate figure of "Uncle Sam," Francis Scott Key's hymn to the "Star-Spangled Banner," Captain James Lawrence's dying cry, "Don't give up the ship!"—all the rich raiment of a proud nationality. Surprisingly, a war which had been but grudgingly supported by the American people led, at its conclusion, to a vigorous renewal of national principles and feelings. The people, Albert Gallatin observed, "are more Americans; they feel and act more as a nation."

The nation's confidence appeared to be well founded. The Peace of Ghent, though it resolved none of the issues which had provoked the war, nevertheless laid the basis for the pacific settlement of differences with Great Britain. At the same time the return of peace at home and abroad obliterated the principal basis of internal opposition to the administration in Washington. The Federalist party never recovered from the fiasco of the Hartford Convention of 1814. In national affairs the Republican party ruled without hindrance except from itself. With the melting of the partisan rivalries inherited from the generation of the founders, and in the absence of new fuel for party warfare, there seemed little reason to doubt that the Republican "era of good feelings" inaugurated with President Monroe would enjoy a long life.

The prospect looked almost as good from the economic standpoint. A Europe famished by the wars of the Napoleonic era was suddenly thrown open to American commerce. As agricultural surpluses found their way once again to foreign markets, commodity prices rose, lands increased in value, and a speculative mania burst upon the West. The looms and spindles of the British industrial revolution consumed American cotton faster than the sprawling lands of the South could produce it. Hundreds of state banks, aided and abetted by the newly chartered Second Bank of the United States, fed the credit hunger of the nation. The general inflationary movement reflected itself as well in the profits of merchants who catered to American tastes—long unsatisfied—for European finery. Only the fledgling native manufactures, which had been born under the protective mantle of European wars, appeared to suffer from the return of peace. Thus, despite some unfavorable currents, the nationalism of the postwar years was floated on a sea of prosperity.

But prosperity ended abruptly in 1819. The panic which struck with full force in the early months of that year was the first great capitalist crisis in American history, and it set the pattern for others to follow at intervals of roughly every twenty years. The Panic of 1819 was unusual only in the rapidity with which the cycle of boom and bust completed itself. After a brief period of soaring prices, active trading, prolific credit, and heavy investment, the economy suffered sharp reverses all along the line. Wholesale prices—a sensitive indicator of economic conditions—declined, on the average, twelve per cent in 1819 and a further thirteen per cent the following year. Many manufacturing companies closed their doors. The total work force in thirty Philadelphia industries fell from 9672 in 1816 to 2137 in 1819. Philadelphia, along with other eastern cities, set up soup kitchens to feed their hungry. Merchants, shipmasters, and seamen were injured by the decline in foreign trade, as recorded in federal revenue collections at the customhouses: thirty-six million dollars in 1816, twenty-one million in 1819, fifteen million in 1820, and—the bottom—thirteen million in 1821.

The depression of 1819, though it broke banks, bankrupted merchants, idled workers and emptied factories, was centered in American agriculture and, more particularly, in the freshly burgeoned lands of the South and West. Prices of most agricultural commodities fell thirty to forty per cent in a few months' time. Cotton, which sold for thirty-three cents a pound before the panic struck, plunged to fourteen in the fall of 1819. The collapse of the cotton market was disastrous for the entire economy, since soaring cotton prices had fed the boom in foreign commerce, virgin land, and bank credit. New Western states took the lead in passing "relief laws" for the benefit of debtors, but the laws, while they caused political havoc, actually gave little relief. Conditions as portrayed in Vincennes, Illinois, in 1823 were fairly typical. "A few years past Vincennes was the very emblem of prosperity: every wind wafted her some good," a local observer wrote.

How sadly is the picture reversed. More than one third of our dwelling houses are destitute of inhabitants, our population has decreased nearly one half, our ready property has suffered a greater diminution. Buildings that a few years ago rented for $200 to $300 per annum now rent for $50 to $100. . . . A universal despondency prevails.

Economic knowledge was in a primitive state: there was little agreement as to what had caused the panic and what might be done to overcome it. Some men felt that time and patience were the best correctives. They were no doubt comforted by President Monroe's assurance to Congress in 1820 that, despite evidences of despondency, the country was in a "prosperous and happy condition." Many more traced the country's ills into the realm of private economy: wasteful spending in articles of fashion and luxury and reckless speculation in lands and stocks. The remedy would be found in return to the simple virtues of honesty and frugality. In some religious quarters the panic was viewed as the judgment of God on a wicked people. The General Assembly of the Presbyterian Church thus called the people back to the ways of Christianity. But much more significant than these exhortations to patience, piety, and frugality were several fundamental responses to the crisis which had far-reaching implications for government policy and which in their different tendencies, renewed the sectional tensions that had so recently been quieted in the "era of good feelings."

One of these responses may be identified with the advocates of the American System. Nationalistic in principle and design, the American System consolidated several specific ideas and policies into a practical program of political economy. It resembled, in some respects, the system Alexander Hamilton had pursued in the Republic's infancy. Its more ardent champions often invoked Hamilton's name in behalf of their cause. But the American System boasted prominent Jeffersonian features as well. Most of its adherents were Jeffersonian in political sympathy and party affiliation. Whereas Hamilton's economic nationalism had been hamstrung by his, and his party's, dependence on Great Britain and discredited by abuses against republican government, the American System was both republican and national in outline. Imbued with the patriotic *élan* of the second war against Britain, addressed to the problems that came in the war's aftermath, the American System was neither Federalist nor Republican in any partisan or doctrinaire sense. Circumstances combined to favor national solutions to urgent economic problems. Friends of American System policies were found in every section of the country, though support for the program as a whole was concentrated in the Middle Atlantic states, with Pennsylvania the keystone. Much of the leadership in Congress came from men who had been "war hawks" in 1811—Henry Clay of Kentucky, who resumed the Speakership of the House of Representatives in 1815, and stern-visaged John C. Calhoun of South Carolina. Especially prominent in mobilizing public sentiment for the American System were Hezekiah Niles, the Baltimore publisher of *Niles' Weekly Register*, and Mathew Carey, indefatigable pamphleteer, of Philadelphia.

From the Peace of Ghent to the Panic of 1819 the United States government moved steadily on the course charted by the American System toward greater power and responsibility for the national welfare. In 1816 the Second Bank of the United States was incorporated by Congress. A new edition of Hamilton's bank, which had been allowed to expire with its charter in 1811, the Second Bank was made necessary by the deplorable state of the country's currency and the government's credit following the war. By virtue not alone of its size but also of its several powers to establish branches, to act as the fiscal agent of the government, and to issue notes that were receivable—in lieu of gold and silver—in payment of taxes and other government dues, the Bank was believed capable of providing the entire nation with a sound and uniform currency and a regulated volume of credit, both important conditions of expanding business enterprise. The passage of the Bank bill signaled the rise of a *national* Republicanism very different from the original variety. The measure was urged upon Congress, and then signed into law, by President Madison, author of the Virginia Resolutions of 1798. It was steered through the House of Representatives by Calhoun, who claimed Jeffersonian lineage, and dramatically advocated by Clay, who five years earlier had taken strict constructionist ground to help defeat the recharter of the first national bank. The new bank was most wanted in the regions that tended to be Jeffersonian in outlook; and, in the final vote, more Federalists than Republicans were recorded against it.

The war had also underscored the need for extensive new arteries of transportation to facilitate movement among different parts of the union, bind it together, and secure its defenses. The rapid development of the South and

West created still further demands for roads and canals to link the interior farm lands with the eastern markets. A national system of internal improvements had been proposed by Jefferson's Secretary of the Treasury, Albert Gallatin, in 1808. Calhoun revived Gallatin's plan in 1816. Seizing upon the $1,500,000 bonus which the Second Bank had paid for its charter privileges, Calhoun's Bonus Bill proposed to establish a permanent fund for financing a vast network of roads, canals, and other improvements. The fund would be continually replenished by the pledge of dividends on the government's holdings of one-fifth of the Bank's stock. In this ingenious way one measure of the American System would service another. Strongly supported by the Middle Atlantic and Western states, the bill passed both houses of Congress only to be vetoed by Madison in the last act of his Presidency. Madison favored a national program of internal improvements; but, in a surprising retreat to the doctrine of strict construction, he called for the explicit sanction of a constitutional amendment. No such amendment was ever passed, or seriously agitated for. The advocates of internal improvements continued to press their case in Congress, but almost nothing was accomplished. In the absence of constructive national action the separate states embarked upon ambitious projects of their own (such as New York's Erie Canal, begun in 1817), which, though they helped to meet the country's need for improved transportation, failed to realize the objectives of a coherent national system.

The protective tariff for the encouragement of domestic manufactures was unquestionably the crucial policy of the American System. The war and the commercial restrictions preceding it had stimulated native industrial production in many lines—textiles, iron, glass, leather, etc. The rage for "homespun" was nationwide, and many expected that the second war against Britain would accomplish, as the first clearly had not, the *economic* independence of the United States. But with the return of peace, the British glutted the American market with the intent of destroying the manufactures of "the youthful Hercules." The experience seemed to prove Hamilton's contention a quarter-century earlier that American manufacturing enterprise would not be able to compete with the more advanced industrial nations of Europe without substantial government assistance.

A sympathetic Congress endeavored to supply the needed support in the Tariff Act of 1816. Modeled on a plan reported by Alexander Dallas, Secretary of the Treasury, the act classified all imported articles in three categories. Articles that could be produced in abundance at home were taxed at prohibitive rates, generally thirty-five per cent of value, in order to secure the market to American manufacturers. The duties on articles not produced at home were fixed with a view to revenue only; they averaged about fifteen per cent of value. The third category included articles which could be manufactured in large quantities but of which the supply was not yet sufficient for American needs; accordingly, duties were adjusted to encourage the domestic product while still leaving the door open to the foreign competitor. The prevailing level was twenty per cent, though special protective devices were employed in the case of cotton textiles, one of the newest and largest branches of American manufacture. Dissatisfied with the Tariff of 1816, manufacturing interests and champions of the American System stepped up their agitation for higher tariffs.

The protective tariff, internal improvements, the national bank—such were the principal measures of the American System. A system, by definition, exhibits its various elements in relationship to each other. Thus the meaning of the American System is to be found less in the specific measures than in their interconnections and in the underlying assumptions that gave coherency to the entire program. The theorists and advocates of the American System assumed, first of all, that the nation is an economic entity unto itself, having interests which are paramount to those of individual citizens and other nations. "The great desideratum in political economy," according to Henry Clay, "is what is the largest application of the aggregate industry of the nation that can be made honestly to produce the largest sum of national wealth." The end, *national wealth*, was more than the sum of individual wealth; and the central government, as the custodian of national interests, had a crucial role in planning, organizing, and channeling economic activities. The ascendant idea of *laissez faire*, which identified individual self-interests with the national interest, was emphatically rejected. Rejected as well was the older idea that a nation becomes rich through foreign commerce. In its place, the American System advocates projected the idea of a "self-contained nation." It was to be brought into being by the balanced organization of the country's immense and varied economic resources. Thus, wealth was no longer equated with money per se, as it had been under mercantilism, where bullion was needed to attract client states, buy armies, and maintain power. Under the American System wealth was redefined as the potential for natural resources to ensure permanent prosperity. The United States appeared as potentially "a world within itself." A country of continental proportions need not, like Britain, look to far-flung markets. Its path of destiny lay in the development of a "territorial division of labor," founded in climate and geography, and in the creation of a "home market" for the productions of its different territories. Manufactures would rise behind the tariff wall, particularly in the Northeast, and absorb the raw materials and surpluses of the agricultural sections. An expanding transportation network would facilitate the internal trade. A national banking system would assure fair and expeditious management of the credit operations in domestic exchange. These were economic considerations, but they were not unrelated to important political objectives. For example, in regard to national defense, the American System promised to strengthen the country by reducing its dependence on foreign markets, sources of supply, and revenue collected at the customhouses; and, in regard to national union, the promotion of internal commerce and communication among the parts of a wide and disparate country seemed likely to consolidate the loyalties of the American people.

The economic collapse of 1819 fortified the friends of the American System in their convictions. Since, as they thought, the disaster flowed from the essentially colonial character of the American economy, the remedy was to be found in the more vigorous application of the principles and policies of the American System. Great Britain had declared war on American manufactories, closed ports to Amercian foodstuffs, and regained much of the world's carrying trade that had been lost to American shippers in the Napoleonic era. As long as Britain, indeed most of Europe, was involved in war and famished by the marchings of armies, the American economy flourished. The United States prospered from Europe's distresses. But peace returned in 1815, the European economies quickly recovered, and after a brief interlude of delusory prosperity the United States was brought to terms with its radically altered position in the international economy. The unhappy condition of the country stemmed from the fact, Henry Clay observed, "that during the whole existence of this government, we have shaped our industry, our navigation, and our commerce, in reference to an extraordinary war in Europe, and to foreign markets which no longer exist." The solution was to exploit the "home market" on a grand scale. Thus, in certain quarters, particularly among manufacturers and allied interests, but including major segments of agriculture as well, the Panic of 1819 increased support for the American System.

In other quarters, however, the result was just the opposite. The coastal merchants and shippers who had made their fortunes in foreign trade naturally saw the protective tariff as a threat to them. Their orientation was seaward rather than landward. They were fundamentally hostile to a system of political economy aimed at the expansion of domestic manufactures, internal commerce, and the home market. While they advocated Adam Smith's principles of *laissez faire* and free trade against the protectionists, they were not at all averse to government assistance in their behalf and, in fact, they had always received such assistance. The revival of foreign commerce after 1815, they said, was largely at the expense of American shippers and merchants. It yielded handsome revenues to the Treasury but small returns to the American economy. European countries had adopted highly discriminatory policies in favor of their own commercial interests. The United States retaliated, as in the Navigation Act of 1818; but American commerce did not revive. In the opinion of those who manned this historic mainstay of the American economy, its weakness contributed to the collapse of 1819 and required the first attention of the government.

In the new agricultural lands of the South and West, where the Panic struck hardest, the blame was laid at the door of the Second Bank of the United States. The prosperity that descended on these lands after 1815 created an insatiable demand for credit. Under provision of the Harrison Land Act of 1800, the public lands could be purchased on credit over a four-year period, which acted as a stimulus to speculators as well as to legitimate planters and farmers. But far more important in the booming economy of the frontier areas was bank credit. At first, numerous and small state-chartered banks attempted to meet the need. Their inability to do so, leading to reckless overexpansion of loans and suspension of payment in specie—that is, gold or silver—on note issues, contributed to the financial disorders that brought the Second Bank into being. It was not greeted with any enthusiasm by the state bankers. Not only was it a much bigger rival for the lucrative banking business of the region; it was also armed with the power to force the state banks to contract their issues and resume specie payment.

But the Bank's managers—a group of profit-seeking incompetents and embezzlers—had no intention either of forcing retrenchment on the state banks, and thus ending the boom, or of ignoring the opportunities for gain in the South and West. The Bank established most of its branches in these areas. The branches—at New Orleans, Cincinnati, Louisville, and elsewhere—issued notes freely and made little attempt to restrain the state banks. The notes issued in the South and West made their way in the normal course of trade to the Northeast, where they were often redeemed in specie, with the two-fold result, first, that most of the Bank's capital was drained from the Northeast and, second, that the pressure to pay in specie was seldom felt south or west of Ohio.

By July, 1818, the time of reckoning had come. The Bank's reserves of gold and silver had dwindled to a dangerous one-tenth of its liabilities. A combination of factors, which included embezzlement on a lavish scale in the Baltimore branch as well as overexpansion in the South and West, had brought the Bank near collapse. In order to save itself the Bank management turned to a policy of retrenchment. Specie was called from the Southern and Western branches to Philadelphia, and these branches were ordered to collect, in specie, the large balances owed by the state banks. The state banks, with little specie in their vaults, pressed their debtors—farmers, merchants, and speculators—to pay up. But they too were overextended. Moreover, the bank pressure coincided with the collapse of agricultural prices. The farmers and planters suffered drastic shrinkage in their incomes precisely when their credit was cut off. The state banks, unable to meet their commitments, closed their doors or suspended specie payments, which once again threw the currency into confusion. The chain of pressures started by the Bank, and transmitted through the branches to the state banks, ended in the bankruptcy and ruin of thousands of farmers, merchants, bankers, and other enterprisers.

The rest of the country did not escape the banking crisis, but it was aggravated in the agricultural areas that had amply tasted both the delights of the boom and the distresses of the bust. The prevailing tendency in these areas, though offset in the grain-growing Ohio Valley by the appeal of the "home market," was to blame the disaster on banks and chiefly on the Bank of the United States. "The Bank was saved and the people were ruined!" As it happened, the people who were ruined were often the very same people who had inflated the Bank bubble for their own profit. Nevertheless, the Bank became in their eyes the monstrous symbol of all evil. Nor was the evil mitigated by the change in the Bank's management early in 1819. Although the new president, Langdon Cheves of South Carolina, and his directors were untainted by corruption, they were responsible for the ruthless contraction of credit that saved the Bank even as it drew the breath of life from the economy.

The reaction against the Bank spread along a wide political front. A House committee investigated; but its report, in January, 1819, while critical, did not support demands from the Western Country for annulment of the Bank's charter. Anger against the Bank was rapidly converted into anger against the East, where the Bank was located, where most of its stock was owned, and where, in the opinion of many inland farmers, the big profits of the American economy were reaped. The revival of these deep-rooted sectional fears and tensions contributed, in turn, to the revival of Jeffersonian doctrines of individual freedom, agrarian simplicity, strict construction, and state rights, which had been welded into a formidable ideology by the original Republicans during their assault on Hamilton's financial system. Perhaps in the agrarian mind the Bank had never overcome the suspicions aroused by its Federalist ancestry. Because the Bank occupied a prominent place in the American System—and because it symbolized the evils of aristocracy, monopoly, and corruption—feelings of enmity against the Bank were transmitted to the other cardinal measures of that system. Its whole tendency, opponents declared, was to force the American economy into unnatural channels of development through Hamiltonian devices of centralization and privilege. In the South particularly, the Panic of 1819 gave the signal for a full-scale retreat from the political and economic nationalism of the postwar years.

While the Panic was at its height, in March, 1819, the Supreme Court delivered its momentous decision in the case of *McCulloch* v. *Maryland*. The question of the constitutionality of a national bank had been debated off and on for thirty years. Chief Justice Marshall decided the issue in favor of the Bank at the moment when public opinion was inflamed as never before against it. Marshall's opinion—the most nationalistic of his long and distinguished career—not only defended the Bank but, even more important, it built on the Hamiltonian doctrine of "implied powers" an impregnable constitutional fortress for the entire American System. In the outcry that rose against the decision, the question of the Bank was subordinated to the more fundamental constitutional issue of national supremacy versus state rights. The court sharpened the issue by striking down state laws in two other cases that came before it in the early months of 1819. In *Dartmouth College* v. *Woodward* Marshall ruled that New Hampshire was barred by the "obligation of contract" clause of the Constitution from interfering with the charter privileges of a corporation. In *Sturges* v. *Crowninshield* Marshall used the same clause to annul a New York statute for the relief of debtors. The State of Virginia, after contesting for several years the authority of the Supreme Court to review the decisions of its own judiciary, now took the lead in reviving the doctrine of the famous Resolutions of 1798. Virginians who called themselves Old Republicans—John Randolph, John Taylor, Spencer Roane, even Thomas Jefferson—all veterans of '98—sounded the alarm for the defense of the states against the encroachments of the national government.

The battle lines had begun to form between the old Republicans and the new when the Sixteenth Congress convened in December, 1819. The issues of the tariff, the Bank, and internal improvements were brought into sharper focus; but no progress was registered in disposing of them, principally because of the Missouri question, first posed in the previous session, agitated for nine months in the press, taken up again in December, and finally settled after four months' debate, on March 3, 1820. The immediate question concerned the status of slavery in Missouri once admitted to statehood. Ultimately it involved much more: the power of Congress to restrict the spread of slavery, the future civilization of the entire territory embraced in the Louisiana Purchase, the balance of power between the two older sections as they competed for favor and advantage in the trans-Mississippi West, and, perhaps, the duration of the Union itself. It rapidly assumed a transcendent importance and overlaid the issues raised by the Panic of 1819 with a new network of political forces. Though enmeshed in the wider economic controversy that surrounded it, the Missouri Compromise aligned sectional feelings and fears on the terrible issue of slavery and dropped a curtain of dread before the nationalist anticipations of 1815.

DOCUMENTS

1] Hezekiah Niles Views "The Prospect Before Us" in 1815

> The editor of *Niles' Weekly Register* was an ardent Jeffersonian Republican who became an equally ardent National Republican after the War of 1812. A printer by trade, largely self-taught, he established at Baltimore in 1812 one of the most influential journals of political commentary in the history of American publishing. Peering down from the gallery of the House of Representatives, Niles once counted as many as forty-seven copies of the *Register* on as many desks. In the following editorial Niles writes on two of his most persistent themes: national unity and independence, domestic industry and the home market.*

THE EXISTING state of things, as well as the "prospect before us," is most happy for the American people. THE REPUBLIC, REPOSING ON THE LAURELS OF A GLORIOUS WAR, GATHERS THE RICH HARVEST OF AN HONORABLE PEACE. Every where the sound of the axe is heard opening the forest to the sun, and claiming for agriculture the range of the buffalo.—Our cities grow and towns rise up as by magic; commerce expands her proud sails in safety, and the "striped bunting" floats with majesty over every sea. The busy hum of ten thousand wheels fills our seaports, and the sound of the spindle and the loom succeeds the yell of the savage or screech of the night owl in the late wilderness of the interior. The *lord of the soil,* who recently deserted the plough to meet the enemies of his country on its threshold, and dispute the possession, has returned in quiet to his fields, exulting that the *republic lives,* and in honor! The hardy hunter, whose deadly rifle lately brought the foeman to the earth, has resumed his former life, and, in the trackless forest, employs the same weapon, with unerring aim, to stop the fleet deer in his course. Plenty crowns the works of peace with abundance, and scatters from her cornucopia all the good things of this life, with prodigal bounty. A high and honorable feeling generally prevails, and the people begin to assume, more and more, a NATIONAL CHARACTER; and to look at home for the only means, under Divine goodness, of preserving their religion and liberty—with all the blessings that flow from their unrestricted enjoyment. The "bulwark" of these is in the sanctity of their principles, and the virtue and valor of those who profess to love them; and need no guarantee from the blood-stained and profligate princes and powers of *Europe.* . . .

The progress of our country in population, wealth and resources, is with-

---

* HEZEKIAH NILES VIEWS "THE PROSPECT BEFORE US" IN 1815: "The Prospect Before Us." From *Niles' Weekly Register* (September 2, 1815).

out parallel. The census of 1820 will give us not less than ten millions of people; of which a large and unexpected portion will be found westward of the *Alleganies,* having emigrated from the *east*—with a tripled proportion of wealth and resources compared with what they were in 1810, the "calamities of the war" notwithstanding. The great ease with which a livelihood is obtained in the republic, will continue a like increase of the first for many generations; and the others will go on with a geometrical ratio. And much assistance to each may be expected from warworn Europeans, seeking a place of rest from oppression and chains. It is hardly possible to imagine with any degree of certainty, the value annually *created* by the recently applied industry of the people to MANUFACTURES, aided by the various labor-saving machinery adapted to large institutions or *household* establishments. . . .

A general spirit of manufacturing was got up with great difficulty, and cannot now be laid aside without immense exertion and sacrifice. The money that has been invested in our various branches of manufacture, including the rearing of sheep and cultivation of the cane to make sugar, within the last 8 or 10 years, and now employed in them, far exceeds that occupied by foreign trade. And happily it is so; for if the weight of the power of the "legitimates" of Europe shall settle the people down into the calm of despotism, and a general peace lasts for five years, the *shipping interest* of the United States, now or recently engaged in trading with that part of the world and its colonies, will suffer a diminution of 40 or 50 *per cent.* and the demand for some of our most valuable and bulky staple articles of agriculture will be exceedingly reduced. The fact is, we had a great deal more of the commerce of the world than our share, as they who would have sold every honorable feeling to *England* for a miserable part of it, will soon ascertain. But this is of little consequence to the bulk of the people; who would rather have peace and quietness than *Boston* memorials, insurrection resolutions, or *Hartford conventions.*

In the general prosperity, we behold the downfall of that faction which would have made a common interest with the British, during the late war . . . a faction that would have raised itself to power on the broken fasces of the union! *It falls as its country rises*—the stability of the republic is arsenic to its hopes and wishes. . . . These men had no pride in the name of an *American,* and it may be right to treat them as *aliens* when we speak of the affairs of the *republic.* But, if they must be considered as of our people, we have the satisfaction to say that they are a small and the only portion of the population whose heart does not leap with gratitude to heaven for its munificence to the UNITED STATES. . . .

Let us then, fellow citizens, cherish our republican institutions, and hold up as "objects for scorn to point her slow unmoving finger at" any one that would jeopardize them, or bring them into disrepute. . . . Let us recollect the saying of the sage who declared, that he who gives up essential liberty to purchase temporary safety, deserves neither liberty nor safety; and, always acting up to it, fix the disposition in our mind as a part of our existence, that these United States are, of God and by our right, free, sovereign and independent; and, in this persuasion, also feel a determination to obey the injunction of *Washington,* "and frown indignantly on the first drawing of an attempt to alienate one portion of our country from the rest, or to enfeeble the sacred ties that now link together the various parts."

2] Alexander J. Dallas Recommends a National Bank

Secretary of the Treasury Dallas first proposed a national bank in 1814. Congress passed a weak bank bill, which President Madison vetoed as unsatisfactory. Eleven months later, in December, 1815, Madison asked Congress to reconsider the matter. It was referred to the House Committee on the National Currency, whose chairman, John C. Calhoun, sought further advice from Dallas. His response, given in part below, explains the crucial features of the proposed bank. It was accompanied by a detailed plan which Calhoun followed closely in the bill he drafted and reported to the House in January. Slightly modified, the bill passed both houses of Congress and was signed into law on April 10, 1816.*

.   .   .   .

IT AFFORDS much satisfaction to find, that the policy of establishing a national bank has received the sanction of the committee; and the decision in this respect, renders it unnecessary to enter into a comparative examination of the superior advantages of such an institution, for the attainment of the objects contemplated by the legislature. Referring, therefore, to the outline of a national bank . . . I proceed, with deference and respect, to offer some explanation of the principles upon which the system is founded.

I. It is proposed, that, under a charter for twenty years, the capital of the national bank shall amount to 35,000,000 of dollars; that congress shall retain the power to raise it to 50,000,000 of dollars, that that it shall consist, three-fourths of public stock, and one-fourth of gold and silver.

1st. With respect to the amount of the capital.—The services to be performed by the capital of the bank, are important, various, and extensive. They will be required through a period, almost as long as is usually assigned to a generation. They will be required for the accommodation of the government, in the collection and distribution of its revenue; as well as for the uses of commerce, agriculture, manufactures, and the arts, throughout the Union. They will be required to restore and maintain the national currency. And, in short, they will be required, under every change of circumstances, in a season of war, as well as in the season of peace, for the circulation of the national wealth; which augments with a rapidity beyond the reach of ordinary calculation.

In the performance of these national services, the local and incidental co-operation of the state banks may undoubtedly be expected; but it is the object of the present measure, to create an independent, though not a discordant, institution; and while the government is granting a monopoly for 20 years, it would seem to be improvident and dangerous, to rely upon gratuitous or

* ALEXANDER J. DALLAS RECOMMENDS A NATIONAL BANK: "Letter from the Secretary of the Treasury to the Chairman of the Committee on the National Currency, December 24, 1815." From the *Annals of Congress* (*Debates and Proceedings in the Congress of the United States*), 14 Cong., 1 Sess., pp. 505–08.

casual aids for the enjoyment of those benefits, which can be effectually secured by positive stipulation.

. . . The competition which exists at present among the state banks will, it is true, be extended to the national bank; but competition does not imply hostility. The commercial interests and the personal associations of the stockholders, will generally be the same, in the state banks, and in the national bank. The directors of both institutions will naturally be taken from the same class of citizens. And experience has shown not only the policy, but the existence of those sympathies, by which the intercourse of a national bank and the state banks has been, and always ought to be, regulated for their common credit and security—At the present crisis, it will be peculiarly incumbent upon the national bank, as well as the treasury, to conciliate the state banks, to confide to them, liberally, a participation in the deposits of public revenue; and to encourage them in every reasonable effort, to resume the payment of their notes in coin. But, independent of these considerations, it is to be recollected, that when portions of the capital of the national bank shall be transferred to its branches, the amount invested in each branch, will not, probably, exceed the amount of the capital of any of the principal state banks; and will certainly be less than the amount of the combined capital of the state banks, operating in any of the principal commercial cities. The whole number of the banking establishments in the United States may be stated at 260; and the aggregate amount of their capitals may be estimated at $85,000,000; but the services of the national bank are also required in every state and territory, and the capital proposed is $35,000,000, of which only one-fourth part will consist of gold and silver.

2d. *With respect to the composition of the capital of the bank.*—There does not prevail much diversity of opinion, upon the proposition to form a compound capital for the national bank, partly of public stock, and partly of coin. The proportions now suggested appear, also, to be free from any important objections. Under all the regulations of the charter, it is believed that the amount of gold and silver required will afford an adequate supply for commencing and continuing the payments of the bank in current coin; while the power which the bank will possess, to convert its stock portion of capital into bullion or coin, from time to time, is calculated to provide for any probable augmentation of the demand. . . .

II. It is proposed, that the national bank shall be governed by twenty-five directors, and each of its branches by thirteen directors; that the president of the U. States, with the advice and consent of the senate, shall appoint five of the directors of the bank, one of whom shall be chosen as president of the bank by the board of directors; that the resident stockholders shall elect twenty of the directors of the national bank, who shall be resident citizens of the U. States; and that the national bank shall appoint the directors of each bank . . . one of whom shall be designated by the secretary of the treasury, with the approbation of the president of the United States, to be president of each branch bank. . . .

Upon general principles, wherever a pecuniary interest is to be affected by the operations of a public institution, a representative authority ought to be recognized. The United States will be the proprietors of one-fifth of the capital of the bank, and in that proportion, upon general principles, they should be represented in the direction. But an apprehension has sometimes been expressed, lest the power of the government thus inserted in to the administration of the affairs of the bank, should be employed, eventually, to alienate the funds and destroy the credit of the institution. Whatever may have been the fate of banks in other countries, subject to forms of government essentially different, there can be no reasonable cause for the apprehension here. Independent of the obvious improbability of the attempt, the government of the United States cannot, by any legislative or executive act, impair the rights or multiply the obligations of a corporation constitutionally established, as long as the independence and integrity of the judicial power shall be maintained. Whatever accommodation the treasury may have occasion to ask from the bank, can only be asked under the license of a law; and whatever accommodation shall be obtained, must be obtained from the voluntary assent of the directors, acting under the responsibility of their trust.

Nor can it be doubted that the department of the government, which is invested with the power of appointment to all the important offices of the state, is a proper department to exercise the power of appointment in relation to a national trust of incalculable magnitude. The national bank ought not to be regarded simply as a commercial bank.—It will not operate upon the funds of the stockholders alone, but much more upon the funds of the nation. Its conduct, good or bad, will not affect the corporate credit alone, but much more the credit and resources of the government. In fine, it is not an institution created for the purposes of commerce and profit alone, but much more for the purposes of national policy, as an auxiliary in the exercise of some of the highest powers of the government. Under such circumstances, the public interests cannot be too cautiously guarded, and the guards proposed can never be injurious to the commercial interests of the institution. The rights to inspect the general accounts of the bank may be employed to detect the evils of a maladministration; but an interior agency in the direction of its affairs will best serve to prevent them.

III. It is proposed, that, in addition to the usual privileges of a corporation, the notes of the national bank shall be received in all payments to the United States, unless congress shall hereafter otherwise provide by law; and that in addition to the duties usually required from a corporation of this description, the national bank shall be empowered to receive, transfer and distribute, the public revenue, under the directions of the proper department. . . .

It is not proposed to stipulate that the bank shall in any case be bound to make loans to the government; but, in that respect, whenever a loan is authorized by law, the government will act upon the ordinary footing of an applicant for pecuniary accommodation.

IV. It is proposed, that the organization of the national bank shall be effected with as little delay as possible; and that its operations shall commence and continue, upon the basis of payments in the current coin of the United States, with a qualified power under the authority of the government to suspend such payments.

The proposition, now submitted, necessarily implies an opinion that it is practicable to commence the operations of the national bank upon a circulation of gold and silver coin; and, in support of the opinion, a few remarks are respectfully offered to the consideration of the committee.

1. The actual receipts of the bank at the opening of the subscription, will amount to the sum of 8,400,000 dollars; of which the sum of 1,400,000 dollars will consist of gold and silver, and the sum of 7,000,000 of dollars will consist of public stock convertible by sale into gold and silver. . . . To the fund thus possessed by the bank, the accumulations of the public revenue and the deposits of individuals, being added, there can be no doubt, from past experience and observation in reference to similar establishments, that a sufficient foundation will exist for a gradual and judicious issue of bank notes payable on demand in the current coin. . . .

2. The public confidence cannot be withheld from the institution. The resources of the nation will be intimately connected with the resources of the bank. The notes of the bank are accredited in every payment to the government, and must become familiar in every pecuniary negotiation.—Unless, therefore, a state of things exist in which gold and silver only can command the public confidence, the national bank must command it. But the expression of the public sentiment does not, even at this period, leave the question exposed to difficulty and doubt; it is well known that the wealth of opulent and commercial nations requires for its circulation something more than a medium composed of the precious metals. The incompetency of the existing paper substitutes, to furnish a national currency, is also well known. Hence, throughout the United States, the public hope seems to rest, at this crisis, upon the establishment of a national bank; and every citizen, upon private or upon patriotic motives, will be prepared to support the institution.

3. Sinister combinations to defeat the operations of a national bank ought not to be presumed, and need not be feared. It is true, that the influence of the state banks is extensively diffused; but the state banks and the patrons of the state banks partake of the existing evils; they must be conscious of the inadequacy of state institutions to restore and maintain the national currency; they will perceive that there is sufficient space in the commercial sphere for the movement of the state banks and the national bank, and, upon the whole, they will be ready to act upon the impulse of a common duty and a common interest. If, however, most, unexpectedly, a different course should be pursued, the concurring powers of the national treasury and the national bank, will be sufficient to avert the danger.

4. The demand of an unfavorable balance of trade appears to be much overrated. It is not practicable, at this time, to ascertain either the value of the goods imported since the peace, or the value of the property employed to pay for them.—But when it is considered that a great proportion of the importations arose from the investment of American funds previously in Europe; that a great proportion of the price has been paid by American exports; that a great proportion has been paid by remittances in American stocks; and that a great proportion remains upon credit, to be paid by gradual remittances of goods, as well as in coin—it cannot be justly concluded that the balance of trade has hitherto materially affected the national stock of the precious metals. . . .

V. It is proposed that a bonus be paid to the government by the subscribers to the national bank, in consideration of the emoluments to be derived from an exclusive charter, during a period of twenty years. . . .

VI. It is proposed that the measures suggested by the following considerations be adopted, to aid the national bank in commencing and maintaining its operations upon the basis of payments in current coin.

1. To restore the national currency of gold and silver, it is essential that the quantity of bank paper in circulation should be reduced. . . . The policy, the interest, and the honor of the state banks, will stimulate them to undertake and to prosecute this salutary work. But it will be proper to apprise them that after a specified day, the notes of such banks as have not resumed their payments in the current coin, will not be received in payments, either to the government or to the national bank.

2. The resumption of payments in current coin, at the state banks, will remove every obstacle to the commencement of similar payments at the national bank. . . . The national bank, free from all engagements, will be able to regulate its issues of paper, with a view to the danger as well as to the demand, that may be found to exist. But in addition to the privileges granted by the charter, it will also be proper to apprise the state banks, that after the commencement of the operations of the national bank, the notes of such banks as do not agree to receive, re-issue and circulate, the notes of that institution, shall not be received in payments, either to the government or to the national bank. . . .

3] John C. Calhoun Speaks for Internal Improvements

A statesman of abundant intelligence, liberality, and vision, John C. Calhoun of South Carolina was as ardent a nationalist as could be found in American politics in 1816. In December he turned from his labors on behalf of the Bank and the tariff to devise a federal plan of internal improvements. He had in mind a vast system of roads and waterways similar to the one proposed by Albert Gallatin in 1808. It would be financed by the bonus and the dividends paid to the government by the Bank. Calhoun's Bonus Bill passed both houses of Congress with but one significant amendment, which called for state consent to undertakings by the federal government, only to be vetoed by Madison on constitutional grounds.*

. . . THE MANNER in which facility and cheapness of intercourse, added to the wealth of a nation, had been so often and ably discussed by writers on political economy, that he [1] presumed the House to be perfectly acquainted with the subject. It was sufficient to observe, that every branch of national industry, Agricultural, Manufacturing, and Commercial, was greatly stimulated

---

* JOHN C. CALHOUN SPEAKS FOR INTERNAL IMPROVEMENTS: John C. Calhoun, "Speech on Internal Improvements" (February 4, 1817). From Robert L. Meriwether, ed., *The Papers of John C. Calhoun* (Columbia, S.C., 1959), I [1801–17], 398–407. Reprinted with the permission of the South Carolina Archives Department.

1 That is, Calhoun, the speaker.

and rendered by it more productive. The result is, said he, that it tends to diffuse universal opulence. It gives to the interior the advantages possessed by the parts most eligibly situated for trade. It makes the country price, whether in the sale of the raw product, or in the purchase of the articles for consumption, approximate to that of the commercial towns. In fact, if we look into the nature of wealth we will find, that nothing can be more favorable to its growth than good roads and canals. An article, to command a price, must not only be useful, but must be the subject of demand; and the better the means of commercial intercourse, the larger is the sphere of demand.

The truth of these positions, said Mr. C. is obvious; and has been tested by all countries where the experiment has been made. It has particularly been strikingly exemplified in England and if the result there, in a country so limited and so similar in its products, has been to produce a most uncommon state of opulence, what may we not expect from the same cause in our country, abounding as it does in the greatest variety of products, and presenting the greatest facility for improvements? Let it not be said that internal improvements may be wholly left to the enterprise of the states and of individuals. He knew, he said, that much might justly be expected to be done by them; but in a country so new, and so extensive as ours, there is room enough, said he, for all the general and state governments and individuals, in which to exert their resources. But many of the improvements contemplated, said Mr. C. are on too great a scale for the resources of the states or individuals; and many of such a nature, that the rival jealousy of the states, if left alone, might prevent. They required the resources and the general superintendence of this government to effect and complete them.

But, said Mr. C. there are higher and more powerful considerations why Congress ought to take charge of this subject. If we were only to consider the pecuniary advantages of a good system of roads and canals, it might indeed admit of some doubt whether they ought not to be left wholly to individual exertions; but when we come to consider how intimately the strength and political prosperity of the Republic are connected with this subject, we find the most urgent reasons why we should apply our resources to them. In many respects, no country of equal population and wealth, possesses equal materials of power with ours. The people, in muscular power, in hardy and enterprizing habits, and in a lofty and gallant courage, are surpassed by none. In one respect, and in my opinion, in one only, are we materially weak. We occupy a surface prodigiously great in proportion to our numbers. The common strength is brought to bear with great difficulty on the point that may be menaced by an enemy. It is our duty, then, as far as in the nature of things it can be effected, to counteract this weakness. Good roads and canals judiciously laid out, are the proper remedy. In the recent war, how much did we suffer for the want of them! . . .

But on this subject of national power, what, said Mr. C. can be more important than a perfect unity in every part, in feelings and sentiments? And what can tend more powerfully to produce it, than overcoming the effects of distance? No country, enjoying freedom, ever occupied any thing like as great an extent of country as this Republic. One hundred years ago, the most profound philosophers did not believe it to be even possible. They did not suppose it possible that a pure republic could exist on as great a scale even as the Island of Great Britain. What then was considered as chimerical, said Mr. C. we now have the felicity to enjoy; and, what is most remarkable, such is the happy mould of our government, so well are the state and the general powers blended, that much of our political happiness draws its origin from the extent of our Republic. It has exempted us from the most of the causes which distracted the small republics of antiquity. Let it not however be forgotten; let it, said he, be forever kept in mind, that it exposes us to the greatest of all calamities, next to the loss of liberty, and even to that in its consequence—*disunion*. We are great, and rapidly, he was about to say fearfully, growing. This, said he, is our pride and danger—our weakness and our strength. Little, said Mr. C. does he deserve to be entrusted with the liberties of this people, who does not raise his mind to these truths. We are under the most imperious obligation to counteract every tendency to disunion. . . . Whatever, said Mr. C. impedes the intercourse of the extremes with this, the centre of the Republic, weakens the union. The more enlarged the sphere of commercial circulation, the more extended that of social intercourse; the more strongly are we bound together; the more inseparable are our destinies. Those who understand the human heart best, know how powerfully distance tends to break the sympathies of our nature. Nothing, not even dissimilarity of language, tends more to estrange man from man. Let us then, said Mr. C. bind the Republic together with a perfect system of roads and canals. Let us conquer space. It is thus the most distant parts of the republic will be brought within a few days travel of the centre; it is thus that a citizen of the West will read the news of Boston still moist from the press. The mail and the press, said he, are the nerves of the body politic. By them, the slightest impression made on the most remote parts, is communicated to the whole system; and the more perfect the means of transportation, the more rapid and true the vibration. To aid us in this great work, to maintain the integrity of this Republic, we inhabit a country presenting the most admirable advantages. Belted around, as it is, by lakes and oceans, intersected in every direction by bays and rivers, the hand of industry and art is tempted to improvement. So situated, said he, blessed with a form of government at once combining liberty and strength, we may reasonably raise our eyes to a most splendid future, if we only act in a manner worthy of our advantages. If, however, neglecting them, we permit a low, sordid, selfish, and sectional spirit to take possession of this House, this happy scene will vanish. We will divide, and in its consequences will follow misery and despotism.

To legislate for our country, said Mr. C. requires not only the most enlarged views, but a species of self-devotion, not exacted in any other. In a country so extensive, and so various in its interests, what is necessary for the common good, may apparently be opposed to the interest of particular sections. It must be submitted to as the condition of our greatness. But were we a small republic; were we confined to the ten miles square, the selfish instincts of our nature might in most cases be relied on in the management of public affairs.

Such, then, being the obvious advantages of internal improvements, why, said Mr. C. should the House hesitate to commence the system? He understood there were, with some members, constitutional objections. The power of Congress is objected to, first, that they have none to cut a road or canal through a state without its consent—and next, that the public monies can only be appropriated to effect the particular powers enumerated in the Constitution. The first of these objections, said Mr. C. it is plain does not apply to this bill. No particular road or canal is proposed to be cut through any state. The bill simply appropriates money to the general purpose of improving the means of communication. . . . In fact, he scarcely thought it worth the discussion, since the good sense of the states might be relied on. They will in all cases readily yield their assent. The fear is in a different direction: in a too great a solicitude to obtain an undue share to be expended within their respective limits. In fact, he said he understood that this was not the objection insisted on. It was mainly urged that the Congress can only apply the public money in execution of the enumerated powers. He was no advocate for refined arguments on the Constitution. The instrument was not intended as a thesis for the logician to exercise his ingenuity on. It ought to be construed with plain, good sense; and what can be more express than the Constitution on this very point? The first power delegated to Congress, is comprized in these words: "to lay and collect taxes, duties, imposts and excises; to pay the debts, and provide for the common defence and general welfare of the United States; but all duties, imposts and excises shall be uniform throughout the United States." First—the power is given to lay taxes; next, the objects are enumerated to which the money accruing from the exercise of this power, may be applied—to pay the debts, provide for the defence, and promote the general welfare; and last, the rule for laying the taxes is prescribed—that all duties, imposts and excises shall be uniform. If the framers had intended to limit the use of the money to the powers afterwards enumerated and defined, nothing could be more easy than to have expressed it plainly. . . .

Forced, however, as such a construction was, he might admit it, and urge that the words do constitute a part of the enumerated powers. The Constitution, said he, gives to Congress the power to establish post offices and post-roads. He knew the interpretation which was usually given to these words confined our power to that of designating only the post roads; but it seemed to him that the word "establish" comprehended something more. But suppose the Constitution to be silent, said Mr. C. why should we be confined in the application of money to the enumerated powers? There is nothing in the reason of the thing, that he could perceive, why it should be so restricted; and the habitual and uniform practice of the government coincided with his opinion. Our laws are full of instances of money appropriated without any reference to the enumerated powers. . . .

He believed that the passage of the bill would not be much endangered by a doubt of the power; as he conceived on that point there were not many who were opposed. The mode is principally objected to. A system it is contended ought to be presented before the money is appropriated. He thought differently. To set apart the fund appeared to him to be naturally the first act; at least he took it to be the only practicable course. A bill filled with details would have but a faint prospect of passing. The enemies to any possible system in detail and those who are opposed in principle, would unite and defeat it. Though he was unwilling to incorporate details in the bill, yet he was not adverse to presenting his views on that point. The first great object was to perfect the communication from Maine to Louisiana. This might be fairly considered as the principal artery of the whole system. The next was the connection of the Lakes with the Hudson River. In a political, commercial and military point of view, few objects could be more important. The next object of chief importance was to connect all the great commercial points on the Atlantic, Philadelphia, Baltimore, Washington, Richmond, Charleston and Savannah, with the Western States; and finally, to perfect the intercourse between the West and New Orleans. These seem to him to be the great objects. There were others no doubt of great importance which would receive the aid of government. The fund proposed to be set apart in this bill was about 650,000 dollars a year, which was doubtless, too small to effect such great objects of itself; but it would be a good beginning; and he had no doubt when it was once begun, the great work will be finished. If the bill succeeds, at the next session the details can be arranged, and the system commenced. . . . The money cannot be appropriated to a more exalted use. Every portion of the community, the farmer, mechanic and merchant will feel its good effects; and, what is of the greatest importance, the strength of the community will be augmented, and its political prosperity rendered more secure.

4] Henry Clay Champions Domestic Industry

> The political career of Henry Clay was inseparable from that of the American System. Rising to eminence in the Western metropolis and aspiring manufacturing center of Lexington, Kentucky, Clay was one of the earliest Republican converts to the gospel of home industry. He contributed to the agitation that led to the proposed tariff of 1820, though as Speaker of the House of Representatives he had no direct hand in drafting it. Its principal author was Henry Baldwin, congressman from depression-ridden Pittsburgh and chairman of the newly established Committee on Manufactures. In order to obtain much higher levels of protection and at the same time meet the revenue needs of the government, the Baldwin Tariff boldly proposed shifting the base of the revenue system from the impost to the internal, or excise, tax. The bill passed the House but was defeated by two votes in the Senate.*

.   .   .   .

IN CONSIDERING the subject, the first important inquiry that we should make is, whether it be desirable that such a portion of the capital and labor of the country should be employed in the business of manufacturing, as would furnish a supply of our necessary wants? Since the first colonization of America, the principal direction of the labor and capital of the inhabitants has been to produce raw materials for the consumption or fabrication of foreign nations. We have always had, in great abundance, the means of subsistence, but we have derived chiefly from other countries our clothes, and the instruments of defense. Except during those interruptions of commerce arising from a state of war,

* HENRY CLAY CHAMPIONS DOMESTIC INDUSTRY: Henry Clay, "On the Protection of Home Industry" (April 26, 1820). From Calvin Colton, ed., *The Works of Henry Clay* (New York, 1857), VI, 219–37.

or from measures adopted for vindicating our commercial rights, we have experienced no very great inconvenience heretofore from this mode of supply. The limited amount of our surplus produce, resulting from the smallness of our numbers, and the long and arduous convulsions of Europe, secured us good markets for that surplus in her ports, or those of her colonies. But those convulsions have now ceased, and our population has reached nearly ten millions. A new epoch has arisen; and it becomes us deliberately to contemplate our own actual condition, and the relations which are likely to exist between us and the other parts of the world. The actual state of our population, and the ratio of its progressive increase, when compared with the ratio of the increase of the population of the countries which have hitherto consumed our raw produce, seem, to me, alone to demonstrate the necessity of diverting some portion of our industry from its accustomed channel. We double our population in or about the term of twenty-five years. If there be no change in the mode of exerting our industry, we shall double, during the same term, the amount of our exportable produce. Europe, including such of her colonies as we have free access to, taken altogether, does not duplicate her population in a shorter term, probably, than one hundred years. The ratio of the increase of her capacity of consumption, therefore, is, to that of our capacity of production, as one is to four. And it is manifest, from the simple exhibition of the powers of the consuming countries, compared with those of the supplying country, that the former are inadequate to the latter. It is certainly true, that a portion of the mass of our raw produce, which we transmit to her, reverts to us in a fabricated form, and that this return augments with our increasing population. This is, however, a very inconsiderable addition to her actual ability to afford a market for the produce of our industry.

I believe that we are already beginning to experience the want of capacity in Europe to consume our surplus produce. Take the articles of cotton, tobacco, and bread-stuffs. For the latter we have scarcely any foreign demand. And is there not reason to believe that we have reached if we have not passed, the maximum of the foreign demand for the other two articles? . . . It appears to me, then, that, if we consult our interests merely, we ought to encourage home manufactures. But there are other motives to recommend it, of not less importance.

The wants of man may be classed under three heads: food, raiment, and defense. They are felt alike in the state of barbarism and of civilization. He must be defended against the ferocious beast of prey in the one condition, and against the ambition, violence, and injustice incident to the other. If he seeks to obtain a supply of those wants without giving an equivalent, he is a beggar or a robber; if by promising an equivalent which he can not give, he is fraudulent, and if by commerce, in which there is perfect freedom on his side, while he meets with nothing but restrictions on the other, he submits to an unjust and degrading inequality. What is true of individuals is equally so of nations. The country, then, which relies upon foreign nations for either of those great essentials, is not, in fact, independent. Nor is it any consolation for our dependence upon other nations that they are also dependent upon us, even were it true. Every nation should anxiously endeavor to establish its absolute independence, and consequently be able to feed, and clothe, and defend itself.

If it rely upon a foreign supply, that may be cut off by the caprice of the nation yielding it, by war with it, or even by war with other nations; it can not be independent. But it is not true that any other nations depend upon us in a degree any thing like equal to that of our dependence upon them for the great necessaries to which I have referred. Every other nation seeks to supply itself with them from its own resources; and so strong is the desire which they feel to accomplish this purpose, that they exclude the cheaper foreign article for the dearer home production. Witness the English policy in regard to corn. So selfish, in this respect, is the conduct of other powers that, in some instances, they even prohibit the produce of the industry of their own colonies when it comes into competition with the produce of the parent country. All other countries but our own exclude by high duties, or absolute prohibitions, whatever they can respectively produce within themselves. The truth is, and it is in vain to disguise it, that we are a sort of independent colonies of England—politically free, commercially slaves. Gentlemen tell us of the advantage of a free exchange of the produce of the world. But they tell us of what has never existed, does not exist, and perhaps never will exist. They invoke us to give perfect freedom on our side, while, in the ports of every other nation, we are met with a code of odious restrictions, shutting out entirely a great part of our produce, and letting in only so much as they can not possibly do without. I will hereafter examine their favorite maxim, of leaving things to themselves, more particularly. At present I will only say that I too am a friend to free trade, but it must be a free trade of perfect reciprocity. If the governing consideration were cheapness; if national independence were to weigh nothing; if honor nothing; why not subsidize foreign powers to defend us? why not hire Swiss or Hessian mercenaries [sic] to protect us? why not get our arms of all kinds, as we do in part, the blankets and clothing of our soldiers, from abroad? We should probably consult economy by these dangerous expedients.

But, say gentlemen, there are to the manufacturing system some inherent objections, which should induce us to avoid its introduction into this country; and we are warned by the example of England, by her pauperism, by the vices of her population, her wars, and so forth. It would be a strange order of Providence, if it were true, that he should create necessary and indispensable wants, and yet should render us unable to supply them without the degradation or contamination of our species.

Pauperism is, in general, the effect of an overflowing population. Manufactures may undoubtedly produce a redundant population; but so may commerce, and so may agriculture. In this respect they are alike; and from whatever cause the disproportion of a population to the subsisting faculty of a country may proceed, its effect on pauperism is the same. Many parts of Asia would exhibit, perhaps, as afflicting effects of an extreme prosecution of the agricultural system, as England can possibly furnish respecting the manufacturing. It is not, however, fair to argue from these extreme cases against either the one system or the other. There are abuses incident to every branch of industry, to every profession. It would not be thought very just or wise to arraign the honorable professions of law and physic, because the one produces the pettifogger, and the other the quack. Even in England it has been established, by the diligent search of Colquhoun, from the most authentic evidence, the judicial records of the country, that the instances of crime were much more numerous in the agricultural than in the manufacturing districts; thus proving that the cause of wretchedness and vice, in that country, was to be sought for, not in this or that system, so much as in the fact of the density of its population. . . . I am aware, that while the public domain is an acknowledged security against the abuses of the manufacturing, or any other system, it constitutes, at the same time, an impediment, in the opinion of some, to the success of manufacturing industry, by its tendency to prevent the reduction of the wages of labor. Those who urge this objection have their eyes too much fixed on the ancient system of manufacturing, when manual labor was the principal instrument which it employed. During the last half century, since the inventions of Arkwright, and the long train of improvements which followed, the labor of machinery is principally used. I have understood, from sources of information which I believe to be accurate, that the combined force of all the machinery employed by Great Britain, in manufacturing, is equal to the labor of one hundred millions of able-bodied men. If we suppose the aggregate of the labor of all the individuals which she employs, in that branch of industry, to be equal to the united labor of two millions of able-bodied men (and I should think it does not exceed it), machine labor will stand to manual labor in the proportion of one hundred to two. There can not be a doubt that we have skill and enterprise enough to command the requisite amount of machine power.

There are, too, some checks to emigration from the settled parts of our country to the waste lands of the west. Distance is one, and it is every day becoming greater and greater. There exists, also a natural repugnance (felt less, it is true, in the United States than elsewhere, but felt even here), to abandoning the place of our nativity. Women and children who could not migrate, and who would be comparatively idle if manufactures did not exist, may be profitably employed in them. This is a very great benefit. I witnessed the advantage resulting from the employment of this description of our population, in a visit which I lately made to the Waltham manufactory, near Boston. There, some hundreds of girls and boys were occupied in separate apartments. The greatest order, neatness, and apparent comfort, reigned throughout the whole establishment. The daughters of respectable farmers, in one instance, I remember, the daughter of a senator in the State Legislature, were usefully employed. They would come down to the manufactory, remain perhaps some months, and return, with their earnings, to their families, to assist them throughout the year. But one instance had occurred, I was informed by the intelligent manager, of doubtful conduct on the part of any of the females, and, after she was dismissed, there was reason to believe that injustice had been done her. Suppose that establishment to be destroyed, what would become of all the persons who are there engaged so beneficially to themselves, and so usefully to the State? Can it be doubted that, if the crowds of little mendicant boys and girls who infest this edifice, and assail us, every day, at its very thresholds, as we come in and go out, begging for a cent, were employed in some manufacturing establishment, it would be better for them, and the city? Those who object to the manufacturing system should recollect, that constant occupation is the best security for innocence and virtue, and that idleness is the parent of vice and crime. They should contemplate the laboring poor with employment, and ask themselves what would be their condition without it. . . .

In one respect there is a great difference in favor of manufactures, when compared with agriculture. It is the rapidity with which the whole manufacturing community avail themselves of an improvement. It is instantly communicated and put in operation. There is an avidity for improvement in the one system, an aversion to it in the other. The habits of generation after generation pass down the long track of time in perpetual succession without the slightest change in agriculture. The plowman who fastens his plow to the tails of his cattle, will not own that there is any other mode equal to his. . . .

It is objected, that the effect of the encouragement of home manufacture, by the proposed tariff, will be, to diminish the revenue from the customs. The amount of the revenue from that source will depend upon the amount of importations, and the measure of these will be the value of the exports from this country. The quantity of the exportable produce will depend upon the foreign demand; and there can be no doubt that, under any distribution of the labor and capital of this country, from the greater allurements which agriculture presents than any other species of industry, there would be always a quantity of its produce sufficient to satisfy that demand. If there be a diminution in the ability of foreign nations to consume our raw produce, in the proportion of our diminished consumption of theirs, under the operation of this system, that will be compensated by the substitution of a home for a foreign market, in the same proportion. . . .

Can any one doubt the impolicy of government resting solely upon the precarious resource of such a revenue? It is constantly fluctuating. It tempts us, by its enormous amount, at one time, into extravagant expenditure; and we are then driven, by its sudden and unexpected depression, into the opposite extreme. We are seduced by its flattering promises into expenses which we might avoid; and we are afterward constrained by its treachery, to avoid expenses which we ought to make. It is a system under which there is a sort of perpetual war, between the interest of the government and the interest of the people. Large importations fill the coffers of government, and empty the pockets of the people. Small importations imply prudence on the part of the people, and leave the treasury empty. In war, the revenue disappears; in peace it is unsteady. On such a system the government will not be able much longer exclusively to rely. We all anticipate that we shall have shortly to resort to some additional supply of revenue within ourselves. I was opposed to the total repeal of the internal revenue. I would have preserved certain parts of it at least, to be ready for emergences such as now exist. . . . By the encouragement of home industry, you will lay a basis of internal taxation, when it gets strong, that will be steady and uniform yielding alike in peace and in war. We do not derive our ability from abroad, to pay taxes. That depends upon our wealth and our industry; and it is the same, whatever may be the form of levying the public contributions.

But it is urged, that you tax other interests of the State to sustain manufacturers. The business of manufacturing, if encouraged, will be open to all. It is not for the sake of the particular individuals who may happen to be engaged in it, that we propose to foster it; but it is for the general interest. We think that it is necessary to the comfort and well-being of society, that fabrication, as well as the business of production and distribution, should be supported and taken care of. Now, if it be even true, that the price of the home fabric will be somewhat higher, in the first instance, than the rival foreign articles, that consideration ought not to prevent our extending reasonable protection to the home fabric. Present temporary inconvenience may be well submitted to for the sake of future permanent benefit. If the experience of all other countries be not utterly fallacious; if the promises of the manufacturing system be not absolutely illusory; by the competition which will be elicited in consequence of your parental care, prices will be ultimately brought down to a level with that of the foreign commodity. Now, in a scheme of policy which is devised for a nation, we should not limit our views to its operation during a single year, or for even a short term of years. We should look at its operation for a considerable time, and in war as well as in peace. Can there be a doubt, thus contemplating it, that we shall be compensated by the certainty and steadiness of the supply in all seasons, and the ultimate reduction of the price for any temporary sacrifices we make? . . .

The manufacturing system is not only injurious to agriculture, but, say its opponents, it is injurious also to foreign commerce. We ought not to conceal from ourselves our present actual position in relation to other powers. During the protracted war which has so long convulsed all Europe, and which will probably be succeeded by a long peace, we transacted the commercial business of other nations, and largely shared with England the carrying trade of the world. Now, every other nation is anxiously endeavoring to transact its own business, to rebuild its marine, and to foster its navigation. The consequence of the former state of things was, that our mercantile marine, and our commercial employment were enormously disproportionate to the exchangeable domestic produce of our country. And the result of the latter will be, that, as exchanges between this country and other nations will hereafter consist principally, on our part, of our domestic produce, that marine and that employment will be brought down to what is necessary to effect those exchanges. I regret exceedingly this reduction. I wish the mercantile class could enjoy the same extensive commerce that they formerly did. But, if they can not, it would be a folly to repine at what is irrecoverably lost, and we should seek rather to adapt ourselves to the new circumstances in which we find ourselves. If, as I think, we have reached the maximum of our foreign demand for our three great staples, cotton, tobacco, and flour, no man will contend that we should go on to produce more and more, to be sent to the glutted foreign market, and consumed by devouring expenses, merely to give employment to our tonnage and to our foreign commerce. It would be extremely unwise to accommodate our industry to produce, not what is wanted abroad, but cargoes for our unemployed ships. I would give our foreign trade every legitimate encouragement, and extend it whenever it can be extended profitably. Hitherto it has been stimulated too highly, by the condition of the world, and our own policy acting on that condition. And we are reluctant to believe that we must submit to its necessary abridgment. The habits of trade, the tempting instances of enormous fortunes which have been made by the successful prosecution of it, are such, that we turn with regret from its pursuit; we still cherish a lingering hope; we persuade ourselves that something will occur, how and what it may be, we know not, to revive its former activity; and we would push into every untried channel, grope through the Dardanelles into the Black Sea, to restore its former profits. I repeat it, let us proclaim to the people of the United States the incontestable truth, that our foreign trade must be circumscribed by the altered state of the world; and, leaving it in the possession of all the gains which it can now possibly make, let us present motives to the capital and labor of our country, to employ themselves in fabrication at home. . . .

The manufacturing system is favorable to the maintenance of peace. Foreign commerce is the great source of foreign wars. The eagerness with which we contend for every branch of it, the temptations which it offers, operating alike upon us and our foreign competitors, produce constant collisions. No country on earth, by the extent of its superfices, the richness of its soil, the variety of its climate, contains within its own limits more abundant facilities for supplying all our rational wants than ours does. . . .

The tendency of reasonable encouragement to our home industry is favorable to the preservation and strength of our confederacy. Now our connection is merely political. For the sale of the surplus of the produce of our agricultural labor, all eyes are constantly turned upon the markets of Liverpool. There is scarcely any of that beneficial intercourse, the best basis of political connection, which consists in the exchange of the produce of our labor. On our maritime frontier there has been too much stimulus, an unnatural activity; in the great interior of the country, there exists a perfect paralysis. Encourage fabrication at home, and there will instantly arise animation and a healthful circulation throughout all the parts of the republic. The cheapness, fertility, and quantity of our waste lands, offer such powerful inducements to cultivation, that our countrymen are constantly engaging in it. I would not check this disposition, by hard terms in the sale of it. Let it be easily accessible to all who wish to acquire it. But I would countervail this predilection, by presenting to capital and labor motives for employment in other branches of industry. . . .

I am sensible, Mr. Chairman, if I have even had a success, which I dare not presume, in the endeavor I have been making to show that sound policy requires a diversion of so much of the capital and labor of this country from other employments as may be necessary, by a different application of them, to secure, within ourselves, a steady and adequate supply of the great necessaries of life, I shall have only established one half of what is incumbent upon me to prove. It will still be required by the other side, that a second proposition be supported, and that is, that government ought to present motives for such a diversion and new application of labor and capital, by that species of protection which the tariff holds out. Gentlemen say, We agree with you; you are right in your first proposition; but, "let things alone," and they will come right in the end. Now, I agree with them, that things would ultimately get right; but not until after a long period of disorder and distress, terminating in the impoverishment, and perhaps ruin, of the country. Dissolve government, reduce it to its primitive elements, and without any general effort to reconstruct it, there would arise, out of the anarchy which would ensue, partial combinations for the purpose of individual protection, which would finally lead to a social form, competent to the conservation of peace within, and the repulsion of force from without. Yet no one would say, in such a state of anarchy, Let things alone! If gentlemen, by their favorite maxim, mean only that, within the bosom of the State, things are to be left alone, and each individual, and each branch of industry, allowed to pursue their respective interests, without giving a preference to either, I subscribe to it. But if they give it a more comprehensive import; if they require that things be left alone, in respect not only to interior action, but to exterior action also; not only as regards the operation of our own government upon the mass of the interests of the State, but as it relates to the operation of foreign governments upon that mass, I dissent from it.

In this maxim, in this enlarged sense, it is indeed everywhere proclaimed; but nowhere practiced. It is truth in the books of European political economists. It is error in the practical code of every European State. It is not applied where it is most applicable; it is attempted to be introduced here, where it is least applicable; and even here its friends propose to limit it to the single branch of manufacturing industry, while every other interest is encouraged and protected according to the policy of Europe. The maxim would best suit Europe, when each interest is adjusted and arranged to every other, by causes operating during many centuries. Every thing there has taken and preserved its ancient position. . . . But the policy of the European States is otherwise. Here every thing is new and unfixed. Neither the State, nor the individuals who compose it, have settled down in their permanent positions. There is a constant tendency, in consequence of the extent of our public domain, toward production for foreign markets. The maxim, in the comprehensive sense in which I am considering it, requires, to entitle it to observation, two conditions, neither of which exists. First, that there should be perpetual peace, and secondly, that the maxim should be everywhere respected. When war breaks out, that free and general circulation of the produce of industry among the nations which it recommends, is interrupted, and the nation that depends upon a foreign supply for its necessaries, must be subjected to the greatest inconvenience. If it be not everywhere observed, there will be, between the nation that does not, and the nation that does, conform to it, an inequality alike condemned by honor and by interest. If there be no reciprocity; if, on the one side, there is perfect freedom of trade, and on the other a code of odious restrictions, will gentlemen still contend that we are to submit to such an unprofitable and degrading intercourse? Will they require that we shall act upon the social system, while every other power acts upon the selfish? . . .

But this maxim, according to which gentlemen would have us abandon the home industry of the country, to the influence of the restrictive systems of other countries, without an effort to protect and preserve it, is not itself observed by the same gentlemen, in regard to the great interests of the nation. We protect our fisheries by bounties and drawbacks. We protect our tonnage, by excluding or restricting foreign tonnage, exactly as our tonnage is excluded or restricted by foreign States. We passed, a year or two ago, the bill to prohibit British navigation from the West India colonies of that power to the United States, because ours is shut out from them. . . . We protect our foreign trade by consuls, by foreign ministers, by embargoes, by non-intercourse, by a navy, by fortifications, by squadrons constantly acting abroad, by war, and by a variety of commercial regulations in our statute-book. The whole system of the general government, from its first formation to the present time, consists, almost exclusively, in one unremitting endeavor to nourish, and protect, and defend the foreign trade. Why have not all these great interests been left to the operation of the gentlemen's favorite maxim? . . .

But, sir, friendly as I am to the existence of domestic manufactures, I would not give to them unreasonable encouragement, by protecting duties. Their growth ought to be gradual but sure. I believe all the circumstances of the present period highly favorable to their success. But they are the youngest and the weakest interest of the State. . . . Our great mistake has been in the irregularity of the action of the measures of this government upon manufacturing industry. At one period it is stimulated too high, and then, by an opposite course of policy, it is precipitated into a condition of depression too low. First there came the embargo; then non-intercourse, and other restrictive measures followed; and finally, that greatest of all stimuli to domestic fabrication, war. During all that long period we were adding to the positive effect of the measures of government, all the moral encouragement which results from popular resolves, legislative resolves, and other manifestations of the public will and the public wish to foster our home manufactures, and to render our confederacy independent of foreign powers. The peace ensued, and the country was flooded with the fabrics of other countries; and we, forgetting all our promises, coolly and philosophically talk of leaving things to themselves—making up our deficiency of practical good sense, by the stores of learning which we collect from theoretical writers. I, too, sometimes amuse myself with the visions of these writers (as I do with those of metaphysicians and novelists), and, if I do not forget, one of the best among them enjoins it upon a country to protect its industry against the injurious influence of the prohibitions and restrictions of foreign countries, which operate upon it.

Monuments of the melancholy effects upon our manufactures, and of the fluctuating policy of the councils of the Union in regard to them, abound in all parts of the country. Villages, and parts of villages, which sprang up but yesterday in the western country, under the excitement to which I have referred, have dwindled into decay, and are abandoned. In New England, in passing along the highway, one frequently sees large and spacious buildings, with the glass broken out of the windows, the shutters hanging in ruinous disorder, without any appearance of activity, and enveloped in solitary gloom. Upon inquiring what they are, you are almost always informed that they were some cotton or other factory, which their proprietors could no longer keep in motion against the overwhelming pressure of foreign competition. Gentlemen ask for facts to show the expediency and propriety of extending protection to our manufactures. Do they want stronger evidence than the condition of things I have pointed out? They ask, why the manufacturing industry is not resumed under the encouraging auspices of the present time? Sir, the answer is obvious, there is a general dismay; there is a want of heart; there is the greatest moral discouragement experienced throughout the nation. A man who engages in the manufacturing business is thought by his friends to be deranged. Who will go to the ruins of Carthage or Baalbec to rebuild a city there? Let government commence a systematic but moderate support of this important branch of our industry; let it announce its fixed purpose, that the protection of manufactures against the influence of the measures of foreign governments, will enter into the scope of our national policy; let us substitute, for the irregular action of our measures, one that shall be steady and uniform; and hope, and animation, and activity, will again revive. . . .

Mr. Chairman, I frankly own that I feel great solicitude for the success of this bill. The entire independence of my country of all foreign States, as it respects a supply of our essential wants, has ever been with me a favorite object. The war of our Revolution effected our political emancipation. The last war contributed greatly toward accomplishing our commercial freedom. But our complete independence will only be consummated after the policy of this bill shall be recognized and adopted. We have, indeed, great difficulties to contend with—old habits, colonial usages, the obduracy of the colonial spirit, the enormous profits of a foreign trade, prosecuted under favorable circumstances, which no longer continue. I will not despair; the cause, I verily believe, is the cause of the country. It may be posponed [*sic*]; it may be frustrated for the moment, but it must finally prevail. Let us endeavor to acquire for the present Congress the merit of having laid this solid foundation of the national prosperity. . . .

5] Merchants and Planters Attack the Tariff

Opposition to the protective tariff was centered in two sections of the country which otherwise had little in common: New England and the South. But merchants and planters, the dominant groups in these respective sections, shared a compelling interest in foreign markets, although this was already in 1820 a waning interest in New England. Many societies and associations of citizens sent memorials to Congress either for or against the new tariff. The first selection below emanated from Fredericksburg, Virginia; the second, from Salem, Massachusetts.*

A] THE FREDERICKSBURG REMONSTRANCE

To the Congress of the United States:

The remonstrance of the Virginia Agricultural Society of Fredericksburg against the attempts now making, by our domestic manufacturers and their friends, to increase the duties upon foreign goods, wares, and merchandise, respectfully represents:

That it is the indisputable right of every free people to petition and remonstrate . . .

That hostility, resulting from true republican principles, to partial taxation, exclusive privileges, and monopolies created by law, was the primary cause of our glorious and ever memorable Revolution.

That, although most of us are only the descendants of those patriots who achieved that Revolution, by the lavish expenditure of their treasure and their

---

* MERCHANTS AND PLANTERS ATTACK THE TARIFF: From the *Annals of Congress*, 16 Cong., 1 Sess., Appendix, pp. 2296–99, 2335–48.

blood, yet that we inherit enough of their spirit to feel equal aversion to similar oppressions; at the same time, we confidently trust that neither we, nor our sons after us, will ever be found backward or reluctant in offering up at the shrine of national good and national happiness any sacrifices, however great, which their promotion and preservation may obviously and necessarily require. But we have been taught to believe that a parental Government—a Government founded upon the immutable and sacred principles of truth, justice, and liberty—if she required sacrifices at all from those whom she is so solemnly bound to protect, would make them such as should operate equally upon every member of the community.

That we view with great concern, both nationally and individually, certain late attempts, on the part of various descriptions of domestic manufacturers, to induce your honorable body to increase the duties upon imports, already so high as to amount, upon many articles, nearly to a prohibition. The increased cost upon some of these may truly be designated a tax upon knowledge, if not a bounty to ignorance; such, for example, as the duty upon books in foreign languages, and upon philosophical, mathematical, surgical, and chemical instruments.

That, although, these attempts are sustained under the plausible pretext of "promoting national industry," they are calculated (we will not say in *design,* but certainly in *effect*) to produce a tax highly impolitic in its nature, partial in its operation, and oppressive in its effect; a tax, in fact, to be levied principally on the great body of agriculturists, who constitute a large majority of the whole American people, and who are the chief consumers of all foreign imports.

That such a tax would be a flagrant violation of the soundest and most important principles of political economy, amongst which we deem the following to be incontrovertibly true; that, as the interests of dealers and consumers necessarily conflict with each other, the first always aiming to *narrow,* whilst the latter, who form the majority of every nation, as constantly endeavor to *enlarge* competition; by which enlargement alone extravagant prices and exorbitant profits are prevented, it is the duty of every wise and just Government to secure the consumers against both exorbitant profits and extravagant prices, by leaving competition as free and open as possible.

That in this way alone can the benefits of good government be equalized among the various orders and classes of society, the prosperity and happiness of which depend not upon immunities, privileges, and monopolies granted to one class or order at the expense of another, but upon the unfettered exercise of talent, skill, and industry, directed and employed in whatever manner and upon whatsoever objects of pursuit, each individual may select for himself; provided, always, that such objects be not incompatible with the public good; for so to use your own rights as not to injure the rights of others, is not less the dictate of common sense and common honesty than it is a cardinal maxim of all legitimate government.

That national industry is best promoted by leaving every member of society free to apply his labor and his knowledge according to his own choice, exempt from all restraints but such as the public good requires, and burdened with no tax but such as shall be both impartial, and as moderate as the exigencies of the State will permit.

That, according to the natural progress of society in every country favorably situated for agriculture, the class of manufacturers is the last to spring up; but that it will necessarily do so, as soon as either the natural or artificial wants of the people create a demand for their labors.

That any legislative interference to force either this or any other class into existence by the strong arm of power, exercised in levying taxes to support the forced class, contrary to the wishes and interests of the other members of the community, is not only bad policy, but oppression; because taxes of any kind, to be rightfully levied, should be equal, and should be imposed, not for the emolument of any one portion of society at the expense of the rest, but for the support of Government alone.

That either to exclude foreign manufacturers, or to tax them very heavily, under a notion of improving those of domestic fabric, lessens the profits of agriculture; diminishes the public revenue, either by augmenting the number of smugglers, or by enabling the domestic manufacturer to pocket that sum which otherwise would go into the public treasury, under the form of an import duty; and at the same time secures to him the power of practising upon the community the double imposition of deteriorating his goods, and selling them at a higher price; because that competition which constitutes the only security for skill, industry, and moderate prices, is either entirely removed, or so limited as not to be felt.

"That all free trade, of whatever description, must be a mutual benefit to the parties engaged in it." . . .

"That, instead of struggling against the dictates of reason and nature, and madly attempting to produce every thing at home, countries should study to direct their labors to those departments of industry for which their situation and circumstances are best adapted."

"That the use of capital should be left, as much as possible, to the care of those to whom it belongs; because they will be most likely to discover in what line it can be employed to the greatest advantage."

And that the best regulated and happiest communities are those wherein all the various trades, professions, and callings, enjoy equal rights, and contribute equally to the necessary support of their common Government; but that if any one should be thought to have superior claims to the fostering care of the National Legislature, it should be "the tillers of the earth—the fountain-head of all wealth, of all power, and of all prosperity." . . .

Your petitioners have thus freely, but respectfully, endeavored to represent to your honorable body their views of a policy which you are so importunately urged to adopt. . . . We ask no tax upon manufacturers for our benefit; neither do we desire any thing of Government to enable us to cultivate the soil as profitably as we could wish, but to leave us free, so far as it depends on them, to carry our products to the best market we can find, and to purchase what we want in return, on the best terms we can, either at home or abroad. We will ever support the Government of our choice in all just and rightful undertakings, both with our fortunes and our lives; but we will never voluntarily contribute to maintain either manufacturers, or any other class of citizens, by the payment of unequal and partial taxes, by awarding to them exclusive privileges, or by sustaining them in the enjoyment of oppressive monopolies, which are ultimately to grind both us and our children after us "into dust and ashes."

All which is respectfully submitted.

JAS. M. GARNETT, *Pres't.*

b] THE SALEM MEMORIAL

To the honorable the Senate and the House of Representatives of the United States of America in Congress assembled:

The undersigned memorialists, merchants and inhabitants of Salem, in the Commonwealth of Massachusetts, and of the towns in its vicinity, beg leave most respectfully to represent: That they have seen, with unfeigned regret and surprise, some propositions recently brought forward in Congress . . . which, in their humble opinions, are calculated seriously to injure, if not eventually to destroy, some of the most important branches of the commerce and navigation of the United States. . . .

Under a wise and enlightened revenue system, the commerce of our country has hitherto advanced with a rapidity and force which have exceeded the most sanguine expectations of its friends. This commerce has contributed largely to the employment of the capital, the industry, and the enterprise of our citizens. It has quickened the march of agriculture, and, by increasing the value as well as amount of its products, has given to the planter and husbandman a reward in solid profit for their toils. It has also materially sustained the credit and finances of the nation, by insuring a regular and growing revenue through a taxation scarcely felt, and cheerfully bourne by all classes of our citizens. It has also given birth to our naval power, by fostering a hardy race of seamen, and patronizing those arts which are essential to the building, preservation, and equipment of ships. It has greatly enlarged, and the memorialists had almost said created, the moneyed capital of the country. And the memorialists believe that it cannot be too frequently or deeply inculcated as an axiom in political economy, that productive capital, in whatever manner added to the stock of the country, is equally beneficial to its best interests. Its real value can never be ascertained by the sources from whence it flows, but from the blessings which it dispenses. A million dollars added to the productive capital by commerce is at least as useful as the same sum added by manufactures.

The benefits of the commerce of the United States, which have been enumerated, are not deduced from theoretical reasoning; they are established by thirty years' experience, since the Constitution was adopted. . . . On the seaboard we have everywhere flourishing towns and cities, the busy haunts of industry, where the products of our soil are accumulated on their transit to foreign countries. In the interior, hundreds of towns have arisen, which but a few years since were desolate wastes or dreary forests. The agriculture of the old States has grown up and spread itself into a thousand new directions; and our cotton and our wheat, our tobacco and our provisions, are administering to the wants of millions, to whom even our very name was but a short time ago utterly unknown.

. . . Cases may possibly arise in which the interests of a respectable portion of the community may be justly sacrificed; but they are cases of extreme public necessity, not cases where the rivalry and the interest of one class of men seek to sustain themselves by destruction to another. In a free country too it may well be asked if it be a legitimate end of government to control the ordinary occupations of men, and compel them to confine themselves to pursuits in which their habits, their feelings, or their enterprise, forbid them to engage. While the manufacturers are left free to engage in their own peculiar pursuits, enjoying in common with others a reasonable protection from the Government, the memorialists trust it is no undue claim on their own part to plead for the freedom of commerce also, as the natural ally of agriculture and naval greatness. Nothing, however, can be more obvious than that many of the manufacturers and their friends are attempting, by fallacious statements, founded on an interested policy, or a misguided zeal, or very short-sighted views, to uproot some of the fundamental principles of our revenue policy, and to compel our merchants to abandon some of the most lucrative branches of commerce—branches which alone enable us to contend with success against the monopoly and the competition of foreign nations. . . .

There is another consideration which the memorialists would respectfully suggest . . . and that is, the dangers and inconveniences which fluctuations in the commercial policy of a nation unavoidably produce. . . . No nation ever prospered in commerce until its own policy became settled, and the channels of its trade were worn deep and clear. It is to this state of things that the capitalist looks with confidence; because he may conclude that, if his profits are but small, they are subject to a reasonable certainty of calculation. Another state of things may suit the young and enterprising speculators; but it can never be safe for a nation to found its revenue upon a trade that is not uniform in its operations. The memorialists most sincerely believe that it is a sound political maxim, that the more free trade is, and the more widely it circulates, the more sure will be its prosperity and that of the nation. Every restriction, which is not indispensable for purposes of revenue, is a shoal which will impede its progress, and not unfrequently jeopard its security. . . .

The memorialists are no enemies to manufactures; but they most sincerely express it as their deliberate judgment that no manufactures ought to be patronized in the country which will not grow up and support themselves in every competition in the market, under the ordinary protecting duty; that the only manufactures which can ultimately flourish here are those which are of slow growth and moderate profit, such as can be carried on by capitalists with economy and steadiness; and that a change of system, which should suddenly introduce great profits, by encouraging undue speculation, and the expectation of inordinate gain, would end in the deepest injuries even to manufacturing establishments. The history of the cotton manufactories in New England completely demonstrates the truth of these positions. They grew up gradually, under the protection of our ordinary duties, in a time of peace, and were profitable to those engaged in them. But when the embargo and non-importation systems produced a deficiency in the foreign supply, a feverish excitement was produced; manufactories were established without sufficient capital; extravagant expenditures in buildings and machinery followed; for a while the demand was great, and the profits high, but, upon the return of the ordinary state of things, many of these establishments sunk, one after another, and involved their owners in ruin. And such, in the opinion of the memorialists, would be the scene acted over again in a few years, if the manufacturers could not succeed in accomplishing their present objectives. . . .

Salem, January, 1820

6] Offenses of Banks and the Paper System

> The newspapers of the time were filled with complaints against banks generally and the Bank of the United States in particular. In the first of the items collected below, the anonymous author of a series of articles contributed to *Niles' Register* denounces the "Paper System" for its corruption of the agricultural population, which he regards as the bulwark of republican liberty. The second item is an editorial appearing in the *Argus of Western America* (Frankfort, Kentucky) after the contraction induced by the National Bank was felt by the numerous banks of Kentucky. (The editor of this newspaper, Amos Kendall, later played a prominent role in President Jackson's war on the Bank.) This is followed by several miscellaneous items on different aspects of the banking and currency problem from *Niles' Register*.*

A] THE PAPER SYSTEM

THE TWO boasted benefits which the farmers are said to derive from the paper-rag system, are the facility of procuring money, from the banks, wherewith to improve their lands, and the increased price of the land, as well as of its produce. As to the first, sir, I am one of those desperate unbelievers, who doubt whether the virtue, the happiness, or the prosperity of a people, are enhanced by the facility of running in debt. I believe that the only true and lasting basis of honorable and salutary independence, to the laboring classes, is industry and frugality; for I know, by experience, that a dependence on any other props is sure to be followed by idleness, debauchery, extravagance and ruin.—Whenever a state of public feeling is produced, where men are not ashamed of being in debt, the mind loses its proper sense of manly independence; and whenever the salutary obstacles to borrowing money are removed, and men are *invited* to become debtors by the facility of borrowing, the axe is laid to the root of national industry, which is the foundation of national virtue and prosperity. . . .

There *was* a time—I speak in the melancholy *past tense* when recurring to the days of agricultural prosperity—There was a time, when it was disgraceful in a farmer to borrow money, and his respectability was seriously injured by becoming a dependent on banks. . . . Such however was the situation of the

* OFFENSES OF BANKS AND THE PAPER SYSTEM: From *Niles' Weekly Register* (May 9, 1818); *The Argus of Western America* (November 13, 1818); *Niles' Weekly Register* (July 11, 1818; October 9, November 20, 1819).

agricultural interest, previous to THE GRAND CONSPIRACY OF DESPERATE SPECU-
LATORS, AGAINST THE LABORING CLASSES, AND HOLDERS OF REAL PROPERTY, IN THE
UNITED STATES. . . .

Since then the decline of the landed interest has been exactly in proportion
to the increase of the means of trading, speculating, monopolizing, and lending, by the agency of paper banks—to the increase of bank dividends, and the
rate of depreciation in the paper currency. The temptation of nine or ten per
cent. per annum, obtained by investing money in the banks, no matter whether
gained honestly or not, has caused all the floating capital of the country to be
embarked in banks, which are now become the only lenders of money, through
discounts, or through the channel of usurers, brokers, and bank directors. To
the banks then the farmer is courteously invited to borrow money, whether
he wants it or not. There is no difficulty in his getting loans to the amount
of nearly the value of his farm. Nay, it appears by a report of a committee of
the assembly of the state of New York, that he is actually *coaxed,* seduced,
into borrowing, by the cunning jackalls of the country banks. . . . Thus instead of the country prospering by its pure and genuine sources of prosperity,
these are in fact destroyed by fictitious substitutes, that possess no other attribute of reality, than the means of scattering ruin around them.

All suffer more or less by this substitution of ideal, for real wealth, but none
so vitally as the great landed interest, which is the back-bone of this country.
The means which formerly sufficed to make the farmer independent, are now
no longer so, because the value of money is decreased, in a much greater ratio,
than the rise in the price of his land and its produce; and above all, because,
a mode of living extravagant beyond all former example, is introduced; every
where in this country, by the brokers, bank directors, and speculators, to which
the revenues and the gains of every other class of people are entirely inadequate. The natural, and therefore the inevitable consequences of this state of
things, may be readily anticipated.—Either the farmer, is tempted to sell his
land, and invest it in some neighboring bank, lured by the irresistible argument of nine or ten per cent. or he is tempted to borrow money which he does
not want, to speculate, and grow rich of a sudden, like his neighbor the bank
director. If he takes the first course—the stock of capital invested in the cultivation of the land, is diminished in proportion to the recruits thus lured from
honest and permanent independence, to take the chances of banking and
speculation, and deposit their real riches in the same fate with the ideal wealth
of pennyless adventurers. From a useful citizen adding every day to the wealth
of his country and the happiness of his fellow beings, he sinks into a useless
drone, nay, a mischievous tempter—an animal who preys on the unsuspecting,
and grows rich on the distresses of his neighbors.

If, on the contrary, the farmer is tempted, and *coaxed* to accept of a discount,
and this is done continually by the country and village banks, which are of
course ever on the alert to procure the security of real property for their *rags*—
what then is the common effect of such imprudence? He obtains a temporary
accommodation for SIXTY DAYS, which cannot be useful to him in the slow
progress of agricultural economy, and which the assurance of his *friend,* the
bank director, that his note will be renewed forever if he wishes it, renders
him careless in repaying. Nine times out of ten he is not ready to pay the

note—which is renewed a decent number of times, until the favorable period for refusing all further accommodation arrives.—Banks never want a decent excuse for this—but the real reason generally is, that some hungry bank director, has cast the eyes of longing on the good man's farm, which, in process of time, is sold at public vendue, and sacrificed for half or one-third its value,—because the little country bank, having every body in debt, has only to draw in its discounts suddenly, to make money so scarce in their neighborhood, that there is no competition of purchasers. . . .

Alas! where shall they go to find . . . asylum from brokers and speculators? The borders of the Mississippi, the Missouri, Illinois, Ohio, Kentucky, and Tennessee, are infested by this pernicious *fry*—and the depths of the forests swarm with paper banks, that lend their money at *par,* to miserable dupes, who pass it away at a depreciation of ten or fifteen per cent. A moment's consideration will let us into the manner in which this operates on the borrower. Every time he goes to the bank, he loses ten or fifteen per cent. on the money he procures—and in this way his property, as the honest farmer expresses it, is *"eaten up,"* by ten and fifteen per cent. at a time.—It may be urged by the ingenious abstract reasoners, on the mysteries of financiering and banking, that the farmers are not *obliged* to borrow of the banks; they can let alone if they please—and for the consequences of his voluntary acts, a man can blame none but himself. The position is true, provided no *coaxing* or temptations are used. Yet after all, "Lead us not into temptation" is the wisest prayer ever put into the mouth of man. Nothing that offers an extensive allurement to folly, imprudence, and extravagance, ought ever to receive the sanction of a wise and virtuous legislator, whose first duty it is to guard a people against factitious, and unnecessary temptations, and shield them from those arts which cunning and unprincipled men use to deceive and ruin the simple and the unwary. . . .

B] THE FRANKFORT *Argus:* EDITORIAL

THE United States' Banch Banks, it is understood, have received another mandate from the mother at Philadelphia and are now directed not to keep any interest account with the local banks; but to settle every month and demand the balances due in specie or their own paper. This is but another specimen of that variable policy which pays no respect to the public good or the interests of trade; but is regulated by whim, caprice, or some other principle unknown to the people.

When the late arrangement of the U.S. Bank was published, it was vauntingly proclaimed in this State, that our local banks would be entirely relieved from the pressure of the western Branches. We then gave it as our opinion that such would not be the fact. The event has verified our prediction. The Branches do not issue their paper at all, or if they do, it is in such small quantities, that it does not travel out of the immediate vicinity of the banks.—For months past we have not seen a single U.S. Bank note of any description, and we believe that ninety-nine in one hundred of the people of Kentucky are equally strangers to it.

What is the consequence? The local banks being utterly unable to obtain their paper to meet balances every thirty days, will be compelled in self-defence to call in their debts and stop discounting. The Bank of Kentucky has already found it necessary to adopt this course, and such must be the plan pursued by every one of the local banks in the Western Country, whose paper is taken by these branches, or they will soon find themselves drained of specie. There is no Branch Bank paper in the country to pay the debts which are due to those institutions, and consequently they are paid entirely in the notes of the local banks. These immediately return upon the banks which issued them, and they being equally unable to obtain U.S. Branch Bank notes are obliged to pay them in specie. To save their specie then, they are obliged to cease issuing their notes.

Much has been said about the U.S. Branches *checking* the extravagance of the local Banks. How do they check them? They take the notes of a few of the best and most substantial among us and oblige them to curtail their business and withdraw their paper from circulation, leaving us inundated with the depreciated paper of less substantial institutions. This is *checking* with a vengence! It is *checking* the substantial well-managed banks, leaving those which are less honest, to luxuriate on the ruin of better institutions and fill the country with depreciated paper. . . . Scarcely a hundred dollars can be raised on an emergency to pay a debt in bank, while thousands may be obtained within an hour's notice on the little banks in distant towns and counties. . . . The good banks are checked, the bad ones are left to themselves. . . .

But let the U.S. Branches leave the state and we shall find the Bank of Kentucky and the sound independent banks, furnishing us a currency which will be as good as gold and silver, and soon confine the paper of the less prudent or less sound institutions to their own neighborhood.

c] MISCELLANY

Illegitimate Rag-manufacturers. Since our catalogue of frauds last week, springing from excessive banking, we have the following:

A *Plattsburg* paper of June 27, contains an account of the condemnation of two persons for dealing in forged notes. One of them had an assortment of wares and several new articles. He had no less than TWENTY different kinds of notes, some of them said to be "well executed!" . . .

The Baltimore Telegraph, of yesterday, has the following "caution."—"A letter has been received by one of the police officers of this city, apprising him of the apprehension in New York, of an old offender, having no less than 80,000 dollars of counterfeit money in his possession, principally of southern banks—He further informs that when the culprit left Canada, two accomplices left there for Baltimore, with large sums of counterfeit paper on the Baltimore and southern banks. This information may be relied on, and the public are desired to examine strictly bank bills before receiving them."

☞ From what we have lately seen and heard, it may fairly be estimated that more, much more, perhaps, than a *million of dollars* in counterfeit and altered notes, have very *recently* been manufactured. If suffered to circulate, the loss will, nine times in ten, fall upon that part of the community which is least able to bear it. *Farmers, mechanics, manufacturers and laborers—all you who work with your hands for a living,* refuse, absolutely refuse, to receive the bills of banks with which you are unacquainted, unless you know of whom you receive them.

The times. The *Aurora* [Philadelphia] of the 16th inst. contains, under an anonymous signature, some remarkable instances of what the writer justly styles the odious effects of the banking and usury systems; for example, it is stated that a person near Easton, mortgaged property which cost him 12,500 dollars, for 2,500 dollars, which the mortgagee forced the owner to dispose of at a sheriff's sale, and became the purchaser. Another is the case of a druggist, who had his stock seized for rent, and to raise 400 dollars, the landlord sold what was worth in ordinary times, at wholesale prices, $2,000, and at retail prices probably $10,000.

The times. A writer in the Richmond *Enquirer,* thus describes the state of the times—"I confine my views to a single county, in order that they may be more striking, though I know full well there must be the same distress every where. Of gold and silver we have next kin to none; of Virginia and United States bank paper but little—of North Carolina money, if it had credit, enough to pay taxes, buy necessaries, and discharge debts: but it has lost its credit—the merchant will not take it; the sheriff demands a discount when he takes it for taxes—the creditor takes it when he doubts the solvency of his debtor; it circulates freely among professional men for their professional services, and a few independent farmers, in whose hands some predict it is destined to perish an emblem of their folly, and in better days the remembrance of an iron age that has passed away. . . . Thus, from the nature of things, the money here must be that in common circulation in North Carolina, and you are prepared to estimate our difficulties from the depreciation of the Carolina paper. The iron business languishes; the waggon shops are shut up; taxes cannot be paid in the required money; the flinty creditor asks Virginia paper, or gold and silver, for his debt: the debtor, unable to raise either, gives up his land, and, ruined and undone, seeks a home for himself and his family in the western wilderness. The picture is sometimes realized. A tract of land, of 300 acres, sold a few days ago, about 25 miles from my house, for $300 only. The improvements on this land I have heard variously represented; some say they were worth $1,500, some much more. A horse valued at $80, was sold the other day near my house for $10; and two waggon horses were sold about the same time for $40, which I well know cost nearly $200. If the state of the currency was calculated only to ruin the knave, it might be endured without complaining; but alas! it is calculated to ruin the honest man also."

7] Three Views of the Panic

Although there was a wide spectrum of opinion on the causes of the Panic of 1819, most observers agreed on the effects. The three selections printed below offer different but characteristic views and interpretations. The first is an editorial from the *Federal Republican* of Baltimore, the city that probably suffered more than any other from the depression. The observations of a Scotsman, James Flint, who was traveling in the Western Country when the Panic struck, are offered in the second selection. Finally, the recollection of Thomas Ford, who grew to manhood in frontier Illinois and later became governor of the state, places the money problem in the larger context of the problem of Western commerce.*

A] DISTRESSES

WE HAVE several times adverted to the distresses of the day, and should feel timid in resuming the subject, were it not the paramount topic in all papers—in all places—and on all occasions. The famous South Sea scheme in England—the execrated Mississippi scheme in France—each produced in their turns the same terror, the same ruin, and the same distress which our city feels at this juncture. The fallacy of our banking systems was never more obvious as now—and while we see our monied institutions on the verge of ruin—our wealthiest and some of our worthiest citizens falling about us—their tributaries without subsistence, and their creditors without redress, we cannot wonder that so many rapid revolutions are made in our systems of finance and economy; nor can we be surprised that so many are stripping off the tawdry trimmings of dishonorable vanity, and mourning, though too late, that their pride has carried them beyond their resources, and has left them beyond the dearth of relief. The gay crowd of fashionists that but yesterday were strolling in market street, in all the haughty pomp of ostentation, are no more seen. The streets are now thronged only with astonished victims, studying their various modes of ruin or remedy.

The sober reality has at last found its way to the toilette; wives and daughters now hear the story of distress, and are told that their gew-gaws must be laid aside . . . that industry must take the place of luxurious indolence; and that pride *must* yield to poverty, or the drawing room be exchanged for the *gaol*. Our whole city presents an aspect of gloom which would hardly be equalled during the reign of pestilence; and, though we are far from wishing to give strangers the alarm, we feel a conviction that the shock of this period will carry us back with a retrogression more rapid than our advance, and will for years shroud many a face with mourning that has always been a stranger to care. Long will our industry toil in vain to repair this vast wreck of its efforts, and long will it mourn over our crumbling places before the word of redemption is accomplished.

B] OBSERVATIONS OF A SCOTSMAN IN INDIANA

Jeffersonville, (Indiana,) May 4, 1820

THE ACCOUNTS given in my last letter of the depredations committed by bankers, will make you suppose that affairs are much deranged here. Bank-

---

* THREE VIEWS OF THE PANIC: From the Baltimore *Federal Republican* (May 28, 1819); James Flint, *Letters from America*, in Reuben Gold Thwaites, ed., *Early Western Travels*, IX (Cleveland, 1904), 224–29; Thomas Ford, *A History of Illinois*, Milo M. Quaife, ed. (Chicago, 1945), I, 44–48.

ruptcy is now a sin prohibited by law. In the Eastern States, and in Europe, our condition must be viewed as universal insolvency. Who, it may be asked, would give credit to a people whose laws tolerate the violation of contracts? Mutual credit and confidence are almost torn up by the roots. It is said that in China, knaves are openly commended in courts of law for the adroitness of their management. In the interior of the United States, law has removed the necessity of being either acute or honest.

The money in circulation is puzzling to traders, and more particularly to strangers; for besides the multiplicity of banks, and the diversity in supposed value, fluctuations are so frequent, and so great, that no man who holds it in his possession can be safe for a day. The merchant, when asked the price of an article, instead of making a direct answer, usually puts the question, "What sort of money have you got?" Supposing that a number of bills are shown, and one or more are accepted of, it is not till then, that the price of the goods is declared; and an additional price is uniformly laid on, to compensate for the supposed defect in the quality of the money. Trade is stagnated—produce cheap—and merchants find it difficult to lay in assortments of foreign manufactures. . . .

Agriculture languishes—farmers cannot find profit in hiring labourers. The increase of produce in the United States is greater than any increase of consumpt[ion] that may be pointed out elsewhere. To increase the quantity of provisions, then, without enlarging the numbers of those who eat them, will be only diminishing the price farther. Land in these circumstances can be of no value to the capitalist who would employ his funds in farming. The spare capital of farmers is here chiefly laid out in the purchase of lands.

Labourers and mechanics are in want of employment. I think that I have seen upwards of 1500 men in quest of work within eleven months past, and many of these declared, that they had no money. Newspapers and private letters agree in stating, that wages are so low as eighteen and three-fourths cents . . . per day, with board, at Philadelphia, and some other places. Great numbers of strangers lately camped in the open field near Baltimore, depending on the contributions of the charitable for subsistence. You have no doubt heard of emigrants returning to Europe without finding the prospect of a livelihood in America. Some who have come out to this part of the country do not succeed well. Labourers' wages are at present a dollar and an eighth part per day. Board costs them two [and] three-fourths or three dollars per week, and washing three-fourths of a dollar for a dozen pieces. On these terms, it is plain that they cannot live two days by the labour of one, with the other deductions which are to be taken from their wages. Clothing, for example, will cost about three times its price in Britain: and the poor labourer is almost certain of being paid in depreciated money; perhaps from thirty to fifty per cent under par. I have seen several men turned out of boarding houses, where their money would not be taken. They had no other resource left but to lodge in the woods, without any covering except their clothes. They set fire to a decayed log, spread some boards alongside of it for a bed, laid a block of timber across for a pillow, and pursued their labour by day as usual. A still greater misfortune than being paid with bad money is to be guarded against, namely, that of not being paid at all. Public improvements are frequently executed by subscription, and subscribers do not in every case consider themselves dishonoured by non-payment of the sum they engage for. I could point out an interesting work, where a tenth part of the amount on the subscription book cannot now be realized. The treasurer of a company so circumstanced, has only to tell the undertakers or labourers that he cannot pay them. . . . It is understood that persons who are agents for others, frequently exchange the money put into their hands for worse bills, and reserve the premium obtained for themselves. Employers are also in the habit of deceiving their workmen, by telling them that it is not convenient to pay wages in money, and that they run accounts with the storekeeper, the tailor, and the shoemaker, and that from them they may have all the necessaries they want very cheap. The workman who consents to this mode of payment, procures orders from the employer, on one or more of these citizens, and is charged a higher price for the goods than the employer actually pays for them. This is called *paying in trade.*

You have often heard that extreme poverty does not exist in the United States. For some time after my arrival in the country supposed to be exempt from abject misery, I never heard the term poor, (a word, by the by, not often used,) without imagining that it applied to a class in moderate circumstances, who had it not in their power to live in fine houses, indulge in foreign luxuries, and wear expensive clothing; and on seeing a person whose external appearance would have denoted a beggar in Britain, I concluded that the unfortunate must have been improvident or dissipated, or perhaps possessed of both of these qualities. My conjectures may have on two or three occasions been just, as people of a depressed appearance are very rarely to be seen, but I now see the propriety of divesting myself of such a hasty and ungenerous opinion. Last winter a Cincinnati newspaper advertised a place where old clothes were received for the poor, and another where castoff shoes were collected for children who could not, for want of them, attend Sunday schools. The charitable measure of supplying the poor with public meals, has lately been resorted to at Baltimore; but there is reason to believe, that most of the people who are relieved in this way, are Europeans recently come into America. In the western country, poor rates are raised in the form of a county tax. . . . The operations of bankers, and the recent decline in trade, have been effective causes of poverty; and it seems probable that the introduction of manufacturing industry, and a reduction of base paper, would soon give effectual relief.

c] RECOLLECTIONS OF THE PANIC IN ILLINOIS

SUCH a thing as regular commerce was nearly unknown [in Illinois]. Until 1817 everything of foreign growth or manufacture had been brought from New Orleans in keel boats towed with ropes or pushed with poles by the hardy race of boatmen of that day up the current of the Mississippi; or else wagoned across the mountains from Philadelphia to Pittsburgh, and from thence floated down the Ohio to its mouth in keel boats; and from there shoved, pushed, and towed up the Mississippi, as from New Orleans. Upon the conclusion of the war of 1812 the people from the old States began to come in and settle in the country. They brought some money and property with them and introduced some changes in the customs and modes of living. Before the war such a thing as money was scarcely ever seen in the country, the skins of the deer and raccoon supplying the place of a circulating medium. The money which was now brought in, and which had before been paid by the United States to the militia during the war, turned the heads of all the people and gave them new ideas and aspirations; so that by 1819 the whole country was in a rage for speculating in lands and town lots. The States of Ohio and Kentucky, a little before, had each incorporated a batch of about forty independent banks. The Illinois territory had incorporated two at home, one at Edwardsville and the other at Shawneetown; and the territory of Missouri added two more at St. Louis. These banks made money very plenty; emigrants brought it to the State in great abundance. The owners of it had to use it in some way; and as it could not be used in legitimate commerce in a State where the material for commerce did not exist, the most of it was used to build houses in towns which the limited business of the country did not require, and to purchase land which the labor of the country was not sufficient to cultivate. This was called "developing the infant resources of a new country."

The United States government was then selling land at two dollars per acre; eighty dollars on the quarter section to be paid down on the purchase, with a credit of five years for the residue. For nearly every sum of eighty dollars there was in the country, a quarter section of land was purchased; for in those days there were no specie circulars to restrain unwarrantable speculations; [1] but, on the contrary, the notes of most of the numerous banks in existence were good in the public land offices. The amount of land thus purchased was increased by the general expectation that the rapid settlement of the country would enable the speculator to sell it for a high price before the expiration of the credit. This great abundance of money also, about this time, made a vast increase in the amount of merchandise brought into the State. When money is plenty every man's credit is good. The people dealt largely with the stores on credit, and drew upon a certain fortune in prospect for payment. Every one was to get rich out of the future emigrant. The speculator was to sell him houses and lands; and the farmer was to sell him everything he wanted to begin with and to live upon until he could supply himself. Towns were laid out all over the country and lots were purchased by every one on a credit; the town maker received no money for his lots, but he received notes of hand which he considered to be as good as cash; and he lived and embarked in other ventures, as if they had been cash in truth. In this mode, by the year 1820 nearly the whole people were irrecoverably involved in debt. The banks in Ohio and Kentucky broke, one after another, leaving the people of those States covered with indebtedness and without the means of extrication. The banks at home and in St. Louis ceased business. The great tide of immigrants from abroad, which had been looked for by every one, failed to come. Real estate was unsaleable; the lands purchased of the United States were unpaid for, and likely to be forfeited. Bank notes had driven out specie, and when these notes became worthless there was no money of any description left in the country. And

1 The allusion is to the several Specie Circulars issued during President Jackson's administration, more especially the one of July 11, 1836, requiring payments for public lands to be made in gold or silver coin.

there was absolutely no commerce by means of which a currency could be restored. For in those days we exported nothing; and if there had been any property fit for exportation there was no market for it abroad, and if there had been a market there was no capital with which to purchase it and take it to market. The people began to sue one another for their debts; and as there was absolutely no money in the country it was evident that scarcely any amount of property would pay the indebtedness. . . .

8] Chief Justice Marshall Expounds the Constitution

> During the outrage against the National Bank, the legislatures of several Southern and Western states levied huge taxes on the branches operating within their borders in order to curtail, or perhaps destroy, the Bank's business. When a Maryland law of this character was ignored by the Baltimore branch of the Bank, the state brought suit against the cashier, James W. McCulloch. He appealed from the Maryland decision to the Supreme Court of the United States. Chief Justice Marshall spoke for a unanimous court in invalidating the Maryland statute and in upholding the constitutionality of the Second Bank of the United States.*

.   .   .   .

THE FIRST question made in the cause is, has Congress power to incorporate a bank? . . .

In discussing this question, the counsel for the state of Maryland have deemed it of some importance, in the construction of the constitution, to consider that instrument not as emanating from the people, but as the act of sovereign and independent states. The powers of the general government, it has been said, are delegated by the states, who alone are truly sovereign; and must be exercised in subordination to the states, who alone possess supreme dominion.

It would be difficult to sustain this proposition. The convention which framed the constitution was indeed elected by the state legislatures. But the instrument, when it came from their hands, was a mere proposal, without obligation, or pretensions to it. It was reported to the then existing Congress of the United States, with a request that it might 'be submitted to a convention of delegates, chosen in each state by the people thereof, under the recommendation of its legislature, for their assent and ratification.' This mode of proceeding was adopted; and by the convention, by Congress, and by the state legislatures, the instrument was submitted to the people. They acted upon it in the only manner in which they can act safely, effectively, and wisely, on such a subject, by assembling in convention. . . .

From these conventions the constitution derives its whole authority. The government proceeds directly from the people; is 'ordained and established' in the name of the people; and is declared to be ordained, 'in order to form

---

* CHIEF JUSTICE MARSHALL EXPOUNDS THE CONSTITUTION: From *McCulloch* v. *Maryland*, 4 Wheat. 316.

a more perfect union, establish justice, insure domestic tranquillity, and secure the blessings of liberty to themselves and to their posterity.' The assent of the states, in their sovereign capacity, is implied in calling a convention, and thus submitting that instrument to the people. But the people were at perfect liberty to accept or reject it; and their act was final. It required not the affirmance, and could not be negatived, by the state governments. The constitution, when thus adopted, was of complete obligation, and bound the state sovereignties. . . .

If any one proposition could command the universal assent of mankind, we might expect it would be this—that the government of the Union, though limited in its powers, is supreme within its sphere of action. This would seem to result necessarily from its nature. It is the government of all; its powers are delegated by all; it represents all, and acts for all. Though any one state may be willing to control its operations, no state is willing to allow others to control them. The nation, on those subjects on which it can act, must necessarily bind its component parts. But this question is not left to mere reason; the people have, in express terms, decided it by saying, 'this constitution, and the laws of the United States, which shall be made in pursuance thereof,' 'shall be the supreme law of the land,' and by requiring that the members of the state legislatures, and the officers of the executive and judicial departments of the states shall take the oath of fidelity to it. . . .

Among the enumerated powers, we do not find that of establishing a bank or creating a corporation. But there is no phrase in the instrument which, like the articles of confederation, excludes incidental or implied powers; and which requires that everything granted shall be expressly and minutely described. Even the 10th amendment, which was framed for the purpose of quieting the excessive jealousies which had been excited, omits the word 'expressly,' and declares only that the powers 'not delegated to the United States, nor prohibited to the states, are reserved to the states or to the people'; thus leaving the question, whether the particular power which may become the subject of contest has been delegated to the one government, or prohibited to the other, to depend on a fair construction of the whole instrument. The men who drew and adopted this amendment had experienced the embarrassments resulting from the insertion of this word in the articles of confederation, and probably omitted it to avoid those embarrassments. A constitution, to contain an accurate detail of all the subdivisions of which its great powers will admit, and of all the means by which they may be carried into execution, would partake of a prolixity of a legal code, and could scarcely be embraced by the human mind. It would probably never be understood by the public. Its nature, therefore, requires that only its great outlines should be marked, its important objects designated, and the minor ingredients which compose those objects be deduced from the nature of the objects themselves. . . . In considering this question, then, we must never forget that it is a constitution we are expounding.

Although, among the enumerated powers of government, we do not find the word 'bank' or 'incorporation,' we find the great powers to lay and collect taxes; to borrow money; to regulate commerce; to declare and conduct a war; and to raise and support armies and navies. The sword and the purse, all the external relations, and no inconsiderable portion of the industry of the nation, are entrusted to its government. It can never be pretended that these vast powers draw after them others of inferior importance, merely because they are inferior. Such an idea can never be advanced. But it may with great reason be contended, that a government, entrusted with such ample powers, on the due execution of which the happiness and prosperity of the nation so vitally depends, must also be entrusted with ample means for their execution. The power being given, it is the interest of the nation to facilitate its execution. It can never be their interest, and cannot be presumed to have been their intention, to clog and embarrass its execution by withholding the most appropriate means. . . . Can we adopt that construction (unless the words imperiously require it) which would impute to the framers of that instrument, when granting these powers for the public good, the intention of impeding their exercise by withholding a choice of means? If, indeed, such be the mandate of the constitution, we have only to obey; but that instrument does not profess to enumerate the means by which the powers it confers may be executed; nor does it prohibit the creation of a corporation, if the existence of such a being be essential to the beneficial exercise of those powers. It is, then, the subject of fair inquiry, how far such means may be employed. It is not denied that the powers given to the government imply the ordinary means of execution. . . .

The creation of a corporation, it is said, appertains to sovereignty. This is admitted. But to what portion of sovereignty does it appertain? Does it belong to one more than to another? In America, the powers of sovereignty are divided between the government of the Union, and those of the States. They are each sovereign, with respect to the objects committed to it, and neither sovereign with respect to the objects committed to the other. . . . The power of creating a corporation, though appertaining to sovereignty, is not, like the power of making war, or levying taxes, or of regulating commerce, a great substantive and independent power, which cannot be implied as incidental to other powers, or used as a means of executing them. It is never the end for which other powers are exercised, but a means by which other objects are accomplished. . . . No city was ever built with the sole object of being incorporated, but is incorporated as affording the best means of being well governed. The power of creating a corporation is never used for its own sake, but for the purpose of effecting something else. No sufficient reason is, therefore, perceived, why it may not pass as incidental to those powers which are expressly given, if it be a direct mode of executing them.

But the constitution of the United States has not left the right of Congress to employ the necessary means for the execution of the powers conferred on the government to general reasoning. To its enumeration of powers is added that of making 'all laws which shall be necessary and proper, for carrying into execution the foregoing powers, and all other powers vested by this constitution, in the government of the United States, or in any department thereof.'

The counsel for the State of Maryland have urged various arguments, to prove that this clause, though in terms a grant of power, is not so in effect. . . .

But the argument on which most reliance is placed, is drawn from the peculiar language of this clause. Congress is not empowered by it to make all laws, which may have relation to the powers conferred on the government, but such only as may be 'necessary and proper' for carrying them into execution. The word 'necessary' is considered as controlling the whole sentence, and as limiting the right to pass laws for the execution of the granted powers, to such as are indispensable, and without which the power would be nugatory. That it excludes the choice of means, and leaves to Congress, in each case, that only which is most direct and simple.

Is it true that this is the sense in which the word 'necessary' is always used? Does it always import an absolute physical necessity, so strong that one thing, to which another may be termed necessary, cannot exist without that other? We think it does not. . . . A thing may be necessary, very necessary, absolutely or indispensably necessary. To no mind would the same idea be conveyed to these several phrases. . . . This word, then, like others, is used in various senses; and, in its construction, the subject, the context, the intention of the person using them, are all to be taken into view.

Let this be done in the case under consideration. The subject is the execution of those great powers on which the welfare of a nation essentially depends. It must have been the intention of those who gave these powers, to insure, as far as human prudence could insure, their beneficial execution. This could not be done by confiding the choice of means of such narrow limits as not to leave it in the power of Congress to adopt any which might be appropriate, and which were conducive to the end. This provision is made in a constitution intended to endure for ages to come, and, consequently, to be adapted to the various crises of human affairs. To have prescribed the means by which government should, in all future time, execute its powers, would have been to change, entirely, the character of the instrument, and give it the properties of a legal code. . . .

We admit, as all must admit, that the powers of the government are limited, and that its limits are not to be transcended. But we think the sound construction of the constitution must allow to the national legislature that discretion, with respect to the means by which the powers it confers are to be carried into execution, which will enable that body to perform the high duties assigned to it, in the manner most beneficial to the people. Let the end be legitimate, let it be within the scope of the constitution, and all means which are appropriate, which are plainly adapted to that end, which are not prohibited, but consist with the letter and spirit of the constitution, are constitutional. . . .

If a corporation may be employed indiscriminately with other means to carry into execution the powers of the government, no particular reason can be assigned for excluding the use of a bank, if required for its fiscal operations. To use one, must be within the discretion of Congress, if it be an appropriate mode of executing the powers of government. That it is a convenient, a useful, and essential instrument in the prosecution of its fiscal operations, is not now a subject of controversy. . . .

It being the opinion of the court that the act incorporating the bank is constitutional, and that the power of establishing a branch in the state of Maryland might be properly exercised by the bank itself, we proceed to inquire:

2. Whether the state of Maryland may, without violating the constitution, tax that branch?

That the power of taxation is one of vital importance; that it is retained by the states; that it is not abridged by the grant of a similar power to the government of the Union; that it is to be concurrently exercised by the two governments: are truths which have never been denied. But, such is the paramount character of the constitution that its capacity to withdraw any subject from the action of even this power, is admitted. . . .

On this ground the counsel for the bank place its claim to be exempted from the power of a state to tax its operations. There is no express provision for the case, but the claim has been sustained on a principle which so entirely pervades the constitution, is so intermixed with the materials which compose it, so interwoven with its web, so blended with its texture, as to be incapable of being separated from it without rending it into shreds.

This great principle is, that the constitution and the laws made in pursuance thereof are supreme; that they control the constitution and laws of the respective states, and cannot be controlled by them. From this, which may be almost termed an axiom, other propositions are deduced as corollaries, on the truth or error of which, and on their application to this case, the cause has been supposed to depend. These are 1st. that a power to create implies a power to preserve. 2d. That a power to destroy, if wielded by a different hand, is hostile to, and incompatible with these powers to create and to preserve. 3d. That where this repugnancy exists, that authority which is supreme must control, not yield to that over which it is supreme. . . .

That the power to tax involves the power to destroy; that the power to destroy may defeat and render useless the power to create; that there is a plain repugnance, in conferring on one government a power to control the constitutional measures of another, which other, with respect to those very measures, is declared to be supreme over that which exerts the control, are propositions not to be denied. . . .

If we apply the principle for which the state of Maryland contends, to the constitution generally, we shall find it capable of changing totally the character of that instrument. We shall find it capable of arresting all the measures of the government, and of prostrating it at the foot of the states. The American people have declared their constitution, and the laws made in pursuance thereof, to be supreme; but this principle would transfer the supremacy, in fact, to the states.

If the states may tax one instrument, employed by the government in the execution of its powers, they may tax any and every other instrument. They may tax the mail; they may tax the mint; they may tax patent-rights; they may tax the papers of the custom-house; they may tax judicial process; they may tax all the means employed by the government, to an excess which would defeat all the ends of government. . . .

This is not all. If the controlling power of the states be established; if their supremacy as to taxation be acknowledged; what is to restrain their exercising this control in any shape they may please to give it? Their sovereignty is not confined to taxation. That is not the only mode in which it might be displayed. The question is, in truth, a question of supremacy; and if the right of the states to tax the means employed by the general government be conceded, the declaration that the constitution, and the laws made in pursuance thereof, shall be the supreme law of the land, is empty and unmeaning declamation. . . .

9] A Virginia Judge Expounds the Constitution

Spencer Roane, the head of Virginia's highest court, had been challenging the authority of the United States Supreme Court for several years before 1819. He insisted that the Supreme Court could not rightfully overturn the decisions of the Virginia judiciary—a militant state rights position. Jefferson and other leading Virginians supported Roane's futile claim. The court's decision in *McCulloch* v. *Maryland* occupied much higher national ground which, if it was to be resisted, called for an equivalent assertion of state rights principles. A marked revival of these principles of 1798 commenced in Virginia in 1819. Writing as "Hampden," Roane sparked the revival with his elaborate analysis of the court's opinion in the pages of the *Richmond Enquirer*. Only two small segments are printed below.*

IT HAS been the happiness of the American people to be connected together in a confederate republic: to be united by a system, which extends the sphere of popular government, and reconciles the advantages of monarchy with those of a republic: a system which combines all the internal advantages of the latter, with all the force of the former. It has been our happiness to believe, that in the partition of powers between the general and State governments, the former possessed only such as were expressly granted, or passed therewith as necessary incidents, while all the residuary powers were reserved by the latter. It was deemed by the enlightened founders of the Constitution, as essential to the internal happiness and welfare of their constituents, to reserve some powers to the State governments. As to their external safety, to grant others to the government of the union. This, it is believed, was done by the Constitution, in its original shape; but such were the natural fears and jealousies of our citizens, in relation to this all-important subject, that it was deemed necessary to quiet those fears by the tenth amendment to the Constitution. It is not easy to devise stronger terms to effect that object than those used in that amendment.

Such, however, is the proneness of all men to extend and abuse their power, —to "feel power and forget right,"—that even this article has afforded us no security. That legislative power which is everywhere extending the sphere of its activity and drawing all power into its impetuous vortex, has blinked even the strong words of this amendment. That judicial power, which according to Montesquieu is, "in some measure, next to nothing"; and whose province this great writer limits to "punishing criminals and determining the disputes which arise between individuals"; that judiciary which . . . in England, has only invaded the constitution in the worst of times, and then, always, on the

* A VIRGINIA JUDGE EXPOUNDS THE CONSTITUTION: "Hampden," "Rights of the States and of the People." From *The John P. Branch Historical Papers of Randolph-Macon College* (Ashland, Va., 1905), IV, 357–73, *passim*.

side of arbitrary power, has also deemed its interference necessary, in our country. It will readily be perceived that I allude to the decision of the supreme court of the United States, in the case of M'Culloh [*sic*] against the State of Maryland.

The warfare carried on by the legislature of the Union, against the rights of "the States" and of "the people" has been with various success and always by detachment. *They* have not dared to break down the barriers of the Constitution, by a *general* act declaratory of their power. That measure was too bold for these ephemeral deputies of the people. That people hold them in check by a short rein, and would consign them to merited infamy, at the next election. . . .

The warfare waged by the judicial body has been of a bolder tone and character. It was not enough for them to sanction, in former times, the detestable doctrines of Pickering and Co.: . . . it was not enough for them to annihilate the freedom of the press, by incarcerating all those who dared, with a manly freedom, to canvass the conduct of their public agents: it was not enough for the predecessors of the present judges to preach political sermons from the bench of justice and bolster up the most unconstitutional measures of the most abandoned of our rulers: it did not suffice to do the business in detail, and ratify, one by one, the legislative infractions of the Constitution. That process would have been too slow, and perhaps too troublesome. . . . They resolved, therefore, to put down all discussions of the kind, in future, by a judicial *coup de main:* to give a *general* letter of attorney to the future legislators of the Union; and to tread under foot all those parts and articles of the Constitution which had been, heretofore, deemed, to set limits to the power of the federal legislature. That man must be a deplorable idiot who does not see that there is no earthly difference between an *unlimited* grant of power and a grant limited in its terms, but accompanied with *unlimited* means of carrying it into execution.

The Supreme Court of the United States have not only granted this *general* power of attorney to Congress, but they have gone out of the record to do it, in the case in question. It was only necessary, in that case, to decide whether or not the bank law was "necessary and proper" . . . for carrying into effect some of the granted powers; but the court have, in effect, expunged those words from the Constitution. There is no essential difference between expunging words from an instrument, by erasure, and reading them in a sense entirely arbitrary with the reader, and which they do not naturally bear. Great as is the confidence of the nation in all its tribunals, they are not at liberty to change the meaning of our language. I might therefore justly contend that this opinion of the court, in so far as it outgoes the actual case depending before it, and so far as it established a *general* and *abstract* doctrine, was entirely extrajudicial and without authority. I shall not, however, press this point, as it is entirely merged in another, which I believe will be found conclusive,— namely, that that court had no power to adjudicate away the *reserved* rights of a sovereign member of the confederacy, and vest them in the general government. . . .

I address you, Mr. Editor, on this great subject with no sanguine presages of success. I must say to my fellow citizens that they are sunk in apathy, and that a torpor has fallen upon them. Instead of that noble and magnanimous spirit which achieved our independence, and has often preserved us since, we are sodden in the *luxuries* of banking. A money-loving, funding, stock-jobbing spirit has taken foothold among us. We are almost prepared to sell our liberties for "a mess of pottage." If Mason or Henry could lift their patriot heads from prophesies! they would almost exclaim with Jugurtha, "Venal people! you will soon perish, if you can find a purchaser."

.   .   .   .

I beg leave to lay down the following propositions, as being . . . incontestable in themselves, and assented to by the enlightened *advocates* of the Constitution, at the time of its adoption.

1. That that Constitution conveyed only a limited grant of powers to the general government, and reserved the residuary powers to the governments of the States, and to the people: and that the tenth amendment was merely declaratory of this principle, and inserted only to quiet what the court is pleased to call "the excessive jealousies of the people."

2. That the limited grant to Congress of certain enumerated powers only carried with it such additional powers as were *fairly incidental* to them, or, in other words, were necessary and proper for their execution.

And 3. That the insertion of the words "necessary and proper," in the last part of the eighth section of the first article, did not enlarge the powers previously given, but were inserted only through abundant caution. . . .

. . . They were only added (says *The Federalist*) for greater caution, and are tautologous and redundant, though *harmless*. It is also said in the *report* aforesaid [Madison's *Report* of 1799], that these words *do not amount* to a grant of *new* power, but for the removal of all uncertainty the declaration was made that the means were included in the grant. I might multiply authorities on this point to infinity; but if these do not suffice, neither would one were he to arise from the dead. If this power existed in the government, before these words were used, its repetition or reduplication, in the Constitution, does not increase it. The "expression of that which before existed in the grant, has no operation." So these words "necessary and proper," have no power or other effect than if they had been annexed to and repeated in every specific grant; and in that case they would have been equally unnecessary and harmless. As a friend, however, to the just powers of the general government, I do not object to them, considered as merely declaratory words, and inserted for greater caution: I only deny to them an extension to which they are not entitled, and which may be fatal to the reserved rights by the States and of the people.

10] A Federalist Argues for Slavery Restriction

When the bill to admit Missouri to statehood came before Congress in February, 1819, James Tallmadge of New York offered an amendment to prohibit the introduction of more slaves into Missouri and to bring about a gradual emancipation of the slaves already residing there. The amendment passed the House but was defeated in the Senate; thus the question was carried over to the next session. Rufus King, senator from New York and long a leader of the Federalist party, delivered the most effective speeches for the Missouri restriction. The speeches went unreported, though not unnoticed, at the time; but on November 22, 1819, just prior to the resumption of the Missouri debate, King wrote from his memory and his notes "the substance" of what he had said in Congress in order to comply with the request of a committee of New York citizens interested in the passage of the Missouri restriction. The document was then released to the press and widely circulated.*

. . . . - . .

THE CONSTITUTION declares "that congress shall have power to dispose of, and make all needful rules and regulations respecting the territory and other property of the United States." Under this power, congress have passed laws for the survey and sale of the public lands, for the division of the same into separate territories; and have ordained for each of them a constitution, a place of temporary government, whereby the civil and political rights of the inhabitants are regulated, and the rights of conscience and other natural rights are protected.

The power to make all needful regulations, includes the power to determine what regulations are needful: and if a regulation prohibiting slavery within any territory of the United States be, as it has been, deemed needful, congress possess the power to make the same, and moreover to pass all laws necessary to carry this power into execution.

The territory of Missouri is a portion of Louisiana, which was purchased of France, and belongs to the United States in full dominion; in the language of the constitution, Missouri is their territory, or property, and is subject, like other territories of the United States, to the regulations and temporary government which has been, or shall be, prescribed by congress. The clause of the constitution, which grants this power to congress, is so comprehensive and unambiguous, and its purpose so manifest, that commentary will not render the power, or the object of its establishment, more explicit or plain.

The constitution further provides, that "new states may be admitted by congress into the union." As this power is conferred without limitation, the time, terms, and circumstances of the admission of new states are referred to the discretion of congress—which may admit new states, but are not obliged to do so—of right no new state can demand admission into the union, unless such demand be founded upon some previous engagement with the United States. . . .

The question respecting slavery in the old thirteen states had been decided and settled before the adoption of the constitution, which grants no power to congress to interfere with, or to change what had been previously settled—the slave states, therefore, are free to continue or to abolish slavery. Since the year 1808, congress have possessed power to prohibit, and have prohibited, the further importation of slaves into any of the old thirteen states, and at all

* A FEDERALIST ARGUES FOR SLAVERY RESTRICTION: Rufus King, "The Substance of Two Speeches on the Missouri Bill." From *Niles' Weekly Register* (December 4, 1819).

times under the constitution have had power to prohibit such migration or importation, into any of the new states or territories of the United States. The constitution contains no express provisions respecting slavery in a new state that may be admitted into the union: every regulation upon this subject, belongs to the power whose consent is necessary to the formation and admission of such state. Congress may, therefore, make it a condition of the admission of a new state, that slavery shall be forever prohibited within the same. We may, with the more confidence, pronounce this to be the construction of the constitution, as it has been so amply confirmed by the past decisions of congress. . . .

It is . . . objected, that the article of the act of admission into the union, by which slavery should be excluded from Missouri, would be nugatory, as the new state, in virtue of its sovereignty, would be at liberty to revoke its consent, and annul the article by which slavery should be excluded.

Such revocation would be contrary to the obligations of good faith, which enjoins the observance of our engagements—it would be repugnant to the principles upon which government itself is founded. Sovereignty in every lawful government is a limited power, and can do only what is lawful to do—sovereigns, like individuals, are bound by their engagements, and have no moral power to break them. Treaties between nations repose on this principle. If the new state can revoke and annul an article constructed between itself and the United States, by which slavery is excluded from it, it may revoke and annul any other article of the compact; it may for example annul the article respecting public lands, and in virtue of its sovereignty, assume the right to tax and to sell the lands of the United States.

There is yet a more satisfactory answer to this objection. The judicial power of the United States is co-extensive with their legislative power, and every question arising under the constitution, or laws of the United States, is cognizable by the judiciary thereof. Should the new state rescind any of the articles of compact contained in the act of admission into the union, that for example by which slavery is excluded, and should pass a law authorizing slavery, the judiciary of the United States, on proper application, would immediately deliver from bondage any person detained as a slave in said state; and in like manner, in all instances affecting individuals, the judiciary might be employed to defeat every attempt to violate the constitution and laws of the United States.

If congress possess the power to exclude slavery from Missouri, it still remains to be shown that they ought to do so. . . .

Slavery unhappily exists within the United States. Enlightened men in the states where it is permitted, and every where out of them, regret its existence among us, and seek for the means of limiting and of mitigating it.—The first introduction of slaves is not imputable to the present generation nor even to their ancestors. Before the year 1642, the trade and ports of the colonies were open to foreigners equally as those of the mother country, and as early as 1620, a few years only after planting the colony of Virginia, and the same in which the first settlement was made in the old colony of Plymouth, a cargo of negroes was brought into, and sold as slaves in Virginia, by a foreign ship. From this beginning the importation of slaves was continued for nearly two centuries. . . . The laws and customs of the states in which slavery has existed for so long a period, must have had their influence on the opinions and habits of the citizens, which ought not to be disregarded on the present occasion.

Omitting therefore the arguments which might be urged, and which by all of us might be deemed conclusive, were this an original question, the reasons which shall be offered in favor of the interpretation of the power of congress to exclude slavery from Missouri, shall be only such as respect the common defence, the general welfare, and that wise administration of government which as far as possible may produce the impartial distribution of benefits and burdens throughout the union.

By the articles of confederation, the common treasury was to be supplied by the several states according to the value of the land, with the houses and improvements thereon, within the respective states. . . .

When the general convention that formed the constitution took the subject into their consideration, the whole question was once more examined, and while it was agreed that all contributions to the common treasury should be made according to the ability of the several states to furnish the same, the old difficulty recurred in agreeing upon a rule whereby such ability should be ascertained, there being no simple standard by which the ability of individuals to pay taxes can be ascertained. A diversity in the selection of taxes has been deemed requisite to their equalization. Between communities this difficulty is less considerable, and although the rule of relative numbers would not accurately measure the wealth of nations, in states in the circumstances of the United States, whose institutions, laws and employment are so much alike, the rule of number is probably as nearly equal as any other simple and practicable rule can be expected to be, (though between the old and new states its equity is defective); these considerations, added to the approbation which had already been given to the rule by a majority of the states, induced the convention to agree, that direct taxes should be apportioned to the whole number of free persons, and three-fifths of the slaves which they might respectively contain.

The rule for apportionment of taxes, is not necessarily the most equitable rule for the apportionment of representatives among the states;—property must not be disregarded in the composition of the first rule, but frequently is overlooked in the establishment of the second; a rule which might be approved in respect to taxes, would be disapproved in respect to representatives; one individual, possessing twice as much property as another, might be required to pay double the taxes of such other; but no man has two votes to another's one; rich or poor, each has but one vote in the choice of representatives. . . . If three-fifths of the slaves are virtually represented, or their owners obtain a disproportionate power in legislation, and in the appointment of the president of the United States, why should not other property be virtually represented, and its owners obtain a like power in legislation, and in the choice of the president. Property is not confined to slaves, but exists in houses, stores, ships, capital in trade and manufactures. To secure to the owners of property in slaves, greater political power than is allowed to the owners of other and equivalent property, seems to be contrary to our theory of the equality of personal rights, inasmuch as the citizens of some states thereby become entitled to other and greater political power than citizens of other states. The present house of representatives consists of one hundred and eighty-one members, which are apportioned among the states in a ratio of one representative for every thirty-five thousand federal numbers, which are ascertained by adding to the whole number of free persons three-fifths of the slaves. According to the last census, the whole number of slaves within the United States was 1,191,364, which entitled the states possessing the same, to twenty representatives and twenty presidential electors more than they would be entitled to, were the slaves excluded. By the last census, Virginia contained 582,104 free persons, and 392,518 slaves. In any of the states where slavery is excluded, 582,104 free persons would be entitled to elect only sixteen representatives, while in Virginia, 582,104 free persons, by the addition of three-fifths of her slaves, become entitled to elect, and do in fact elect, twenty-three representatives, being seven additional ones on account of her slaves. Thus . . . five free persons in Virginia have as much power in the choice of representatives to congress, and in the appointment of presidential electors, as seven free persons in any of the states in which slavery does not exist.

This inequality in the apportionment of representatives was not misunderstood at the adoption of the constitution—but as no one anticipated the fact that the whole of the revenue of the United States would be derived from indirect taxes, (which cannot be supposed to spread themselves over the several states, according to the rule for the apportionment of direct taxes,) but it was believed that a part of the contribution to the common treasury would be apportioned among the states by the rule for the apportionment of representatives. The states in which slavery is prohibited, ultimately, though with reluctance, acquiesced in the disproportionate number of representatives and electors that was secured to the slave holding states. The concession was, at the time, believed to be a great one, and has proved to have been the greatest which was made to secure the adoption of the constitution.

Great, however, as this concession was, it was definite, and its full extent was comprehended. It was a settlement between the thirteen states. The considerations arising out of their actual conditions, their past connexion, and the obligation which all felt to promote a reformation in the federal government, were peculiar to the time and to the parties; and are not applicable to the new states, which congress may now be willing to admit into the union.

The equality of rights, which includes an equality of burdens, is a vital principle in our theory of government, and its jealous preservation is the best security of public and individual freedom; the departure from this principle in the disproportionate power and influence, allowed to the slave holding states, was a necessary sacrifice to the establishment of the constitution. The effect of this constitution has been obvious to the preponderance it has given to the slave holding states over the other states. Nevertheless, it is an ancient settlement, and faith and honor stand pledged not to disturb it. But the extension of this disproportionate power to the new states would be unjust and odious. The states whose power would be abridged, and whose burdens would be increased by the measure, cannot be expected to consent to it; and we may hope that the other states are too magnanimous to insist on it. . . .

The motives for the admission of new states into the union, are the extension of the principles of our free government, the equalizing of the public burdens, and the consolidation of the power of the confederated nation. Unless these objects be promoted by the admission of new states, no such admission can be expedient or justified.

The states in which slavery already exists are contiguous to each other, they are also the portion of the United States nearest to the European colonies in the West Indies; colonies whose future condition can hardly be regarded as problematical. If Missouri, and the other states that may be formed to the west of the river Mississippi, are permitted to introduce and establish slavery, the repose, if not the security of the union may be endangered; all the states south of the river Ohio and west of Pennsylvania and Delaware, will be peopled with slaves, and the establishment of new states west of the river Mississippi, will serve to extend slavery instead of freedom over that boundless region.

Such increase of the states, whatever other interests it may promote, will be sure to add nothing to the security of the public liberties; and can hardly fail hereafter to require and produce a change in our government. . . .

If slavery be permitted in Missouri, with the climate and soil, and in the circumstances of this territory, what hope can be entertained that it will ever be prohibited in any of the new states that will be formed in the immense region west of the Mississippi. Will the co-extensive establishment of slavery and of new states throughout this region, lessen the danger of domestic insurrection, or of foreign oppression? Will this manner of executing the great trust of admitting new states into the union, contribute to assimilate our manners and usages, to increase our mutual affection and confidence, and to establish that equality of benefits and burthens which constitutes the true basis of our strength and union? Will the militia of the nation, which must furnish our soldiers and seamen, increase as slaves increase; will the actual disproportion in the military service of the nation be thereby diminished: a disproportion that will be, as it has been, readily borne, as between the original states, because it arises out of their compact of union, but which may become a badge of inferiority, if required for the protection of those who, being free to choose, persist in the establishment of maxims, the inevitable effect of which will deprive of the power to contribute to the common defence, and even to the ability to protect themselves. There are limits within which our federal system must stop; no one has supposed that it could be indefinitely extended—we are now about to pass our original boundary; if this can be done without affecting the principles of our free government, it can be accomplished only by the most vigilant attention to plant, cherish and sustain the principles of liberty in the new states that may be formed beyond our ancient limits: with out utmost caution in this respect, it may still be justly apprehended that the general government must be made stronger as we become more extended.

But if, instead of freedom, slavery is to prevail, and spread as we extend out dominion, can any reflecting man fail to see the necessity of giving to the general government greater powers; to enable it to afford the protection that will be demanded of it: powers that will be difficult to control, and which may prove fatal to the public liberties.

11] "A Southron" Denounces Restriction

It was said in the North that slaveholders could not hear of King's speeches "without being seized with cramps." Thomas Ritchie, editor of the Richmond *Enquirer*, the most influential newspaper south of the Potomac, thought King's argument worthy of a detailed rebuttal, which ran through several numbers of the newspaper. Briefer and more pointed was the answer of a contributor to the *Enquirer's* columns over the signature of "A Southron." Especially significant was his opinion that the Missouri question was a political stalking-horse for disappointed politicians and disgruntled interests in the North.*

THE CONGRESS of the United States have again before them the deeply interesting Missouri question. In my judgment, the petty concern of an acquisition of barren territory and even the danger of a war with a decrepit foe, in comparison with it, sink into insignificance. The matter is to preserve the happiness we already possess; to perpetuate this noble confederacy; to brighten the chain which binds together a band of brothers, instead of lighting up the torch of discord which will blaze like a vale fire from one end of the continent to the other. The harmony of the present moment, the happiness of the future, the independence of the states, the continuance of their union, even the preservation of the unimpaired sovereignty of this ancient and venerable member [Virginia] of the confederacy, may perhaps hang upon the decision to this interesting question. . . .

It were charity to hope that the motives which have dictated the late attempt to introduce restrictions into the constitution of Missouri were as praiseworthy as they affect to be. But we cannot "wink so hard" as to be insensible to the political object, which some of the statesmen of the east would fain conceal. The pretexts of humanity, and a love of liberty, are too flimsy a veil to hide from our views the political hostility which governs these. Humanity!— where is the humanity of resisting the only feasible plan of future emancipation? Can we expect an event so desirable in the southern states, while their numbers so far exceed the numbers of whites? Shall we oppose that dispersion of them through the western states, which by lessening the excess, may at a future day render practicable the schemes of philanthropy for their relief? Shall we adopt the barbarous principles of affected benevolence, in imposing a check on the increase of black population by excluding them from an emigration to a country more salubrious and fertile than they now inhabit, and affording more abundantly the means of subsistence and comfort? Admirable philanthropists! who have religion and humanity on their lips, and look to the diminution of slave population from the combined operations of pestilence and famine.

But while humanity cannot offer an apology for this outrage upon the rights of the south, it is easily explained by the antipathies of certain politicians, and

* "A SOUTHRON" DENOUNCES RESTRICTION: "A Southron." From the Richmond *Enquirer* (December 23, 1819).

their jealousy of the influence of the southern states in the councils of the nation. Rob us of our just portion of the territory which has been jointly purchased by the treasures of the nation, and the valley of the Mississippi will be settled by the sons of the eastern people, the inheritors of the fathers' prejudices; new states will spring up, emulous of setting new limits to southern domination; swarms of "southern slave holders" will no longer crowd the halls of congress and "sear the eyeballs" of their jealous countrymen;—"the sceptre will depart from Judah"; and Virginia influence—so magnified and deprecated —will be heard of no more!

If rumour has not deceived us, there may be other objects more immediate to be attained by this modern crusade against the rights of the people of the south. Some master spirit of the north may expect to ride on this popular wave to the lofty pinnacle of his ambition.—Whatever is indecorous in personality or unparliamentary in abuse, has been abundantly poured forth by those frothy declaimers against the unavoidable domestic slavery of the south. They have assumed to themselves the power of making a form of government for others, and have supported so insolent a pretension, by arguments and language no less insolent and offensive.

And when they have succeeded in excluding from the western settlements every southern man, and shall have sent forth in every direction swarms from the northern hive, and missionary preachers against the cruelties and inhumanities of southern slavery, an universal emancipation may be the next scheme suggested by visionary philanthropists or promoted by designing politicians.

With dangers such as these in prospect, can Virginia look on with stoical indifference because it is not her own case? . . . Shall she be silent when the great principles of the constitution are assailed, when the rights of her sons, now peopling a western clime, are invaded, and principles asserted which may one day be turned with fatal effect against her own institutions? . . . It behooves us to contest at the threshold, a pretension which violates the compact of the states; which sets at nought the great principle of self government; which will prove to be an apple of discord among the sisters of this confederacy, and threaten to subvert our free and happy constitution by a deadly blow at the rights of a part of the nation, and a destruction of the harmony and tranquility of the whole.

12] Thomas Jefferson and John Quincy Adams Fear for the Union

In retirement at Monticello since 1809, Thomas Jefferson was swept into the rising stream of nationalism. In 1816 he retracted his earlier agrarian opinions and endorsed domestic manufactures. But Jefferson was forced back upon his original principles in 1819. Many misfortunes, public and private, contributed to this result, but the crowning blow was the Missouri Compromise. He confided his fears of John Holmes, a Massachusetts congressman who was one of the handful of Northerners to vote against the Tallmadge amendment.

The Massachusetts son of the Federalist President, Secretary of State in

1820, John Quincy Adams was also badly shaken by the Missouri Compromise. He confided his innermost thoughts to his diary.*

A] THOMAS JEFFERSON TO JOHN HOLMES

MONTICELLO, April 22, 1820.

I THANK you, dear Sir, for the copy you have been so kind as to send me of the letter to your constituents on the Missouri question. It is a perfect justification to them. I had for a long time ceased to read newspapers, or pay any attention to public affairs, confident they were in good hands, and content to be a passenger in our bark to the shore from which I am not distant. But this momentous question, like a fire bell in the night, awakened and filled me with terror. I considered it at once as the knell of the Union. It is hushed, indeed, for the moment. But this is a reprieve only, not a final sentence. A geographical line, coinciding with a marked principle, moral and political, once conceived and held up to the angry passions of men, will never be obliterated; and every new irritation will mark it deeper and deeper. I can say, with conscious truth, that there is not a man on earth who would sacrifice more than I would to relieve us from this heavy reproach, in any *practicable* way. The cession of that kind of property, for so it is misnamed, is a bagatelle which would not cost me a second thought, if, in that way, a general emancipation and *expatriation* could be effected; and gradually, and with due sacrifices, I think it might be. But as it is, we have the wolf by the ears, and we can neither hold him, nor safely let him go. Justice is in one scale, and self-preservation in the other. Of one thing I am certain, that as the passage of slaves from one State to another, would not make a slave of a single human being who would not be so without it, so their diffusion over a greater surface would make them individually happier, and proportionally facilitate the accomplishment of their emancipation, by dividing the burthen on a greater number of coadjutors. An abstinence too, from this act of power, would remove the jealousy excited by the undertaking of Congress to regulate the condition of the different descriptions of men composing a State. This certainly is the exclusive right of every State, which nothing in the constitution has taken from them and given to the General Government. Could Congress, for example, say, that the non-freemen of Connecticut shall be freemen, or that they shall not emigrate into any other State?

I regret that I am now to die in the belief, that the useless sacrifice of themselves by the generation of 1776, to acquire self-government and happiness to their country, is to be thrown away by the unwise and unworthy passions of their sons, and that my only consolation is to be, that I live not to weep over it. If they would but dispassionately weigh the blessings they will throw away, against an abstract principle more likely to be effected by union than by scis-

---

* THOMAS JEFFERSON AND JOHN QUINCY ADAMS FEAR FOR THE UNION: Thomas Jefferson to John Holmes, April 22, 1820, and John Quincy Adams' Diary, March 3, 1820. From Paul Leicester Ford, ed., *Writings of Thomas Jefferson* (New York, 1892–99), X, 157, and Charles Francis Adams, ed., *Memoirs of John Quincy Adams* (Boston, 1874–77), V, 11–12.

sion, they would pause before they would perpetrate this act of suicide on themselves, and of treason against the hopes of the world. To yourself, as the faithful advocate of the Union, I tender the offering of my high esteem and respect.

B] JOHN QUINCY ADAMS' DIARY

March 3, 1820

... It is among the evils of slavery that it taints the very sources of moral principle. ... The impression produced upon my mind by the progress of this discussion is, that the bargain between freedom and slavery contained in the Constitution of the United States is morally and politically vicious, inconsistent with the principles upon which alone our revolution can be justified; cruel and oppressive, by riveting the chains of slavery, by pledging the faith of freedom to maintain and perpetuate the tyranny of the master; and grossly unequal and impolitic, by admitting that slaves are at once enemies to be kept in subjection, property to be secured or restored to their owners, and persons not to be represented themselves, but for whom their masters are privileged with nearly a double share of representation. The consequence has been that this slave representation has governed the Union. Benjamin portioned above his brethren has ravined as a wolf. In the morning he has devoured the prey, and at night he has divided the spoil. It would be no difficult matter to prove, by reviewing the history of the Union under this Constitution, that almost everything which has contributed to the honor and welfare of the nation has been accomplished in despite of them or forced upon them, and that everything unpropitious and dishonorable, including the blunders and follies of their adversaries, may be traced to them. I have favored this Missouri compromise, believing it to be all that could be effected under the present Constitution, and from extreme unwillingness to put the Union at hazard. But perhaps it would have been a wiser as well as a bolder course to have persisted in the restriction upon Missouri, till it should have terminated in a convention of the States to revise and amend the Constitution. This would have produced a new Union of thirteen or fourteen States unpolluted with slavery, with a great and glorious object to effect, namely that of rallying to their standard the other States by the universal emancipation of their slaves. If the Union must be dissolved, slavery is precisely the question upon which it ought to break. For the present, however, this contest is laid asleep.

CONCLUSION

THE MISSOURI question was settled by the admission of Missouri as a slave state, Maine as a free state, and the prohibition of slavery in the Louisiana Purchase north of the 36°30′ line. The balance of free and slave states was thus maintained, while slavery was excluded from most, if not quite all, of the Western lands. It was a compromise many Southerners swallowed with difficulty. To Old Republicans, it was part of a pattern of Northern aggression—as deliberate a blow at the South as the protective tariff. In their eyes the presumption of Congressional authority to restrict slavery grew out of the loose constitutional morality that had accompanied the growth of national power, and there could be no protection for slavery anywhere until the federal government was forced back within the rigid confines of the Constitution.

The prominence of Old Federalists like Rufus King in the ranks of the restrictionists gave some semblance of reality to Southern fears. The grievances which such men expressed against the three-fifths clause, one of the original compromises of the Constitution, suggests that their compassion for the slave veiled a still deeper passion for political power. Was it possible that the Northeast sought to check the addition of new slave states in order to vanquish Southern power in the Union? Was it possible that the Northern appeal to the sympathies of the free states of the Ohio Valley, which opposed slavery, was intended to cut across their economic ties with the South and create new bonds of attachment to the Northeast? Whatever the answers to these questions, the solidarity that the Northeast and the Northwest demonstrated on the Missouri question was to be followed in subsequent years by their concurrence on the policies of the American System, above all the protective tariff, which drove the minority South into deeper and deeper reaction.

As Thomas Jefferson reflected at Monticello, the Missouri Compromise established a new and portentous line of sectional division, which endured long after the depression of 1819 was overcome. Yet the significance of the breach cannot be appreciated except in the context of other events which superficially had nothing to do with it. The occurrences of 1819 and 1820 profoundly conditioned the events to come. The problem of the historian is not only to describe the events themselves but also to explain their hidden interrelationships and tendencies.

STUDY QUESTIONS

1] Discuss the origins of the American System. Did that system offer a sound and practical approach to the problems that confronted American government and economy after the War of 1812?

2] Discuss the following proposition: That the significance of the major events of the years 1819 and 1820 is to be found less in the individual events themselves than in their interrelationships.

3] How do you account for the fact that, with seeming irony, the upsurge of nationalism after 1815 actually contributed to the revival of sectional feelings and conflicts?

4] Discuss the Panic of 1819 as an economic crisis, a constitutional crisis, and a political crisis. If it was a genuine crisis in these different aspects, how do you explain President Monroe's re-election in 1820 with only one electoral vote cast against him?

RECOMMENDED READINGS

PRIMARY SOURCES

CALLENDER, GUY S. *Selections from the Economic History of the United States, 1765–1860* (Boston, 1909).

CAREY, MATHEW. *Addresses of the Philadelphia Society for the Promotion of National Industry* (Philadelphia, 1819).

COOPER, THOMAS. *Lectures on the Elements of Political Economy* (Columbia, S.C., 1826).

FLINT, JAMES. *Letters from America*, in Reuben Gold Thwaites, ed., *Early Western Travels: 1784–1846*, IX (Cleveland, 1904).

LIST, FRIEDRICH. *Outlines of American Political Economy* (Philadelphia, 1827).

Niles' Weekly Register, IX–XVII (Baltimore, 1815–20).

PITKIN, TIMOTHY. *A Statistical View of the Commerce of the United States of America* (New York, 1834).

RAYMOND, DANIEL. *Thoughts on Political Economy* (Baltimore, 1820).

TAYLOR, JOHN. *Construction Construed, and Constitutions Vindicated* (Philadelphia, 1820).

U.S. CONGRESS. *Annals of Congress* (*Debates and Proceedings in the Congress of the United States*), 14–16 Cong. (Washington, 1855).

SECONDARY SOURCES

BEVERIDGE, ALBERT J. *Life of John Marshall*, 4 vols. (Boston, 1919), Vol. IV.

CATTERALL, RALPH C. H. *The Second Bank of the United States* (Chicago, 1903).

DANGERFIELD, GEORGE. *The Era of Good Feelings* (New York, 1953).

DORFMAN, JOSEPH. *The Economic Mind in American Civilization*, 5 vols. (New York, 1946–59), Vol. II.

HAMMOND, BRAY. *Banks and Politics in America from the Revolution to the Civil War* (Princeton, 1957).

MAYO, BERNARD. *Henry Clay: Spokesman of the New West* (Boston, 1937).

REZNECK, SAMUEL. "The Depression of 1819–1822: A Social History," *American Historical Review*, XXXIX (1933), 28–47.

SYDNOR, CHARLES S. *The Development of Southern Sectionalism, 1819–1848* (Baton Rouge, La., 1948).

TAYLOR, GEORGE R. *The Transportation Revolution, 1815–1860* (New York, 1951).

TURNER, FREDERICK JACKSON. *The Rise of the New West, 1819–1829* (Boston, 1906).

WILTSE, CHARLES M. *John C. Calhoun, Nationalist, 1782–1828* (Indianapolis, 1944).

Jacksonian Democracy and the Bank War: The Crisis of 1830–1834

ALFRED D. CHANDLER, JR.

MASSACHUSETTS INSTITUTE OF TECHNOLOGY

CONTENTS

CHRONOLOGY

1829

DECEMBER 8   Jackson raises the Bank issue in his first annual message.

1830

APRIL 13   Report of House Ways and Means Committee defends the Bank.

1831

FEBRUARY 2   Benton attacks the Bank in the Senate.
DECEMBER 12   Clay nominated for the Presidency.

1832

JANUARY   Biddle decides to apply for recharter.
MARCH–MAY   Congressional committee investigates the Bank.
JULY 3   Bill for recharter passes Congress.
JULY 10   Jackson vetoes the bill.
JULY 11   Webster replies to Jackson.
DECEMBER 5   Jackson re-elected.

1833

MAY 29   Duane appointed Secretary of the Treasury.
SEPTEMBER 23   Taney appointed Secretary of the Treasury.
SEPTEMBER 26   Removal of deposits begun.
OCTOBER   Biddle begins extensive contraction.
DECEMBER 26   Clay introduces censuring resolutions.

1834

APRIL 15   Jackson answers Clay's charges.
AUTUMN   End of the Bank War.

1836

MARCH 4   The Bank becomes a state-chartered bank.
JULY 11   The Specie Circular issued.

1840

JULY 4   Independent Treasury Act passed.

INTRODUCTION

MORE THAN any other issue of its day, the clash between the President and the Bank of the United States highlights the history of the exuberant age of Jacksonian democracy. The "Bank War" reveals the dynamics of political, constitutional, economic, and even ideological change at the time when the United States first became a full-fledged democracy and developed a continental economy. In fact, the controversy between Jackson and the Bank grew out of an underlying incompatibility between the economic needs of a continental nation and the beliefs of the new democracy. Once the tension between needs and values erupted into open conflict, the resulting "war" immediately sharpened latent economic, political, constitutional, and class conflicts. The Bank War hastened a reformation of the American party system, a redefinition of the role of the Presidency, and a clearer awareness of regional, occupational, and class interests. Finally, it strengthened the American commitment to democratic ideas and values.

The election of Andrew Jackson in 1828 marked the culmination of a strong impulse toward broadening American democracy, which rapid settlement in the Mississippi Valley had helped to produce. The new Western states, entering the Union in quick succession, gave the vote and opened political offices to all white males. Eastern states somewhat hesitantly followed suit. After 1815 they removed religious and property qualifications for voting and office holding, redistricted states so as to assure more equitable representation, and provided, as had the Western states, for more directly elected officials—including presidential electors. Jackson was historically correct when he boasted that he was the first popularly elected President.

The spread of democratic practices intensified democratic beliefs. Faith grew in the competence of the common man to handle any and all of the intricate affairs of the political or business world. And a clamor rose against any special privilege or status that might prevent any man from proving his ability. The appointed administrative officeholder became suspect; so did incorporated business enterprise. Jackson and his supporters expected to expand political opportunities by destroying what they considered a monopoly in appointive positions through a drastic "rotation" of offices. They hoped to enlarge economic opportunities by eliminating or reducing corporate privileges.

After 1800 the corporation had become widely used for business ventures. A persistent shortage of capital in the United States led to the use of the corporate device in such fields as utilities (e.g., waterworks, turnpikes, canals), manufacturing, and, above all, banking in order to raise funds through the sale of shares to a number of investors. The corporate device also allowed individuals to spread risks and permitted state governments to help finance economic enterprises by purchasing shares of their stock. Incorporation required a special act of a state legislature, and the incorporators often convinced legislators that the difficulty of raising capital or the need to protect public as well as private investments required the granting of monopolistic franchises, limited liability, and other special privileges. When the democratic surge of the 1820's brought the corporation increasingly under attack, many Americans began to urge its abolition. Others more aware of its usefulness advocated the democratizing of the institution by the passage of general incorporation laws that would permit the routine granting of charters to anyone who paid a small fee.

In 1828 the most powerful corporation in the country—and the only one chartered by the national legislature—was the Second Bank of the United States. The Bank's enormous power rested, however, more on the brilliant banking innovations of its able president, Nicholas Biddle, than on any specific monopolistic grants. Biddle's innovations derived for the most part from his skill in meeting the needs of the flourishing commercial community that created the rapid growth and westward expansion of the nation in the years after 1815. In answering these enlarged demands Biddle fashioned the country's first central banking system. In so doing he collided squarely with the prevalent democratic ideas and principles. An understanding of the significance of the Bank War, therefore, calls for an awareness of why and how Biddle met new economic needs and how and why his activities came into conflict with Jacksonian democracy.

Chartered in 1816, the Second Bank was, it should be remembered, the direct descendant of the Bank that Alexander Hamilton had done so much to found in 1791. Like the First Bank, it was essentially a private institution with many public functions. It was privately owned and managed, although the United States held one-fifth of its stock and appointed five of its twenty-five directors. As did any bank, it made long- and short-term loans and took deposits. As did any other incorporated bank, it issued its own notes which promised to pay the bearer on demand their face value in gold and silver. Bank notes were, it needs to be stressed, the primary source of currency in the United States during the first half of the nineteenth century. When a borrower or depositor drew funds from an incorporated bank, he received its notes rather than specie (gold and silver) or paper currency issued by the United States Treasury.

The national bank differed from all state incorporated banks in that it had branches throughout the country and acted as the government's fiscal agent. Moreover, it had been founded and rechartered for the specific purpose of providing a uniform and stable currency. Failure to recharter the First Bank in 1811 immediately demonstrated the country's need for a national bank. After 1811 the rapid issuing of state bank notes and Treasury notes, along with the coming of the war of 1812, brought a runaway inflation. At the same time the transferring of government funds became costly and exceedingly difficult. As a result the Second Bank was chartered shortly after the war's end. At first, under incompetent management, it failed to provide either sound currency or credit. In fact, by overextending and then sharply contracting its loans and notes, it brought financial ruin to many Americans, particularly in the South and West, and so earned their bitter enmity.

After Nicholas Biddle, an urbane and polished scion of an old Philadelphia family, became its president in 1823, the Second Bank began to provide exceptionally stable and uniform currency and exceptionally efficient and inexpensive credit facilities. It maintained a sound currency in two ways: by issuing its own notes and by controlling those of the state banks. Because the Bank had branches throughout the nation (twenty-five by 1830) where its notes could be redeemed, because of its close connection with the federal government, and because of its large capital and specie reserves, its notes were accepted at their face value from Mexico City to Montreal. The task of maintaining state bank notes at par was much more difficult, for these banks were constantly tempted to print notes that circulated as money far beyond the limits set by their specie reserves. Control over such issues became increasingly difficult as the number of state banks rose rapidly with the swift settlement of the West after 1815.

Biddle was able to achieve this control because the Bank had a network of branches and because it was the depository for government funds. Since the currency was made up largely of bank notes, the Bank received many state bank notes when customers deposited funds at its headquarters in Philadelphia or in one of its many branches. An even larger source of these notes were the government deposits. Custom duties, purchases of public lands, post office fees, and other charges were paid for in state bank notes and were then deposited by the government in the Bank or one of its branches. State banks, of course, received the notes of the Second Bank in deposits, as payment for private loans and so forth, but because of its size and geographical spread the balance was nearly always in the national bank's favor. As the Bank cleared its accounts with the state banks every week, the local banks had to be constantly ready to redeem their notes in specie and therefore dared not overextend their note issues. Because the public was well aware of this control, local bank notes tended to stay at par within their own area, although, unlike those of the national bank, they were usually taken at a discount in more distant places.

Besides assuring the country of a sound currency, the Bank provided it with cheap and efficient short-term commercial credit facilities. The need for such facilities increased enormously as the population poured into the Mississippi Valley after 1815. The difference between short-term commercial credit and long-term loans needs to be noted. The latter were and still are loans to pay for land, buildings, and equipment, usually secured by a mortgage with principal and interest to be paid back at regular intervals over a period of many years. Short-term credit, on the other hand, is used to finance goods and commodities in transit from plantation, farm, or factory to the place where they are to be processed or consumed. Short-term notes or loans, commonly termed bills of exchange, or drafts, are normally for sixty or ninety days and secured by the commodity itself. In the 1820's the planter, merchant, or manufacturer who was paid by a bill of exchange and who did not want to wait sixty or ninety days for his money could obtain cash immediately by "selling" the bill to a bank or a broker at a small discount. Before 1815 the business of "buying" and "selling" of short-term bills at a discount had been small because the trade on which it was based was small. But after 1815 the rapid growth of the cotton trade for the great new textile industry in Britain and the swift expansion of domestic commerce following westward migration demanded a large-scale increase in short-term credit facilities.

In 1823 Biddle decided to put the Bank into "the business of exchange." His institution could provide this credit more cheaply than any other bank because the buying and selling of bills at a discount could be largely handled as accounting transactions between its many branches. No state-chartered bank had a comparable network of branches, because all other incorporated banks were state-chartered and could only do business in the state in which they were incorporated. Moreover, Biddle used these bills drawn on goods in transit as a new base for issuing bank notes. He realized, as would the founders of the Federal Reserve System many years later, that bills which would be paid as soon as goods on which they were drawn reached their destination were as sound a security for notes as gold and silver. For these reasons the Bank charged less than 1 per cent, and sometimes nothing at all, for providing this credit. To give similar services to businessmen in foreign trade, Biddle set up large balances in the banks of major European commercial centers. No other American bank had the capital necessary to imitate the Second Bank and so be able to offer as low rates in handling foreign exchange.

Because the Second Bank took over the financing of both domestic and foreign trade, Biddle was able to affect the flow of goods and funds within the United States as well as between the United States and Europe. This control, as well as that over note issues, gave Biddle the means to mobilize the nation's financial resources in much the same way as the Federal Reserve System was enabled after 1914 to meet potentially dangerous money shortages caused by the complexities of international trade and economic growth. His institution became in the words of a contemporary "the balance wheel of the banking system." Finally, the Bank was able to carry on the government's financial business at a low cost and in a way that did not interfere with the requirements of American commerce and finance. Even the transferal of large sums involved in paying off the national debt and in meeting payments required by treaties was done with the least possible disturbance to the nation's money supply. In giving the Second Bank these broad commercial functions, Biddle created a central banking system, which any large, modern commercial economy requires and which every economically advanced nation has quickly acquired.

Few men, even Biddle's most enthusiastic admirers, completely understood his many banking innovations, and as few, even among his harshest critics, claimed that he failed to provide a stable currency and inexpensive credit. Indeed, the complaint underlying much of the economic opposition to the Bank was precisely that it was too efficient. Merchants, brokers, and private bankers could hardly compete with the Second Bank for the lucrative domestic and foreign exchange business when the latter charged less than 1 per cent for discounting bills. New Yorkers, whose city had taken over since

1815 much of the nation's new international commerce, were particularly unhappy at being deprived of this business. Martin Van Buren and other Jackson supporters in the Empire State were quite sympathetic to the desires of this powerful group of constituents. Nevertheless most merchants, even those in New York, realized that higher profits for bill brokers and bankers on the exchange business could only increase the costs of their own particular importing or exporting trade.

Western businessmen, farmers, and planters disliked the Bank for these and other reasons. Brokers and bankers in New Orleans, Nashville, St. Louis, and other commercial cities would have also profited from the buying and selling of bills of exchange. The West's major grievance, however, was the control the Bank held over the notes of state banks. Short on credit and on cash, Western and Southern banks were under constant pressure to issue notes far beyond the safe limits set by their existing reserves. What right, they demanded, had a rich, conservative, Eastern institution to control their money supply and so control their whole economy? The resentment of both the recently settled West and the merchants and brokers of New York and other seaports participating in the great new commerce ran higher when they were reminded that the Bank's monopoly of domestic and foreign exchange and its control over state bank issues rested on its unique privileges of having branches and holding government moneys.

Bankers and businessmen in both West and East were further irritated by the Bank's competition in local business for mortgages and other long-term loans. Despite Biddle's announced policies of not making loans on mortgages and of letting state banks handle local needs, the national bank and its branches did carry on an extensive business in granting long-term loans and in receiving deposits from individuals, state banks, and other corporations. Its vast resources, the prestige of its connection with the national government, and its ability to charge low interest rates gave it a decisive advantage in competing for such local accounts.

Yet economic self-interest can account for only a small share of the hostility to the Bank. Only a relatively few Americans felt directly oppressed by the Bank in their business affairs and they were certainly outnumbered by those businessmen who appreciated its usefulness. Moreover the backbone of Jackson's support came from farmers and artisans who rarely had any personal contact with the Bank, for good or bad. Ideas, beliefs, and values were undoubtedly more significant in creating hostility to the Bank than economic self-interest. Surely the reason many Americans disliked the Bank was simply that it was undemocratic. To men who had helped extend the franchise and who had worked to elect a Westerner, a man of the people, to the Presidency, the Bank's concentrated financial power and control seemed to pose a potent threat to economic and even political freedom and opportunity.

If a strong commitment to democratic practices and principles gave impetus to the protest against the Bank, the arguments used to define this protest reflected older concepts and values. Men of one generation often view their new and quite different problems in terms of the ideas and beliefs of the preceding generation. Not surprisingly then the arguments used in the 1830's were often phrased in terms that are usually associated with Thomas Jefferson.

The economic concepts of those men who distrusted the Bank were certainly Jeffersonian. Their views belonged to a simpler age when the country still hugged the Atlantic, when the volume of trade was small and the need for extensive credit facilities much less. They were skeptical of paper money and credit instruments. Operations involving the transfer of bills and the issuing of notes seemed little more than tricky, dishonest manipulation. That the money and bill changers made high profits by such manipulations proved the inherent evil of the system. That the stockholders of the national and some incorporated state banks enjoyed the privileges of limited liability for any loss their institution incurred seemed to compound this evil. If a bank failed, the stockholders were not responsible for its debts; they only lost the value of the stock they owned. But if a farmer or laborer was unable to pay a bank the interest on his mortgage, he lost his house and land. The surest way to return to an honest and pure economy, many argued, was to get rid of all banks, all paper currencies, and all corporations. Commercial transactions must be carried on with "metallic currency" issued by the Treasury. The first step in such a hard money program was clearly to eliminate the greatest and most manipulative financial institution of them all—the Second Bank of the United States.

The Bank's opponents also found justification for their views in Jeffersonian political and constitutional concepts. The Bank was a centralizing, nationalizing institution for which the Constitution had never provided. It violated state rights; it denied the "strict construction" interpretation of the Constitution. These beliefs had already raised controversy. In 1816, citizens sensitive to the encroachment of federal power or control saw the Bank as a threat to the sovereignty of their states. Maryland, Kentucky, Tennessee, Georgia, North Carolina, and Ohio all passed laws levying taxes on the branches of the Bank with the intent of preventing them from doing business within their boundaries. Two new states, Indiana and Illinois, in setting up their state constitutions, prohibited the establishment of the Bank's branches within their borders. These laws were annulled in 1819 when Chief Justice John Marshall declared that the Bank was constitutional and the tax on its branches unconstitutional in the case of *McCulloch* v. *Maryland*. Many Americans, however, long continued to disagree with Marshall's interpretation of the Constitution.

Economic and constitutional positions were argued then, as now, with strong moral conviction. In identifying the Bank with what was good or bad, both its attackers and defenders spoke to the older values that had Jeffersonian overtones. "The effort to destroy the Monster Bank and its vicious brood—privileged corporations, paper money," writes Marvin Meyers perceptively in *The Jacksonian Persuasion* (1957), "enlisted moral passions in a drama of social justice and self-justification." Meyers continues:

Broadly speaking, the Jacksonians blamed the Bank for the transgressions committed by the people of their era against the political, social, and economic values of the Old Republic. The Bank carried the bad seed of Hamilton's first Monster, matured all the old evils, and created some new ones. To the Bank's influence Jacksonians traced constitutional impiety, consolidated national power, aristocratic privilege, and plutocratic corruption. Social inequality, impersonal and intangible business relations, economic instability, perpetual debt and taxes, all issued from the same source.

The manipulation of money, banking, and particularly the workings of the Bank all challenged Jeffersonian virtues of simplicity, stability, self-reliance, useful toil, plain living, and plain dealing.

The Bank's defenders appealed quite naturally to the same values. They preferred candidates with the older log-cabin virtues and they too had their monster. This monster was not an institution but a man—King Andrew the First, who centralized the power of the national executive, spat upon the Constitution, debauched the polity with his corrupt spoils system, and ruined the economy with his "pet banks." As his opponents banded together into a political organization, they chose the name Whig to indicate that they, like an earlier generation, were opposing dictatorial tyranny in a fight for republican and democratic principles.

There were, of course, genuine differences between the words and actions of the Whigs and the Democrats. The Whigs spoke for economic expansion. They wanted to enlarge the continental economy through a system of banks, tariffs, and a publicly financed transportation network through the American System (see pp. 270–73). Their views made sense to businessmen, merchants, and manufacturers, just as Jackson's opposition to these policies was more meaningful to planters, farmers, mechanics, and laborers.

It took the Bank War, however, to clarify fully these differences in actions and ideas. The controversy brought out the latent hostility to the Bank by reminding the farmers and mechanics of its immense power. It restored the two-party system after nearly a generation of personal politics. The resulting debate clarified the divergent aims and interests of different economic and regional groups and brought into sharper focus the economic, constitutional, and ideological arguments used to defend these interests.

And it took Jackson's veto of the bill to recharter to bring on the Bank War. Biddle's institution was not an issue in the election of 1828. Some of Jackson's supporters opposed the Bank. Others agreed to its value. The issue was first raised by a brief reference in Jackson's first annual message to Congress concerning the Bank's expediency and constitutionality. A Westerner, a planter, a self-made man, imbued with Jeffersonian economic and constitutional beliefs, Andrew Jackson had long had a deep distrust of corporations, banks, and paper money. Yet in his message he made it clear that he was willing enough to have a national bank if it more closely fitted his constitutional and economic views. In the following spring the House Committee on Ways and Means answered the President with a long defense of the Bank that included most of the arguments its defenders were to use in the coming years. There the matter rested for ten months. Then in February, 1831, Thomas Hart Benton of Missouri, one of the ablest spokesmen for the West, opened the attack on the Bank in Congress. His bitter condemnation of the institution summarized effectively many of the charges which were used again and again during the Bank War. Although Benton's assault troubled Biddle, neither Congress nor the President said much more about the Bank in the following months.

In December, 1831, Jackson in his annual message suggested that Congress dispose of the matter as it saw fit. Then his Secretary of the Treasury, Louis McLane, in his annual report recommended rechartering. In this same month Jackson's opponents nominated Henry Clay to the Presidency. At this time too, Biddle, still concerned by Benton's blast, asked the supporters of both Clay and Jackson about the advisability of applying for recharter before next November's election. While McLane and other Jacksonians urged Biddle to wait, Clay and his ally Daniel Webster advised him to apply before November. They argued that if Jackson was re-elected, his approval would be more difficult to obtain. They also suggested that a veto would provide an excellent campaign issue.

Convinced that Jackson would be more likely to sign the bill before than after the election, Biddle decided in January to apply for recharter. During the subsequent Congressional hearings the Philadelphian clearly explained the functions of his institution. However, as the Congressional committee consisted largely of the Bank's opponents, it raised many of the old complaints, including the charge that Biddle was attempting to influence politics by lending funds to politicians and editors. The committee's report revived Jackson's distrust and dashed all hopes of Presidential approval. After Congress passed the act to recharter on July 3, Jackson returned it to Congress with his famous veto message. The issue was drawn; the Bank War was on.

The veto message, saying little about the economic functions of the Bank, concentrated more on constitutional points. Jackson not only explained why he considered the Bank unconstitutional and why its status had not been decided by *McCulloch* v. *Maryland*, but also outlined his views on the President's role in interpreting the Constitution. "The opinion of the judges," he emphasized, "has no more authority over Congress than the opinion of Congress has over the judges, and on that point the President is independent of both."

On the very next day, Daniel Webster rose in the Senate to condemn the veto message. His economic and constitutional arguments for the Bank, while eloquently expressed, had been made before. But Webster, like Jackson, added a new note to the controversy. The President's veto message, Webster charged, challenged the prerogatives of the legislative branch of the government and struck at the very fabric of the Constitution. Webster's reply and Jackson's message became the key campaign documents in the fall electioneering.

The people spoke for Jackson. The President's substantial victory at the polls dimmed still further any chances of rechartering. Incensed by the political role the Bank seemed to be playing, Jackson was determined to break its power even before its charter expired in 1836. Following the advice of Roger B. Taney, his Attorney-General, who had helped to draft the veto message, the President decided to remove the government's deposits from the Bank and place them in a number of specified state banks. McLane, Secretary of the Treasury, strongly opposed the removal. Jackson reshuffled his Cabinet in the late spring of 1833 by appointing McLane Secretary of State and William J. Duane, an articulate foe of the Bank, to head the Treasury. To Jackson's embarrassment, Duane refused to carry out the President's orders and then even refused to resign. Finally on September 23 Jackson replaced Duane with Taney, who three days later began the withdrawal of the government funds.

The Bank forces responded quickly with Clay attacking on the political front and Biddle on the economic one. Shortly after Congress met in December, the Kentuckian introduced two resolutions in the Senate—one criticizing the action of the Treasury, the other condemning Jackson. "The President in the late executive proceedings," read the second, "has assumed upon himself authority and power not conferred by the Constitution and the laws, but in derogation of both." By March when Congress passed both resolutions, Biddle had been for some time restricting credit, calling in loans, and reducing note issues. Such a contraction was essential if the Bank was to remain financially sound after the government deposits were withdrawn. But Biddle, hoping to demonstrate the value of the Bank to the nation's economy and to arouse hostility to Jackson, carried the contraction further than conservative banking practices demanded. Because they helped to precipitate a financial crisis, the Bank's actions undoubtedly convinced more Americans of the danger of centralized economic power in the hands of the Bank than Clay's speeches in Congress worried them about the threat of centralized political power in the hands of the President. Jackson increased his popularity still further by an eloquent defense of his actions and use of the Presidency in a message to Congress in April at the height of the Biddle panic.

The counterattack failed. Neither the efforts of the Whigs in Congress nor of Biddle in the market place were able to bring the public to their side or cause a change in the administration's course. By summer Biddle called off the contraction. In the November elections the Whigs failed to cut down the Democratic majorities in Congress. Biddle then prepared to close the Bank when its charter expired in March, 1836. At that time the Bank became a state institution operating under a charter from Pennsylvania.

By the fall of 1834 the Bank War was over. Jackson had won. By then the status of the President's office had been greatly enlarged, the two-party system revived, the social and economic bases of the parties clarified, constitutional and economic issues sharpened, and ideological differences made more distinct. Difficult problems remained. These revolved around providing the country with essential central banking services without the aid of a national bank. While Jackson and his successors made several attempts to solve these problems, they were only fully answered eighty years later with the formation of the Federal Reserve System in 1914.

DOCUMENTS

1] The Issue Raised

> Since the crisis of 1819 there had been relatively little outspoken criticism of the Bank. It had not been an issue in the 1828 campaign. President Jackson first brought the Bank into the political arena by referring to it in two short paragraphs at the end of his initial annual message to Congress. He had asked James A. Hamilton, a son of Alexander Hamilton, to draft the statement on the Bank. When Hamilton read it to him, Jackson asked, "Do you think that is all I ought to say?" Hamilton answered, "I think you ought to say nothing for the present about the Bank." To this Jackson replied, "My friend, I am pledged against the Bank, but if you think that is enough, so let it be." *

THE CHARTER of the Bank of the United States expires in 1836, and its stockholders will most probably apply for a renewal of their privileges. In order to avoid the evils resulting from precipitancy in a measure involving such important principles and such deep pecuniary interests, I feel that I can not, in justice to the parties interested, too soon present it to the deliberate consideration of the Legislature and the people. Both the constitutionality and the expediency of the law creating this bank are well questioned by a large portion of our fellow-citizens, and it must be admitted by all that it has failed in the great end of establishing a uniform and sound currency.

Under these circumstances, if such an institution is deemed essential to the fiscal operations of the Government, I submit to the wisdom of the Legislature whether a national one, founded upon the credit of the Government and its revenues, might not be devised which would avoid all constitutional difficulties and at the same time secure all the advantages to the Government and country that were expected to result from the present bank. . . .

2] The Bank Defended

> The House of Representatives routinely referred the President's comments on the Bank to its Committee of Ways and Means, whose chairman, George McDuffie of South Carolina, and the majority of whose members were enthusiastic supporters of Jackson. The report was submitted to the House on April 13, 1830. Although written by McDuffie, who had long been a hard money

---

* THE ISSUE RAISED: Jackson's First Annual Message, December 8, 1829. From James D. Richardson, ed., *A Compilation of the Messages and Papers of the Presidents, 1789–1897* (Washington, 1896–99), II, 462.

man and a strong state rights advocate, it effectively outlined most of the
constitutional and economic arguments that continued to be used to defend
the Bank.*

THE COMMITTEE of Ways and Means, to whom was referred so much of the
Message of the President as relates to the Bank of the United States, beg
leave to report:

That they have bestowed upon the subject all the attention demanded by
its intrinsic importance, and now respectfully submit the result of their deliberations to the consideration of the House. There are few subjects, having
reference to the policy of an established Government, so vitally connected with
the health of the body politic, or in which the pecuniary interests of society
are so extensively and deeply involved. No one of the attributes of sovereignty
carries with it a more solemn responsibility, or calls in requisition a higher
degree of wisdom, than the power of regulating the common currency, and
thus fixing the general standard of value for a great commercial community,
composed of confederated States.

Such being, in the opinion of the committee, the high and delicate trust
exclusively committed to Congress by the federal constitution, they have proceeded to discharge the duty assigned to them, with a corresponding sense of
its magnitude and difficulty.

The most simple and obvious analysis of the subject, as it is presented by
the message of the President, exhibits the following questions for the decision
of the National Legislature:

1. Has Congress the constitutional power to incorporate a bank, such as
that of the United States?

2. Is it expedient to establish and maintain such an institution?

3. Is it expedient to establish "a national bank, founded upon the credit of
the Government and its revenues?"

I. If the concurrence of all the departments of the Government, at different
periods of our history, under every administration, and during the ascendency
of both the great political parties, into which the country was divided, soon
after the adoption of the present constitution, shall be regarded as having the
authority ascribed to such sanctions by the common consent of all well regulated
communities, the constitutional power of Congress to incorporate a bank, may
be assumed as a postulate no longer open to controversy. . . .

This brief history of the former and present bank forcibly suggests a few
practical reflections. It is to be remarked, in the first place, that, since the
adoption of the constitution, a bank has existed, under the authority of the
Federal Government, for thirty three out of forty years; during which time,
public and private credit have been maintained at an elevation fully equal to
what has existed in any nation in the world: whereas, in the two short intervals,
during which no national bank existed, public and private credit were greatly

---

* THE BANK DEFENDED: *Report of the House Committee of Ways and Means* (April 13,
1830). From M. St. Clair Clarke and D. A. Hall, eds., *Legislative and Documentary History of the Bank of the United States* (Washington, 1832), pp. 735–57.

impaired, and, in the latter instance, the fiscal operations of the Government were almost entirely arrested. In the second place, it is worthy of special notice, that, in both the instances in which Congress has created a bank, it has been done under circumstances calculated to give the highest authority to the decision. The first instance, as has been already remarked, was in the primitive days of the republic, when the patriots of the Revolution, and the sages of the Federal Convention, were the leading members both of the Executive and Legislative councils; and when General Washington, who, at the head of her armies, had conducted his country to independence, and, as the head of the convention, had presided over those deliberations which resulted in the establishment of the present constitution, was the acknowledged President of a People, undistracted by party divisions. The second instance was under circumstances of a very different but equally decisive character. We find the very party, which had so recently defeated the proposition to renew the charter of the old bank, severely schooled both by adversity and experience, magnanimously sacrificing the pride of consistency, and the prejudices of party, at the shrine of patriotism. . . .

That may be said of the bank charter, which can be said of few contested questions of constitutional power. Both the great political parties that have so long divided the country have solemnly pronounced it to be constitutional, and there are but very few of the prominent men of either party, who do not stand committed in its favor. When, to this imposing array of authorities, the committee add the solemn and unanimous decision of the Supreme Court, in a case which fully and distinctly submitted the constitutional question to their cognizance, may they not ask, in the language of Mr. Dallas,[1] "can it be deemed a violation of the right of private opinion to consider the constitutionality of a national bank as a question forever settled and at rest?" . . .

The committee will now submit a few remarks, with the design of showing, that, viewing the constitutionality of the bank as an original question, the arguments in its favor are, at least, as strong as those against it.

The earliest, and the principal objection urged against the constitutionality of a national bank, was, that Congress had not the power to create corporations. That Congress has a distinct and substantive power to create corporations, without reference to the objects entrusted to its jurisdiction, is a proposition which never has been maintained, within the knowledge of the committee; but, that any one of the powers, expressly conferred upon Congress, is subject to the limitation that it shall not be carried into effect by the agency of a corporation, is a proposition which cannot be maintained, in the opinion of the committee. . . .

It now remains for the committee to show that the Bank of the United States is a "necessary and proper," or, in other words, a natural and appropriate means of executing the powers vested in the Federal Government. In the discussion of 1791, and also in that before the Supreme Court, the powers of raising, collecting, and disbursing the public revenue, of borrowing money on the credit of the United States, and paying the public debt, were those which

---

1 Alexander J. Dallas, Secretary of the Treasury under Madison, played an important role in the formation of the Second Bank.

were supposed most clearly to carry with them the incidental right of incorporating a bank, to facilitate these operations. There can be no doubt that these fiscal operations are greatly facilitated by a bank, and, it is confidently believed, that no person has presided twelve months over the treasury, from its first organization to the present time, without coming to the conclusion that such an institution is exceedingly useful to the public finances in time of peace, but indispensable in time of war. But, as this view of the question has been fully unfolded in former discussions, familiar to the House, the committee will proceed to examine the relation which the Bank of the United States bears to another of the powers of the Federal Government, but slightly adverted to in former discussions of the subject.

The power to "coin money and fix the value thereof," is expressly and exclusively vested in Congress. This grant was evidently intended to invest Congress with the power of regulating the circulating medium. "Coin" was regarded, at the period of framing the constitution, as synonymous with "currency;" as it was then generally believed that bank notes could only be maintained in circulation by being the true representative of the precious metals. The word "coin," therefore, must be regarded as a particular term, standing as the representative of a general idea. . . .

But, even if it should be conceded, that the grant of power to "coin money and fix the value thereof," does not, in its terms, give Congress the power of regulating any other than the "coined" currency of the Union, may not the power of regulating any substituted currency, and especially one which is the professed representative of coin, be fairly claimed as an incidental power—as an essential means of carrying into effect the plain intention of the constitution, in clothing Congress with the principal power? This power was granted in the same clause with that to regulate weights and measures, and for similar reasons. The one was designed to ensure a uniform measure of value, as the other was designed to ensure a uniform measure of quantity. The former is decidedly the more important, and belongs essentially to the General Government, according to every just conception of our system. A currency of uniform value is essential to what every one will admit to be of cardinal importance —the equal action of our revenue system upon the different parts of the Union. The state of things which existed when the bank was incorporated, furnished a most pregnant commentary on this clause of the constitution. The currency of the country consisted of the paper of local banks, variously depreciated. At one of the principal sea ports the local currency was twenty per cent. below par. Now it was in vain for Congress to regulate the value of coin, when the actual currency, professing to be its equivalent, bore no fixed relation to it. This great and essential power of fixing the standard of value, was, in point of fact, taken from Congress, and exercised by some hundreds of irresponsible banking corporations, with the strongest human motives to abuse it, because their enormous profits resulted from the abuse. The power of laying and collecting imposts and excises is expressly subject to the condition, that they "shall be uniform throughout the United States;" and it is also provided, that "no preference shall be given, by any regulation of commerce or *revenue,* to the ports of one State over those of another." Now, when it is known that the circulating medium of Baltimore was twenty per cent. below the value of the circulating medium of Boston, is it not apparent that an impost duty, though nominally uniform, would, in effect, make a discrimination in favor of Baltimore, proportioned to the depreciation of the local currency? Congress, therefore, not only had the power, but, as it seems to the committee, were under the most solemn constitutional obligations to restore the disordered currency; and the Bank of the United States was not only an appropriate means for the accomplishment of that end, but, in the opinion of the committee, the only safe and effectual means that could have been used. . . .

Such are the authorities, and such the arguments, which have brought the committee to the conclusion, that the power to incorporate a bank is incidental to the powers of collecting and disbursing the public revenue; of borrowing money on the credit of the United States; of paying the public debt; and, above all, of fixing and regulating the standard of value, and thereby ensuring, at least so far as the medium of payment is concerned, the uniformity and equality of taxation.

II. The next question proposed for consideration, is the expediency of establishing an incorporated bank, with a view to promote the great ends already indicated. In discussing the constitutionality of such a measure, some of the considerations which render it expedient have been slightly unfolded. But these require a more full and complete development, while others remain to be presented.

It must be assumed as the basis of all sound reasoning on this subject, that the existence of a paper currency, issued by banks deriving their charters from the State Governments, cannot be prohibited by Congress. Indeed, bank credit and bank paper are so extensively interwoven with the commercial operations of society, that, even if Congress had the constitutional power, it would be utterly impossible to produce so entire a change in the monetary system of the country, as to abolish the agency of banks of discount, without involving the community in all the distressing embarrassments usually attendant on great political revolutions, subverting the titles to private property. The sudden withdrawal of some hundred millions of bank credit, would be equivalent, in its effects, to the arbitrary and despotic transfer of the property of one portion of the community to another, to the extent, probably, of half that amount. Whatever, therefore, may be the advantages of a purely metallic currency, and whatever the objections to a circulating medium, partly composed of bank paper, the committee consider that they are precluded, by the existing state of things, from instituting a comparison between them, with a view to any practical result.

If they were not thus precluded, and it were submitted to them as an original question, whether the acknowledged and manifold facilities of bank credit and bank paper are not more than counterbalanced by the distressing vicissitudes in trade incident to their use, they are by no means prepared to say, that they would not give a decided preference to the more costly and cumbersome medium.

But the question really presented for their determination, is not between a metallic and a paper currency, but between a paper currency of uniform value, and subject to the control of the only power competent to its regulation, and a paper currency of varying and fluctuating value, and subject to no common or adequate control whatever. On this question, it would seem that there could scarcely exist a difference of opinion; and that this is substantially the question involved in considering the expediency of a national bank, will satisfactorily appear by a comparison of the state of the currency previous to the establishment of the present bank, and its condition for the last ten years.

Soon after the expiration of the charter of the first Bank of the United States, an immense number of local banks sprung up under the pecuniary exigencies produced by the withdrawal of so large an amount of bank credit, as necessarily resulted from the winding up of its concerns—an amount falling very little short of fifteen millions of dollars. These banks being entirely free from the salutary control which the Bank of the United States had recently exercised over the local institutions, commenced that system of imprudent trading and excessive issues, which speedily involved the country in all the embarrassments of a disordered currency. The extraordinary stimulus of a heavy war expenditure, derived principally from loans, and a corresponding multiplication of local banks, chartered by the double score in some of the States, hastened the catastrophe which must have occurred, at no distant period, without these extraordinary causes. The last year of the war presented the singular and melancholy spectacle of a nation abounding in resources, a people abounding in self-devoting patriotism, and a Government reduced to the very brink of avowed bankruptcy, solely for the want of a national institution, which, at the same time that it would have facilitated the Government loans and other treasury operations, would have furnished a circulating medium of general credit in every part of the Union. . . .

But the principal loss which resulted from the relative depreciation of bank paper at different places, and its want of general credit, was that sustained by the community in the great operations of commercial exchange. The extent of these operations annually, may be safely estimated at sixty millions of dollars. Upon this sum, the loss sustained by the merchants, and planters, and farmers, and manufacturers, was not probably less than an average of ten per cent., being the excess of the rate of exchange between its natural rate in a sound state of the currency, and beyond the rate to which it has been actually reduced by the operations of the Bank of the United States. It will be thus perceived, that an annual tax of six millions of dollars was levied from the industrious and productive classes, by the large moneyed capitalists in our commercial cities, who were engaged in the business of brokerage. A variously depreciated currency, and a fluctuating state of the exchanges, open a wide and abundant harvest to the money brokers; and it is not, therefore, surprising, that they should be opposed to an institution, which, at the same time that it has relieved the community from the enormous tax just stated, has deprived them of the enormous profits which they derived from speculating in the business of exchange. In addition to the losses sustained by the community, in the great operations of exchange, extensive losses were suffered throughout the interior of the country in all the smaller operations of trade, as well as by the failure of the numerous paper banks, puffed into a factitious credit by fraudulent artifices, and having no substantial basis of capital to ensure the redemption of their bills. . . .

But it is impossible to exhibit any thing like a just view of the beneficial operations of the bank, without adverting to the great reduction it has effected, and the steadiness it has superinduced, in the rate of the commercial exchanges of the country. Though this branch of the business of the bank has been the subject of more complaint, perhaps, than any other, the committee have no hesitation in saying, it has been productive of the most signal benefits to the community, and deserves the highest commendation. It has been already stated that it has saved the community from the immense losses resulting from a high and fluctuating state of the exchanges. It now remains to show its effect in equalizing the currency. In this respect, it has been productive of results more salutary than were anticipated by the most sanguine advocates of the policy of establishing the bank. *It has actually furnished a circulating medium more uniform than specie.* . . .

For all the purposes of the revenue, it gives to the national currency that perfect uniformity, that ideal perfection, to which a currency of gold and silver, in so extensive a country, could have no pretensions. A bill issued at Missouri is of equal value with specie at Boston, in payment of duties; and the same is true of all other places, however distant, where the bank issues bills, and the Government collects its revenue. When it is, moreover, considered, that the bank performs, with the most scrupulous punctuality, the stipulation to transfer the funds of the Government to any point where they may be wanted, free of expense, it must be apparent that the committee are correct, to the very letter, in stating that the bank has furnished, both to the Government and to the People, *a currency of absolutely uniform value in all places, for all the purposes of paying the public contributions, and disbursing the public revenue.* And when it is recollected that the Government annually collects and disburses more than twenty-three millions of dollars, those who are at all familiar with the subject will at once perceive that bills, which are of absolutely uniform value for this vast operation, must be very nearly so for all the purposes of general commerce.

Upon the whole, then, it may be confidently asserted, that no country in the world has a circulating medium of greater uniformity than the United States, and that no country, of any thing like the same geographical extent, has a currency at all comparable to that of the United States, on the score of uniformity. . . .

But the salutary agency of the Bank of the United States, in furnishing a sound and uniform currency, is not confined to that portion of the currency which consists of its own bills. One of the most important purposes which the bank was designed to accomplish, and which, it is confidently believed, no other human agency could have effected, under our federative system of Government, was the enforcement of specie payments on the part of numerous local banks, deriving their charters from the several States, and whose paper, irredeemable in specie, and illimitable in its quantity, constituted the almost entire currency of the country. Amidst a combination of the greatest difficulties, the bank has almost completely succeeded in the performance of this arduous, delicate, and painful duty. With exceptions, too inconsiderable to merit notice, all the State banks in the Union have resumed specie payments. Their bills, in the respective spheres of their circulation, are of equal value with gold and silver; while, for all the operations of commerce beyond that sphere, the bills or the checks of the Bank of the United States are even more valuable than specie. And even in the very few instances in which the paper of State banks is depreciated, those banks are winding up their concerns; and it may be safely said, that no citizen of the Union is under the necessity of taking depreciated paper, because a sound currency cannot be obtained. North Carolina is believed to be the only State where paper of the local banks is irredeemable in specie, and, consequently, depreciated. Even there, the depreciation is only one or two per cent., and, what is more important, the paper of the Bank of the United States can be obtained by all those who desire it, and have an equivalent to give for it. . . .

In connexion with this branch of the subject, the committee will briefly examine the grounds of a complaint, sometimes made against the Bank of the United States. It is alleged that this bank, availing itself of the Government deposites, consisting in some places principally of local paper, makes heavy and oppressive draughts on the local banks for specie, and thus compels them to curtail their discounts, to the great injury of the community. In the first place, it is to be remarked, that one of the highest duties of the bank—the great object for which it was established—was to prevent the excessive issues of local paper; and this duty can only be performed, by enforcing upon the State banks the payment of specie for any excess in their issues. But the committee are induced to believe, that this complaint is principally owing, so far as it now exists, to the fact, that the operations of the federal treasury are mistaken for the operations of the bank, because the bank is the agent by whom those operations are performed. This institution receives the Government deposites in the paper of the local banks, certainly in no spirit of hostility to those banks. On the contrary, it tends to give them credit, and is designed to have that effect. But the Bank of the United States is not only bound to pay in specie, or its own bills, what it receives for the Government in local paper, but to transfer the funds to any part of the Union where they may be required for disbursement. Let it be assumed, that the Government collects annually, at the custom house in Charleston, one million of dollars in local bank notes, and disburses in South Carolina only one hundred thousand, it would result from this, that the Government would have nine hundred thousand dollars of local bank paper deposited in the Charleston branch, which the bank would be bound by its charter, and for the national benefit, to transfer perhaps to Washington or Norfolk. As this paper would not answer the purposes of the Government at those places, the bank would be, of course, compelled to provide specie, or bills that will command specie at those places. It is obvious, then, that it is the inequality in the collection and disbursement of the revenue that produces the evil in question. If all the revenue collected in Charleston were disbursed in the State, no draughts would be made upon the local banks for specie. The Bank of the United States, so far from being justly obnoxious to any complaint on this score, has greatly mitigated the action of the treasury upon the local banks, by means of the liberal arrangements which its large capital and numerous branches have enabled it to make with them. The degree in which that institution has reduced the rate of exchange, may be fairly assumed as that in which it has mitigated the action of the treasury upon the State banks. If, for example, there existed no national bank, and the deposites of the revenue collected in Charleston were made in one of the local banks, what would be the effect of transferring, annually, nine hundred thousand dollars to Washington or Norfolk? The local banks, having no branches at either of those places, instead of transmitting drafts, as is now generally done, would be compelled to transmit specie. The bank in which the Government deposites were made, would consequently be under the necessity of demanding specie from all the other banks, in a manner, and to an extent, much more oppressive than any thing that can be imputed to the Bank of the United States. If, to avoid these specie drafts, the local banks should purchase bills on Washington or Norfolk, they would probably cost five or six per cent. even in a tolerable state of the currency, which would be a loss to the banks almost to the full extent of the premium. . . .

It is sometimes alleged that the present stockholders are large capitalists, and, as the stock of the bank is some twenty per cent. above par, that a renewal of the charter would be equivalent to a grant to them of twenty per cent. upon their capital. It is true, that a small proportion of the capital of the company belongs to very wealthy men. Something more than two millions of that owned in the United States belongs to persons holding upwards of one hundred thousand dollars each. It is also true, that foreigners own seven millions, or one-fifth of the capital. But, on the other hand, it is to be remarked that the Government, in trust for the People of the United States, holds seven millions; that persons owning less than five thousand dollars each, hold four millions six hundred and eighty-two thousand; and that persons owning between five and ten thousand dollars each, hold upwards of three millions. It is also worthy of remark, that a very considerable portion of the stock, very nearly six millions, is held by trustees and guardians, for the use of females and orphan children, and charitable and other institutions. Of the twenty-eight millions of the stock which is owned by individuals, only three millions four hundred and fifty-three thousand is now held by the original subscribers. All the rest has been purchased at the market prices—a large portion of it, probably, when those prices were higher than at present. Most of the investments made by wills, and deeds, and decrees in equity, for the use of females and minors, are believed to have been made when the stock was greatly above par. From this brief analysis, it will appear that there is nothing in the character or situation of the stockholders, which should make it desirable to deprive them of the advantage which they have fairly gained, by an application of their capital to purposes highly beneficial, as the committee have attempted to show, to the Government and People of the United States. If foreigners own seven millions of the stock of the bank, our own Government owns as much; if wealthy men own more than two millions, men in moderate circumstances own between seven and eight millions; and widows, orphans, and institutions devoted to charitable and other purposes, own nearly six millions.

But, the objection that the stock is owned by men of large capital, would apply with equal, if not greater force, to any bank that could be organized. In the very nature of things, men who have large surplus capitals are the principal subscribers at the first organization of a bank. Farmers and planters, merchants and manufacturers, having an active employment for their capitals, do not choose to be the first adventurers in a bank project. Accordingly, when the present bank went into operation, it is believed that most of the capital was owned by large capitalists, and under a much more unequal distribution than exists at present. The large amount of stock now held in trust for females and minors, has been principally, if not entirely, purchased since the bank went into operation; and the same remark is generally applicable to the stock in the hands of small holders. It is only when the character of a bank is fully established, and when its stock assumes a steady value, that these descriptions of persons make investments in it.

It is morally certain, therefore, that, if another distinct institution were created, on the expiration of the present charter, there would be a much greater portion of its capital subscribed by men of large fortunes, than is now owned by persons of this description, of the stock of the United States' Bank. Indeed, it might be confidently predicted, that the large capitalists who now hold stock in that bank, would, from their local position and other advantages, be the first to forestall the subscriptions to the new bank, while the small stockholders, scattered over the country, would be probably excluded, and the females and minors, and others interested in trust investments made by decrees in equity, would be almost necessarily excluded, as the sanction of a court could scarcely be obtained, after the passage of the new act of incorporation, in time to authorize a subscription.

To destroy the existing bank, therefore, after it has rendered such signal services to the country, merely with a view to incorporate another, would be an act rather of cruelty and caprice, than of justice and wisdom, as it regards the present stockholders. It is no light matter to depreciate the property of individuals, honestly obtained, and usefully employed, to the extent of five millions six hundred thousand dollars, and the property of the Government, to the extent of one million four hundred thousand dollars, purely for the sake of change. It would indicate a fondness for experiment, which a wise Government will not indulge upon slight considerations.

But the great injury which would result from the refusal of Congress to renew the charter of the present bank, would, beyond all question, be that which would result to the community at large. It would be difficult to estimate the extent of the distress which would naturally and necessarily result from the sudden withdrawal of more than forty millions of credit, which the community now enjoys from the bank. But this would not be the full extent of the operation. The Bank of the United States, in winding up its concerns, would not only withdraw its own paper from circulation, and call in its debts, but would unavoidably make such heavy draughts on the local institutions for specie as very greatly to curtail their discounts. The pressure upon the active, industrious, and enterprising classes, who depend most on the facilities of bank credit, would be tremendous. A vast amount of property would change hands at half its value, passing, under the hammer, from the merchants, manufacturers, and farmers, to the large moneyed capitalists, who always stand ready to avail themselves of the pecuniary embarrassments of the community. The large stockholders of the present bank, the very persons whose present lawful gains it would be the object of some to cut off, having a large surplus money capital thrown upon their hands, would be the very first to speculate upon the distresses of the community, and build up princely fortunes upon the ruins of the industrious and active classes. On the other hand, the females and minors, and persons in moderate circumstances, who hold stock in the institution, would sustain an injury, in no degree mitigated by the general distress of the community. . . .

If the Bank of the United States were destroyed, and the local institutions left without its restraining influence, the currency would almost certainly relapse into a state of unsoundness. The very pressure which the present bank, in winding up its concerns, would make upon the local institutions, would compel them either to curtail their discounts, when most needed, or to suspend specie payments. It is not difficult to predict which of these alternatives they would adopt, under the circumstances in which they would be placed. The imperious wants of a suffering community would call for discounts, in language which could not be disregarded. The public necessities would demand, and public opinion would sanction, the suspension, or at least an evasion of specie payments.

But, even if this desperate resort could be avoided in a period of peace and general prosperity, neither reason nor experience will permit use to doubt that a state of war would speedily bring about all the evils which so fatally affected the credit of the Government and the national currency, during the late war with Great Britain. We should be again driven to the same miserable round of financial expedients, which, in little more than two years, brought a wealthy community almost to the very brink of a declared national bankruptcy, and placed the Government completely at the mercy of speculating stockjobbers. . . .

III. Having said thus much on the constitutionality and expediency of an incorporated National Bank, the only question which remains to be examined by the committee is, the expediency of establishing "a National Bank founded upon the credit of the Government and its revenues."

It is presumed to have been the intention of the President, in suggesting the inquiry as to a bank founded upon the credit and revenues of the Government, to be understood as having allusion to a bank of discount and deposite. Such a bank, it is taken for granted, would have branches established in various parts of the Union, similar to those now established by the Bank of the United States, and co-extensive with them. The great object of furnishing a national currency could not be accomplished, with an approach to uniformity, without the agency of such branches; and another object, second only in importance to the one just stated, the extension of the commercial facilities of bank accommodations to the different parts of the Union, could not be at all effected without such agency. If there should be simply a great central bank established at the seat of Government, without branches to connect its operations with the various points of the commerce of the Union, the promise to pay specie for its notes, whenever presented, would be almost purely nominal. Of what consequence would it be to a merchant or planter of Louisiana, or a manufacturer or farmer of Maine, that he could obtain specie for bills of the National Bank, on presenting them at the city of Washington—a place wholly unconnected either with Louisiana or Maine, by any sort of commercial inter-course, and where, consequently, these bills would never come in the regular course of trade? A promise to pay specie at a place so remote from the place of circulation, and where the bills would never come but at a great expense, and for the sole purpose of being presented for payment, would neither give credit to the notes, nor operate as an effective check upon excessive issues. Whatever credit such notes might have at a distance from the place of issue, would not be because they were redeemable at the pleasure of the holder, for such would not be the fact; but principally because of the ultimate responsi-bility of the Government, and of their being receivable in payment of all dues to the treasury. They would rest, therefore, upon almost precisely the same basis of credit as the paper money of our Revolution, the assignats of revolu-tionary France, and the treasury notes of the late war. These were receivable in discharge of debts due to the treasury, and the Government was of course ultimately responsible for their payment; yet the two former depreciated almost to nothing, and the latter, though bearing interest, sunk to twenty per cent. below par. But the notes of a central Government Bank, without branches, would be subject to depreciation from a cause which constitutes a conclusive objection to such an institution. *There would be nothing to limit excessive issues but the discretion and prudence of the Government or of the direction*. Human wisdom has never devised any adequate security against the excessive issues, and, consequently, the depreciation of bank paper, but its actual, and easy, and prompt convertibility into specie, at the pleasure of the holder. . . .

But a Government Bank, without branches, would be obnoxious to another objection, which could not be obviated. Its loans would be confined to the District of Columbia or, if extended to the various parts of the Union, to say nothing of the inconvenience to which it would expose those at a distance, who obtained accommodations, they would be unavoidably granted without any knowledge of the circumstances of the persons upon whose credit the Govern-ment would depend for re-payment. It would, in fact, be, for all useful pur-poses, a mere District Bank.

These views of the subject have brought the committee to the conclusion, that, if a Government Bank should be established, it would have at least as many branches as the Bank of the United States, and probably a much greater number. Few administrations would have the firmness to resist an application to establish a branch, coming from any quarter of the Union, however injudi-cious the location might be, upon correct principles of commerce and banking.

The Bank of the United States now employs five hundred agents, in the various parts of the Union, where its offices are established. From this fact some idea may be formed of the very great addition which would be made to the patronage of the Executive Government, by the establishment of such a bank as the one under consideration.

But the patronage resulting from the appointment, the annual appointment, of these agents, great as it would doubtless be, would be insignificant and harmless, when compared to that which would result from the dispensation of bank accommodations to the standing amount of at least fifty millions of dollars! The mind almost instinctively shrinks from the contemplation of an idea so ominous to the purity of the Government, and the liberties of the People. No government of which the committee have any knowledge, except, perhaps, the despotism of Russia, was ever invested with a patronage at once so prodigious in its influence, and so dangerous in its character. In the most desperate financial extremities, no other European government has ever ventured upon an experiment so perilous. If the whole patronage of the English monarchy were concentrated in the hands of the American Executive, it may be well doubted whether the public liberty would be so much endangered by it, as it would by this vast pecuniary machine, which would place in the hands of every administration fifty millions of dollars, as a fund for rewarding political partizans. . . .

3] Biddle Explains the Bank's Exchange Business

Even though Nicholas Biddle had supplied them with information, McDuffie and the members of the Ways and Means Committee remained relatively untutored in the intricacies of commercial banking. Biddle explained more fully the activities of his bank in this important financial business when he testified in April, 1832, before the Congressional committee which was investigating the Bank after its application for recharter.*

THE CAPITAL is now distributed among the branches as follows: To some of the branches, recently established, no definite capital has yet been assigned; the board preferring to wait the progressive development of their business before fixing, finally, their capital, and, in the mean time, regulating the amount of their loans by particular instructions. But the general distribution of capital, and the amount of the investments, will be seen in the following sketch [p. 356].

It will be perceived, from this statement, that, in the great abundance of capital employed in banking in the northern and middle States, the funds of the bank have naturally sought a temporary employment in those sections of the Union where there is less banking capital, and where the productions of the great staples of the country seem to require most assistance in bringing them into the commercial market. This observation applies especially to New Orleans, the centre and the depository of all the trade of the Mississippi and its tributaries. The course of the western business is to send the produce to New Orleans, and to draw bills on the proceeds, which bills are purchased at the several branches, and remitted to the branch at New Orleans. When the notes issued by the several branches find their way in the course of trade to the Atlantic branches, the western branches pay the Atlantic branches by

---

* BIDDLE EXPLAINS THE BANK'S EXCHANGE BUSINESS: From *House Reports*, No. 460, 22 Cong., 1 Sess. (1832), pp. 316–18, 322–23.

OFFICES.	Discounts. [Loans]	Domestic bills.	Totals.	Capitals.
Portland, - -	$189,802 14	43,943 03	233,745 17	
Portsmouth, - -	113,292 97	98,850 03	212,143	300,000
Boston, - -	896,877 34	1,671,065 47	2,567,942 81	1,500,000
Providence, - -	637,440 14	381,218 72	1,018,658 86	800,000
Hartford, - -	422,794 97	50,936 54	473,731 51	300,000
New York, - -	4,869,189 44	1,060,744 01	5,929,933 45	2,500,000
Philadelphia, - -	6,682,322 10	2,127,140 93	8,809,463 03	16,450,000
Baltimore, - -	1,962,355 83	340,184 42	2,302,540 25	1,500,000
Washington, - -	1,082,124 54	178,898 13	1,261,022 67	500,000
Richmond, - -	807,136 29	780,341 49	1,587,477 78	1,000,000
Norfolk, - -	655,170 91	254,392 15	909,563 06	500,000
Fayetteville, - -	525,076 68	171,061 82	606,138 50	500,000
Charleston, - -	2,931,036 40	963,554 12	3,894,590 52	1,500,000
Savannah, - -	767,464 28	543,502 84	1,310,967 12	1,000,000
Mobile, - -	1,400,188 14	1,098,667 20	2,498,855 34	
New Orleans, - -	6,763,758 80	2,975,056 09	9,738,814 89	1,000,000
Natchez, - -	1,336,609 50	1,236,066 07	2,572,675 57	
St. Louis, - -	677,504 80	77,078 36	754,583 16	
Nashville, - -	2,170,240 16	2,677,902 51	4,848,142 67	1,000,000
Louisville, - -	2,567,900 96	1,333,430 59	3,901,331 55	1,250,000
Lexington, - -	1,150,121 03	636,595 77	1,786,716 80	1,000,000
Cincinnati, - -	3,320,306 94	716,454 82	4,036,761 76	1,700,000
Pittsburg, - -	1,167,217 68	598,070 64	1,765,288 32	700,000
Buffalo, - -	597,310 98	351,786 77	949,097 75	
Utica, - -	504,822 18	184,543 18	689,865 36	
Burlington, - -	448,539 52	213,364 55	661,904 07	
	$44,646,604 72	20,764,850 25	65,411,454 97	35,000,000

drafts on their funds accumulated at the branch in New Orleans, which there pay the Atlantic branches by bills growing out of the purchases made in New Orleans on account of the northern merchants or manufacturers, thus completing the circle of the operations. This explains the large amount of business done at that branch.

The committee will also perceive that, while the local discounts [loans] of the bank amount to forty-four millions, the domestic bills of exchange amount to nearly twenty-one millions of dollars. This is the most striking feature in the condition of the bank.

It has been deemed by the bank that, next to the preservation of the currency, the most important service it could render, would be to facilitate the internal exchanges of the produce and labor of the citizens of every part of the Union. No merely physical improvement in the means of communication between them can so effectually approximate them; no facilities of travelling and transportation can so completely abridge the wide spaces which separate the parts of this extensive country, as the removal of those great barriers which the want of easy commercial exchanges interpose to their prosperity. The great object, therefore, to which the bank has, for many years, directed its anxious attention, has been to identify itself thoroughly with the real business of the country, and more especially to melt down, into one uniform and healthy mass, all the depreciated currencies with which some parts of the country were afflicted; and having thus established the exchanges throughout the whole on their true basis, the interchange of equal values at each place, to bring down these exchanges to the lowest cost to them all. By such an effort, the bank has thought that it assumed its true and federal character, as the great channel of intercommunication for the business of the Union; and that, leaving to local institutions as much as they desired or could accomplish of the local business in every section of the Union, its more appropriate sphere was the general communication between them all.

Of the nature and extent of these operations, the committee can form the best estimate by inspecting the weekly reports from the branches during the last week, which are now lying on the table, and which will exhibit the commercial map of the interior trade of the United States at the present moment. It will be seen that, during the last week, there has been purchased by the bank and its branches, the amount of $1,081,335 88 of domestic bills, at the following places:

At Portland,	-	-	$6,076 63	At Mobile	-	-	102,082 61
Portsmouth,		-	3,637 68	New Orleans,	-	145,555 80
Boston,	-	-	92,221 22	Natchez,	-	-	42,183 43
Providence,	-	-	21,539 22	St. Louis,	-	-	9,603 63
Hartford,	-	-	4,671 51	Nashville,	-	-	30,790 33
New York,	-	-	50,019 80	Louisville,	-	-	60,152 36
Baltimore,	-	-	27,174 26	Lexington,	-	-	25,185 25
Washington,		-	21,145 16	Cincinnati,	-	-	42,907 71
Richmond,	-	-	28,662 15	Pittsburg,	-	-	35,685 69
Norfolk,	-	-	19,009 16	Buffalo,	-	-	32,105 64
Fayetteville,		-	13,911 30	Utica,	-	-	18,791 44
Charleston,	-	-	66,401 36	Burlington,	-	-	12,550 69
Savannah,	-	-	66,302 50	Bank United States,		102,970 30
					$1,081,335 88

It may not be uninteresting to illustrate this movement of the internal exchanges, by showing the points from which this $20,776,916 of bills come, and where they are tending. This will be seen in the annexed table, marked A: among the objects of interest presented in it, it will be seen that the amount of bills from the waters of the Mississippi amount to $10,212,905, and that the amount payable within an average, probably, of sixty days, at New York, is $4,096,410; and at Baltimore, Philadelphia, Providence, and Boston, $4,387,059, making an aggregate of $8,483,469. The extent of these operations during the last year, amounted to $48,562,185 32, as will be seen in the following table.

Bills purchased					
At Bank U. States,	-	$5,267,675 48	At Savannah,	- -	$2,128,574 37
Portland,	- -	167,915 36	Mobile,	- -	1,777,043 07
Portsmouth,	-	128,871 95	New Orleans,	- -	9,470,184 38
Boston,	-	3,444,815 88	Natchez,	- -	1,379,698 93
Providence,	-	1,218,332 62	St. Louis,	- -	274,390 04
Hartford,	-	111,288 83	Nashville,	- -	3,022,647 19
New York,	-	4,497,183 80	Louisville,	- -	2,220,824 46
Baltimore,	-	1,048,228 07	Lexington,	- -	1,684,563 83
Washington,	-	864,532 22	Cincinnati,	- -	1,291,721 48
Richmond,	-	1,939,108 83	Pittsburg,	- -	1,371,686 94
Norfolk,	-	845,957 12	Buffalo,	- -	819,343 29
Fayetteville,	-	801,542 63	Utica,	- -	279,590 05
Charleston,	-	2,210,393 56	Burlington,	- -	296,071 94
					$48,562,185 32

Of the security with which these operations, based as they are on the real transactions of the country, are conducted, an estimate may be formed by this circumstance, that, of this amount of $48,562,185 32, the whole sum which as yet has been under protest, has been $43,521 06, and the whole amount of loss which will probably be incurred on these amounts to $17,038.

For the distribution of the proceeds of these bills, the bank gives its drafts, which are given at the lowest rates. These extensive operations have enabled the bank to reduce the rate of its exchanges so low that, throughout the Union, they are in many places without any charge, in others scarcely forming a perceptible charge on the operations of trade, and almost always, if not quite without exception, within the limit of the transportation of the precious metals. We may indeed repeat with confidence what is said by a most competent judge, Mr. Gallatin,[1] that "there is not, it is believed, a single country where the community is, in that respect, served with less risk or expense." . . .

In reference to the general operations of the bank in foreign exchanges, it has been considered that the connection of the bank with the business of the country would be incomplete, if it did not contribute its aid in facilitating the foreign intercourse of its citizens. When, in the southern States, the crops are shipped to the northern States, their transmission is rendered easy on the part of the bank, by purchasing the bills drawn on the north to accompany them. If the same parties, instead of shipping their produce to the north, ship it to Europe, there is no reason why the bank should not afford them the same facility by the purchase of their bills on Europe. While in the south, the presence of a large and constant purchaser thus gives greater steadiness and uniformity to the demand for bills, on which the profit of the southern merchant and planter depends, the appearance in the north of the same purchaser, as a large seller, gives equal advantage to those who have remittances to make to Europe.

1 Albert Gallatin, Secretary of the Treasury for Jefferson and Madison, was in the 1830's one of the nation's most respected bankers.

There is, however, a strong reason of general policy why the bank should engage largely in the foreign exchanges. The state of the currency of this country depends mainly on its relations with Europe; and whenever commercial or other circumstances create an adverse exchange, such are the great facilities of intercourse with France and England, that an immediate shipment of coin takes place, which necessarily occasions abrupt transitions in the business of the banks, and which, in turn, affect the community. It seems, therefore, to belong essentially to the conservative power of the bank over the currency, to have the ability of interposing on these occasions, of breaking the shock of any sudden demand, and of giving time to the State institutions to adopt protective measures for their own security. This power is to be acquired only by a large participation in the foreign exchanges, so as to enable it, on any emergency, out of its own accumulations in Europe, or out of its established credits there, to supply the most urgent wants of commerce. This it has often done to great advantage, and eminently on the late occasion, when these demands might have pressed with injurious, if not fatal consequences on the community. The total amount of foreign exchanges drawn by the bank from the first of January, 1831, to the first of March, 1832, amounted to $11,166,743 10. Of these, the amount paid for the Mediterranean squadron, and for diplomatic expenses on account of Government, was $583,082 42. . . .

4] The Bank Attacked

> On February 2, 1831, Thomas Hart Benton, the broad-shouldered, stocky senator from Missouri, launched the attack on the Bank in Congress. Vain, pompous, and pedantic, Benton was always an honest, able, and ardent advocate of Western interests. His slashing condemnation makes clear both the economic and the ideological nature of the resentment against the Bank and spells out many of the arguments that long were used against it.*

. . . "*First:* Mr. President, I object to the renewal of the charter of the Bank of the United States, because I look upon the bank as an institution too great and powerful to be tolerated in a government of free and equal laws. Its power is that of the purse; a power more potent than that of the sword; and this power it possesses to a degree and extent that will enable this bank to draw to itself too much of the political power of this Union; and too much of the individual property of the citizens of these States. The money power of the bank is both direct and indirect. . . .

"Mr. B. resumed. The direct power of the bank is now prodigious, and in the event of the renewal of the charter, must speedily become boundless and uncontrollable. The bank is now authorized to own effects, lands inclusive, to the amount of fifty-five millions of dollars, and to issue notes to the amount of thirty-five millions more. This makes ninety millions; and, in addition to this vast sum, there is an opening for an unlimited increase: for there is a dis-

* THE BANK ATTACKED: Benton's Speech in the Senate, February 2, 1831. From Thomas Hart Benton, *Thirty Years' View* (New York, 1854), pp. 191–202.

pensation in the charter to issue as many more notes as Congress, by law, may permit. This opens the door to boundless emissions; for what can be more unbounded than the will and pleasure of successive Congresses? The indirect power of the bank cannot be stated in figures; but it can be shown to be immense. In the first place, it has the keeping of the public moneys, now amounting to twenty-six millions per annum (the Post Office Department included), and the gratuitous use of the undrawn balances, large enough to constitute, in themselves, the capital of a great State bank. In the next place, its promissory notes are receivable, by law, in purchase of all property owned by the United States, and in payment of all debts due them; and this may increase its power to the amount of the annual revenue, by creating a demand for its notes to that amount. In the third place, it wears the name of the United States, and has the federal government for a partner; and this name, and this partnership, identifies the credit of the bank with the credit of the Union. In the fourth place, it is armed with authority to disparage and discredit the notes of other banks, by excluding them from all payments to the United States; and this, added to all its other powers, direct and indirect, makes this institution the uncontrollable monarch of the moneyed system of the Union. To whom is all this power granted? To a company of private individuals, many of them foreigners, and the mass of them residing in a remote and narrow corner of the Union, unconnected by any sympathy with the fertile regions of the Great Valley, in which the natural power of this Union—the power of numbers— will be found to reside long before the renewed term of a second charter would expire. By whom is all this power to be exercised? By a directory of seven (it may be), governed by a majority, of four (it may be); and none of these elected by the people, or responsible to them. Where is it to be exercised? At a single city, distant a thousand miles from some of the States, receiving the produce of none of them (except one); no interest in the welfare of any of them (except one); no commerce with the people; with branches in every State; and every branch subject to the secret and absolute orders of the supreme central head: thus constituting a system of centralism, hostile to the federative principle of our Union, encroaching upon the wealth and power of the States, and organized upon a principle to give the highest effect to the greatest power. This mass of power, thus concentrated, thus ramified, and thus directed, must necessarily become, under a prolonged existence, the absolute monopolist of American money, the sole manufacturer of paper currency, and the sole authority (for authority it will be) to which the federal government, the State governments, the great cities, corporate bodies, merchants, traders, and every private citizen, must, of necessity apply, for every loan which their exigencies may demand. 'The rich ruleth the poor, and the borrower is the servant of the lender.' Such are the words of Holy Writ; and if the authority of the Bible admitted of corroboration, the history of the world is at hand to give it.

"*Secondly.* I object to the continuance of this bank, because its tendencies are dangerous and pernicious to the government and the people.

"What are the tendencies of a great moneyed power, connected with the government, and controlling its fiscal operations? Are they not dangerous to every interest, public and private—political as well as pecuniary? I say they are; and briefly enumerate the heads of each mischief.

"1. Such a bank tends to subjugate the government, as I have already shown in the history of what happened to the British minister in the year 1795.

"2. It tends to collusions between the government and the bank in the terms of the loans, as has been fully experienced in England in those frauds upon the people, and insults upon the understanding, called three per cent. loans, in which the government, for about £50 borrowed, became liable to pay £100.

"3. It tends to create public debt, by facilitating public loans, and substituting unlimited supplies of paper, for limited supplies of coin. The British debt is born of the Bank of England. That bank was chartered in 1694, and was nothing more nor less in the beginning, than an act of Parliament for the incorporation of a company of subscribers to a government loan. The loan was £1,200,000; the interest £80,000; and the expenses of management £4,000. And this is the birth and origin, the germ and nucleus of that debt, which is now £900,000,000 (the unfunded items included), which bears an interest of £30,000,000, and costs £260,000 for annual management.

"4. It tends to beget and prolong unnecessary wars, by furnishing the means of carrying them on without recurrence to the people. England is the ready example for this calamity. . . .

"5. It tends to aggravate the inequality of fortunes; to make the rich richer, and the poor poorer; to multiply nabobs and paupers; and to deepen and widen the gulf which separates Dives from Lazarus. A great moneyed power is favorable to great capitalists; for it is the principle of money to favor money. It is unfavorable to small capitalists; for it is the principle of money to eschew the needy and unfortunate. It is injurious to the laboring classes; because they receive no favors, and have the price of the property they wish to acquire raised to the paper maximum, while wages remain at the silver minimum.

"6. It tends to make and to break fortunes, by the flux and reflux of paper. Profuse issues, and sudden contractions, perform this operation, which can be repeated, like planetary and pestilential visitations, in every cycle of so many years; at every periodical return, transferring millions from the actual possessors of property to the Neptunes who preside over the flux and reflux of paper. . . .

"This is what was done in England five years ago, it is what may be done here in every five years to come, if the bank charter is renewed. Sole dispenser of money, it cannot omit the oldest and most obvious means of amassing wealth by the flux and reflux of paper. The game will be in its own hands, and the only answer to be given is that to which I have alluded: 'The Sultan is too just and merciful to abuse his power.'

"*Thirdly*. I object to the renewal of the charter, on account of the exclusive privileges, and anti-republican monopoly, which it gives to the stockholders. It gives, and that by an act of Congress, to a company of individuals, the exclusive legal privileges: . . .

"1. The name, the credit, and the revenues of the United States are given up to the use of this company, and constitute in themselves an immense capital to bank upon. The name of the United States, like that of the King, is a tower of strength; and this strong tower is now an outwork to defend the citadel of a moneyed corporation. The credit of the Union is incalculable; and, of this credit, as going with the name, and being in partnership with the United

States, the same corporation now has possession. The revenues of the Union are twenty-six millions of dollars, including the post-office; and all this is so much capital in the hands of the bank, because the revenue is received by it, and is payable in its promissory notes.

"2. To pay the revenues of the United States in their own notes, until Congress, by law, shall otherwise direct. This is a part of the charter, incredible and extraordinary as it may appear. The promissory notes of the bank are to be received in payment of every thing the United States may have to sell—in discharge of every debt due to her, until Congress, by law, shall otherwise direct; so that, if this bank, like its prototype in England, should stop payment, its promissory notes would still be receivable at every custom-house, land-office, post-office, and by every collector of public moneys, throughout the Union, until Congress shall meet, pass a repealing law, and promulgate the repeal. Other banks depend upon their credit for the receivability of their notes; but this favored institution has law on its side, and a chartered right to compel the reception of its paper by the federal government. The immediate consequence of this extraordinary privilege is, that the United States becomes virtually bound to stand security for the bank, as much so as if she had signed a bond to that effect; and must stand forward to sustain the institution in all emergencies, in order to save her own revenue. This is what has already happened, some ten years ago, in the early progress of the bank, and when the immense aid given it by the federal government enabled it to survive the crisis of its own overwhelming mismanagement.

"3. To hold the moneys of the United States in deposit, without making compensation for the use of the undrawn balances.—This is a right which I deny; but, as the bank claims it, and, what is more material, enjoys it; and as the people of the United States have suffered to a vast extent in consequence of this claim and enjoyment, I shall not hesitate to set it down to the account of the bank. Let us then examine the value of this privilege, and its effect upon the interest of the community; and, in the first place, let us have a full and accurate view of the amount of these undrawn balances, from the establishment of the bank to the present day. Here it is! Look! Read! . . .

"4. To discredit and disparage the notes of all other banks, by excluding them from the collection of the federal revenue. This results from the collection—no, not the collection, but the receipt of the revenue having been communicated to the bank, and along with it the virtual execution of the joint resolution of 1816, to regulate the collection of the federal revenue. The execution of that resolution was intended to be vested in the Secretary of the Treasury —a disinterested arbiter between rival banks; but it may be considered as virtually devolved upon the Bank of the United States, and powerfully increases the capacity of that institution to destroy, or subjugate, all other banks. This power to disparage the notes of all other banks, is a power to injure them; and, added to all the other privileges of the Bank of the United States, is a power to destroy them! If any one doubts this assertion, let him read the answers of the president of the bank to the questions put to him by the chairman of the Finance Committee. These answers are appended to the committee's report of the last session in favor of the bank, and expressly declare the capacity of the federal bank to destroy the State banks. The worthy chairman [Mr.

Smith, of Md.] puts this question; 'Has the bank at any time oppressed any of the State banks.' The president [Mr. Biddle], answers, as the whole world would answer to a question of oppression, that it never had; and this response was as much as the interrogatory required. But it did not content the president of the bank; he chose to go further, and to do honor to the institution over which he presided, by showing that it was as just and generous as it was rich and powerful. He, therefore, adds the following words, for which, as a seeker after evidence, to show the alarming and dangerous character of the bank, I return him my unfeigned thanks: 'There are very few banks which might not have been destroyed by an exertion of the power of the bank.'

"This is enough! proof enough! not for me alone, but for all who are unwilling to see a moneyed domination set up—a moneyed oligarchy established in this land, and the entire Union subjected to its sovereign will. The power to destroy all other banks is admitted and declared; the inclination to do so is known to all rational beings to reside with the power! Policy may restrain the destroying faculties for the present; but they exist; and will come forth when interest prompts and policy permits. They have been exercised; and the general prostration of the Southern and Western banks attest the fact. They will be exercised (the charter being renewed), and the remaining State banks will be swept with the besom of destruction. Not that all will have their signs knocked down, and their doors closed up. Far worse than that to many of them. Subjugation, in preference to destruction, will be the fate of many. Every planet must have its satellites; every tyranny must have its instruments; every knight is followed by his squire; even the king of beasts, the royal quadruped, whose roar subdues the forest, must have a small, subservient animal to spring his prey. Just so of this imperial bank, when installed anew in its formidable and lasting power. The State banks, spared by the sword, will be passed under the yoke. They will become subordinate parts in the great machine. Their place in the scale of subordination will be one degree below the rank of the legitimate branches; their business, to perform the work which it would be too disreputable for the legitimate branches to perform. This will be the fate of the State banks which are allowed to keep up their signs, and to set open their doors; and thus the entire moneyed power of the Union would fall into the hands of one single institution, whose inexorable and invisible mandates, emanating from a centre, would pervade the Union, giving or withholding money according to its own sovereign will and absolute pleasure. To a favored State, to an individual, or a class of individuals, favored by the central power, the golden stream of Pactolus would flow direct. To all such the munificent mandates of the High Directory would come, as the fabled god made his terrestrial visit of love and desire, enveloped in a shower of gold. But to others—to those not favored—and to those hated—the mandates of this same directory would be as 'the planetary plague which hangs its poison in the sick air;' death to them! death to all who minister to their wants! What a state of things! What a condition for a confederacy of States! What grounds for alarm and terrible apprehension, when in a confederacy of such vast extent, so many independent States, so many rival commercial cities, so much sectional jealousy, such violent political parties, such fierce contests for power, there should be but one moneyed tribunal, before which all the rival and contending elements must appear! but one single dispenser of money, to which every citizen, every trader, every merchant, every manufacturer, every planter, every corporation, every city, every State, and the federal government itself, must apply, in every emergency, for the most indispensable loan! and this, in the face of the fact, that, in every contest for human rights, the great moneyed institutions of the world have uniformly been found on the side of kings and nobles, against the lives and liberties of the people.

"5. To hold real estate, receive rents, and retain a body of tenantry. This privilege is hostile to the nature of our republican government, and inconsistent with the nature and design of a banking institution. Republics want free-holders, not landlords and tenants; and, except the corporators in this bank, and in the British East India Company, there is not an incorporated body of landlords in any country upon the face of the earth whose laws emanate from a legislative body. Banks are instituted to promote trade and industry, and to aid the government and its citizens with loans of money. The whole argument in favor of banking—every argument in favor of this bank—rests upon that idea. No one, when this charter was granted, presumed to speak in favor of incorporating a society of landlords, especially foreign landlords, to buy lands, build houses, rent tenements, and retain tenantry. Loans of money was the object in view, and the purchase of real estate is incompatible with that object. Instead of remaining bankers, the corporators may turn land speculators: instead of having money to lend, they may turn you out tenants to vote. To an application for a loan, they may answer, and answer truly, that they have no money on hand; and the reason may be, that they have laid it out in land. This seems to be the case at present. A committee of the legislature of Pennsylvania has just applied for a loan; the president of the bank, nothing loth to make a loan to that great State, for twenty years longer than the charter has to exist, expresses his regret that he cannot lend but a limited and inadequate sum. The funds of the institution, he says, will not permit it to advance more than eight millions of dollars. And why? because it has invested three millions in real estate! To this power to hold real estate, is superadded the means to acquire it. The bank is now the greatest moneyed power in the Union; in the event of the renewal of its charter, it will soon be the sole one. Sole dispenser of money, it will soon be the chief owner of property. To unlimited means of acquisition, would be united perpetuity of tenure, for a corporation never dies, and is free from the operation of the laws which govern the descent and distribution of real estate in the hands of individuals. The limitations in the charter are vain and illusory. They insult the understanding, and mock the credulity of foolish believers. The bank is first limited to such acquisitions of real estate as are necessary to its own accommodation; then comes a proviso to undo the limitation, so far as it concerns purchases upon its own mortgages and executions! This is the limitation upon the capacity of such an institution to acquire real estate. As if it had any thing to do but to make loans upon mortgages, and push executions upon judgments! Having all the money, it would be the sole lender; mortgages being the road to loans, all borrowers must travel that road. When birds enough are in the net, the fowler draws his string, and the heads are wrung off. So when mortgages enough are taken, the loans are called in; discounts cease; curtailments are made; failures to pay ensue; writs issue; judgments and executions follow; all the mortgaged premises are for sale at once; and the attorney of the bank appears at the elbow of the marshal, sole bidder and sole purchaser. . . .

"6. To deal in pawns, merchandise, and bills of exchange. I hope the Senate will not require me to read dry passages from the charter to prove what I say. I know I speak a thing nearly incredible when I allege that this bank, in addition to all its other attributes, is an incorporated company of pawnbrokers! The allegation staggers belief, but a reference to the charter will dispel incredulity. The charter, in the first part, forbids a traffic in merchandise; in the after part, permits it. For truly this instrument seems to have been framed upon the principles of contraries; one principle making limitations, and the other following after with provisos to undo them. Thus is it with lands, as I have just shown; thus is it with merchandise, as I now show. The bank is forbidden to deal in merchandise—proviso, unless in the case of goods pledged for money lent, and not redeemed to the day; and, proviso, again, unless for goods which shall be the proceeds of its lands. With the help of these two provisos, it is clear that the limitation is undone; it is clear that the bank is at liberty to act the pawnbroker and merchant, to any extent that it pleases. It may say to all the merchants who want loans, Pledge your stores, gentlemen! They must do it, or do worse; and, if any accident prevents redemption on the day, the pawn is forfeited, and the bank takes possession. On the other hand, it may lay out its rents for goods; it may sell its real estate, now worth three millions of dollars, for goods. Thus the bank is an incorporated company of pawnbrokers and merchants, as well as an incorporation of landlords and land-speculators; and this derogatory privilege, like the others, is copied from the old Bank of England charter of 1694. Bills of exchange are also subjected to the traffic of this bank. It is a traffic unconnected with the trade of banking, dangerous for a great bank to hold, and now operating most injuriously in the South and West. It is the process which drains these quarters of the Union of their gold and silver, and stifles the growth of a fair commerce in the products of the country. The merchants, to make remittances, buy bills of exchange from the branch banks, instead of buying produce from the farmers. The bills are paid for in gold and silver; and, eventually, the gold and silver are sent to the mother bank, or to the branches in the Eastern cities, either to meet these bills, or to replenish their coffers, and to furnish vast loans to favorite States or individuals. The bills sell cheap, say a fraction of one per cent.; they are, therefore, a good remittance to the merchant. To the bank the operation is doubly good; for even the half of one per cent. on bills of exchange is a great profit to the institution which monopolizes that business, while the collection and delivery to the branches of all the hard money in the country is a still more considerable advantage. Under this system, the best of the Western banks—I do not speak of those which had no foundations, and sunk under the weight of neighborhood opinion, but those which deserved favor and confidence—sunk ten years ago. Under this system, the entire West is now undergoing a silent, general, and invisible drain of its hard money; and, if not quickly arrested, these States will soon be, so far as the precious metals are concerned, no more than the empty skin of an immolated victim.

"7. To establish branches in the different States without their consent, and in defiance of their resistance. No one can deny the degrading and injurious tendency of this privilege. It derogates from the sovereignty of a State; tramples upon her laws; injures her revenue and commerce; lays open her government to the attacks of centralism; impairs the property of her citizens; and fastens a vampire on her bosom to suck out her gold and silver. 1. It derogates from her sovereignty, because the central institution may impose its intrusive branches upon the State without her consent, and in defiance of her resistance. This has already been done. The State of Alabama, but four years ago, by a resolve of her legislature, remonstrated against the intrusion of a branch upon her. She protested against the favor. Was the will of the State respected? On the contrary, was not a branch instantaneously forced upon her, as if, by the suddenness of the action, to make a striking and conspicuous display of the omnipotence of the bank, and the nullity of the State? 2. It tramples upon her laws; because, according to the decision of the Supreme Court, the bank and all its branches are wholly independent of State legislation; and it tramples on them again, because it authorizes foreigners to hold lands and tenements in every State, contrary to the laws of many of them; and because it admits of the *mortmain* tenure, which is condemned by all the republican States in the Union. 3. It injures her revenue, because the bank stock, under the decision of the Supreme Court, is not liable to taxation. And thus, foreigners, and non-resident Americans, who monopolize the money of the State, who hold its best lands and town lots, who meddle in its elections, and suck out its gold and silver, and perform no military duty, are exempted from paying taxes, in proportion to their wealth, for the support of the State whose laws they trample upon, and whose benefits they usurp. 4. It subjects the State to the dangerous manœuvres and intrigues of centralism, by means of the tenants, debtors, bank officers, and bank money, which the central directory retain in the State, and may embody and direct against it in its elections, and in its legislative and judicial proceedings. 5. It tends to impair the property of the citizens, and, in some instances, that of the States, by destroying the State banks in which they have invested their money. 6. It is injurious to the commerce of the States (I speak of the Western States), by substituting a trade in bills of exchange, for a trade in the products of the country. 7. It fastens a vampire on the bosom of the State, to suck away its gold and silver, and to co-operate with the course of trade, of federal legislation, and of exchange, in draining the South and West of all their hard money. The Southern States, with their thirty millions of annual exports in cotton, rice, and tobacco, and the Western States, with their twelve millions of provisions and tobacco exported from New Orleans, and five millions consumed in the South, and on the lower Mississippi,—that is to say, with three fifths of the marketable productions of the Union, are not able to sustain thirty specie paying banks; while the minority of the States north of the Potomac, without any of the great staples for export, have above four hundred of such banks. These States, without rice, without cotton, without tobacco, without sugar, and with less flour and provisions, to export, are saturated with gold and silver; while the Southern and Western States, with all the real sources of wealth, are in a state of the utmost destitution. For this calamitous reversal of the natural order of things, the Bank of the United States stands forth pre-eminently culpable. Yes, it is pre-eminently culpable! and a statement in the 'National Intelligencer' of this morning (a paper which would overstate no fact to the prejudice of the bank), cites and proclaims the fact which proves this culpability. It dwells, and exults, on the quantity of gold and silver in the vaults of the United States Bank. It declares that institution to be 'overburdened' with gold and silver; and well may it be so overburdened, since it has lifted the load entirely from the South and West. It calls these metals 'a drug' in the hands of the bank; that is to say, an article for which no purchaser can be found. Let this 'drug,' like the treasures of the dethroned Dey of Algiers, be released from the dominion of its keeper; let a part go back to the South and West, and the bank will no longer complain of repletion, nor they of depletion.

"8. Exemption of the stockholders from individual liability on the failure of the bank. This privilege derogates from the common law, is contrary to the principle of partnerships, and injurious to the rights of the community. It is a peculiar privilege granted by law to these corporators, and exempting them from liability, except in their corporate capacity, and to the amount of the assets of the corporation. Unhappily these assets are never *assez,* that is to say, enough, when occasion comes for recurring to them. When a bank fails, its assets are always less than its debts; so that responsibility fails the instant that liability accrues. Let no one say that the bank of the United States is too great to fail. One greater than it, and its prototype, has failed, and that in our own day, and for twenty years at a time: the Bank of England failed in 1797, and the Bank of the United States was on the point of failing in 1819. The same cause, namely, stockjobbing and overtrading, carried both to the brink of destruction; the same means saved both, namely, the name, the credit, and the helping hand of the governments which protected them. Yes, the Bank of the United States may fail; and its stockholders live in splendor upon the princely estates acquired with its notes, while the industrious classes, who hold these notes, will be unable to receive a shilling for them. This is unjust. It is a vice in the charter. The true principle in banking requires each stockholder to be liable to the amount of his shares; and subjects him to the summary action of every holder on the failure of the institution, till he has paid up the amount of his subscription. This is the true principle. It has prevailed in Scotland for the last century, and no such thing as a broken bank has been known there in all that time.

"9. To have the United States for a partner. Sir, there is one consequence, one result of all partnerships between a government and individuals, which should of itself, and in a mere mercantile point of view, condemn this association on the part of the federal government. It is the principle which puts the strong partner forward to bear the burden whenever the concern is in danger. The weaker members flock to the strong partner at the approach of the storm, and the necessity of venturing more to save what he has already stated, leaves him no alternative. He becomes the Atlas of the firm, and bears all upon his own shoulders. This is the principle: what is the fact? Why, that the United States has already been compelled to sustain the federal bank; to prop it with her revenues and its credit in the trials and crisis of its early administration. I pass over other instances of the damage suffered by the United States on account of this partnership; the immense standing deposits for which we receive no compensation; the loan of five millions of our own money, for which we have paid a million and a half in interest; the five per cent. stock note, on which we have paid our partners four million seven hundred and twenty-five thousand dollars in interest; the loss of ten millions on the three per cent. stock, and the ridiculous catastrophe of the miserable *bonus,* which has been paid to us with a fraction of our own money: I pass over all this, and come to the point of a direct loss, as a partner, in the dividends upon the stock itself. Upon this naked point of profit and loss, to be decided by a rule in arithmetic, we have sustained a direct and heavy loss. The stock held by the United States, as every body knows, was subscribed, not paid. It was a stock note, deposited for seven millions of dollars, bearing an interest of five per cent. The inducement to this subscription was the seductive conception that, by paying five per cent. on its note, the United States would clear four or five per cent. in getting a dividend of eight or ten. This was the inducement; now for the realization of this fine conception. Let us see it. Here it is; an official return from the Register of the Treasury of interest paid, and of dividends received. The account stands thus:

Interest paid by the United States,	$4,725,000
Dividends received by the United States,	4,629,426
Loss to the United States,	$95,574

"Disadvantageous as this partnership must be to the United States in a moneyed point of view, there is a far more grave and serious aspect under which to view it. It is the political aspect, resulting from the union between the bank and the government. This union has been tried in England, and has been found there to be just as disastrous a conjunction as the union between church and state. It is the conjunction of the lender and the borrower, and Holy Writ has told us which of these categories will be master of the other. But suppose they agree to drop rivalry, and unite their resources. Suppose they combine, and make a push for political power: how great is the mischief which they may not accomplish! . . .

"10. To have foreigners for partners. This, Mr. President, will be a strange story to be told in the West. The downright and upright people of that unsophisticated region believe that words mean what they signify, and that 'the Bank of the United States' is the Bank of the United States. How great then must be their astonishment to learn that this belief is a false conception, and that this bank (its whole name to the contrary notwithstanding) is just as much the bank of foreigners as it is of the federal government. Here I would like to have the proof—a list of the names and nations, to establish this almost incredible fact. But I have no access except to public documents, and from one of these I learn as much as will answer the present pinch. It is the report of the Committee of Ways and Means, in the House of Representatives, for the last session of Congress. That report admits that foreigners own seven millions of the stock of this bank; and every body knows that the federal government owns seven millions also.

"Thus it is proved that foreigners are as deeply interested in this bank as the United States itself. In the event of a renewal of the charter they will be much more deeply interested than at present; for a prospect of a rise in the stock to two hundred and fifty, and the unsettled state of things in Europe, will induce them to make great investments. It is to no purpose to say that the foreign stockholders cannot be voters or directors. The answer to that suggestion is this: the foreigners have the money; they pay down the cash, and want no accommodations; they are lenders, not borrowers; and in a great moneyed institution, such stockholders must have the greatest influence. The name of this bank is a deception upon the public. It is not the bank of the federal government, as its name would import, nor of the States which compose this Union; but chiefly of private individuals, foreigners as well as natives, denizens, and naturalized subjects. They own twenty-eight millions of the stock, the federal government but seven millions, and these seven are precisely balanced by the stock of the aliens. The federal government and the aliens are equal, owning one fifth each; and there would be as much truth in calling it the English Bank as the Bank of the United States. . . .

"11. Exemption from due course of law for violations of its charter.—This is a privilege which affects the administration of justice, and stands without example in the annals of republican legislation. In the case of all other delinquents, whether persons or corporations, the laws take their course against those who offend them. It is the right of every citizen to set the laws in motion against every offender; and it is the constitution of the law, when set in motion, to work through, like a machine, regardless of powers and principalities, and cutting down the guilty which may stand in its way. Not so in the case of this bank. In its behalf, there are barriers erected between the citizen and his oppressor, between the wrong and the remedy, between the law and the offender. Instead of a right to sue out a *scire facias* or a *quo warranto,* the injured citizen, with an humble petition in his hand, must repair to the President of the United States, or to Congress, and crave their leave to do so. If leave is denied (and denied it will be whenever the bank has a peculiar friend in the President, or a majority of such friends in Congress, the convenient pretext being always at hand that the general welfare requires the bank to be sustained), he can proceed no further. The machinery of the law cannot be set in motion, and the great offender laughs from behind his barrier at the impotent resentment of its helpless victim. Thus the bank, for the plainest violations of its charter, and the greatest oppressions of the citizen, may escape the pursuit of justice. Thus the administration of justice is subject to be strangled in its birth for the shelter and protection of this bank. But this is not all. Another and most alarming mischief results from the same extraordinary privilege. It gives the bank a direct interest in the presidential and congressional elections: it gives it need for friends in Congress and in the presidential chair. Its fate, its very existence, may often depend upon the friendship of the President and Congress; and, in such cases, it is not in human nature to avoid using the immense means in the hands of the bank to influence the elections of these officers. Take the existing fact—the case to which I alluded at the commencement of this speech. There is a case made out, ripe with judicial evidence, and big with the fate of the bank. It is a case of usury at the rate of forty-six per cent., in violation of the charter, which only admits an interest of six. The facts were admitted, in the court below, by the bank's demurrer; the law was decided, in the court above, by the supreme judges. The admission concludes the facts; the decision concludes the law. The forfeiture of the charter is established; the forfeiture is incurred; the application of the forfeiture alone is wanting to put an end to the institution. An impartial President or Congress might let the laws take their course; those of a different temper might interpose their veto. What a crisis for the bank! It beholds the sword of Damocles suspended over its head! What an interest in keeping those away who might suffer the hair to be cut!

"12. To have all these unjust privileges secured to the corporators as a monopoly, by a pledge of the public faith to charter no other bank.—This is the most hideous feature in the whole mass of deformity. If these banks are beneficial institutions, why not several? one, at least, and each independent of the other, to each great section of the Union? If malignant, why create one? The restriction constitutes the monopoly, and renders more invidious what was sufficiently hateful in itself. It is, indeed, a double monopoly, legislative as well as banking; for the Congress of 1816 monopolized the power to grant these monopolies. It has tied up the hands of its successors; and if this can be done on one subject, and for twenty years, why not upon all subjects, and for all time? Here is the form of words which operate this double engrossment of our rights: 'No other bank shall be established by any future law of Congress, during the continuance of the corporation hereby enacted, for which the faith of Congress is hereby pledged;' with a proviso for the District of Columbia. And that no incident might be wanting to complete the title of this charter, to the utter reprobation of whig republicans, this compound monopoly, and the very form of words in which it is conceived, is copied from the charter of the Bank of England!—not the charter of William and Mary, as granted in 1694 (for the Bill of Rights was then fresh in the memories of Englishmen), but the charter as amended, and that for money, in the memorable reign of Queen Anne, when a tory queen, a tory ministry, and a tory parliament, and the apostle of toryism, in the person of Dr. Sacheverell, with his sermons of divine right, passive obedience, and non-resistance, were riding and ruling over the prostrate liberties of England! This is the precious period, and these the noble authors, from which the idea was borrowed, and the very form of words copied, which now figure in the charter of the Bank of the United States, constituting that double monopoly, which restricts at once the powers of Congress and the rights of the citizens.

"These, Mr. President, are the chief of the exclusive privileges which constitute the monopoly of the Bank of the United States. I have spoken of them, not as they deserved, but as my abilities have permitted. I have shown you that they are not only evil in themselves, but copied from an evil example. . . ."

5] Gouge Explains the Hard Money Position

Benton's arguments had powerful political and ideological appeal, but they included few carefully thought out economic ideas. Nor did they stress the hard money views which had more of an appeal to the Eastern laborers and artisans than to Western farmers. During the same spring when Biddle was explaining the operations of his Bank to a Congressional committee, another Philadelphian, William M. Gouge, was starting to write *A Short History of Paper Money and Banking in the United States,* an analysis that was to become the Bible of the hard money advocates. In the following excerpt Gouge summarizes his position.*

To PLACE the subject fairly before the reader, we shall bring together the principal propositions that have been supported in this essay and leave the decision to his candid judgment.

We have maintained:

1. That real money is that valuable by reference to which the value of other articles is estimated, and by the instrumentality of which they are circulated. It is a *commodity,* done up in a particular form to serve a particular use, and does not differ *essentially* from other items of wealth.

2. That silver, owing to its different physical properties, the universal and incessant demand for it, and the small proportion the annual supply bears to the stock on hand, is as good a practical standard of value as can reasonably be desired. It has no variations except such as *necessarily* arise from the nature of value.

3. That real money diffuses itself through different countries and through different parts of a country in proportion to the demands of commerce. No prohibitions can prevent its departing from countries where wealth and trade are declining; and no obstacle except spurious money can prevent its flowing into countries where wealth and trade are increasing.

4. That money is the tool of all trades and is, as such, one of the most useful of productive instruments and one of the most valuable of labor saving machines.

5. That bills of exchange and promissory notes are a *mere commercial medium* and are, as *auxiliaries* of gold and silver money, very useful; but they differ from metallic money in having no inherent value and in being evidences of debt. The expressions of value in bills of exchange and promissory notes are according to the article which law or custom has made the standard; and the failure to pay bills of exchange and promissory notes does not affect the value of the currency or the standard by which all contracts are regulated.

6. That bank notes are *mere evidences of debt* due by the banks and in this respect differ not from the promissory notes of the merchants; but, being re-

* GOUGE EXPLAINS THE HARD MONEY POSITION: From William M. Gouge, *A Short History of Paper Money and Banking in the United States* (Philadelphia, 1833), pp. 135–40.

ceived in full of all demands, they become to all intents and purposes the money of the country.

7. That banks owe their credit to their charters; for, if these were taken away, not even their own stockholders would trust them.

8. That the circulating quality of bank notes is in part owing to their being receivable in payment of dues to government, in part to the interest which the debtors to banks and bank stockholders have in keeping them in circulation, and in part to the difficulty, when the system is firmly established, of obtaining metallic money.

9. That so long as specie payments are maintained, there is a limit on bank issues; but this is not sufficient to prevent successive "expansions" and "contractions" which produce ruinous fluctuations of prices; while the means by which bank medium is kept "convertible" inflict great evils on the community.

10. That no restriction which can be imposed on banks and no discretion on the part of the directors can prevent these fluctuations; for bank credit, as a branch of commercial credit, is affected by all the causes, natural and political, that affect trade, or that affect the confidence man has in man.

11. That the "flexibility" or "elasticity" of bank medium is not an excellence, but a defect, and that "expansions" and "contractions" are not made to suit the wants of the community but from a simple regard to the profits and safety of the banks.

12. That the uncertainty of trade produced by these successive "expansions" and "contractions" is but *one* of the evils of the present system. That the banks cause credit dealings to be carried to an extent that is highly pernicious; that they cause credit to be given to men who are not entitled to it, and deprive others of credit to whom it would be useful.

13. That the granting of exclusive privileges to companies or the exempting of companies from liabilities to which individuals are subject is repugnant to the fundamental principles of American government; and that the banks, inasmuch as they have exclusive privileges and exemptions and have the entire control of credit and currency, are the most pernicious of money corporations.

14. That a nominal responsibility may be imposed on such corporations but that it is impossible to impose on them an effective responsibility. They respect the laws and public opinion so far only as is necessary to promote their own interest.

15. That on the supposition most favorable to the friends of the banking system, the whole amount gained by the substitution of bank medium for gold and silver coin is equal only to about 40 cents per annum for each individual in the country; but that it will be found that nothing is in reality gained *by the nation,* if due allowance be made for the expense of supporting three or four hundred banks, and for the fact that bank medium is a machine which performs its work badly.

16. That some hundreds of thousands of dollars are annually extracted from the people of Pennsylvania and some millions from the people of the United States for the support of the banks, insomuch as through banking the natural order of things is reversed and interest paid to the banks on evidences of debt due by them, instead of interest being paid to those who part with commodities in exchange for bank notes.

17. That into the formation of the bank capital of the country very little substantial wealth has ever entered, that capital having been formed principally out of the promissory notes of the original subscribers, or by other means which the operations of the banks themselves have facilitated. They who have bought the script of the banks at second hand may have honestly paid cent. per cent. for it; but what they have paid has gone to those from whom they bought the script and does not form any part of the capital of the banks.

18. That if it was the wish of the Legislature to promote usurious dealings, it could not well devise more efficient means than incorporating paper money banks. That these banks, moreover, give rise to many kinds of stock-jobbing, by which the simple-minded are injured and the crafty benefited.

19. That many legislators have, in voting for banks, supposed that they were promoting the welfare of their constituents; but the prevalence of false views in legislative bodies in respect to money corporations and paper money is to be attributed chiefly to the desire certain members have to make money for themselves, or to afford their political partisans and personal friends opportunities for speculation.

20. That the banking interest has a pernicious influence on the periodical press, on public elections, and the general course of legislation. This interest is so powerful that the establishment of a system of sound currency and sound credit is impracticable, except one or other of the political parties into which the nation is divided makes such an object its primary principle of action.

21. That through the various advantages which the system of incorporated paper-money banking has given to some men over others, the foundation has been laid of an *artificial* inequality of wealth, which kind of inequality is, when once laid, increased by all the subsequent operations of society.

22. That this artificial inequality of wealth adds nothing to the substantial happiness of the rich and detracts much from the happiness of the rest of the community. That its tendency is to corrupt one portion of society and debase another.

23. That the sudden dissolution of the banking system without suitable preparation would put an end to the collection of debts, destroy private credit, break up many productive establishments, throw most of the property of the industrious into the hands of speculators, and deprive laboring people of employment.

24. That the system can be got rid of, without difficulty, by prohibiting, after a certain day, the issue of small notes and proceeding gradually to those of the highest denomination.

25. That the feasibility of getting rid of the system is further proved by the fact that the whole amount of bank notes and bank credits is, according to Mr. Gallatin's calculation, only about one hundred and nine million dollars. By paying ten or eleven millions a year, the whole can be liquidated in the term of ten years. If, however, twenty or thirty years should be required for the operation, the longest of these is but a short period in the lifetime of a nation.

26. That it has not been through the undervaluation of gold at the mint that eagles and half-eagles have disappeared; but from the free use of bank notes. Nevertheless, a new coinage of pieces containing four and eight, or five and

ten dollars worth of gold is desirable to save the trouble of calculating fractions. The dollar being the money of contract and account, no possible confusion or injustice can be produced by an adjustment of the gold coinage to the silver standard.

27. That incorporating a paper-money bank is not the "necessary and proper" or "natural and appropriate" way of managing the fiscal concerns of the Union; but that the "necessary and proper" or "natural and appropriate" way is by sub-treasury offices.

28. That incorporating a paper-money bank is not "the necessary and proper" or "natural and appropriate" way of correcting the evils occasioned by the State banks, inasmuch as a national bank, resting on the same principles as the State banks, must produce similar evils.

29. That "convertible" paper prevents the accumulation of such a stock of the precious metals as will enable the country to bear transitions from peace to war and insure the punctual payment of war taxes, and that the "necessary and proper" or "natural and appropriate" way of providing for all public exigencies is by making the Government *a solid money Government* as was intended by the framers of the Constitution.

30. That if Congress should, from excessive caution or some less commendable motive, decline passing the acts necessary to insure the gradual withdrawal of bank notes, they may greatly diminish the evils of the system by declaring that nothing but gold and silver shall be received in payment of duties and by making the operations of the Government entirely distinct from those of the banks.

31. That, on the abolition of incorporated paper-money banks, private bankers will rise up who will receive money on deposit and allow interest on the same, discount promissory notes, and buy and sell bills of exchange. Operating on sufficient funds and being responsible for their engagements in the whole amount of their estates, these private bankers will not by sudden and great "expansions" and "curtailments" derange the whole train of mercantile operations. In each large city an office of deposit and transfer similar to the Bank of Hamburg will be established, and we shall thus secure all the good of the present banking system and avoid all its evils.

32. That, if the present system of banking and paper money shall continue, the wealth and population of the country will increase from natural causes till they shall be equal for each square mile to the wealth and population of Europe. But, with every year, the state of society in the United States will more nearly approximate to the state of society in Great Britain. Crime and pauperism will increase. A few men will be inordinately rich, some comfortable, and a multitude in poverty. This condition of things will naturally lead to the adoption of that policy which proceeds on the principle that a legal remedy is to be found for each social evil, and nothing left for the operations of nature. This kind of legislation will increase the evils it is intended to cure.

33. That there is reason to *hope* that, on the downfall of moneyed corporations and the substitution of gold and silver for bank medium, sound credit will take the place of unsound, and legitimate enterprise the place of wild speculation. That the moral and intellectual character of the people will be sensibly, though gradually, raised, and the causes laid open of a variety of evils

under which society is now suffering. That the sources of legislation will to a certain extent be purified, by taking from members of legislative bodies inducements to pass laws for the special benefit of themselves, their personal friends, and political partisans. That the operation of the natural and just causes of wealth and poverty will no longer be inverted, but that each cause will operate in its natural and just order and produce its natural and just effect: wealth becoming the reward of industry, frugality, skill, prudence, and enterprise; and poverty the punishment of few except the indolent and prodigal.

6] The Issue Drawn

The bill to recharter the Bank had passed the Senate (28–20) on June 11, 1832, and the House (107–86) on July 3. Jackson had already made up his mind to veto the bill, but he found little support in his Cabinet. Only Roger B. Taney, the Attorney-General, strongly advocated a veto. The others urged him to return the bill unsigned and to say that this would leave the way open for its passage at some later date. Jackson therefore asked Taney to revise and amplify the draft of the veto message already penned by Amos Kendall, the Kentucky editor and politician who was a key figure in the President's informal "kitchen cabinet." The final version reflected Taney's interests and training by concentrating on constitutional rather than economic matters.*

WASHINGTON, *July 10, 1832.*

To the Senate:

The bill "to modify and continue" the act entitled "An act to incorporate the subscribers to the Bank of the United States" was presented to me on the 4th July instant. Having considered it with that solemn regard to the principles of the Constitution which the day was calculated to inspire, and come to the conclusion that it ought not to become a law, I herewith return it to the Senate, in which it originated, with my objections.

A bank of the United States is in many respects convenient for the Government and useful to the people. Entertaining this opinion, and deeply impressed with the belief that some of the powers and privileges possessed by the existing bank are unauthorized by the Constitution, subversive of the rights of the States, and dangerous to the liberties of the people, I felt it my duty at an early period of my Administration to call the attention of Congress to the practicability of organizing an institution combining all its advantages and obviating these objections. I sincerely regret that in the act before me I can perceive none of those modifications of the bank charter which are necessary, in my opinion, to make it compatible with justice, with sound policy, or with the Constitution of our country.

The present corporate body, denominated the president, directors, and company of the Bank of the United States, will have existed at the time this act

* THE ISSUE DRAWN: Jackson's Veto Message. From James D. Richardson, ed., *Messages and Papers of the Presidents* (Washington, 1896), II, 576–91.

is intended to take effect twenty years. It enjoys an exclusive privilege of banking under the authority of the General Government, a monopoly of its favor and support, and, as a necessary consequence, almost a monopoly of the foreign and domestic exchange. The powers, privileges, and favors bestowed upon it in the original charter, by increasing the value of the stock far above its par value, operated as a gratuity of many millions to the stockholders.

An apology may be found for the failure to guard against this result in the consideration that the effect of the original act of incorporation could not be certainly foreseen at the time of its passage. The act before me proposes another gratuity to the holders of the same stock, and in many cases to the same men, of at least seven millions more. This donation finds no apology in any uncertainty as to the effect of the act. On all hands it is conceded that its passage will increase at least 20 or 30 per cent more the market price of the stock, subject to the payment of the annuity of $200,000 per year secured by the act, thus adding in a moment one-fourth to its par value. It is not our own citizens only who are to receive the bounty of our Government. More than eight millions of the stock of this bank are held by foreigners. By this act the American Republic proposes virtually to make them a present of some millions of dollars. For these gratuities to foreigners and to some of our own opulent citizens the act secures no equivalent whatever. They are the certain gains of the present stockholders under the operation of this act, after making full allowance for the payment of the bonus.[1]

Every monopoly and all exclusive privileges are granted at the expense of the public, which ought to receive a fair equivalent. The many millions which this act proposes to bestow on the stockholders of the existing bank must come directly or indirectly out of the earnings of the American people. It is due to them, therefore, if their Government sell monopolies and exclusive privileges, that they should at least exact for them as much as they are worth in open market. The value of the monopoly in this case may be correctly ascertained. The twenty-eight millions of stock would probably be at an advance of 50 per cent, and command in market at least $42,000,000, subject to the payment of the present bonus. The present value of the monopoly, therefore, is $17,000,000, and this the act proposes to sell for three millions, payable in fifteen annual installments of $200,000 each.

It is not conceivable how the present stockholders can have any claim to the special favor of the Government. The present corporation has enjoyed its monopoly during the period stipulated in the original contract. If we must have such a corporation, why should not the Government sell out the whole stock and thus secure to the people the full market value of the privileges granted? Why should not Congress create and sell twenty-eight millions of stock, incorporating the purchasers with all the powers and privileges secured in this act and putting the premium upon the sales into the Treasury?

But this act does not permit competition in the purchase of this monopoly.

---

1 The bill to recharter for fifteen years required the Bank to pay for its privileges. The price was $200,000 a year, to be paid to the United States government. The 1816 charter had called for a comparable "bonus" of $1,500,000, to be paid in a lump sum rather than annually.

It seems to be predicated on the erroneous idea that the present stockholders have a prescriptive right not only to the favor but to the bounty of Government. It appears that more than a fourth part of the stock is held by foreigners and the residue is held by a few hundred of our own citizens, chiefly of the richest class. For their benefit does this act exclude the whole American people from competition in the purchase of this monopoly and dispose of it for many millions less than it is worth. This seems the less excusable because some of our citizens not now stockholders petitioned that the door of competition might be opened, and offered to take a charter on terms much more favorable to the Government and country.

But this proposition, although made by men whose aggregate wealth is believed to be equal to all the private stock in the existing bank, has been set aside, and the bounty of our Government is proposed to be again bestowed on the few who have been fortunate enough to secure the stock and at this moment wield the power of the existing institution. I can not perceive the justice or policy of this course. If our Government must sell monopolies, it would seem to be its duty to take nothing less than their full value, and if gratuities must be made once in fifteen or twenty years let them not be bestowed on the subjects of a foreign government nor upon a designated and favored class of men in our own country. It is but justice and good policy, as far as the nature of the case will admit, to confine our favors to our own fellow-citizens, and let each in his turn enjoy an opportunity to profit by our bounty. In the bearings of the act before me upon these points I find ample reasons why it should not become a law.

It has been urged as an argument in favor of rechartering the present bank that the calling in its loans will produce great embarrassment and distress. The time allowed to close its concerns is ample, and if it has been well managed its pressure will be light, and heavy only in case its management has been bad. If, therefore, it shall produce distress, the fault will be its own, and it would furnish a reason against renewing a power which has been so obviously abused. But will there ever be a time when this reason will be less powerful? To acknowledge its force is to admit that the bank ought to be perpetual, and as a consequence the present stockholders and those inheriting their rights as successors be established a privileged order, clothed both with great political power and enjoying immense pecuniary advantages from their connection with the Government.

The modifications of the existing charter proposed by this act are not such, in my view, as make it consistent with the rights of the States or the liberties of the people. The qualification of the right of the bank to hold real estate, the limitation of its power to establish branches, and the power reserved to Congress to forbid the circulation of small notes are restrictions comparatively of little value or importance. All the objectionable principles of the existing corporation, and most of its odious features, are retained without alleviation.

The fourth section provides "that the notes or bills of the said corporation, although the same be, on the faces thereof, respectively made payable at one place only, shall nevertheless be received by the said corporation at the bank or at any of the offices of discount and deposit thereof if tendered in liquidation or payment of any balance or balances due to said corporation or to such office of discount and deposit from any other incorporated bank." This provision secures to the State banks a legal privilege in the Bank of the United States which is withheld from all private citizens. If a State bank in Philadelphia owe the Bank of the United States and have notes issued by the St. Louis branch, it can pay the debt with those notes, but if a merchant, mechanic, or other private citizen be in like circumstances he can not by law pay his debt with those notes, but must sell them at a discount or send them to St. Louis to be cashed. This boon conceded to the State banks, though not unjust in itself, is most odious because it does not measure out equal justice to the high and the low, the rich and the poor. To the extent of its practical effect it is a bond of union among the banking establishments of the nation, erecting them into an interest separate from that of the people, and its necessary tendency is to unite the Bank of the United States and the State banks in any measure which may be thought conducive to their common interest.

The ninth section of the act recognizes principles of worse tendency than any provision of the present charter.

It enacts that "the cashier of the bank shall annually report to the Secretary of the Treasury the names of all stockholders who are not resident citizens of the United States, and on the application of the treasurer of any State shall make out and transmit to such treasurer a list of stockholders residing in or citizens of such State, with the amount of stock owned by each." Although this provision, taken in connection with a decision of the Supreme Court, surrenders, by its silence, the right of the States to tax the banking institutions created by this corporation under the name of branches throughout the Union, it is evidently intended to be construed as a concession of their right to tax that portion of the stock which may be held by their own citizens and residents. In this light, if the act becomes a law, it will be understood by the States, who will probably proceed to levy a tax equal to that paid upon the stock of banks incorporated by themselves. In some States that tax is now 1 per cent, either on the capital or on the shares, and that may be assumed as the amount which all citizen or resident stockholders would be taxed under the operation of this act. As it is only the stock *held* in the States and not that *employed* within them which would be subject to taxation, and as the names of foreign stockholders are not to be reported to the treasurers of the States, it is obvious that the stock held by them will be exempt from this burden. Their annual profits will therefore be 1 per cent more than the citizen stockholders, and as the annual dividends of the bank may be safely estimated at 7 per cent, the stock will be worth 10 or 15 per cent more to foreigners than to citizens of the United States. To appreciate the effects which this state of things will produce, we must take a brief review of the operations and present condition of the Bank of the United States.

By documents submitted to Congress at the present session it appears that on the 1st of January, 1832, of the twenty-eight millions of private stock in the corporation, $8,405,500 were held by foreigners, mostly of Great Britain. The amount of stock held in the nine Western and Southwestern States is $140,200, and in the four Southern States is $5,623,100, and in the Middle and Eastern

States is about $13,522,000. The profits of the bank in 1831, as shown in a statement to Congress, were about $3,455,598; of this there accrued in the nine Western States about $1,640,048; in the four Southern States about $352,507, and in the Middle and Eastern States about $1,463,041. As little stock is held in the West, it is obvious that the debt of the people in that section to the bank is principally a debt to the Eastern and foreign stockholders; that the interest they pay upon it is carried into the Eastern States and into Europe, and that it is a burden upon their industry and a drain of their currency, which no country can bear without inconvenience and occasional distress. To meet this burden and equalize the exchange operations of the bank, the amount of specie drawn from those States through its branches within the last two years, as shown by its official reports, was about $6,000,000. More than half a million of this amount does not stop in the Eastern States, but passes on to Europe to pay the dividends of the foreign stockholders. In the principle of taxation recognized by this act the Western States find no adequate compensation for this perpetual burden on their industry and drain of their currency. The branch bank at Mobile made last year $95,140, yet under the provisions of this act the State of Alabama can raise no revenue from these profitable operations, because not a share of the stock is held by any of her citizens. Mississippi and Missouri are in the same condition in relation to the branches at Natchez and St. Louis, and such, in a greater or less degree, is the condition of every Western State. The tendency of the plan of taxation which this act proposes will be to place the whole United States in the same relation to foreign countries which the Western States now bear to the Eastern. When by a tax on resident stockholders the stock of this bank is made worth 10 or 15 per cent more to foreigners than to residents, most of it will inevitably leave the country.

Thus will this provision in its practical effect deprive the Eastern as well as the Southern and Western States of the means of raising a revenue from the extension of business and great profits of this institution. It will make the American people debtors to aliens in nearly the whole amount due to this bank, and send across the Atlantic from two to five millions of specie every year to pay the bank dividends.

In another of its bearings this provision is fraught with danger. Of the twenty-five directors of this bank five are chosen by the Government and twenty by the citizen stockholders. From all voice in these elections the foreign stockholders are excluded by the charter. In proportion, therefore, as the stock is transferred to foreign holders the extent of suffrage in the choice of directors is curtailed. Already is almost a third of the stock in foreign hands and not represented in elections. It is constantly passing out of the country, and this act will accelerate its departure. The entire control of the institution would necessarily fall into the hands of a few citizen stockholders, and the ease with which the object would be accomplished would be a temptation to designing men to secure that control in their own hands by monopolizing the remaining stock. There is danger that a president and directors would then be able to elect themselves from year to year, and without responsibility or control manage the whole concerns of the bank during the existence of its charter.

It is easy to conceive that great evils to our country and its institutions might flow from such a concentration of power in the hands of a few men irresponsible to the people.

Is there no danger to our liberty and independence in a bank that in its nature has so little to bind it to our country? The president of the bank has told us that most of the State banks exist by its forbearance. Should its influence become concentered, as it may under the operation of such an act as this, in the hands of a self-elected directory whose interests are identified with those of the foreign stockholders, will there not be cause to tremble for the purity of our elections in peace and for the independence of our country in war? Their power would be great whenever they might choose to exert it; but if this monopoly were regularly renewed every fifteen or twenty years on terms proposed by themselves, they might seldom in peace put forth their strength to influence elections or control the affairs of the nation. But if any private citizen or public functionary should interpose to curtail its powers or prevent a renewal of its privileges, it can not be doubted that he would be made to feel its influence.

Should the stock of the bank principally pass into the hands of the subjects of a foreign country, and we should unfortunately become involved in a war with that country, what would be our condition? Of the course which would be pursued by a bank almost wholly owned by the subjects of a foreign power, and managed by those whose interests, if not affections, would run in the same direction there can be no doubt. All its operations within would be in aid of the hostile fleets and armies without. Controlling our currency, receiving our public moneys, and holding thousands of our citizens in dependence, it would be more formidable and dangerous than the naval and military power of the enemy.

If we must have a bank with private stockholders, every consideration of sound policy and every impulse of American feeling admonishes that it should be *purely American*. Its stockholders should be composed exclusively of our own citizens, who at least ought to be friendly to our Government and willing to support it in times of difficulty and danger. So abundant is domestic capital that competition in subscribing for the stock of local banks has recently led almost to riots. To a bank exclusively of American stockholders, possessing the powers and privileges granted by this act, subscriptions for $200,000,000 could be readily obtained. Instead of sending abroad the stock of the bank in which the Government must deposit its funds and on which it must rely to sustain its credit in times of emergency, it would rather seem to be expedient to prohibit its sale to aliens under penalty of absolute forfeiture.

It is maintained by the advocates of the bank that its constitutionality in all its features ought to be considered as settled by precedent and by the decision of the Supreme Court. To this conclusion I can not assent. Mere precedent is a dangerous source of authority, and should not be regarded as deciding questions of constitutional power except where the acquiescence of the people and the States can be considered as well settled. So far from this being the case on this subject, an argument against the bank might be based on precedent. One Congress, in 1791, decided in favor of a bank; another, in 1811, decided against it. One Congress, in 1815, decided against a bank; another, in 1816, decided in its favor. Prior to the present Congress, therefore, the precedents drawn from that source were equal. If we resort to the States, the expressions of legislative, judicial, and executive opinions against the bank have been probably to those in its favor as 4 to 1. There is nothing in precedent, therefore, which, if its authority were admitted, ought to weigh in favor of the act before me.

If the opinion of the Supreme Court covered the whole ground of this act, it ought not to control the coordinate authorities of this Government. The Congress, the Executive, and the Court must each for itself be guided by its own opinion of the Constitution. Each public officer who takes an oath to support the Constitution swears that he will support it as he understands it, and not as it is understood by others. It is as much the duty of the House of Representatives, of the Senate, and of the President to decide upon the constitutionality of any bill or resolution which may be presented to them for passage or approval as it is of the supreme judges when it may be brought before them for judicial decision. The opinion of the judges has no more authority over Congress than the opinion of Congress has over the judges, and on that point the President is independent of both. The authority of the Supreme Court must not, therefore, be permitted to control the Congress or the Executive when acting in their legislative capacities, but to have only such influence as the force of their reasoning may deserve.

But in the case relied upon the Supreme Court have not decided that all the features of this corporation are compatible with the Constitution. It is true that the court have said that the law incorporating the bank is a constitutional exercise of power by Congress; but taking into view the whole opinion of the court and the reasoning by which they have come to that conclusion, I understand them to have decided that inasmuch as a bank is an appropriate means for carrying into effect the enumerated powers of the General Government, therefore the law incorporating it is in accordance with that provision of the Constitution which declares that Congress shall have power "to make all laws which shall be necessary and proper for carrying those powers into execution." Having satisfied themselves that the word *"necessary"* in the Constitution means *"needful," "requisite," "essential," "conducive to,"* and that "a bank" is a convenient, a useful, and essential instrument in the prosecution of the Government's "fiscal operations," they conclude that to "use one must be within the discretion of Congress" and that "the act to incorporate the Bank of the United States is a law made in pursuance of the Constitution;" "but," say they, *"where the law is not prohibited and is really calculated to effect any of the objects intrusted to the Government, to undertake here to inquire into the degree of its necessity would be to pass the line which circumscribes the judicial department and to tread on legislative ground."*

The principle here affirmed is that the "degree of its necessity," involving all the details of a banking institution, is a question exclusively for legislative consideration. A bank is constitutional, but it is the province of the Legislature to determine whether this or that particular power, privilege, or exemption is "necessary and proper" to enable the bank to discharge its duties to the Government, and from their decision there is no appeal to the courts of justice. Under the decision of the Supreme Court, therefore, it is the exclusive prov-

ince of Congress and the President to decide whether the particular features
of this act are *necessary* and *proper* in order to enable the bank to perform
conveniently and efficiently the public duties assigned to it as a fiscal agent,
and therefore constitutional, or *unnecessary* and *improper*, and therefore unconstitutional.

Without commenting on the general principle affirmed by the Supreme
Court, let us examine the details of this act in accordance with the rule of
legislative action which they have laid down. It will be found that many of
the powers and privileges conferred on it can not be supposed necessary for
the purpose for which it is proposed to be created, and are not, therefore,
means necessary to attain the end in view, and consequently not justified by
the Constitution. . . .

On two subjects only does the Constitution recognize in Congress the power
to grant exclusive privileges or monopolies. It declares that "Congress shall
have power to promote the progress of science and useful arts by securing for
limited times to authors and inventors the exclusive right to their respective
writings and discoveries." Out of this express delegation of power have grown
our laws of patents and copyrights. As the Constitution expressly delegates to
Congress the power to grant exclusive privileges in these cases as the means
of executing the substantive power "to promote the progress of science and
useful arts," it is consistent with the fair rules of construction to conclude that
such a power was not intended to be granted as a means of accomplishing any
other end. On every other subject which comes within the scope of Congressional power there is an ever-living discretion in the use of proper means, which
can not be restricted or abolished without an amendment of the Constitution.
Every act of Congress, therefore, which attempts by grants of monopolies or
sale of exclusive privileges for a limited time, or a time without limit, to restrict or extinguish its own discretion in the choice of means to execute its
delegated powers is equivalent to a legislative amendment of the Constitution,
and palpably unconstitutional.

This act authorizes and encourages transfers of its stock to foreigners and
grants them an exemption from all State and national taxation. So far from
being *"necessary and proper"* that the bank should possess this power to make
it a safe and efficient agent of the Government in its fiscal operations, it is calculated to convert the Bank of the United States into a foreign bank, to im-
poverish our people in time of peace, to disseminate a foreign influence through
every section of the Republic, and in war to endanger our independence.

The several States reserved the power at the formation of the Constitution
to regulate and control titles and transfers of real property, and most, if not all,
of them have laws disqualifying aliens from acquiring or holding lands within
their limits. But this act, in disregard of the undoubted right of the States to
prescribe such disqualifications, gives to aliens stockholders in this bank an
interest and title, as members of the corporation, to all the real property it may
acquire within any of the States of this Union. This privilege granted to
aliens is not *"necessary"* to enable the bank to perform its public duties, nor in
any sense *"proper,"* because it is vitally subversive of the rights of the States. . . .

The Government is the only *"proper"* judge where its agents should reside and keep their offices, because it best knows where their presence will be *"neces-sary."* It can not, therefore, be *"necessary"* or *"proper"* to authorize the bank to locate branches where it pleases to perform the public service, without consult-ing the Government, and contrary to its will. The principle laid down by the Supreme Court concedes that Congress can not establish a bank for purposes of private speculation and gain, but only as a means of executing the delegated powers of the General Government. By the same principle a branch bank can not constitutionally be established for other than public purposes. The power which this act gives to establish two branches in any State, without the in-junction or request of the Government and for other than public purposes, is not *"necessary"* to the due *execution* of the powers delegated to Congress.

The bonus which is exacted from the bank is a confession upon the face of the act that the powers granted by it are greater than are *"necessary"* to its character of a fiscal agent. . . .

It is maintained by some that the bank is a means of executing the constitu-tional power "to coin money and regulate the value thereof." Congress have established a mint to coin money and passed laws to regulate the value thereof. The money so coined, with its value so regulated, and such foreign coins as Congress may adopt are the only currency known to the Constitution. But if they have other power to regulate the currency, it was conferred to be exercised by themselves, and not to be transferred to a corporation. If the bank be established for that purpose, with a charter unalterable without its consent, Congress have parted with their power for a term of years, during which the Constitution is a dead letter. It is neither necessary nor proper to transfer its legislative power to such a bank, and therefore unconstitutional.

By its silence, considered in connection with the decision of the Supreme Court in the case of McCulloch against the State of Maryland, this act takes from the States the power to tax a portion of the banking business carried on within their limits, in subversion of one of the strongest barriers which secured them against Federal encroachments. Banking, like farming, manufacturing, or any other occupation or profession, is *a business,* the right to follow which is not originally derived from the laws. . . . These corporations, unless there be an exemption in their charter, are, like private bankers and banking com-panies, subject to State taxation. The manner in which these taxes shall be laid depends wholly on legislative discretion. It may be upon the bank, upon the stock, upon the profits, or in any other mode which the sovereign power shall will.

Upon the formation of the Constitution the States guarded their taxing power with peculiar jealousy. They surrendered it only as it regards imports and exports. In relation to every other object within their jurisdiction, whether persons, property, business, or professions, it was secured in as ample a manner as it was before possessed. All persons, though United States officers, are liable to a poll tax by the States within which they reside. The lands of the United States are liable to the usual land tax, except in the new States, from whom agreements that they will not tax unsold lands are exacted when they are admitted into the Union. Horses, wagons, any beasts or vehicles, tools, or property belonging to private citizens, though employed in the service of the

United States, are subject to State taxation. Every private business, whether carried on by an officer of the General Government or not, whether it be mixed with public concerns or not, even if it be carried on by the Government of the United States itself, separately or in partnership, falls within the scope of the taxing power of the State. Nothing comes more fully within it than banks and the business of banking, by whomsoever instituted and carried on. Over this whole subject-matter it is just as absolute, unlimited, and uncontrollable as if the Constitution had never been adopted, because in the formation of that instrument it was reserved without qualification.

The principle is conceded that the States can not rightfully tax the operations of the General Government. They can not tax the money of the Government deposited in the State banks, nor the agency of those banks in remitting it; but will any man maintain that their mere selection to perform this public service for the General Government would exempt the State banks and their ordinary business from State taxation? Had the United States, instead of establishing a bank at Philadelphia, employed a private banker to keep and transmit their funds, would it have deprived Pennsylvania of the right to tax his bank and his usual banking operations? It will not be pretended. . . .

It can not be *necessary* to the character of the bank as a fiscal agent of the Government that its private business should be exempted from that taxation to which all the State banks are liable, nor can I conceive it *"proper"* that the substantive and most essential powers reserved by the States shall be thus attacked and annihilated as a means of executing the powers delegated to the General Government. It may be safely assumed that none of those sages who had an agency in forming or adopting our Constitution ever imagined that any portion of the taxing power of the States not prohibited to them nor delegated to Congress was to be swept away and annihilated as a means of executing certain powers delegated to Congress.

If our power over means is so absolute that the Supreme Court will not call in question the constitutionality of an act of Congress the subject of which "is not prohibited, and is really calculated to effect any of the objects intrusted to the Government," although, as in the case before me, it takes away powers expressly granted to Congress and rights scrupulously reserved to the States, it becomes us to proceed in our legislation with the utmost caution. Though not directly, our own powers and the rights of the States may be indirectly legislated away in the use of means to execute substantive powers. We may not enact that Congress shall not have the power of exclusive legislation over the District of Columbia, but we may pledge the faith of the United States that as a means of executing other powers it shall not be exercised for twenty years or forever. We may not pass an act prohibiting the States to tax the banking business carried on within their limits, but we may, as a means of executing our powers over other objects, place that business in the hands of our agents and then declare it exempt from State taxation in their hands. Thus may our own powers and the rights of the States, which we can not directly curtail or invade, be frittered away and extinguished in the use of means employed by us to execute other powers. That a bank of the United States, competent to all the duties which may be required by the Government, might be so organized as not to infringe on our own delegated powers or the reserved rights of the States I do not entertain a doubt. Had the Executive been called upon to furnish the project of such an institution, the duty would have been cheerfully performed. In the absence of such a call it was obviously proper that he should confine himself to pointing out those prominent features in the act presented which in his opinion make it incompatible with the Constitution and sound policy. A general discussion will now take place, eliciting new light and settling important principles; and a new Congress, elected in the midst of such discussion, and furnishing an equal representation of the people according to the last census, will bear to the Capitol the verdict of public opinion, and, I doubt not, bring this important question to a satisfactory result.

Under such circumstances the bank comes forward and asks a renewal of its charter for a term of fifteen years upon conditions which not only operate as a gratuity to the stockholders of many millions of dollars, but will sanction any abuses and legalize any encroachments.

Suspicions are entertained and charges are made of gross abuse and violation of its charter. An investigation unwillingly conceded and so restricted in time as necessarily to make it incomplete and unsatisfactory discloses enough to excite suspicion and alarm. In the practices of the principal bank partially unveiled, in the absence of important witnesses, and in numerous charges confidently made and as yet wholly uninvestigated there was enough to induce a majority of the committee of investigation—a committee which was selected from the most able and honorable members of the House of Representatives—to recommend a suspension of further action upon the bill and a prosecution of the inquiry. As the charter had yet four years to run, and as a renewal now was not necessary to the successful prosecution of its business, it was to have been expected that the bank itself, conscious of its purity and proud of its character, would have withdrawn its application for the present, and demanded the severest scrutiny into all its transactions. In their declining to do so there seems to be an additional reason why the functionaries of the Government should proceed with less haste and more caution in the renewal of their monopoly.

The bank is professedly established as an agent of the executive branch of the Government, and its constitutionality is maintained on that ground. Neither upon the propriety of present action nor upon the provisions of this act was the Executive consulted. It has had no opportunity to say that it neither needs nor wants an agent clothed with such powers and favored by such exemptions. There is nothing in its legitimate functions which makes it necessary or proper. Whatever interest or influence, whether public or private, has given birth to this act, it can not be found either in the wishes or necessities of the executive department, by which present action is deemed premature and the power conferred upon its agent not only unnecessary, but dangerous to the Government and country.

It is to be regretted that the rich and powerful too often bend the acts of government to their selfish purposes. Distinctions in society will always exist under every just government. Equality of talents, of education, or of wealth can not be produced by human institutions. In the full enjoyment of the gifts of Heaven and the fruits of superior industry, economy, and virtue, every man is equally entitled to protection by law; but when the laws undertake to add to these natural and just advantages artificial distinctions, to grant titles, gratuities, and exclusive privileges, to make the rich richer and the potent more powerful, the humble members of society—the farmers, mechanics, and laborers —who have neither the time nor the means of securing like favors to themselves, have a right to complain of the injustice of their Government. There are no necessary evils in government. Its evils exist only in its abuses. If it would confine itself to equal protection, and, as Heaven does its rains, shower its favors alike on the high and the low, the rich and the poor, it would be an unqualified blessing. In the act before me there seems to be a wide and unnecessary departure from these just principles.

Nor is our Government to be maintained or our Union preserved by invasions of the rights and powers of the several States. In thus attempting to make our General Government strong we make it weak. Its true strength consists in leaving individuals and States as much as possible to themselves—in making itself felt, not in its power, but in its beneficence; not in its control, but in its protection; not in binding the States more closely to the center, but leaving each to move unobstructed in its proper orbit.

Experience should teach us wisdom. Most of the difficulties our Government now encounters and most of the dangers which impend over our Union have sprung from an abandonment of the legitimate objects of Government by our national legislation, and the adoption of such principles as are embodied in this act. Many of our rich men have not been content with equal protection and equal benefits, but have besought us to make them richer by act of Congress. By attempting to gratify their desires we have in the results of our legislation arrayed section against section, interest against interest, and man against man, in a fearful commotion which threatens to shake the foundations of our Union. It is time to pause in our career to review our principles, and if possible revive that devoted patriotism and spirit of compromise which distinguished the sages of the Revolution and the fathers of our Union. If we can not at once, in justice to interests vested under improvident legislation, make our Government what it ought to be, we can at least take a stand against all new grants of monopolies and exclusive privileges, against any prostitution of our Government to the advancement of the few at the expense of the many, and in favor of compromise and gradual reform in our code of laws and system of political economy.

I have now done my duty to my country. If sustained by my fellow-citizens, I shall be grateful and happy; if not, I shall find in the motives which impel me ample grounds for contentment and peace. In the difficulties which surround us and the dangers which threaten our institutions there is cause for neither dismay nor alarm. For relief and deliverance let us firmly rely on that kind Providence which I am sure watches with peculiar care over the destinies of our Republic, and on the intelligence and wisdom of our countrymen. Through *His* abundant goodness and *their* patriotic devotion our liberty and Union will be preserved.

7] Webster Replies to the Veto Message

On the following day, the eloquent orator from Massachusetts, the implacable foe of President Jackson, rose in the Senate to deliver a hastily prepared reply to the veto message. In defending the Bank, Webster added
little of substance to arguments made earlier; but in his final peroration he
emphasized a point which was to be, like the Bank itself, a major issue in
the coming Presidential campaign.*

. . . WHEN THE message denies, as it does, the authority of the Supreme Court
to decide on constitutional questions, it effects, so far as the opinion of the President and his authority can effect it, a complete change in our government. It
does two things, first, it converts constitutional limitations of power into mere
matters of opinion, and then it strikes the judicial department, as an efficient
department, out of our system. But the message by no means stops even at
this point. Having denied to Congress the authority of judging what powers
may be constitutionally conferred on a bank, and having erected the judgment
of the President himself into a standard by which to try the constitutional
character of such powers, and having denounced the authority of the Supreme
Court to decide finally on constitutional questions, the message proceeds to
claim for the President, not the power of approval, but the primary power,
the power of originating laws. The President informs Congress, that *he* would
have sent them such a charter, if it had been properly asked for, as they ought
to confer. He very plainly intimates, that, in his opinion, the establishment
of all laws, of this nature at least, belongs to the functions of the executive
government; and that Congress ought to have waited for the manifestation of
the executive will, before it presumed to touch the subject. Such, Mr. President,
stripped of their disguises, are the real pretences set up in behalf of the executive power in this most extraordinary paper.

Mr. President, we have arrived at a new epoch. We are entering on experi-
ments, with the government and the Constitution of the country, hitherto untried, and of fearful and appalling aspect. This message calls us to the contemplation of a future which little resembles the past. Its principles are at war
with all that public opinion has sustained, and all which the experience of the
government has sanctioned. It denies first principles; it contradicts truths,
heretofore received as indisputable. It denies to the judiciary the interpretation
of law, and claims to divide with Congress the power of originating statutes.
It extends the grasp of executive pretension over every power of the government. But this is not all. It presents the chief magistrate of the Union in the
attitude of arguing away the powers of that government over which he has
been chosen to preside; and adopting for this purpose modes of reasoning
which, even under the influence of all proper feeling towards high official station, it is difficult to regard as respectable. It appeals to every prejudice which
may betray men into a mistaken view of their own interests, and to every

* WEBSTER REPLIES TO THE VETO MESSAGE: Speech in the Senate, July 11, 1832. From
Edward Everett, ed., *The Works of Daniel Webster* (Boston, 1851), III, 446–47.

passion which may lead them to disobey the impulses of their understanding. It urges all the specious topics of State rights and national encroachment against that which a great majority of the States have affirmed to be rightful, and in which all of them have acquiesced. It sows, in an unsparing manner, the seeds of jealousy and ill-will against that government of which its author is the official head. It raises a cry, that liberty is in danger, at the very moment when it puts forth claims to powers heretofore unknown and unheard of. It affects alarm for the public freedom, when nothing endangers that freedom so much as its own unparalleled pretences. This, even, is not all. It manifestly seeks to inflame the poor against the rich; it wantonly attacks whole classes of the people, for the purpose of turning against them the prejudices and the resentments of other classes. It is a state paper which finds no topic too exciting for its use, no passion too inflammable for its address and its solicitation.

Such is this message. It remains now for the people of the United States to choose between the principles here avowed and their government. These cannot subsist together. The one or the other must be rejected. If the sentiments of the message shall receive general approbation, the Constitution will have perished even earlier than the moment which its enemies originally allowed for the termination of its existence. It will not have survived to its fiftieth year.

8] Clay Condemns the Removal of Deposits

The people chose Jackson. Encouraged by his victory, the President decided to speed the separation of bank from state by removing the government deposits, even though he had to get rid of two Secretaries of the Treasury before he found one, Roger B. Taney, who would carry out his request. After Congress met in the following December, 1833, Henry Clay introduced on the 26th of that month resolutions that condemned both the Secretary of the Treasury and the President. In concluding his arguments for these resolutions, Clay defined the views of the emerging Whig party on the Bank and on the President. The basis for Clay's condemnation of the President was that Jackson, by his arbitrary dismissal of Duane and his appointment of a Secretary who would carry out his will, had violated both the Constitution and a statute. Since the Constitution gives the power of the purse to Congress, Clay maintained that the Secretary of the Treasury is responsible to Congress and not to the President. The argument was specious, as Jackson would later point out. Although the law creating the Treasury Department did name it an "Executive Department," and although the Secretary did report to Congress, not the President, every Secretary since Washington's day had been appointed by the President. Moreover, the law specifically recognized the President's power to remove the Secretary from office, and the Bank's charter permitted the Secretary to remove deposits at his own discretion.*

. . . WE HAVE, Mr. President, a most wonderful financier at the head of our treasury department. He sits quietly by in the cabinet, and witnesses the contests between his colleague and the President; sees the conflict in the mind

* CLAY CONDEMNS THE REMOVAL OF DEPOSITS: Speech in the Senate, December 26, 1833. From James B. Swain, *The Life and Speeches of Henry Clay* (New York, 1842), II, 228–30.

of that colleague between his personal attachment to the President on the one hand, and his solemn duty to the public on the other. Beholds the triumph of conscientious obligation; contemplates the noble spectacle of an honest man, preferring to surrender an exalted office with all its honors and emoluments, rather than betray the interests of the people. Sees the contemptuous and insulting expulsion of that colleague from office; and then coolly enters the vacated place, without the slightest sympathy or the smallest emotion. He was installed on the 23d of September, and by the 26th, the brief period of three days, he discovers that the government of the United States had been wrong from its origin; that every one of his predecessors from Hamilton down including Gallatin (who, whatever I said of him on a former occasion, and that I do not mean to retract, possessed more practical knowledge of currency, banks, and finance, than any man I have ever met in the public councils,) Dallas, and Crawford[1] had been mistaken about both the expediency and constitutionality of the bank, that every chief magistrate, prior to him whose patronage he enjoyed, had been wrong; that the supreme court of the United States, and the people of the United States, during the thirty-seven years that they had acquiesced in or recognised the usefulness of a bank, were all wrong. And opposing his single opinion to their united judgments, he dismisses the bank, scatters the public money, and undertakes to regulate and purify the public morals, the public press, and popular elections.

If we examine the operations of this modern Turgot, in their financial bearing merely, we shall find still less for approbation.

1. He withdraws the public moneys, where, by his own deliberate admission, they were perfectly safe, with a bank of thirty-five millions of capital, and ten millions of specie, and places them at great hazard with banks of comparatively small capital, and but little specie, of which the Metropolis bank is an example.

2. He withdraws them from a bank created by, and over which the federal government had ample control, and puts them in other banks, created by different governments, and over which it has no control.

3. He withdraws them from a bank in which the American people as a stockholder, were drawing their fair proportion of interest accruing on loans, of which those deposites formed the basis, and puts them where the people of the United States draw no interest.

4. From a bank which has paid a bonus of a million and a half, which the people of the United States may be now liable to refund, and puts them in banks which have paid to the American people no bonus.

5. Depreciates the value of stock in a bank, where the general government holds seven millions, and advances that of banks in whose stock it does not

---

1 William H. Crawford, as Secretary of the Treasury under Madison and Monroe, actively supported, as did Dallas, the chartering of the Second Bank in 1816.

hold a dollar; and whose aggregate capital does not probably much exceed that very seven millions. And, finally,

6. He dismisses a bank whose paper circulates, in the greatest credit throughout the Union and in foreign countries, and engages in the public service banks whose paper has but a limited and local circulation in their "immediate vicinities."

These are immediate and inevitable results. How much that large and longstanding item of unavailable funds, annually reported to Congress, will be swelled and extended, remains to be developed by time.

And now, Mr. President, what, under all these circumstances, is it our duty to do? Is there a senator, who can hesitate to affirm, in the language of the resolution, that the President has assumed a dangerous power over the treasury of the United States not granted to him by the constitution and the laws; and that the reasons assigned for the act, by the Secretary of the treasury, are insufficient and unsatisfactory?

The eyes and the hopes of the American people are anxiously turned to Congress. They feel that they have been deceived and insulted; their confidence abused; their interests betrayed; and their liberties in danger. They see a rapid and alarming concentration of all power in one man's hands. They see that, by the exercise of the positive authority of the executive, and his negative power exerted over Congress, the will of one man alone prevails, and governs the Republic. The question is no longer what laws will Congress pass, but what will the executive not veto? The President, and not Congress, is addressed for legislative action. We have seen a corporation, charged with the execution of a great national work, dismiss an experienced, faithful and zealous President, afterwards testify to his ability by a voluntary resolution, and reward his extraordinary services by a large gratuity, and appoint in his place an executive favorite, totally inexperienced and incompetent, to propitiate the President. We behold the usual incidents of approaching tyranny. The land is filled with spies and informers; and detraction and denunciation are the orders of the day. People, especially official incumbents in this place, no longer dare speak in the fearless tones of manly freemen, but in the cautious whispers of trembling slaves. The premonitory symptoms of despotism are upon us; and if Congress do not apply an instantaneous and effective remedy, the fatal collapse will soon come on, and we shall die—ignobly die! base, mean, and abject slaves —the scorn and contempt of mankind—unpitied, unwept, unmourned!

9] The Biddle Contraction

While Clay attacked in Congress, Biddle began action on the economic front. Because of the withdrawal of the government deposits, Biddle had to contract credit and notes and call in loans. But as a letter he wrote to

William Appleton, president of the Bank's Boston branch, on January 27, 1834, suggests, his intentions were more than just to carry out sound banking practices.*

(private)   B. U S

Jany 27th 1834

DEAR SIR

. . . My own view of the whole matter is simply this. The projectives of this last assault on the Bank regret, and are alarmed at it—but the ties of party allegiance can only be broken by the actual conviction of existing distress in the community. Nothing but the evidence of suffering abroad will produce any effect in Congress. If the Bank remains strong & quiet, the course of events will save the Bank & save all the institutions of the country which are now in great peril. But if, from too great a sensitiveness—from the fear of offending or the desire of conciliating, the Bank permits itself to be frightened or coaxed into any relaxation of its present measures, the relief will itself be cited as evidence that the measures of the Gov^t. are not injurious or oppressive, and the Bank will inevitably be prostrated. Our only safety is in pursuing a steady course of firm restriction—and I have no doubt that such a course will ultimately lead to restoration of the currency and the recharter of the Bank. How soon this will take place, it is of course difficult to conjecture—but I have little apprehension as to the ultimate result.

10] Jackson Answers Clay

Clay's censuring resolutions passed the Senate on March 28, 1834. On April 15 Jackson sent a "protest" to the Senate asserting he had been accused of an impeachable offense but had not been allowed an opportunity to defend himself. In this defense, written with the aid of Amos Kendall and Benjamin Butler, the Attorney-General, Jackson presents a persuasive case for a strong and independent Executive. In January, 1837, through the continuing efforts of Senator Benton, Clay's resolutions were finally expunged from the Senate Journal.†

DURING the last year the approaching termination, according to the provisions of its charter and the solemn decision of the American people, of the Bank of the United States made it expedient, and its exposed abuses and corruptions made it, in my opinion, the duty of the Secretary of the Treasury, to place the moneys of the United States in other depositories. The Secretary did not concur in that opinion, and declined giving the necessary order and direction. . . .

---

* THE BIDDLE CONTRACTION: Nicholas Biddle to William Appleton, January 27, 1834. From Reginald C. McGrane, ed., *The Correspondence of Nicholas Biddle* (New York, 1919), pp. 219–20. Reprinted by permission of Reginald C. McGrane.

† JACKSON ANSWERS CLAY: Message to Congress, April 15, 1834. From James D. Richardson, ed., *Messages and Papers of the Presidents* (Washington, 1896–99), III, 85–87.

His place I supplied by one whose opinions were well known to me, and whose frank expression of them in another situation and generous sacrifices of interest and feeling when unexpectedly called to the station he now occupies ought forever to have shielded his motives from suspicion and his character from reproach. In accordance with the views long before expressed by him he proceeded, with my sanction, to make arrangements for depositing the moneys of the United States in other safe institutions.

The resolution of the Senate as originally framed and as passed, if it refers to these acts, presupposes a right in that body to interfere with this exercise of Executive power. If the principle be once admitted, it is not difficult to perceive where it may end. If by a mere denunciation like this resolution the President should ever be induced to act in a matter of official duty contrary to the honest convictions of his own mind in compliance with the wishes of the Senate, the constitutional independence of the executive department would be as effectually destroyed and its power as effectually transferred to the Senate as if that end had been accomplished by an amendment of the Constitution. But if the Senate have a right to interfere with the Executive powers, they have also the right to make that interference effective, and if the assertion of the power implied in the resolution be silently acquiesced in we may reasonably apprehend that it will be followed at some future day by an attempt at actual enforcement. The Senate may refuse, except on the condition that he will surrender his opinions to theirs and obey their will, to perform their own constitutional functions, to pass the necessary laws, to sanction appropriations proposed by the House of Representatives, and to confirm proper nominations made by the President. It has already been maintained (and it is not conceivable that the resolution of the Senate can be based on any other principle) that the Secretary of the Treasury is the officer of Congress and independent of the President; that the President has no right to control him, and consequently none to remove him. With the same propriety and on similar grounds may the Secretary of State, the Secretaries of War and the Navy, and the Postmaster-General each in succession be declared independent of the President, the subordinates of Congress, and removable only with the concurrence of the Senate. Followed to its consequences, this principle will be found effectually to destroy one coordinate department of the Government, to concentrate in the hands of the Senate the whole executive power, and to leave the President as powerless as he would be useless—the shadow of authority after the substance had departed.

The time and the occasion which have called forth the resolution of the Senate seem to impose upon me an additional obligation not to pass it over in silence. Nearly forty-five years had the President exercised, without a question as to his rightful authority, those powers for the recent assumption of which he is now denounced. The vicissitudes of peace and war had attended our Government; violent parties, watchful to take advantage of any seeming usurpation on the part of the Executive, had distracted our councils; frequent removals, or forced resignations in every sense tantamount to removals, had been made of the Secretary and other officers of the Treasury, and yet in no one instance is it known that any man, whether patriot or partisan, had raised his voice against it as a violation of the Constitution. The expediency and justice of such changes in reference to public officers of all grades have frequently been the topic of discussion, but the constitutional right of the President to appoint, control, and remove the head of the Treasury as well as all other Departments seems to have been universally conceded. And what is the occasion upon which other principles have been first officially asserted? The Bank of the United States, a great moneyed monopoly, had attempted to obtain a renewal of its charter by controlling the elections of the people and the action of the Government. The use of its corporate funds and power in that attempt was fully disclosed, and it was made known to the President that the corporation was putting in train the same course of measures, with the view of making another vigorous effort, through an interference in the elections of the people, to control public opinion and force the Government to yield to its demands. This, with its corruption of the press, its violation of its charter, its exclusion of the Government directors from its proceedings, its neglect of duty and arrogant pretensions, made it, in the opinion of the President, incompatible with the public interest and the safety of our institutions that it should be longer employed as the fiscal agent of the Treasury. A Secretary of the Treasury appointed in the recess of the Senate, who had not been confirmed by that body, and whom the President might or might not at his pleasure nominate to them, refused to do what his superior in the executive department considered the most imperative of his duties, and became in fact, however innocent his motives, the protector of the bank. And on this occasion it is discovered for the first time that those who framed the Constitution misunderstood it; that the First Congress and all its successors have been under a delusion; that the practice of near forty-five years is but a continued usurpation; that the Secretary of the Treasury is not responsible to the President, and that to remove him is a violation of the Constitution and laws for which the President deserves to stand forever dishonored on the journals of the Senate. . . .

11] "The One Party Is for a Popular Government; the Other for an Aristocracy"

By the fall of 1834 the Bank War was over. Party and class lines had become more clearly defined. The following editorial by William Leggett, an editor of the New York *Evening Post* and spokesman for the more radical Democrats, particularly New York workingmen, suggests the sharpening lines. It also indicates the ideological as well as constitutional basis of the Democratic position.*

SINCE THE organization of the Government of the United States the people of this country have been divided into two great parties. One of these parties

* "THE ONE PARTY IS FOR A POPULAR GOVERNMENT; THE OTHER FOR AN ARISTOCRACY": William Leggett, "The Division of Parties." From the New York *Evening Post* (November 4, 1834).

has undergone various changes of name; the other has continued steadfast alike to its appellation and to its principles and is now, as it was at first, the *Democracy*. Both parties have ever contended for the same opposite ends which originally caused the division, whatever may have been, at different times, the particular means which furnished the immediate subject of dispute. The great object of the struggles of the Democracy has been to confine the action of the General Government within the limits marked out in the Constitution; the great object of the party opposed to the Democracy has ever been to overleap those boundaries and give to the General Government greater powers and a wider field for their exercise. The doctrine of the one party is that all power not expressly and clearly delegated to the General Government remains with the States and with the people; the doctrine of the other party is that the vigor and efficacy of the General Government should be strengthened by a free construction of its powers. The one party sees danger from the encroachments of the General Government; the other affects to see danger from the encroachments of the States.

This original line of separation between the two great political parties of the Republic, though it existed under the old Confederation and was distinctly marked in the controversy which preceded the formation and adoption of the present Constitution, was greatly widened and strengthened by the project of a National Bank, brought forward in 1791. This was the first great question which occurred under the new Constitution to test whether the provisions of that instrument were to be interpreted according to their strict and literal meaning; or whether they might be stretched to include objects and powers which had never been delegated to the General Government and which consequently still resided with the States as separate sovereignties. . . .

. . . The Bank question stands now on precisely the same footing that it originally did; it is now, as it was at first, a matter of controversy between the two great parties of this country, between parties as opposite as day and night, between parties which contend, one for the consolidation and enlargement of the powers of the General Government, and the other for strictly limiting that Government to the objects for which it was instituted and to the exercise of the means with which it was entrusted. The one party is for a popular government; the other for an aristocracy. The one party is composed, in a great measure, of the farmers, mechanics, laborers, and other producers of the middling and lower classes, according to the common gradation by the scale of wealth, and the other of the consumers, the rich, the proud, the privileged, of those who, if our Government were converted into an aristocracy, would become our dukes, lords, marquises, and baronets. The question is still disputed between these two parties; it is ever a new question; and whether the democracy or the aristocracy shall succeed in the present struggle, the fight will be renewed whenever the defeated party shall be again able to muster strength enough to take the field. The privilege of self-government is one which the people will never be permitted to enjoy unmolested. Power and wealth are continually stealing from the many to the few. There is a class continually gaining ground in the community who desire to monopolize the advantage of the Government, to hedge themselves round with exclusive privileges and elevate themselves at the expense of the great body of the people. These, in our society, are emphatically the aristocracy; and these, with all such as their means of persuasion or corruption or intimidation can move to act with them, constitute the party which are now struggling against the democracy for the perpetuation of an odious and dangerous moneyed institution.

Putting out of view, for the present, all other objections to the United States Bank,—that it is a monopoly, that it possesses enormous and overshadowing power, that it has been most corruptly managed, and that it is identified with political leaders to whom the people of the United States must ever be strongly opposed—the constitutional objection alone is an insurmountable objection to it.

The Government of the United States is a limited sovereignty. The powers which it may exercise are expressly enumerated in the Constitution. None not thus stated, or that are not "necessary and proper" to carry those which are stated into effect, can be allowed to be exercised by it. The power to establish a bank is not expressly given; neither is it incidental; since it cannot be shown to be "necessary" to carry the powers which are given, or any of them, into effect. That power cannot therefore be exercised without transcending the constitutional limits.

This is the *democratic* argument stated in its briefest form. The *aristocratic* argument in favor of the power is founded on the dangerous heresy that the Constitution says one thing and means another. That "necessary" does not mean *necessary* but simply *convenient*. By a mode of reasoning not looser than this it would be easy to prove that our Government ought to be changed into a monarchy, Henry Clay crowned king, and the opposition members of the Senate made peers of the realm; and power, place, and perquisites given to them and their heirs forever. . . .

And what, we ask, is the power against which the people not only of this country but of almost all Europe are called upon to array themselves, and the encroachment on their rights they are summoned to resist? It is not emphatically the power of monopoly and the encroachments of corporate privileges of every kind which the cupidity of the rich engenders to the injury of the poor?

It was to guard against the encroachments of power, the insatiate ambition of wealth, that this government was instituted by the people themselves. But the objects which call for the peculiar jealousy and watchfulness of the people are not now what they once were. The cautions of the early writers in favor of the liberties of mankind have in some measure become obsolete and inapplicable. We are menaced by our old enemies, avarice and ambition, under a new name and form. The tyrant is changed from a steel-clad feudal baron or a minor despot, at the head of thousands of ruffian followers, to a mighty civil gentleman who comes mincing and bowing to the people with a quill behind his ear, at the head of countless millions of magnificent *promises*. He promises to make everybody rich; he promises to pave cities with gold; and he promises to pay. In short he is made up of promises. He will do wonders such as never were seen or heard of, provided the people will only allow him to make his promises equal to silver and gold and human labor, and grant him the exclusive benefits of all the great blessings he intends to confer on them. He is the sly, selfish, grasping, and insatiable tyrant the people are now to guard against. A *concentrated money power;* a usurper in the disguise of a benefactor; an agent exercising privileges which his principal never possessed; an impostor who, while he affects to wear chains, is placed above those who are free; a chartered libertine that pretends to be manacled only that he may the more safely pick our pockets and lord it over our rights. This is the enemy we are now to encounter and overcome before we can expect to enjoy the substantial realities of freedom.

12] The Issue Evaluated

When Harriet Martineau, a perceptive, well-informed Englishwoman, began an extended visit to the United States in August, 1834, most Americans had come to hold as strong views on the Bank issue as Clay or Leggett. As an outsider, a humanitarian, and a writer versed in the best economic thinking of the day, Miss Martineau presented one of the few balanced contemporary evaluations of the Bank War and the questions it raised in a widely read book that she wrote on her return to England.*

THE FUNDAMENTAL difficulty of this great question, now one of the most prominent in the United States, is indicated by the fact that, while the practice of banking is essential to a manufacturing and commercial nation, a perfect system of banking remains to be discovered.

When it is remembered that the question of the Currency has never yet been practically mastered in the countries of the Old World; that in America it has fallen into the hands of a young and inexperienced people; that it is implicated with constitutional questions, and has to be reconciled with democratic principles, it will not be expected that a passing stranger will be able to present a very clear view of its present aspect, or any decided opinion upon difficulties which perplex the wisest heads in the country. The mere history of banking in the United States would fill more than a volume: and the speculations which arise out of it, a library. . . .

In countries differently governed from the United States, it appears as if it would be most reasonable either to have the currency made a national affair, transacted wholly by the government, on determined principles, or to leave banking entirely free. In neither case, probably, would the evils be so great as those which have happened under the mixture of the two systems. But in the United States, the committing the management of the currency to the general government is now wholly out of the question. Free banking will be the method, some time or other; but not yet. There is not yet knowledge enough; nor freedom enough of production and commerce to render such a policy safe. Meantime, various doctrines are afloat. Some persons are for no banking whatsoever: but mere money-lending by individuals. Some are for the abolition of paper-money, and the establishment of one public bank of deposit and transfer in each State. Some are for private banking only, with or without paper money. Some are for State incorporations, with no central bank. Others are for restoring the United States Bank.

* THE ISSUE EVALUATED: "The Currency." From Harriet Martineau, *Society in America* (London, 1837), II, 76–87.

No objections against banking and paper-money altogether will avail any-thing, while commerce is conducted on its present principles. It answers no practical purpose to object to any useful thing on the ground of its abuse: and while the commerce of the United States is daily on the increase, and the only check on its prosperity is the want of capital, there is no possibility of a return to the use of private money-lending and rouleaus. . . .

Private banking is, in the present state of affairs, necessary and inevitable; so that there is little use in arguments for or against it. Capital is grievously wanted, in all the commercial cities. There must be some place of resort for small amounts, and for foreign capital, whence money may issue to supply the need of commercial men. There must, in other words, be money stores; and, in the absence of others, private banks must serve the purpose. The amount of good or harm which, in the present state of things, they are able to do, depends mainly on the discretion or indiscretion of their customers; who, in common prudence, must look well whom they trust.

As for State incorporations, it cannot be said that they are absolutely neces-sary; though the arguments in favour of their expediency are very strong. . . . The incorporation of a bank is not always to be considered in the light of a monopoly; it may be the reverse. It may enable a number of individuals, by no means the most wealthy in the community, to compete, by an union of forces, with the most wealthy. Corporations may be multiplied, as occasion arises, and, by competition, give the public the benefit of the greatest possible amount of service done at the least cost.

Such are the leading arguments in favour of State Banks. The objections to them are in part applicable to faulty methods of incorporation, and not to the principle itself. The special exemption from liabilities to which individuals are subject; the imposing of such inhibitions elsewhere as render the affair a monopoly; the making responsibility a mere abstraction, are great, but perhaps avoidable evils. So are the methods by which charters have been obtained and renewed; the method of "log-rolling" bills through the legislature; and other such corruption.

An objection less easily disposed of is, that by the creation of any great moneyed power, means are afforded of controlling the fortunes of individuals, and of influencing the press and the political constituency. If these objections cannot be obviated, they are fatal to banking corporations. If, however, any means can be devised, either by causing a sufficient publicity of proceedings, or by granting charters for a short term, renewable on strict conditions, or by any other plan for establishing a true responsibility, of uniting the benefits of incorporated banks with republican principles, it seems as if it would be a great benefit to all parties in the community.

The difference of opinion which has made the most noise in the world, is about a National Bank. . . . This bank was believed to be wanted for another purpose;—to watch over and control the State Banks. . . .

Its purpose was presently answered. The local banks had, in three years, re-sumed cash payments. The management of the United States Bank, during the rest of its term, has been, upon the whole, prudent and moderate. That a power has not been abused is not, however, a reason for its continued exercise, if it be really unconstitutional. President Jackson thinks, and the majority thinks with him, that it is contrary to the spirit of the constitution, (as it is certainly unauthorised by its letter,) that any institution should have the power, unchecked for a long term of years, of affecting the affairs of individuals, from the further corners of Maine or Missouri, down to the shores of the Gulf of Mexico; of influencing elections; of biassing the press; and of acting strongly either with or against the administration. The majority considers, that if the United States Bank has great power for good, it has also great power for harm; and that the general government cannot be secure of working naturally in its limited functions, while this great power subsists, to be either its enemy or its ally.

This seems to be proved by the charges brought against the late Bank by President Jackson. Whether they are true or false, (and the gravest of them do not appear to have been substantiated,) they indicate that power is in the hands of a central institution, which no federal establishment ought to have, otherwise than by the express permission of the constitution.

As for President Jackson's mode of proceeding against the Bank—it is an affair of merely temporary interest, unless he should be found to have exceeded the authority conferred on him by his office. He does seem to have done so, in one particular, at least. His first declaration against the renewal of the charter, was honest and manly. His re-election, after having made this avowal, was a sufficient evidence of the desire of the majority to extinguish the Bank. It was, no doubt, in reliance on the will of the majority, thus indicated, that the President removed the deposits in a peculiarly high-handed manner; and also exercised the veto, when the two Houses had passed a bill to renew the charter of the United States Bank.

With the last of these measures, no one has any right to quarrel. He exercised a constitutional power, according to his long-declared convictions. His sudden removal of the deposits is not to be so easily justified.

The President has the power of removing his Secretaries from office, and of appointing others, whose appointment must be sanctioned by the Senate. The Secretaries of State are enjoined by law to execute such orders as shall be imposed on them by the President of the United States:—all the Secretaries but the Secretary of the Treasury. In his case, no such specification is made; obviously because it would not be wise to put the whole power of the Treasury into the hands of the President. President Jackson, however, contrived to obtain this power by using with adroitness his other power of removal from office. Mr. Duane was appointed Secretary of the Treasury on the 29th of May, 1833; his predecessor having been offered a higher office. It is known that the predecessor had given his opinion in the cabinet against removing the Treasury deposits from the Bank; and that Mr. Duane was an acknowledged enemy of the Bank. On the 3rd of June, the President opened to the new Secretary his scheme of removing the deposits. Mr. Duane was opposed to the act, as being a violation of the government contract with the Bank. He refused to sign the necessary order. While he was still in office, on the 20th of September, the intended removal of the deposits was announced in the government news paper. On the 23rd, Mr. Duane was dismissed from office; and Mr. Taney who had previously promised to sign the order, was installed in the office. On the 26th, the official order for the removal of the deposits was given. No plea o impending danger to the national funds, if such could have been substantiated, could justify so high-handed a deed as this. No such plea has been substantiated; and the act remains open to strong censure.

Just before the expiration of its charter, the United States Bank accepted a charter from the Legislature of Pennsylvania. It remains to be seen what effects will arise from the operation of the most powerful State Bank which has yet existed.

The problem now is to keep a sound currency, in the absence of an institution, believed to be unconstitutional, but hitherto found the only means of establishing order and safety in this most important branch of economy. Here is a deficiency, which cannot but be the cause of much evil and perplexity. It must be supplied, either by increased knowledge and improved philosophy and practice among the people, or by an amendment of the Constitution. Meanwhile, it is only time and energy lost to insist upon the return to a mere metallic currency. Society cannot be set back to a condition which could dispense with so great an improvement as paper-money, with all its abuses, undoubtedly is.

The singular order which last year emanated from the Treasury, compelling the payments for the public lands to be made in specie, will not have the effect of making the people in love with a metallic currency. If this measure is intended to be an obstacle to the purchase of large quantities of land, or virtually to raise the price,—these are affairs with which the Treasury has nothing to do. If it is intended merely to compel cash payments, as far as the administration has power to do so, it seems a pity that those who undertake to meddle with the currency should not know better what they are about. The scarcity of money in the eastern States has been well nigh ruinous, while large amounts of specie have been accumulated in the west, where they are not wanted. . . .

CONCLUSION

THE PROBLEM posed by Harriet Martineau proved to be an exceedingly difficult one. As a Pennsylvania bank without a network of branches and deprived of government deposits, Biddle's institution could no longer provide inexpensive and efficient short-term credit nor maintain control of state bank issues. The state banks, their restraints struck off, expanded their note issues with happy abandon. The government deposits which many received permitted them to expand credit as generously. Government banking policy thus swept forward the already growing speculation in land, cotton, canals, railroads, and shipping. Then in July, 1836, Jackson, true to his hard money convictions, issued the famous Specie Circular that required all land to be paid for in gold and silver. As Harriet Martineau indicated, the resulting scarcity of money proved ruinous. Just as Jackson left office, the speculative boom collapsed, ushering in one of the most severe depressions of the nineteenth century. While there were many deep-seated causes for the boom and bust of the 1830's, the administration's banking policy certainly intensified the cycle.

Jackson's successor and protégé, Martin Van Buren, took the final step in the separation of banking from the national government when he obtained the Independent Treasury Act from Congress in July, 1840. Under this law, re-enacted in 1846, all government moneys were taken from private institutions and placed in subtreasuries. Located in the major cities, they handled all government financial activities. The National Banking Act of 1864 finally provided a uniform national currency by incorporating national banks that could issue notes on the basis of specie and government securities and by placing a 10 per cent tax on all state bank notes. But the return of inexpensive commercial credit and of a central banking system that could mobilize the financial resources of the nation in times of economic trouble had to wait until the passage of the Federal Reserve Act in December, 1913. Until then Wall Street continued to finance American commerce at a sizable profit and at the cost of chronic financial and economic instability. Bray Hammond has justly evaluated the long-range economic result of the Bank War: "Destruction of the Bank ended federal regulation of bank credit and shifted the money center from Chestnut Street to Wall Street. It left the poor agrarian as poor as he had been before and it left the money power possessed of more money and more power than ever."

STUDY QUESTIONS

1] Could a national bank have been devised to serve the dual purpose of providing the services given by the Second

Bank and satisfying the economic, constitutional, and ideological objections of its opponents?

2] Do you think Jackson, Benton, and Leggett, or Clay and Webster really believed their opponents were subverting the Constitution and the American way of life? If they did not, why did they make the point? If they did believe what they said, how did they account for their opponents' sinister motives?

3] A basic assumption of economics is that men are motivated by self-interest. Does the controversy over the Bank indicate that men are so motivated? If so, do they always know what is in their own economic interest?

4] Historians have called Jackson's veto message "legalistic," "demagogic," and "full of sham" and have said that its economic reasoning was "beneath contempt." Discuss.

RECOMMENDED READINGS

PRIMARY SOURCES

BASSETT, JOHN S., ed. Correspondence of Andrew Jackson, 6 vols. (Washington, 1926–33), Vols. IV and V.

BENTON, THOMAS HART. Thirty Years' View, 2 vols. (New York, 1854–56).

BLAU, JOSEPH L., ed. Social Theories of Jacksonian Democracy: Some Representative Writings of the Period 1825–1850 (New York, 1947).

CLARKE, M. ST. CLAIR, AND D. A. HALL, eds. Legislative and Documentary History of the Bank of the United States (Washington, 1832).

EVERETT, EDWARD, ed. The Works of Daniel Webster, 6 vols. (Boston, 1851), Vol. III.

GOUGE, WILLIAM M. A Short History of Paper Money and Banking in the United States (Philadelphia, 1833).

McGRANE, REGINALD C., ed. The Correspondence of Nicholas Biddle (New York, 1919).

RICHARDSON, JAMES D., ed. A Compilation of the Messages and Papers of the Presidents, 1789–1897, 10 vols. (Washington, 1896–99), Vols. II and III.

SWAIN, JAMES B. The Life and Speeches of Henry Clay, 2 vols. (New York, 1842), Vol. II.

U.S. CONGRESS, Congressional Debates (Register of Debates in Congress), 21 Cong., 2 Sess.; 22 Cong., 1 Sess.; 23 Cong., 1 Sess.

SECONDARY SOURCES

BASSETT, JOHN S. Life of Andrew Jackson (New York, 1928).

CATTERALL, RALPH C. H. The Second Bank of the United States (Chicago, 1903).

GOVAN, THOMAS P. Nicholas Biddle: Nationalist and Public Banker, 1786–1844 (New York, 1959).

HAMMOND, BRAY. *Banks and Politics in America from the Revolution to the Civil War* (Princeton, 1957).

JAMES, MARQUIS. *The Life of Andrew Jackson* (Indianapolis, 1938).

MEYERS, MARVIN. *The Jacksonian Persuasion: Politics and Belief* (Stanford, Cal., 1957).

SCHLESINGER, ARTHUR M., JR. *The Age of Jackson* (Boston, 1945).

SELLERS, CHARLES G. "Andrew Jackson versus the Historians," *Mississippi Valley Historical Review*, XLIV (March, 1958), 615–34.

SMITH, WALTER B. *Economic Aspects of the Second Bank of the United States* (Cambridge, Mass., 1953).

SWISHER, CARL B. *Roger B. Taney* (New York, 1935).

Slavery and Expansion: The Crisis and Compromise of 1850

HOLMAN HAMILTON

UNIVERSITY OF KENTUCKY

CONTENTS

CHRONOLOGY

1849

MARCH 5 Zachary Taylor is inaugurated as the twelfth President of the United States.

DECEMBER 3 The Thirty-first Congress assembles.

1850

JANUARY 21 Taylor sends to Congress his special message on California and New Mexico.

JANUARY 29 Henry Clay presents eight resolutions to the United States Senate.

FEBRUARY 5–6 Clay speaks in support of his resolutions.

FEBRUARY– Many important Senate speeches are delivered, including those of John C. Calhoun, Daniel Webster, and William H. Seward.
MARCH

FEBRUARY– Scores of speeches in the House of Representatives.
JULY The legislative impasse there is related to the California debate.

APRIL 17 The Benton-Foote dramatics on the Senate floor.

MAY 8 Report of the Senate Committee of Thirteen.

MAY 13 and 21 Major speeches by Senator Clay.

MAY 27 The Washington *Republic* replies on Taylor's behalf.

JULY 9 Death of Taylor. Millard Fillmore succeeds to the Presidency.

JULY 30–31 Defeat in the Senate of the Committee of Thirteen's "Omnibus Bill."

AUGUST 9– The Senate passes compromise legislation under
SEPTEMBER 16 Stephen A. Douglas' leadership.

SEPTEMBER 6–17 Compromise bills also pass in the House.

SEPTEMBER 9, The Compromise of 1850 becomes law.
18, and 20

INTRODUCTION

HISTORIANS and biographers have subjected the coming of the Civil War to a dozen or more interpretations. Among "causes" of the conflict listed by the "experts" are hate, zeal, drift, intolerance, pride, the slavery institution, slavery plus race, race alone, and avoidable errors committed by a "blundering generation." The breakdown of democratic processes from 1861 to 1865 has been attributed to cultural, economic, moral, constitutional, philosophical, political, and psychological preliminaries. A century after it occurred, not all Americans can agree on a suitable name for the epic struggle. The "War Between the States," the "War Against the States," the "Brothers' War," the "War of the Rebellion," and simply the "Civil War"— each label has its sponsors. Nor is there unanimity of opinion whether the four-year slaughter was repressible or irrepressible, needless or necessary. If chaos and confusion obtained in that era, echoes of controversy linger today. There still is a degree of misunderstanding between citizens of South and North. Distortions persist. Ignorance abides. Because of currently conflicting viewpoints, scholarly observers of sectional differences now may be better equipped to comprehend the tensions of the ante bellum era than were the people of, say, 1930—or those of 1900.

If the elderly Thomas Jefferson regarded the Missouri Controversy as "a fire bell in the night," other warnings alarmed younger leaders from 1821 to 1860. The tariff contests of the 1820's, the Vesey and Turner slave insurrections, the nullification crisis in South Carolina, and the abolitionists' petitions submitted to Congress engendered bitterness and taxed the skill of firm men who were also moderates. *Prigg* v. *The Commonwealth of Pennsylvania* (1842) and *Dred Scott* v. *Sanford* (1857) were two Supreme Court decisions that, ultimately in the first case and immediately in the second, set off incendiary sparks. The questions of slavery and the slave trade in the District of Columbia, the annexation of Texas (1845), the Mexican War, and the Wilmot Proviso eventually yielded the spotlight to *Uncle Tom's Cabin* (1852), the Kansas-Nebraska Law, "Bleeding" Kansas, the caning of Charles Sumner, and the hanging of John Brown. One is tempted to tarry at almost any of those mileposts, crying: "Harken ye, brethren. Bend near, and bear witness. This is the single match and this the particular kindling which ignited a holocaust snuffing out the lives and ambitions and loves and dreams of 600,000 uniformed civilians in battle areas stretching from First Manassas through an agony of space and time to Cold Harbor and Five Forks." That, of course, would be an oversimplification of the sort which cautious chroniclers shun. Perhaps a person stressing the significance of the Compromise of 1850 likewise may be fairly accused of exaggerating the importance of one set of laws. The 1850 national crisis, however, deserves scrutiny not only for itself but also for the light it sheds on earlier and later spasms and convulsions.

Three developments of 1848—a discovery, a treaty, and a triumph at the polls—set the stage for one of the most famous debates in all the annals of America. In January, a Jersey wheelwright named James W. Marshall found loose flakes of gold in a California river; the news did not reach the Atlantic seaboard for months, but spectacular events (including the memorable Gold Rush of the Forty-niners) had been set in motion by the drama of the mill-race. In February, at the suburban Mexican village of Guadalupe Hidalgo, negotiators for the United States and Mexico ended their nations' twenty-one-month-old war; the loser then ceded to her northern neighbor what eventually became the modern states of California, Nevada, Utah, most of Arizona and New Mexico, and parts of Colorado and Wyoming. Although the figure usually given for the acquisition's area is 529,189 square miles, some Americans and especially Texans disputed the total then and thereafter by reason of Texas' land claims. Even prior to the enormous cession, and long before visions of golden nuggets transfixed Eastern eyes, it was evident that the extension or containment of slavery exerted an influence on the thoughts and emotions of both politicians and voters. Gold, Guadalupe, and the shapes of things to come hovered on the horizon during the 1848 Presidential campaign, from which Zachary Taylor emerged victorious over Lewis Cass and Martin Van Buren.

Taylor's inauguration in March, 1849, ushered into the White House a professional soldier who was also a cotton planter and the owner of more than a hundred Negroes. Nominated by the Whigs because of his popularity as a hero in the Mexican War, "Old Rough and Ready" had never held civil office, nor had he so much as voted. Although the Thirty-first Congress did not assemble until nine months after Taylor's term began, observers knew in March that on a partisan basis Democrats would certainly control the Senate and possibly dominate the House of Representatives. It was clear, moreover, that rival sectional and nationalistic attitudes impinged tellingly on party discipline and that the wide variety of views was sure to complicate resolutions, bills, and laws. To the assumption that slavery's Western fate would be the main theme of speeches in Congress was added the prospect that at least four major proposals were bound to be debated in both chambers. As each of these plans had been projected in the relatively recent past, House and Senate leaders and lieutenants were familiar with them all.

At one Congressional extreme, Senator John C. Calhoun of South Carolina had taken the stand that Washington held no power over slavery in the West. Masters, he asserted, were therefore entitled to transport their chattels anywhere they pleased in the length and breadth of the new domain. A contrasting proposition was primarily identified with David Wilmot, a Free-soiler. Vehemently dissenting from Calhoun's thesis, the Pennsylvania representative had demanded that slavery be specifically prohibited everywhere in the area. Among the large number of Americans adamantly opposing both Wilmot and Calhoun, Southerners tended to favor the westward extension of the Missouri Compromise line—with slavery legal below 36°30′ all the way to the Pacific Ocean. Most moderate Northerners, on the other hand, subscribed to the doctrine of popular sovereignty; reduced to its essence, this amounted to the principle that—when the Southwest and Far

West were carved into new territories—the admission or exclusion of slavery should be determined by actual residents. In the spring and autumn of 1849, Taylor sponsored a fifth alternative. Encouraging California and New Mexico to draw up state constitutions, the President hoped that their speedy admission to the Union as states (avoiding territorial complications) would appreciably reduce the charge in dangerous emotional currents.

It is problematical whether such a reduction was immediately possible under prevailing conditions. As 1849 drew to a close, the political atmosphere was electric. Intensely aware of the delicate balance between fifteen slave states and fifteen free ones, Southern realists feared that the addition of extra stars to the flag would mean the end of the Senate "equilibrium" and jeopardize Southern influence forever. In October the call had gone out from Mississippi for a section-wide convention to be held at Nashville, Tennessee, the following June; inevitably, the action to be taken by the delegates would depend on the record of the federal government in the intervening eight months. Would secession result? Might the South insist on Northern acceptance of Calhoun's policy, or on the 36°30′ division? In a sense, a Damoclean sword seemed suspended over Washington.

Congress, like the South, was also far from oblivious to developments above the Mason-Dixon Line. Many hitherto conciliatory Northerners were heeding abolitionist assertions that the Mexican War stemmed from a plot to tighten the grip of an insidious "Slave Power" on free and freedom-loving citizens. Residents of the Cotton Belt were alarmed because the legislatures of all Northern states except Iowa instructed their senators and requested their representatives to support the Wilmot Proviso. President Taylor's course also aroused suspicions in the region he had long called home. Representative Alexander H. Stephens summarized the forebodings of Georgia Whigs. "I find," Stephens wrote on December 5, "the feeling among Southern members for a dissolution of the Union—if anti-slavery should be pressed to extremity—is becoming much more general. . . . Men are now beginning to talk of it seriously, who, twelve months ago, hardly permitted themselves to think of it." Three days later, Calhoun confided to his son-in-law: "The South is more united than I ever knew it to be, and more bold and decided. The North must give away, or there will be a rupture." If a less violent reaction came from Senator Henry Clay, the comments sent by the Kentuckian to a devoted friend reveal tribulations in their author: "The feeling for disunion among some intemperate Southern politicians, is stronger than I hoped or supposed it could be. The masses generally, even at the South, are, I believe sound; but they may become influenced and perverted."

Unlike extremists from Boston to Charleston, the temperate men of America moved with amazing silence (if they moved at all) during the preceding weeks. A search of forty manuscript collections and fifty newspaper files reveals little of a tangible nature respecting 1849 plans to reach a comprehensive adjustment of the North-South differences. There was no convention of compromisers. It has not even been hinted by most historians that there may have been informal meetings of middle-roaders regarding a legislative compromise, months before the congressmen left their farms and cities for the capital. Circumstantial evidence suggests, nevertheless, that Democrats and Whigs of considerable Congressional stature had been engaged in evaluating combinations well in advance of 1850.

These people could anticipate a Congressional response to the "State of Deseret," which Mormons under Brigham Young formed at Salt Lake City in 1849 and which encompassed all the country between the Sierra Nevada Mountains and the Rockies and between Mexico and Oregon, plus a slice of California's seacoast. Senators and representatives likewise could be reasonably certain that a stronger fugitive slave law than the one virtually nullified by the Prigg Decision would be favored by James M. Mason of Virginia or by other Southerners. District of Columbia legislation, affecting either slavery or the slave trade or both, had been introduced in the past and almost surely would be broached again. Most promising of all, as a potential catalyst, was the *quid pro quo* feature associated with Texas boundaries and Texas debts.

Most details of the boundary question need not concern us here. But it is vital to realize that a vast expanse north of the Mexican border and east of the Rio Grande, including the community of Santa Fe, was claimed by Texas for herself and by the United States for New Mexico. If the disputed region became a permanent part of Texas, it would all be open to slavery. If Texas relinquished it to a New Mexico Territory formed on a popular-sovereignty basis, the institution would be seriously threatened. While the American public was hardly aware of the fiscal problems of the Lone Star State, practical politicians knew that the former Republic of Texas had bequeathed to its fledgling successor a curious complex of financial burdens. Still, sharply defined was the demarcation between two broad types of Texan liabilities. In the first group were small sums, due active participants in the Texas Revolution and suppliers of the Texas army in the grim days when Mexico menaced the republic. The second category consisted of the republic's bonds and notes, relatively few of which had been issued at face value and most at substantial discounts.

When Texas had been annexed, the customhouses of the republic were automatically supplanted by American ones. The state and the owners of the notes and bonds pleaded that, Texas being deprived of customs revenue with which to redeem the paper, it was incumbent on the United States to assume the debts. In 1849 and 1850, although James Hamilton of Texas and South Carolina served as attorney for a majority of the investors, the bulk of the securities reposed in non-Texans' hands. Wealthy bankers and businessmen were influential members of the bondholders' lobby. They are introduced into our story with the warning that most writers omit or barely mention this politico-economic consideration. But the possibility of Washington's assumption of the debts, in return for Austin's relinquishment of land, was tantalizing in its implications.

Matters having less to do with special-interest elements than with personalities are markedly less controversial. Respecting the celebrities of Capitol Hill there was minimal disagreement. No Congress of Jefferson's day, of Andrew Jackson's or Abraham Lincoln's or Woodrow Wilson's, surpassed the color of the one enacting the Compromise of 1850. That was a year when generations joined heart and hand and energy and effort in what has been described as a meeting of "rising, risen, and setting suns."

On the Senate floor, three brilliant old men—Calhoun, Clay, and Daniel Webster—shared the limelight and the twilight for the final time. Observers could pick out Thomas Hart Benton's rugged form as the Missourian industriously pored over documents at a desk piled high with books. Sam Houston in his leopardskin waistcoat was seen sending the little wooden hearts, which the tall and romantic Texan whittled, to lovely ladies in the galleries. Jefferson Davis, one of the younger men, leaned on a cane in deference to a wound inflicted in the battle of Buena Vista. Evident also were the shiny bald head and ceaseless energy of Davis' fellow Mississippian and waspish foe, the vocal and volatile Henry S. Foote. Salmon P. Chase, Stephen A. Douglas, William H. Seward all were there. Youth was served more obviously in the House, where thirty-four-year-old Howell Cobb vigorously wielded the gavel. Linn Boyd, Robert Toombs, and Robert C. Winthrop were numbered with Cobb among the able representatives. Senatorial strategy and tactics, however, proved far more spectacular and important in the aggregate. So it is from seats overlooking the more dignified chamber that we shall witness most of the high moments in the ensuing drama.

One of the first specific propositions submitted to the Senate was a fugitive slave bill, which Mason sponsored (and later altered). Then came Benton with a plan limited to the Texas problem. Advocating the eventual division of Texas into two states on a basis unattractive to the Austin authorities, the Missouri Democrat offered them fifteen million dollars for their debts but was unsympathetic with respect to their land claims. More comprehensive than either of these proposals was Foote's series of stipulations that California, Deseret, and New Mexico be given territorial governments—and that any future dividing of Texas be predicated on boundaries with which he thought Texans would be in full accord. In a medium-length speech bristling with invective, Foote attacked Benton and compared him with "that degenerate Roman senator," Cataline. The thrusts of the diminutive Mississippian signaled the start of a furious, session-long, personal controversy between two mutually hostile Southerners.

Superficially, there was nothing so theatrical about Zachary Taylor's special message of January 21, 1850. Congressmen heard it read by a mere clerk in a rather humdrum manner. But the fact that the message summarized administration policy on California and New Mexico made it one of several springboards for the debates of a critical session. The Presidential report immediately touched off oratorical reactions from Thomas L. Clingman of North Carolina, Volney E. Howard of Texas, and James A. Seddon of Virginia. In contrast to the fiery phrases of the three perfervid representatives were the cool tones of Senator Clay. On January 29, the Kentuckian offered eight resolutions which resembled—and, therefore, have often been confused with—what ultimately became the Compromise. On February 5 and 6, pausing for breath as he climbed the Capitol steps, the seventy-two-year-old "Sage of Ashland" again entered the Senate to deliver a well received address underscoring the need for moderation.

With Clay now seeming to dominate developments and providing much of the suspense, the Capitol was the focus of attention. Small wonder that slight notice was diverted from the forensics by an advertised meeting of Texas bondholders at the National Hotel on Pennsylvania Avenue; what the investors and speculators then decided has been shrouded in doubt from that day to this. Even less criticized were the mistakes made by Henry Foote in attempting to define his boundaries; the senator's lines simply did not meet, but friends and enemies skimmed over the discrepancies. Strangest of all has been posterity's ignorance of a Foote-Clay interchange on February 14. Pushing a general scheme of pacification and compromise, incorporating features from Clay's January resolutions, Foote averred that Clay formerly championed a procedure that he currently deserted. The latter, however, poked a bit of fun at the "worthy Senator from Mississippi," who "made a sort of omnibus speech, in which he introduced all sorts of things and every kind of passenger, and myself among the number." An important subsequent recommendation (which Clay enthusiastically backed) came to be known as the "Omnibus Bill." Although a legend developed that the "omnibus" term originated with President Taylor, we see that Clay apparently was the first to use the disparaging expression.

There was much talk of firearms in Capitol corridors during the latter half of February and the first part of March. Tempers were brittle in the House, where a Wisconsin man's attempt to promote the Wilmot Proviso led to a verbal battle royal. Physical violence was feared, and correspondents telegraphed their editors that not a few of the members carried weapons. "The breach is widening," a Minnesotan warned. The "apprehension . . . that a separation of the Union would take place . . . is now universal." Edward Everett of Massachusetts wrote: "There never was a period when the continuance of the Union seemed to me so precarious." Two senators scuffled on a Washington street, one hitting the other in the face. Another quarrel, involving Jefferson Davis and an Illinois congressman, threatened to terminate in a duel. When Taylor visited his native Virginia for a Washington's Birthday celebration, the President alluded inferentially to the turmoil and exhorted his fellow Southerners to "preserve the Union at all hazards."

On February 28, Senator John Bell of Tennessee spoke at length and submitted a set of compromise resolutions as an alternative to Clay's. Tension still was high. From March 4 through March 14, five significant Senate addresses—including two of the most famous in our annals—reflected almost every shade of the political spectrum. One of the most frequently quoted was Calhoun's; too sick to enunciate the crisp sentences he had composed, the dying lion listened attentively as Mason read them for him. Hannibal Hamlin, a Maine Democrat, replied to the Carolinian and upheld the President. Webster, the Massachusetts Whig, delivered the celebrated Seventh of March Speech that extended an olive branch to moderate Southerners. Seward stressed moral aspects of the sectional controversy; sympathetic toward Taylor, the New York Whig advanced beyond the White House position and identified himself with explicit Provisoists. Douglas, the Illinois Democrat, at first seemed to differ with Webster but proceeded to a position approximating Webster's and Clay's.

Nothing occurring in Washington from that time until the second week in July did much to succor the adjustment cause. Calhoun died the last morning in March. His death was a sentimental loss to his section, but it strengthened extremists' efforts to secure the 36°30' arrangement. When Benton rose on April 8, the Missouri Democrat (who, like Taylor, was regarded as a renegade by Southern critics) made remarks commanding the approval of the administration and most Northern Whigs. Nine days later there occurred a shocking episode. Foote brandished a pistol in the Senate, pointing it at Benton who exclaimed: "Stand out of the way, and let the assassin fire!" Foote did not fire, and order was restored—Foote insisting that he had sought to defend himself against a bigger man who menaced him. An immediate hubbub permeated the press, and there were seethings in private letters of public men.

On May 8, Clay made the majority report of a Senate Committee of Thirteen, which he headed and which had been appointed to resolve the nation's difficulties. Twice in mid-May the Kentucky Nestor spoke formally on behalf of the Committee's three bills, criticizing Taylor as an obstructionist. Within a week the Washington *Republic*, journalistic organ of the Whig administration, blasted Clay—whose very name and leadership long had been synonymous with Whiggery. Symptomatic of trouble, too, were the opinions of Webster, Douglas, Benton, and others that Clay and the Committee erred tactically in lumping four of their compromise components in a single "Omnibus Bill"—a method Clay had earlier condemned. The Nashville Convention, meeting in June, adopted milder resolutions than expected. But reassuring developments in Tennessee were offset by the news from Texas. There resentment erupted over the Taylor-approved drive to bring New Mexico into the Union as a state with a constitution excluding slavery. A special session of the Texas Legislature was called, with a military march on Santa Fe anticipated. Texas Governor P. H. Bell sent a letter to Taylor demanding an explanation of the President's New Mexico policy. Congress called for similar information, Taylor replying that the Santa Fe region was held by the United States (not by Texas) and "ought so to remain" until the boundary problem was settled.

Taylor suddenly died on the night of July 9. When Vice-President Millard Fillmore took the Presidential oath, compromise prospects noticeably brightened—Webster heading the new Cabinet as Secretary of State. Clay's floor strategy, however, met with final failure at the end of July when three-fourths of the Omnibus Bill went down to defeat. The sole measure then surviving was the one creating Utah Territory for part of the region embraced by the Mormons in their provisional state of Deseret. With the exhausted Clay leaving Washington for a respite in Rhode Island, Douglas now strode from the wings to the center of the Capitol stage. On August 3, in a letter exuding confidence, the Illinoisan reviewed the recent past and outlined his sanguine expectations for the future. Fillmore helped appreciably on August 6 with a deftly phrased message to Congress, enclosing a copy of a firm but pacifying communication from Secretary Webster to Governor Bell. Under Douglas' dynamic direction, Texas boundary-and-debt legislation passed the Senate on August 9. Admission of California as a free state was approved by that body four days later. On August 15, nineteen Democrats and eight Whigs supplied the winning total for New Mexico Territory. A new, stronger, and harsher fugitive slave bill swept through the Senate before the month was over. Then, on September 16, the abolition of the District of Columbia slave trade (except for intra-District sales) also received the Senate's blessing.

Compromisers in the House were equally diligent, though paradoxically they reverted to a modified form of the omnibus technique. Linn Boyd of Kentucky took the lead in shepherding through the chamber a combination of the Texas boundary-and-debt bill and the measure establishing New Mexico Territory. After a series of resourceful maneuvers, passage of this "little omnibus" occurred on Friday, September 6, and the Senate ratified the union on Monday. Meanwhile, in separate Saturday votes, the representatives had likewise endorsed the Senate's California and Utah legislation. September 12 saw the fugitive slave bill speed to House victory by a four-to-three margin. Finally, on September 17, the District slave-trade reform triumphed overwhelmingly. President Fillmore appended his signature to the various acts on three September days. And the Compromise of 1850 was law.

DOCUMENTS

1] Clay Introduces a Compromise Project

Henry Clay's maneuvers of January and February, 1850, brought the Senate spotlight to bear on a veteran statesman whose reputation for parliamentary genius is an enviable one. Slender, willowy, resourceful, magnetic, the Kentuckian was not a handsome man. Yet so penetrating was the glance of his eyes, so winning his smile, so compelling his manner that his very homeliness seemed attractive. Old as Clay was, his voice was silvery when—after preliminary business was disposed of—the graceful figure of the master rose, first (January 29) to offer his resolutions and then (February 5 and 6) to support them in a memorable speech.*

I NOW ASK every Senator, I entreat you, gentlemen, in fairness and candor, to examine the plan of accommodation which this series of resolutions proposes. . . . I move that the resolutions be read and received. . . .

It being desirable for the peace, concord, and harmony of the Union of these States, to settle and adjust amicably all existing questions of controversy between them, arising out of the institution of slavery, upon a fair, equitable, and just basis: Therefore,

1st. *Resolved,* That California, with suitable boundaries, ought upon her application to be admitted as one of the States of this Union, without the imposition by Congress of any restriction in respect to the exclusion or introduction of slavery within those boundaries.

2d. *Resolved,* That as slavery does not exist by law, and is not likely to be introduced into any of the territory acquired by the United States from the Republic of Mexico, it is inexpedient for Congress to provide by law either for its introduction into or exclusion from any part of the said territory; and that appropriate Territorial governments ought to be established by Congress in all of the said territory, not assigned as the boundaries of the proposed State of California, without the adoption of any restriction or condition on the subject of slavery.

3d. *Resolved,* That the western boundary of the State of Texas ought to be fixed on the Rio del Norte [Rio Grande], commencing one marine league from its mouth, and running up that river to the southern line of New Mexico; thence with that line eastwardly, and so continuing in the same direction to the line as established between the United States and Spain, excluding any portion of New Mexico, whether lying on the east or west of that river.

4th. *Resolved,* That it be proposed to the State of Texas that the United States will provide for the payment of all that portion of the legitimate and *bona fide* public debt of that State contracted prior to its annexation to the United States, and for which duties on foreign imports were pledged by the said State to its creditors, not exceeding the sum of $———, in consideration of the said duties so pledged

---

* CLAY INTRODUCES A COMPROMISE PROJECT: From the *Congressional Globe*, 31 Cong., 1 Sess., pp. 244–47, and the *Congressional Globe Appendix*, pp. 115–27.

having been no longer applicable to that object after the said annexation, but having henceforward become payable to the United States; and upon the condition also that the said State of Texas shall, by some solemn and authentic act of her Legislature, or of a convention, relinquish to the United States any claim which it has to any part of New Mexico.

5th. *Resolved,* That it is inexpedient to abolish slavery in the District of Columbia, whilst that institution continues to exist in the State of Maryland, without the consent of that State, without the consent of the people of the District, and without just compensation to the owners of slaves within the District.

6th. *But Resolved,* That it is expedient to prohibit within the District the slave-trade, in slaves brought into it from States or places beyond the limits of the District, either to be sold therein as merchandise, or to be transported to other markets without the District of Columbia.

7th. *Resolved,* That more effectual provision ought to be made by law, according to the requirements of the Constitution, for the restitution and delivery of persons bound to service or labor in any State, who may escape into any other State or Territory in the Union.

And 8th. *Resolved,* That Congress has no power to prohibit or obstruct the trade in slaves between the slaveholding States; but that the admission or exclusion of slaves brought from one into another of them, depends exclusively upon their own particular laws.

. . . If in this struggle of power and empire between two classes of States a decision of California has taken place adverse to the wishes of the southern States . . . , it is a decision made by California herself, and which California had incontestibly a right to make under the Constitution of the United States. There is, then, in that first resolution . . . a case where neither party concedes; where the question of slavery, either of its introduction or interdiction, is silent as respects the action of this Government; and if it has been decided, it has been decided by a different body—by a different power—by California herself, who had a right to make that decision.

Mr. President, the next resolution of the series which I have offered, I beg gentlemen candidly now to look at. I was aware, perfectly aware, of the perseverance with which the Wilmot proviso was insisted upon. I knew that every one of the free States of this Union—I believe without exception—had, by its legislative bodies, passed resolutions instructing its Senators and requesting its Representatives to get that restriction incorporated into any territorial bill that might be offered under the auspices of Congress. . . . But . . . what do you want?—what do you want?—you who reside in the free States? Do you want that there shall be no slavery introduced into the territories acquired by the war with Mexico? Have you not your desire in California? And in all human probability you will have it in New Mexico also. What more do you want? You have got what is worth more than a thousand Wilmot provisos. You have nature on your side—facts upon your side—and this truth staring you in the face, that there is no slavery in those territories. . . . We will act upon this altered state of facts which were unknown to our constituents, and appeal to their justice and magnanimity to concur with us in this action for peace, concord, and harmony. . . .

I pass from the second resolution to the third and fourth, which relate to the Texas question. . . . I have said that I thought the power has been concentrated in the United States to fix upon the limits of Texas. . . . What is proposed? To confine her to the Nueces? No, sir. To extend it from the Sabine to the mouth of the Rio Grande—and thence up the Rio Grande to the southern limits of New Mexico, and thence, with that limit, to the boundary between the United States and Spain, as marked out under the treaty of 1819. Why, sir, here is a vast country . . . sufficiently large, with her consent hereafter, to carve out of it some two or three additional States, when the condition and number of the population may render it expedient to make new States. Well, sir, is not that concession, liberality, and justice?

But, sir, that is not all we propose to give. . . . We propose to offer . . . a sum which the worthy Senator from Texas, in my eye, thinks will not be less than about three millions of dollars—the exact amount neither he nor I yet possesses the requisite materials to ascertain. Well, you get this large boundary and three millions of your debt paid. . . . The United States, having appropriated . . . the duties arising from imports which have been pledged to the creditor by Texas, as an honorable and just Power, ought now to pay the debt for which these duties were solemnly pledged by a Power independent and competent to make the pledge. . . .

The next resolution in the series . . . neither affirms nor disaffirms the constitutionality of the exercise of the power of abolition in the District. It is silent upon the subject. It says that it is inexpedient to do it but upon certain conditions. . . . The North has contended that the power exists under the Constitution to abolish slavery here. I am aware that the South, or a greater portion of the South, have contended for the opposite doctrine. What does this resolution ask? It asks of both parties to forbear urging their respective opinions the one to the exclusion of the other. But it concedes to the South all that the South . . . ought in reason to demand, inasmuch as it requires such conditions as amount to an absolute security for the property in slaves within the District. . . .

Mr. President, if it be conceded that Congress has the power of legislation—exclusive legislation—in all cases whatsoever, how can it be doubted that Congress has the power to prohibit what is called the slave trade within the District of Columbia? . . . I really do not think that this resolution, which proposes to abolish that trade, ought to be considered as a concession by either class of States to the other class. I think it should be regarded as an object, acceptable to both, conformable to the wishes and feelings of both. . . .

I think that the existing laws for the recovery of fugitive slaves, and the restoration and delivering of them to their owners, being often inadequate and ineffective, it is incumbent upon Congress . . . to assist in allaying this subject, so irritating and disturbing to the peace of this Union. . . . It is our duty to make the laws more effective; and I will go with the furthest Senator from the South in this body to make penal laws, to impose the heaviest sanctions from the recovery of fugitive slaves, and the restoration of them to their owners.

. . . The last resolution . . . is a concession—not, I admit, of any real constitutional provision, but a concession—of what is understood, I believe, by a great number at the North to be a constitutional provision—from the North to the South. . . . There is a great deal that might be said on both sides of the subject in relation to the right of Congress to regulate the trade between the States. But I believe the decision of the Supreme Court has been founded upon correct principles; and I hope it will forever put an end to the question whether Congress has or has not the power to regulate the slave trade between the different States. . . .

We are told now, and it is rung throughout this entire country, that the Union is threatened with subversion and destruction. . . . Suppose your rights to be violated; suppose wrongs to be done you, aggressions to be perpetuated upon you, cannot you better fight and vindicate them, if you have occasion to resort to that last necessity of the sword, within the Union . . . than you can fight and vindicate your rights, expelled from the Union, and driven from it without ceremony and without authority?

. . . I solemnly believe—that the dissolution of the Union and war are identical and inseparable; that they are convertible terms. Such a war, too, as that would be, following the dissolution of the Union! Sir, we may search the pages of history, and none so furious, so bloody, so implacable, so exterminating . . . none, none of them rages with such violence . . . as will that war which shall follow that disastrous event—if that event ever happens—of dissolution. . . . Finally, Mr President, I implore, as the best blessing which Heaven can bestow upon me upon earth, that if the direful and sad event of the dissolution of the Union shall happen, I may not survive to behold the sad and heart-rending spectacle.

2] Texas Bondholders Plan to Meet

Meanwhile, holders of Texas bonds were responding to advertisements like this.*

A MEETING of the holders of the bonds of the late Republic of Texas, in which revenues of the Republic are specially pledged for their payment, is requested to meet, either in person or by proxy, on Monday the 11th day of February next at 12 o'clock, m., at the National Hotel, Washington City, D.C., to take into consideration matters of essential importance to their interests.

J. HAMILTON,

Galveston, Dec. 13. On his own behalf, and as Att'y for a majority in amount

3] Calhoun Assails the Record of the North

At sixty-seven, John C. Calhoun was in the last stages of tuberculosis. Disciplined, severe, and devoted to his section, the Carolinian had long been hailed as one of Congress' giant intellects. Now, on March 4, sagging shoulders and faltering steps betrayed his physical debility. The "incarnation of

* TEXAS BONDHOLDERS PLAN TO MEET: "Notice." From the Austin *Texas State Gazette* (January 19, 1850).

the wrath of God" looked burned out, like the ash of a man, as, swathed in flannels, he listened intently while his incisive sentences were intoned by Mason.*

I HAVE, Senators, believed from the first that the agitation of the subject of slavery would, if not prevented by some timely and effective measure, end in disunion. . . . Agitation has been permitted to proceed, with almost no attempt to resist it, until it has reached a period when it can no longer be disguised or denied that the Union is in danger. You have thus had forced upon you the greatest and the gravest question that can ever come under your consideration: How can the Union be preserved?

To give a satisfactory answer to this mighty question, it is indispensable to have an accurate and thorough knowledge of the nature and the character of the cause by which the Union is endangered. . . . The first question . . . in the investigation I propose to make, in order to obtain such knowledge, is: What is it that has endangered the Union? To this question there can be but one answer: that the immediate cause is the almost universal discontent which pervades all the States composing the southern section of the Union. . . . What is the cause of this discontent? It will be found in the belief of the people of the southern States, as prevalent as the discontent itself, that they cannot remain, as things now are, consistently with honor and safety, in the Union. The next question to be considered is: What has caused this belief?

One of the causes is, undoubtedly, to be traced to the long-continued agitation of the slave question on the part of the North, and the many aggressions which they have made on the rights of the South. . . . There is another, lying back of it, with which this is intimately connected, that may be regarded as the great and primary cause. That is to be found in the fact that the equilibrium between the two sections in the Government, as it stood when the constitution was ratified and the Government put into action, has been destroyed. . . . One section has the exclusive power of controlling the Government, which leaves the other without any adequate means of protecting itself against its encroachment and oppression. . . .

The prospect then, is, that the two sections in the Senate, should the efforts now made to exclude the South from the newly-acquired territories succeed, will stand, before the end of the decade, twenty northern States to twelve southern, (considering Delaware as neutral,) and forty northern Senators to twenty-four southern. This great increase of Senators, added to the great increase of members of the House of Representatives and the electoral college on the part of the North, which must take place under the next decade, will effectually and irretrievably destroy the equilibrium which existed when the Government commenced.

Had this destruction been the operation of time, without the interference of Government, the South would have had no reason to complain; but such was not the fact. It was caused by the legislation of this Government, which was

---

* CALHOUN ASSAILS THE RECORD OF THE NORTH: From the *Congressional Globe*, 31 Cong., 1 Sess., pp. 451–55.

appointed as the common agent of all, and charged with the protection of the interests and security of all. The legislation by which it has been effected may be classed under three heads. The first is, that series of acts by which the South has been excluded from the common territory belonging to all of the States. . . . It is to be found in the provision of the ordinance of 1787. . . . The next is the system of revenue and disbursements which has been adopted. . . . The South, as the great exporting portion of the Union, has in reality paid vastly more than her due proportion of the revenue. . . . A far greater portion of the revenue has been disbursed at the North than its due share. . . . Under the most moderate estimate, it would be sufficient to add greatly to the wealth of the North, and thus greatly increase her population by attracting emigration from all quarters to that section. . . .

But while these measures were destroying the equilibrium between the two sections, the action of the Government was leading to a radical change in its character, by concentrating all the power of the system in itself. . . . The character of the Government has been changed . . . from a Federal Republic, as it originally came from the hands of its framers, and . . . into a great national consolidated Democracy. . . .

How can the Union be saved? There is but one way by which it can with any certainty; and that is, by a full and final settlement, on the principle of justice, of all the questions at issue between the two sections. . . . But can this be done? Yes, easily; not by the weaker party, for it can of itself do nothing —not even protect itself—but by the stronger. The North has only to will it to accomplish it—to do justice by conceding to the South an equal right in the acquired territory, and to do her duty by causing the stipulations relative to fugitive slaves to be faithfully fulfilled—to cease the agitation of the slave question, and to provide for the insertion of a provision in the Constitution, by an amendment, which will restore to the South in substance the power she possessed of protecting herself, before the equilibrium between the sections was destroyed by the action of this Government. There will be no difficulty in devising such a provision—one that will protect the South, and which at the same time will improve and strengthen the Government, instead of impairing and weakening it.

But will the North agree to do this? It is for her to answer this question. But, I will say, she cannot refuse, if she has half the love of the Union which she professes to have, or without justly exposing herself to the charge that her love of power and aggrandizement is far greater than her love of the Union. At all events, the responsibility of saving the Union rests on the North, and not the South. The South cannot save it by any act of hers, and the North may save it without any sacrifice whatever, unless to do justice, and to perform her duties under the Constitution, should be regarded by her as a sacrifice.

It is time, Senators, that there should be an open and manly avowal on all sides, as to what is intended to be done. If the question is not now settled, it is uncertain whether it ever can hereafter be; and we, as the representatives of the States of this Union, regarded as governments, should come to a distinct understanding as to our respective views, in order to ascertain whether the great questions at issue can be settled or not. If you, who represent the stronger portion, cannot agree to settle them on the broad principle of justice and duty, say so; and let the States we both represent agree to separate and part in peace. If you are unwilling we should part in peace, tell us so, and we shall know what to do, when you reduce the question to submission or resistance. If you remain silent, you will compel us to infer by your acts what you intend. In that case, California will become the test question. If you admit her, under all the difficulties that oppose her admission, you compel us to infer that you intend to exclude us from the whole of the acquired territories, with the intention of destroying irretrievably the equilibrium between the two sections. We would be blind not to perceive, in that case, that your real objects are power and aggrandizement, and infatuated not to act accordingly.

I have now, Senators, done my duty in expressing my opinions fully, freely, and candidly, on this solemn occasion. In doing so, I have been governed by the motives which have governed me in all the stages of the agitation of the slavery question since its commencement. I have exerted myself, during the whole period, to arrest it, with the intention of saving the Union, if it could be done; and, if it could not, to save the section where it has pleased Providence to cast my lot, and which I sincerely believe has justice and the Constitution on its side. Having faithfully done my duty to the best of my ability, both to the Union and my section, throughout this agitation, I shall have the consolation, let what will come, that I am free from all responsibility.

4] Webster Calls for Harmony and Peace

No other American of his day surpassed Daniel Webster as a public speaker. There was something about his swarthy face and noble brow that enhanced the golden tones of the man from the seaside acres at Marshfield. Sixty-eight years old that winter, Webster was a victim of insomnia and—like Calhoun and Clay—suffered from poor health. Yet his personality remained powerful and winning. And the crowds, cramming the corridors and clamoring for admittance to the galleries for this speech on March 7, remembered that Webster's "air of Imperial strength" had been compared to Julius Caesar's, his eyes to great "anthracite furnaces," his mouth to a mastiff's, and his cadences to thunder.*

MR. PRESIDENT, I wish to speak to-day, not as a Massachusetts man, nor as a northern man, but as an American, and a member of the Senate of the United States. . . . I speak to-day for the preservation of the Union. "Hear me for my cause." I speak to-day, out of a solicitous and anxious heart, for the restoration to the country of that quiet and that harmony which make the blessings of this Union so rich and so dear to us all. These are the topics that I propose to myself to discuss; these are the motives, and the sole motives, that influence me in the wish to communicate my opinions to the Sen-

* WEBSTER CALLS FOR HARMONY AND PEACE: From the *Congressional Globe Appendix* 31 Cong., 1 Sess., pp. 269–76.

ate and the country; and if I can do anything, however little, for the promotion of these ends, I shall have accomplished all that I desire. . . .

As to California and New Mexico, I hold slavery to be excluded from those territories by a law even superior to that which admits and sanctions it in Texas—I mean the law of nature—of physical geography—the law of the formation of the earth. That law settles forever, with a strength beyond all terms of human enactment, that slavery cannot exist in California or New Mexico. Understand me, sir—I mean slavery as we regard it; slaves in gross, of the colored race, transferable by sale and delivery, like other property. . . . If a resolution, or a law, were now before us, to provide a territorial government for New Mexico, I would not vote to put any prohibition into it whatever. . . . I would not take pains to reaffirm an ordinance of nature, nor to reënact the will of God. And I would put in no Wilmot proviso, for the purpose of a taunt or a reproach. I would put into it no evidence of the votes of superior power, to wound the pride, even whether a just pride, a rational pride, or an irrational pride—to wound the pride of the gentlemen who belong to the southern States. . . .

Mr. President, in the excited times in which we live, there is found to exist a state of crimination and recrimination between the North and the South. There are lists of grievances produced by each. . . . Especially one complaint of the South . . . has in my opinion just foundation; and that is, that there has been found at the North, among individuals and among the Legislatures of the North, a disinclination to perform, fully, their constitutional duties, in regard to the return of persons bound to service, who have escaped into the free States. In that respect, it is my judgment that the South is right, and the North is wrong. . . . I put it to all the sober and sound minds at the North, as a question of morals and a question of conscience, What right have they, in all their legislative capacity, or any other, to endeavor to get round this Constitution, to embarrass the free exercise of the rights secured by the Constitution, to the persons whose slaves escape from them? None at all—none at all. . . .

I hear with pain, and anguish, and distress, the word secession, especially when it falls from the lips of those who are eminently patriotic, and known to the country, and known all over the world, for their political services. Secession! Peaceable secession! Sir, your eyes and mine are never destined to see that miracle. . . . Why, what would be the result? Where is the line to be drawn? What States are to secede? What is to remain American? What am I to be?—an American no longer? Where is the flag of the Republic to remain? Where is the eagle still to tower? or is he to cower, and shrink, and fall to the ground? Why, sir, our ancestors—our fathers, and our grandfathers, those of them that are yet living among us with prolonged lives—would rebuke and reproach us; and our children, and our grandchildren, would cry out, Shame upon us! if we, of this generation, should dishonor these ensigns of the power of the Government, and the harmony of the Union, which is every day felt among us with so much joy and gratitude. What is to become of the army? What is to become of the navy? What is to become of the public lands? How is each of the thirty States to defend itself? I know, although the idea has not been stated distinctly, there is to be a southern Confederacy. I do not mean, when I allude to this statement, that any one seriously contemplates such a state of things. I do not mean to say that it is true, but I have heard it suggested elsewhere, that that idea has originated in a design to separate. I am sorry, sir, that it has ever been thought of, talked of, dreamed of, in the wildest flights of human imagination. But the idea must be of a separation, including the slave States upon one side, and the free States on the other. Sir, there is not—I may express myself too strongly perhaps—but some things, some moral things, are almost impossible, as other natural or physical things; and I hold the idea of a separation of these States—those that are free to form one government, and those that are slaveholding to form another—as a moral impossibility. We could not separate the States by any such line, if we were to draw it. We could not sit down here to-day, and draw a line of separation that would satisfy any five men in the country.

. . . Sir, I wish to . . . hasten to a conclusion. I wish to say, in regard to Texas, that if it should be hereafter at any time the pleasure of the Government of Texas to cede to the United States a portion, larger or smaller, of her territory which lies adjacent to New Mexico and north of the 34° of north latitude, to be formed into free States, for a fair equivalent in money, or in the payment of her debt, I think it an object well worthy the consideration of Congress, and shall be happy to concur in it myself, if I should be in the public counsels of the country at the time. . . .

Never did there devolve, on any generation of men, higher trusts than now devolve upon us for the preservation of this Constitution, and the harmony and peace of all who are destined to live under it. Let us make our generation one of the strongest, and the brightest link, in that golden chain which is destined, I fully believe, to grapple the people of all the States to this Constitution, for ages to come. It is a great popular Constitutional Government, guarded by legislation, by law, by judicature, and defended by the whole affections of the people. . . . Its daily respiration, is liberty and patriotism; its yet youthful veins are full of enterprise, courage, and honorable love of glory and renown. It has received a vast addition of territory. Large before, the country has now, by recent events, become vastly larger. This Republic now extends, with a vast breadth, across the whole continent. The two great seas of the world wash the one and the other shore. We realize on a mighty scale, the beautiful description of the ornamental edging of the buckler of Achilles—

> "Now the broad shield complete the artist crowned,
> With his last hand, and poured the ocean round;
> In living silver seemed the waves to roll,
> And beat the buckler's verge, and bound the whole."

5] The "Higher Law" Is Invoked by Seward

Four days after the seventh of March, a fellow Whig challenged the Webster presentation. William H. Seward was shrewd, ambitious, energetic, and socially charming. With his tousled, straw-colored, red-tinged hair, his gray-blue eyes, now keen, now dreamy, his protruding beak of a nose and receding pinpoint of a chin, he held his head like a wise macaw and cocked it birdlike in conversation. Seward had a husky voice. On March 11 he read from a manuscript, contrary to the prevailing fashion. Not a few senators stayed away. But, valuing content more than manner, the New Yorker appealed to a larger audience than that contained by the Senate's walls.*

CALIFORNIA is already a State—a complete and fully-appointed State. She never again can be less than that; she can never again be a province or a colony; nor can she be made to shrink and shrivel into the proportions of a Federal dependent territory. California, then, henceforth and forever, must be, what she is now, a State.

. . . But it is insisted that the admission of California shall be attended by a COMPROMISE of questions which have arisen out of SLAVERY.

I AM OPPOSED TO ANY SUCH COMPROMISE, IN ANY AND ALL THE FORMS IN WHICH IT HAS BEEN PROPOSED, because . . . I think all legislative compromises radically wrong and essentially vicious. They involve the surrender of the exercise of judgment and conscience on distinct and separate questions, at distinct and separate times, with the indispensable advantages it affords for ascertaining truth. . . .

What is proposed, is a political equilibrium. . . . The theory of a new political equilibrium claims that it once existed, and has been lost. When lost, and how? It began to be lost in 1787, when preliminary arrangements were made to admit five new free States in the Northwest territory, two years before the Constitution was finally adopted—that is, it began to be lost two years before it began to exist!

. . . But there is yet another aspect in which this principle [of compromise] must be examined. It regards the domain only as a possession, to be enjoyed, either in common or by partition, by the citizens of the old States. It is true, indeed, that the national domain is ours; it is true, it was acquired by the valor and with the wealth of the whole nation; but we hold, nevertheless, no arbitrary power over it. We hold no arbitrary authority over anything, whether acquired lawfully, or seized by usurpation. The Constitution regulates our stewardship; the Constitution devotes the domain to union, to justice, to defence, to welfare, and to liberty.

But there is a higher law than the Constitution, which regulates our authority over the domain, and devotes it to the same noble purposes. The territory is a part—no inconsiderable part—of the common heritage of mankind, bestowed upon them by the Creator of the universe. We are his stewards, and must so discharge our trust as to secure, in the highest attainable degree, their happiness. . . . And now the simple, bold, and even awful question which presents itself to us, is this: Shall we, who are founding institutions, social and political, for countless millions—shall we, who know by experience the wise and the just, and are free to choose them, and to reject the erroneous and

* THE "HIGHER LAW" IS INVOKED BY SEWARD: From the *Congressional Globe Appendix*, 31 Cong., 1 Sess., pp. 260–69.

unjust—shall we establish human bondage, or permit it, by our sufferance, to be established? Sir, our forefathers would not have hesitated an hour. . . .

The argument is, that the *proviso is unnecessary*. I answer, then there can be no error in insisting upon it. But why is it unnecessary? It is said—*first*, by reason of *climate*. I answer, if this be so, why do not the Representatives of the slave States concede the proviso? . . . I find no authority for the position, that climate prevents slavery anywhere. It is the indolence of mankind, in any climate, and not the natural necessity, that introduces slavery in any climate. . . .

You insist that you cannot submit to the freedom with which slavery is discussed in the free States. Will war—a war for slavery—arrest, or even moderate, that discussion? No, sir; that discussion will not cease; war would only inflame it to a greater height. . . . There will be no disunion and no secession. I do not say that there may not be disturbance, though I do not apprehend even that. . . .

I have heard somewhat here—and almost for the first time in my life—of divided allegiance—of allegiance to the South and to the Union—of allegiance to States severally and to the Union. Sir, if sympathies with State emulation and pride of achievement could be allowed to raise up another sovereign to divide the allegiance of a citizen of the United States, I might recognize the claims of the State to which, by birth and gratitude, I belong—to the State of Hamilton and Jay, of Schuyler, of the Clintons, and of Fulton—the State which, with less than two hundred miles of natural navigation connected with the ocean, has, by her own enterprize, secured to herself the commerce of the continent, and is steadily advancing to the command of the commerce of the world. But for all this, I know only one country and one sovereign—the United States of America and the American people. And such as my allegiance is, is the loyalty of every other citizen of the United States. As I speak, he will speak when his time arrives. He knows no other country, and no other sovereign. He has life, liberty, property, and precious affections, and hopes for himself and for his posterity, treasured up in the ark of the Union. He knows as well, and feels as strongly, as I do, that this Government is his own Government; that he is a part of it; that it was established for him, and that it is maintained by him; that it is the only truly wise, just, free, and equal Government that has ever existed; that no other Government could be so wise, just, free, and equal; and that it is safer and more beneficent than any which time or change could bring into its place.

You may tell me, sir, that although all this may be true, yet the trial of faction has not yet been made. Sir, if the trial of faction has not been made, it has not been because faction has not always existed, and has not always menaced a trial, but because faction could find no fulcrum on which to place the lever to subvert the Union, as it can find no fulcrum now; and in this is my confidence. I would not rashly provoke the trial, but I will not suffer a fear which I have not, to make me compromise one sentiment—one principle of truth or justice—to avert a danger that all experience teaches me is purely chimerical. Let, then, those who distrust the Union, make compromises to save it. I shall not impeach their wisdom, as I certainly cannot their patriotism; but indulging no such apprehensions myself, I shall vote for the admission of California directly, without conditions, without qualifications, and without compromise.

For the vindication of that vote, I look not to the verdict of the passing hour, disturbed as the public mind now is by conflicting interests and passions, but to that period, happily not far distant, when the vast regions over which we are now legislating shall have received their destined inhabitants.

While looking forward to that day, its countless generations seem to me to be rising up, and passing in dim and shadowy review before us; and a voice comes forth from their serried ranks, saying, "Waste your treasures and your armies, if you will; raze your fortifications to the ground; sink your navies into the sea; transmit to us even a dishonored name, if you must; but the soil you hold in trust for us, give it to us free. You found it free, and conquered it to extend a better and surer freedom over it. Whatever choice you have made for yourselves, let us have no partial freedom; let us all be free; let the reversion of your broad domain descend to us unincumbered, and free from the calamities and the sorrows of human bondage."

6] A Pistol Is Brandished on the Senate Floor

Of all the 1850 senatorial quarrels, none developed more rudely than the mutual antipathy of Benton and Foote. Aristocratic in appearance, fairly tall, forehead high, and his strong jaw the mark of a determined leader, Benton was tireless, egotistical, scholarly, and impervious to pressure. The short, slight, bald, vigorous Foote was equally gifted in several ways. A four-time duelist, forcible and fluent, he set out full-tilt after the Missourian and caught him and whipped him with abuse. For all his emotionalism the Mississippi Democrat was a compromiser at heart, while Benton sided with President Taylor. On April 17, the controversy reached its climax. Benton having denounced the extreme Southernism of the late Calhoun, Foote (who himself had deserted Calhoun's leadership) posed as the Carolinian's champion in the process of attacking Benton.*

Mr. FOOTE. The Senate will bear witness to the fact that I have endeavored to avoid discussion and controversy on this question. I have believed, and I yet believe, that the time has come when all true patriots should unite in the true spirit of fraternal conciliation and compromise for the settlement of these questions; and that they should feel it their bounden and imperious duty to do all in their power to quiet excitement, and save the Republic from that danger which all of us do know has environed it for the last six or eight months. I repeat, that I did not come here this morning in the expectation of saying a word; and especially would I not be heard referring to anything emanating from a certain quarter, after what has occurred here, but for what I conceive to be a direct attack upon myself and others with whom I am proud to stand

* A PISTOL IS BRANDISHED ON THE SENATE FLOOR: From the *Congressional Globe*, 31 Cong., 1 Sess., pp. 762–64.

associated. We all know the history of the Southern Address, and the world knows its history. It is the history of the action of a band of patriots, worthy of the highest laudation, and who will be held in veneration when their calumniators, no matter who they may be, will be objects of general loathing and contempt. Who is the author of the Southern Address? He is known to the world. The late illustrious Senator from South Carolina, whose decease a nation now mourns, and over whose untimely death every good man in all Christian countries, at the present time, is now lamenting—is the author, and the sole author, of that address. In our presence here to-day, in the hearing of the friends of that distinguished statesman associated with him in that holy work, that address is denounced with great appearance of deliberation, as fraught with mischief, and as having supplied food for the agitation and excitement which has involved our institutions in dangers from which they had to be rescued by the efforts of others hostile to the propositions of that address, and who did not participate in its preparation. Those who were associated with and sanctioned that address, are charged with being agitators. And by whom? With whom does such an accusation as this originate? I shall not be personal, after the lesson I have already received here. I intend to be, in a parliamentary sense, perfectly decorous in all things. But by whom in this extraordinary denunciation hurled against all those individuals who subscribed this address? By a gentleman long denominated the oldest member of the Senate—the father of the Senate. By a gentleman who, on a late occasion—.

[Here Mr. Foote, who occupies a seat on the outer circle, in front of the Vice President's chair, retreated backwards down the aisle, towards the chair of the Vice President, with a pistol in his hand. Mr. Benton, a moment before, having suddenly risen from his seat and advanced by the aisle, outside the bar, towards him, following him into the aisle down which the Senator from Mississippi had retreated. In a moment almost every Senator was on his feet, and calls to "order;" demands for the Sergeant-at-Arms; requests that Senators would take their seats, from the Chair and from individual Senators, were repeatedly made. Mr. Benton was followed and arrested by Mr. Dodge, of Wisconsin, and, in the confusion and excitement which prevailed, he was heard to exclaim, from time to time: "I have no pistols!" "Let him fire!" "Stand out of the way!" "I have no pistols!" "I disdain to carry arms!" "Stand out of the way, and let the assassin fire!" While making these exclamations, Mr. Benton was brought back to his seat; but, breaking away from Mr. Dodge, of Wisconsin, who sought forcibly to detain him, he advanced again towards Mr. Foote, who stood near the Vice President's chair, on the right-hand side, surrounded by a number of Senators, and others not members of the Senate. Mr. Dickinson took the pistol from the hand of Mr. Foote, and locked it up in his desk, and Mr. Foote, on the advice of Mr. Butler, returned to his seat.] * 1

The Vice President directed that Senators and spectators should be seated; and order was partially restored.

Mr. Dickinson. Mr. President, what is the question before the Senate?

The Vice President. The question is on the appeal from the decision of the Chair.

1 The asterisk refers to the card from Senator Foote printed following the end of the debate. [See p. 428.]

Mr. DICKINSON. I should like to hear the question again stated, as I do not remember precisely what it was.

[There was still much confusion prevailing at this time in the Senate.]

Mr. CLAY. I hope that order will be preserved.

Mr. BENTON. We are not going to get off in this way. A pistol has been brought here to assassinate me. The scoundrel had no reason to think I was armed, for I carry nothing of the kind, sir.

Mr. FOOTE. I brought it here to defend myself.

Mr. BENTON. Nothing of the kind, sir. It is a false imputation. I carry nothing of the kind, and no assassin has a right to draw a pistol on me.

Several SENATORS. "Order," "order."

Mr. BENTON. It is a mere pretext of the assassin. Will the Senate take notice of it, or shall I be forced to take notice of it by going and getting a weapon myself? A pistol has been brought here and drawn upon me by an assassin.

The VICE PRESIDENT. Senators will be seated.

Mr. FOOTE. Mr. President—

The VICE PRESIDENT. Senators will be pleased to suspend their remarks until order is restored. Senators are requested to be seated.

Mr. CLAY. Mr. President—

The VICE PRESIDENT. Business cannot proceed until order is restored.

Mr. HALE. I hope order will be kept in the galleries.

The VICE PRESIDENT. There is too much noise in the galleries. Quiet and order must be restored.

Mr. FOOTE. May I proceed in order?

Mr. BENTON. I demand that the Senate shall take immediate cognizance of the fact of this pistol having been brought here to assassinate me, under the villainous pretext that I was armed—the pretext of every assassin who undertakes to constitute a case of self-defence when laying out the death of his victim. Will the Senate notice it, or shall I myself, for it shall not pass. I will not be satisfied here.

Mr. FOOTE. If my presenting a pistol here has been understood as anything except the necessary means of self-defence, after threats of personal chastisement, it is doing me a wrong. I saw him advancing towards me, and I took it for granted he was armed; for had I thought otherwise, I should have stopped to meet him in that narrow alley. But I supposed that he was armed, and therefore I determined to take ground where I could meet him more fairly, and I drew out the pistol and was ready to fire it in self-defence. I have never sought any man's life, nor gone in quest of any man with a view of taking his life. No, sir, never. My life has been a defensive one from my boyhood. I mention it, not from the imputations that have been thrown out here, but that all the Senators present and the American public, who may hear of this thing, may be witnesses of the fact, that whilst I was making a perfectly parliamentary speech, threatening language was used, menacing gestures indulged in, and an advance made toward me, with the view, as I supposed, of putting violent designs into effect. I therefore retreated a few steps, with a view to get elbow room to act in my own defence, and not to shoot him. So help me God, such alone was my intention. . . .

Mr. DODGE, of Wisconsin. . . . I move you, then, sir, that a committee of five be appointed by the Chair to investigate the whole matter, and report all the facts to the Senate.

Mr. MANGUM. . . . I have drawn up a resolution proposing that a committee of seven should be appointed. . . . The resolution is:

Resolved, That a committee of seven be appointed to investigate the disorder of to-day in the Senate, and that they report to the Senate what befits the occasion, and have power to examine witnesses and take testimony in the case. . . .

Mr. CLAY. . . . I think the two Senators . . . ought to be placed under an obligation to keep the peace, and for that purpose that they should either voluntarily or otherwise go before some magistrate of the city, or that both of them in their places here should pledge themselves—which would be more gratifying to me—not to pursue this matter, at any rate, during the session of the Senate, further than what occurred to-day. If the Senators will make such promise to the Senate, I shall be extremely happy.

Mr. BENTON. I have done nothing upon God Almighty's earth to authorize any man to charge me with a breach of the peace, and I will rot in jail before I will give a promise admitting that the charge is true. I regret nothing. It is lying and cowardly to undertake to impute to me the bearing of arms here, in order to justify the use of them upon me. . . .

The resolution proposed by Mr. MANGUM was adopted.

. . . It was accordingly ordered that the Chair appoint the committee.

* * *

* A CARD.—In the report of the unhappy occurrence which took place on yesterday in the Senate, I regret to perceive one or two slight inaccuracies, which I hope you will promptly correct. . . . As to the *"retreat"* spoken of, it was simply a movement in a line—which made something like a right angle with the one along which the Senator from Missouri was advancing. On seeing him advance, I simply glided towards the alley leading from the Secretary's chair to the door, intending to take a defensive attitude, and then await any assault which might be made. I could not have done otherwise, without, in a certain event, endangering the lives of unoffending persons. You seem to represent myself as being pursued by my antagonist down a narrow alley. If you allude to the alley along which I walked in order to take my defensive attitude alluded to, you are in error, as the person alluded to did not even reach my seat, nor even get more than something like half-way from his seat to mine. The fact is, that I neither retreated from, nor advanced upon, the Senator referred to: I simply advanced to a convenient position for purposes of *defence.* You say "Mr. DICKINSON took the pistol from the hand of Mr. FOOTE." This is true, but I would add, that it was cheerfully surrendered on application being made for it, and upon seeing that I was no longer in danger of being assaulted. I regret that I have deemed it necessary to make this explanation, but I did not know how to avoid it.

H. S. FOOTE.

April 18, 1850.

7] Clay as Spokesman for the Committee of Thirteen

Clay again was the center of attention in May. Presenting the majority report of the Committee of Thirteen, he also delivered two formal addresses ardently urging the report's adoption.*

[On May 8]

MR. PRESIDENT, I have risen to present to the Senate a report from the Committee of Thirteen, which was appointed some weeks ago. . . .

"The views and recommendations contained in this report may be recapitulated in a few words:

"1. The admission of any new State or States formed out of Texas to be postponed until they shall hereafter present themselves to be received into the Union, when it will be the duty of Congress fairly and faithfully to execute the compact with Texas by admitting such new State or States.

"2. The admission forthwith of California into the Union with the boundaries which she has proposed.

"3. The establishment of territorial governments without the Wilmot proviso for New Mexico and Utah, embracing all the territory recently acquired by the United States from Mexico not contained in the boundaries of California.

"4. The combination of these two last-mentioned measures in the same bill.

"5. The establishment of the western and northern boundary of Texas, and the exclusion from her jurisdiction of all New Mexico, with the grant to Texas of a pecuniary equivalent; and the section for that purpose to be incorporated in the bill admitting California and establishing territorial governments for Utah and New Mexico.

"6. More effectual enactments of law to secure the prompt delivery of persons bound to service or labor in one State, under the laws thereof, who escape into another State.

"And, 7. Abstaining from abolishing slavery; but, under a heavy penalty, prohibiting the slave trade in the District of Columbia.

". . . The committee have endeavored to present to the Senate a comprehensive plan of adjustment, which, removing all causes of existing excitement and agitation, leaves none open to divide the country and disturb the general harmony. The nation has been greatly convulsed, not by measures of general policy, but by questions of a sectional character, and, therefore, more dangerous and more to be deprecated. It wants repose. It loves and cherishes the Union. And it is most cheering and gratifying to witness the outbursts of deep and abiding attachment to it which have been exhibited in all parts of it, amidst all the trials through which we have passed and are passing. A people so patriotic as those of the United States will rejoice in an accommodation of all troubles and difficulties by which the safety of that Union might have been brought into the least danger. And, under the blessings of that Providence who, amidst all vicissitudes, has never ceased to extend to them His

---

* CLAY AS SPOKESMAN FOR THE COMMITTEE OF THIRTEEN: From the *Congressional Globe*, 31 Cong., 1 Sess., pp. 944–48, and the *Congressional Globe Appendix*, pp. 567–73, 612–16.

protecting care, His smiles, and His blessings, they will continue to advance in population, power, and prosperity, and work out triumphantly the glorious problem of man's capacity for self-government."

[On May 13]
. . . I have risen, as I announced, more particularly for the purpose of entering into some further explanations of the course of the committee, and of throwing out some few observations in support of the measures which they have recommended to be adopted by the Senate. The first measure which they reported, Mr. President, was that of the true exposition of the compact between the United States and Texas upon the occasion of the admission of that State into the Union. . . . But I will not dwell longer upon that part of the subject.

I will now, Mr. President, approach that subject which in the committee and the two Houses of Congress has given most trouble, and created the most anxiety of all the measures upon which the committee have reported—I mean, the admission of California into the Union. . . . With regard to the limits of California . . . an effort was made in the committee to extend a line through California at 36°30′ of north latitude, and one member who was not satisfied with that line proposed 35°30′. A majority of the committee, I believe, were in favor of that amendment; but, on the question being taken for the line of 35°30′, a majority was found to be against it. . . . With respect to the population of California, with respect to the limits of California, and with respect to the circumstances under which she presents herself to Congress for admission as a State into the Union, all are favorable to grant her what she solicits, and we can find neither in the one nor in the other a sufficient motive to reject her, and to throw her back into the state of lawless confusion and disorder from which she has emerged.

Sir, with the committee I unite in saying on this occasion that all the considerations which call upon Congress to admit California as a State, and to sanction what she has done, and to give her the benefit of self-government, apply with equal force to the territories of Utah and New Mexico.

Mr. President, allow me, at this stage of the few observations which I propose to address to the Senate, to contrast the plans which have been presented for the settlement of these questions. One has come to us from a very high authority, recommending, as I understand it, the admission of California, and doing nothing more, leaving the question of the boundary unsettled between New Mexico and Texas, and leaving the people who inhabit Utah and New Mexico unprovided for by Government. Mr. President, I will take occasion to say that I came to Washington with the most anxious desire—a desire which I still entertain—to coöperate in my legislative position in all cases in which I could conscientiously coöperate with the Executive branch of the Government. I need not add, however, sir, that I came here also with a settled purpose to follow the deliberate dictates of my own judgment, wherever that judgment might carry me. Sir, it is with great pleasure that we do coöperate with the President of the United States to the extent which he recommends. He recommends the admission of California. The committee propose this. There the President's recommendation stops, and there we take up the subject, and proceed to act upon the other parts of the territory acquired from Mexico.

Now, which of these two courses commends itself best to the judgment of those who are to act in the case? . . . I will go further with reference to the message in relation to California—which I am sorry it is my duty to contrast with the plan of the committee now under consideration—and say that I have no doubt that there were strong, or at least plausible reasons for the adoption of the recommendation contained in the message of the President, at the time it was sent to Congress, at the beginning of the session. . . . But, sir, I am happy to be able to recognize, what all have seen, that since the commencement of the session a most gratifying change has taken place. The North, the glorious North, has come to the rescue of this Union of ours. She has displayed a disposition to abate in her demands.

The South, the glorious South—not less glorious than her neighbor section of the Union—has also come to the rescue. The minds of men have moderated; passion has given place to reason everywhere. Everywhere, in all parts of the Union, there is a demand—a demand, I trust, the force and effect of which will be felt in both Houses of Congress—for an amicable adjustment of those questions, for the relinquishment of those extreme opinions, whether entertained on the one side or on the other, and coming together once more as friends, as brethren, living in a common country and enjoying the benefits of freedom and happiness flowing from a common Government.

. . . Well, then, there is the boundary question with Texas. Why, sir, at this very moment we learn through the public papers that Texas has sent her civil commissioners to Santa Fé, or into New Mexico for the purpose, of bringing them under authority; and if you leave the Texas boundary question unsettled, and establish no government for Utah and New Mexico, I venture to say that, before we meet again next December, we shall hear of some civil commotion, perhaps the shedding of blood, in the contest between New Mexico and Texas with respect to the boundary; for, without meaning to express at this time, or at any time, any positive opinion on that question, we know that the people of Santa Fé are as much opposed to the government of Texas, and as much convinced that they do not belong to Texas, that they constitute no portion of the territory of Texas, as we know Texas to be earnest in asserting the contrary, and affirming her right to the country from the mouth of the Rio Grande to its uppermost sources. Is it right, then, to leave these territories unprovided for? Is it right to leave this important question of boundary between New Mexico and Texas unsettled? Is it right that it should be left unsettled to produce possibly the fearful consequences to which I have adverted?

Sir, on these questions I believe—though I do not recollect the exact state of the vote in committee—that there was no serious diversity of opinion. . . . The next question which arose before the committee, after having agreed upon the proposal to be made to Texas for the settlement of the boundary between her and New Mexico, was the question of the union of these three measures in one bill. And upon that subject, sir, the same diversity of opinion which had developed itself in the Senate displayed itself in the committee.

A SENATOR, in his seat. What of the amount to be paid to Texas?

Mr. CLAY. Ah; I am reminded that I have said nothing about the amount proposed to be given to Texas for the relinquishment of her title to the United

States of the territory north of the proposed line. The committee, I hope with the approbation of the Senate, thought it best not to fill up that blank until the last moment, upon the final reading of the bill; that if it were inserted in the bill it would go out to the country, and might lead to improper speculation in the stock markets; and that therefore it was better to leave it out until the final passage of the bill. When we arrive at that point, which I hope we shall do in a short time, I shall be most happy to propose the sum which has been thought of by the committee. . . .

I will pass on, with a single observation on an amendment introduced by the committee into the territorial bill. To that amendment I was opposed, but it was carried in the committee. It is an amendment which is to be found in the tenth section of one of the bills limiting the power of the territorial legislature upon the subject of laws which it may pass. Amongst other limitations, it declares "that the territorial legislature shall have no power to pass any law in respect to African slavery." I did not then, and do not now attach much importance to the amendment. . . . The effect of that amendment will at once be seen. If the territorial legislature can pass no law with respect to African slavery, the state of the law as it exists now in the Territories of Utah and New Mexico will continue to exist until the people form a constitution for themselves, when they can settle the question of slavery as they please. . . .

The next subject upon which the committee acted was that of fugitive slaves. The committee have proposed two amendments to be offered to the bill introduced by the Senator from Virginia, [Mr. MASON,] whenever that bill is taken up. The first of these amendments provides that the owner of a fugitive slave, when leaving his own State, and whenever it is practicable . . . shall carry with him a record from the State from which the fugitive has fled; which record shall contain an adjudication of two facts, first, the fact of slavery, and secondly the fact of an elopement; and, in the third place, such a general description of the slave as the court shall be enabled to give upon such testimony as shall be brought before it. It also provides that this record, taken from the county court, or from the court record in the slaveholding State, shall be carried to the free State, and shall be there held to be competent and sufficient evidence of the facts which it avows. . . .

The other amendment provides, that when the owner of a slave shall arrest his property in a non-slaveholding State, and shall take him before the proper functionary to obtain a certificate to authorize the return of that property to the State from which he fled, if he declares to that functionary at the time that he is a free man and not a slave, what does the provision require the officer to do? Why, to take a bond from the agent or owner, without surety, that he will carry the black person back to the county of the State from which he fled; and that at the first court which may sit after his return, he shall be carried there, if he again assert the right to his freedom; the court shall afford, and the owner shall afford to him all the facilities which are requisite to enable him to establish his right to freedom. Now, no surety is even required of the master. The committee thought, and in that I believe they all concurred, that it would be wrong to demand of a stranger, hundreds of miles from home, surety to take back the slave to the State from which he fled. The trial by jury is what is demanded by the non-slaveholding States. Well, we put the party claimed to be a fugitive back to the State from which he fled, and give him trial by jury in that State.

Well, sir, ought we not to make this concession? It is but very little inconvenience. I will tell you, sir, what will be the practical operation. It will be this: When a slave has escaped from the master and taken refuge in a free State, and that master comes to recapture him and take him back to the State from which he fled, the slave will cry out, "I do not know the man; I never saw him in my life; I am a free man." He will say anything and will do anything to preserve to himself that freedom of which he is for a moment in possession. He will assert most confidently before the judge that he is a free man. But take him back to the State from which he fled, to his comrades, and he will state the truth, and will disavow all claim to freedom. The practical operation, therefore, of the amendment which we have proposed, will be attended with not the least earthly inconvenience to the party claiming the fugitive. . . . Is this unreasonable? Is it not a proper and rational concession to the prejudices, if you please, which exist in the non-slaveholding States? Sir, our rights are to be asserted; our rights are to be maintained. But they ought to be asserted and maintained in a manner not to wound unnecessarily the sensibilities of others. And in requiring such a bond as this amendment proposes to exact from the owner, I do not think there is the slightest inconvenience imposed upon him, of which he ought to complain.

Sir, there is one opinion prevailing—I hope not extensively—in some of the non slaveholding States, which nothing we can do will conciliate. I allude to that opinion that asserts that there is a higher law—a divine law—a natural law—which entitles a man, under whose roof a runaway has come, to give him assistance, and succor, and hospitality. Where is the difference between receiving and harboring a known fugitive slave, and going to the plantation of his master and stealing him away? A divine law, a natural law! And who are they that venture to tell us what is divine and what is natural law? Where are their credentials of prophecy? Why, sir, we are told that the other day, at a meeting of some of these people at New York, Moses and all of the prophets were rejected, and that the name even of our blessed Saviour was treated with blasphemy and contempt by these propagators of a divine law, of a natural law, which they have discovered, above all human laws and constitutions. If Moses and the prophets, and our Saviour and all others, are to be rejected, will they condescend to show us their authority for propagating this new law, this new divine law of which they speak? The law of nature, sir! Look at it as it is promulgated, and even admitted or threatened to be enforced, in some quarters of the world. Well, sir, some of these people have discovered another plausible law of nature. There is a large class who say that if a man has acquired, no matter whether by his own exertions or by inheritance, a vast estate, much more than is necessary for the subsistence of himself and family, I, who am starving, am entitled by a law of nature to have a portion of these accumulated goods to save me from the death which threatens me. Here are you, with your barns full, with your warehouses full of goods, collected from all quarters of the globe; your kitchens, and laundries, and pantries all full of that which conduces to the subsistence and comfort of man; and here am I standing by, as Lazarus at the gate of the rich man, perishing from hunger—will not the law of nature allow me to take enough of your superabundance to save me a little while from that death which is inevitable without I do it? Another modern law of nature is that the possession of more land than you can cultivate, is a forbidden monopoly; and that the parchment from Heaven supersedes the parchment from Government! Wild, reckless, and abominable theories, which strike at the foundations of all property, and threaten to crush in ruins the fabric of civilized society. Why, sir, trace this pretended law of nature, about which, seriously, none of the philosophers are agreed, and apply it to one of the most interesting and solemn ceremonies of life. Go to a Mahometan country, and the Mahometan will tell you that you are entitled to as many wives as you can get. Come next to a Christian country, and you will be told that you are entitled to but one. Go to our friends the Shakers, and they will tell you that you are entitled to none. But there are persons in this age of enlightenment and progress, and civilization, who will rise up in public assemblages, and, denouncing the church and all that is sacred that belongs to it—denouncing the founders of the religion which we all profess and revere—will tell you that, notwithstanding the solemn oath which they have taken by kissing the sacred book to carry out into full effect all the provisions of the Constitution of our country, there is a law of their God—a divine law, which they have found out and nobody else has—superior and paramount to all human law; and that they do not mean to obey this human law, but the divine law, of which, by some inspiration, by some means undisclosed, they have obtained a knowledge. This is the class of persons which we do not propose to conciliate by any amendments, by any concession which we can make.

But the committee, in considering this delicate subject, and looking at the feelings and interests on both sides of the question, thought it best to offer these two provisions—that which requires the production of a record in the non-slaveholding States, and that which requires a bond to grant to the real claimant of his freedom a trial by jury, in the place where that trial ought to take place, according to a just interpretation of the Constitution of the United States, if it takes place anywhere. . . .

Mr. President, the only measure remaining upon which I shall say a word now, is the abolition of the slave trade in the District of Columbia. There is, I believe, precious little of it. I believe the first man in my life that I ever heard denounce that trade was a southern man—John Randolph, of Roanoke. I believe there has been no time within the last forty years, when, if earnestly pressed upon Congress, there would not have been found a majority—perhaps a majority from the slaveholding States themselves—in favor of the abolition of the slave trade in this District. . . . Sir, some years ago it would have been thought a great concession to the feelings and wishes of the North to abolish this slave trade. Now, I have seen some of the rabid abolition papers denounce it as amounting to nothing. It is nothing that slavery is interdicted in California! They do not care for that. And will my friends—some of my friends on the other side of the house—allow me to say a word or two with respect to their course in relation to this measure? At the beginning of this session, as you know, that offensive proviso, called the "Wilmot proviso," was what was the most apprehended, and what all the slaveholding States were most desirous to get rid of. Well, sir, by the operation of causes upon the northern mind friendly to the Union, hopes are inspired, which I trust will not be frustrated in the progress of this measure, that the North, or at least a sufficient portion of the North, are now willing to dispense with the proviso. When, the other day, on the coming in of the report to these measures, it was objected, by way of reproach, that they were simply carrying out my own plan, my honorable friend from North Carolina at the moment justly pointed out the essential differences between the plan, as contained in the resolutions offered by me, and that now presented by the committee. At the time I offered those resolutions, knowing what consequences, and, as I sometimes feared, fatal consequences, might result from the fact of the North insisting on that proviso, by way of compensation, in one of the resolutions which I offered— the second one—I stated two truths, one of law and one of fact, which I thought ought to satisfy the North that it ought no longer to insist on the Wilmot proviso. Those truths were not incorporated in the bill reported by the committee, but they exist, nevertheless, as truths. I believe them both now as much as I did in February last. I know there are others who do not concur with me in opinion. Every Senator must decide for himself, as the country will decide for itself, when the question comes to be considered. Well, when our southern friends found they were rid of the proviso, they were highly satisfied, and I shared with them in their satisfaction. If I am not much mistaken, a great majority of them would have said, "If, Mr. CLAY, you had not put those two obnoxious truths in them, we should have been satisfied with your series of resolutions." Well, sir, we have got rid of the Wilmot proviso; we have got rid of the enactment into laws of the two truths to which I refer; but I fear there are some of our southern brethren who are not yet satisfied. There are some who say that there is yet the Wilmot proviso, under another form, lurking in the laws of Mexico, or lurking in the mountains of Mexico, in that natural fact to which my honorable friend from Massachusetts adverted, as I myself did when I hinted that the law of nature was adverse to the introduction of slavery there. Now, as you find in the progress of events that all is obtained which was desired or expected three months ago, there is something further, there are other difficulties in the way of the adjustment of these unhappy subjects of difference, and of obtaining that which is most to be desired—the cementing of the bonds of this Union.

Mr. President, I do not despair, I will not despair, that the measure will be carried. And I would almost stake my existence, if I dared, that if these measures which have been reported by the committee of thirteen were submitted to the people of the United States to-morrow, and their vote were taken upon them, there would be nine-tenths of them in favor of the pacification which is imbodied in that report. . . . I trust that the feelings of attachment to the Union, of love for its past glory, of anticipation of its future benefits and happiness; a fraternal feeling which ought to be common throughout all parts of the country; the desire to live together in peace and harmony, to prosper as we have prospered heretofore, to hold up to the civilized world the example of one great and glorious Republic fulfilling the high destiny that belongs to it, demonstrating beyond all doubt man's capacity for self-government; these motives and these considerations will, I confidently hope and fervently pray, animate us all, bringing us together to discuss alike questions of abstraction and form, and consummating the act of concord, harmony, and peace, in such a manner as to heal not one only, but all the wounds of the country.

[On May 21]

. . . Let me call the attention of the Senate to a very painful duty, which I am constrained to perform, and which I shall perform let it subject me to what misinterpretation it may, here or elsewhere. I mean the duty of contrasting the plan proposed by the Executive of the United States with the plan proposed by the committee of thirteen. If the Executive has a friend—(I do not mean exactly that, because I believe and wish myself to be a friend of the Executive, feeling most anxious to coöperate with him)—but if there be a friend of the Executive who supports his measure *to the exclusion of that of the committee,* will he stand up here, and meet us face to face upon the question of superiority of the one measure to the other? Let us here, and not in the columns of newspapers, have a fair, full, and manly interchange of argument and opinion. I shall be ready to bear my humble part in such a mental contest. Allow me to premise by assuming, in the first place, that every friend of his country must be anxious that all our difficulties be settled; and that we should once more restore concord and harmony to this country.

Now, what is the plan of the President? I will describe it by a simile, in a manner which cannot be misunderstood. Here are five wounds—one, two, three, four, five—bleeding and threatening the well being, if not the existence of the body politic. What is the plan of the President? Is it to heal all these wounds? No such thing. It is only to heal one of the five, and to leave the other four to bleed more profusely than ever, by the sole admission of California, even if it should produce death itself. I have said that five wounds are open and bleeding. What are they? First, there is California; there are the territories second; there is the question of the boundary of Texas the third; there is the fugitive slave bill the fourth; and there is the question of the slave trade in the District of Columbia fifth. The President, instead of proposing a plan comprehending all the diseases of the country, looks only at one. His recommendation does not embrace, and he says nothing about the fugitive slave bill or the District bill; but he recommends that the other two subjects, of territorial government and Texas boundary, remain and be left untouched, to cure themselves by some law of nature, by the *vis medicatrix naturae,*[1] or some self remedy, in the success of which I cannot perceive any ground of the least confidence. I have seen with profound surprise and regret, the persistence—for so I am painfully compelled to regard the facts around us—of the Chief Magistrate of the country in his own peculiar plan. I think that in the spirit of compromise, the President ought to unite with us. He recommends the admission of California. We are willing to admit California. We go with him as far as he goes, and we make its admission compose a part of a general plan

1 *vis medicatrix naturae:* the force of nature as a physician, or nature's healing power.

of settlement and compromise, which we propose to the consideration of the Senate. . . . After the observations which I addressed to the Senate a week ago, I did hope and trust there would have been a reciprocation from the other end of the avenue, as to the desire to heal, not one wound only, which being healed alone would exasperate and aggravate instead of harmonizing the country, but to heal them all. I did hope that we should have had some signification in some form or other, of the Executive contentment and satisfaction with the entire plan of adjustment. But, instead of concurrence with the committee on the part of the Executive, we have an authentic assurance of his adherence exclusively to his own particular scheme. . . .

Mr. President, with regard to Utah, there is no government whatever, unless it is such as necessity has prompted the Mormons to institute; and when you come to New Mexico, what government have you? A military government, by a lieutenant colonel of the army! A lieutenant colonel—a mere subordinate of the army of the United States—holds the governmental power there, in a time of profound peace! Stand up, Whig who can—stand up, Democrat who can, and defend the establishment of a military government in this free and glorious Republic, in a time of profound peace! Sir, we had doubts about the authority of the late President [James K. Polk] to do this in time of war, and it was cast as a reproach against him. But here, in a time of profound peace, it is proposed by the highest authority, that this government, that this military government—and by what authority it has continued since peace ensued, I know not—should be continued indefinitely, till New Mexico is prepared to come as a State into the Union. And when will that be? There are now about ten thousand people there, composed of Americans, Spaniards, and Mexicans; and about eighty thousand or ninety thousand Indians, civilized, half civilized, and barbarous people; and when will they be ready to come in as a State? Sir, I say it under a full sense of the responsibility of my position, that if to-morrow, with such a population, and such a constitution as such a population might make, they were to come here for admission as a State, I, for one, would not vote for it. It would be ridiculous; it would be farcical; it would bring into contempt the grave matter of forming commonwealths as sovereign members of this glorious Union. She has no population, in sufficient numbers, morally capable of self-government; nor will she have, for many years to come, such a population as will make it proper to admit her as a State. And yet the plan of the President is to leave this military government under this lieutenant colonel in full operation, declaring, as he does, in opposition to evidence, that they have a very good government there now. . . .

In what circumstances will this country be, if Congress adjourns without a settlement of this boundary question, and without establishing territorial governments for Utah and New Mexico? In what condition would the people of New Mexico be, east of the Rio del Norte [Rio Grande], in their conflict with Texas? Sir, I need not remind you of what everybody knows—of the settled dislike, the insuperable antipathy existing on the part of the people of New Mexico towards Texas, denouncing and denying her authority, contravening the existence of her laws, and ready, if they had the power to do it, to resist her claim of jurisdiction to the last extremity. And yet they are to be left to

take care of themselves! They have got a government good enough for them!
. . . I will close this part of what I have to say by grouping, comparing, and
contrasting the features of the respective plans of the Executive and the committee, which I shall be glad if the reporters will publish in parallel columns:

The President's plan proposes an adjustment of only one of the five subjects which agitate and divide the country.

The committee's plan recommends an amicable settlement of all five of them.

The President's plan proposes the admission of California as a State.

That of the committee also pro- poses the admission of California as a State.

He proposes non-intervention as to slavery.

They also propose non-interven- tion as to slavery.

But he proposes, further, non-in- tervention in the establishment of territorial governments; that is to say, that we shall neglect to execute the obligation of the United States in the treaty of Hidalgo; fail to govern those whom we are bound to govern; leave them without the protection of the civil authority of any general government; leave Utah without any government at all, but that which the Mormons may institute; and leave New Mexico under the military gov- ernment of a lieutenant colonel.

They propose action and interven- tion, by the establishment of civil government for the Territories, in conformity with treaty and constitu- tional obligations; to give the super- intending and controlling power of our general government, in place of that of Mexico, which they have lost; and to substitute a civil instead of that military government which de- clares it will assume an attitude of neutrality in the boundary contest be- tween New Mexico and Texas.

His plan fails to establish the limits of New Mexico east of the Rio Grande, and would expose the people who inhabit it to civil war, already threatened, with Texas.

Theirs proposes a settlement of the boundary question, and, being settled, a civil war with Texas would be averted.

He proposes no adjustment of the fugitive slave subject.

They offer amendments, which will make the recovery of fugitives more effectual, and at the same time, it is believed, will be generally satis- factory to the North.

He proposes no arrangement of the subject of slavery or the slave trade in the District of Columbia.

They propose to interdict the slave trade in the District, and to leave slavery there undisturbed.

Thus, of the five subjects of disturbance and agitation—to wit: California, territorial governments, the boundary question with Texas, the fugitive bill, and the subject of slavery in the District—

They propose to adjust all five of them on a basis which, it is confidently believed, is just, fair, and honorable, and will be satisfactory to the people of the United States.

His plan settles but one, leaving the other four unadjusted, to inflame and exasperate the public mind, I fear, more than ever.

They offer the olive branch of peace, harmony, and tranquillity.

Under his plan, one party, flushed with success in the admission of California alone, will contend with new hopes and fresh vigor, for the application of the Wilmot proviso to all the remaining territory; whilst the other party, provoked and chagrined by obtaining no concession whatever, may be urged and animated to extreme and greater lengths than have yet been manifested.

Under their plan, all questions being settled in a spirit of mutual concession and compromise, there will be general acquiescence, if not satisfaction; and the whole country will enjoy once more the blessing of domestic peace, concord, and reconciliation.

Whilst the President's plan is confined to a single measure, leaving the governments of Utah and New Mexico unprovided for, and the boundary between Texas and New Mexico unsettled, another, and one of the most irritating questions, is left by him, without any recommendation or any provision, to harass and exasperate the country.

He fails to recommend any plan for the settlement of the important and vexatious subject of fugitive slaves. He proposes no plan of settlement of the agitating questions which arise out of this subject. I will repeat, let him who can stand up here and tell the country, and satisfy his own conscience—when the whole country is calling out for peace, peace, peace; when it is imploring its rulers above and its rulers below to bring once more to this agitated and distracted people some broad and comprehensive scheme of healing, and to settle all these questions which agitate this afflicted people—let any man who can, not in the public press, but in the Senate of the United States, stand up and show that the plan which is proposed by executive authority is such a one as is demanded by the necessities of the case and the condition of the country. I should be glad to hear that man. Ay, Mr. President, I wish I had the mental power commensurate with my fervent wishes for the adjustment of these unhappy questions—commensurate to urge upon you and upon the country forbearance, conciliation, the surrender of extreme opinions, the avoidance of attempting impossibilities.

Sir, I know there is a floating idea in the southern mind, such as we have heard before, of the necessity of an equilibrium of power between the two sections of the Union—of a balancing authority. However desirable such a state of political arrangement might be, we all know it is utterly impracticable. We all know that the rapid growth and unparalleled progress of the northern portion of this country is such that it is impossible for the South to keep pace with it; and unless the order of all republics shall be reversed, and the majority shall be governed by the minority, the equilibrium is unattainable. But, sir, because there is not and cannot be, and in the nature of things it is impossible that there should be, this equilibrium of power between the two sections of this country, does it therefore follow that the southern portion is in any danger with respect to that great institution which exists there, and is cherished with so much solicitude? I think not; I believe not. . . .

Nor is this great interest of the South, this institution of slavery, the only one to be affected by the fact that it is in a minority. Is it peculiar to that interest? No, sir. How is it with the fishing interest? How with the navigating interest? They are both greatly in the minority. How is it with the manufacturing interest? In the minority. How is it with the commercial interest? In the minority. In short, without continuing the enumeration, every interest in this country is in the minority, except that great and all-pervading interest of agriculture, which extends from one end of the country to the other. We must be reconciled to the condition which is inevitable. There is all reasonable security against any abuses which may be inflicted in the progress of events, which you can no more arrest than you can seize and hold the beams which are poured forth from that great luminary of the system of which we compose a part, or than you can stop, in its onward course, the flowing of the Mississippi river, and compel it to turn back to its sources in the Rocky and Alleghany mountains. It is utterly vain to suppose you can acquire that equilibrium of which we have heard so much, between the slaveholding and the non-slaveholding portions of the Union. It is not necessary, I hope; it is not necessary, I believe; but, whether it is or not, it is unattainable, by the operation of causes beyond all human or earthly control. And to oppose the immutable and irrevocable laws of population and of nature is equivalent to a demand for the severance of the Union.

I conclude by repeating that here are five wounds which, by the committee of compromise, are proposed to be closed. Sir, I know what may be said. I know it will be said that agitators will, even after the passage of all these measures, continue to agitate; that the two extremes will still cry out for their respective favorite measures; that the Wilmot proviso, although territorial governments will be established, will be pressed, to be added by a supplementary act, or to be incorporated in the constitutions which these territories may establish. I know it may be urged—indeed, I have heard it stated on this floor—"Pass all your measures, and we will cry out for repeal." I know something, I think, of the nature of man. I know something of the nature of my own countrymen. I speak, also, with the authority and with the aid of history. At the time of the memorable Missouri compromise, as at this—and I have been unable to determine in my own mind whether more solicitude and anxiety existed then than now—the whole country was in an uproar, on the one side, for the admission of Missouri, and, on the other, for her exclusion. Every legislative body throughout the country—I believe there were twenty-four then—had denounced or approved the measure of the admission of Missouri. The measure was finally carried by a small majority; only six in the House of Representatives, where the great struggle—where the long-continued exertion—was carried on. And what were the consequences—the tranquillizing consequences —which ensued throughout this distracted country? The act was everywhere received with joy, and exultation, and triumph; and the man who would have dared to interrupt the universal, and deep-felt, and all-pervading harmony which prevailed throughout the country, in consequence of that adjustment, would have stood rebuked, and repudiated, and reproached by the indignant voice of his countrymen. And I venture to say, if this measure of compromise goes to the country with all the high sanctions which it may carry—sanctions of both houses of Congress, and of the Executive, and of the great body of the American people—to a country bleeding at every pore—to a country imploring us to settle their difficulties, and give once more peace and happiness to them—I venture to say that the agitation will be at an end, though a few may croak and halloo as they please. There are a few miserable men who live upon agitation—men who are never satisfied until they can place themselves at the head of a little clique of agitators, and, fastening them to their tails, go to the Democratic party and say, "Take me—I am a good Democrat, and I will bring to you this capital which I have, and insure your success;" or go to the Whig party and say, "Take this little balancing power which I possess, and I will enable your party to triumph over their adversaries." I venture to say they will be hushed into silence, by the indignation they will meet everywhere, in their vain and futile attempt to prolong that agitation which has threatened this country with the most direful calamity which, in all the dispensations of God, could befall it.

Sir, I am done. I would say much more, but I cannot longer trespass upon your time. I did not expect to have said so much, and my physical powers will not permit me to say more.

8] Clay Is Attacked and Taylor Defended

Clay's May 21 speech was mainly an assault on Zachary Taylor, whose Washington newspaper—the *Republic*—had differed sharply with Clay the day before. Antagonisms were white-hot the final week in May, when in turn the Whig senator once more was answered by the Whig President's *Republic* spokesman.*

IT IS NOW more than six months since the President of the United States, in a message to Congress transmitting information in answer to a resolution of the House of Representatives on the subject of California and New Mexico . . . ,

* CLAY IS ATTACKED AND TAYLOR DEFENDED: From the Washington *Republic* (May 27, 1850).

pointed out the course of policy which, in his opinion, under all the circumstances of the case, it would be most wise to pursue in reference to the government of the territory acquired from Mexico by the treaty of Guadalupe Hidalgo. To that subject, and that subject alone, did the recommendations contained in his message refer. To none other did he conceive it to be his duty, on that occasion, to call the attention of Congress. That the line of policy then recommended by him was, at the time, most favorably received by the people of the United States . . . we presume no one will pretend to deny.

After the PRESIDENT had recommended to Congress the plan of proceeding which he deemed best, various other plans were offered by individual members of the Senate, and more recently another has emanated from a committee of thirteen members of the Senate, to whom the subject had been referred. This is known as the Compromise. During the discussions . . . it began to be rumored that the PRESIDENT had *changed his opinion* in regard to the policy originally recommended by him, and that he thought better of some other plan. Positive statements to that effect were made in the public prints, and began to obtain a very general credence. Under these circumstances, it was alike due to the PRESIDENT, to the public, and, in a particular manner, to those members of Congress who preferred the line of policy recommended by him to any other, and who had from the beginning stood ready to support it, that the misapprehension should be corrected. He accordingly authorized us to say that no such change of opinion as that attributed to him had taken place, and that he was still firm in the belief that the policy recommended by him was . . . the best that was practicable. This simple correction of current misapprehensions and misrepresentations . . . has, it appears, been singularly misconceived as to its object, and as strangely received in certain quarters. The *Union* newspaper, the sole organ, in this city, of the Democratic party, construes it into an indication that the PRESIDENT is opposed to "the Compromise"—which means the Compromise in all its parts and provisions—and that he is "against the settlement of the slavery question."

The enunciation was also received, it appears, "with profound surprise and regret" by a distinguished Whig Senator, Mr. CLAY, who . . . on Tuesday the 21st instant, in the discharge of "a *painful duty,*" felt himself called upon to contrast the plan proposed by the PRESIDENT with the compromise plan. This he did by a "simile." "Here," said he, "are five wounds—one, two, three, four, and five—bleeding and threatening the well-being, if not the existence of the body politic. What is the plan of the PRESIDENT? Is it to heal all these wounds? No such thing. It is only to heal one of the five, and to leave the others to bleed more profusely than ever, by the sole admission of California, even if it should produce death itself."

. . . In this contrast, which the Senator proceeds to carry out at considerable length, it appears to us, and we doubt not it will so appear to the public, that he has done the PRESIDENT very great injustice. . . .

The injustice of the contrast in part lies here—that while the course of policy recommended by the PRESIDENT had reference only to the government of the people of the territory acquired from Mexico; whilst he expressed no opinion, and was called upon to express no opinion on the subject of the fugitive slave bill and the question of the slave trade in the District of Columbia, that policy is held up by the Senator as antagonistic to these two last-mentioned measures. . . . Who has the shadow of a right to assume, from any thing the PRESIDENT has anywhere said, that he is opposed or indifferent to the adoption of either of those measures? We are not aware that he has expressed an opinion favorable or adverse to those measures, or either of them. How can either be in anywise affected by the adherence of the PRESIDENT to his plan in respect to California and New Mexico? Could they not both as well go hand in hand with the policy recommended by him, in reference to our newly acquired Mexican territory, as with the policy recommended in "the Compromise" in reference to the same territory? These two "wounds," it may be sufficient here to say, the PRESIDENT did not open; he has not recommended that they should be left open; nor has he offered the slightest impediment to their being healed up.

The subjects of the government of the Territories, and the question of the boundary of Texas—the second and third "wounds" in the order enumerated —we will consider together. . . . The Senator says: "The PRESIDENT's plan proposes the admission of California. He proposes non-intervention as to slavery. But he proposes further non-intervention in the establishment of territorial government; that is to say, that we shall neglect to execute the obligation of the treaty of Hidalgo—fail to govern those whom we are bound to govern— leave them without the protection of the civil authority of any general government—leave Utah without any government at all, but that which the Mormons may institute—and leave New Mexico under the military government of a Lieutenant Colonel. His plan fails to establish the limits of New Mexico east of the Rio Grande, and would expose the people who inhabit it to civil war, already threatened, with Texas."

A formidable array of alleged defects and omissions in the PRESIDENT's plan! Let us turn for a few moments to the plan itself, and see whether it is justly liable to the grave objections urged by the Senator. That plan contemplated the *immediate* formation of State constitutions by the people of California and New Mexico, and their early admission into the Union as States. . . . California, accordingly, proceeded to form a State constitution, and is now applying to Congress for admission into the Union as a State. Nothing has existed, or now exists, to prevent New Mexico from following the example of California. She may, and probably will, do so before the close of the present session of Congress, unless she is deterred by the declaration of the Senator that he will not vote for her admission into the Union at present as a State. With what fairness and justice, then, can it be charged upon the PRESIDENT, that he proposes to leave New Mexico under the military government of a Lieutenant Colonel, without the protection of the civil authority of any general government, and in utter disregard of the obligation of the United States in the treaty of Guadalupe Hidalgo? Leave them in that condition? For how long a period? For such brief space only as will be requisite for the formation of a State constitution, and their admission into the Union as a State. . . .

Another of the objections of the Senator to the PRESIDENT's plan is, as he alleges, that the PRESIDENT recommends that the subject, or "wound," of the

Texas boundary, along with that of the Territorial government, should remain, and be left untouched, to cure itself by some law of nature. . . . And this in the face of the following extract from the message of the PRESIDENT!

"A claim has been advanced by the State of Texas to a very large portion of the most populous district of the Territory commonly designated by the name of New Mexico. If the people of New Mexico had formed a plan of a State government for that Territory, as ceded by the treaty of Guadalupe Hidalgo, and had been admitted by Congress as a State, our Constitution would have afforded the means of obtaining an adjustment of the question of boundary with Texas by a judicial decision. At present, however, no judicial tribunal has the power of deciding that question, and *it remains for Congress to devise some mode of adjustment.*"

Is this express submission of the Texas boundary question to *Congress,* with whom the subject properly belonged, "to devise some mode of adjustment?" —is this proposing to leave it "untouched, to cure itself by some law of nature, by the *vis medicatrix naturae,* or some self remedy?" New Mexico being admitted into the Union as a State, the Supreme Court would then have jurisdiction over the question of boundary between that State and Texas, and its adjudication would be competent to heal that wound.

With regard to Utah, the people of that portion of the territory acquired from Mexico have emigrated thither of their own free volition, and now constitute an isolated people. They have adopted a provisional form of government, perhaps as well or better suited to their condition and wants than any which Congress could devise for them. They are in the full enjoyment of the great right of self-government. They are well armed, and, if we are correctly informed, abundantly able to protect themselves from the Indian tribes in the vicinity. Should they at any time need additional military protection, the PRESIDENT will no doubt take care that it be promptly extended to them. . . .

Non-action by Congress in respect to the establishment of territorial governments is an important feature in the PRESIDENT's policy. He is not in favor of the establishment of territorial governments, while the compromise plan insists upon their necessity. Now, without desiring or intending to assail any plan, we may be permitted, we hope, without offence, to examine this feature of the PRESIDENT's plan, in connexion with the antagonistic feature in the compromise plan.

In recommending the course of policy he did, the PRESIDENT had in view the early and final settlement of the slavery question, so far as it concerned the territory acquired from Mexico; his object was to put a stop to all agitation, in Congress and out of it, on the subject of the prohibition of the introduction of the institution of slavery into that territory, and to relieve Congress from the necessity of legislating on that subject at all. For, if that body legislated at all on the subject, it must needs bring itself into conflict with the passions, prejudices, and opinions of both sections of the Union. Now, it was evident that no bill establishing territorial governments over the territory could pass Congress without bringing up the Wilmot proviso question—if, indeed, any such bill could pass without having that proviso incorporated into it. The mere discussion of that question in Congress, and the necessity of having to vote upon it, were to be deprecated and avoided, if possible, because such discussion, and such a vote, even if the proviso should be voted down, would, in all probability, sow the seeds of future agitation and excitement broadcast over the whole of the free States.

In the South, too, what evidence have we that there will be general acquiescence and satisfaction with so much of the compromise as relates to the government of the territory acquired from Mexico? Are the Southern members of Congress united on that subject? It is well known that they are not. . . . While at the South it is held by distinguished men to secure all that the South desires, other equally distinguished men in the same section maintain that it surrenders all that the South has contended for. Equally conflicting views of its effect are held at the North—some contending that it will open the whole of New Mexico and Utah to the admission of slavery; whilst its supporters from that section contend that slavery is now prohibited by the local law in those Territories, which will not be abrogated by the compromise, and thus that it will have all the effect of the Wilmot proviso. Is it not, then, manifest that Northern men who support it will be arraigned for surrendering the principle of the proviso, and that Southern men who support it will be arraigned for surrendering the rights of the South, for which they had pledged themselves to contend so strenuously? Can a measure like this give harmony and tranquillity to the country? Is it not rather to be feared that, if adopted, it will prove a prolific fountain, from which will flow continued agitation and discord?

. . . The PRESIDENT's plan, if adopted and carried out, can be attended with no such consequences. It will leave nothing behind it to agitate about. It gives finality to this vexed question of the inhibition or admission of slavery into the territory acquired from Mexico, and in no wise conflicts with the other measures contemplated in reference to fugitive slaves and the slave trade in the District of Columbia—both of them subjects of high and grave importance, and neither of which is any more dependent upon the adoption of the territorial portion of the compromise plan than it is upon the adoption of the PRESIDENT's plan. Either or both may possibly be defeated, though the Compromise bill should pass. If the Compromise bill should pass, and the fugitive slave bill be lost, will not the Southern supporters of the former impute bad faith to its Northern supporters? And if the bill respecting the slave trade in the District of Columbia should fail to become a law, will not those Northern members of Congress who support the Compromise as a whole, make loud complaints against its Southern supporters? Will there not, in either of these cases, be mutual imputations of bad faith, and mutual criminations and recriminations? Where, then, will be the harmony, the absence of which the Senator from Kentucky so eloquently deplores? May there not, in either case, be a startling addition to the five bleeding wounds so graphically described by the Senator?

Upon a full view of the whole question, and upon a candid consideration of the reasons on both sides, we are wholly unable to see that superior remedial potency in the compromise plan over that of the PRESIDENT, which is claimed for the former by its supporters. Certainly such superiority, if it indeed exists, is not so manifest as to justify its supporters in *requiring* the PRESIDENT to abandon his own opinions, deliberately formed and expressed, and actively exert his influence to defeat the principle of adjustment which he has deliberately recommended, and which he still believes to be the best calculated to overcome all the difficulties growing out of our acquisition of territory from Mexico. Such a course, on his part, would be incompatible with self-respect, and could not fail to diminish the confidence of the country in his firmness and wisdom. . . .

9] Douglas' Private Comments on Strategy and Tactics

It was after Taylor's death and Clay's departure that Stephen A. Douglas forged to the front. Only thirty-seven, the Chicagoan was chubby and chunky but impressive none the less. A "steam engine in britches" he had been called, and the title "the Little Giant" became him. Now we read the letter he sent to friends in early August, revealing 1850 realities more accurately than most Congressional speeches.*

Washington, Aug 3d 1850

(Private)
Messrs. Lanphier & Walker,
Dr Sirs

You have doubtless heard of the defeat of the Compromise of the Committee of thirteen. I regret it very much, altho I must say that I never had very strong hopes of its passage. By combining the measures into one Bill the Committee united the opponents of each measure instead of securing the friends of each. I have thought from the beginning that they made a mistake in this respect. I declined being a member of the Committee of 13 for this reason & for the same reasons opposed the appointment of the Committee. It was as well known before the Committee were appointed what they were to do as after they reported. I had previously written & reported as Chmn of the Com. on Territories two Bills—one for the admission of California & the other providing territorial Governments for Utah & New Mexico also providing for the settlement of the Texas Boundary. Before I reported these Bills I consulted Mr. Clay & Gen'l Cass whether I should put them in one or separate Bills. They both advised me to keep them separate & both expressed the same opinions in debate about that time. I took their advice & reported the measures in two Bills instead of one. About two weeks afterward they changed their minds & concluded to appoint a committee for the purpose of uniting them. I opposed the movement as unwise & unnecessary as they declared they did not intend to change any feature in my Bills. The Committee was appointed & took my two printed Bills & put a wafer between & reported them back without changing or writing a single word except one line. The one line inserted prohibited the Territorial Legislatures from legislating upon the subject of slavery. This amendment was written in by the Com. in opposition to the wishes of Gen'l

* DOUGLAS' PRIVATE COMMENTS ON STRATEGY AND TACTICS: From a letter from Stephen A. Douglas to Charles H. Lanphier and George Walker, August 3, 1850; original in possession of Dr. Charles L. Patton, Springfield, Illinois. Reprinted by permission.

Cass & Mr. Clay, and they gave notice that they should move to strike it out in the Senate, & it was stricken out. So you see that the difference between Mr. Clay's Compromise Bill & my two Bills was a wafer & that he did not write one word of it & that I did write every word. After the majority of the Senate decided that they would act upon the measures jointly instead of separately[,] I gave the Bill of Mr. Clay my active & unswerving support down to its final defeat. The same remark is true of my colleague Gen'l Shields and it is also proper to remark that all our [Illinois] representatives, except Baker & Wentworth were anxious for the passage of the Bill & were ready to support it if it passed the Senate. It is true Col. McClernand, at one time, thought that he could get up a better one, but soon gave it up. His Bill was substantially the same as Mr. Clay's, differing a little in the details. The Compromise Bill was defeated by a union between the Free Soilers & Disunionists & the administration of Gen'l Taylor. All the power & patronage of the Govt was brought to bear against us & at the last the allied forces were able to beat us. The Utah Bill has passed the Senate in the precise words in which I wrote it. We are now engaged on my California Bill & I trust you will hear of its passage through the Senate before you receive this. We shall then take up a Bill for the Texas Boundary which Mr. Pearce of Md. & myself are now preparing & he will introduce on Monday next. We shall then take up the Bill for New Mexico & pass it just as I reported it four months ago. Thus will all the Bills pass the Senate & I believe the House also. When they are all passed you see they will be collectively Mr. Clay's Compromise & separately the Bills reported by the committee on Territories four months ago. Col. Benton has done much to delay action & to defeat all the measures. In my opinion no justification, no excuse can be made for his conduct. On the other hand I must say that if Mr. Clay's name had not been associated with the Bills they would have passed long ago. The Administration were jealous of him & hated him & some democrats were weak enough to fear that the success of his Bill would make him President. But let it always be said of old Hal that he fought a glorious & a patriotic battle. No man was ever governed by higher or finer motives. The same remark is true of Gen'l Cass. Many of our friends talk hard of Buchanan. It is supposed that he encouraged the nullifiers & disunionists to oppose the measure out of jealousy of Gen'l Cass. I hope this will turn out not to be true. I have now given you a pretty full history of the Compromise—of its rise and fall. We have great confidence that we will yet be able to settle the whole difficulty before we adjourn. Excuse this long epistle.

> Your friend
> S. A. DOUGLAS

10] The Military Readiness of Captain Jacob Roberts

Jacob Roberts of Plum Creek, Texas, would have been consigned to oblivion long ago if his reply to Governor Bell did not give him a certain kind of immortality. How astounded Roberts' ghost must be to find his composition bracketed with the polished utterances of Webster and Calhoun. Here is the delightfully illiterate response of an obscure militia captain to his chief executive's call to arms.*

the
August   1850
      27

Goveneor P H Bell

SIR I tak this oppertunity of riting to you informing you that I have about got my company rased for Santafee and will note your order I seen Capt McCullock the other day and he tolde me that he wood not go and I ask him his reason for not going and his anser was to me that he thought you did not treate him rite in given me an order and told sum others pursons that he exspected to git an order to rase men for the frunt teers survis as for my part I am perfectley willing to surve my contry Goveneor if the Santafee expadision dos not go on and the is a chance to git in to the Survis on the frunt teers and you think me worthey of a companey and wood give me an order it wood be a favor thankfulley recieved so nothing moor at present but remandes your true frende and brother Solder

JACOB ROBERTS

11] Linn Boyd Cries, "In God's Name Let Us Act"

It remained for a member of the House to summarize the weariness and determination many congressmen felt after eight months of wrangling. A tall, handsome, white-haired, seven-term idol of western Kentucky, Linn Boyd usually held his tongue. But on August 29 the Democrat spoke out with a hint of desperation in his language, which proved extraordinarily effective.†

THE AMENDMENT . . . which I had the honor to introduce yesterday . . . is now upon the table of every member of this House. . . . Sir, the path is beaten. We have all investigated each and every proposition contained either in the bill or in the amendment. . . . I take it for granted that every member of this House is as well prepared this moment as he will be next week, or next year, to say how he will vote in relation to these propositions. Everything we do—every movement that we make in relation to the delicate and important questions involved in the propositions before us, has a consequence in it of the gravest concern. It has become a matter of importance whether we shall consider the [Texas and New Mexico] bills in a connected or in a separate form.

* THE MILITARY READINESS OF CAPTAIN JACOB ROBERTS: Jacob Roberts to Governor P. H. Bell, August 27, 1850. From Governor's Letters, Texas State Archives, Austin.
† LINN BOYD CRIES, "IN GOD'S NAME LET US ACT": From the *Congressional Globe*, 31 Cong., 1 Sess., pp. 1696–97.

. . . We have had in another branch of this Capitol, a measure which has been called the omnibus. Piece by piece it broke down; and there are many gentlemen here who are unwilling, after it shall have been coopered up, to take passage in it. There are many gentlemen who think that every measure sent us from the Senate may be passed through this House if the vote shall be taken singly upon them. Other gentlemen think that it is impossible to come to any settlement of the question, unless the California and other bills shall be connected together, so as to help each other on. For my own part, I avow what my object is in offering this amendment. It is to test the sense of the House in relation to the establishment of territorial governments upon the non-intervention principle. . . . It is, in my humble judgment, the principle of the Constitution itself. It is the principle which has been sanctioned and advocated by the Democratic party through the entire country, North and South. It is acknowledged to be a just principle by very many persons, even outside of that party. Shall we abandon it now—especially at a time when it seems to be, and in fact is, the only principle upon which we can settle the question of territorial governments?

. . . Mr. Speaker, I have thus stated the object of my amendment. I do not desire to see this omnibus coopered up again; but if we can settle all these questions better in that form, I should rejoice to see it done. If gentlemen are indisposed to attempt to pass all these measures in a single bill, I shall be content. And, in proof of the sincerity of that declaration, I propose to withdraw all that portion of my amendment which relates to the Territory of Utah. My object is to satisfy every gentleman on all sides of this House that I am earnestly and in good faith seeking to test the sense of the House upon the doctrine of non-intervention. I want to see that principle carried out—I want to see it carried out in good faith. I want to see peace restored to the country. I am for the Union. I am for the Constitution as it is—I want no amendment to it. . . . In the name of God, let us save that Constitution.

I said—though I fear I have in some degree violated the strict letter of my word—that I did not intend to make a speech—

[Cries, "Go on, Boyd—go on."]

I do not intend it. We have already been listening to speeches for nine long months. It is time we should act. I am astonished at the patience with which our constituents have borne our procrastination. I think we have talked enough —in God's name let us act. If the result of our action should be, that we cannot settle these questions upon the only principle on which . . . I believe they can be settled, then I, for one, shall be in favor of an immediate adjournment after the passage of the necessary appropriation bills. Nay, I will go further, and say, that I should be pleased, in that event, to see every man of this House resign his commission into the hands of the people who gave it, and leave it to them to send here Representatives better disposed to do their duty and to save the Union.

I have not another word to say. I withdraw that portion of my amendment which relates to the Territory of Utah.

12] Out of Crisis, Compromise in the Form of Five Laws

And what of the Compromise itself? One of its components is reproduced *in toto*. Some were long, but their essence remains even after drastic excisions. In examining the territorial laws in particular, the reader is asked to compare their provisions with Clay's original resolutions and also with the work of the Committee of Thirteen. Some historians have been inclined to consider them all identical, which obviously they were not.*

An Act proposing to the State of Texas the Establishment of her Northern and Western Boundaries, the Relinquishment by the said State of all Territory claimed by her exterior to said Boundaries, and of all her Claims upon the United States, and to establish a territorial Government for New Mexico.

Be it enacted by the Senate and House of Representatives of the United States of America in Congress assembled, That the following propositions shall be, and the same hereby are, offered to the State of Texas, which, when agreed to by the said State, in an act passed by the general assembly, shall be binding and obligatory upon the United States, and upon the said State of Texas: *Provided,* The said agreement by the said general assembly shall be given on or before the first day of December, eighteen hundred and fifty:

FIRST. The State of Texas will agree that her boundary on the north shall commence at the point at which the meridian of one hundred degrees west from Greenwich is intersected by the parallel of thirty-six degrees thirty minutes north latitude, and shall run from said point due west to the meridian of one hundred and three degrees west from Greenwich; thence her boundary shall run due south to the thirty-second degree of north latitude; thence on the said parallel of thirty-two degrees of north latitude to the Rio Bravo del Norte [Rio Grande], and thence with the channel of said river to the Gulf of Mexico.

SECOND. The State of Texas cedes to the United States all her claim to territory exterior to the limits and boundaries which she agrees to establish by the first article of this agreement.

THIRD. The State of Texas relinquishes all claim upon the United States for liability of the debts of Texas, and for compensation or indemnity for the surrender to the United States of her ships, forts, arsenals, custom-houses, custom-house revenue, arms and munitions of war, and public buildings with their sites, which became the property of the United States at the time of the annexation.

FOURTH. The United States, in consideration of said establishment of boundaries, cession of claim to territory, and relinquishment of claims, will pay to

---

* OUT OF CRISIS, COMPROMISE IN THE FORM OF FIVE LAWS: The Compromise of 1850. From *The Statutes at Large and Treaties of the United States of America* (Boston, 1845–   ), IX, 447–58, 462–65, 467–68.

the State of Texas the sum of ten millions of dollars in a stock bearing five per cent. interest, and redeemable at the end of fourteen years, the interest payable half-yearly at the treasury of the United States.

FIFTH. Immediately after the President of the United States shall have been furnished with an authentic copy of the act of the general assembly of Texas accepting these propositions, he shall cause the stock to be issued in favor of the State of Texas, as provided for in the fourth article of this agreement: *Provided, also,* That no more than five millions of said stock shall be issued until the creditors of the State holding bonds and other certificates of stock of Texas for which duties on imports were specially pledged, shall first file at the treasury of the United States releases of all claim against the United States for or on account of said bonds or certificates in such form as shall be prescribed by the Secretary of the Treasury and approved by the President of the United States: *Provided,* That nothing herein contained shall be construed to impair or qualify any thing contained in the third article of the second section of the "joint resolution for annexing Texas to the United States," approved March first, eighteen hundred and forty-five, either as regards the number of States that may hereafter be formed out of Texas, or otherwise.

SEC. 2. *And be it further enacted,* That all that portion of the Territory of the United States bounded as follows: Beginning at a point in the Colorado River where the boundary line with the republic of Mexico crosses the same; thence eastwardly with the said boundary line to the Rio Grande; thence following the main channel of said river to the parallel of the thirty-second degree of north latitude; thence east with said degree to its intersection with the one hundred and third degree of longitude west of Greenwich; thence north with said degree of longitude to the parallel of thirty-eighth degree of north latitude; thence west with said parallel to the summit of the Sierra Madre; thence south with the crest of said mountains to the thirty-seventh parallel of north latitude; thence west with said parallel to its intersection with the boundary line of the State of California; thence with said boundary line to the place of beginning—be, and the said is hereby, erected into a temporary government, by the name of the Territory of New Mexico: *Provided, . . .* That, when admitted as a State, the said Territory, or any portion of the same, shall be received into the Union, with or without slavery, as their constitution may prescribe at the time of their admission. . . .

SEC. 7. *And be it further enacted,* That the legislative power of the Territory shall extend to all rightful subjects of legislation, consistent with the Constitution of the United States and the provisions of this act; but . . . all the laws passed by the legislative assembly and governor shall be submitted to the Congress of the United States, and, if disapproved, shall be null and of no effect. . . .

SEC. 10. *And be it further enacted,* That the judicial power of said Territory shall be vested in a Supreme Court, District Courts, Probate Courts, and in justices of the peace. . . . Writs of error and appeals from the final decisions of said Supreme Court shall be allowed, and may be taken to the Supreme Court of the United States. . . .

SEC. 17. *And be it further enacted,* That the Constitution, and all laws of the United States which are not locally inapplicable, shall have the same force and effect within the said Territory of New Mexico as elsewhere within the United States.

Sec. 18. *And be it further enacted,* That the provisions of this act be, and they are hereby, suspended until the boundary between the United States and the State of Texas shall be adjusted; and when such adjustment shall have been effected, the President of the United States shall issue his proclamation, declaring this act to be in full force and operation. . . .

An Act for the Admission of the State of California into the Union.

Whereas the people of California have presented a constitution and asked admission into the Union, which constitution was submitted to Congress by the President of the United States, by message dated February thirteenth, eighteen hundred and fifty, and which, on due examination, is found to be republican in its form of government:

Be it enacted by the Senate and House of Representatives of the United States of America in Congress assembled, That the State of California shall be one, and is hereby declared to be one, of the United States of America, and admitted into the Union on an equal footing with the original States in all respects whatever. . . .

An Act to Establish a Territorial Government for Utah.

Be it enacted by the Senate and House of Representatives of the United States of America in Congress assembled, That all that part of the territory of the United States included within the following limits, to wit: bounded on the west by the State of California, on the north by the Territory of Oregon, and on the east by the summit of the Rocky Mountains, and on the south by the thirty-seventh parallel of north latitude, be, and the same is hereby, created into a temporary government, by the name of the Territory of Utah; and, when admitted as a State, the said Territory, or any portion of the same, shall be received into the Union, with or without slavery, as their constitution may prescribe at the time of their admission. . . .

Sec. 6. *And be it further enacted,* That the legislative power of said Territory shall extend to all rightful subjects of legislation, consistent with the Constitution of the United States and the provisions of this act; but . . . all the laws passed by the legislative assembly and governor shall be submitted to the Congress of the United States, and, if disapproved, shall be null and of no effect. . . .

Sec. 9. *And be it further enacted,* That the judicial power of said Territory shall be vested in a Supreme Court, District Courts, Probate Courts, and in justices of the peace. . . . Writs of error, and appeals from the final decisions of said Supreme Court, shall be allowed, and may be taken to the Supreme Court of the United States. . . .

Sec. 17. *And be it further enacted,* That the Constitution and laws of the United States are hereby extended over and declared to be in force in said Territory of Utah, so far as the same, or any provision thereof, may be applicable. . . .

An Act to amend, and supplementary to, the Act entitled "An Act respecting Fugitives from Justice, and Persons escaping from the Service of their Masters," approved February twelfth, one thousand seven hundred and ninety-three.

Be it enacted by the Senate and House of Representatives of the United States of America in congress assembled, That the persons who have been, or may hereafter be, appointed commissioners, in virtue of any act of Congress, by the Circuit Courts of the United States, and who, in consequence of such appointment, are authorized to exercise the powers that any justice of the peace, or other magistrate of any of the United States, may exercise in respect to offenders for any crime or offence against the United States, by arresting, imprisoning, or bailing the same under and by virtue of the thirty-third section of the act of the twenty-fourth of September seventeen hundred and eighty-nine, entitled "An Act to establish the judicial courts of the United States," shall be, and are hereby, authorized and required to exercise and discharge all the powers and duties conferred by this act.

Sec. 2. *And be it further enacted,* That the Superior Court of each organized Territory of the United States shall have the same power to appoint commissioners . . . who . . . shall moreover exercise and discharge all the powers and duties conferred by this act.

Sec. 3. *And be it further enacted,* That the Circuit Courts of the United States, and the Superior Courts of each organized Territory of the United States, shall from time to time enlarge the number of commissioners, with a view to afford reasonable facilities to reclaim fugitives from labor, and to the prompt discharge of the duties imposed by this act.

Sec. 4. *And be it further enacted,* That the commissioners above named shall have concurrent jurisdiction with . . . judges . . . and shall grant certificates to such claimants, upon satisfactory proof being made, with authority to take and remove such fugitives from service or labor, under the restrictions herein contained, to the State or Territory from which such persons may have escaped or fled.

Sec. 5. *And be it further enacted,* That it shall be the duty of all marshals and deputy marshals to obey and execute all warrants and precepts issued under the provisions of this act, when to them directed; and should any marshal or deputy marshal refuse to receive such warrant, or other process, when tendered, or to use all proper means diligently to execute the same, he shall, on conviction thereof, be fined in the sum of one thousand dollars, to the use of such claimant, on the motion of such claimant, by the Circuit or District Court for the district of such marshal; and after arrest of such fugitive, by such marshal or his deputy, or whilst at any time in his custody under the provisions of this act, should such fugitive escape, whether with or without the assent of such marshal or his deputy, such marshal shall be liable, on his official bond, to be prosecuted for the benefit of such claimant, for the full value of the service or labor of said fugitive in the State, Territory, or District whence he escaped; and the better to enable the said commissioners, when thus appointed, to execute their duties faithfully and efficiently, in conformity with the requirements of the Constitution of the United States and of this act, they are hereby authorized and empowered, within their counties respectively, to appoint, in writing under their hands, any one or more suitable persons . . . to execute all such warrants and other process as may be issued by them in the lawful performance of their respective duties; with authority to such commissioners, or the persons to be appointed by them, to execute process as aforesaid, to summon and call to their aid the bystanders, or *posse comitatus*[1] of the proper county, when necessary to ensure a faithful observance of the clause of the Constitution referred to, in conformity with the provisions of this act; and all good citizens are hereby commanded to aid and assist in the prompt and efficient execution of this law, whenever their services may be required, as aforesaid, for that purpose; and said warrants shall run, and be executed by said officers, any where in the State within which they are issued.

SEC. 6. *And be it further enacted,* That when a person held to service or labor in any State or Territory of the United States, has heretofore or shall hereafter escape into another State or Territory of the United States, the person or persons to whom such service or labor may be due, or his, her, or their agent or attorney, duly authorized, by power of attorney, in writing, acknowledged and certified under the seal of some legal officer or court of the State or Territory in which the same may be executed, may pursue and reclaim such fugitive person, either by procuring a warrant from some one of the courts, judges, or commissioners aforesaid, of the proper circuit, district or county, for the apprehension of such fugitive from service or labor, or by seizing and arresting such fugitive, where the same can be done without process, and by taking, or causing such person to be taken, forthwith before such court, judge, or commissioner, whose duty it shall be to hear and determine the case of such claimant in a summary manner; and upon satisfactory proof being made . . . , to use such reasonable force and restraint as may be necessary, under the circumstances of the case, to take and remove such fugitive person back to the State or Territory whence he or she may have escaped as aforesaid. In no trial or hearing under this act shall the testimony of such alleged fugitive be admitted in evidence. . . .

SEC. 7. *And be it further enacted,* That any person who shall knowingly and willingly obstruct, hinder, or prevent such claimant, his agent or attorney, or any person or persons lawfully assisting him, her, or them, from arresting such a fugitive from service or labor, either with or without process as aforesaid, or shall rescue, or attempt to rescue, such fugitive from service or labor, from the custody of such claimant, his or her agent or attorney, or other person or persons lawfully assisting as aforesaid, when so arrested, pursuant to the authority herein given and declared; or shall aid, abet, or assist such person . . . to escape from such claimant, his agent or attorney, or other person or persons legally authorized as aforesaid; or shall harbor or conceal such fugitive, so as to prevent the discovery and arrest of such person, after notice or knowledge of the fact that such person was a fugitive from service or labor as aforesaid, shall, for either of said offences, be subject to a fine not exceeding one thousand dollars, and imprisonment not exceeding six months . . . ; and shall moreover forfeit and pay, by way of civil damages to the party injured by such

---

1 *posse comitatus:* literally, "the power of the county"; hence, the entire body of those who may be summoned—also the body of persons so summoned—to assist in preserving the public peace or in executing any legal precept that is forcibly opposed.

illegal conduct, the sum of one thousand dollars, for each fugitive so lost as aforesaid, to be recovered by action of debt. . . .

SEC. 8. *And be it further enacted,* That the marshals, their deputies, and the clerks of the said District and Territorial Courts, shall be paid, for their services, the like fees as may be allowed to them for similar services in other cases; and where such services are rendered exclusively in the arrest, custody, and delivery of the fugitive to the claimant, his or her agent or attorney, or where such supposed fugitive may be discharged out of custody for the want of sufficient proof as aforesaid, then such fees are to be paid in the whole by such claimant, his agent or attorney; and in all cases where the proceedings are before a commissioner, he shall be entitled to a fee of ten dollars . . . upon the delivery of the said certificate to the claimant, his or her agent or attorney; or a fee of five dollars in cases where the proof shall not, in the opinion of such commissioner, warrant such certificate and delivery. . . . The person or persons authorized to execute the process . . . shall also be entitled to a fee of five dollars each for each person he or they may arrest and take before any such commissioner. . . .

SEC. 9. *And be it further enacted,* That, upon affidavit made by the claimant of such fugitive, his agent or attorney, after such certificate has been issued, that he has reason to apprehend that such fugitive will be rescued by force from his or their possession before he can be taken beyond the limits of the State in which the arrest is made, it shall be the duty of the officer making the arrest to retain such fugitive in his custody, and to remove him to the State whence he fled, and there to deliver him to said claimant, his agent, or attorney. And to this end, the officer aforesaid is hereby authorized and required to employ so many persons as he may deem necessary to overcome such force, and to retain them in his service so long as circumstances may require. . . .

An Act to suppress the Slave Trade in the District of Columbia.

Be it enacted by the Senate and House of Representatives of the United States of America in Congress assembled, That from and after the first day of January, eighteen hundred and fifty-one, it shall not be lawful to bring into the District of Columbia any slave whatever, for the purpose of being sold, or for the purpose of being placed in depot, to be subsequently transferred to any other State or place to be sold as merchandize. And if any slave shall be brought into the said District by its owner, or by the authority or consent of its owner, contrary to the provisions of this act, such slave shall thereupon become liberated and free.

SEC. 2. *And be it further enacted,* That it shall and may be lawful for each of the corporations of the cities of Washington and Georgetown, from time to time, and as often as may be necessary, to abate, break up, and abolish any depot or place of confinement of slaves brought into the said District as merchandize, contrary to the provisions of this act, by such appropriate means as may appear to either of the said corporations expedient and proper. And the same power is hereby vested in the Levy Court of Washington county, if any attempt shall be made, within its jurisdictional limits, to establish a depot or place of confinement for slaves brought into the said District as merchandize for sale contrary to this act.

MAPS

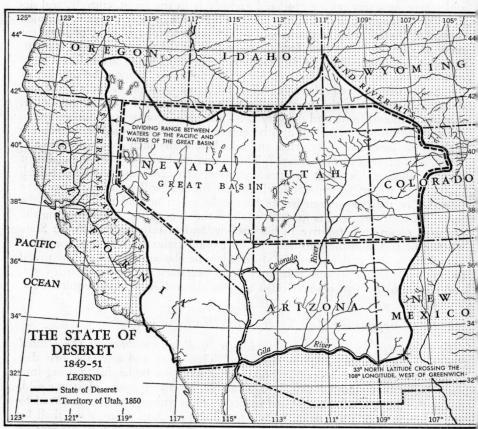

THE STATE OF
DESERET
1849-51
LEGEND
——— State of Deseret
- - - Territory of Utah, 1850

Adapted from the *Utah Historical Quarterly*, Volume VIII. Compiled by E. R. Varner 1940 from the map by Charles Preuss 1848 and other original sources.
Reprinted by permission of the *Utah Historical Quarterly*.

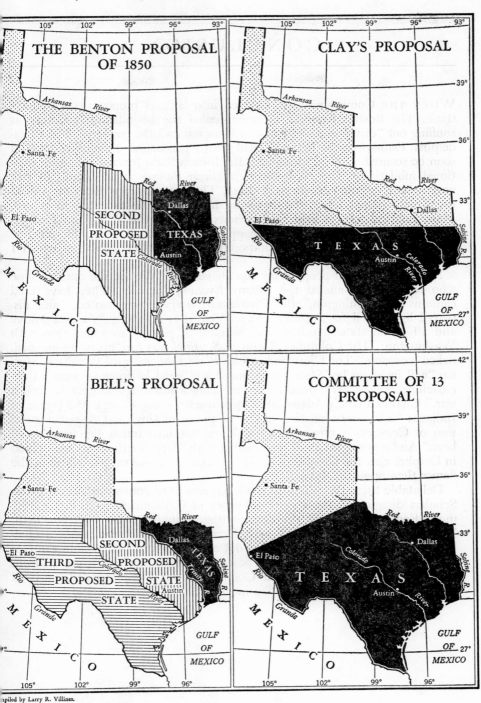

Four Proposals for Dividing Texas Soil

mpiled by Larry R. Villines.

CONCLUSION

WHEN THE Compromise was enacted into law, its proponents waxed ecstatic. The Boston *Evening Traveller* hailed the boundary bill victory as snuffing out "disunion and treason in Congress and the country." The Philadelphia *Pennsylvanian* felt confident that "peace and tranquility" would soon be secured. Out in Springfield, the *Illinois State Journal* called for "national jubilation." The Nashville *Republican Banner* urged friends of free government to congratulate each other. The New Orleans *Picayune* voiced the widely shared hope that harmony might now be expected to return. Many political leaders held similar views. Fillmore the Whig and Douglas the Democrat acknowledged their happiness and relief. Recent achievements, Webster declared, surpassed in importance "any acts of legislation which I have known for thirty years."

Not all papers and people were equally certain. "We are not among those who rejoice," announced the Albany *Evening Journal*. "They have fired cannons in Washington," the Charleston *Mercury* commented, "and displayed lights as if for a great victory. Well, it is a victory . . . over justice and all sound statesmanship. The burning of powder may not stop with Washington." The Columbus (Georgia) *Sentinel* was for "open, unqualified, naked *secession*." The Cleveland (Ohio) *Plain Dealer* hoped that New Mexico "will insist on her State Government and resist by force of arms all encroachments. . . . We should glory in being a humble volunteer in such a war." Charles Francis Adams of Massachusetts wrote George W. Julian of Indiana: "The consummation of the iniquities of this most disgraceful session of Congress is now reached—I know not how much the people will bear." And a young Kentuckian, familiar with Deep South reactions, opined in October that the Compromise "has proven more like oil poured upon the flames than upon the waves."

Debatable then, the adjusters' work has remained controversial ever since. Scholars disagree on the relative influence of Calhoun, Clay, Douglas, Fillmore, Foote, Taylor, and Webster. Southern emphasis vies with Northern, Western with Eastern, Whig with Democratic. Legislative nuances challenge the specialist. To what extent did economic forces determine the fate of the states and the nation? Did "peace and tranquility" really prevail from late 1850 until 1853? Perhaps the Compromise of 1850 postponed the Civil War. Perhaps it made Armageddon inevitable.

STUDY QUESTIONS

1] What difficult problems confronted Congress in late 1849 and early 1850? What was the President's attitude toward them?

2] What proposed solutions did Henry Clay project in January and February, 1850? How did the plan of the Senate Committee of Thirteen differ from them?

3] To what 1850 developments may the victory of the compromisers be attributed?

4] Did the Compromise of 1850 serve a useful purpose? Was there a more sensible alternative? Give specific reasons to buttress your answers to these two questions.

5] Examine five college textbooks in United States history. To what extent is each of them correct in its statements about the Compromise of 1850?

RECOMMENDED READINGS

PRIMARY SOURCES

COLTON, CALVIN, ed. *The Works of Henry Clay*, 10 vols. (New York, 1904), Vols. III and V.

JAMESON, J. FRANKLIN, ed. *Correspondence of John C. Calhoun*, American Historical Association *Annual Report . . . for the Year 1899*, II (Washington, 1900).

RICHARDSON, JAMES D., ed. *A Compilation of the Messages and Papers of the Presidents, 1789–1897*, 10 vols. (Washington, 1901), Vol. V.

U.S. CONGRESS. *Congressional Globe*, 31 Cong., 1 Sess.

————. *Congressional Globe Appendix*, 31 Cong., 1 Sess.

The Writings and Speeches of Daniel Webster, 18 vols. (Boston, 1903), Vols. X and XVIII.

SECONDARY SOURCES

BINKLEY, WILLIAM C. *The Expansionist Movement in Texas, 1836–1850* (Berkeley, Cal., 1925).

CAPERS, GERALD M. *Stephen A. Douglas: Defender of the Union* (Boston, 1959).

CRAVEN, AVERY O. *The Growth of Southern Nationalism, 1848–1861* (Baton Rouge, La., 1953).

FUESS, CLAUDE M. *Daniel Webster*, 2 vols. (Boston, 1930), Vol. II.

GANAWAY, LOOMIS M. *New Mexico and the Sectional Controversy, 1846–1861* (Albuquerque, N.M., 1944).

GOODWIN, CARDINAL. *The Establishment of State Government in California, 1848–1850* (New York, 1914).

HAMILTON, HOLMAN. "Texas Bonds and Northern Profits," *Mississippi Valley Historical Review*, XLIII (March, 1957), 579–94.

HAMILTON, HOLMAN. *Zachary Taylor: Soldier in the White House* (Indianapolis, 1951).

HODDER, FRANK H. "The Authorship of the Compromise of 1850," *Mississippi Valley Historical Review*, XXII (March, 1936), 525–36.

JOHNSON, ALLEN. "The Constitutionality of the Fugitive Slave Acts," *Yale Law Journal*, XXXI (December, 1921), 161–82.

MILTON, GEORGE F. *The Eve of Conflict: Stephen A. Douglas and the Needless War* (Boston, 1934).

MORGAN, DALE L. "The State of Deseret," *Utah Historical Quarterly*, VIII (April–July–October, 1940), 65–251.

NEVINS, ALLAN. *Ordeal of the Union*, 2 vols. (New York, 1947), Vol. I.

RAYBACK, ROBERT J. *Millard Fillmore: Biography of a President* (Buffalo, 1959).

RUSSEL, ROBERT R. "What Was the Compromise of 1850?" *Journal of Southern History*, XXII (August, 1956), 292–309.

SHRYOCK, RICHARD H. *Georgia and the Union in 1850* (Durham, N.C., 1926).

VAN DEUSEN, GLYNDON G. *The Life of Henry Clay* (Boston, 1937).

————. *Thurlow Weed: Wizard of the Lobby* (Boston, 1947).

WILTSE, CHARLES M. *John C. Calhoun: Sectionalist* (Indianapolis, 1951).

Disruption of the Union: The Secession Crisis, 1860–1861

T. HARRY WILLIAMS

LOUISIANA STATE UNIVERSITY

CONTENTS

CHRONOLOGY

1860

NOVEMBER   6   Abraham Lincoln elected President of the United States.

DECEMBER   3   James Buchanan sends message to Congress on the state of the Union.

DECEMBER   4   House of Representatives creates a committee to study plans of compromise.

DECEMBER 18   Senate creates a committee to study plans of compromise and John J. Crittenden presents a plan to the Senate.

DECEMBER 20   South Carolina secedes from the Union.

DECEMBER 28   The Senate committee reports it can reach no agreement.

1861

JANUARY 5–8   Buchanan sends the *Star of the West* to reinforce Fort Sumter, but the ship is turned back.

JANUARY   9–   Six more Lower South states secede.
FEBRUARY   1

JANUARY 16   Crittenden's proposal to submit his plan to a popular vote fails in the Senate.

FEBRUARY   4   Delegates from the seceded states meet in Montgomery, Alabama, to create the Confederate States of America.

FEBRUARY   4   The Peace Convention called by Virginia meets in Washington and presents plan to Congress on February 27.

FEBRUARY   The House committee presents resolutions, some of
27–28   which are adopted, including a constitutional amendment forbidding future interference with slavery.

MARCH   4   Lincoln inaugurated as President.

MARCH   29–   Lincoln, after much deliberation, decides to send re-
APRIL   4   lief expedition to Fort Sumter.

APRIL 12–14   Confederate forces bombard Sumter and it surrenders.

APRIL   15   Lincoln calls for troops to repress an insurrection.

APRIL   17–   Four Upper South states secede and join the Con-
MAY   20   federacy.

INTRODUCTION

R OBERT TOOMBS knew without a doubt what his state of Georgia and his beloved South should do if the Republicans—the Black Republicans, Toombs and most Southerners called them—won the Presidential election of 1860. Like so many American leaders in that fateful year, the huge and hearty Toombs approached all problems with a terrible certainty of opinion. If the Republicans won, he now advised, there could be no safety for the South "except in breaking up the concern." And when in November of 1860 the news came that the Republicans had indeed carried the election and that Abraham Lincoln would enter the White House on the next fourth of March, Toombs went before the Georgia legislature to thunder a warning. "Withdraw your sons from the Army, the Navy and every department of the Federal public service," he cried.

Keep your own taxes in your own coffers—buy arms with them and throw the bloody spear into this den of incendiaries and assassins, and let God defend the right. . . . Nothing but ruin will follow delay. . . . Twenty years of labor and toil and taxes all expended upon preparation would not make up for the advantage your enemies would gain if the rising sun on the fifth of March should find you in the Union. Then strike, strike while it is yet time.

"They are your enemies." This note struck by Toombs is the motif running through the public pronouncements of most of the political leaders North and South, in 1860 and in that following year which would witness the long-dreaded disruption of the Union. How had Americans got themselves into a mental condition where they could look on other Americans as enemies to be met with hostility and possibly with force? Why did Southerners consider the government in Washington as something distant and dangerous and essentially alien? And why did Northerners regard the section below the Potomac as a region apart from the mainstream of national life and incompatible with the American ethic and the American dream? These are fundamental questions, and if we knew the answers to them we would know why there was an American Civil War. And knowing that, we would know a lot more. Using the conflict of 1860–61 as a case study, we might then achieve a fuller understanding of the causes of war generally.

That the events of 1860–61 were only the culmination of a decade or more of controversy and merely registered a result that had been determined long before might be demonstrable. But whether or not such a generalization is true, it is obvious that the secession crisis cannot be understood without reference to the divisive issues and forces that had been at work in American society since the 1830's. The election of 1860 and its result may have sparked the fire of secession, but the fuel for division was already abundantly stacked and had threatened to erupt into flame on previous occasions. That is, the causes of the dissolution of the Union were both short- and long-range in na-

ture and have to be considered as parts of the same piece. However, the
scholarly writing about the long-range causes is even more controversial than
that covering any other subject in our history.

A convenient way to get at the possible causes of the war is to examine
what historians have written over the years about the causes. And a convenient
summary of the various schools of historical thought on the subject is found
in Thomas J. Pressly's book, *Americans Interpret Their Civil War* (1954),
a history of the ways in which historians have treated the war's causation.
Professor Pressly's arrangement of "schools" may be presented in tabular
form:

1. *The Nationalists.* This first genuine historical school to deal with the
war's causes emerged in the 1890's, in a period of expanding nationalism.
The Nationalists said that the war was fought for fundamental causes, notably slavery and the issue of union, and they at least implied that it was
an irrepressible conflict. Their interpretation was almost universally accepted
until the era of World War I.

2. *The Beardians.* Arising in the 1920's, in the period of frustration following the First World War and the abeyance of the Progressive movement in
politics, was a school that emphasized the determining influence of economics on history. Its founder, Charles A. Beard, agreed with the Nationalists that the Civil War was the irrepressible result of fundamental causes.
But these causes had nothing to do with slavery or concepts of government.
Rather, two rival economic societies, the industrial North and the agricultural
South, had clashed in a struggle that finally ended in war and the total triumph of the industrial order.

3. *The Southern Vindicators.* Challenging the Beardian version was a
group of Southern historians who came forward in the 1930's at a moment
when sectional and racial tensions were being revived. These men too believed the war had fundamental causes, but not of a moral, political, or
economic nature. Perhaps the words cultural and psychological best describe
their approach. The North and the South represented diverse civilizations
and the war had resulted from the aggressive drives of the majority North to
impose its culture on the minority South, from, in the phrase of one of the
Vindicators, "egocentric sectionalism."

4. *The Revisionists.* Appearing concurrently with the Vindicators but reflecting a different cultural influence, the liberal disillusionment with war
as an instrument of national policy, the Revisionist school was the first to
deny that the war had fundamental causes. In the Revisionist presentation
there was nothing fundamental about the resort to war. Instead, the war
had come because the men of the time were intolerant, inept, too much devoted to politics, and too little committed to compromise. It was a needless
war fought for artificial reasons. The Revisionist thesis won wide acceptance
and was not challenged until after World War II.

5. *The New Nationalists.* In the era of international tensions after 1945,
when both intellectuals and laymen came to concede new values to nationalism and specifically to the values represented by the American nation, the
most recent of the schools emerged. Attacking the Revisionists, these historians asserted that it was not enough to say the men of the 1860's had been

needlessly excited; it was the job of the historian to explain why those men had thought certain issues were important enough to get excited about. The view of the latest school bore close resemblance to that of the first Nationalists. The New Nationalists returned to the thesis that the war had fundamental causes, slavery and the Union, but they put more emphasis on slavery as part of a continuing race problem than had the first Nationalists.

All of these formulas throw some light on the nature of the sectional controversy, but the question arises: would any one of the issues defined under those rubrics have caused the Northern and Southern peoples to resort to the arbitration of war? Would they have fought over the tariff? Or over the comparative merits of their societies? Or even over their concepts of government? Was there not another issue that symbolized and dramatized and drew together all the points of difference and dispute between the sections? It will occur to the student that the explanations we have been considering—diverse economic systems, diverse civilizations, diverse notions of government—may be related parts of a whole. But what ties them together? Would the South have had the kind of economic system it had if slavery had not existed? Or the kind of cultural order? Without the presence of slavery, would the South have been a sensitive minority? Except for slavery, would the North have felt that the South was so different it had to be reformed? Was slavery then the only serious difference between the sections? And was it because of slavery that the war finally came?

The answers to these questions will hinge on the student's evaluation of two factors. (1) Was slavery a profitable economic institution, capable of expansion, and hence at least potentially aggressive? Some historians have argued that slavery was not profitable and could not expand, if for no other reason than that there was no place for cotton to expand. Therefore, the agitation of the antislavery people was without cause, much ado about nothing. Other historians contend that slavery was as profitable as any other form of enterprise, that it was exceedingly variable and could be employed in various economic activities, and thus that it was capable of limited and possibly unlimited expansion. And here a related question intrudes. Regardless of the condition of slavery, how did it appear to Lincoln and other antislavery men? Though we may think slavery could not expand, did they think that it could? The truth of history may not be what was true but what men thought was true.

(2) Was the issue of slavery, or of slavery and race, a moral one or one with moral overtones? Or was the whole business a front for power groups seeking more material objectives? For example, were Northern businessmen who professed hostility to slavery really opposed to the institution or were they after a high tariff? Were politicians who talked about the evil or the good of slavery really concerned or were they recklessly playing with an emotional subject to win votes? In short, was the slavery issue a real issue? Those historians who think that it was can point to much supporting evidence. They can quote from countless speeches and newspaper editorials on both sides. More important, they can indicate the final and tragic outcome of the controversy. In a democracy such as ours the true function of politicians and parties is to blunt differences and to reconcile conflicting interests. Nearly

always have our parties and politicians been marvelously successful in executing their function. Only once have they been unable to bring it off—in
the crisis of 1860–61 that eventuated in war. Why the one great failure
then? Was it because slavery was a moral issue and moral issues cannot be
settled by the ordinary political process of compromise? Or was it because
slavery was a race question and the race question releases emotions that
jeopardize the democratic process?

By 1860 it would seem that the division over slavery and the issues related
to it had reached a point where some kind of settlement had to be made.
The controversy was too dangerous and distracting to be permitted to continue indefinitely. The majority North had to be satisfied that some plan or
method would be found to get rid of slavery. This need not have been an
immediately effective plan—indeed, Northern opinion inclined strongly
against immediacy and toward graduation—but some such scheme as proposed by Lincoln to prevent slavery from expanding to the territories and
by confinement to place it in a state of ultimate extinction. The South had
to recognize the will of the majority on slavery and nerve itself to pay the
price of racial adjustment. The only other possibilities were that the North
would admit slavery was a permanent institution and stop attacking it, a
highly unlikely result, or that the South would, to protect its way of life,
secede from the Union, a much more likely eventuality than Northerners
realized as the election of 1860 approached.

Four parties offered candidates and programs in 1860. At their convention
the Democrats split into two factions, one essentially a Northern wing and
the other a Southern. The Southern Democrats nominated John C. Breckinridge and demanded a Congressional slave code recognizing the rights of
slavery in the territories. The Northern Democrats nominated Stephen A.
Douglas and proposed to refer the question of slavery in the territories to
the courts. Actually they were committed to the doctrine of popular sovereignty, whereby the people of a territory would decide the status of slavery.
Popular sovereignty, however evasive it seemed, was in reality an antislavery device: presumably the majority of settlers in a territory would be
from the North and would vote to bar slavery. The Republicans, their
strength centered entirely in the North, put forward Abraham Lincoln and
advocated legislation to aid Northern economic groups and the exclusion of
slavery from the territories by Congressional fiat. The Constitutional Union
party, newly formed by remnants of the old Whig party, named John Bell
and merely said they stood for the Constitution. They hoped to throw the
election into the House of Representatives.

When the votes were counted in November, Lincoln emerged as the
winner. Although he had a minority of the popular vote, he polled a decisive majority of the electoral vote and would probably have won even if
his opposition had been unified. The meaning of the election may be interpreted in various ways. But one fact stands out. Lincoln and Douglas, who
by one formula or another were committed to keeping slavery out of the
territories, amassed approximately seventy per cent of the popular vote. If
the results meant anything, they indicated that a majority disapproved of
slavery. This was something the South knew it must face up to.

The Lower, or "cotton," South reacted with furious and fearful haste. Beginning with South Carolina on December 20, seven states seceded from the Union by the first day of February. The others were Mississippi, Florida, Alabama, Georgia, Louisiana, and Texas. These states went out proclaiming a doctrine almost universally accepted in most of the South, the right of a sovereign state to withdraw from the federal compact. In some states there was opposition; but it was not grounded on the right of secession, only on the expediency of it at the moment. Probably most people in these states, whether leaders or ordinary men, would have had some difficulty in defining exactly why they felt the interests of the South were no longer safe in the Union. Southerners voiced many reasons, possibly to explain their actions to themselves, but all of them boiled down to one overriding conviction: the election of a Republican President portended an attack on the Southern way of life. Perhaps Lincoln meant it when he said that his party proposed no interference with slavery in the states where it already existed. But perhaps he did not. And if the attack did not come now it would surely come later; for majority opinion in the country was against the continued existence of slavery. In Toombs's words, the enemy was at the gate, and the South must hasten to bar it.

While the adventure of secession was unfolding, Lincoln, Republican President-elect, waited at Springfield, Illinois, and James Buchanan, Democrat incumbent, sat in the White House. Not even his greatest admirers ever thought to call the venerable and white-haired "Old Buck" a strong man. Easily perturbed by untoward events, he was cruelly shaken by the crisis of which he found himself the center. Nevertheless, he acted with more resolution than is sometimes credited to him. When he delivered his message to Congress on December 3, not a state had left the Union; but it was known that preparations to secede were being made by at least five states. Buchanan denied that a state had a right to secede, but he added that it was doubtful if the national government had the power to coerce a seceded state back into the Union. His thinking was not quite as confused as it seems. Even if he had been disposed to use force, he had almost none to employ; the small regular army of sixteen thousand troops was scattered at posts all over the country. By a policy of nonaggression he hoped to avert secession except by a few states, to maintain the symbolic authority of the government, and to hand the problem over to Lincoln and the Republicans, who presumably had a mandate from the people to deal with it. Immediately after she seceded, South Carolina subjected the President's policy to a severe test. As the various states seceded, they had taken possession of federal installations within their borders, but they were unable to seize the offshore forts of Sumter at Charleston, South Carolina, and Pickens at Pensacola, Florida. South Carolina sent commissioners to Washington to negotiate for the surrender of Fort Sumter, but Buchanan refused to yield it. He even sent a ship, the *Star of the West*, to reinforce Sumter and its small garrison commanded by Major Robert Anderson; but when this vessel attempted to enter Charleston harbor early in January, it was fired on by South Carolina forces and had to retire. Slowly and painfully, as he saw conciliation was not halting secession, Buchanan assumed a stronger nationalistic stand.

In the crisis of 1860–61 it was natural that men should remember the crisis of 1850 and the great compromise that then had averted disunion. Buchanan in his December message recommended that Congress act to frame compromise measures, urging large concessions to the South; and the legislators, while not in as yielding a mood as the President, were ready to act on their own initiative. Both chambers appointed committees to study plans of adjustment, the House naming the Committee of Thirty-three on December 4 and the Senate the Committee of Thirteen on December 18. Although the House body was created first, the Senate committee was the first to consider a specific plan. On the day the Senate committee came into being, one of its members, John J. Crittenden, regarded as the heir of Henry Clay, introduced a proposal in the Senate that became the basis of the committee's deliberations. Known as the Crittenden Compromise, this measure called for a series of constitutional amendments. All were designed to satisfy Southern demands on one issue or another, but the heart of the plan was its attempt to settle the question of slavery in the territories, the one issue that had to be settled before all others. Crittenden proposed to establish the Missouri Compromise line of 36°30′ in all the territory of the United States then held or thereafter acquired. North of the line slavery was to be prohibited; south of it, slavery was to be recognized and protected.

The Southern members indicated they would accept this division if the Republicans, who were not averse to Crittenden's other recommendations, would agree to it. But the five Republican members, after sounding out Lincoln, voted against the Missouri line. Lincoln felt that to compromise on the territories would abrogate the party platform, and he feared that to divide the territories on a line would incite the South to embark on imperialist ventures in Latin America. As the committee had agreed it would report nothing not supported by a majority of the Democrats and Republicans, it now had to announce it could not agree on a compromise. Later, Crittenden tried unsuccessfully to bring his plan before the Senate. He wanted it submitted to a national referendum and believed it would carry in a popular vote. Many thought it would at the time, and many historians have thought so since.

Meanwhile, the House committee, unwieldy in size and with a Republican majority, began its labors. The Republican members were willing to concede Southern demands on such matters as the rendition of fugitive slaves and even to support an amendment guaranteeing the existence of slavery in the states. But on the key issue of slavery in the territories the Republicans voted down the Missouri Compromise line proposal. As the committee deliberated, it steadily decreased in size, the Southern members dropping off as their states seceded, and by the time it was ready to report it had lost much of its authority to speak. Nevertheless, in late February, the remnant presented a series of propositions which were adopted by the House, including a constitutional amendment stating that the Constitution could never be amended to give Congress the power to interfere with slavery in the states. This measure, also approved by the Senate, posed an interesting legal question: Could one generation chain all future generations not to alter the fundamental law? But despite this and other concessions the committee report was not acceptable to the South because it did not meet the issue of slavery in the territories. Moreover, it came too late, after most of the states had seceded, to affect the course of events. A similar fate befell the third attempt at compromise. Early in February Virginia invited the other states to send delegates to a conference in Washington, and twenty-one responded. Known as the Peace Convention, this body produced by the end of the month a plan that followed closely Crittenden's proposal. It attempted to satisfy Lincoln's objection to the Missouri Compromise line by stipulating that no new territory should be acquired without the consent of a majority of senators from both sections. Rejected by the Senate, it was not even considered by the House.

Before Lincoln was inaugurated, then, seven states had seceded from the Union. Not only that, but in February representatives from these states met in Montgomery, Alabama, and formed a new, a Southern Union—the Confederate States of America. Lincoln faced a terrible crisis. How would he deal with it? Did he come to Washington with a policy already framed? Historians differ as to what was in Lincoln's mind. The principal issue is: did he think before March 4 that the Union could not be restored except by force? And was he prepared to use force? Or did he believe that the seceded states were not serious in their resolve and that they could be coaxed back by conciliation? Aside from some remarks in letters, he stated his policy only in the inaugural address. This remarkable state paper offers many clues to what he intended, but it is not completely revealing. He denied the right of secession and said he would execute the laws in all the states and maintain possession of federal property in the seceded states. Was this his way of saying that he would, if necessary, resort to coercion or war to preserve the nation?

Whatever Lincoln's policy was, he found immediately after his inauguration that he had to take specific action. The garrison at Sumter was running short of provisions and unless supplied would have to evacuate the fort. After much deliberation, Lincoln decided to send a naval relief expedition to Sumter, notifying the South Carolina authorities that relief was on the way. (He would not recognize the Confederate government.) Lincoln's move faced the Confederacy with a dilemma of diplomacy. If the Southern government permitted the ships to land, it would be placed in the position of bowing to federal authority. But the only alternative was to reduce Sumter before the expedition arrived—to invoke war. After anguished discussion, the government decided on the latter choice. The Confederate commander at Charleston was directed to demand the surrender of Sumter, and, if the demand was refused, to attack the fort. The summons was served and rejected, the Confederates bombarded Sumter on April 12–13, and on the fourteenth the garrison surrendered. Lincoln then called on the states for troops to repress what the government would officially term an insurrection, but in reality his proclamation amounted to a Presidential declaration of war. This was a display of national power that forced the states of the Upper South to choose sides. Committed to the doctrine of state sovereignty, they had considered secession before Sumter but had decided Lincoln's election was not sufficient reason to act. Coercion, however, was something else. At this juncture four of them—Virginia, North Carolina, Tennessee, and Arkansas—seceded and joined the Confederacy. Again with the Sumter episode, as with earlier stages of the crisis, fascinating questions arise. What were Lincoln's motives in the affair? Was he merely attempting to hold the fort until he could conciliate the South to return to the fold? Or had he decided war was inevitable, and did he provoke the Confederacy into starting it?

Historians provide different answers to these questions. Two related issues are at stake. What was Lincoln's purpose or policy, from the beginning of the secession movement to the developing crisis at Sumter? And what specifically was he trying to do at Sumter, preserve peace or instigate war? David M. Potter argues cogently, in *Lincoln and His Party in the Secession Crisis* (1942), that Lincoln's policy was peaceful in intent and that compromise was possible. Potter thinks that Lincoln would have drawn the support of Southern moderates by endorsing compromise. Just as cogently, Kenneth M. Stampp contends in *And the War Came* (1950) that Lincoln intended neither war nor peace but adopted a policy of "calculated risk" to preserve the Union. Stampp doubts that compromise was possible and he at least implies that Lincoln was ready to use force if necessary to maintain the nation. Charles W. Ramsdell, in the *Journal of Southern History* (1937), presents the case that in the Sumter affair Lincoln maneuvered to provoke the South into starting a war. His thesis is denied by Potter and also by James G. Randall in *Lincoln the President* (1945) and other writings. Randall believes that Lincoln's policy was one of peace. The evidence to support all these views is of so complex a nature as to permit legitimate divergence of opinion, and the divergence bids fair to continue.

DOCUMENTS

1] Robert Toombs Shouts for the South to Act

> Southerners of the Lower South reacted to Lincoln's election with feelings
> that were at once similar and different. None liked the prospect of a Re-
> publican administration, and all had some apprehension of alarm. But men
> divided on what to do about the situation. Some, the ardent secessionists,
> said the South must secede before Lincoln took office. Others, more moder-
> ate, said the South should wait and see, should not move before an overt
> act was committed. These two Southern attitudes were perfectly embodied
> in speeches made to the Georgia legislature by the state's two leading states-
> men, Robert Toombs and Alexander H. Stephens. When the news of Lin-
> coln's election arrived, the legislature took under consideration a proposal to
> call a special convention to decide if the state should secede. But first it
> asked some of the political figures to address it on the crisis. Toombs spoke
> on November 13. A huge, mastiff-like man, Toombs had a brilliant mind
> and a thunderous voice. He cried that Georgia must leave the Union.*

GENTLEMEN OF THE GENERAL ASSEMBLY: I very much regret, in appearing before you at your request, to address you on the present state of the country,
and the prospect before us, that I can bring you no good tidings. The stern,
steady march of events has brought us in conflict with our non-slaveholding
confederates upon the fundamental principles of our compact of Union. We
have not sought this conflict; we have sought too long to avoid it; our forbearance has been construed into weakness, our magnanimity into fear, until
the vindication of our manhood, as well as the defence of our rights, is required
at our hands. The door of conciliation and compromise is finally closed by our
adversaries, and it remains only to us to meet the conflict with the dignity and
firmness of men worthy of freedom. We need no declaration of independence.
Above eighty-four years ago our fathers won that by the sword from Great
Britain, and above seventy years ago Georgia, with the twelve other confederates, as free, sovereign, and independent States, having perfect governments
already in existence, for purposes and objects clearly expressed, and with powers
clearly defined, erected a common agent for the attainment of these purposes
by the exercise of those powers, and called this agent the United States of
America. . . .

The instant the Government was organized, at the very first Congress, the
Northern States evinced a general desire and purpose to use it for their own
benefit, and to pervert its powers for sectional advantage, and they have steadily
pursued that policy to this day. They demanded a monopoly of the business
of ship-building, and got a prohibition against the sale of foreign ships to
citizens of the United States, which exists to this day.

---

* ROBERT TOOMBS SHOUTS FOR THE SOUTH TO ACT: From Frank Moore, ed., *The Rebellion Record, Supplement* (Washington, 1869), XII, 362–68.

They demanded a monopoly of the coasting trade, in order to get higher freights than they could get in open competition with the carriers of the world. Congress gave it to them, and they yet hold this monopoly. . . .

The North, at the very first Congress, demanded and received bounties under the name of protection, for every trade, craft, and calling which they pursue, and there is not an artisan in brass, or iron, or wood, or weaver, or spinner in wool or cotton, or a calico-maker, or iron-master, or a coal-owner, in all the Northern or Middle States, who has not received what he calls the protection of his government on his industry to the extent of from fifteen to two hundred per cent from the year 1791 to this day. They will not strike a blow, or stretch a muscle, without bounties from the government. No wonder they cry aloud for the glorious Union; they have the same reason for praising it, that craftsmen of Ephesus had for shouting, "Great is Diana of the Ephesians," whom all Asia and the world worshipped. By it they got their wealth; by it they levy tribute on honest labor. . . .

With these vast advantages, ordinary and extraordinary, one would have supposed the North would have been content, and would have at least respected the security and tranquillity of such obedient and profitable brethren; but such is not human nature. They despised the patient victims of their avarice, and they very soon began a war upon our political rights and social institutions, marked by every act of perfidy and treachery which could add a darker hue to such a warfare. . . . The South at all times demanded nothing but equality in the common territories, equal enjoyment of them with their property, to that extended to Northern citizens and their property—nothing more. They said, we pay our part in all the blood and treasure expended in their acquisition. Give us equality of enjoyment, equal right to expansion—it is as necessary to our prosperity as yours. In 1790 we had less than eight hundred thousand slaves. Under our mild and humane administration of the system they have increased above four millions. The country has expanded to meet this growing want, and Florida, Alabama, Mississippi, Louisiana, Texas, Arkansas, Kentucky, Tennessee, and Missouri, have received this increasing tide of African labor; before the end of this century, at precisely the same rate of increase, the Africans among us in a subordinate condition will amount to eleven millions of persons. What shall be done with them? We must expand or perish. We are constrained by an inexorable necessity to accept expansion or extermination. Those who tell you that the territorial question is an abstraction, that you can never colonize another territory without the African slave-trade, are both deaf and blind to the history of the last sixty years. All just reasoning, all past history, condemn the fallacy. The North understand it better—they have told us for twenty years that their object was to pen up slavery within its present limits—surround it with a border of free States, and like the scorpion surrounded with fire, they will make it sting itself to death. One thing at least is certain, that whatever may be the effect of your exclusion from the Territories, there is no dispute but that the North mean it, and adopt it as a measure hostile to slavery upon this point. They all agree, they are unanimous in Congress, in the States, on the rostrum, in the sanctuary—everywhere they declare that slavery shall not go into the Territories. They took up arms to drive it out of

Kansas; and Sharpe's rifles were put into the hands of assassins by Abolition preachers to do their work. Are they mistaken? No; they are not. The party put it into their platform at Philadelphia—they have it in the corner-stone of their Chicago platform; Lincoln is on it—pledged to it. Hamlin is on it, and pledged to it; every Abolitionist in the Union, in or out of place, is openly pledged, in some manner, to drive us from the common Territories. The conflict, at least, is irrepressible—it is easily understood—we demand the equal right with the North to go into the common Territories with all of our property, slaves included, and to be there protected in its peaceable enjoyment by the Federal Government, until such Territories may come into the Union as equal States—then we admit them with or without slavery, as the people themselves may decide for themselves. Will you surrender this principle? The day you do this base, unmanly deed, you embrace political degradation and death. . . .

I have shown you what this party has done, and declared in the national councils, in the State Legislatures, by and through their executive departments. Let us examine what they are at as private citizens. By the laws of nations, founded on natural justice, no nation, nor the subject or citizens of any nation, have the right to disturb the peace or security of any other nation or people, much less to conspire, excite insurrection, discontent, or the commission of crimes among them, and all these are held to be good causes of war. For twenty years this party has, by Abolition societies, by publications made by them, by the public press, through the pulpit and their own legislative halls, and every effort—by reproaches, by abuse, by vilification, by slander—to disturb our security, our tranquillity—to excite discontent between the different classes of our people, and to excite our slaves to insurrection. No nation in the world would submit to such conduct from any other nation. I will not willingly do so from this Abolition party. I demand the protection of my State government, to whom I owe my allegiance. I wish it distinctly understood that it is the price of my allegiance. You are here, constitutional legislators—I make the demand to-day of you. Gentlemen, I have thus shown you the violations of our constitutional rights by our confederates; I have shown you that they are plain, palpable, deliberate, and dangerous; that they are committed by the executive, legislative, and judicial departments of the State governments of our confederates—that all their wrongs are approved by the people of these States. I say the time has come to redress these acknowledged wrongs, and to avert even greater evils, of which these are but the signs and symbols. But I am asked, why do you demand action now? The question is both appropriate and important; it ought to be frankly met. The Abolitionists say you are raising a clamor because you were beaten in the election. The falsity of this statement needs no confirmation. Look to our past history for its refutation. Some excellent citizens and able men in Georgia say the election of any man constitutionally is no cause for a dissolution of the Union. That position is calculated only to mislead, and not to enlighten. It is not the issue. I say the election of Lincoln, with all of its surroundings, is sufficient. What is the significance of his election? It is the indorsement, by the non-slaveholding States, of all those acts of aggression upon our rights by all these States, legislatures, governors, judges, and people. He is elected by the perpetrators of these wrongs with the purpose and intent to aid and support them in wrong-doing.

Hitherto the Constitution has had on its side the Federal Executive, whose duty it is to execute the laws and Constitution against these malefactors. It has earnestly endeavored to discharge that duty. Relying upon its power and good faith to remedy these wrongs, we have listened to conservative counsels, trusting to time, to the Federal Executive, and to a returning sense of justice in the North. The Executive has been faithful—the Federal judiciary have been faithful—the President has appointed sound judges, sound marshals, and other subordinate officers to interpret and to execute the laws. With the best intentions, they have all failed—our property has been stolen, our people murdered; felons and assassins have found sanctuary in the arms of the party which elected Mr. Lincoln. The Executive power, the last bulwark of the Constitution to defend us against these enemies of the Constitution, has been swept away, and we now stand without a shield, with bare bosoms presented to our enemies, and we demand at your hands the sword for our defence, and if you will not give it to us, we will take it—take it by the divine right of self-defence, which governments neither give nor can take away. Therefore, redress for past and present wrongs demands resistance to the rule of Lincoln and his Abolition horde over us; he comes at their head to shield and protect them in the perpetration of these outrages upon us, and, what is more, he comes at their head to aid them in consummating their avowed purposes by the power of the Federal Government. Their main purpose, as indicated by all their acts of hostility to slavery, is its final and total abolition. His party declare it; their acts prove it. He has declared it; I accept his declaration. The battle of the irrepressible conflict has hitherto been fought on his side alone. We demand service in this war. Surely no one will deny that the election of Lincoln is the indorsement of the policy of those who elected him, and an indorsement of his own opinions. The opinions of those who elected him are to be found in their solemn acts under oath—in their State governments, indorsed by their constituents. To them I have already referred. They are also to be found in the votes of his supporters in Congress—also indorsed by the party, by their return. Their opinions are to be found in the speeches of Seward, and Sumner, and Lovejoy, and their associates and confederates in the two Houses of Congress. Since the promotion of Mr. Lincoln's party, all of them speak with one voice, and speak trumpet-tongued their fixed purpose to outlaw four thousand millions of our property in the Territories, and to put it under the ban of the empire in the States where it exists. They declare their purpose to war against slavery until there shall not be a slave in America, and until the African is elevated to a social and political equality with the white man. Lincoln indorses them and their principles, and in his own speeches declares the conflict irrepressible and enduring, until slavery is everywhere abolished.

Hitherto they have carried on this warfare by State action, by individual action, by appropriation, by the incendiary's torch and the poisoned bowl. They were compelled to adopt this method because the Federal executive and the Federal judiciary were against them. They will have possession of the Federal executive with its vast power, patronage, prestige of legality, its army, its navy, and its revenue on the fourth of March next. Hitherto it has been on the side of the Constitution and the right; after the fourth of March it will be in the hands of your enemy. Will you let him have it? [Cries of "No, no. Never."] Then strike while it is yet to-day. Withdraw your sons from the army, from the navy, and every department of the Federal public service. Keep your own taxes in your own coffers—buy arms with them and throw the bloody spear into this den of incendiaries and assassins, and let God defend the right. But you are advised to wait, send soft messages to their brethren, to beg them to relent, to give you some assurances of their better fidelity for the future. What more can you get from them under this Government? You have the Constitution—you have its exposition by themselves for seventy years—you have their oaths—they have broken all these, and will break them again. They tell you everywhere, loudly and defiantly, you shall have no power, no security until you give up the right of governing yourselves according to your own will—until you submit to theirs. For this is the meaning of Mr. Lincoln's irrepressible conflict—this is his emphatic declaration to all the world. Will you heed it? For myself, like the Athenian ambassador, I will take no security but this, that it shall not be in the power of our enemies to injure my country if they desire it. Nothing but ruin will follow delay. The enemy on the fourth of March will intrench himself behind a quintuple wall of defence. Executive power, judiciary, (Mr. Seward has already proclaimed its reformation,) army, navy, and treasury. Twenty years of labor and toil and taxes all expended upon preparation would not make up for the advantage your enemies would gain if the rising sun on the fifth of March should find you in the Union. Then strike, strike while it is yet time.

But we are told that secession would destroy the fairest fabric of liberty the world ever saw, and that we are the most prosperous people in the world under it. The arguments of tyranny as well as its acts, always reënact themselves. The arguments I now hear in favor of this Northern connection are identical in substance, and almost in the same words as those which were used in 1775 and 1776 to sustain the British connection. We won liberty, sovereignty, and independence by the American Revolution—we endeavored to secure and perpetuate these blessings by means of our Constitution. The very men who use these arguments admit that this Constitution, this compact, is violated, broken and trampled under foot by the abolition party. Shall we surrender the jewels because their robbers and incendiaries have broken the casket? Is this the way to preserve liberty? I would as lief surrender it back to the British crown as to the abolitionists. I will defend it from both. Our purpose is to defend those liberties. What baser fate could befall us or this great experiment of free government than to have written upon its tomb: "Fell by the hands of abolitionists and the cowardice of its natural defenders." If we quail now, this will be its epitaph.

We are said to be a happy and prosperous people. We have been, because we have hitherto maintained our ancient rights and liberties—we will be until we surrender them. They are in danger; come, freemen, to the rescue. If we are prosperous, it is due to God, ourselves, and the wisdom of our State government. We have an executive, legislative, and judicial department at home, possessing and entitled to the confidence of the people. I have already vainly asked for the law of the Federal Government that promotes our prosperity. I have shown you many that retard that prosperity—many that drain our coffers for the benefit of our bitterest foes. I say bitterest foes—show me the nation in the world that hates, despises, vilifies, or plunders us like our abolition "brethren" in the North. There is none. I can go to England or France, or any other country in Europe with my slave, without molestation or violating any law. I can go anywhere except in my own country, whilom called "the glorious Union;" here alone am I stigmatized as a felon; here alone am I an outlaw; here alone am I under the ban of the empire; here alone I have neither security nor tranquillity; here alone are organized governments ready to protect the incendiary, the assassin who burns my dwelling or takes my life or those of my wife and children; here alone are hired emissaries paid by brethren to glide through the domestic circle and intrigue insurrection with all of its nameless horrors. My countrymen, "if you have nature in you, bear it not." Withdraw yourselves from such a confederacy; it is your right to do so—your duty to do so. I know not why the abolitionists should object to it, unless they want to torture and plunder you. If they resist this great sovereign right, make another war of independence, for that then will be the question; fight its battles over again—reconquer liberty and independence. As for me, I will take any place in the great conflict for rights which you may assign. I will take none in the Federal Government during Mr. Lincoln's administration.

2] Alexander H. Stephens Begs the South to Be Prudent

> On the day following Toombs's speech, Stephens, Georgia's other great leader, spoke to the legislature. "Little Ellick," that "queer-looking bundle," as one man descibed him, weighed only about ninety pounds, and he spoke in a shrill voice. But he had a mind as brilliant as Toombs's, and of a more scholarly cast. A devoted believer in state rights and later Vice-President of the Confederacy, he yet loved the Union and did not think that Lincoln's election justified secession.*

. . . FELLOW-CITIZENS: I appear before you tonight at the request of members of the Legislature and others to speak of matters of the deepest interest that can possibly concern us all of an earthly character. There is nothing—no question or subject connected with this life—that concerns a free people so intimately as that of the Government under which they live. We are now, indeed, surrounded by evils. Never since I entered upon the public stage has the country been so environed with difficulties and dangers that threatened the public peace and the very existence of society as now. . . .

My object is not to stir up strife, but to allay it; not to appeal to your passions, but to your reason. Good governments can never be built up or sustained by

* ALEXANDER H. STEPHENS BEGS THE SOUTH TO BE PRUDENT: From Frank Moore, ed., *The Rebellion Record* (New York, 1861–65), I, 219–27.

the impulse of passion. I wish to address myself to your good sense, to your good judgment, and if after hearing you disagree, let us agree to disagree, and part as we met, friends. We all have the same object, the same interest. That people should disagree in republican governments, upon questions of public policy, is natural. That men should disagree upon all matters connected with human investigation, whether relating to science or human conduct, is natural. Hence, in free governments parties will arise. But a free people should express their different opinions with liberality and charity, with no acrimony toward those of their fellows, when honestly and sincerely given. These are my feelings to-night. . . .

The first question that presents itself is shall the people of the South secede from the Union in consequence of the election of Mr. Lincoln to the presidency of the United States? My countrymen, *I tell you frankly, candidly, and earnestly, that I do not think that they ought.* In my judgment, the election of no man, constitutionally chosen to that high office, is sufficient cause for any State to separate from the Union. It ought to stand by and aid still in maintaining the constitution of the country. To make a point of resistance to the Government, to withdraw from it because a man has been constitutionally elected, puts us in the wrong. We are pledged to maintain the Constitution. Many of us have sworn to support it. Can we, therefore, for the mere election of a man to the Presidency, and that too in accordance with the prescribed forms of the Constitution, make a point of resistance to the Government without becoming the breakers of that sacred instrument ourselves, by withdrawing ourselves from it? Would we not be in the wrong? Whatever fate is to befall this country, let it never be laid to the charge of the people of the South, and especially to the people of Georgia, that we were untrue to our national engagements. Let the fault and the wrong rest upon others. If all our hopes are to be blasted, if the Republic is to go down, let us be found to the last moment standing on the deck, with the Constitution of the United States waving over our heads. [Applause.] Let the fanatics of the North break the Constitution, if such is their fell purpose. Let the responsibility be upon them. I shall speak presently more of their acts; but let not the South, let us not be the ones to commit the aggression. We went into the election with this people. The result was different from what we wished; but the election has been constitutionally held. Were we to make a point of resistance to the Government and go out of the Union on that account, the record would be made up hereafter against us.

But it is said Mr. Lincoln's policy and principles are against the Constitution, and that if he carries them out it will be destructive of our rights. Let us not anticipate a threatened evil. If he violates the Constitution then will come our time to act. Do not let us break it because, forsooth, he may. If he does, that is the time for us to strike. [Applause.] I think it would be injudicious and unwise to do this sooner. I do not anticipate that Mr. Lincoln will do any thing to jeopard our safety or security, whatever may be his spirit to do it; for he is bound by the constitutional checks which are thrown around him, which at this time renders him powerless to do any great mischief. This shows the wisdom of our system. The President of the United States is no emperor, no dictator—he is clothed with no absolute power. He can do nothing unless he is backed by power in Congress. The House of Representatives is largely in the majority against him.

In the Senate he will also be powerless. There will be a majority of four against him. . . . Mr. Lincoln cannot appoint an officer without the consent of the Senate—he cannot form a Cabinet without the same consent. He will be in the condition of George III., (the embodiment of Toryism,) who had to ask the Whigs to appoint his ministers, and was compelled to receive a cabinet utterly opposed to his views; and so Mr. Lincoln will be compelled to ask of the Senate to choose for him a cabinet, if the Democracy of that body choose to put him on such terms. He will be compelled to do this or let the Government stop, if the National Democratic men—for that is their name at the North—the conservative men in the Senate, should so determine. Then, how can Mr. Lincoln obtain a cabinet which would aid him, or allow him to violate the Constitution:

Why then, I say, should we disrupt the ties of this Union when his hands are tied, when he can do nothing against us? . . .

My honorable friend who addressed you last night, (Mr. Toombs,) and to whom I listened with the profoundest attention, asks if we would submit to Black Republican rule? I say to you and to him, as a Georgian, I never would submit to any Black Republican *aggression* upon our constitutional rights. I will never consent myself, as much as I admire this Union for the glories of the past, or the blessings of the present, as much as it has done for the people of all these States, as much as it has done for civilization, as much as the hopes of the world hang upon it, I would never submit to aggression upon my rights to maintain it longer; and if they cannot be maintained in the Union, standing on the Georgia platform, where I have stood from the time of its adoption, I would be in favor of disrupting every tie which binds the States together.

I will have equality for Georgia and for the citizens of Georgia in this Union, or I will look for new safeguards elsewhere. This is my position. The only question now is, can they be secured in the Union? That is what I am counselling with you to-night about. Can it be secured? In my judgment it may be, but it may not be; but let us do all we can, so that in the future, if the worst come, it may never be said we were negligent in doing our duty to the last.

My countrymen, I am not of those who believe this Union has been a curse up to this time. True men, men of integrity, entertain different views from me on this subject. I do not question their right to do so; I would not impugn their motives in so doing. Nor will I undertake to say that this Government of our fathers is perfect. There is nothing perfect in this world of a human origin. Nothing connected with human nature, from man himself to any of his works. You may select the wisest and best men for your judges, and yet how many defects are there in the administration of justice? You may select the wisest and best men for your legislators, and yet how many defects are apparent in your laws? And it is so in our Government.

But that this Government of our fathers, with all its defects, comes nearer the objects of all good Governments than any other on the face of the earth is my settled conviction. . . .

When I look around and see our prosperity in every thing, agriculture, commerce, art, science, and every department of education, physical and mental, as well as moral advancement, and our colleges, I think, in the face of such an exhibition, if we can without the loss of power, or any essential right or interest, remain in the Union, it is our duty to ourselves and to posterity to do so. Let us not too readily yield to this temptation. Our first parents, the great progenitors of the human race, were not without a like temptation when in the garden of Eden. They were led to believe that their condition would be bettered—that their eyes would be opened—and that they would become as gods. They in an evil hour yielded—instead of becoming gods they only saw their own nakedness.

I look upon this country with our institutions as the Eden of the world, the paradise of the universe. It may be that out of it we may become greater and more prosperous, but I am candid and sincere in telling you that I fear if we rashly evince passion and without sufficient cause shall take that step, that instead of becoming greater or more peaceful, prosperous, and happy— instead of becoming gods, we will become demons, and at no distant day commence cutting one another's throats. This is my apprehension. Let us, therefore, whatever we do, meet these difficulties, great as they are, like wise and sensible men, and consider them in the light of all the consequences which may attend our action. Let us see first clearly where the path of duty leads, and then we may not fear to tread therein. . . .

My honorable friend said last night, "I ask you to give me the Sword, for if you do not give it to me, as God lives, I will take it myself."

Mr. Toombs—I will. [Applause on the other side.]

Mr. Stephens—I have no doubt that my honorable friend feels as he says. It is only his excessive ardor that makes him use such an expression; but this will pass off with the excitement of the hour. When the people in their majesty shall speak, I have no doubt that he will bow to their will, whatever it may be, upon the "sober second thought." [Applause.]

Should Georgia determine to go out of the Union, I speak for one, though my views might not agree with them, whatever the result may be, I shall bow to the will of her people. Their cause is my cause, and their destiny is my destiny; and I trust this will be the ultimate course of all. The greatest curse that can befall a free people is civil war. . . .

I am for exhausting all that patriotism can demand before taking the last step. I would invite, therefore, South Carolina to a conference. I would ask the same of all the other Southern States, so that if the evil has got beyond our control, which God, in his mercy, grant may not be the case, we may not be divided among ourselves—[cheers,]—but, if possible, secure the united coöperation of all the Southern States; and then, in the face of the civilized world, we may justify our action; and, with the wrong all on the other side, we can appeal to the God of battles to aid us in our cause. [Loud applause.] But let us do nothing in which any portion of our people may charge you with rash or hasty action. It is certainly a matter of great importance to tear this Government asunder. You were not sent here for that purpose. I would wish the whole South to be united if this is to be done; and I believe if we pursue the policy which I have indicated, this can be effected. . . .

3] A Southern Newspaper Warns of the Record of the Republicans

Many Southerners were convinced that the Republicans would, after taking power, move to change in some way the Southern social system. Here the New Orleans *Daily Crescent* on November 13, 1860, points to the Republican record as indicating what may be expected in the future.*

THE HISTORY of the Abolition or Black Republican party of the North is a history of repeated injuries and usurpations, all having in direct object the establishment of absolute tyranny over the slaveholding States. And all without the smallest warrant, excuse or justification. We have appealed to their generosity, justice and patriotism, but all without avail. From the beginning, we have only asked to be let alone in the enjoyment of our plain, inalienable rights, as explicitly guaranteed in our common organic law. We have never aggressed upon the North, nor sought to aggress upon the North. Yet every appeal and expostulation has only brought upon us renewed insults and augmented injuries. They have robbed us of our property, they have murdered our citizens while endeavoring to reclaim that property by lawful means, they have set at naught the decrees of the Supreme Court, they have invaded our States and killed our citizens, they have declared their unalterable determination to exclude us altogether from the Territories, they have nullified the laws of Congress, and finally they have capped the mighty pyramid of unfraternal enormities by electing Abraham Lincoln to the Chief Magistracy, on a platform and by a system which indicates nothing but the subjugation of the South and the complete ruin of her social, political and industrial institutions.

All these statements are not only true, but absolutely indisputable. The facts are well known and patent. Under these circumstances, in view of the dark record of the past, the threatening aspect of the present, and the very serious contingencies which the future holds forth, we submit and appeal to a candid and honorable world, whether the Southern people have not been astonishingly patient under gross provocation—whether they have not exhibited remarkable forbearance—whether they have not been long suffering, slow to anger and magnanimous, on numerous occasions where indignation was natural, and severe measures of retaliation justifiable? There can be no doubt on this point. For the sake of peace, for the sake of harmony, the South has compromised until she can compromise no farther, without she is willing to compromise away character, political equality, social and individual interest, and every right and franchise which freemen hold dear.

* A SOUTHERN NEWSPAPER WARNS OF THE RECORD OF THE REPUBLICANS: From Dwight L. Dumond, ed., *Southern Editorials on Secession* (New York, 1931), pp. 235–38. Reprinted by permission of the American Historical Association.

4] James Buchanan Foresees the Crisis

On December 3 President Buchanan sent his annual message to Congress. He devoted his main attention to the crisis that he feared would develop. At the time no state had seceded, but preparations for secession were in the making in the Lower South. Buchanan's message was a plea to the South not to act and a warning to the North to satisfy the South's grievances. Although Buchanan's policy seems to add up to nothing, it should be noted that some of his passages exalting the power of the American government are as compelling as those written by Abraham Lincoln.*

Fellow-Citizens of the Senate and House of Representatives:

Throughout the year since our last meeting the country has been eminently prosperous in all its material interests. The general health has been excellent, our harvests have been abundant, and plenty smiles throughout the land. Our commerce and manufactures have been prosecuted with energy and industry, and have yielded fair and ample returns. In short, no nation in the tide of time has ever presented a spectacle of greater material prosperity than we have done until within a very recent period.

Why is it, then, that discontent now so extensively prevails, and the Union of the States, which is the source of all these blessings, is threatened with destruction?

The long-continued and intemperate interference of the Northern people with the question of slavery in the Southern States has at length produced its natural effects. The different sections of the Union are now arrayed against each other, and the time has arrived, so much dreaded by the Father of his Country, when hostile geographical parties have been formed.

I have long foreseen and often forewarned my countrymen of the now impending danger. This does not proceed solely from the claim on the part of Congress or the Territorial legislatures to exclude slavery from the Territories, nor from the efforts of different States to defeat the execution of the fugitive-slave law. All or any of these evils might have been endured by the South without danger to the Union (as others have been) in the hope that time and reflection might apply the remedy. The immediate peril arises not so much from these causes as from the fact that the incessant and violent agitation of the slavery question throughout the North for the last quarter of a century has at length produced its malign influence on the slaves and inspired them with vague notions of freedom. Hence a sense of security no longer exists around the family altar. This feeling of peace at home has given place to apprehensions of servile insurrections. Many a matron throughout the South retires at night in dread of what may befall herself and children before the morning. Should this apprehension of domestic danger, whether real or imaginary,

* JAMES BUCHANAN FORESEES THE CRISIS: From James D. Richardson, ed., *A Compilation of the Messages and Papers of the Presidents, 1789–1897* (Washington, 1896–99), V, 626–39.

extend and intensify itself until it shall pervade the masses of the Southern people, then disunion will become inevitable. Self-preservation is the first law of nature, and has been implanted in the heart of man by his Creator for the wisest purpose; and no political union, however fraught with blessings and benefits in all other respects, can long continue if the necessary consequence be to render the homes and the firesides of nearly half the parties to it habitually and hopelessly insecure. Sooner or later the bonds of such a union must be severed. It is my conviction that this fatal period has not yet arrived, and my prayer to God is that He would preserve the Constitution and the Union throughout all generations.

But let us take warning in time and remove the cause of danger. It can not be denied that for five and twenty years the agitation at the North against slavery has been incessant. In 1835 pictorial handbills and inflammatory appeals were circulated extensively throughout the South of a character to excite the passion of the slaves, and, in the language of General Jackson, "to stimulate them to insurrection and produce all the horrors of a servile war." This agitation has ever since been continued by the public press, by the proceedings of State and county conventions and by abolition sermons and lectures. The time of Congress has been occupied in violent speeches on this never-ending subject, and appeals, in pamphlet and other forms, indorsed by distinguished names, have been sent forth from this central point and spread broadcast over the Union.

How easy would it be for the American people to settle the slavery question forever and to restore peace and harmony to this distracted country! They, and they alone, can do it. All that is necessary to accomplish the object, and all for which the slave States have ever contended, is to be let alone and permitted to manage their domestic institutions in their own way. As sovereign States, they, and they alone, are responsible before God and the world for the slavery existing among them. For this the people of the North are not more responsible and have no more right to interfere than with similar institutions in Russia or in Brazil.

Upon their good sense and patriotic forbearance I confess I still greatly rely. Without their aid it is beyond the power of any President, no matter what may be his own political proclivities, to restore peace and harmony among the States. Wisely limited and restrained as is his power under our Constitution and laws, he alone can accomplish but little for good or for evil on such a momentous question.

And this brings me to observe that the election of any one of our fellow-citizens to the office of President does not of itself afford just cause for dissolving the Union. This is more especially true if his election has been effected by a mere plurality, and not a majority of the people, and has resulted from transient and temporary causes, which may probably never again occur. In order to justify a resort to revolutionary resistance, the Federal Government must be guilty of "a deliberate, palpable, and dangerous exercise" of powers not granted by the Constitution. The late Presidential election, however, has been held in strict conformity with its express provisions. How, then, can the result justify a revolution to destroy this very Constitution? Reason, justice, a regard for the Constitution, all require that we shall wait for some overt and dangerous act on the part of the President elect before resorting to such a remedy. It is said, however, that the antecedents of the President elect have been sufficient to justify the fears of the South that he will attempt to invade their constitutional rights. But are such apprehensions of contingent danger in the future sufficient to justify the immediate destruction of the noblest system of government ever devised by mortals? From the very nature of his office and its high responsibilities he must necessarily be conservative. The stern duty of administering the vast and complicated concerns of this Government affords in itself a guaranty that he will not attempt any violation of a clear constitutional right.

After all, he is no more than the chief executive officer of the Government. His province is not to make but to execute the laws. And it is a remarkable fact in our history that, notwithstanding the repeated efforts of the antislavery party, no single act has ever passed Congress, unless we may possibly except the Missouri compromise, impairing in the slightest degree the rights of the South to their property in slaves; and it may also be observed, judging from present indications, that no probability exists of the passage of such an act by a majority of both Houses, either in the present or the next Congress. Surely under these circumstances we ought to be restrained from present action by the precept of Him who spake as man never spoke, that "sufficient unto the day is the evil thereof." The day of evil may never come unless we shall rashly bring it upon ourselves.

It is alleged as one cause for immediate secession that the Southern States are denied equal rights with the other States in the common Territories. But by what authority are these denied? Not by Congress, which has never passed, and I believe never will pass, any act to exclude slavery from these Territories; and certainly not by the Supreme Court, which has solemnly decided that slaves are property, and, like all other property, their owners have a right to take them into the common Territories and hold them there under the protection of the Constitution.

So far, then, as Congress is concerned, the objection is not to anything they have already done, but to what they may do hereafter. It will surely be admitted that this apprehension of future danger is no good reason for an immediate dissolution of the Union. . . .

Only three days after my inauguration the Supreme Court of the United States solemnly adjudged that this power did not exist in a Territorial legislature. Yet such has been the factious temper of the times that the correctness of this decision has been extensively impugned before the people, and the question has given rise to angry political conflicts throughout the country. Those who have appealed from this judgment of our highest constitutional tribunal to popular assemblies would, if they could, invest a Territorial legislature with power to annul the sacred rights of property. This power Congress is expressly forbidden by the Federal Constitution to exercise. Every State legislature in the Union is forbidden by its own constitution to exercise it. It can not be exercised in any State except by the people in their highest sovereign capacity, when framing or amending their State constitution. In like manner it can only be exercised by the people of a Territory represented in a convention of delegates for the purpose of framing a constitution preparatory to admission as a State into the Union. Then, and not until then, are they invested with power to decide the question whether slavery shall or shall not exist within their limits. This is an act of sovereign authority, and not of subordinate Territorial legislation. Were it otherwise, then indeed would the equality of the States in the Territories be destroyed, and the rights of property in slaves would depend not upon the guaranties of the Constitution, but upon the shifting majorities of an irresponsible Territorial legislature. Such a doctrine, from its intrinsic unsoundness, can not long influence any considerable portion of our people, much less can it afford a good reason for a dissolution of the Union.

The most palpable violations of constitutional duty which have yet been committed consist in the acts of different State legislatures to defeat the execution of the fugitive-slave law. It ought to be remembered, however, that for these acts neither Congress nor any President can justly be held responsible. Having been passed in violation of the Federal Constitution, they are therefore null and void. All the courts, both State and national, before whom the question has arisen have from the beginning declared the fugitive-slave law to be constitutional. . . . Here, then, a clear case is presented in which it will be the duty of the next President, as it has been my own, to act with vigor in executing this supreme law against the conflicting enactments of State legislatures. Should he fail in the performance of this high duty, he will then have manifested a disregard of the Constitution and laws, to the great injury of the people of nearly one-half of the States of the Union. But are we to presume in advance that he will thus violate his duty? This would be at war with every principle of justice and of Christian charity. Let us wait for the overt act. The fugitive-slave law has been carried into execution in every contested case since the commencement of the present Administration, though often, it is to be regretted, with great loss and inconvenience to the master and with considerable expense to the Government. Let us trust that the State legislatures will repeal their unconstitutional and obnoxious enactments. Unless this shall be done without unnecessary delay, it is impossible for any human power to save the Union.

The Southern States, standing on the basis of the Constitution, have a right to demand this act of justice from the States of the North. Should it be refused, then the Constitution, to which all the States are parties, will have been willfully violated by one portion of them in a provision essential to the domestic security and happiness of the remainder. In that event the injured States, after having first used all peaceful and constitutional means to obtain redress, would be justified in revolutionary resistance to the Government of the Union.

I have purposedly confined my remarks to revolutionary resistance, because it has been claimed within the last few years that any State, whenever this shall be its sovereign will and pleasure, may secede from the Union in accordance with the Constitution and without any violation of the constitutional rights of the other members of the Confederacy; that as each became parties to the Union by the vote of its own people assembled in convention, so any one of them may retire from the Union in a similar manner by the vote of such a convention.

In order to justify secession as a constitutional remedy, it must be on the principle that the Federal Government is a mere voluntary association of States, to be dissolved at pleasure by any one of the contracting parties. If this be so, the Confederacy is a rope of sand, to be penetrated and dissolved by the first adverse wave of public opinion in any of the States. In this manner our thirty-three States may resolve themselves into as many petty, jarring, and hostile republics, each one retiring from the Union without responsibility whenever any sudden excitement might impel them to such a course. By this process a Union might be entirely broken into fragments in a few weeks which cost our forefathers many years of toil, privation, and blood to establish.

Such a principle is wholly inconsistent with the history as well as the character of the Federal Constitution. After it was framed with the greatest deliberation and care it was submitted to conventions of the people of the several States for ratification. Its provisions were discussed at length in these bodies, composed of the first men of the country. Its opponents contended that it conferred powers upon the Federal Government dangerous to the rights of the States, whilst its advocates maintained that under a fair construction of the instrument there was no foundation for such apprehensions. In that mighty struggle between the first intellects of this or any other country it never occurred to any individual, either among its opponents or advocates, to assert or even to intimate that their efforts were all vain labor, because the moment that any State felt herself aggrieved she might secede from the Union. What a crushing argument would this have proved against those who dreaded that the rights of the States would be endangered by the Constitution. . . .

It was intended to be perpetual, and not to be annulled at the pleasure of any one of the contracting parties. The old Articles of Confederation were entitled "Articles of Confederation and Perpetual Union between the States," and by the thirteenth article it is expressly declared that "the articles of this Confederation shall be inviolably observed by every State, and the Union shall be perpetual." The preamble to the Constitution of the United States, having express reference to the Articles of Confederation, recites that it was established "in order to form a more perfect union." And yet it is contended that this "more perfect union" does not include the essential attribute of perpetuity.

But that the Union was designed to be perpetual appears conclusively from the nature and extent of the powers conferred by the Constitution on the Federal Government. These powers embrace the very highest attributes of national sovereignty. They place both the sword and the purse under its control. Congress has power to make war and to make peace, to raise and support armies and navies, and to conclude treaties with foreign governments. It is invested with the power to coin money and to regulate the value thereof, and to regulate commerce with foreign nations and among the several States. It is not necessary to enumerate the other high powers which have been conferred upon the Federal Government. In order to carry the enumerated powers into effect, Congress possesses the exclusive right to lay and collect duties on imports, and, in common with the States, to lay and collect all other taxes. . . .

In order to carry into effect these powers, the Constitution has established a perfect Government in all its forms—legislative, executive, and judicial; and this Government to the extent of its powers acts directly upon the individual citizens of every State, and executes its own decrees by the agency of its own officers. In this respect it differs entirely from the Government under the old Confederation, which was confined to making requisitions on the States in their sovereign character. This left it in the discretion of each whether to obey or to refuse, and they often declined to comply with such requisitions. It thus became necessary for the purpose of removing this barrier and "in order to form a more perfect union" to establish a Government which could act directly upon the people and execute its own laws without the intermediate agency of the States. This has been accomplished by the Constitution of the United States. In short, the Government created by the Constitution, and deriving its authority from the sovereign people of each of the several States, has precisely the same right to exercise its power over the people of all these States in the enumerated cases that each one of them possesses over subjects not delegated to the United States, but "reserved to the States respectively or to the people."

To the extent of the delegated powers the Constitution of the United States is as much a part of the constitution of each State and is as binding upon its people as though it had been textually inserted therein.

This Government, therefore, is a great and powerful Government, invested with all the attributes of sovereignty over the special subjects to which its authority extends. Its framers never intended to implant in its bosom the seeds of its own destruction, nor were they at its creation guilty of the absurdity of providing for its own dissolution. It was not intended by its framers to be the baseless fabric of a vision, which at the touch of the enchanter would vanish into thin air, but a substantial and mighty fabric, capable of resisting the slow decay of time and of defying the storms of ages. Indeed, well may the jealous patriots of that day have indulged fears that a Government of such high powers might violate the reserved rights of the States, and wisely did they adopt the rule of a strict construction of these powers to prevent the danger. But they did not fear, nor had they any reason to imagine, that the Constitution would ever be so interpreted as to enable any State by her own act, and without the consent of her sister States, to discharge her people from all or any of their Federal obligations.

It may be asked, then, Are the people of the States without redress against the tyranny and oppression of the Federal Government? By no means. The right of resistance on the part of the governed against the oppression of their governments can not be denied. It exists independently of all constitutions, and has been exercised at all periods of the world's history. Under it old governments have been destroyed and new ones have taken their place. It is embodied in strong and express language in our own Declaration of Independence. But the distinction must ever be observed that this is revolution against an established government, and not a voluntary secession from it by virtue of an inherent constitutional right. In short, let us look the danger fairly in the face. Secession is neither more nor less than revolution. It may or it may not be a justifiable revolution, but still it is revolution.

What, in the meantime, is the responsibility and true position of the Executive? He is bound by solemn oath, before God and the country, "to take care that the laws be faithfully executed," and from this obligation he can not be absolved by any human power. But what if the performance of this duty, in whole or in part, has been rendered impracticable by events over which he could have exercised no control? Such at the present moment is the case throughout the State of South Carolina so far as the laws of the United States to secure the administration of justice by means of the Federal judiciary are concerned. All the Federal officers within its limits through whose agency alone these laws can be carried into execution have already resigned. We no longer have a district judge, a district attorney, or a marshal in South Carolina. In fact, the whole machinery of the Federal Government necessary for the distribution of remedial justice among the people has been demolished, and it would be difficult, if not impossible, to replace it. . . .

Apart from the execution of the laws, so far as this may be practicable, the Executive has no authority to decide what shall be the relations between the Federal Government and South Carolina. He has been invested with no such discretion. He possesses no power to change the relations heretofore existing between them, much less to acknowledge the independence of that State. This would be to invest a mere executive officer with the power of recognizing the dissolution of the confederacy among our thirty-three sovereign States. It bears no resemblance to the recognition of a foreign *de facto* government, involving no such responsibility. Any attempt to do this would, on his part, be a naked act of usurpation. It is therefore my duty to submit to Congress the whole question in all its bearings. The course of events is so rapidly hastening forward that the emergency may soon arise when you may be called upon to decide the momentous question whether you possess the power by force of arms to compel a State to remain in the Union. I should feel myself recreant to my duty were I not to express an opinion on this important subject.

The question fairly stated is, Has the Constitution delegated to Congress the power to coerce a State into submission which is attempting to withdraw or has actually withdrawn from the Confederacy? If answered in the affirmative, it must be on the principle that the power has been conferred upon Congress to declare and to make war against a State. After much serious reflection I have arrived at the conclusion that no such power has been delegated to Congress or to any other department of the Federal Government. It is manifest upon an inspection of the Constitution that this is not among the specific and enumerated powers granted to Congress, and it is equally apparent that its exercise is not "necessary and proper for carrying into execution" any one of these powers. So far from this power having been delegated to Congress, it was expressly refused by the Convention which framed the Constitution. . . .

Without descending to particulars, it may be safely asserted that the power to make war against a State is at variance with the whole spirit and intent of the Constitution. Suppose such a war should result in the conquest of a State; how are we to govern it afterwards? Shall we hold it as a province and govern it by despotic power? In the nature of things, we could not by physical force control the will of the people and compel them to elect Senators and Representatives to Congress and to perform all the other duties depending upon their own volition and required from the free citizens of a free State as a constituent member of the Confederacy.

But if we possessed this power, would it be wise to exercise it under existing circumstances? The object would doubtless be to preserve the Union. War would not only present the most effectual means of destroying it, but would vanish all hope of its peaceable reconstruction. Besides, in the fraternal conflict a vast amount of blood and treasure would be expended, rendering future reconciliation between the States impossible. In the meantime, who can foretell what would be the sufferings and privations of the people during its existence?

The fact is that our Union rests upon public opinion, and can never be cemented by the blood of its citizens shed in civil war. If it can not live in the affections of the people, it must one day perish. Congress possesses many means of preserving it by conciliation, but the sword was not placed in their hand to preserve it by force.

But may I be permitted solemnly to invoke my countrymen to pause and deliberate before they determine to destroy this the grandest temple which has ever been dedicated to human freedom since the world began? It has been consecrated by the blood of our fathers, by the glories of the past, and by the hopes of the future. The Union has already made us the most prosperous, and ere long will, if preserved, render us the most powerful, nation on the face of the earth. In every foreign region of the globe the title of American citizen is held in the highest respect, and when pronounced in a foreign land it causes the hearts of our countrymen to swell with honest pride. Surely when we reach the brink of the yawning abyss we shall recoil with horror from the last fatal plunge.

By such a dread catastrophe the hopes of the friends of freedom throughout the world would be destroyed, and a long night of leaden despotism would enshroud the nations. Our example for more than eighty years would not only be lost, but it would be quoted as a conclusive proof that man is unfit for self-government.

It is not every wrong—nay, it is not every grievous wrong—which can justify a resort to such a fearful alternative. This ought to be the last desperate remedy of a despairing people, after every other constitutional means of conciliation had been exhausted. We should reflect that under this free Government there is an incessant ebb and flow in public opinion. The slavery question, like everything human, will have its day. I firmly believe that it has reached and passed the culminating point. But if in the midst of the existing excitement the Union shall perish, the evil may then become irreparable.

Congress can contribute much to avert it by proposing and recommending to the legislatures of the several States the remedy for existing evils which the Constitution has itself provided for its own preservation. This has been tried at different critical periods of our history, and always with eminent success. It is to be found in the fifth article, providing for its own amendment. . . .

This is the very course which I earnestly recommend in order to obtain an "explanatory amendment" of the Constitution on the subject of slavery. This might originate with Congress or the State legislatures, as may be deemed most advisable to attain the object. The explanatory amendment might be confined to the final settlement of the true construction of the Constitution on three special points:

1. An express recognition of the right of property in slaves in the States where it now exists or may hereafter exist.

2. The duty of protecting this right in all the common Territories throughout their Territorial existence, and until they shall be admitted as States into the Union, with or without slavery, as their constitutions may prescribe.

3. A like recognition of the right of the master to have his slave who has escaped from one State to another restored and "delivered up" to him, and of the validity of the fugitive-slave law enacted for this purpose, together with a declaration that all State laws impairing or defeating this right are violations of the Constitution, and are consequently null and void. It may be objected that this construction of the Constitution has already been settled by the Supreme Court of the United States, and what more ought to be required? The answer is that a very large proportion of the people of the United States still contest the correctness of this decision, and never will cease from agitation and admit its binding force until clearly established by the people of the several States in their sovereign character. Such an explanatory amendment would, it is believed, forever terminate the existing dissensions, and restore peace and harmony among the States.

It ought not to be doubted that such an appeal to the arbitrament established by the Constitution itself would be received with favor by all the States of the Confederacy. In any event, it ought to be tried in a spirit of conciliation before any of these States shall separate themselves from the Union.

5] Extreme Southerners Spurn Compromise

> On December 13, 1860, just as the House Committee of Thirty-three was about to begin its labors, thirty Southern senators and representatives met at the rooms of Reuben Davis of Mississippi and issued a statement to their people advocating secession.*

To our Constituents: The argument is exhausted. All hope of relief in the Union, through the agency of committees, Congressional legislation, or constitutional amendments, is extinguished, and we trust the South will not be deceived by appearances or the pretence of new guarantees. The Republicans are resolute in the purpose to grant nothing that will or ought to satisfy the South. We are satisfied the honor, safety, and independence of the Southern

---

* EXTREME SOUTHERNERS SPURN COMPROMISE: From Edward McPherson, *Political History of the Great Rebellion* (Washington, 1865), p. 37.

people are to be found only in a Southern Confederacy—a result to be obtained only by separate State secession—and that the sole and primary aim of each slaveholding State ought to be its speedy and absolute separation from an unnatural and hostile Union.

6] A Northern Republican Spurns Compromise

Among the Republicans, Senator Benjamin F. Wade of Ohio was one of the firmest opponents of compromise. Known as "Bluff Ben," he had won fame in the fifties by offering to meet Southern hotheads in duels, if he could choose the weapons—squirrel rifles at twenty paces. On December 17, 1860, as the Committee of Thirteen was about to be authorized, he spoke his mind on compromise, and spoke in his usual blunt fashion. His speech was widely circulated in the South as an example of Republican intolerance. Significantly, Wade was named a member of the Committee of Thirteen.*

WE BEAT you on the plainest and most palpable issue ever presented to the American people, and one which every man understood; and now, when we come to the capital, we tell you that our candidates must and shall be inaugurated—must and shall administer this Government precisely as the Constitution prescribes. It would not only be humiliating, but highly dishonorable to us, if we listened to any compromise by which we should set aside the honest verdict of the people. When it comes to that, you have no government, but anarchy intervenes, and civil war may follow; and all the evils that human imagination can raise may be consequent on such a course as that. The American people would lose the sheet-anchor of their liberties whenever it is denied on this floor that a majority, fairly given, shall rule. I know not what others may do; but I tell you that, with that verdict of the people in my pocket, and standing on the platform on which these candidates were elected, I would suffer anything before I would compromise in any way. I deem it no case where we have a right to extend courtesy and generosity. The absolute right, the most sacred that a free people can bestow upon any man, is their verdict that gives him a full title to the office he holds. If we cannot stand there, we cannot stand anywhere; and, my friends, any other verdict would be as fatal to you as to us.

7] Crittenden Offers Some Peace Resolutions

Senator John J. Crittenden of Kentucky looked upon himself, and was regarded by others, as the heir of Henry Clay and the spirit of compromise. And representing a border state, he viewed with particular and profound alarm the possibility of disunion and civil conflict. Able, conservative, dignified, he rose in the Senate on December 18, 1860, to offer a set of resolutions

---

* A NORTHERN REPUBLICAN SPURNS COMPROMISE: From Horace Greeley, *The American Conflict* (Hartford, 1864–67), I, 375–76.

that he hoped would allay the crisis. His plan, known to history as the Crittenden Compromise, was considered by the Senate Committee of Thirteen but was not adopted. As here presented, article 5, which dealt with a highly technical phase of the rendition of fugitive slaves, is omitted.*

WHEREAS, serious and alarming dissensions have arisen between the Northern and Southern States, concerning the rights and security of the rights of the slave-holding States, and especially their rights in the common territory of the United States; and whereas it is eminently desirable and proper that these dissensions which now threaten the very existence of this Union, should be permanently quieted and settled, by constitutional provision, which shall do equal justice to all sections, and thereby restore to the people that peace and good will which ought to prevail between all the citizens of the United States: Therefore,

Resolved by the Senate and House of Representatives of the United States of America in Congress Assembled, That the following articles be, and are hereby, proposed and submitted as amendments to the Constitution of the United States, . . .

ARTICLE 1. In all the territory of the United States now held, or hereafter acquired, situate North of Latitude 36°30', slavery or involuntary servitude, except as a punishment for crime, is prohibited while such territory shall remain under territorial government. In all the territory south of said line of latitude, slavery of the African race is hereby recognized as existing, and shall not be interfered with by Congress, but shall be protected as property by all the departments of the territorial government during its continuance. And when any Territory, north or south of said line, within such boundaries as Congress may prescribe, shall contain the population requisite for a member of Congress according to the then Federal ratio, of representation of the people of the United States, it shall, if its form of government be republican, be admitted into the Union, on an equal footing with the original States, with or without slavery, as the constitution of such new State may provide.

ART. 2. Congress shall have no power to abolish slavery in places under its exclusive jurisdiction, and situate within the limits of States that permit the holding of slaves.

ART. 3. Congress shall have no power to abolish slavery within the District of Columbia so long as it exists in the adjoining States of Virginia and Maryland, or either, nor without the consent of the inhabitants, nor without just compensation first made to such owners of slaves as do not consent to such abolishment. Nor shall Congress at any time prohibit officers of the Federal Government, or members of Congress, whose duties require them to be in said District, from bringing with them their slaves, and holding them as such during the time their duties may require them to remain there, and afterwards taking them from the District.

ART. 4. Congress shall have no power to prohibit or hinder the transportation of slaves from one State to another, or to a Territory in which slaves are by

* CRITTENDEN OFFERS SOME PEACE RESOLUTIONS: From Edward McPherson, *Political History of the Great Rebellion* (Washington, 1865), pp. 64–65.

law permitted to be held, whether that transportation be by land, navigable rivers, or by the sea. . . .

ART. 6. No future amendment of the Constitution shall affect the five preceding articles . . . and no amendment shall be made to the Constitution which shall authorize or give to Congress any power to abolish or interfere with slavery in any of the States by whose laws it is, or may be, allowed or permitted.

And whereas, also, besides these causes of dissension embraced in the foregoing amendments proposed to the Constitution of the United States, there are others which come within the jurisdiction of Congress, and may be remedied by its legislative power; Therefore

1. *Resolved.* . . . That the laws now in force for the recovery of fugitive slaves are in strict pursuance of the plain and mandatory provisions of the Constitution, and have been sanctioned as valid and constitutional by the judgment of the Supreme Court of the United States; that the slave-holding States are entitled to the faithful observance and execution of those laws, and that they ought not to be repealed, or so modified or changed as to impair their efficiency; and that laws ought to be made for the punishment of those who attempt by rescue of the slave, or other illegal means, to hinder or defeat the due execution of said laws.

2. That all State laws which conflict with the fugitive slave acts of Congress, or any other Constitutional acts of Congress, or which, in their operation, impede, hinder, or delay, the free course and due execution of any of said acts, are null and void by the present provisions of the Constitution of the United States; yet those State laws, void as they are, have given color to practices, and led to consequences which have obstructed the due administration and execution of acts of Congress, and especially the acts for the delivery of fugitive slaves, and have thereby contributed much to the discord and commotion now prevailing. Congress, therefore, in the present perilous juncture, does not deem it improper, respectfully and earnestly to recommend the repeal of those laws to the several States which have enacted them, or such legislative corrections or explanations of them as may prevent their being used or perverted to such mischievous purposes.

3. That the Act of the 18th of September, 1850, commonly called the fugitive slave law, . . . the last clause of the fifth section of said act, which authorizes a person holding a warrant for the arrest or detention of a fugitive slave, to summon to his aid the *posse comitatus,*[1] and which declares it to be the duty of all good citizens to assist him in its execution, ought to be so amended as to expressly limit the authority and duty to cases in which there shall be resistance or danger of resistance or rescue.

4. That the laws for the suppression of the African slave trade, and especially those prohibiting the importation of slaves in the United States, ought to be made effectual, and ought to be thoroughly executed: and all further enactments necessary to those ends ought to be promptly made.

1 *posse comitatus:* See p. 454n.

8] Lincoln Refuses to Compromise the Vital Issue

> Early in December Senator Trumbull and Representative Kellogg, both of Illinois, wrote Lincoln that talk of compromise was rife in Congress. The President-elect warned them that, whatever Republicans might yield on other issues, they must be adamant in refusing to extend slavery to the territories. Lincoln feared that some of his party might take up Democrat Senator Stephen A. Douglas' popular sovereignty, which would let the people of a territory decide the status of slavery.*

Private, & confidential
Hon. L. Trumbull.

Springfield, Ills. Dec. 10. 1860

MY DEAR SIR: Let there be no compromise on the question of *extending* slavery. If there be, all our labor is lost, and, ere long, must be done again. The dangerous ground—that into which some of our friends have a hankering to run—is Pop. Sov. Have none of it. Stand firm. The tug has to come, & better now, than any time hereafter. Yours as ever

A. LINCOLN.

Private, & confidential
Hon. William Kellogg.

Springfield, Ills. Dec. 11. 1860

MY DEAR SIR—

Entertain no proposition for a compromise in regard to the *extension* of slavery. The instant you do, they have us under again; all our labor is lost, and sooner or later must be done over. Douglas is sure to be again trying to bring in his "Pop. Sov." Have none of it. The tug has to come & better now than later.

You know I think the fugitive slave clause of the constitution ought to be enforced—to put it on the mildest form, ought not to be resisted. In haste Yours as ever

A. LINCOLN.

9] South Carolina Secedes from the Union

> In the first seven states that seceded, a common procedure was followed. First, the state government, usually the legislature and governor acting together, authorized and called an election to choose delegates to a convention to decide if the state should secede. Because such a convention represented the sovereign will of the state and came directly from the people, it

* LINCOLN REFUSES TO COMPROMISE THE VITAL ISSUE: From Roy P. Basler, ed., *The Collected Works of Abraham Lincoln* (New Brunswick, N.J., 1953), IV, 149–50. Reprinted by permission of the Rutgers University Press.

was not thought necessary to refer its decision to a popular referendum. South Carolina led off the secession parade, its convention voting unanimously on December 20 to take the state out of the Union.*

WE, THE PEOPLE of the State of South Carolina, in Convention assembled, do declare and ordain, and it is hereby declared and ordained, that the ordinance adopted by us in Convention, on the 23rd day of May, in the year of our Lord 1788, whereby the Constitution of the United States of America was ratified, and also all Acts and parts of Acts of the General Assembly of this State ratifying the amendments of the said Constitution, are hereby repealed, and that the union now subsisting between South Carolina and other States under the name of the United States of America is hereby dissolved.

10] South Carolina Explains Why She Seceded

On December 21, the day following the adoption of the secession ordinance, the South Carolina convention issued a statement justifying its action. This document was not intended for domestic consumption but for the world outside—the rest of the South, the North, Europe. It was a declaration of independence, like the one promulgated by the American colonies in 1776.†

. . . AND NOW the State of South Carolina having resumed her separate and equal place among nations, deems it due to herself, to the remaining United States of America, and to the nations of the world, that she should declare the immediate causes which have led to this act.

In the year 1765, that portion of the British Empire embracing Great Britain undertook to make laws for the Government of that portion composed of the thirteen American Colonies. A struggle for the right of self-government ensued, which resulted, on the 4th of July, 1776, in a Declaration, by the Colonies, "that they are, and of right ought to be, FREE AND INDEPENDENT STATES; and that, as free and independent States, they have full power to levy war, conclude peace, contract alliances, establish commerce, and to do all other acts and things which independent States may of right do."

They further solemnly declared that whenever any "form of government becomes destructive of the ends for which it was established, it is the right of the people to alter or abolish it, and to institute a new government." Deeming the Government of Great Britain to have become destructive of these ends, they declared that the Colonies "are absolved from all allegiance to the British Crown, and that all political connection between them and the State of Great Britain is, and ought to be, totally dissolved." . . .

Thus were established the two great principles asserted by the Colonies,

* SOUTH CAROLINA SECEDES FROM THE UNION: From Frank Moore, ed., *The Rebellion Record* (New York, 1861–65), I, 2.

† SOUTH CAROLINA EXPLAINS WHY SHE SECEDED: From Frank Moore, ed., *The Rebellion Record* (New York, 1861–65), I, 3–4.

namely, the right of a State to govern itself; and the right of a people to abolish a Government when it becomes destructive of the ends for which it was instituted. And concurrent with the establishment of these principles, was the fact, that each Colony became and was recognized by the mother country as a FREE, SOVEREIGN AND INDEPENDENT STATE.

In 1787, Deputies were appointed by the States to revise the articles of Confederation; and on 17th September, 1787, these Deputies recommended, for the adoption of the States, the Articles of Union, known as the Constitution of the United States.

The parties to whom this constitution was submitted were the several sovereign States; they were to agree or disagree, and when nine of them agreed, the compact was to take effect among those concurring; and the General Government, as the common agent, was then to be invested with their authority. . . .

Thus was established, by compact between the States, a Government with defined objects and powers, limited to the express words of the grant. This limitation left the whole remaining mass of power subject to the clause reserving it to the States or the people, and rendered unnecessary any specification of reserved rights. We hold that the Government thus established is subject to the two great principles asserted in the Declaration of Independence; and we hold further, that the mode of its formation subjects it to a third fundamental principle, namely, the law of compact. We maintain that in every compact between two or more parties, the obligation is mutual; that the failure of one of the contracting parties to perform a material part of the agreement, entirely releases the obligation of the other; and that, where no arbiter is provided, each party is remitted to his own judgment to determine the fact of failure, with all its consequences.

In the present case, the fact is established with certainty. We assert that fourteen of the States have deliberately refused for years past to fulfil their constitutional obligations, and we refer to their own statutes for the proof.

The Constitution of the United States, in its fourth Article, provides as follows: "No person held to service or labor in one State under the laws thereof, escaping into another, shall, in consequence of any law or regulation therein, be discharged from such service or labor, but shall be delivered up, on claim of the party to whom such service or labor may be due."

This stipulation was so material to the compact that without it that compact would not have been made. The greater number of the contracting parties held slaves, and they had previously evinced their estimate of the value of such a stipulation by making it a condition in the Ordinance for the government of the territory ceded by Virginia, which obligations, and the laws of the General Government, have ceased to effect the objects of the Constitution. The States of Maine, New Hampshire, Vermont, Massachusetts, Connecticut, Rhode Island, New York, Pennsylvania, Illinois, Indiana, Michigan, Wisconsin, and Iowa, have enacted laws which either nullify the acts of Congress, or render useless any attempt to execute them. In many of these States the fugitive is discharged from the service of labor claimed, and in none of them has the State Government complied with the stipulation made in the Constitution. . . .

Thus the constitutional compact has been deliberately broken and disregarded by the non-slaveholding States; and the consequence follows that South Carolina is released from her obligation.

The ends for which this Constitution was framed are declared by itself to be "to form a more perfect union, establish justice, insure domestic tranquillity, provide for the common defence, promote the general welfare, and secure the blessings of liberty to ourselves and our posterity."

These ends it endeavored to accomplish by a Federal Government, in which each State was recognized as an equal, and had separate control over its own institutions. The right of property in slaves was recognized by giving to free persons distinct political rights; by giving them the right to represent, and burdening them with direct taxes for, three-fifths of their slaves; by authorizing the importation of slaves for twenty years; and by stipulating for the rendition of fugitives from labor.

We affirm that these ends for which this Government was instituted have been defeated, and the Government itself has been destructive of them by the action of the non-slaveholding States. Those States have assumed the right of deciding upon the propriety of our domestic institutions; and have denied the rights of property established in fifteen of the States and recognized by the Constitution; they have denounced as sinful the institution of Slavery; they have permitted the open establishment among them of societies, whose avowed object is to disturb the peace of and eloin the property of the citizens of other States. They have encouraged and assisted thousands of our slaves to leave their homes; and those who remain, have been incited by emissaries, books, and pictures, to servile insurrection.

For twenty-five years this agitation has been steadily increasing, until it has now secured to its aid the power of the common Government. Observing the *forms* of the Constitution, a sectional party has found within that article establishing the Executive Department, the means of subverting the Constitution itself. A geographical line has been drawn across the Union, and all the States north of that line have united in the election of a man to the high office of President of the United States whose opinions and purposes are hostile to Slavery. He is to be intrusted with the administration of the common Government, because he has declared that that "Government cannot endure permanently half slave, half free," and that the public mind must rest in the belief that Slavery is in the course of ultimate extinction.

This sectional combination for the subversion of the Constitution has been aided, in some of the States, by elevating to citizenship persons who, by the supreme law of the land, are incapable of becoming citizens; and their votes have been used to inaugurate a new policy, hostile to the South, and destructive of its peace and safety.

On the 4th of March next this party will take possession of the Government. It has announced that the South shall be excluded from the common territory, that the Judicial tribunal shall be made sectional, and that a war must be waged against Slavery until it shall cease throughout the United States.

The guarantees of the Constitution will then no longer exist; the equal rights of the States will be lost. The Slaveholding States will no longer have the power of self-government, or self-protection, and the Federal Government will have become their enemy.

Sectional interest and animosity will deepen the irritation; and all hope of remedy is rendered vain, by the fact that the public opinion at the North has invested a great political error with the sanctions of a more erroneous religious belief.

We, therefore, the people of South Carolina, by our delegates in Convention assembled, appealing to the Supreme Judge of the world for the rectitude of our intentions, have solemnly declared that the Union heretofore existing between this State and the other States of North America is dissolved, and that the State of South Carolina has resumed her position among the nations of the world, as a separate and independent state, with full power to levy war, conclude peace, contract alliances, establish commerce, and to do all other acts and things which independent States may of right do.

11] A Southern Analysis of the Economics of Secession

> As the crisis deepened, men on both sides found reasons why they should act as they wanted to act. The New Orleans *Daily Crescent*, on January 21, 1861, five days before the secession of Louisiana, thus depicted the results of Southern economic subjection to the North and indicated the fair prospects for an independent South.*

. . . THEY KNOW that the South is the main prop and support of the Federal system. They know that it is Southern productions that constitute the surplus wealth of the nation, and enables us to import so largely from foreign countries. They know that it is their import trade that draws from the people's pockets sixty or seventy millions of dollars per annum, in the shape of duties, to be expended mainly in the North, and in the protection and encouragement of Northern interests. They know that it is the export of Southern productions, and the corresponding import of foreign goods, that gives profitable employment to their shipping. They know that the bulk of the duties is paid by the Southern people, though first collected at the North, and that, by the iniquitous operation of the Federal Government, these duties are mainly expended among the Northern people. They know that they can plunder and pillage the South, as long as they are in the same Union with us, by other means, such as fishing bounties, navigation laws, robberies of the public lands, and every other possible mode of injustice and peculation. . . . And, above and beyond all this, is the Puritanic love of mean tyranny and cold-blooded, inexorable oppression, which the Union enables them to cherish and reduce to practice—coupled with the Pharisaical boast of "holier than thou,"

* A SOUTHERN ANALYSIS OF THE ECONOMICS OF SECESSION: From Dwight L. Dumond, ed., *Southern Editorials on Secession* (New York, 1931), pp. 408–09. Reprinted by permission of the American Historical Association.

which they are constantly uttering as a reproach to the South—both of which feelings are innate in the descendants of the Pilgrims, and have become a part of their nature, which they could not get rid of if they wished.

These are the reasons why these people do not wish the South to secede from the Union. They are enraged at the prospect of being despoiled of the rich feast upon which they have so long fed and fattened, and which they were just getting ready to enjoy with still greater *goût*[1] and gusto. They are mad as hornets because the prize slips them just as they are ready to grasp it. Their fruitless wailing and frantic rage only serve to confirm the South in her inflexible determination to break up an alliance which is as unnatural as it is, to us, oppressive and degrading.

12] A Northern Intellectual Analyzes the Constitutional Issues of Secession

> To James Russell Lowell in New England, the crisis appeared starkly simple—the South was refusing to accept the decision of the majority as registered in the election of 1860. Indeed, as Lowell saw it, the question went even deeper. The South was refusing to accept the basic principle of democracy, and the North now had to vindicate that principle.*

. . . THE COUNTRY is weary of being cheated with plays upon words. The United States are a nation, and not a mass-meeting; theirs is a government, and not a caucus,—a government that was meant to be capable, and is capable, of something more than the helpless *please don't* of a village constable; they have executive and administrative officers that are not mere puppet-figures to go through the motions of an objectless activity, but arms and hands that become supple to do the will of the people so soon as that will becomes conscious and defines its purpose. It is time that we turned up our definitions in some more trustworthy dictionary than that of avowed disunionists and their more dangerous because more timid and cunning accomplices. Rebellion smells no sweeter because it is called Secession, nor does Order lose its divine precedence in human affairs because a knave may nickname it Coercion. "Secession means chaos, and Coercion the exercise of legitimate authority." . . .

It cannot be too distinctly stated or too often repeated that the discontent of South Carolina is not one to be allayed by any concessions which the Free States can make with dignity or even safety. It is something more radical and of longer standing than distrust of the motives or probable policy of the Republican party. It is neither more nor less than a disbelief in the very principles on which our government is founded. So long as they practically retained the government of the country, and could use its power and patronage

---

1 *goût*: relish.
* A NORTHERN INTELLECTUAL ANALYZES THE CONSTITUTIONAL ISSUES OF SECESSION: From James Russell Lowell, *Political Essays* (Boston, 1871), pp. 45–74.

to their own advantage, the plotters were willing to wait; but the moment they lost that control, by the breaking up of the Democratic party, and saw that their chance of ever regaining it was hopeless, they declared openly the principles on which they have all along been secretly acting. Denying the constitutionality of special protection to any other species of property or branch of industry, and in 1832 threatening to break up the Union unless their theory of the Constitution in this respect were admitted, they went into the late Presidential contest with a claim for extraordinary protection to a certain kind of property already the only one endowed with special privileges and immunities. Defeated overwhelmingly before the people, they now question the right of the majority to govern, except on their terms, and threaten violence in the hope of extorting from the fears of the Free States what they failed to obtain from their conscience and settled convictions of duty. Their quarrel is not with the Republican party, but with the theory of Democracy. . . .

We have been so long habituated to a kind of local independence in the management of our affairs, and the central government has fortunately had so little occasion for making itself felt at home and in the domestic concerns of the States, that the idea of its relation to us as a power, except for protection from without, has gradually become vague and alien to our ordinary habits of thought. We have so long heard the principle admitted, and seen it acted on with advantage to the general weal, that the people are sovereign in their own affairs, that we must recover our presence of mind before we see the fallacy of the assumption, that the people, or a bare majority of them, in a single State, can exercise their right of sovereignty as against the will of the nation legitimately expressed. When such a contingency arises, it is for a moment difficult to get rid of our habitual associations, and to feel that we are not a mere partnership, dissolvable whether by mutual consent or on the demand of one or more of its members, but a nation, which can never abdicate its right, and can never surrender it while virtue enough is left in the people to make it worth retaining. It would seem to be the will of God that from time to time the manhood of nations, like that of individuals, should be tried by great dangers or by great opportunities. If the manhood be there, it makes the great opportunity out of the great danger; if it be not there, then the great danger out of the great opportunity. The occasion is offered us now of trying whether a conscious nationality and a timely concentration of the popular will for its maintenance be possible in a democracy, or whether it is only despotisms that are capable of the sudden and selfish energy of protecting themselves from destruction. . . .

Slavery is no longer the matter in debate, and we must beware of being led off upon that side-issue. The matter now in hand is the reëstablishment of order, the reaffirmation of national unity, and the settling once for all whether there can be such a thing as a government without the right to use its power in self-defence. . . .

13] The House Accepts Part of the Report of Its Committee

On February 27, 1861, the Committee of Thirty-three reported to the House of Representatives two propositions designed to assure the South that slavery was secure in the states where it existed. Both were adopted. But the Committee could come to no agreement and could not report on the vital issue— whether or not slavery could expand to the territories.*

Resolved by the Senate and House of Representatives of the United States of America in Congress assembled, That all attempts on the part of the Legislatures of any of the States to obstruct or hinder the recovery and surrender of fugitives from service or labor, are in derogation of the Constitution of the United States, inconsistent with the comity and good neighborhood that should prevail among the several States, and dangerous to the peace of the Union.

Resolved, That the several States be respectfully requested to cause their statutes to be revised, with a view to ascertain if any of them are in conflict with or tend to embarrass or hinder the execution of the laws of the United States, made in pursuance of the second section of the fourth article of the Constitution of the United States for the delivery up of persons held to labor by the laws of any State and escaping therefrom; and the Senate and House of Representatives earnestly request that all enactments having such tendency be forthwith repealed, as required by a just sense of constitutional obligations, and by a due regard for the peace of the Republic; and the President of the United States is requested to communicate these resolutions to the Governors of the several States, with a request that they will lay the same before the Legislatures thereof respectively.

Resolved, That we recognize slavery as now existing in fifteen of the United States by the usages and laws of those States; and we recognize no authority, legally or otherwise, outside of a State where it so exists, to interfere with slaves or slavery in such States, in disregard of the rights of their owners or the peace of society.

Resolved, That we recognize the justice and propriety of a faithful execution of the Constitution, and laws made in pursuance thereof on the subject of fugitive slaves, or fugitives from service or labor, and discountenance all mobs or hindrances to the execution of such laws, and that citizens of each State shall be entitled to all the privileges and immunities of citizens in the several States.

Resolved, That we recognize no such conflicting elements in its composition, or sufficient cause from any source, for a dissolution of this Government; that we were not sent here to destroy, but to sustain and harmonize the institutions of the country, and to see that equal justice is done to all parts of

---

* THE HOUSE ACCEPTS PART OF THE REPORT OF ITS COMMITTEE: From Edward McPherson, *Political History of the Great Rebellion* (Washington, 1865), pp. 58–59.

the same; and finally, to perpetuate its existence on terms of equality and justice to all the States.

Resolved, That a faithful observance, on the part of all the States, of all their constitutional obligations to each other and to the Federal Government, is essential to the peace of the country.

Resolved, That it is the duty of the Federal Government to enforce the Federal laws, protect the Federal property, and preserve the Union of these States.

Resolved, That each State be requested to revise its statutes, and if necessary, so to amend the same as to secure, without legislation by Congress, to citizens of other States travelling therein, the same protection as citizens of such State enjoy; and also to protect the citizens of other States travelling or sojourning therein against popular violence or illegal summary punishment, without trial in due form of law, for imputed crimes.

Resolved, That each State be also respectfully requested to enact such laws as will prevent and punish any attempt whatever in such State to recognize or set on foot the lawless invasion of any other State or Territory.

Resolved, That the President be requested to transmit copies of the foregoing resolutions to the Governors of the several States, with a request that they be communicated to their respective Legislatures. . . .

Be it resolved by the Senate and House of Representatives of the United States of America in Congress assembled, two-thirds of both Houses concurring, That the following article be proposed to the Legislatures of the several States as an amendment to the Constitution of the United States, which when ratified by three-fourths of said Legislatures, shall be valid, to all intents and purposes, as a part of the said Constitution, namely:

ART. XII. No amendment of this Constitution having for its object any interference within the States with the relation between their citizens and those described in section second of the first article of the Constitution as "all other persons," shall originate with any State that does not recognize that relation within its own limits, or shall be valid without the assent of every one of the States composing the Union.

Before the vote was taken Mr. Corwin offered the following substitute for the above article:

ART. XII. No amendment shall be made to the Constitution which will authorize or give to Congress the power to abolish or interfere, within any State, with the domestic institutions thereof, including that of persons held to labor or service by the laws of said State.

14] The Compromise Plan of the Peace Convention

Meeting in Washington at the invitation of Virginia, the Peace Convention labored to produce a plan that would meet the requirements of Republicans and secessionists. Its final proposal followed closely the Crittenden Compromise but contained an addition on the acquisition of territory designed to satisfy Lincoln. The Convention worked under severe handicaps. Not all the states were represented (only twenty-one sent delegates), neither the

Republicans nor the secessionists were sympathetic to its aims, and its plan
was not produced until after secession had run its course.*

.   .   .   .

SECTION 1. In all the present territory of the United States north of the
parallel of 36°30′ of north latitude, involuntary servitude, except in punishment
of crime, is prohibited. In all the present territory south of that line, the *status*
of persons held to involuntary service or labor, as it now exists, shall not be
changed; nor shall any law be passed by Congress or the Territorial Legislature to hinder or prevent the taking of such persons from any of the States
of this Union to said territory, nor to impair the rights arising from said relation; but the same shall be subject to judicial cognizance in the Federal courts,
according to the course of the common law. When any Territory north or
south of said line, within such boundary as Congress may prescribe, shall contain a population equal to that required for a member of Congress, it shall,
if its form of Government be republican, be admitted into the Union on an
equal footing with the original States, with or without involuntary servitude,
as the constitution of such State may provide.

SEC. 2. No territory shall be acquired by the United States, except by discovery, and for naval and commercial stations, depots, and transit routes, without the concurrence of a majority of all the Senators from States which allow
involuntary servitude, and a majority of all the Senators from States which prohibit that relation; nor shall territory be acquired by treaty, unless the votes of
a majority of the Senators from each class of States hereinbefore mentioned
be cast as a part of the two-thirds majority necessary to the ratification of such
treaty.

SEC. 3. Neither the constitution nor any amendment thereof, shall be construed to give Congress power to regulate, abolish, or control within any State
the relation established or recognized by the laws thereof touching persons held
to labor or involuntary service therein, nor to interfere with or abolish involuntary service in the District of Columbia without the consent of Maryland, and
without the consent of the owners, or making the owners who do not consent
just compensation; nor the power to interfere with or prohibit representatives
and others from bringing with them to the District of Columbia, retaining,
and taking away, persons so held to labor or service; nor the power to interfere with or abolish involuntary service in places under the exclusive jurisdiction of the United States, within those States and Territories where the
same is established or recognized; nor the power to prohibit the removal or
transportation of persons held to labor or involuntary service in any State or
Territory of the United States to any other State or Territory thereof, where
it is established or recognized by law or usage; and the right during transportation, by sea or river, of touching at ports, shores, and landings, and of landing
in case of distress, shall exist; but not the right of transit in or through any
State or Territory, or of sale or traffic, against the laws thereof. Nor shall

* THE COMPROMISE PLAN OF THE PEACE CONVENTION: From Frank Moore, ed., *The Rebellion Record* (New York, 1861–65), I, 35–36.

Congress have power to authorize any higher rate of taxation on persons held to labor or service than on land. The bringing into the District of Columbia of persons held to labor or service, for sale, or placing them in depots to be afterwards transferred to other places for sale as merchandise, is prohibited.

Sec. 4. The third paragraph of the second section of the fourth article of the constitution shall not be construed to prevent any of the States, by appropriate legislation, and through the action of their judicial and ministerial officers, from enforcing the delivery of fugitives from labor to the person to whom such service or labor is due.

Sec. 5. The foreign slave trade is hereby forever prohibited; and it shall be the duty of Congress to pass laws to prevent the importation of slaves, coolies, or persons held to service or labor, into the United States and Territories from places beyond the limits thereof.

Sec. 6. The first, third, and fifth sections, together with this section, of these amendments, and the third paragraph of the second section of the first article of the constitution, and third paragraph of the second section of the fourth article thereof, shall not be amended or abolished without the consent of all the States.

Sec. 7. Congress shall provide by law that the United States shall pay to the owner the full value of his fugitive from labor, in all cases where the marshal, or other officer, whose duty it was to arrest such fugitive, was prevented from so doing by violence or intimidation from mobs or riotous assemblages, or when, after arrest, such fugitive was rescued by like violence or intimidation, and the owner thereby deprived of the same; and the acceptance of such payment shall preclude the owner from further claim to such fugitive. Congress shall provide by law for securing to the citizens of each State the privileges and immunities of citizens in the several States.

15] A Michigander Is Not Averse to a Little "Blood-Letting"

> Senator Zachariah Chandler, extreme Republican of Michigan, feared that the Peace Convention might fix up a compromise that would undermine Republican principles. He urged Governor Austin Blair of his state to send firm delegates to the convention. Chandler's letter reveals the explosive elements of aggression under the surface of the secession crisis.*

Washington, Feb. 11, 1861.

My Dear Governor:

Governor Bingham and myself telegraphed you on Saturday, at the request of Massachusetts and New York, to send delegates to the Peace or Compromise Congress. They admit that we were right and that they were wrong; that no Republican States should have sent delegates but they are here, and cannot get

---

* A MICHIGANDER IS NOT AVERSE TO A LITTLE "BLOOD-LETTING": From the *Congressional Globe*, 36 Cong., 2 Sess., p. 1247.

away. Ohio, Indiana and Rhode Island are caving in, and there is danger of
Illinois; and now they beg of us for God's sake to come to their rescue, and
save the Republican party from rupture. I hope you will send *stiff-backed* men
or none. The whole thing was gotten up against my judgment and advice,
and will end in thin smoke. Still I hope as a matter of courtesy to some of our
erring brethren, that you will send the delegates. Truly your friend,

Z. CHANDLER.

P.S. Some of the manufacturing States think a fight would be awful. Without a little blood-letting, this Union will not, in my estimation, be worth a
rush.

16] Crittenden Pleads, "Hold Fast to the Union"

On March 2, 1861, on the eve of the adjournment of Congress, Senator
Crittenden, knowing his plan had failed, still pleaded with his colleagues
to devise some measure to save the Union.*

. . . MR. PRESIDENT, the cause of this great discontent in the country, the
cause of the evils which we now suffer and which we now fear, originates
chiefly from questions growing out of the respective territorial rights of the
different States and the unfortunate subject of slavery. I have said before to
my brother Senators that I do not appear on this occasion as the advocate
of slavery; I appear here as the advocate of the Union. I want to preserve that
from overthrow; and I am suggesting that policy, which, according to my
poor judgment, is adequate to the object.

What is the great question out of which this mighty mischief has grown;
what is this question about territory? Practically, it is reduced to a very small
matter. We have passed through many of these territorial difficulties; we have
now arrived at the very last one of them. Neither the climate nor the wishes
of any portion of this Union have induced the people anywhere to desire really
to extend slavery above the line of $36°30'$ north latitude. . . . We have now
much territory north of that line; but there is no pretension to any rights there
by those who hold slaves. We have, since that compromise line was first established, acquired territory south of it. That territory south of it is composed of
the Territory of New Mexico, and nothing else; and there slavery now exists
by law. . . . These points of controversy have reference practically now to no
other Territory which we have except the Territory of New Mexico; and to
show how infinitely small that is, there is another consideration to which I
wish to advert. What are the worth and value of that Territory to white or to
black? It is the most sterile region of country belonging to the United States,
the least happy. It has been open to slavery for ten years, and there is a controversy, I believe, whether there are twenty-four or twenty-six or twenty-eight

* CRITTENDEN PLEADS, "HOLD FAST TO THE UNION": From the *Congressional Globe*,
36 Cong., 2 Sess., pp. 1357–80.

slaves within the whole Territory. As I believe, it can never be made a slave State. It is not a country where slaves can be profitably employed; and that great law of profit and loss governs with invariable power and invariable efficacy. Here is a mere question of abstract right, in the deprivation of which the South has supposed itself to be offended. . . .

Thirty-seven thousand men from the noble old State of Massachusetts have said, "Let there be no compromise." Nothing is more justly boasted of by Massachusetts than her school-houses and her churches. Her churches and her school-houses were the first houses she built; and now here have arisen out of these churches over thirty thousand men who, when a great controversy arises in the country, when revolution is seizing arms on every side, and brethren are ready to slay and destroy each other, and when such terms as those which I have endeavored to explain can settle the whole matter, with an apparently pious and religious cry, say: "No compromise; let blood flow; but no com- promise." . . . I have no doubt, sir, there are many venerable and good men among them, because they are neighbors to at least forty thousand Massachu- setts men who have petitioned in a very different tone, and say: "Compromise, I pray; make peace with them; let us not slay and destroy one another." That is the language of the petition which I presented.

Sir, if old Bunker Hill now had a voice, it would be, of course, as it should be, a voice like thunder; and what would she proclaim from her old and triumphant heights? No compromise with your brethren? No, sir; that would not be her voice; but I fancy to myself, if that venerated and honored old scene of American bravery, hallowed by the blood of the patriots who stood there, hand in hand, brethren of the North and South, could but speak, it would be but one voice, a great and patriotic voice: peace with thy brethren; be recon- ciled with thy brethren. It is less than the value of a straw that is asked from you as compromise, and you will not give a straw. You prefer the bloody doctrine of "No compromise; battle first;" and woe be to those who first draw the sword. . . .

I fear for further revolution—for revolution to such an extent as to destroy, in effect, this Union. I hope not. I would advise against it. I would say to the people [of the South], the distraction which exists in the opinions of those that constitute Congress are such that they cannot agree upon any measures now; you may think and feel that justice is denied you; it may be so; but is denied you by whom? In a time of high party excitement, by one Congress. Your Constitution is so framed as to give you, in a short period, many Con- gresses. The power returns to the people of electing their representatives; and this Government is worth being patient for, and worth bearing a great deal for. Be patient and bear it, even though you think you are wronged. . . . Hold fast to the Union. The Union is the instrument by which you may obtain re- dress, by which you will in the end obtain redress. Congress may err. It may err from error of judgment, from passion, from excitement, from party heats; they will not last always. The principles upon which your Government was founded recognize all these frailties, recognize all these sources of occasional and temporary wrong and injustice, but they furnish a remedy for it. They furnish a remedy in the often-recurring elections which the people make. It is not for the first offense that dismemberment and disunion are justified. Hold fast to the Union. There is safety, tried safety, known safety; and that same Union is the best assurance you can have of eventually obtaining from your fellow-citizens a generous recompense for all the wrongs you have received, and a generous remedy against any wrongs hereafter. . . .

Through this great nation common blood flows. What man is there here that is not of a blood, flowing—meandering—perhaps through every State in the Union? and we talk about not compromising a family quarrel; and that is to be held up as patriotism, or party fidelity. In the name of God, who is it that will adopt that policy? We are one people in blood; in language one; in thoughts one; we read the same books; we feed on the same meats; we go to the same school; we belong to the same communion. If, as we go through this quarrelsome world, we meet with our little difficulties, if we wish to carry with us grateful hearts of the blessings we have enjoyed, we shall be bound to compromise with the difficulties that must occur on all the ways of the world that are trodden by Governments on earth. It is our infirmity to have such difficulties. Let it be our magnanimity and our wisdom to compromise and settle them. . . .

My principle, and the doctrine I teach, is, take care of the Union; compromise it; do anything for it; it is the palladium—so General Washington called it—of your rights; take care of it, and it will take care of you. Yes, sir; let us take care of the Union, and it will certainly take care of us. That is the proposition which I teach.

17] Lincoln Delivers His First Inaugural Address

> On March 4, 1861, Lincoln spoke to a divided nation that awaited his words with mingled feelings of anxiety, hope, and hostility. This address was the first of the many great state papers that would come from Lincoln during the war. Already he was demonstrating his matchless talent for the use of words. But what exactly was he saying—or not saying? Was he threatening force or promising conciliation? Was he hiding his real purpose? Or, like any sensible political leader, was he leaving to himself several possible avenues of action? *

FELLOW CITIZENS OF THE UNITED STATES;

In compliance with a custom as old as the government itself, I appear before you to address you briefly, and to take, in your presence, the oath prescribed by the Constitution of the United States, to be taken by the President "before he enters on the execution of his office."

I do not consider it necessary, at present, for me to discuss those matters of administration about which there is no special anxiety, or excitement.

Apprehension seems to exist among the people of the Southern states, that

---

* LINCOLN DELIVERS HIS FIRST INAUGURAL ADDRESS: From Roy P. Basler, ed., *The Collected Works of Abraham Lincoln* (New Brunswick, N.J., 1953), IV, 262–71. The student who wishes to consult the original draft and Lincoln's revisions is urged to read pages 249–62 of this work.

by the accession of a Republican administration, their property, and their peace, and personal security, are to be endangered. There has never been any reasonable cause for such apprehension. Indeed, the most ample evidence to the contrary has all the while existed, and been open to their inspection. It is found in nearly all the published speeches of him who now addresses you. I do but quote from one of those speeches when I declare that "I have no purpose, directly or indirectly, to interfere with the institution of slavery in the states where it exists. I believe I have no lawful right to do so, and I have no inclination to do so." Those who nominated and elected me did so with full knowledge that I had made this and many similar declarations, and had never recanted them. And more than this, they placed in the platform, for my acceptance, and as a law to themselves, and to me, the clear and emphatic resolution which I now read:

"*Resolved,* That the maintenance inviolate of the rights of the states, and especially the right of each state to order and control its own domestic institutions according to its own judgment exclusively, is essential to that balance of power on which the perfection and endurance of our political fabric depend; and we denounce the lawless invasion by armed force of the soil of any state or territory, no matter under what pretext, as among the gravest of crimes."

I now reiterate these sentiments: and in doing so, I only press upon the public attention the most conclusive evidence of which the case is susceptible, that the property, peace and security of no section are to be in anywise endangered by the now incoming administration. I add too, that all the protection which, consistently with the Constitution and the laws, can be given, will be cheerfully given to all the states when lawfully demanded, for whatever cause —as cheerfully to one section, as to another.

There is much controversy about the delivering up of fugitives from service or labor. The clause I now read is as plainly written in the Constitution as any other of its provisions:

"No person held to service or labor in one state, under the law thereof, escaping into another, shall, in consequence of any law or regulation therein, be discharged from such service or labor, but shall be delivered up on claim of the party to whom such service or labor may be due."

It is scarcely questioned that this provision was intended by those who made it, for the reclaiming of what we call fugitive slaves; and the intention of the lawgiver is the law. All members of Congress swear their support to the whole Constitution—to this provision as much as to any other. To the proposition, then, that slaves whose cases come within the terms of this clause, "shall be delivered up," their oaths are unanimous. Now, if they would make the effort in good temper, could they not, with nearly equal unanimity, frame and pass a law, by means of which to keep good that unanimous oath?

There is some difference of opinion whether this clause should be enforced by national or by state authority; but surely that difference is not a very material one. If the slave is to be surrendered, it can be of but little consequence to him, or to others, by which authority it is done. And should anyone, in any case, be content that his oath shall go unkept, on a merely unsubstantial controversy as to *how* it shall be kept?

510 Disruption of the Union

Again, in any law upon this subject, ought not all the safeguards of liberty known in civilized and humane jurisprudence to be introduced, so that a free man be not, in any case, surrendered as a slave? And might it not be well, at the same time, to provide by law for the enforcement of that clause in the Constitution which guaranties that "The citizen of each state shall be entitled to all privileges and immunities of citizens in the several states?"

I take the official oath today, with no mental reservations, and with no purpose to construe the Constitution or laws, by any hypercritical rules. And while I do not choose now to specify particular acts of Congress as proper to be enforced, I do suggest, that it will be much safer for all, both in official and private stations, to conform to, and abide by, all those acts which stand unrepealed, than to violate any of them, trusting to find impunity in having them held to be unconstitutional.

It is seventy-two years since the first inauguration of a President under our national Constitution. During that period fifteen different and greatly distinguished citizens, have, in succession, administered the executive branch of the government. They have conducted it through many perils; and, generally, with great success. Yet, with all this scope for precedent, I now enter upon the same task for the brief constitutional term of four years, under great and peculiar difficulty. A disruption of the federal Union heretofore only menaced, is now formidably attempted.

I hold, that in contemplation of universal law, and of the Constitution, the Union of these states is perpetual. Perpetuity is implied, if not expressed, in the fundamental law of all national governments. It is safe to assert that no government proper, ever had a provision in its organic law for its own termination. Continue to execute all the express provisions of our national Constitution, and the Union will endure forever—it being impossible to destroy it, except by some action not provided for in the instrument itself.

Again, if the United States be not a government proper, but an association of states in the nature of contract merely, can it, as a contract, be peaceably unmade, by less than all the parties who made it? One party to a contract may violate it—break it so to speak; but does it not require all to lawfully rescind it?

Descending from these general principles, we find the proposition that, in legal contemplation, the Union is perpetual, confirmed by the history of the Union itself. The Union is much older than the Constitution. It was formed in fact, by the Articles of Association in 1774. It was matured and continued by the Declaration of Independence in 1776. It was further matured and the faith of all the then thirteen states expressedly plighted and engaged that it should be perpetual, by the Articles of Confederation in 1778. And finally, in 1787, one of the declared objects for ordaining and establishing the Constitution, was *"to form a more perfect union."*

But if destruction of the Union, by one, or by a part only, of the states, be lawfully possible, the Union is *less* perfect than before the Constitution, having lost the vital element of perpetuity.

It follows from these views that no state, upon its own mere motion, can lawfully get out of the Union—that *resolves* and *ordinances* to that effect are legally void; and that acts of violence, within any state or states, against the authority of the United States, are insurrectionary or revolutionary, according to circumstances.

I therefore consider that, in view of the Constitution and the laws, the Union is unbroken; and, to the extent of my ability, I shall take care, as the Constitution itself expressly enjoins upon me, that the laws of the Union be faithfully executed in all the states. Doing this I deem to be only a simple duty on my part; and I shall perform it, so far as practicable, unless my rightful masters, the American people, shall withhold the requisite means, or, in some authoritative manner, direct the contrary. I trust this will not be regarded as a menace, but only as the declared purpose of the Union that it *will* constitutionally defend, and maintain itself.

In doing this there needs to be no bloodshed or violence; and there shall be none, unless it be forced upon the national authority. The power confided to me, will be used to hold, occupy, and possess the property, and places belonging to the government, and to collect the duties and imposts; but beyond what may be necessary for these objects, there will be no invasion—no using of force against, or among the people anywhere. Where hostility to the United States, in any interior locality, shall be so great and so universal, as to prevent competent resident citizens from holding the federal offices, there will be no attempt to force obnoxious strangers among the people for that object. While the strict legal right may exist in the government to enforce the exercise of these offices, the attempt to do so would be so irritating, and so nearly impracticable with all, that I deem it better to forego, for the time, the uses of such offices.

The mails, unless repelled, will continue to be furnished in all parts of the Union. So far as possible, the people everywhere shall have that sense of perfect security which is most favorable to calm thought and reflection. The course here indicated will be followed, unless current events, and experience, shall show a modification, or change, to be proper; and in every case and exigency, my best discretion will be exercised, according to circumstances actually existing, and with a view and a hope of a peaceful solution of the national troubles, and the restoration of fraternal sympathies and affections.

That there are persons in one section, or another who seek to destroy the Union at all events, and are glad of any pretext to do it, I will neither affirm or deny; but if there be such, I need address no word to them. To those, however, who really love the Union, may I not speak?

Before entering upon so grave a matter as the destruction of our national fabric, with all its benefits, its memories, and its hopes, would it not be wise to ascertain precisely why we do it? Will you hazard so desperate a step, while there is any possibility that any portion of the ills you fly from, have no real existence? Will you, while the certain ills you fly to, are greater than all the real ones you fly from? Will you risk the commission of so fearful a mistake?

All profess to be content in the Union, if all constitutional rights can be maintained. Is it true, then, that any right, plainly written in the Constitution, has been denied? I think not. Happily the human mind is so constituted, that no party can reach to the audacity of doing this. Think, if you can, of a single instance in which a plainly written provision of the Constitution has ever been denied. If, by the mere force of numbers, a majority should deprive a minority of any clearly written constitutional right, it might, in a moral point of view, justify revolution—certainly would, if such right were a vital one. But such is not our case. All the vital rights of minorities, and of individuals, are so plainly assured to them, by affirmations and negations, guaranties and prohibitions, in the Constitution, that controversies never arise concerning them. But no organic law can ever be framed with a provision specifically applicable to every question which may occur in practical administration. No foresight can anticipate, nor any document of reasonable length contain express provisions for all possible questions. Shall fugitives from labor be surrendered by national or by state authority? The Constitution does not expressly say. *May* Congress prohibit slavery in the territories? The Constitution does not expressly say. *Must* Congress protect slavery in the territories? The Constitution does not expressly say.

From questions of this class spring all our constitutional controversies, and we divide upon them into majorities and minorities. If the minority will not acquiesce, the majority must, or the government must cease. There is no other alternative; for continuing the government, is acquiescence on one side or the other. If a minority, in such case, will secede rather than acquiesce, they make a precedent which in turn, will divide and ruin them; for a minority of their own will secede from them, whenever a majority refuses to be controlled by such minority. For instance, why may not any portion of a new confederacy, a year or two hence, arbitrarily secede again, precisely as portions of the present Union now claim to secede from it. All who cherish disunion sentiments, are now being educated to the exact temper of doing this. Is there such perfect identity of interests among the states to compose a new Union, as to produce harmony only, and prevent renewed secession?

Plainly, the central idea of secession, is the essence of anarchy. A majority, held in restraint by constitutional checks, and limitations, and always changing easily, with deliberate changes of popular opinions and sentiments, is the only true sovereign of a free people. Whoever rejects it, does, of necessity, fly to anarchy or to despotism. Unanimity is impossible; the rule of a minority, as a permanent arrangement, is wholly inadmissible; so that, rejecting the majority principle, anarchy, or despotism in some form, is all that is left.

I do not forget the position assumed by some, that constitutional questions are to be decided by the Supreme Court; nor do I deny that such decisions must be binding in any case, upon the parties to a suit, as to the object of that suit, while they are also entitled to very high respect and consideration, in all parallel cases, by all other departments of the government. And while it is obviously possible that such decision may be erroneous in any given case, still the evil effect following it, being limited to that particular case, with the chance that it may be overruled, and never become a precedent for other cases, can better be borne than could the evils of a different practice. At the same time the candid citizen must confess that if the policy of the government, upon vital questions, affecting the whole people, is to be irrevocably fixed by decisions of the Supreme Court, the instant they are made, in ordinary litigation between parties, in personal actions, the people will have ceased, to be their own rulers, having, to that extent, practically resigned their government, into the hands of that eminent tribunal. Nor is there, in this view, any assault upon the court, or the judges. It is a duty, from which they may not shrink, to decide cases properly brought before them; and it is no fault of theirs, if others seek to turn their decisions to political purposes.

One section of our country believes slavery is *right,* and ought to be extended, while the other believes it is *wrong,* and ought not to be extended. This is the only substantial dispute. The fugitive slave clause of the Constitution, and the law for the suppression of the foreign slave trade, are each as well enforced, perhaps, as any law can ever be in a community where the moral sense of the people imperfectly supports the law itself. The great body of the people abide by the dry legal obligation in both cases, and a few break over in each. This, I think, cannot be perfectly cured; and it would be worse in both cases *after* the separation of the sections, than before. The foreign slave trade, now imperfectly suppressed, would be ultimately revived without restriction, in one section; while fugitive slaves, now only partially surrendered, would not be surrendered at all, by the other.

Physically speaking, we cannot separate. We cannot remove our respective sections from each other, nor build an impassable wall between them. A husband and wife may be divorced, and go out of the presence, and beyond the reach of each other; but the different parts of our country cannot do this. They cannot but remain face to face; and intercourse, either amicable or hostile, must continue between them. Is it possible then to make that intercourse more advantageous, or more satisfactory, *after* separation than *before?* Can aliens make treaties easier than friends can make laws? Can treaties be more faithfully enforced between aliens, than laws can among friends? Suppose you go to war, you cannot fight always; and when, after much loss on both sides, and no gain on either, you cease fighting, the identical old questions, as to terms of intercourse, are again upon you.

This country, with its institutions, belongs to the people who inhabit it. Whenever they shall grow weary of the existing government, they can exercise their *constitutional* right of amending it, or their *revolutionary* right to dismember, or overthrow it. I cannot be ignorant of the fact that many worthy, and patriotic citizens are desirous of having the national Constitution amended. While I make no recommendation of amendments, I fully recognize the rightful authority of the people over the whole subject, to be exercised in either of the modes prescribed in the instrument itself; and I should, under existing circumstances, favor, rather than oppose, a fair opportunity being afforded the people to act upon it.

I will venture to add that, to me, the convention mode seems preferable, in that it allows amendments to originate with the people themselves, instead of only permitting them to take, or reject, propositions, orginated by others, not especially chosen for the purpose, and which might not be precisely such, as they would wish to either accept or refuse. I understand a proposed amendment to the Constitution—which amendment, however, I have not seen, has passed Congress, to the effect that the federal government, shall never interfere with the domestic institutions of the states, including that of persons held to service. To avoid misconstruction of what I have said, I depart from my purpose not to speak of particular amendments, so far as to say that, holding such a provision to now be implied constitutional law, I have no objection to its being made express, and irrevocable.

The chief magistrate derives all his authority from the people, and they have conferred none upon him to fix terms for the separation of the states. The people themselves can do this also if they choose; but the executive, as such, has nothing to do with it. His duty is to administer the present government, as it came to his hands, and to transmit it, unimpaired by him, to his successor.

Why should there not be a patient confidence in the ultimate justice of the people? Is there any better, or equal hope, in the world? In our present differences, is either party without faith of being in the right? If the Almighty Ruler of nations, with his eternal truth and justice, be on your side of the North, or on yours of the South, that truth, and that justice, will surely prevail, by the judgment of this great tribunal, the American people.

By the frame of the government under which we live, this same people have wisely given their public servants but little power for mischief; and have, with equal wisdom, provided for the return of that little to their own hands at very short intervals.

While the people retain their virtue, and vigilance, no administration, by any extreme of wickedness or folly, can very seriously injure the government, in the short space of four years.

My countrymen, one and all, think calmly and well, upon this whole subject. Nothing valuable can be lost by taking time. If there be an object to *hurry* any of you, in hot haste, to a step which you would never take deliberately, that object will be frustrated by taking time; but no good object can be frustrated by it. Such of you as are now dissatisfied, still have the old Constitution unimpaired, and, on the sensitive point, the laws of your own framing under it; while the new administration will have no immediate power, if it would, to change either. If it were admitted that you who are dissatisfied, hold the right side in the dispute, there still is no single good reason for precipitate action. Intelligence, patriotism, Christianity, and a firm reliance on Him, who has never yet forsaken this favored land, are still competent to adjust, in the best way, all our present difficulty.

In *your* hands, my dissatisfied fellow-countrymen, and not in *mine,* is the momentous issue of civil war. The government will not assail *you.* You can have no conflict, without being yourselves the aggressors. *You* have no oath registered in Heaven to destroy the government, while *I* shall have the most solemn one to "preserve, protect and defend" it.

I am loath to close. We are not enemies, but friends. We must not be enemies. Though passion may have strained, it must not break our bonds of affection. The mystic chords of memory, stretching from every battlefield, and patriot grave, to every living heart and hearthstone, all over this broad land, will yet swell the chorus of the Union, when again touched, as surely they will be, by the better angels of our nature.

18] Two Southern Newspapers Interpret Lincoln's Inaugural Address

Newspapers all over the country placed different interpretations on Lincoln's policy as outlined in the inaugural address. Those in the South generally took the line that he intended war. Those in the North took almost as many positions as there were editors. It would seem that at this stage the Northern press reflected completely the state of Northern opinion—the people were not sure what their government should do and they were not sure what Lincoln was going to do. Southern opinion, on the other hand, was more assured. In the following editorials (1), the Richmond *Dispatch* on March 5, 1861, charges that Lincoln means war. But (2), the Raleigh *Standard,* March 9, immediately following, is not so sure.*

THE Inaugural Address of ABRAHAM LINCOLN inaugurates civil war, as we have predicted it would from the beginning. The Black Republicans have played their deep, temporizing game with profound address and subtlety; but there is no longer any need of concealment, and the veil drops from the false prophet. The Demon of Coercion stands unmasked. The sword is drawn and the scabbard thrown away. If the fifteen Slave States had gone out in a body, this would have never been. But, as it is, the Border States lie almost at the mercy of an invader. Their forts are filled with Federal troops, whilst they have not raised a finger for defence. No doubt Fortress Monroe, in a month, will be powerfully reinforced, and ere long Virginia may be engaged in a life and death struggle for independence, honor, and for all that makes existence worth living.

We have no intention of arguing the points raised by his Sable Excellency upon the right of secession. That is a subject upon which there is the most radical disagreement between the North and South, a disagreement which he proposes to reconcile by the sword. . . .

There is but one power under Heaven that can keep this man from executing his purpose, THE AMERICAN PEOPLE, which he recognizes as his Master, and in order to secure the interposition of that power, every Border State ought to go out of the Union within twenty-four hours. Even this movement, which would once have been effectual, may now be too late to avert the catastrophe, but it will at all events mitigate its force. It will increase the difficulties of the ferocious enterprise which these enemies of humanity propose; it is the only alternative, except the most abject humiliation. . . .

* * *

OUR opinions in relation to the Chicago platform, Abraham Lincoln, and the Black Republican party are well known. We are as hostile to Mr. Lincoln and to the sectional party that elected him as any reasonable man in the South.

* TWO SOUTHERN NEWSPAPERS INTERPRET LINCOLN'S INAUGURAL ADDRESS: From Dwight L. Dumond, ed., *Southern Editorials on Secession* (New York, 1931), pp. 475–79. Reprinted by permission of the American Historical Association.

We will never submit to the administration of the government on the principles of that party so far as they relate to slavery in the Territories; but while we say this for the hundredth time, we also hold that justice should be done even to Mr. Lincoln and his party, and that he who would deliberately fan the flame of sectional strife, instead of doing all he can to put out the fires of discord which threaten to consume the temple of the Union, is guilty of an inexpiable crime. We want peace, not war. We want Union, not disunion. We want justice for the South, but we must do justice to the North. We long for light, not darkness. We believe that the Union can be preserved, and we are willing to bear and forbear—to watch and wait—to labor in a fraternal spirit to achieve this most desirable result. When the enemy offers us the olive branch we will not reject it. When he approaches us pointing to his oath, yet in a spirit of amity, we will not rush upon him with the sword. When he pleads for the Union we will point to the Constitution; and if both of us should then pause, we would then go with him to the fountain of all power, the people of the States, and seek there, and establish there, if possible, new foundations for equality and brotherhood.

So far as coercion is concerned, Mr. Lincoln occupies the very ground occupied by Mr. Buchanan.—We have compared the Inaugural in this respect with Mr. Buchanan's message, and the fact is so.—We cannot, as an honest man, denounce in Mr. Lincoln what we approved in Mr. Buchanan. The man had just taken an oath to support the Constitution and to enforce the laws. What was he to do? Was he to say to the seven cotton States, you are out of the Union? Who gave him that authority? Has Congress said it? . . .

If Mr. Lincoln were mad enough to attempt to subjugate the Southern States, or even if he were disposed to do so—as his Inaugural shows he is not—he has no army at his command. He might spare a thousand troops from the forts and frontiers, but what could these do against the armies of the fifteen slaveholding States? Then he has no money. The Treasury is empty. Then he has no authority for raising troops, even if he had money to pay them with. The "force bill" so-called, was defeated in the House of Representatives. What then? He is powerless. He is not only powerless at present, but the tone of his Inaugural shows that he is alarmed in view of the calamities that impend. Will he be stronger in future? We do not believe he will.—His party is already demoralized, and in addition to this, the great body of the Northern people will never consent to an aggressive war on the South.—If the seven cotton States had remained in the Union, both branches of Congress would have been against Mr. Lincoln by large majorities, and the Senate could have dictated all his important appointments. But they abandoned the Union—abandoned it selfishly and for no sufficient cause, and left us at the mercy, *as they say,* of a dominant sectional party. Shall we go out simply because they did? We trust not. Have we of the middle States no self-respect—no will of our own? We think we have *some* will of our own, for we are still in the Union. . . .

We do not propose to comment further on this document. It is before our readers, and each one of them will read and study it carefully for himself.— We approve portions of it, and we disapprove other portions. *It is not a war message.* It is not, strictly speaking, a Black Republican message; for while he recognizes slavery in the States as perpetual, and as never to be interfered with in any way by the abolitionists, he deliberately refrains from pressing the main principle in his platform, to wit, the exclusion of the South from all the Territories of the Union. It is not unfriendly to the South. It deprecates war, and bloodshed, and it pleads for the Union. That any portion of it will be approved by the Disunionists we have no idea. If it had breathed violence and war—if it had claimed the government for the North exclusively, and had threatened the South with subjugation, the Disunionists would have shouted for joy, as they did in Charleston when they learned that Lincoln was elected, for they would then have been sure of the attainment of their darling purpose, the permanent and final disruption of the Union.

19] A Virginian Urges South Carolina to Strike a Blow

> Roger A. Pryor of Virginia, an ardent secessionist, was irritated that his own state was delaying action. Proceeding to Charleston, where things were evidently about to happen, Pryor made this address on April 10, 1861. If there were men in the North who wanted war, there were also some in the South.*

GENTLEMEN, I thank you, especially that you have at last annihilated this accursed Union, [applause,] reeking with corruption, and insolent with excess of tyranny. Thank God, it is at last blasted and riven by the lightning wrath of an outraged and indignant people. [Loud applause.] Not only is it gone, but gone forever. [Cries of 'You're right,' and applause.] In the expressive language of Scripture, it is water spilt upon the ground, which cannot be gathered up. [Applause.] Like Lucifer, son of the morning, it has fallen, never to rise again. [Continued applause.] *For my part, gentlemen, if Abraham Lincoln and Hannibal Hamlin to-morrow were to abdicate their offices and were to give me a blank sheet of paper to write the condition of reannexation to the defunct Union, I would scornfully spurn the overture.* . . . I invoke you, and I make it in some sort a personal appeal—personal so far as it tends to our assistance in Virginia —I do invoke you, in your demonstrations of popular opinion, in your exhibitions of official intent, to give no countenance to this idea of reconstruction. [Many voices, emphatically, 'Never,' and applause.] In Virginia they all say, if reduced to the dread dilemma of the memorable alternative, they will espouse the cause of the South as against the interest of the Northern Confederacy, but they whisper of reconstruction, and they say Virginia must abide in the Union, with the idea of reconstructing the Union which you have annihilated. *I pray you, gentlemen, rob them of that idea.* Proclaim to the world that upon no condition, and under no circumstance, will South Carolina ever again enter into political association with the Abolitionists of New England. [Cries of 'Never,' and applause.] Do not distrust Virginia. As sure as to-morrow's sun will rise

---

* A VIRGINIAN URGES SOUTH CAROLINA TO STRIKE A BLOW: From Edward McPherson, *Political History of the Great Rebellion* (Washington, 1865), p. 112.

upon us, just so sure will Virginia be a member of this Southern Confederation. [Applause.] *And I will tell you, gentlemen, what will put her in the Southern Confederation in less than an hour by Shrewsbury clock*—STRIKE A BLOW! [Tremendous applause.] *The very moment that blood is shed, old Virginia will make common cause with her sister of the South.* [Applause.] It is impossible she should do otherwise.

20] A Northern Editor Rejoices That Sumter Has Resolved the Crisis

> The Confederate seizure of Fort Sumter snapped a tension that had become unbearable, a tension that had been built up over twenty years. Now all the debating was over—men would act instead of talk. To many in both sections the situation after Sumter came as a relief. Here Horace Greeley's New York *Tribune*, in an April issue, expresses the Northern reaction.*

FORT SUMTER is lost, but freedom is saved. There is no more thought of bribing or coaxing the traitors who have dared to aim their cannon balls at the flag of the Union, and those who gave their lives to defend it. It seems but yesterday that at least two-thirds of the journals of this city were the virtual allies of the Secessionists, their apologists, their champions. The roar of the great circle of batteries pouring their iron hail upon devoted Sumter, has struck them all dumb. It is as if one had made a brilliant and effective speech, setting forth the innocence of murder, and having just bidden adieu to the cheers and the gaslight, were to be confronted by the gory form and staring eyes of a victim of assassination, the first fruit of his oratorical success. For months before the late Presidential election, a majority of our journals predicted forcible resistance to the government as the natural and necessary consequence of a Republican triumph; for months since they have been cherishing and encouraging the Slaveholder's Rebellion, as if it were a very natural and proper proceeding. Their object was purely partisan—they wished to bully the Republican Administration into shameful recreancy to Republican principle, and then call upon the people to expel from power a party so profligate and cowardly. They did not succeed in this; they *have* succeeded in enticing their Southern *protegés* and some time allies into flagrant treason.

There cannot be a rational doubt that every man who aided or abetted the attack on Fort Sumter is involved in the guilt of treason. That all the besiegers of Forts Sumter and Pickens have incurred the penalty of treason—which is death—is indisputable.

Most of our journals lately parading the pranks of the Secessionists with scarcely disguised exultation, have been suddenly sobered by the culmination of the slaveholding conspiracy. They would evidently like to justify and en-

---

* A NORTHERN EDITOR REJOICES THAT SUMTER HAS RESOLVED THE CRISIS: From Frank Moore, ed., *The Rebellion Record* (New York, 1861–65), I, 57–58.

courage the traitors further, but they dare not; so the Amen sticks in their throat. The aspect of the people appalls them. Democrat as well as Republican, Conservative and Radical, instinctively feel that the guns fired at Sumter were aimed at the heart of the American Republic. Not even in the lowest groggery of our city would it be safe to propose cheers for Beauregard and Gov. Pickens. The Tories of the Revolution were relatively ten times as numerous here as are the open sympathizers with the Palmetto Rebels. It is hard to lose Sumter; it is a consolation to know that in losing it we have gained a united people. Henceforth, the loyal States are a unit in uncompromising hostility to treason, wherever plotted, however justified. Fort Sumter is temporarily lost, but the country is saved. Live the Republic! . . .

21] Virginia Secedes from the Union

Virginia's response to Lincoln's election and the developing secession crisis may be taken as typical of the Upper, or border, South. In essence, Virginia was not pleased with the prospect of a Republican President and it did not approve Lincoln's policy as announced in his inaugural. But it was not going to secede until there was evidence that Lincoln meant to do something menacing the South or state rights. A convention elected to consider the situation met in February, 1861, and marked time, watching events and encouraging compromise. When after Sumter Lincoln called for troops to repress the "insurrection," Virginia acted. On April 17 the convention voted to secede. Even then opinion was not unanimous. Eighty-eight delegates voted for secession and fifty-five against.*

THE PEOPLE of Virginia, in the ratification of the Constitution of the United States of America, adopted by them in convention, on the 25th day of June, in the year of our Lord one thousand seven hundred and eighty-eight, having declared that the powers granted under the said constitution were derived from the people of the United States, and might be resumed whensoever the same should be perverted to their injury and oppression, and the Federal Government having perverted said powers, not only to the injury of the people of Virginia, but to the oppression of the Southern slaveholding States;

Now, therefore, we, the people of Virginia, do declare and ordain, that the ordinance adopted by the people of this State in convention on the twenty-fifth day of June, in the year of our Lord one thousand seven hundred and eighty-eight, whereby the Constitution of the United States of America was ratified, and all acts of the General Assembly of this State ratifying or adopting amendments to said constitution, are hereby repealed and abrogated; that the Union between the State of Virginia and the other States under the constitution aforesaid is hereby dissolved, and that the State of Virginia is in the full possession and exercise of all the rights of sovereignty which belong and appertain to a free and independent State. And they do further declare that

* VIRGINIA SECEDES FROM THE UNION: From Frank Moore, ed., *The Rebellion Record* (New York, 1861–65), I, 70.

said Constitution of the United States of America is no longer binding on any of the citizens of this State.

This ordinance shall take effect and be an act of this day, when ratified by a majority of the votes of the people of this State, cast at a poll to be taken thereon, on the fourth Thursday in May next, in pursuance of a schedule hereafter to be enacted.

Done in convention in the city of Richmond, on the seventeenth day of April, in the year of our Lord, one thousand eight hundred and sixty-one, and in the eighty-fifth year of the Commonwealth of Virginia.

22] Abraham Lincoln Reviews the Events That Led to War

> After the fall of Fort Sumter Lincoln acted on his own initiative to put the country on a war footing. Then he convened Congress in special session, and in a message on July 4, 1861, presented his version of the Sumter crisis and defined the purpose of the war.*

FELLOW-CITIZENS OF THE SENATE AND HOUSE OF REPRESENTATIVES:

Having been convened on an extraordinary occasion, as authorized by the Constitution, your attention is not called to any ordinary subject of legislation.

At the beginning of the present presidential term, four months ago, the functions of the Federal government were found to be generally suspended within the several states of South Carolina, Georgia, Alabama, Mississippi, Louisiana, and Florida, excepting only those of the Post Office Department.

Within these states, all the forts, arsenals, dockyards, custom-houses, and the like, including the movable and stationary property in, and about them, had been seized, and were held in open hostility to this government, excepting only Forts Pickens, Taylor, and Jefferson, on, and near the Florida coast, and Fort Sumter, in Charleston harbor, South Carolina. The forts thus seized had been put in improved condition; new ones had been built; and armed forces had been organized, and were organizing, all avowedly with the same hostile purpose.

The forts remaining in the possession of the Federal government, in and near, these states, were either besieged or menaced by warlike preparations; and especially Fort Sumter was nearly surrounded by well-protected hostile batteries, with guns equal in quality to the best of its own, and outnumbering the latter as perhaps ten to one. A disproportionate share, of the Federal muskets and rifles, had somehow found their way into these states, and had been seized, to be used against the government. Accumulations of the public revenue, lying within them, had been seized for the same object. The navy was scattered in distant seas; leaving but a very small part of it within the im-

* ABRAHAM LINCOLN REVIEWS THE EVENTS THAT LED TO WAR: From Roy P. Basler, ed., *The Collected Works of Abraham Lincoln* (New Brunswick, N.J., 1953), IV, 421–41.

mediate reach of the government. Officers of the Federal army and navy, had resigned in great numbers; and, of those resigning, a large proportion had taken up arms against the government. Simultaneously, and in connection, with all this, the purpose to sever the Federal Union, was openly avowed. In accordance with this purpose, an ordinance had been adopted in each of these states, declaring the states, respectively, to be separated from the national Union. A formula for instituting a combined government of these states had been promulgated; and this illegal organization, in the character of Confederate States was already invoking recognition, aid, and intervention, from foreign powers.

Finding this condition of things, and believing it to be an imperative duty upon the incoming executive, to prevent, if possible, the consummation of such attempt to destroy the Federal Union, a choice of means to that end became indispensable. This choice was made; and was declared in the inaugural address. The policy chosen looked to the exhaustion of all peaceful measures, before a resort to any stronger ones. It sought only to hold the public places and property, not already wrested from the government, and to collect the revenue; relying for the rest, on time, discussion, and the ballot box. It promised a continuance of the mails, at government expense, to the very people who were resisting the government; and it gave repeated pledges against any disturbance to any of the people, or any of their rights. Of all that which a president might constitutionally, and justifiably, do in such a case, everything was forborne, without which, it was believed possible to keep the government on foot.

On the 5th of March (the present incumbent's first full day in office) a letter of Major Anderson, commanding at Fort Sumter, written on the 28th of February, and received at the War Department on the 4th of March, was, by that department, placed in his hands. This letter expressed the professional opinion of the writer, that reinforcements could not be thrown into that fort within the time for his relief, rendered necessary by the limited supply of provisions, and with a view of holding possession of the same, with a force of less than twenty thousand good, and well-disciplined men. This opinion was concurred in by all the officers of his command; and their *memoranda* on the subject, were made enclosures of Major Anderson's letter. The whole was immediately laid before Lieutenant General Scott, who at once concurred with Major Anderson in opinion. On reflection, however, he took full time, consulting with other officers, both of the army and the navy; and at the end of four days, came reluctantly, but decidedly, to the same conclusion as before. He also stated at the same time that no such sufficient force was then at the control of the government, or could be raised, and brought to the ground, within the time when the provisions in the fort would be exhausted. In a purely military point of view, this reduced the duty of the administration, in the case, to the mere matter of getting the garrison safely out of the fort.

It was believed, however, that to so abandon that position, under the circumstances, would be utterly ruinous; that the *necessity* under which it was to be done, would not be fully understood—that, by many, it would be construed as a part of a *voluntary* policy—that, at home, it would discourage the friends of the Union, embolden its adversaries, and go far to insure to the latter, a recognition abroad—that, in fact, it would be our national destruction consummated. This could not be allowed. Starvation was not yet upon the garrison; and ere it would be reached, *Fort Pickens* might be reinforced. This last, would be a clear indication of *policy,* and would better enable the country to accept the evacuation of Fort Sumter, as a military *necessity.* An order was at once directed to be sent for the landing of the troops from the steamship Brooklyn, into Fort Pickens. This order could not go by land, but must take the longer, and slower route by sea. The first return news from the order was received just one week before the fall of Fort Sumter. The news itself was, that the officer commanding the Sabine, to which vessel the troops had been transferred from the Brooklyn, acting upon some *quasi* armistice of the late administration (and of the existence of which, the present administration, up to the time the order was despatched, had only too vague and uncertain rumors, to fix attention), had refused to land the troops. To now reinforce Fort Pickens, before a crisis would be reached at Fort Sumter was impossible—rendered so by the near exhaustion of provisions in the latter-named fort. In precaution against such a conjuncture, the government had, a few days before, commenced preparing an expedition, as well adapted as might be, to relieve Fort Sumter, which expedition was intended to be ultimately used, or not, according to circumstances. The strongest anticipated case, for using it, was now presented; and it was resolved to send it forward. As had been intended, in this contingency, it was also resolved to notify the governor of South Carolina, that he might expect an attempt would be made to provision the fort; and that, if the attempt should not be resisted, there would be no effort to throw in men, arms, or ammunition, without further notice, or in case of an attack upon the fort. This notice was accordingly given; whereupon the fort was attacked, and bombarded to its fall, without even awaiting the arrival of the provisioning expedition.

It is thus seen that the assault upon, and reduction of, Fort Sumter, was, in no sense, a matter of self-defence on the part of the assailants. They well knew that the garrison in the fort could, by no possibility, commit aggression upon them. They knew—they were expressly notified—that the giving of bread to the few brave and hungry men of the garrison, was all which would on that occasion be attempted, unless themselves, by resisting so much, should provoke more. They knew that this government desired to keep the garrison in the fort, not to assail them, but merely to maintain visible possession, and thus to preserve the Union from actual, and immediate dissolution—trusting, as hereinbefore stated, to time, discussion, and the ballot box, for final adjustment; and they assailed, and reduced the fort, for precisely the reverse object —to drive out the visible authority of the Federal Union, and thus force it to immediate dissolution.

That this was their object, the executive well understood; and having said to them in the inaugural address, "You can have no conflict without being yourselves the aggressors," he took pains, not only to keep this declaration good, but also to keep the case so free from power of ingenious sophistry, as that the world should not be able to misunderstand it. By the affair at Fort Sumter, with its surrounding circumstances, that point was reached. Then, and thereby, the assailants of the government, began the conflict of arms, without a gun in sight, or in expectancy, to return their fire, save only the few in the fort, sent to that harbor, years before, for their own protection, and still ready to give that protection, in whatever was lawful. In this act, discarding all else, they have forced upon the country, the distinct issue: "Immediate dissolution, or blood."

And this issue embraces more than the fate of these United States. It presents to the whole family of man, the question, whether a constitutional republic, or a democracy—a government of the people, by the same people—can, or cannot, maintain its territorial integrity, against its own domestic foes. It presents the question, whether discontented individuals, too few in numbers to control administration, according to organic law, in any case, can always, upon the pretense, break up their government, and thus practically put an end to free government upon the earth. It forces us to ask: "Is there, in all republics, this inherent, and fatal weakness?" "Must a government, of necessity, be too *strong* for the liberties of its own people, or too *weak* to maintain its own existence?"

So viewing the issue, no choice was left but to call out the war power of the government; and so to resist force, employed for its destruction, by force, for its preservation. . . .

It is now recommended that you give the legal means for making this contest a short, and a decisive one; that you place at the control of the government, for the work, at least four hundred thousand men, and four hundred millions of dollars. That number of men is about one tenth of those of proper ages within the regions where, apparently, *all* are willing to engage; and the sum is less than a twenty-third part of the money value owned by the men who seem ready to devote the whole. A debt of six hundred millions of dollars *now*, is a less sum per head, than was the debt of our Revolution, when we came out of that struggle; and the money value in the country now, bears even a greater proportion to what it was *then*, than does the population. Surely each man has as strong a motive *now*, to *preserve* our liberties, as each had *then*, to *establish* them.

A right result, at this time, will be worth more to the world, than ten times the men, and ten times the money. The evidence reaching us from the country, leaves no doubt, that the material for the work is abundant; and that it needs only the hand of legislation to give it legal sanction, and the hand of the executive to give it practical shape and efficiency. One of the greatest perplexities of the government, is to avoid receiving troops faster than it can provide for them. In a word, the people will save their government, if the government itself, will do its part, only indifferently well.

It might seem, at first thought, to be of little difference whether the present movement at the South be called "secession" or "rebellion." The movers, however, well understand the difference. At the beginning, they knew they could never raise their treason to any respectable magnitude, by any name which implies *violation* of law. They knew their people possessed as much of moral sense, as much of devotion to law and order, and as much pride in, and reverence for, the history, and government, of their common country, as any other civilized, and patriotic people. They knew they could make no advancement directly in the teeth of these strong and noble sentiments. Accordingly they commenced by an insidious debauching of the public mind. They invented an ingenious sophism, which, if conceded, was followed by perfectly logical steps, through all the incidents, to the complete destruction of the Union. The sophism itself is, that any state of the Union may, *consistently* with the national Constitution, and therefore *lawfully,* and *peacefully,* withdraw from the Union, without the consent of the Union, or of any other state. The little disguise that the supposed right is to be exercised only for just cause, themselves to be the sole judge of its justice, is too thin to merit any notice.

With rebellion thus sugar-coated, they have been drugging the public mind of their section for more than thirty years; and, until at length, they have brought many good men to a willingness to take up arms against the government the day *after* some assemblage of men have enacted the farcical pretense of taking their state out of the Union, who could have been brought to no such thing the day *before*.

This sophism derives much—perhaps the whole—of its currency, from the assumption, that there is some omnipotent, and sacred supremacy, pertaining to a *state*—to each state of our Federal Union. Our states have neither more, nor less power, than that reserved to them, in the Union, by the Constitution —no one of them ever having been a state *out* of the Union. The original ones passed into the Union even *before* they cast off their British colonial dependence; and the new ones each came into the Union directly from a condition of dependence, excepting Texas. And even Texas, in its temporary independence, was never designated a state. The new ones only took the designation of states, on coming into the Union, while that name was first adopted for the old ones, in, and by, the Declaration of Independence. Therein the "United Colonies" were declared to be "Free and Independent States"; but, even then, the object plainly was not to declare their independence of *one another,* or of the *Union;* but directly the contrary, as their mutual pledge, and their mutual action, before, at the time, and afterwards, abundantly show. The express plighting of faith, by each and all of the original thirteen, in the Articles of Confederation, two years later, that the Union shall be perpetual, is most conclusive. Having never been states, either in substance, or in name, *outside* of the Union, whence this magical omnipotence of "state rights," asserting a claim of power to lawfully destroy the Union itself? Much is said about the "sovereignty" of the states; but the word, even, is not in the national Constitution; nor, as is believed, in any of the state constitutions. What is a "sovereignty," in the political sense of the term? Would it be far wrong to define it "A political community, without a political superior"? Tested by this, no one of our states, except Texas, ever was a sovereignty. And even Texas gave up the character on coming into the Union; by which act, she acknowledged the Constitution of the United States, and the laws and treaties of the United States made in pursuance of the Constitution, to be for her, the supreme law of the land. The states have their *status* in the Union, and they have no other *legal status*. If they break from this, they can only do so against law, and by revolution. The Union, and not themselves separately, procured their independence, and their liberty. By conquest, or purchase, the Union gave each of them, whatever of independence, and liberty, it has. The Union is older than any of the states; and, in fact, it created them as states. Originally, some dependent colonies made the Union; and, in turn, the Union threw off their old dependence, for them, and made them states, such as they are. Not one of them ever had a state constitution, independent of the Union. Of course, it is not forgotten that all the new states framed their constitutions, before they entered the Union; nevertheless, dependent upon, and preparatory to, coming into the Union.

Unquestionably the states have the powers, and rights, reserved to them in, and by the national Constitution; but among these, surely are not included all conceivable powers, however mischievous, or destructive; but, at most, such only, as were known in the world, at the time, as governmental powers; and certainly, a power to destroy the government itself, had never been known as a governmental—as a merely administrative power. This relative matter of national power, and state rights, as a principle, is no other than the principle of *generality,* and *locality.* Whatever concerns the whole, should be confided to the whole—to the general government; while, whatever concerns *only* the state, should be left exclusively, to the state. This is all there is of original principle about it. Whether the national Constitution, in defining boundaries between the two, has applied the principle with exact accuracy, is not to be questioned. We are all bound by that defining, without question.

What is now combatted, is the position that secession is *consistent* with the Constitution—is *lawful,* and *peaceful.* It is not contended that there is any express law for it; and nothing should ever be implied as law, which leads to unjust, or absurd consequences. . . .

The seceders insist that our Constitution admits of secession. They have assumed to make a national constitution of their own, in which, of necessity, they have either *discarded,* or *retained,* the right of secession, as they insist, it exists in ours. If they have discarded it, they thereby admit that, on principle, it ought not to be in ours. If they have retained it, by their own construction of ours they show that to be consistent they must secede from one another, whenever they shall find it the easiest way of settling their debts, or effecting any other selfish, or unjust object. The principle itself is one of disintegration, and upon which no government can possibly endure. . . .

It may be affirmed, without extravagance, that the free institutions we enjoy, have developed the powers, and improved the condition, of our whole people, beyond any example in the world. Of this we now have a striking, and an impressive illustration. So large an army as the government has now on foot, was never before known, without a soldier in it, but who had taken his place there, of his own free choice. But more than this: there are many single regiments whose members one and another, possess full practical knowledge of all the arts, sciences, professions, and whatever else, whether useful or elegant, is known in the world; and there is scarcely one, from which there could not be selected, a president, a cabinet, a congress, and perhaps a court, abundantly competent to administer the government itself. Nor do I say this is not true, also, in the army of our late friends, now adversaries, in this contest; but if it is, so much better the reason why the government, which has conferred such benefits on both them and us, should not be broken up. Whoever, in any section, proposes to abandon such a government, would do well to consider, in deference to what principle it is, that he does it—what better he is likely to get in its stead—whether the substitute will give, or be intended to give, so much of good to the people. There are some foreshadowings on this subject. Our adversaries have adopted some Declarations of Independence; in which, unlike the good old one, penned by Jefferson, they omit the words "all men are created equal." Why? They have adopted a temporary national constitution, in the preamble of which, unlike our good old one, signed by Washington, they omit "We, the people," and substitute "We, the deputies of the sovereign and independent States." Why? Why this deliberate pressing out of view, the rights of men, and the authority of the people?

This is essentially a people's contest. On the side of the Union, it is a struggle for maintaining in the world, that form, and substance of government, whose leading object is, to elevate the condition of men—to lift artificial weights from all shoulders—to clear the paths of laudable pursuit for all—to afford all, an unfettered start, and a fair chance, in the race of life. Yielding to partial, and temporary departures, from necessity, this is the leading object of the government for whose existence we contend.

I am most happy to believe that the plain people understand, and appreciate this. It is worthy of note, that while in this, the government's hour of trial, large numbers of those in the army and navy, who have been favored with the offices, have resigned, and proved false to the hand which had pampered them, not one common soldier, or common sailor is known to have deserted his flag.

Great honor is due to those officers who remain true, despite the example of their treacherous associates; but the greatest honor, and most important fact of all, is the unanimous firmness of the common soldiers, and common sailors. To the last man, so far as known, they have successfully resisted the traitorous efforts of those, whose commands, but an hour before, they obeyed as absolute law. This is the patriotic instinct of the plain people. They understand, without an argument, that destroying the government, which was made by Washington, means no good to them.

Our popular government has often been called an experiment. Two points in it, our people have already settled—the successful *establishing,* and the successful *administering* of it. One still remains—its successful *maintenance* against a formidable attempt to overthrow it. It is now for them to demonstrate to the world, that those who can fairly carry an election, can also suppress a rebellion—that ballots are the rightful, and peaceful, successors of bullets; and that when ballots have fairly, and constitutionally, decided, there can be no successful appeal, back to bullets; that there can be no successful appeal, except to ballots themselves, at succeeding elections. Such will be a great lesson of peace; teaching men that what they cannot take by an election, neither can they take it by a war—teaching all, the folly of being the beginners of a war. . . .

23] Jefferson Davis Reviews the Events That Led to War

> Like Lincoln, the President of the Confederate States felt constrained to review for his people the crisis that had ended in war. Here is his summary, presented to the Confederate Congress in a message of April 29, 1861. As in all his state papers, Davis stressed the constitutionality of the doctrine of state rights.*

GENTLEMEN OF CONGRESS:—It is my pleasing duty to announce to you that the Constitution framed for the establishment of a permanent government of the Confederate States of America has been ratified by the several conventions of each of those States to which it was referred. To inaugurate the said Government in its full proportions and upon its own substantial basis of the popular will, it only remains that elections should be held for the designation of the officers to administer it.

There is every reason to believe that at no distant day other States, identical in political principles and community of interests with those which you represent, will join this Confederacy, giving to its typical constellation increased splendor—to its government of free, equal and sovereign States, a wider sphere of usefulness, and to the friends of constitutional liberty a greater security for its harmonious and perpetual existence.

It was not, however, for the purpose of making this announcement that I have deemed it my duty to convoke you at an earlier day than that fixed by yourselves for your meeting.

The declaration of war made against this Confederacy, by Abraham Lincoln, President of the United States, in his proclamation, issued on the 15th day of the present month, renders it necessary, in my judgment, that you should convene at the earliest practicable moment to devise the measures necessary for the defence of the country.

The occasion is, indeed, an extraordinary one. It justifies me in a brief review of the relations heretofore existing between us and the States which now unite in warfare against us, and a succinct statement of the events which have resulted to the end, that mankind may pass intelligent and impartial judgment on our motives and objects. . . .

The people of the Southern States, whose almost exclusive occupation was agriculture, early perceived a tendency in the Northern States to render a common government subservient to their own purposes by imposing burthens on commerce as protection to their manufacturing and shipping interests.

Long and angry controversies grew out of these attempts, often successful,

---

* JEFFERSON DAVIS REVIEWS THE EVENTS THAT LED TO WAR: From Frank Moore, ed., *The Rebellion Record* (New York, 1861–65), I, 166–72. The text of the message has been collated with the version in Dunbar Rowland, ed., *Jefferson Davis, Constitutionalist* (Jackson, Miss., 1923), V, 567–78.

to benefit one section of the country at the expense of the other, and the danger of disruption arising from this cause was enhanced by the fact that the Northern population was increasing, by emigration and other causes, more than the population of the South.

By degrees, as the Northern States gained preponderance in the National Congress, self-interest taught their people to yield ready assent to any plausible advocacy of their right as a majority to govern the minority without control. They learned to listen with impatience to the suggestion of any constitutional impediment to the exercise of their will, and so utterly have the principles of the Constitution been corrupted in the Northern mind that, in the inaugural address delivered by President Lincoln in March last, he asserts a maxim which he plainly deems to be undeniable, that the theory of the Constitution requires, in all cases, that the majority shall govern. And in another memorable instance the same Chief Magistrate did not hesitate to liken the relations between States and the United States to those which exist between the county and the State in which it is situated and by which it was created.

This is the lamentable and fundamental error in which rests the policy that has culminated in his declaration of war against these Confederate States.

In addition to the long-continued and deep-seated resentment felt by the Southern States at the persistent abuse of the powers they had delegated to the Congress for the purpose of enriching the manufacturing and shipping classes of the North at the expense of the South, there has existed for nearly half a century another subject of discord, involving interests of such transcendent magnitude as at all times to create the apprehension in the minds of many devoted lovers of the Union that its permanence was impossible.

When the several States delegated certain powers to the United States Congress, a large portion of the laboring population were imported into the colonies by the mother country. In twelve out of the fifteen States, negro slavery existed, and the right of property existing in slaves was protected by law; this property was recognized in the Constitution, and provision was made against its loss by the escape of the slave.

The increase in the number of slaves by foreign importation from Africa was also secured by a clause forbidding Congress to prohibit the slave trade anterior to a certain date, and in no clause can there be found any delegation of power to the Congress to authorize it in any manner to legislate to the prejudice, detriment or discouragement of the owners of that species of property, or excluding it from the protection of the Government.

The climate and soil of the Northern States soon proved unpropitious to the continuance of slave labor, while the converse was the case at the South. Under the unrestricted free intercourse between the two sections, the Northern States consulted their own interests by selling their slaves to the South and prohibiting slavery between their limits. The South were willing purchasers of property suitable to their wants, and paid the price of the acquisition, without harboring a suspicion that their quiet possession was to be disturbed by those who were not only in want of constitutional authority, but by good faith as vendors, from disquieting a title emanating from themselves.

As soon, however, as the Northern States, that prohibited African slavery within their limits, had reached a number sufficient to give their representation a controlling vote in the Congress, a persistent and organized system of hostile measures against the rights of the owners of slaves in the Southern States was inaugurated and gradually extended. A continuous series of measures was devised and prosecuted for the purpose of rendering insecure the tenure of property in slaves.

Fanatical organizations, supplied with money by voluntary subscriptions, were assiduously engaged in exciting amongst the slaves a spirit of discontent and revolt. Means were furnished for their escape from their owners, and agents secretly employed to entice them to abscond.

The constitutional provision for their rendition to their owners was first evaded, then openly denounced as a violation of conscientious obligation and religious duty. Men were taught that it was a merit to elude, disobey, and violently oppose the execution of the laws enacted to secure the performance of the promise contained in the constitutional compact. Often owners of slaves were mobbed and even murdered in open day solely for applying to a magistrate for the arrest of a fugitive slave.

The dogmas of the voluntary organization soon obtained control of the Legislatures of many of the Northern States, and laws were passed for the punishment, by ruinous fines, and long-continued imprisonment in jails and penitentiaries, of citizens of the Southern States who should dare to ask aid of the officers of the law for the recovery of their property. Emboldened by success, the theater of agitation and aggression . . . was transferred to the Congress. Senators and Representatives were sent to the common councils of the nation, whose chief title to this distinction consisted in the display of a spirit of ultra fanaticism, and whose business was not "to promote the general welfare, or ensure domestic tranquillity," but to awaken the bitterest hatred against the citizens of sister States by violent denunciations of their institutions.

The transaction of public affairs was impeded by repeated efforts to usurp powers not delegated by the Constitution, for the purpose of impairing the security of property in slaves, and reducing those States which held slaves to a condition of inferiority.

Finally, a great party was organized for the purpose of obtaining the administration of the Government, with the avowed object of using its power for the total exclusion of the slave States from all participation in the benefits of the public domain acquired by all the States in common, whether by conquest or purchase; of surrounding them entirely by States in which slavery should be prohibited; of thus rendering the property in slaves so insecure as to be comparatively worthless, and thereby annihilating in effect property worth thousands of millions of dollars.

This party, thus organized, succeeded in the month of November last in the election of its candidate for the Presidency of the United States.

In the meantime, under the mild and genial climate of the Southern States, and the increasing care for the well-being and comfort of the laboring classes, dictated alike by interest and humanity, the African slaves had augmented in number from about six hundred thousand, at the date of the adoption of the constitutional compact, to upwards of four millions.

In moral and social condition they had been elevated from brutal savages into docile, intelligent, and civilized agricultural laborers, and supplied not only with bodily comforts, but with careful religious instruction. Under the supervision of a superior race, their labor had been so directed as not only to allow a gradual and marked amelioration of their own condition, but to convert hundreds of thousands of square miles of the wilderness into cultivated lands covered with a prosperous people. Towns and cities had sprung into existence, and had rapidly increased in wealth and population under the social system of the South.

The white population of the Southern slaveholding States had augmented from about 1,250,000, at the date of the adoption of the Constitution, to more than 8,500,000 in 1860, and the productions of the South in cotton, rice, sugar and tobacco, for the full development and continuance of which the labor of African slaves was and is indispensable, had swollen to an amount which formed nearly three-fourths of the export of the whole United States, and had become absolutely necessary to the wants of civilized man.

With interests of such overwhelming magnitude imperiled, the people of the Southern States were driven by the conduct of the North to the adoption of some course of action to avoid the dangers with which they were openly menaced. With this view, the Legislatures of the several States invited the people to select delegates to conventions to be held for the purpose of determining for themselves what measures were best to be adopted to meet so alarming a crisis in their history. . . .

Scarce had you assembled in February last, when, prior even to the inauguration of the chief-magistrate you had elected, you [expressed] your desire for the appointment of commissioners to be sent to the Government of the United States [to negotiate] "all questions of disagreement between the two governments upon principles of right, justice, equity and good faith."

It was my pleasure as well as my duty to coöperate with you in this work of peace. Indeed, in my address to you on taking the oath of office, and before receiving from you the communication of this resolution, I had said "as a necessity, not a choice, we have resorted to the remedy of separating, and henceforth our energies must be directed to the conduct of our own affairs, and the perpetuity of the Confederacy which we have formed. If a just perception of mutual interest shall permit us to peaceably pursue our separate political career, my most earnest desire will then have been fulfilled."

It was in furtherance of these accordant views of the Congress and the Executive that I made choice of three discreet, able and distinguished citizens, who repaired to Washington. Aided by their cordial coöperation and that of the Secretary of State, every effort compatible with self-respect and the dignity of the Confederacy was exhausted before I allowed myself to yield to the conviction that the Government of the United States was determined to attempt the conquest of this people, and that our cherished hopes of peace were unattainable.

On the arrival of our commissioners in Washington on the 5th of March, they postponed, at the suggestion of a friendly intermediator, doing more than giving informal notice of their arrival. This was done with a view to afford time to the President of the United States, who had just been inaugurated, for the discharge of other pressing official duties in the organization of his administration, before engaging his attention in the object of their mission.

It was not until the 12th of the month that they officially addressed the Secretary of State, informing him of the purpose of their arrival, and stating in the language of their instructions their wish "to make to the Government of the United States overtures for the opening of negotiations, assuring the Government of the United States that the President, Congress, and people of the Confederate States desired a peaceful solution of these great questions, that it is neither their interest nor their wish to make any demand which is not founded on the strictest principles of justice, nor to do any act to injure their late confederates."

To this communication no formal reply was received until the 8th of April. During the interval, the commissioners had consented to waive all questions of form. With the firm resolve to avoid war if possible, they went so far even as to hold, during that long period, unofficial intercourse through an intermediary, whose high position and character inspired the hope of success, and through whom constant assurances were received from the Government of the United States of its peaceful intentions; of its determination to evacuate Fort Sumter; and further, that no measure changing the existing status prejudicially to the Confederate States, especially at Fort Pickens, was in contemplation, but that in the event of any change of intention on the subject, notice would be given to the commissioners.

The crooked path of diplomacy can scarcely furnish an example so wanting in courtesy, in candor and directness, as was the course of the United States Government toward our commissioners in Washington. For proof of this I refer to the annexed documents marked, taken in connection with further facts which I now proceed to relate.

Early in April the attention of the whole country was attracted to extraordinary preparations for an extensive military and naval expedition in New York and other Northern ports. These preparations commenced in secrecy, for an expedition whose destination was concealed, and only became known when nearly completed, and on the 5th, 6th, and 7th of April, transports and vessels of war with troops, munitions and military supplies, sailed from Northern ports bound southward.

Alarmed by so extraordinary a demonstration, the commissioners requested the delivery of an answer to their official communication of the 12th of March, and thereupon received on the 8th of April a reply dated on the 15th of the previous month, from which it appears that during the whole interval, whilst the commissioners were receiving assurances calculated to inspire hope of the success of their mission, the Secretary of State and the President of the United States had already determined to hold no intercourse with them whatever; to refuse even to listen to any proposals they had to make, and had profited by the delay created by their own assurances, in order to prepare secretly the means for effective hostile operations.

That these assurances were given, has been virtually confessed by the Government of the United States, by its act of sending a messenger to Charleston to give notice of its purpose to use force if opposed in its intention of supplying Fort Sumter.

No more striking proof of the absence of good faith in the confidence of the Government of the United States toward the Confederacy can be re-

[handwritten annotation: "whole argument is circular / me should be free because are free. / are free because should be free"]

quired, than is contained in the circumstances which accompanied this notice.

According to the usual course of navigation, the vessels composing the expedition, and designed for the relief of Fort Sumter, might be expected to reach Charleston harbor on the 9th of April. Yet, with our commissioners actually in Washington, detained under assurances that notice should be given of any military movement, the notice was not addressed to them, but a messenger was sent to Charleston to give notice to the Governor of South Carolina, and the notice was so given at a late hour on the 8th of April, the eve of the very day on which the fleet might be expected to arrive.

That this manoeuvre failed in its purpose was not the fault of those who contrived it. A heavy tempest delayed the arrival of the expedition, and gave time to the commander of our forces at Charleston to ask and receive instructions of the government. Even then, under all the provocation incident to the contemptuous refusal to listen to our commissioners, and the tortuous course of the Government of the United States, I was sincerely anxious to avoid the effusion of blood, and directed a proposal to be made to the commander of Fort Sumter, who had avowed himself to be nearly out of provisions, that we would abstain from directing our fire on Fort Sumter if he would promise to not open fire on our forces unless first attacked. This proposal was refused, and the conclusion was reached that the design of the United States was to place the besieging force at Charleston between the simultaneous fire of the fleet and the fort. [The only alternative was to direct that] the fort should at once be reduced. This order was executed by Gen. Beauregard with the skill and success, which were naturally to be expected from the well-known character of that gallant officer; and, although the bombardment lasted but thirty-three hours, our flag did not wave over the battered walls until after the appearance of the hostile fleet off Charleston. . . .

Scarcely had the President of the United States received intelligence of the failure of the scheme which he had devised for the reinforcement of Fort Sumter, when he issued the declaration of war against this Confederacy, which has prompted me to convoke you. In this extraordinary production, that high functionary affects total ignorance of the existence of an independent Government, which, possessing the entire and enthusiastic devotion of its people, is exercising its functions without question over seven sovereign States—over more than five millions of people—and over a territory whose area exceeds five hundred thousand square miles.

He terms sovereign States "combinations too powerful to be suppressed by the ordinary course of judicial proceedings, or by the powers vested in the marshals by law."

He calls for an army of seventy-five thousand men to act as the *posse comitatus* [1] in aid of the process of the courts of justice in States where no courts exist whose mandates and decrees are not cheerfully obeyed and respected by a willing people.

He avows that "the first service to be assigned to the forces which have been called out" will not be to execute the processes of courts, but to capture forts and strongholds situated within the admitted limits of this Confederacy, and

---

1 *posse comitatus*: See p. 454n.

garrisoned by its troops, and declares that "this effort" is intended "to maintain the perpetuity of popular government."

He concludes by commanding the persons composing the "combinations" aforesaid—to wit, the five millions of inhabitants of these States—"to retire peaceably to their respective abodes within twenty days."

Apparently contradictory as are the terms of this singular document, one point was unmistakably evident. The President of the United States calls for an army of 75,000 men, whose first service was to be to capture our forts. It was a plain declaration of war which I was not at liberty to disregard. . . .

"O ur forts"
— built by U. S. Gov't,
so are "our forts."

TABLES

1] The Election of 1860

	ELECTORAL VOTE	POPULAR VOTE	PER CENT OF POPULAR VOTE
Lincoln	180	1,866,452	40
Douglas	12	1,375,157	29
Breckinridge	72	847,953	18
Bell	39	590,631	13
TOTAL	303	4,680,193	100

2] Dates of Secession of the Southern States

South Carolina	December 20, 1860
Mississippi	January 9, 1861
Florida	January 10, 1861
Alabama	January 11, 1861
Georgia	January 19, 1861
Louisiana	January 26, 1861
Texas	February 1, 1861
Virginia	April 17, 1861
Arkansas	May 6, 1861
Tennessee	May 7, 1861
North Carolina	May 20, 1861

CONCLUSION

THE CRISIS of 1860–61 poses some of the most perplexing questions in all the range of American history. Perhaps the most important one concerns the fate of the compromise proposals. Why did all the plans put forward fail? Was it because the plans themselves were inadequate? Or were the politicians who handled them inadequate to the demands of the moment? Undoubtedly many of the politicians were bumbling and too narrowly devoted to party and sectional interests. And some of them, notably the secessionists and the extreme Republicans, wanted compromise to fail, either for partisan or personal reasons. Many leaders on both sides passionately believed that they could compromise no longer on basic principles. Lincoln, for example, felt that for the Republicans to yield on the territorial question would be to repudiate the platform on which the party had been elected and would postpone a realistic approach to the whole problem of slavery indefinitely. Southerners, on the other hand, sensed that none of the plans went to the heart of the difficulty, the minority status of their section.

Finally, the question arises, was it, in fact, possible in 1860–61 to settle the crisis; to settle it, that is, in some way that would be considered permanent? What the South demanded was a cessation of agitation on slavery. This, the North would never concede. What the North demanded was some assurance that ultimately slavery would become extinct. The North also wanted to be assured that the minority section would not be permitted to exercise a veto on national development. In their reviews of the immediate background of the war, the rival Presidents, Lincoln and Davis, each threw the blame for the conflict on the other. Regardless of where it rested, war was at last a reality. Perhaps it had been inevitable. Lincoln seemed to catch the fatal drift of the time in one of his apt phrases of summary: "And the war came."

STUDY QUESTIONS

1] Compare the policies of Buchanan and Lincoln with respect to the secession crisis. How do you account for their differences and/or similarities?

2] Which of the compromise proposals was best designed to settle the crisis? Why did the efforts at compromise fail?

3] Southerners and Northerners held different views on "the right of secession." Explain and account for these differences, and show what bearing they had on the coming of the war.

4] All of the issues that divided the North and the South had been present for many years. Why did they erupt in disunion and war in 1860–61?

RECOMMENDED READINGS

PRIMARY SOURCES

BASLER, ROY P., ed. *The Collected Works of Abraham Lincoln,* 8 vols. (New Brunswick, N.J., 1953), Vol. IV.

DUMOND, DWIGHT L., ed. *Southern Editorials on Secession* (New York, 1931).

GREELEY, HORACE. *The American Conflict,* 2 vols. (Hartford, 1864–67), Vol. I.

LOWELL, JAMES RUSSELL. *Political Essays* (Boston, 1871).

McPHERSON, EDWARD. *Political History of the Great Rebellion* (Washington, 1865).

MOORE, FRANK, ed. *The Rebellion Record,* 11 vols. (New York, 1861–65), Vol. I; *Supplement,* XII (Washington, 1869).

PERKINS, HOWARD C., ed. *Northern Editorials on Secession,* 2 vols. (New York, 1942).

RICHARDSON, JAMES D., ed. *A Compilation of the Messages and Papers of the Presidents, 1789–1897,* 10 vols. (Washington, 1896–99), Vol. V.

ROWLAND, DUNBAR, ed. *Jefferson Davis, Constitutionalist,* 10 vols. (Jackson, Miss., 1923), Vol. V.

STEPHENS, ALEXANDER H. *A Constitutional View of the War Between the States,* 2 vols. (Philadelphia, 1868).

U.S. CONGRESS. *Congressional Globe,* 36 Cong., 2 Sess.

SECONDARY SOURCES

AUCHAMPAUGH, PHILIP G. *James Buchanan and His Cabinet on the Eve of Secession* (Lancaster, Pa., 1926).

BEALE, HOWARD K. "What Historians Have Said About the Causes of the Civil War," *Theory and Practice in Historical Study* (New York, 1946), pp. 55–102.

CATTON, BRUCE. *The Coming Fury,* "The Centennial History of the Civil War," I, E. B. Long, director of research (New York, 1961).

COLE, A. C. "Lincoln's Election an Immediate Menace to Slavery in the States?" *American Historical Review,* XXXVI (July, 1931), 740–67.

COLEMAN, MRS. CHAPMAN. *Life of John J. Crittenden,* 2 vols. (Philadelphia, 1871).

CRAVEN, AVERY. *The Coming of the Civil War* (Chicago, 1957).

DUMOND, DWIGHT L. *The Secession Movement, 1860–1861* (New York, 1931).

HAMILTON, J. G. DE R. "Lincoln's Election an Immediate Menace to Slavery in the States?" *American Historical Review,* XXXVII (July, 1932), 700–11.

NEVINS, ALLAN. *The Emergence of Lincoln,* 2 vols. (New York, 1950).

OWSLEY, FRANK L. "The Fundamental Cause of the Civil War: Egocentric Sectionalism," *Journal of Southern History,* VII (February, 1941), 3–18.

PHILLIPS, U. B. *The Course of the South to Secession* (New York, 1939).

POTTER, DAVID M. *Lincoln and His Party in the Secession Crisis* (New Haven, 1942).

PRESSLY, THOMAS J. *Americans Interpret Their Civil War* (Princeton, 1954).

RAMSDELL, CHARLES W. "Lincoln and Fort Sumter," *Journal of Southern History*, III (August, 1937), 259–88.
RANDALL, J. G. *Lincoln the President*, 2 vols. (New York, 1945), Vol. I.
STAMPP, KENNETH M. *And the War Came* (Baton Rouge, La., 1950).
SWANBERG, W. A. *First Blood* (New York, 1957).

Historical Aids

HISTORICAL AIDS

TAKEN in its widest sense, history is the unreliable memory of the human race; it embraces everything that has happened in human experience. In a narrower sense, history is the *written* record of man's past. As a scholar's discipline or learned craft, as historians know and practice it, history is a method of thinking, learning, and writing. It is best studied and understood by gathering at first hand the facts of the past, evaluating their validity and reliability, critically selecting among them for relevance and significance, organizing that selection to convey meaning, and presenting the result in an independent and readable synthesis. The task calls for hard work on a sustained basis, for orderly and systematic thinking, for intellectual imagination, and for literary talent. Above all, it calls for careful evaluation of sources, towering skepticism toward every shred of evidence, and ability to work as dispassionately and objectively as is humanly possible—these are indispensable attributes of the historian. Because a critical and judicial mind is as essential for him as for the judge in the courtroom or the physicist in the laboratory, he must know how to distinguish facts from probabilities or possibilities. He must also develop a capacity for generalization and interpretation that is restricted by the evidence available to him. In short, the job of the historian demands complete intellectual honesty, an honesty that directs and informs an ability to function both as a discoverer of the past and an interpreter for the present.

Not the only way, but certainly the best way, to learn and appreciate history, as well as to insure that one is exposed to the best methods of learning what a liberal education can offer, is to act out the role of the historian to the extent that an undergraduate can. By participating in the process of understanding the nature and value of the sources, and by using them as the basis of his own writing of history, the student will not only learn far more effectively; the chances are enhanced that he will develop critical faculties that in the long run are more important in his education than the mere learning of the data.

The time required for sustained research in the gathering of facts from original or primary sources on a single topic is unfortunately not available to most students, even when the sources are at hand. *Major Crises in American History* therefore places before students a small but representative sampling of the source materials for a number of critical episodes in American history, which when read and understood will enable the student to write his own narratives and to make his own judgments about the events described. The book itself is but a point of departure, an immediate tool for the task. The bibliographical references to each chapter will guide students to additional materials, both primary and secondary in nature. But a variety of other tools will be necessary—guides to reference works, bibliographies, accounts of the technical apparatus used in historical writing, and statements of historical method and theories of history. The following list of books, chosen for students beginning the college study of American history, will prove of value.

The *Harvard Guide to American History,* by Oscar Handlin and five other distinguished Harvard historians (Cambridge, Mass.: The Belknap Press, 1955), is the most valuable single reference book. The first section is a series of essays and bibliographies on the nature of history, research methods, and literary presentation. It is organized under such headings as "Theories of Historical Interpretation," "Principles of Historical Criticism," "Methods of Note-Taking," "The Mechanics of Citation," and "History as a Literary Art." The second section is a list of materials and tools of history, such as maps, bibliographies, and guides to manuscript collections, government documents, newspapers, biographies, and encyclopedias. The rest of the book is an excellent bibliography of books and articles on American history organized by chronological topics from pre-Columbian times to "Social and Intellectual History, 1945–1953."

For a fuller treatment of the subjects covered by the first section of the *Harvard Guide,* refer to Homer Carey Hockett, *The Critical Method in Historical Research and Writing,* 3rd ed. (New York: Macmillan Co., 1955), or Jacques Barzun and Henry F. Graff, *The Modern Researcher* (New York: Harcourt, Brace & World, 1957). Hockett's book is a practical manual that places great stress on historical methodology, source materials, and the mechanics of writing. Barzun and Graff, who are more readable, stress history as a literary art and the means of effectively presenting the findings of one's research. Wood Gray's *Historian's Handbook: A Key to the Study and Writing of History* (Boston: Houghton Mifflin Co., 1959), is an inexpensive booklet that serves as a useful, although abbreviated, primer. *The Gateway to History,* by Allan Nevins (Boston: Little, Brown & Co., 1938), is a lively introduction to the nature and subject matter of history and its relations to biography, literature, and philosophy, by one of the greatest of American historians. Carl Becker's *Everyman His Own Historian* (New York: Appleton-Century-Crofts, 1935), is a series of provocative essays on relativism in history; the title essay is especially recommended. *Historians and Their Craft,* by Herman Ausubel (New York: Columbia University Press, 1950), is an interesting study of changing theories of history as revealed by an analysis of presidential addresses before the American Historical Association from 1884 to 1945. Edward Hallett Carr's *What Is History?* (New York: Alfred A. Knopf, 1962) passes in masterly and polemical review the major issues of modern historiography.

For interpretative introductions to the history of the writing of the history of the United States, consult Harvey Wish, *The American Historian: A Social-Intellectual History of the Writing of the American Past* (New York: Oxford University Press, 1960); Michael Kraus, *The Writing of American History* (Norman, Okla.: University of Oklahoma Press, 1953); and William T. Hutchinson, ed., *The Marcus W. Jernegan Essays in American Historiography* (Chicago: University of Chicago Press, 1937, paperback, 1962).

A Guide to the Study of the United States of America, edited by Roy Basler et al. (Washington: Library of Congress, 1960), is an excellent critical bibliography of secondary works on all aspects of the history of life in America. organized by subject matter. More advanced students will find indispensable

Philip M. Hamer, ed., *A Guide to Archives and Manuscripts in the United
States* (New Haven: Yale University Press, 1961), which covers the manu-
script holdings of more than thirteen hundred depositories in all the states.
For the fullest bibliographical guide to articles and books on American history,
one must consult, with considerable inconvenience, the *Writings on American
History*, edited by Grace G. Griffin et al. in annual volumes since 1902. *The
Index to the "Writings on American History," 1920–1940* (Washington:
American Historical Association, 1956), facilitates the use of these volumes.
Volume III of Robert E. Spiller et al., eds., *Literary History of the United
States*, 3 vols. (New York: Macmillan Co., 1948), is a bibliography of the
primary and secondary works in the field of literary history, including the
writings of American statesmen. A *Bibliographical Supplement* to the same
work, edited by Richard M. Ludwig, was published in 1959.

Richard B. Morris, ed., *Encyclopaedia of American History*, 2nd ed. (New
York: Harper & Bros., 1961), is a reliable chronological and topical guide.
Students should make a habit of consulting historical atlases. The best is still
Charles O. Paullin's *Atlas of the Historical Geography of the United States*
(Washington: Carnegie Institution, 1932). Others of value are James Truslow
Adams and R. V. Coleman, eds., *Atlas of American History* (New York:
Charles Scribner's Sons, 1943; and Clifford Lee Lord and Elizabeth H. Lord,
Historical Atlas of the United States (New York: Holt, Rinehart & Winston,
1944).

An indispensable reference tool for biographical information is the *Dictionary of American Biography*, edited by Allen Johnson and Dumas Malone
(New York: Charles Scribner's Sons, 1928–37), a monumental achievement
of American historical scholarship in twenty-one volumes, including the Index
volume. Harris E. Starr, ed., *Dictionary of American Biography: Supplement
One*, published in 1944, and Robert Livingston Schuyler and Edward T.
James, eds., *Supplement Two*, published in 1958, bring the project up to date
by including biographies of persons who died after 1935.

There are a number of major scholarly journals in the field of American
history with which students should make an effort to familiarize themselves.
The leading ones are: *The American Historical Review, The Mississippi
Valley Historical Review, The New England Quarterly, The William and
Mary Quarterly, The Journal of Southern History, The Pacific Historical
Review*, and *The Pennsylvania Magazine of History and Biography*. In addition, most state historical societies publish periodicals that cover, primarily,
state and local history. Scholarly journals publish articles summarizing recent
research and reinterpretation, book reviews, and bibliographies of current
literature.

B
C
D
E
F
G
H
I